ELEMENTS OF LITERATURE

SECOND EDITION

Bethany Harris
Barbara J. Rooks
Kimberly Y. Stegall

bju press
Greenville, South Carolina

Elements of Literature
Second Edition

Bethany Harris, MA, MEd
Barbara J. Rooks, MEd
Kimberly Y. Stegall, MEd

Contributing Writers
Michael Pope, MA
Elizabeth Rose, MEd, MA

Bible Integration
Mark L. Ward Jr., PhD

Editor
Rebecca S. Moore

Concept Design
Drew Fields

Page Design
John Cunningham

Page Layout
Bonnijean Marley

Project Coordinator
Benjamin Sinnamon

Permissions
Sylvia Gass
Ashley Hobbs
Lilia Kielmeyer

Based in part on original materials from *Elements of Literature*, First Edition, by Ronald A. Horton, PhD, and Donnalynn Hess, MA.

Acknowledgments begin on page iv, which is an extension of this copyright page. Illustrators and Photograph Credits appear on pages 478–80.

Produced in cooperation with the Bob Jones University Division of English Language and Literature of the College of Arts and Science, the School of Religion, and Bob Jones Academy.

ISBN: 978-1-60682-167-1

15 14 13 12 11 10 9 8 7 6 5 4 3 2

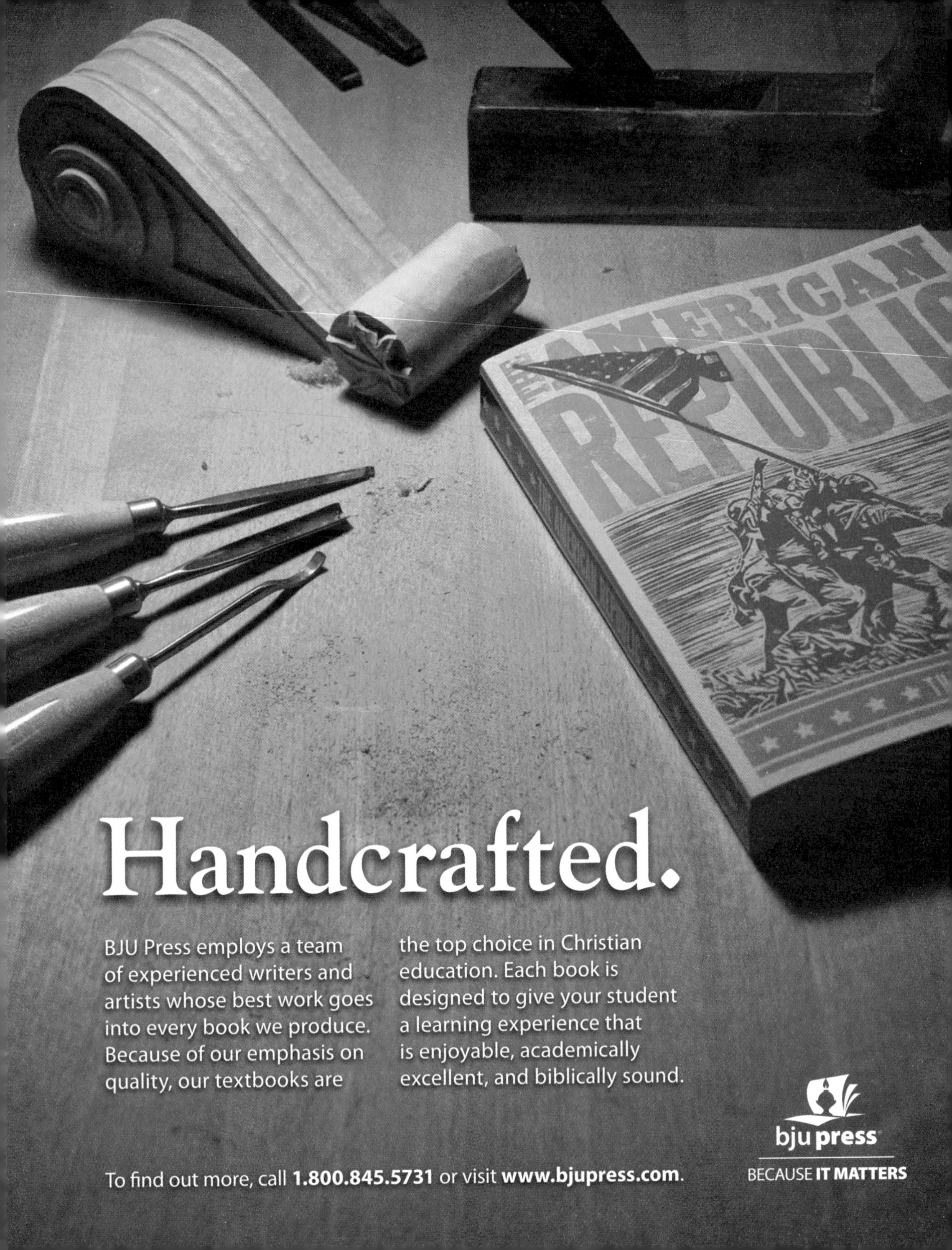
AMERICAN
Handcrafted.
BJU Press employs a team of experienced writers and artists whose best work goes into every book we produce. Because of our emphasis on quality, our textbooks are the top choice in Christian education. Each book is designed to give your student a learning experience that is enjoyable, academically excellent, and biblically sound.
To find out more, call 1.800.845.5731 or visit www.bjupress.com.
bju press
BECAUSE IT MATTERS

ACKNOWLEDGMENTS

Unit I

(Print Edition)
Harvard University Press: "A bird came down the walk" from THE POEMS OF EMILY DICKINSON: VARIORUM EDITION, edited by Ralph W. Franklin, Cambridge, Mass.: The Belknap Press of Harvard University Press, Copyright © 1998 by the President and Fellows of Harvard College. Copyright © 1951, 1955, 1979, 1983 by the President and Fellows of Harvard College.

Scientific American: "The Spider and the Wasp" by Alexander Petrunkevitch. Reproduced with permission. Copyright © 1952 Scientific American, a division of Nature America, Inc. All rights reserved.

Random House, Inc.: "Mother to Son" from THE COLLECTED POEMS OF LANGSTON HUGHES by Langston Hughes, edited by Arnold Rampersad with David Roessel, Associate Editor, copyright © 1994 by the Estate of Langston Hughes. Used by permission of Alfred A. Knopf, a division of Random House, Inc. (US, its territories & possessions, Canada, P.I., Open Market, E.U.) Reprinted by permission of **Harold Ober Associates Incorporated** (UK and British Commonwealth, South Africa, and Ireland.)

(E-book Edition)
Harvard University Press: "A bird came down the walk" from THE POEMS OF EMILY DICKINSON: VARIORUM EDITION, edited by Ralph W. Franklin, Cambridge, Mass.: The Belknap Press of Harvard University Press, Copyright © 1998 by the President and Fellows of Harvard College. Copyright © 1951, 1955, 1979, 1983 by the President and Fellows of Harvard College.

Scientific American: "The Spider and the Wasp" by Alexander Petrunkevitch. Reproduced with permission. Copyright © 1952 Scientific American, a division of Nature America, Inc. All rights reserved.

Harold Ober Associates Inc.: "Mother to Son" from THE COLLECTED POEMS OF LANGSTON HUGHES by Langston Hughes, edited by Arnold Rampersad with David Roessel, Associate Editor, copyright © 1994 by the Estate of Langston Hughes. Used by permission of Harold Ober Associates Incorporated.

Unit II

(Print Edition)
Little, Brown and Company: "March for a One-Man Band" from FIRST LIGHT by David Wagoner. Copyright © 1983 by David Wagoner. By permission of Little, Brown and Company.

Weekly Reader Corporation: "Foul Shot" by Edwin A. Hoey. Special permission granted by *Weekly Reader,* published and copyrighted by Weekly Reader Corporation. All rights reserved.

Random House, Inc.: "Winter Ocean" from COLLECTED POEMS 1953-1993 by John Updike, copyright © 1993 by John Updike. Used by permission of Alfred A. Knopf, a division of Random House, Inc.

Graywolf Press: William Stafford, "Traveling through the Dark" from *The Way It Is: New and Selected Poems.* Copyright © 1962, 1998 by William Stafford and the Estate of William Stafford. Reprinted with the permission of Graywolf Press, Minneapolis, Minnesota, www.graywolfpress.org.

Writers House LLC: "I Have a Dream" by Martin Luther King, Jr. Reprinted by arrangement with The Heirs to the Estate of Martin Luther King Jr., c/o Writers House as agent for the proprietor New York, NY. *Copyright 1963 Dr. Martin Luther King Jr; copyright renewed 1991 Coretta Scott King.*

(E-book Edition)
Little, Brown and Company: "March for a One-Man Band" from FIRST LIGHT by David Wagoner. Copyright © 1983 by David Wagoner. By permission of Little, Brown and Company.

Weekly Reader Corporation: "Foul Shot" by Edwin A. Hoey. Special permission granted by *Weekly Reader,* published and copyrighted by Weekly Reader Corporation. All rights reserved.

Random House, Inc.: "Winter Ocean" from COLLECTED POEMS 1953-1993 by John Updike, copyright © 1993 by John Updike. Used by permission of Alfred A. Knopf, a division of Random House, Inc. For online information about other Random House, Inc. books and authors, see the Internet web site at http://www.randomhouse.com.

Graywolf Press: William Stafford, "Traveling through the Dark" from *The Way It Is: New and Selected Poems.* Copyright © 1962, 1998 by William Stafford and the Estate of William Stafford. Reprinted with the permission of Graywolf Press, Minneapolis, Minnesota, www.graywolfpress.org.

Writers House LLC: "I Have a Dream" by Martin Luther King, Jr. Reprinted by arrangement with The Heirs to the Estate of Martin Luther King Jr., c/o Writers House as agent for the proprietor New York, NY. *Copyright 1963 Dr. Martin Luther King Jr; copyright renewed 1991 Coretta Scott King.*

Unit III

(Print Edition)
Wright's Media: "Outta My Way, Grandpa!" by Hugh O'Neill. From *Runner's World*, July 2010. By permission of Wright's Media on behalf of *Runner's World.*

Liveright Publishing Corporation: "maggie and milly and molly and may". Copyright © 1956, 1984, 1991 by the Trustees for the E. E. Cummings Trust, from COMPLETE POEMS: 1904-1962 by E. E. Cummings, edited by George J. Firmage. Used by permission of Liveright Publishing Corporation.

Random House, Inc.: "Afterglow", from JORGE LUIS BORGES SELECTED POEMS 1923-1967 by Jorge Luis Borges, copyright © 1968, 1969, 1970, 1971, 1972 by Jorge Luis Borges, Emeces Editores, S. A. and Norman Thomas Di Giovanni. Used by permission of Dell Publishing, a division of Random House, Inc.

The Society of Authors: "The Listeners" by Walter de la Mare. By permission of The Trustees of Walter de la Mare and the Society of Authors as their representative.

(E-book Edition)
Wright's Media: "Outta My Way, Grandpa!" by Hugh O'Neill. From *Runner's World*, July 2010. By permission of Wright's Media on behalf of *Runner's World*.

Liveright Publishing Corporation: "maggie and milly and molly and may". Copyright © 1956, 1984, 1991 by the Trustees for the E. E. Cummings Trust, from COMPLETE POEMS: 1904-1962 by E. E. Cummings, edited by George J. Firmage. Used by permission of Liveright Publishing Corporation. This selection may not be reproduced, stored in a retrieval system, or transmitted in any form or by any means without the prior written permission of the publisher.

Random House, Inc.: "Afterglow", from JORGE LUIS BORGES SELECTED POEMS 1923-1967 by Jorge Luis Borges, copyright © 1968, 1969, 1970, 1971, 1972 by Jorge Luis Borges, Emeces Editores, S. A. and Norman Thomas Di Giovanni. Used by permission of Dell Publishing, a division of Random House, Inc. For online information about other Random House, Inc. books and authors, see the Internet website at http://www.randomhouse.com.

The Society of Authors: "The Listeners" by Walter de la Mare. By permission of The Trustees of Walter de la Mare and the Society of Authors as their representative.

Unit IV

(Print and E-book Editions)
New Directions Publishing Corp.: "Jade Flower Palace" by Kenneth Rexroth, from the original by Tu Fu, from ONE HUNDRED POEMS FROM THE CHINESE, copyright © 1971 by Kenneth Rexroth. Reprinted by permission of New Directions Publishing Corp.

Henry Holt and Company, LLC: "A Considerable Speck," from the book, THE POETRY OF ROBERT FROST edited by Edward Connery Lathem. Copyright 1969 by Henry Holt and Company. Copyright 1942 by Robert Frost, copyright 1970 by Lesley Frost Ballantine. **Reprinted by permission of Henry Holt and Company, LLC.**

The Barbara Hogenson Agency, Inc.: "The Day the Dam Broke" from *My Life and Hard Times* by James Thurber. Copyright © 1933 by Rosemary A. Thurber. Reprinted by arrangement with Rosemary A. Thurber and The Barbara Hogenson Agency, Inc. All rights reserved.

Simon and Schuster, Inc.: "Earth" by John Hall Wheelock. Reprinted with the permission of Scribner, a Division of Simon and Schuster, Inc., from THE GARDENER AND OTHER POEMS by John Hall Wheelock. Copyright © 1961 by John Hall Wheelock; copyright renewed © 1989 by Sally Wheelock Brayton. All rights reserved.

C.S. Lewis Pte. Ltd.: Chapters I, II, VIII, and XXV from THE SCREWTAPE LETTERS by C.S. Lewis copyright © C.S. Lewis Pte. Ltd. 1942. Extract reprinted by permission.

Unit V

(Print Edition)
Pollinger Limited: "The Tortoise and the Osprey" from *Where the Leopard Passes: A Book of African Folktales* by Geraldine Elliot. London: Routledge and Kegan Paul Ltd., 1949. Reproduced by permission of Pollinger Limited and The Estate of Geraldine Elliot.

Tuttle Publishing: "Pumpkin Seeds" from *Korean Children's Favorite Stories* by Kim-so Un. Copyright © 1955. Used by permission of Tuttle Publishing, a member of Periplus Publishing Group.

Little, Brown and Company: "Pyramus and Thisbe" from MYTHOLOGY by Edith Hamilton. Copyright © 1942 by Edith Hamilton. By permission of Little, Brown and Company.

The University of Chicago Press: Excerpts from *The Iliad of Homer, Translated with an Introduction by Richmond Lattimore*, Books One, Six, and Twenty-Two. The University of Chicago Press, Ltd., London. Copyright 1951 by The University of Chicago Press. All rights reserved.

(E-book Edition)
Pollinger Limited: "The Tortoise and the Osprey" from *Where the Leopard Passes: A Book of African Folktales* by Geraldine Elliot. London: Routledge and Kegan Paul Ltd., 1949. Reproduced by permission of Pollinger Limited and The Estate of Geraldine Elliot.

Tuttle Publishing: "Pumpkin Seeds" from *Korean Children's Favorite Stories* by Kim-so Un. Copyright © 1955. Used by permission of Tuttle Publishing, a member of Periplus Publishing Group.

Alice Reid Abbott: "Pyramus and Thisbe" from MYTHOLOGY by Edith Hamilton. Copyright © 1942 by Edith Hamilton. Non-exclusive electronic rights granted by Alice Reid Abbott.

The University of Chicago Press: Excerpts from *The Iliad of Homer, Translated with an Introduction by Richmond Lattimore*, Books One, Six, and Twenty-Two. The University of Chicago Press, Ltd., London. Copyright 1951 by The University of Chicago Press. All rights reserved.

Unit VI

(Print Edition)
PARS International: "How to Get Things Done" from Chicago Tribune, © 1930 Chicago Tribune. All rights reserved. Used by permission and protected by the Copyright Laws of the United States. The printing, copying, redistribution, or retransmission of the Material without express written permission is prohibited.

Houghton Mifflin Harcourt Publishing Company: "A Miserable Merry Christmas" from THE AUTOBIOGRAPHY OF LINCOLN STEFFENS, copyright 1931 by Harcourt, Inc. and renewed 1959 by Peter Steffens, reproduced by permission of Houghton Mifflin Harcourt Publishing Company.

Random House, Inc.: "Why the Leaves Turn Color in the Fall", copyright © 1990 by Diane Ackerman, from A NATURAL HISTORY OF THE SENSES by Diane Ackerman. Used by permission of Random House, Inc.

"Civil Peace" from GIRLS AT WAR AND OTHER STORIES by Chinua Achebe. Copyright © 1972, 1973 by Chinua Achebe. Used with permission of Doubleday, a division of Random House, Inc. (World excluding UK and British Commonwealth.) Reprinted with permission of **The Wylie Agency LLC**. (UK and British Commonwealth.)

Houghton Mifflin Harcourt Publishing Company: "A Visit of Charity" from A CURTAIN OF GREEN AND OTHER STORIES, copyright 1941 and renewed 1969 by Eudora Welty, reprinted by permission of Houghton Mifflin Harcourt Publishing Company (World excluding British Commonwealth.) Reprinted by the permission of **Russell & Volkening** as agents for the author. Copyright © 1941 by Eudora Welty, renewed in 1983 by Eudora Welty (British Commonwealth.)

(E-book Edition)
PARS International: "How to Get Things Done" from Chicago Tribune, © 1930 Chicago Tribune. All rights reserved. Used by permission and protected by the Copyright Laws of the United States. The printing, copying, redistribution, or retransmission of the Material without express written permission is prohibited. (www.chicagotribune.com)

William Morris Endeavor Entertainment: "Why the Leaves Turn Color in the Fall" from A NATURAL HISTORY OF THE SENSES by Diane Ackerman. Copyright © 1990 by Diane Ackerman. Used by permission.

Russell & Volkening: "A Visit of Charity" from A CURTAIN OF GREEN AND OTHER STORIES. Reprinted by the permission of Russell & Volkening as agents for the author. Copyright © 1941 by Eudora Welty, renewed in 1983 by Eudora Welty.

The Wylie Agency LLC: "Civil Peace" from GIRLS AT WAR AND OTHER STORIES by Chinua Achebe. Copyright © 1972, 1973 by Chinua Achebe, reprinted with permission of The Wylie Agency LLC.

Unit VII

(Print Edition)
Random House, Inc.: "The Panther", copyright © 1982 by Stephen Mitchell, from THE SELECTED POETRY OF RAINER MARIA RILKE by Rainer Maria Rilke, translated by Stephen Mitchell. Used by permission of Random House, Inc.

"The Wise Old Apple Tree in Spring" copyright 1933 and renewed 1961 by Robert Hillyer, from COLLECTED POEMS by Robert Hillyer. Used by permission of Alfred A. Knopf, a division of Random House, Inc.

Haymarket Books: "Nightsong: City" from *Sirens, Knuckles, Boots* by Dennis Brutus. © 1963. Reprinted in *Poetry and Protest: A Dennis Brutus Reader*, edited by Aisha Karim and Lee Sustar (Chicago: Haymarket Books, 2006). Used by permission of Haymarket Books.

Rhina P. Espaillat: "Landscape with Cows" from *Rehearsing Absence: Poems* by Rhina P. Espaillat. © 2001. Used by permission.

(E-book Edition)
Stephen Mitchell: "The Panther", copyright © 1982 by Stephen Mitchell, from THE SELECTED POETRY OF RAINER MARIA RILKE by Rainer Maria Rilke, translated by Stephen Mitchell. Permission granted by Stephen Mitchell.

Random House, Inc.: "The Wise Old Apple Tree in Spring" copyright 1933 and renewed 1961 by Robert Hillyer, from COLLECTED POEMS by Robert Hillyer. Used by permission of Alfred A. Knopf, a division of Random House, Inc. For online information about other Random House, Inc. books and authors, see the Internet web site at http://www.randomhouse.com.

Haymarket Books: "Nightsong: City" from *Sirens, Knuckles, Boots* by Dennis Brutus. © 1963. Reprinted in *Poetry and Protest: A Dennis Brutus Reader*, edited by Aisha Karim and Lee Sustar (Chicago: Haymarket Books, 2006). Used by permission of Haymarket Books.

Rhina P. Espaillat: "Landscape with Cows" from *Rehearsing Absence: Poems* by Rhina P. Espaillat. © 2001. Used by permission.

CONTENTS

Unit II: Sound and Syntax

UNIT III: ALLUSION AND SYMBOL

Unit IV: Irony

PART TWO: GENRES OF LITERATURE

UNIT V: FOLKTALE AND EPIC

UNIT VI: ESSAY AND SHORT STORY

Unit VII: Poetry

Unit VIII: Drama

TO THE STUDENT

The apostle Paul is one of history's most influential writers. He wrote with tight logic and intense feeling, and there is a literary quality that shines through his words even in translation. Metaphors, allusions, ironies, and even poetry are all tools in the apostle's literary arsenal, and he wields them with precision and power.

Literary skill like his is not something you get genetically from your parents. Inherited traits may be a factor, but literary gifts are mostly learned skills. But how do you learn the useful skill of expressing yourself well? One writer, Richard Lanham, suggests an answer hard to improve on: "Wide reading. You cannot memorize rules, you will not even want to try, until you have an intuitive knowledge of language, until you have cultivated some taste."[1] You learn the skills of civil engineering or nursing from those who have practiced the skills, not from tinkering in your garage or play-operating on your little brother. Likewise, if you want to write anything of quality, you must expose yourself to good literature.

Paul the Reader

Evidence shows that this is just what the apostle Paul did. In a fallen world full of terrible problems, Paul apparently took time out to read—and to read something other than Scripture and Christian devotionals. How do we know this? We know it, not just through the literary power Paul himself had but through his own testimony in Acts 17. The Bible says that Paul, standing on Mars Hill in the preeminent city of Greece, said,

> Ye men of Athens, I perceive that in all things ye are too superstitious. For as I passed by, and beheld your devotions, I found an altar with this inscription, TO THE UNKNOWN GOD. Whom therefore ye ignorantly worship, him declare I unto you. God that made the world and all things therein, seeing that he is Lord of heaven and earth, dwelleth not in temples made with hands; neither is worshipped with men's hands, as though he needed any thing, seeing he giveth to all life, and breath, and all things; and hath made of one blood all nations of men for to dwell on all the face of the earth, and hath determined the times before appointed, and the bounds of their habitation; that they should seek the Lord, if haply they might feel after him, and find him, though he be not far from every one of us: for in him we live, and move, and have our being (vv. 22–28).

But why should a collection of influential Athenians, living at the center of the Roman intellectual world, listen to someone they believed to be a Jewish babbler preaching strange monotheistic doctrines? Paul anticipated this question, and he appealed to a surprising authority:

> As certain also of your own poets have said, "For we are also his offspring." Forasmuch then as we are the offspring of God, we ought not to think that the Godhead is like unto gold, or silver, or stone, graven by art and man's device (Acts 17: 28–29).

Paul was quoting a Greek poet named Aratus in a poem entitled "Phaenomena." Paul, the former Pharisee, clearly had literary power not only in his pen but also in his tongue. He had at least one commonly-known poetic quotation ready to use for his own purposes.

[1]Richard A. Langham, "The Abusage of Usage," *The Virginia Quarterly Review*, Winter 1997, 32-53, http://www.vqronline.org/articles/1977/winter/lanham-abusage-usage/ (accessed Sept. 21 2011).

Literature and the Power of the Cross

Of course, Paul makes clear in his letter to the Corinthians that he didn't trust this power to be sufficient to persuade his hearers.

> I, brethren, when I came to you, came not with excellency of speech or of wisdom, declaring unto you the testimony of God. For I determined not to know any thing among you, save Jesus Christ, and him crucified. And I was with you in weakness, and in fear, and in much trembling. And my speech and my preaching was not with enticing words of man's wisdom, but in demonstration of the Spirit and of power: That your faith should not stand in the wisdom of men, but in the power of God (1 Cor. 2:1–5).

But notice something: While encouraging believers to place their highest confidence in God's transforming power, Paul uses powerful, well-formed words. In other words, he is not telling Christians to speak truth poorly or with as many grammatical errors as they can. Indeed, Proverbs clearly praises well-placed words, stating, "A man hath joy by the answer of his mouth: and a word spoken in due season, how good is it" (Prov. 15:23) and "A word fitly spoken is like apples of gold in pictures of silver" (Prov. 25:11). Careful biblical study backs up this judgment: the Bible makes full use of literary devices, including many you will study in this book.

Paul knew Scripture, and he obeyed it. He would not have denied the teaching of Proverbs that artfully selected words are a good thing. He just kept literary artistry in its proper place beneath—not above—glorifying God.

Literature and Redemption

According to the Bible, the world is a broken and twisted place. There are far too many pieces lying around for you on your own to glue them all back together. And as Paul said, it's not as if God needs your help or anyone else's. But, gloriously, He has chosen to let you be part of His work! As He fixes things in the world, you can be a tool in His hand, and literature can be a tool in yours.

When objects are broken, glue can help. But the brokenness in this world goes deeper than the physical, down to the bottom of every soul. Words can be keys in your and God's hands, opening up people's view of their own dark places. They can be medicine soothing the soul—or electric shocks jolting it to life. Through the Word of God, we gain the truth that can transform us and set us free from sin and bondage. While no words of ours can match that power, human literature is one of the strongest tools for good in this world. And if we do not use this tool well, who will? The Father of Lies stands all too ready to do so.

Think of what Paul did: he took a work of literature formed by pagan people for pagan purposes and used it to help him convey his Christian message to those pagans. He found a point of contact where their groping in the dark stumbled upon some of God's truth, and he used that truth to challenge their false worship of idols.

You have to be careful with this kind of use of pagan art. You have to remember how fallen you are. Some works of literature are so full of sin that they are simply too dangerous for you. Even if there were something inside of them that you could use for good purposes, the risk would not be worthwhile. Your parents and teachers are an invaluable source of wisdom for decisions like these. But Paul demonstrated that some non-Christian literature can sometimes be used for some very good purposes. And in order to accomplish those purposes, you need literary tools.

This year you will be offered some of those literary tools—and free sharpening of your existing tools. Well, almost free. Your parents are probably paying for it, and you'll have to pay something too—attention. But your motive for paying attention should not be merely to get good grades, but rather to increase your effectiveness in using the God-created tools in the academic field of literature.

UNIT III

THE ARMADA PORTRAIT OF QUEEN ELIZABETH I
George Gower

Each unit begins with a notable piece of artwork whose structure or theme touches on the unit topic in some way.

Several questions are provided to aid your analyses and discussion of these visual texts.

Literature selections are grouped to focus on particular literary elements, aiding your understanding of how these elements function to create literary art.

Introductory essays discuss important literary concepts and bring academic and value-related goals into conformity with biblical principles.

ALLUSION AND SYMBOL

You have now studied two marks of literature—imaginative comparison and the organized use of sound and syntax. With few exceptions, these will always be present in literature of a high caliber. Two additional modes of communication in literature are those of allusion and symbol. Though these need not appear in good literature, they are often present because of the rich possibilities they bring to a work.

Allusion

In **allusion**, a writer intentionally references persons, places, or things outside of the work itself, usually without specifically explaining them. As the following conversational statements exemplify, most often these references are to other works of literature or to history: "In her new boss, Sally met her nemesis." "At the last test, Jordan finally met his waterloo!" The first employs a literary allusion to Greek mythology. Nemesis was the goddess of retribution, particularly toward those suffering from excessive pride. The second draws on history, Waterloo being the battle at which Napoleon was finally conquered. But both allusions convey the same general idea—that Sally and Jordan have encountered their downfall within the specified settings.

Allusions can be either brief or extended, either stressed or so understated as to be nearly invisible. Often they overlap with imaginative comparisons (particularly metaphor and simile). Some reference only one aspect of their subject (e.g., the finality of the battle of Waterloo) or help create a certain tone (e.g., humor at comparing one's boss to a Greek goddess). Others carry subtle or complex ideas. For example, the title of the well-known play *A Raisin in the Sun* alludes to the poem "Harlem" (by Langston Hughes), in which the poet asks whether delayed dreams "dry up like a raisin in the sun." This literary allusion introduces and reinforces the play's main theme, the results of having one's dreams fulfilled or denied.

Allusions and Shared Knowledge

Allusions access an audience's communal know[ledge] and take advantage of well-known facts [or] associations between a topic and certain ideas o[r] emotions. Like imaginative comparisons, they ca[n] compress many ideas into a short statement. The Lord Himself made use of allusion. His sermons and conversations repeatedly refer to what His hearers knew best—Israel's history and the Scriptures. In John 3:14–15, He tells Nicodemus, "As Moses lifted up the serpent in the wilderness, even so must the Son of man be lifted up: that whosoever believeth in him should not perish, but have eternal life." Christ's allusion to the brazen serpent (Num. 21:4–9) both illustrates His message and clarifies His attitude. The story directly parallels God's plan to save mankind, but His reference also accentuates God's loving commitment to His people. Just as He has saved them in the past, so He will in the future.

Writers using allusion anticipate readers with knowledge similar to their own. Remove this bond, and allusions can become difficult to decipher. English literature plainly demonstrates this process. For centuries educated persons were well-versed in the Bible and the ancient classics, so older literature abounds with allusions to both. Unfortunately, modern readers find many of these allusions impenetrable. To forestall this effect, authors writing for the broadest audiences tend to avoid allusion events or pop cultu[re] ...

The book includes interesting selections from a variety of cultures, eras, and genres.

Jade Flower Palace

Tu Fu

Translated by Kenneth Rexroth

The following poem seems to describe a scene that Tu Fu encountered in his travels. He uses verbal irony to give his description a subtle message. Think about what the underlying meaning of the poem might be as you read.

The stream swirls. The wind moans in
The pines. Gray rats scurry over
Broken tiles. What prince, long ago,
Built this palace, standing in
Ruins beside the cliffs? There are
Green ghost fires in the black rooms.
The shattered pavements are all
Washed away. Ten thousand organ
Pipes whistle and roar. The storm
Scatters the red autumn leaves.
His dancing girls are yellow dust.
Their painted cheeks have crumbled
Away. His gold chariots
And courtiers are gone. Only

A stone horse is left of his
Glory. I sit on the grass and
Start a poem, but the pathos of
It overcomes me. The future
Slips imperceptibly away.
Who can say what the years will bring?

Discussion questions guide you toward higher-order thinking skills and ask you to evaluate selections based on a biblical worldview.

About the Poem

Borges describes a sunset in his poem. How does the title of the po
Describe the atmosphere of Borges's poem.
What serves as the major symbol of the poem? What meaning do
In your own words, explain the theme of the poem.
Borges describes a common human reaction. If a person trusts
would his or her reaction differ from what Borges describes?

Full-color illustrations and photographs throughout not only add visual interest but also reinforce theme and tone.

About the Author

Born in Buenos Aires, Jorge Luis Borges (1899–1986) grew up in a middle-class family. He enjoyed a close relationship with his parents and younger sister, Norah. His father's library was made available to him early on, and Borges considered this access the most important experience in his life. He started writing at age six and, because his was a bilingual home, could read Shakespeare in English by age twelve.

In 1914 the family relocated to Geneva, Switzerland, where Borges's father received treatment for an eye disease that eventually claimed his sight. Borges inherited the disease, succumbing in time to the same fate. Once blind, Borges found that he more often wrote poetry because he could retain and modify the whole piece in his head.

After schooling in Geneva, Borges traveled to Spain, where he aligned himself with the avant-garde ultraist literary movement. In 1921 he returned to Argentina and began publishing poems, essays, and short stories. In addition, Borges's writing career included literary criticism, screenplays, and translations. His positions through the years included work as a librarian, a lecturer, and eventually a professor of literature at the University of Buenos Aires.

Borges's works have an element of unreality. They oppose nineteenth century realism/naturalism but combine realistic and fantastic elements, contributing to the genre of magical realism. Borges's first collection of short stories, *The Garden of Forking Paths*, combines text and maze. Though the work was successful, Borges did not receive the literary awards for it that many thought he would. He did, however, among other awards, receive the International Publishers' Prize and the Miguel de Cervantes Literature Award, Spain's highest literary honor. Though Borges was on the forefront of Latin American literature and its spread to the world at large, the Nobel Prize always eluded him, a fact that brought personal disappointment.

When information is available, a brief biographical sketch of the author accompanies the selection, alerting you to author purpose and philosophy.

Both contemporary and classic authors are featured.

Why the Leaves Turn Color in the Fall

DIANE ACKERMAN

The following excerpt is taken from *A Natural History of the Senses*. Though basically explaining a natural phenomenon, this scientific essay, with its imaginative comparisons, sound devices, and concrete imagery, rises to the level of literature. Be alert for points where the essay deviates from science and enters the area of personal opinion. Does the essay make a point?

The stealth of autumn catches one unaware. Was that a goldfinch perching in the early September woods, or just the first turning leaf? A red-winged blackbird or a sugar maple closing up shop for the winter? Keen-eyed as leopards, we stand still and squint hard, looking for signs of movement. Early-morning frost sits heavily on the grass, and turns barbed wire into a string of stars. On a distant hill, a small square of yellow appears to be a lighted stage. At last the truth dawns on us: Fall is staggering in, right on schedule, with its baggage of chilly nights, macabre* holidays, and spectacular, heart-stoppingly beautiful leaves. Soon the leaves will start cringing on the trees, and roll up in clenched fists before they actually fall off. Dry seedpods will rattle like tiny gourds. But first there will be weeks of gushing color so bright, so pastel, so confettilike, that people will travel up and down the East Coast just to stare at it—a whole season of leaves.

macabre: frightful, ghastly

Where do the colors come from? Sunlight rules most living things with its golden edicts. When the days begin to shorten, soon after the summer solstice on June 21, a tree reconsiders its leaves. All summer it feeds them so they can process sunlight, but in the dog days of summer the tree begins pulling nutrients back into its trunk and roots, pares down, and gradually chokes off its leaves. A corky layer of cells forms at the leaves' slender petioles,* then scars over. Undernourished, the leaves stop producing the pigment chlorophyll,* and photosynthesis* ceases. Animals can migrate, hibernate, or store food to prepare for winter. But where can a tree go? It survives by dropping its leaves, and by the end of autumn only a few fragile threads of fluid-carrying xylem* hold leaves to their stems.

petioles: the stalk attaching a leaf to a stem
chlorophyll: green pigment found in plants
photosynthesis: the process by which plants produce food from su...
xylem: the woody, wa...

WHY THE LEAVES TUR...

Each selection includes a brief headnote tying it to literary concepts being studied.

Glosses identify difficult or unfamiliar words and provide definitions or explanations.

Occurring twice in every unit, Thinking Zones introduce additional literary terms valuable to your growing skills in literary criticism.

Questions specifically apply the literary terms and concepts presented in the Thinking Zone to the preceding selections.

THINKING ZONE

In the classic Japanese film *Rashomon*, police trying to solve a murder interview various witnesses. Each witness tells his version of events, but these differ so much that determining the truth is difficult. The film illustrates an important fact: perspective matters. A person's view of life depends on the vantage point—physical, spiritual, or emotional—from which he sees it. In similar fashion, writers can change a story almost beyond recognition simply by changing its point of view.

Literary **point of view** signifies the perspective from which the author presents the conflicts, characters, and events of a story. Generally, point of view is categorized by how much the narrator knows of events and of other characters' inner lives. Critics primarily distinguish between narrators who refer to all the characters in the third person (*she, he, they*) and those who speak from a first-person perspective (i.e., use the pronoun *I*). By choosing one over the other, an author may both expand and contract the kind of information that he is able to relate (or relate reliably) to his audience.

Third-person perspectives (of wh... are two) offer the greatest liberty to rel... mation. In the **omniscient** point of v... storyteller knows all. He can describe ... ting, event, or conversation pertaining... story and can even tell what every cha... thinking and feeling. A narrator with a **li...** **omniscient** viewpoint does the same, ex... can "get inside the head" of only one cha...

In contrast, a **first-person** narrato... character in the story and can see, hea... and know only what that character does... approach limits access to information... events or other characters but deepens... ers' knowledge of one character. A first-p... narrator can be much easier to relate to... everything is seen from his perspective... such narrators can also be unreliable: they... be deceived, blinded by prejudice, or limite... their distance from events or inability to un... stand what others are thinking. In any cas... is clear that an author's chosen point of v... strongly influences the development of cha... ter, conflict, and theme as well as tone.

1. Which of the four short stories in this unit is narrated from a **first-person** perspective?
2. The remaining three stories are all written from which **point of view**?
3. In "The Sire de Maletroit's Door" how does the point of view chosen by the author affect readers' sympathy with the characters?
4. In "The Adventure of th...

Each Unit Review helps you prepare for unit tests through challenging short answer, true/false, and essay questions.

UNIT I REVIEW

Remember the Terms

Review the following terms from "Marks and Modes of Literature," "Imaginative Comparison," and the Thinking Zone pages. Be prepared to discuss their meanings and uses.

theme
figurative language
simile
metaphor
repetition
parallelism
euphony
cacophony
imagery
tenor
vehicle
implied metaphors
extended metaphors
allegory
metonymy
synecdoche
personification
apostrophe
paradox
conceit

Apply the Concepts

Answer the following questions about how the literary concepts you have studied are used in this unit.

1. At the end of Emily Dickinson's poem, "A Bird Came Down the Walk," the poet compares the bird's flight to a ship's sailing and butterflies' flying. What is Dickinson trying to communicate about the bird through these metaphors?
2. Identify the tenor and the vehicle in the following quotation by Emily Dickinson:

   I offered him a Crumb / And he unrolled his feathers / And rowed him softer home—
3. What effect does Dickinson's use of the pronouns *he* and *his* in "A Bird Came Down the Walk" have on the poem?
4. Explain the allegory in "The Nightingale and the Glowworm."
5. Which of the imaginative comparison techniques studied in Unit 1 most effectively enabled Twain to achieve humor in "What Stumped the Bluejays"?
6. What technique studied does the following quotation from "The Return of the Rangers" illustrate?

   "I've often seen you," the man said, swallowing. "It's hard to believe!" He shook his head. "We heard you was dead, Major; and I guess it's true! You was!"
7. What imaginary comparison studied does the following quotation from "The Return of the Rangers" illustrate?

   We hurrie… …ur rusty muskets, our soaked and tattered rags of blankets, …ments that now were rubbish; then, taking Billy by his …d him to the bank, where he lay all asprawl, no better than a

The following quotation from "The Return of the Rangers" illustrates <u>imagery</u>.

I joined Ogden, and together we clung to the rope. The raft plucked insistently at it, as if eager to be gone from us.

As illustrated in the following quotation, Kenneth Roberts's use of <u>parallelism</u> provides rhythm and movement, polishes his style, and accumulates realistic details, all of which aid his effective communication in the story.

Then we inched a log to the bank, tumbled it to the shingle, and worried it into the stream.

25. Langston Hughes in his poem "Mother to Son" makes use of a <u>simile</u> to communicate his theme.
26. Herbert's "The Windows" is an <u>implied metaphor</u>.
27. In "The Windows" the "brittle crazy glass" is the <u>preacher</u>.
28. The following verse from John 1 contains an example of <u>allegory</u>.

    Hereafter ye shall see heaven open, and the angels of God ascending and descending upon the Son of man.

Write a Response

Completely answer each of the following questions.

29. Compare the purpose of personification in Twain's "What Stumped the Bluejays" and Cowper's "The Nightingale and the Glowworm."
30. "The Soul's Dark Cottage" and "Mother to Son" offer either insight or advice from the perspective of age. Summarize the advice or insight briefly and then judge its value.
31. Paraphrase the last stanza of "The Windows" by George Herbert.

    Doctrine and life, colors and light, in one
    When they combine and mingle, bring
    A strong regard and awe: but speech alone
    Doth vanish like a flaring thing,
    And in the ear, not conscience ring.

Practice in essay writing helps you personally synthesize and articulate what you have learned throughout the unit.

PART ONE

THE MARKS AND MODES OF LITERATURE

At some point in your study of literature, you likely have wondered, "What exactly makes literature special? What separates my grocery list or Aunt Betty's poetry or even current bestsellers from the literature I study in school?" Identifying lasting works will always be a complex task, but critics do acknowledge several marks of great literature. The core mark of great writing and one that in many ways governs all other aspects of literature is that of **theme** (recurring or emerging ideas in a work). The previous books in this series—*Explorations in Literature*, *Excursions in Literature*, and *Fundamentals of Literature*—have covered theme in detail. But we will naturally return to this element throughout this book.

Imaginative Comparison, Sound and Syntax

In the following units you will study two additional marks of great literature: the skillful use of imaginative comparison and the deliberate organization of sound and syntax (word order). Using these elements, great writers craft language to clarify and attract attention to their ideas. Both are often achieved by using artful deviations from literal speech or normal word order. These may be collectively referred to as **figurative language**. You are probably already familiar with **simile** (a comparison of two things stated using the words *like*, *as*, or *as if*) and **metaphor** (the stated or implied equivalence of two dissimilar things). Both are figures of thought used in the service of imaginative comparison. While often associated with comparison alone, figurative language also encompasses techniques of sound and syntax.

Organization of Sound and Syntax

Effective organization of the sound and syntax of English occurs in a variety of ways. The techniques employed are usually less obvious than those of comparison, but their effects on readers or listeners can nonetheless be very strong. The principles of **repetition** and **parallelism** (similarity in the structure of two or more phrases, clauses, or sentences) govern many such methods and serve to highlight and emphasize ideas. In fact, many simple proverbs and pithy sayings use these principles to aid memorization. Consider one of Benjamin Franklin's famous sayings: "A penny saved is a penny earned." The repetition of "penny" and the parallel syntax of "penny saved" and "penny earned" make this statement easy to recall. In a more subtle approach, the repetition of sounds can reinforce an author's message by reinforcing a specific mood. Here writers make use of the general principles of euphony and cacophony. **Euphony** refers to words that are pleasant and musical to the ear. **Cacophony** describes language generating the opposite effect, that of harshness or dissonance.

A Biblical Illustration

To illustrate imaginative comparison and sound and syntax, consider the first poem ever created by man. It is recorded in Genesis 2:23 as Adam's response to his first sight of Eve, his wife. Though translation generally diffuses sound devices, the imaginative comparison and carefully calculated syntax remain.

This [lit. "this one"] is now bone of my
  bones, and flesh of my flesh:
she ["this one"] shall be called Woman [lit.
  "From Man"],
because she ["this one"] was taken out of [or
  "from"] Man.

Adam says, "This one is for me. She is from man, and therefore 'From Man' will be her name." His response is scientific, defining and naming a new creature. But it is also imaginative and artful, inspired by love at first sight. We might compare his response to a dictionary-like definition of *woman* as "a human female adult." Adam's definition has a similar meaning but expresses it indirectly through an imaginative comparison. He uses two types of imaginative comparison: metaphor (saying that Eve is his bone and flesh) and synecdoche (using his bone and flesh to stand for all of him). Obviously Eve is not Adam's actual bone and flesh anymore, nor is he bone and flesh alone. But depicting her in this way helps to emphasize an important truth: the spiritual oneness of man and woman in marriage. This truth is restated in direct terms in the next verse.

Notice also that Adam's poem, besides being imaginative, has a pleasing symmetry. The sentence structure divides the poem into halves, each being a complete statement. Each half is divided again into a pair of lines. In the first pair of lines, the idea and syntax of "bone of my bones" is repeated in "flesh of my flesh." In the second pair the phrase "from man" is repeated, and the lines are logically linked as cause (line 4) and effect (line 3). The four lines of the poem therefore are linked by syntax, sound, and sense (meaning). The result is a unified imaginative expression of a great truth. Clearly, well-crafted language can add great beauty and emotional force to the expression of ideas.

Allusion, Symbol, Irony

The three marks of literature (theme, imaginative comparison, and organized sound and syntax) will always be present in serious literature. In addition, several modes of expression often appear with great frequency: allusion, symbol, and irony. These will be covered in units 3 and 4. Each involves ways of speaking in which more meaning is intended than may appear at first glance. These layers of meaning lend subtlety to a writer's theme and add depth and richness to any work. Interestingly, these modes are also frequently used in everyday speech, far more often than techniques of sound and syntax. Carefully controlled and directed, they enrich the imaginative writing we call literature.

These marks and modes of literature appear most frequently in poetry, writing that is imaginative and artfully shaped. In fact, to the extent that writing has imaginative comparisons and patterned syntax, sound, and sense, we say that it is poetic, whether or not it is written in rhymed lines. Units 1–4 illustrate all of these marks and modes with both poetry and prose, for both can display the imagination and artistry of the best literature. As you read, consider the poetic qualities of the prose selections included and note how newly introduced literary elements support the prominent themes of each work. Above all, remember that both poetry and prose are means by which God teaches and persuades us in Scripture.

UNIT I

CHRISTINA'S WORLD
Andrew Wyeth

IMAGINATIVE COMPARISON

American artist Andrew Wyeth (1917–2009) painted Christina's World *in 1948. The work was inspired by Christina Olson, a neighbor who suffered from polio that paralyzed her lower body. In this moving realist-style work, a woman sits stretched on the ground in a golden-brown field, pulling herself toward a weathered house on the horizon.*

Wyeth reinterprets the determination and vigor of the Maine spirit through Christina's disability. His image of Christina's clutching the land and leaning toward home is often seen as a metaphor for the Maine spirit: Wyeth called the message of the painting the "extraordinary conquest of a life which most people would consider hopeless."[†]

Christina's solitary placement in the painting's foreground serves as a metaphor for the isolation of Maine residents. She appears strong and determined despite her frailty. She grips the ground in a way that shows her a possessor of this rugged yet serene landscape.

The painting's palette echoes the tranquility and austerity of Christina's world. She sits in grass dappled with lights and darks, gazing toward the horizon. The nearly glowing field ahead of her leads toward the house—a palette that reveals the subject's bright outlook.

- What do you think is happening in the painting?
- What other imaginative comparisons are evident in *Christina's World*?
- If Christina could talk, what might she say?

[†]"Andrew Wyeth. *Christina's World*. 1948." *MeetMe: Module Three: Modern Portraits*. Museum of Modern Art, n.d. Web. 13 April 2011.

IMAGINATIVE COMPARISON

Have you ever tried to communicate an experience or idea only to find yourself at a loss for words? If so, you probably compared your subject to something familiar that evoked the same feeling or that functioned similarly. In other words, you used imaginative comparison. Though sometimes less clear-cut than literal description, imaginative comparison exceeds it in richness and depth of meaning. Comparisons use **imagery** (words or phrases that appeal to sense perceptions) to describe one thing in terms of another, both delighting readers and bridging gaps of understanding that literal language often cannot. For these reasons, the skillful use of imaginative comparison has become a hallmark of literary writing.

Meaning, Emotion, and Depth

Good comparisons often convey more concrete meanings than purely literal descriptions can. In "Sonnet 18," Shakespeare asks, "Shall I compare thee to a Summer's day?" Since everyone has experienced the beauty and heat of summer, Shakespeare's conclusion—"Thou art more lovely and more temperate"—is a judgment readers can relate to. Referencing such a universal experience evokes a more specific meaning than calling a person beautiful or even-tempered would.

Comparisons also elicit vivid emotions. They allow writers to summon images that carry strong or specific emotions and redirect those emotions to the topic. For example, Shakespeare refers to jealousy, an abstract emotion, as "the green-ey'd monster, which doth mock / The meat it feeds on" (*Othello*, act 3, scene 3). "Monster" becomes the perfect image for jealousy, provoking horror of such a being to reinforce how repulsive, frightening, and destructive that emotion can be.

In addition, comparisons add depth to a writer's message. Each invokes numerous potential meanings since the objects compared may be similar in many ways. And the author may wish to convey more than one of those meanings. Consider Psalm 23. The poem begins with a metaphor—"The Lord is my shepherd"—to which the poet responds "I shall not want." To a reader familiar with shepherding, this response already makes sense. Such a reader can infer many applications of this metaphor even if he does not read on. By leaving the comparison open, an author packs many ideas into a short space of text.

Delight and Symmetry

Finally, imaginative comparisons quite simply delight readers. The humor, aptness, or originality of particular comparisons captures our fancy. These may allow us to see commonplace topics in a new way. An example of all three virtues occurs in Charles Dickens's *A Christmas Carol*. The narrator describes Ebenezer Scrooge as being "as solitary as an oyster." Dickens uses a commonplace object in a unique and comical way, yet it remains startlingly apt as well. Scrooge is in oysterlike isolation within his miser's shell. This inventive comparison adds to our understanding and enjoyment of the story.

Less obviously, comparisons sometimes delight by creating symmetry. Using similar imagery throughout a passage, an author creates a satisfying sense of unity. Even short passages can reflect such unity. In Psalm 84:6, the psalmist calls people who trust in God ones "who passing through the valley of Baca [of tears] make it a well; the rain also filleth the pools." Though God's servant may go through troubles (tears), these will become places of spiritual refreshment (a well) and fruitfulness (rain). Water imagery unifies the message, yet each comparison seems suited to its purpose, not forced. Sometimes similar imagery twines throughout an entire work, reinforcing a larger theme.

Figurative Language

Imaginative comparisons are frequently drawn using various types of figurative language. You have already learned two primary methods of comparison—simile and metaphor. Metaphor can be further studied by examining tenor and vehicle. The **tenor** of a metaphor is the original subject being described. The **vehicle** is the image the tenor is being compared to. Sometimes the tenor of a metaphor remains unstated but can be deduced through the context. For example, the Bible records that, seeing Jesus approach, John the Baptist announced, "Behold the Lamb of God, which taketh away the sin of the world" (John 1:29). John used a vehicle (a lamb) that both evoked the ancient sacrificial system and pointed to Jesus as God's ultimate sacrifice for the sins of the world. Though the tenor (Jesus) remains unstated, the meaning of the metaphor is nonetheless clear. Metaphors like this which are indirectly conveyed are often called **implied metaphors**. These can surface not just in nouns but also in other parts of speech. For example, if two people are said to "fence with words," the verb implies a comparison of each person to a fencer and their conversation to a bout of sword fighting.

Metaphors developed beyond a single sentence or comparison are referred to as **extended metaphor**. Some poems are based entirely on extended metaphor, as in Psalm 23. This approach allows the writer to explore a particularly apt comparison at length and gives unity to the imagery of a work. A particularly complex type of extended metaphor, **allegory**, forms an entire story with two or more levels of meaning. Read literally, the narrative makes sense, but its components also stand for other ideas or even real people and events. George Orwell's novella *Animal Farm* recounts the story of a group of animals that overthrow their oppressive farmer and begin to govern themselves. Sadly, the leaders grow corrupt and eventually surpass the oppressive behavior of the farmer. Written to reflect and to reject the rise of Stalinism, the story accurately represents historical events but remains engaging on the literal level too. Even readers unaware of the underlying history may easily grasp important themes, such as the hypocrisy of the corrupt ideals or the necessity of personal integrity and responsibility.

Several indirect methods of comparison are also available to writers. **Metonymy** is an expression in which a related thing stands for the thing itself. For example, the prophet Nathan uses metonymy to deliver God's judgment on David, saying, "The sword shall never depart from thine [David's] house" (2 Sam. 12:10). Here *sword* stands for intense conflict. David's *house* stands for his family. In similar fashion **synecdoche** uses a part of something to stand for the whole. Ecclesiastes 9:10 provides a familiar example of synecdoche: "Whatsoever thy hand findeth to do, do it with thy might." *Hand* stands for the whole person because it is the part of one's anatomy most associated with hard work.

As you read the selections in this unit, note the way in which literature of imagination differs from literature of information. In particular, try to pinpoint how imaginative comparisons add richness and precision to the ideas they represent. As you note each comparison, ask why an author used it. How does it support the author's message? At the same time, do not forget to enjoy the beauty, ingenuity, and humor reflected in comparisons. After all, they are part of the message too.

A Bird Came Down the Walk

EMILY DICKINSON

In the poems of Emily Dickinson, the common creatures of nature—the birds, butterflies, and other inhabitants of a New England garden—appear as personalities. Obviously Dickinson takes such "personalities" seriously. Her careful selection of detail and her extraordinary imaginative comparisons help to convince us of their importance too. While scrutinizing them through the poet's eyes, we are also examining human life. In the following poem, the poet is not only observing but also being observed, and both perspectives seem valid.

A Bird, came down the Walk—
He did not know I saw—
He bit an Angle Worm in halves
And ate the fellow, raw,

And then, he drank a Dew
From a convenient Grass—
And then hopped sidewise to the Wall
To let a Beetle pass—

He glanced with rapid eyes,
That hurried all abroad—
They looked like frightened Beads, I thought,
He stirred his Velvet Head.—

Like one in danger, Cautious,
I offered him a Crumb,
And he unrolled his feathers,*
And rowed him softer Home—

unrolled . . . feathers: i.e., as mariners unroll sails

Than Oars divide the Ocean,
Too silver for a seam,
Or Butterflies, off Banks of Noon,
Leap, plashless as they swim.

About the Poem

1. Dickinson's poem transforms a seemingly trivial incident into a memorable event. List at least three specific details she gives that capture reader interest and make the event vivid.
2. Did Emily Dickinson's poem make you see anything about God's creation that you had not seen before?
3. What metaphors can be found in the poem? Name the tenor and vehicle for each.
4. Where does Dickinson use synecdoche in the poem?
5. What emotions does Dickinson elicit with her comparisons?

About the Author

The legendary reclusiveness of Emily Dickinson (1830–86) often overshadows other details of her life. In reality, the eccentric poet formed more than a few solid friendships with scholarly men and women who acted as mentors, literary critics, and confidants. For example, Dickinson and Col. T. W. Higginson of the *Atlantic Monthly* enjoyed a lifelong friendship, which provided valuable literary criticism and mental challenges.

Another notable influence in Dickinson's life was Professor Hitchcock, a teacher and unflagging lover of nature. As a young woman, Dickinson loved to take long walks and enjoy the beauty and unique charm of her home in Amherst, Massachusetts. Her best poetry synthesizes the mental images and deep emotions connected with this region, which at that time was still rural. Hitchcock encouraged this quality and often organized field trips for his students and friends. This innovative method of teaching brought him criticism but succeeded in giving those like Dickinson a sound background in scientific observation that later proved useful. Indeed, Dickinson's observation of nature both inspired her and provided her with many imaginative comparisons of great charm and force.

The professor also influenced Dickinson's religious views. Hitchcock believed in the immortality of the soul because of the principle of rebirth he saw in the cycle of seasons. Dickinson absorbed these ideas and later used them in her poems. During her stay at Holyoke Female Seminary, Dickinson learned of Christ but wrote to her friend Abiah Root of her inability to make a decision for Him: she could not settle "the one thing needful." Although she used the Bible as a source of poetic inspiration, a thorough study of Dickinson's works indicates that she likely never made that needful decision. Sadly, she seemed unwilling to accept God's love or Christ's deity, much less the gift of salvation.

The Spider and the Wasp

ALEXANDER PETRUNKEVITCH

The Russian-American zoologist Alexander Petrunkevitch (1875–1964) gave most of his life to the study of spiders. His best-known essay proves that scientific writing can rise to the level of literature. Notice that as literature of information, rather than of imagination, it makes little use of imaginative comparisons. There is one prominent simile, however. Can you find it?

To hold its own struggle for existence, every species of animal must have a regular source of food, and if it happens to live on other animals, its survival may be very delicately balanced. The hunter cannot exist without the hunted; if the latter should perish from the earth, the former would, too. When the hunted also prey on some of the hunters, the matter may become complicated.

This is nowhere better illustrated than in the insect world. Think of the complexity of a situation such as the following: There is a certain wasp, *Pimpla inquisitor*, whose larvae feed on the larvae of the tussock moth. *Pimpla* larvae in turn serve as food for the larvae of a second wasp, and the latter in their turn nourish still a third wasp. What subtle balance between fertility and mortality must exist in the case of each of these four species to prevent the extinction of all of them! An excess of mortality over fertility in a single member of the group would ultimately wipe out all four.

This is not a unique case. The two great orders of insects, Hymenoptera and Diptera, are full of such examples of interrelationship. And the spiders (which are not insects but members of a separate order of arthropods) also are killers and victims of insects.

The picture is complicated by the fact that those species which are carnivorous in the larval stage have to be provided with animal food by a vegetarian mother. The survival of the young depends on the mother's correct choice of a food which she does not eat herself.

In the feeding and safeguarding of their progeny the insects and spiders exhibit some interesting analogies to reasoning and some crass examples of blind instinct. The case I propose to describe here is that of the tarantula spiders and their archenemy, the digger wasps of the genus Pepsis. It is a classic example of what looks like intelligence pitted against instinct—a strange situation in which the victim, though fully able to defend itself, submits unwittingly to its destruction.

Most tarantulas live in the Tropics, but several species occur in the temperate zone and a few are common in the southern U.S. Some varieties are large and have powerful fangs with which they can inflict a deep wound. These formidable looking spiders do not, however, attack man; you can hold one in your hand, if you are gentle, without being bitten. Their bite is dangerous only to insects and small mammals such as mice; for a man it is no worse than a hornet's sting.

Tarantulas customarily live in deep cylindrical burrows, from which they emerge at dusk and into which they retire at dawn. Mature males wander about after dark in search of females and occasionally stray into houses. After mating, the male dies in a few weeks, but a female lives much longer and can mate several years in succession. In a Paris museum is a tropical specimen which is said to have been in captivity for 25 years.

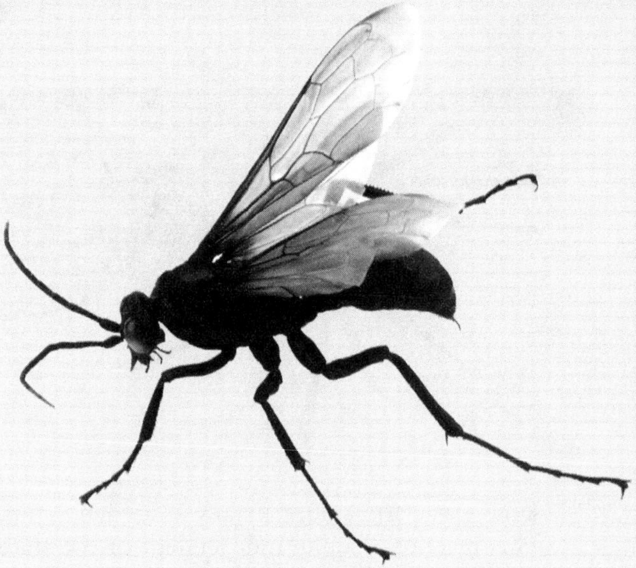

A fertilized female tarantula lays from 200 to 400 eggs at a time; thus it is possible for a single tarantula to produce several thousand young. She takes no care of them beyond weaving a cocoon of silk to enclose the eggs. After they hatch, the young walk away, find convenient places in which to dig their burrows and spend the rest of their lives in solitude. Tarantulas feed mostly on insects and millepedes. Once their appetite is appeased, they digest the food for several days before eating again. Their sight is poor, being limited to sensing a change in the intensity of light and to perception of moving objects. They apparently have little or no sense of hearing, for a hungry tarantula will pay no attention to a loudly chirping cricket placed in its cage unless the insect happens to touch one of its legs.

But all spiders, and especially hairy ones, have an extremely delicate sense of touch. Laboratory experiments prove that tarantulas can distinguish three types of touch: pressure against the body wall, stroking of the body hair and riffling of certain fine hairs on the legs called trichobothria. Pressure against the body by a finger or the end of a pencil, causes the tarantula to move off slowly for a short distance. The touch excites no defensive response unless the approach is from above where the spider can see the motion, in which case it rises on its hind legs, lifts its front legs, opens its fangs and holds this threatening posture as long as the object continues to move. When the motion stops, the spider drops back to the ground, remains quiet for a few seconds and then moves slowly away.

The entire body of a tarantula, especially its legs, is thickly clothed with hair. Some of it is short and woolly, some long and stiff. Touching this body hair produces one of two distinct reactions. When the spider is hungry, it responds with an immediate and swift attack. At the touch of a cricket's antennae the tarantula seizes the insect so swiftly that a motion picture taken at the rate of 64 frames per second shows only the result and not the process of capture. But when the spider is not hungry, the stimulation merely causes it to shake the touched limb.

The trichobothria, very fine hairs growing from disklike membranes on the legs, were once thought to be the spider's hearing organs, but we now know that they have nothing to do with sound. They are sensitive only to air movement. A light breeze makes them vibrate slowly without disturbing the common hair. When one blows gently on the trichobothria, the tarantula reacts with a quick jerk of its four front legs. If the front and hind legs are stimulated at the

same time, the spider makes a sudden jump. This reaction is quite independent of the state of its appetite.

These three tactile responses—to pressure on the body wall, to moving of the common hair and to flexing of the trichobothria—are so different from one another that there is no possibility of confusing them. They serve the tarantula adequately for most of its needs and enable it to avoid most annoyances and dangers. But they fail the spider completely when it meets its deadly enemy, the digger wasp Pepsis.

These solitary wasps are beautiful and formidable creatures. Most species are either a deep shiny blue all over, or a deep blue with rusty wings. The largest have a wing span of about four inches. They live on nectar. When excited, they give off a pungent odor—a warning that they are ready to attack. The sting is much worse than that of a bee or common wasp, and the pain and swelling last longer. In the adult stage the wasp lives only a few months. The female produces but a few eggs, one at a time at intervals of two or three days. For each egg the mother must provide one adult tarantula, alive but paralyzed. The tarantula must be of the correct species to nourish the larva. The mother wasp attaches the egg to the paralyzed spider's abdomen. Upon hatching from the egg, the larva is many hundreds of times smaller than its living but helpless victim. It eats no other food and drinks no water. By the time it has finished its single gargantuan meal and become ready for wasphood, nothing remains of the tarantula but its indigestible chitinous* skeleton.

chitinous: protective material of which insect exoskeletons are made

The mother wasp goes tarantula-hunting when the egg in her ovary is almost ready to be laid. Flying low over the ground late on a sunny afternoon, the wasp looks for its victim or for the mouth of a tarantula burrow, a round hole edged by a bit of silk. The sex of the spider makes no difference, but the mother is highly discriminating as to species. Each species of Pepsis requires a certain species of tarantula, and the wasp will not attack the wrong species. In a cage with a tarantula which is not its normal prey the wasp avoids the spider, and is usually killed by it in the night.

Yet when a wasp finds the correct species, it is the other way about. To identify the species the wasp apparently must explore the spider with her antennae. The tarantula shows an amazing toleration to this exploration. The wasp crawls under it and walks over it without evoking any hostile response. Having satisfied itself that the victim is the right species, the wasp moves off a few inches to dig the spider's grave. Working vigorously with legs and jaws, it excavates a hole 8 to 10 inches deep with a diameter slightly larger than the spider's girth. Now and again the wasp pops out of the hole to make sure that the spider is still there.

When the grave is finished, the wasp returns to the tarantula to complete her ghastly enterprise. First she feels it all over once more with her antennae. Then her behavior becomes more aggressive. She bends her abdomen, protruding her sting, and searches for the soft membrane at the point where the spider's leg joins its body—the only spot where she can penetrate the horny skeleton. From time to time, as the exasperated spider slowly shifts ground, the wasp turns on her back and slides along with the aid of her wings, trying to get under the tarantula for a shot at the vital spot. During all this maneuvering, which can last for several minutes, the tarantula makes no move to save itself. Finally the wasp corners it against some obstruction and grasps one of its legs in her powerful jaws. Now at last the harassed spider tries a desperate but vain defense. The two contestants roll over and over on the ground. It is a terrifying sight and the outcome is always the same. The wasp finally manages to thrust her sting into the soft spot and holds it there for a few seconds while she pumps in the poison. Almost immediately the tarantula falls paralyzed on its back. Its legs stop twitching; its heart stops beating. Yet it is not dead, as is shown by the fact that if taken from the wasp it can be restored to some sensitivity by being kept in a moist chamber for several months.

After paralyzing the tarantula, the wasp cleans herself by dragging her body along the ground and rubbing her feet, sucks the drop of blood oozing from the wound in the spider's abdomen, then grabs a leg of the flabby, helpless animal in her jaws and drags it down to the bottom of the grave. She stays there for many minutes, sometimes for several hours, and what she does all that time in the dark we do not know. Eventually she lays her egg and attaches it to the side of the spider's abdomen with a sticky secretion. Then she emerges, fills the grave with soil carried bit by bit in her jaws, and finally tramples the ground all around to hide any trace of the grave from prowlers. Then she flies away, leaving her descendant safely started in life.

In all this the behavior of the wasp evidently is qualitatively different from that of the spider. The wasp acts like an intelligent animal. This is not to say that instinct plays no part or that she reasons as man does. But her actions are to the point; they are not automatic and can be modified to fit the situation. We do not know for certain how she identifies the tarantula—probably it is by some olfactory* or chemo-tactile sense—but she does it purposefully and does not blindly tackle a wrong species.

olfactory: pertaining to smell

On the other hand, the tarantula's behavior shows only confusion. What makes the tarantula behave as stupidly as it does? No clear, simple answer is available. Possibly the stimulation by the wasp's antennae is masked by a heavier pressure on the spider's body, so that it reacts as when prodded by a pencil. But the explanation may be much more complex. Initiative in attack is not in the nature of tarantulas; most species fight only when cornered so that escape is impossible. Their inherited patterns of behavior apparently prompt them to avoid problems rather than attack them. For example, spiders always weave their webs in three dimensions, and when a spider finds that there is insufficient space to attach certain threads in the third dimension, it leaves the place and seeks another,

instead of finishing the web in a single plane. This urge to escape seems to arise under all circumstances, in all phases of life and to take the place of reasoning. For a spider to change the pattern of its web is as impossible as for an inexperienced man to build a bridge across a chasm obstructing his way.

In a way the instinctive urge to escape is not only easier but more efficient than reasoning. The tarantula does exactly what is most efficient in all cases except in an encounter with a ruthless and determined attacker dependent for the existence of her own species on killing as many tarantulas as she can lay eggs. Perhaps in this case the spider follows its usual pattern of trying to escape, instead of seizing and killing the wasp, because it is not aware of its danger. In any case, the survival of the tarantula species as a whole is protected by the fact that the spider is much more fertile than the wasp.

About the Essay

1. Petrunkevitch states, "For a spider to change the pattern of its web is as impossible as for an inexperienced man to build a bridge across a chasm obstructing his way." What two things are being compared using *as* (simile)?
2. Petrunkevitch states the thesis of his essay in paragraph five. What is this thesis?
3. Informative literature depends greatly on appropriate organization for its clarity. Briefly describe (in the order they occur) the four distinct sections of information apparent in Petrunkevitch's text.
4. From a biblical worldview, what possible answer could you give to Petrunkevitch's question, "What makes the tarantula behave as stupidly as it does?"

Alexander Petrunkevitch is obviously interested in, excited about, and even amazed by the beautiful complexity of nature. He comes close to worship in this piece—but only close. Take a look again at the introductory essay on Paul's use of Greek poets in Acts 17; now write a concluding paragraph for this essay that takes readers all the way to worship.

About the Author

Alexander Petrunkevitch (1875–1967) was one of the twentieth century's greatest experts in the study of spiders. Forced to leave his Russian homeland for political reasons, Petrunkevitch spent most of his life in the United States. This accomplished scholar held positions at Yale and at Indiana University and lectured at Harvard. He authored *A Synonymic Index Catalogue of Spiders of North, Central and South America*, as well as other works of interest to biologists, and in 1954 was elected a member of the National Academy of Science. In addition to his scientific writings, he wrote several philosophical works in German and translated English literature into his native Russian and Russian literature into English.

Little information is available in English about Petrunkevitch's views or lifestyle. It is clear that he was an astute observer capable of analyzing natural processes and explaining them with the flair of a storyteller. His talent in a language not his native tongue is apparent in his well-known essay "The Spider and the Wasp." It exhibits excellent form, smooth transitions between thoughts, and deft suspense-building narrative techniques. Petrunkevitch's meticulous scholarship combined with his ability to make scientific data readable give his works universal value.

The Nightingale and the Glowworm

William Cowper

This meeting of a nightingale with a glowworm is probably intended as a beast fable in the manner of Aesop. The moral is not directly stated, however. Notice that both the nightingale and the glowworm are creatures that "beautify and cheer the night." The one does so by song, the other by light. Probably they are meant to represent two traditional functions of poetry: joyous sound and wise illumination. As you read, think about what the moral of the poem might be.

A nightingale that all day long
Had cheer'd the village with his song,
Nor yet at eve his note suspended,
Nor yet when eventide was ended,
Began to feel, as well he might,
The keen demands of appetite;
When looking eagerly around,
He spied far off, upon the ground,
A something shining in the dark,
And knew the glowworm by his spark;
So, stooping down from hawthorn top,
He thought to put him in his crop.
The worm, aware of his intent,
Harangued him thus, right eloquent:
"Did you admire my lamp," quoth he,
"As much as I your minstrelsy,
You would abhor to do me wrong,
As much as I to spoil your song:
For 'twas the self-same Power Divine
Taught you to sing, and me to shine;
That you with music, I with light,
Might beautify and cheer the night."
The songster heard this short oration,
And warbling out his approbation,
Released him, as my story tells,
And found a supper somewhere else.

About the Poem

1. In your own words, supply a moral for Cowper's "fable."
2. What type of imaginative comparison does the glowworm use when he refers to his light as "my lamp"? What biblical comparison does this echo, and how might that echo contribute to the underlying meaning of the poem (see the headnote on page 14)?
3. What term from the unit introduction does this poem illustrate in an abbreviated form? Briefly explain your answer.
4. Why do you think Cowper chose to portray the nightingale as the one that feels (the pangs of hunger) and the glowworm as the one that reasons (in defense of his right to exist)?

About the Author

"God made the country, and man made the town." This famous quotation by English poet William Cowper (1731–1800) expresses his attitude toward nature and happiness. Like many other evangelical Christians of his day, Cowper asserted that country living was conducive to a virtuous life, for it provided a firsthand view of God's handiwork. Cowper tends to paint the peaceful, benevolent side of nature, and the nature imagery in his poem pictures the power and love of the Creator.

Considered by many the foremost English poet of his time, Cowper aimed for a simple style in his writings. Although he did not always succeed, he came closest to his goal in *The Task*, his longest and most important work. Also known as one of Christianity's great hymnodists, Cowper maintained a long-standing friendship with John Newton, another well-known English hymn writer and the author of "Amazing Grace." The consistency with which Cowper read and studied the Bible affected not only the tone but also the diction of his best poetry. Like many parts of Scripture, Cowper's poems display great power clothed in simple language.

What Stumped the Bluejays

MARK TWAIN

We do not usually think of Mark Twain (Samuel Clemens) as a poet. But much of his prose is highly poetic. In the following selection from *A Tramp Abroad,* Twain uses imaginative comparisons to make his prose vivid and appealing. In this selection, can you find any imaginative comparisons that Twain uses for humor?

Animals talk to each other, of course. There can be no question about that; but I suppose there are very few people who can understand them. I never knew but one man who could. I knew he could, however, because he told me so himself. He was a middle-aged, simple-hearted miner who had lived in a lonely corner of California, among the woods and mountains, a good many years, and had studied the ways of his only neighbors, the beasts and the birds, until he believed he could accurately translate any remark which they made. This was Jim Baker. According to Jim Baker, some animals have only a limited education, and use only very simple words, and scarcely ever a comparison or a flowery figure; whereas, certain other animals have a large vocabulary, a fine command of language and a ready and fluent delivery; consequently these latter talk a great deal; they like it; they are conscious of their talent, and they enjoy "showing off." Baker said, that after long and careful observation, he had come to the conclusion that the bluejays were the best talkers he had found among birds and beasts. Said he:

There's more *to* a bluejay than any other creature. He has got more moods, and more different kinds of feelings than other creatures; and, mind you, whatever a bluejay feels, he can put into language. And no mere commonplace language, either, but rattling, out-and-out book-talk—and bristling with metaphor, too—just bristling! And as for command of language—why *you* never see a bluejay get stuck for a word. No man ever did. They just boil out of him! And another thing: I've noticed a good deal, and there's no bird, or cow, or anything that uses as good grammar as a bluejay. You may say a cat uses good grammar. Well, a cat does—but you let a cat get excited once; you let a cat get to pulling fur with another cat on a shed, nights, and you'll hear grammar that will give you lockjaw. Ignorant people think it's the *noise* which fighting cats make that is so aggravating, but it ain't so; it's the sickening grammar they use. Now I've never heard a jay use bad grammar but very seldom; and when they do, they are as ashamed as a human; they shut right down and leave.

You may call a jay a bird. Well, so he is, in a measure—because he's got feathers on him; but otherwise he is just as much a human as you be. And I'll tell you for why. A jay's gifts, and instincts, and feelings, and interests, cover the whole ground. A jay hasn't got any more principle than a Congressman. A jay will lie, a jay will steal, a jay will deceive, a jay will betray; and four times out of five, a jay will go back on his solemnest promise. The sacredness of an obligation is a thing which you can't cram into no bluejay's head. Now, on top of all this, there's another thing; in the one little particular of scolding, a bluejay can lay over anything, human or divine. Yes, sir, a jay is everything that a man is. A jay can cry, a jay can laugh, a jay can feel shame, a jay can reason and plan and discuss, a jay likes gossip and scandal, a jay has got a sense of humor. If a jay ain't human, he better take in his sign, that's all. Now I'm going to tell you a perfectly true fact about some bluejays. When I first begun to understand jay language correctly, there was a little incident happened here. Seven years ago, the last man in this region but me moved away. There stands his house—been empty ever since; a log house, with a plank roof—just one big room, and no more; no ceiling—nothing between the rafters and the floor. Well, one Sunday morning I was sitting out here in front of my cabin, with my cat, taking the sun, and looking at the blue hills, and listening to the leaves rustling so lonely in the trees, and thinking of the home away yonder in the states, that I hadn't heard from in thirteen years, when a bluejay lit on that house, with an acorn in his mouth, and says, "Hello, I reckon I've struck something." When he spoke, the acorn dropped out of his mouth and rolled down the roof, of course, but he didn't care; his mind was all on the thing he had struck. It was a knothole in the roof. He cocked his head to one side, shut one eye and put the other one to the hole, like a possum looking down a jug; then he glanced up with his bright eyes, gave a wink or two with his wings—which signifies gratification, you understand—and says, "It looks like a hole, it's located like a hole—I believe it *is* a hole!"

Then he cocked his head down and took another look; he glances up perfectly joyful, this time; winks his wings and his tail both, and says, "Oh, no, this ain't no fat thing, I reckon! If I ain't in luck!—why it's a perfectly elegant hole!" So he flew down and got that acorn, and fetched it up and dropped it in, and was just tilting his head back, with the heavenliest smile on his face, when all of a sudden he was paralyzed into a listening attitude and that smile faded gradually out of his countenance like a breath off'n a razor, and the queerest look of surprise took its place. Then he says, "Why, I didn't hear it fall!" He cocked his eye at the hole again, and took a long look; raised up and shook his head; stepped around to the other side of the hole and took another look from that side; shook his head again. He studied awhile, then he just went into the *de*tails—walked round and round the hole and spied into it from every point of the compass. No use. Now he took a thinking attitude on the comb of the roof and scratched the back of his head with his right foot a minute, and finally says, "Well, it's too many for *me*, that's certain; must be a mighty long hole; however, I ain't got no time to fool around here, I got to 'tend to business; I reckon it's all right—chance it, anyway."

So he flew off and fetched another acorn and dropped it in, and tried to flirt his eye to the hole quick enough to see what become of it, but he was too late. He held his eye there as much as a minute; then he raised up and sighed, and says, "Confound it, I don't seem to understand this thing, no way; however, I'll tackle her again." He fetched another acorn, and done his level best to see what become of it, but he couldn't. He says, "Well, I never struck no such hole as this before; I'm of the opinion it's a totally new kind of a hole." Then he begun to get mad. He held in for a spell, walking up and down the comb of the roof and shaking his head and muttering to himself; but his feelings got the upper hand of him, presently, and he broke loose and yelled himself black in the face. I never see a bird take on so about a little thing. When he got through he walks to the hole and looks in again for half a minute; then he says, "Well, you're a long hole, and a deep hole, and a mighty singular hole altogether—but I've started in to fill you, and I *will* fill you, if it takes a hundred years!"

And with that, away he went. You never see a bird work so since you was born. The way he hove acorns into that hole for about two hours and a half was one of the most exciting and astonishing spectacles I ever struck. He never stopped to take a look any more—he just hove 'em in and went for more. Well, at last he could hardly flop his wings, he was so tuckered out. He comes a-drooping down, once more, sweating like an ice-pitcher, drops his acorn in and says, "*Now* I guess I've got the bulge on you by this time!" So he bent down for a look. If you'll believe me, when his head come up again he was just pale with rage. He says, "I've shoveled acorns enough in there to keep the family thirty years, and if I can see a sign of one of 'em I wish I may land in a museum with a belly full of sawdust in two minutes!"

He just had strength enough to crawl up on to the comb and lean his back agin the chimbly, and then he collected his impressions and begun to free his mind. I see in a second what I mistook for a fit o' rage in the mines was only just the rudiments, as you may say.

Another jay was going by, and heard him, and stops to inquire what was up. The sufferer told him the whole circumstance, and says, "Now yonder's the hole, and if you don't believe me, go and look for yourself." So this fellow went and looked, and comes back and says, "How many did you say you put in there?" "Not any less than two tons," says the sufferer. The other jay went and looked again. He couldn't seem to make it out, so he raised a yell, and three more jays come. They all examined the hole, they all made the sufferer tell it over again, then they all discussed it, and got off as many leather-headed opinions about it as an average crowd of humans could have done.

They called in more jays; then more and more, till pretty soon this whole region 'peared to have blue flush about it. There must have been five thousand of them; and such another jawing and disputing, you never heard. Every jay in the whole lot put his eye to the hole and delivered a more chuck-headed opinion about the mystery than the jay that went there before him. They examined the house all over, too. The door was standing half open, and at last one old jay happened to go and light on it and look in. Of course, that knocked the mystery galley-west* in a second. There lay the acorns, scattered all over the floor. He flopped his wings and raised a whoop. "Come here!" he says, "Come here, everybody; hang'd if this fool hasn't been trying to fill up a house with acorns!" They all came a-swooping down like a blue cloud, and as each fellow lit on the door and took a glance, the whole absurdity of the contract that that first jay had tackled hit him home and he fell over backward suffocating with laughter, and the next jay took his place and done the same.

galley-west: to pieces

Well, sir, they roosted around here on the housetop and the trees for an hour, and guffawed over that thing like human beings. It ain't any use to tell me a bluejay hasn't got a sense of humor, because I know better. And memory, too. They brought jays here from all over the United States to look down that hole, every summer for three years. Other birds, too. And they could all see the point, except an owl that come from Nova Scotia to visit Yo Semite, and he took this thing in on his way back. He said he couldn't see anything funny in it. But then he was a good deal disappointed about Yo Semite, too.

About the Story

1. List two similes in Twain's story. What is the effect of each?
2. In this story Twain touches on common human experiences in his use of imaginative comparison. Point out two comparisons that struck you as very true and familiar. Explain your answer.
3. Obviously, the selection is written "tongue-in-cheek." At what point in the story are you convinced of the storyteller's facetious or playful intent? Cite a specific phrase or sentence from the story to support your answer.
4. How does the use of dialect (dialogue written to reflect qualities of a character's speech) affect the tone of Twain's piece?
5. What truth in the first chapter of Genesis best explains the gap between man's abilities and animals' abilities?

About the Author

As a boy, Mark Twain (1835–1910) was the prototype of the central characters he created in his famous novels *Huckleberry Finn* and *Tom Sawyer.* He reveled in the rugged frontier life of his boyhood home, and his childhood adventures in Hannibal, Missouri, live on in the pages of these books. Twain is beloved for his tremendous wit and humor in bringing the American Deep South and West to life. Many of his stories delight by deftly revealing the ridiculous in everyday people and events. Others bend a satiric gaze on the sometimes difficult social issues in the regions he evoked.

Twain's tone, however, is not always good-natured. His cynical side is most clearly stated in his philosophical writings. Twain believed that morality and the Bible were human inventions. He asserts that people are shaped by environment and education. Having denied God's revelation to man through Scripture, Twain naturally denied the individual's accountability to God.

Twain's outlook was both self-centered and ultimately hopeless. Denying that he was created in the image of God, Twain sought to rid himself of feeling any responsibility to his Creator. Unfortunately, Twain's skepticism often seems less the honest questioning of a seeker of truth and more the deliberate defiance of a self-professed rebel.

THINKING ZONE

Two additional techniques of imaginative comparison occur commonly in literature. Both are implied rather than directly stated comparisons. **Personification** gives human characteristics to something that is not human. For example, James Ullman, in his short story "Top Man," describes mountain K3 as seeming "less to tower than to crouch—a white hooded giant, secret and remote, but living. Living and on guard." Using personification, Ullman infuses not only life but also menace into K3. The mountain appears as an enemy that plots and strategizes—watching, waiting, and then malignantly hurling snow at the mountain climbers. The comparison is communicated not only through nouns and adjectives but also through verbs and verbals. Used throughout the story, personification enables Ullman to emphasize a major conflict between the mountain and the expedition.

In "Snow-Bound" John Greenleaf Whittier creates an opposite effect using personification. Whittier creates a scene in which the "throat of the chimney laugh[s]" as the family gravitates to the hearth in the evening to weather the storm amid warmth and inviting smells.

In addition to helping set the mood, personification makes language more lively. In Isaiah 55:12, the mountains and hills "break forth . . . into singing, and all the trees of the field . . . clap their hands." The reference is, of course, figurative.

Apostrophe, a related concept, refers to literature that addresses an absent person, abstraction, or object. Apostrophe can make an abstraction relatable. A good example of both apostrophe and personification is John Donne's "Holy Sonnet 10," which begins with the famous line "Death, be not proud." Throughout the poem, the speaker directly addresses Death (apostrophe), who is personified as a man, proud but powerless to hold those who trust Christ.

Poet John Keats used apostrophe throughout his "Ode on a Grecian Urn," which begins with these lines: "Thou still unravish'd bride of quietness / Thou foster-child of Silence and slow Time." Keats talks to the urn itself. Because the characters are captured in stone, the pursuit of the bride is never ending, her beauty unchanging, and spring perpetual. "Silence" and "Time" are also personified as the parents of the urn.

1. What imaginative comparison does Twain primarily use to create humor throughout "What Stumped the Bluejays"?
2. What figure of speech is Twain using in the following quotation from "What Stumped the Bluejays"?

   > "Well, you're a long hole, and a deep hole, and a mighty singular hole altogether—but I've started in to fill you, and I *will* fill you, if it takes a hundred years!"

3. Explain the **personification** in "A Bird Came Down the Walk."
4. With which of the creatures in "The Spider and the Wasp" do you most identify and why?
5. In "The Spider and the Wasp," why do you think Petrunkevitch didn't use personification?

The Return of the Rangers

Kenneth Roberts

Kenneth Roberts, a well-known staff correspondent for the *Saturday Evening Post*, also wrote novels and travel books. The following selection is taken from his novel *Northwest Passage*, set in the American colonies during the mid-1700s. Notice how his command of details brings the story to life, capturing both the flavor and the perils of the early northern Midwest region.

In the midst of the French and Indian War, Captain Rogers and his Rangers complete an arduous military mission and move to rendezvous with military personnel who will provide them with essential provisions. Only a few of the men are strong enough to make the trip; the rest must stay behind and wait for rescue. When Rogers and his pitiful band finally arrive at the rendezvous point, they discover that the military officers have fled—taking the necessary provisions with them. Despite overwhelming odds, Rogers determines three things: to get himself and his men to the military fort safely, to return with provisions for the men he has left behind, and to discover the names of those who have fled and left the Rangers to die.

I

Somewhere I have heard that after the first three days of fasting a man has no further desire for food, and that after thirty days he feels no discomfort whatever: that his brain is clear, his body pure, and his endurance almost unlimited. I suspect that statement in toto.* I don't believe in the benefits of fasting, and ever since I tried it in the company of Major Robert Rogers on the St. Francis Expedition, I have been strongly opposed to it.

After we had seen the logs of our raft plunge over the edge of the falls, we dragged ourselves higher up the bank, dropped to the ground and lay there. Even Rogers was supine* for a time—though not for long. He got to his knees. "This is no place to stay," he said. "We can't stay anywhere without a fire. We'd freeze. There'll be wood on the bank below the falls." He stood up, swaying. "That's where we go next," he said. "Come on."

in toto: in its entirety; totally

supine: lying on one's back

We crawled after him; and it was as he said. There was wood in plenty along the shore and beyond the falls, though not such wood as would build a raft. There were whole trees, hard wood for the most part, and waterlogged; windrows* of twigs and branches; untold quantities of splintered pines of varying sizes, shattered by the ice-jams of previous springs.

windrows: a row made of twigs, branches, or leaves that have been heaped up by the wind

Rogers shook his head when we had crawled over the largest of those woodheaps. "The only thing we can do today," he told us, "is try to get warm. Maybe tomorrow we can figure out something better."

We built ourselves another fence and a roaring fire of driftwood: then stripped ourselves and dried our shredded blankets and our sorry remnants of garments. So tattered and so rotted were those wretched rags that they were next to worthless as covering, and worse than worthless as protection against the cold.

Our persons, in a way, were as bad as our clothes. I was ashamed, almost, to look at Rogers and Ogden. Their scrawny bodies seemed caricatures of what they ought to be—like bodies formed by a sculptor with no knowledge of anatomy. Their muscles were stringy as those of a skun wildcat: their knees and elbows strangely knobby: their stomachs hollowed and their ribs protuberant* like those of a hake* that has lain for days upon the beach.

protuberant: bulging
hake: a marine fish related to and resembling cod

Rogers was covered with scars—red scars, blue scars, white scars. Some were bullet wounds, while others looked as though made by the claws or teeth of animals. Ogden's two bullet-holes, so recently healed, were flaming purple, rimmed with crimson.

When the strips we called our clothes were dry, we huddled close to the fire, listening to the everlasting roar of White River Falls. The fire warmed me, and drugged by that warmth and the thunder in my ears, I neither knew how we could move from where we were, nor did I care.

II

It was a good thing for us, in a way, that we were wrecked at White River Falls. If the falls had not been there to provide us with the windrows of firewood: if we had spent the night in a spot where we would have had only the fuel that we cut, we would probably have died of exhaustion and cold. Our exertions on the raft had drained us of our last reserves of strength, and it was beyond our power to drive a hatchet into a tree. As for the cold, it was so bitter that in the morning the mist from the falls had cased every branch and rock and dead leaf in a glittering envelope of ice.

We lay beside the fire until the sun had come up to take off the knife-like bite of the air.

"We'll have to eat," Rogers said. "If we don't get something in us we can't stick on the raft."

"What raft?" Ogden asked.

"We'll get a raft," Rogers said.

"I don't know how," Ogden said. "If I try to swing a hatchet, I'll cut off my legs."

"Don't worry about that," Rogers said. "I'll get the raft if you'll find the food. Listen!"

Behind us, on the dark slope of the valley, a red squirrel chirred. Far away another answered. We could hear them chipping and chapping at each other: I knew just how they looked, jerking their tails and sliding spasmodically around tree-trunks with outspread legs.

"There's the food," Rogers said. "There's only one good mouthful to a roasted red squirrel, even if he's hit in the head, but all we need is a few good mouthfuls."

"I guess we can knock down a few," Ogden said. "I don't know about getting 'em back here, if I shoot more than one. One's about all I can carry." He reached for his musket. "We better draw our loads and reload," he told me. "We can't afford to miss."

"Before you go," Rogers told us, "help me with the wood. There's only one way to get trees for a raft, and that's to burn 'em down."

We stacked piles of firewood at the base of six spruces near the water's edge: then dragged ourselves up the bank, leaving Rogers and Billy crawling from pile to pile, kindling the fires that were to fell the trees we no longer had the strength to hack down ourselves.

Ogden and I shot five squirrels during the morning, and found it difficult—not only because we couldn't hurry to a squirrel when we heard one, but because we had to wait for the squirrels to sit still: then shoot from a rest because of being unable to hold the sights steady unless we did so. Hunger cramps caught us with increasing frequency, and if a hunger cramp took hold while we were drawing a bead on a squirrel, there was nothing to do but double up and wait until it went away.

We came back, late in the morning, dividing the fifth one equally; and while we picked the meat from their mouse-like bodies, one of the trees came down with a crash.

Rogers drove us out again as soon as we had eaten. "Keep on hunting," he told us. "Shoot anything you find. I'll have these trees burned into lengths by the time you get back."

It seemed to me I couldn't drag my legs up the slope of that valley again, but somehow we did it, using our muskets as walking sticks and leaning frequently against trees. So far as I could feel, my roast squirrel had done me no good: I needed a side of mutton or a cow's hind-quarter to quiet the aching void within me. I thought bitterly of Cap Huff's idle remark about a goose being a little more than one man could eat alone, but not quite enough for two. How little Cap had known of hunger! A whole goose would not more than take the edge off my appetite.

Not far from us a partridge went out of a thicket with a thunderous roar. From the blundering sound he made among the branches, I was sure he had lit at no greater distance.

"He's in the tree," I whispered to Ogden. Ordinarily, the breast of a partridge makes a toothsome* preliminary to a simple meal; but as a meal itself it's not worth considering. Just now, however, this partridge seemed more desirable than anything on earth.

toothsome: delicious

"Can you see him?" Ogden asked faintly.

I said I couldn't, but knew about where he was.

"Go ahead and get him," Odgen said. "I'll move off to the left and make a noise doing it, so he'll watch me. You sneak around and take him in the rear."

He lowered himself among the dead leaves and threw his arms and legs about, making feeble moaning sounds. I hoped the partridge would find such a noise impressive as I crept around the thicket and stood watching breathlessly. The trees were naked: leafless. In none of them could I see anything that looked like a bird, and I was about to call to Ogden when I saw a movement at one end of a swelling on the branch of an oak. It was the partridge, cocking an eye at Ogden's strange behavior.

I found a good rest, took careful aim and let him have it. When he scaled away from the limb on a long slant, Odgen and I stumbled as fast as we could to where he came down. It was rocky ground, clear of heavy undergrowth, and dotted with an occasional juniper bush and a thin covering of leaves; but the partridge was nowhere in sight.

"You sure he came down here?" Ogden asked.

I said I was; that he was hit hard.

"Yes, I saw him. I guess he was hit all right," Ogden agreed, "but I don't believe he came down here. We'd see him if he had. He must have gone beyond those rocks."

We went there and searched; we walked in circles, sought beneath every juniper: almost looked under every fallen leaf; but we found nothing.

"You're sure he came down at all?" Ogden asked finally.

I just nodded. The thought of losing that partridge shut off my voice completely; I was afraid that if I tried to speak, I'd sob instead.

Ogden, hollow-eyed, stared at the ground. "Guess you—guess you missed him," he said in a whisper. And then his wretched staring eyes seemed to enlarge. "Well, if that don't beat all!"

He was staring at a flat juniper that had a few brown oak leaves on it. Before my eyes the oak leaves magically altered and became a partridge—an enormous cock partridge, with ruff-feathers four inches long and a tail the size of a fan. We must have walked across him and around him twenty times.

I went down on my knees and picked him up. He was still warm—the fattest, most beautiful, angelic partridge I had ever seen. The musket ball had broken his back and left his breast untouched.

I looked up at Ogden. "I'm mighty glad you found him, Captain. Mighty glad."

"I *knew* you hit him," Ogden said. "That was a mighty pretty shot, Langdon—the best shot I ever hope to see."

III

When we returned to the falls, all six trees were down, and under each burned two fires, so to separate them into proper lengths for a raft. Rogers sat at the edge of the stream, his forehead resting on his drawn-up knees, and beside him lay Billy, asleep.

The Major looked up. He was a sight. His face and hands were black with soot: as black as Pomp Whipple's; and his eyes glared at us whitely, looking to see whether we had shot anything. I slipped the partridge's head from under my belt in back and held it up for him to see.

"Let's eat it before our luck changes!" he said.

We ate the intestines first, washed and placed on a hot stone to roast. Then we had half a squirrel apiece, cut along the backbone. The partridge was more difficult to divide evenly. Having agreed that a newly-shot partridge is better raw than cooked, we seared him no more than enough to hold the meat together. Then we took off the breast and, after considerable discussion and measuring, split them in what we agreed were equal parts. The carcass, mattering less, was quartered without argument.

Before we slept that night the twelve fires had done their work, and twelve logs lay on the bank, with nothing more to be done except get them into the water and fasten them together into a raft. To me, that night, the task appeared about as easy as pushing a porcupine through a musket barrel.

IV

Nowadays whenever I dream of the building of that second raft, I wake myself up by whimpering aloud, because I've been straining to move a vast log that will not budge, yet must, or death awaits me.

We drove stakes in shallow water where the bottom was soft. Then we inched a log to the bank, tumbled it to the shingle, and worried it into the stream. We couldn't roll it, because we had to leave protruding branches for binding the raft together.

In moving a log, we worked however we could: leavering it with stakes: sliding it over driftwood: lying on our backs to ease our hunger cramps, and pushing with heels or shoulders, so that from head to foot we were black with soot.

When we had a log in the water, we drew it to the fixed stakes, which held it in place while we went for another log. To each one we fastened a hazel switch, so there might be something by which to seize and guide it if it broke loose; and Billy stood guard at the stakes to do what he could in case they gave way.

It was noon before we had finished our labors, lashed our muskets and other wretched belongings to the uprights, cut new paddles and woven a long rope of hazel shoots.

Rogers insisted on the rope. "We don't want this one to get away from us," he muttered over and over. "We really got to keep hold of *this* one." We thought he was right about that. We couldn't have made a third raft.

Whether it was because of the steadily increasing cold—a cold that threatened snow—or the long struggle with the logs, I cannot say; but whatever advantage we had gained from our mouthful of partridge and two mouthfuls of squirrel had now been lost. We were finished; if our lives depended on our marching a mile, we couldn't have done it.

By the time we started, poor young Billy had bad cramps and couldn't even sit upright, so we laid him on some spruce tips in the middle of the raft. With his sharp nose, his closed eyes, his mouth stretched tight over his teeth, and his dusky color, he looked tragically like a mummy without its wrappings.

We worked free of the stakes, poled ourselves slowly into midstream and sank breathless on the raft, regardless of the icy water that welled up between the logs to soak our trembling bodies. Some day, I thought, I must paint a picture of this and call it Purgatory; and then I realized such a picture would have little meaning: it couldn't show the endlessness of these journeyings—the eternal wetness and shiverings, the aching bruises to the soul and body, the everlasting hunger, everlasting toil, and everlasting exhaustion.

Rogers got to his knees, and I heard him say something about falls. The word shocked me into full consciousness. "Falls?" I asked. "More falls?"

"Not bad ones," he said thickly. "Just little falls. Wattoquitchey Falls, seven miles from here. Fifty yards long. Maybe we can ride 'em."

Ogden and I struggled painfully to our feet.

"Well, why didn't we go there to build the raft?" Ogden asked.

"I said 'seven miles,'" Rogers reminded him. "You couldn't march seven miles. And what about him?" he pointed to Billy. "Why, maybe I couldn't even hardly do it myself."

"Can we see these falls before we're on top of 'em?" I asked.

"See 'em?" Rogers said. "We've *got* to see 'em, haven't we?"

We strained our eyes downstream. A few snowflakes drifted out of the heavy sky, and from the surface of the eddying brown water rose a vapor like a faint ghost of the mist that had billowed up from White River Falls. The thought of more falls was sheerly nauseating, and I knew that if the snow came down too thickly, we might not see them until too late. . . .

Rogers broke the silence at the end of three miles. "Maybe we can ride 'em," he said again. He repeated the words in another quarter-hour. Those falls, I realized, hadn't been out of his mind all day. That was why he had insisted on making the rope of hazel switches. I wondered what would happen if we couldn't ride them; but I didn't dare ask.

V

We sighted the falls through thickening snowflakes at three o'clock, and paddled the raft over toward the left bank, so we might have opportunity to see how they looked.

At first I thought we might indeed possibly ride them, for their total drop was only about ten feet; and the quick water wasn't over fifty yards long. The closer we came, however, the more apparent it was that the raft would never get down safely unless every possible ounce of weight was removed from it. Gouts of foam shot up from the middle of the rapids, proving that the ledges beneath were sharp and dangerous; we could hardly hope to live if the raft broke up or spilled us in that turmoil.

We let the raft drop down to within a few yards of the quick water, laid one end of it against the bank and held it there with our paddles. We could see the pool at the bottom—a brown, deep pool, streaked with streamers of foam.

"I don't believe we'd better try it," Rogers said.

"Somebody's got to," Ogden said wearily. "It's the only chance we've got."

"No it isn't," Rogers said. "The best chance is for me to go down to that pool and try to catch her when she comes down."

Ogden, seized with a cramp, clutched his middle. "You can't!"

Rogers seemed not to hear him. "That's what we'll do. Take Billy ashore. Take the muskets and the rest of the stuff. I'll hold her while you do it."

Ogden hesitated.

"Captain Ogden!" Rogers said sharply. "You heard me!"

Ogden moved quickly to obey. We hurriedly collected our rusty muskets, our soaked and tattered rags of blankets, and all our other accouterments that now were rubbish; then, taking Billy by his pipestem arms, we dragged him to the bank, where he lay all asprawl, no better than a shrivelled little red corpse. At Rogers' orders we made fast the rope of hazel shoots to the stoutest of the uprights; and Ogden tested the rope while I fastened our paddles to the raft's protruding branches. The rope was firm as a cable.

"Now, whatever you do," Rogers said, "don't let go that rope till I give the signal. It'll take some time to reach the pool, and I got to undress. When I hold up my arm, turn her loose. Let the rope trail. If I miss the raft, maybe I can catch the rope." He fastened his own paddle beside ours and went ashore.

I joined Ogden, and together we clung to the rope. The raft plucked insistently at it, as if eager to be gone from us.

Picking up his musket, powder-horn and other belongings, Rogers went slowly from our sight into the dark woods, walking crouched over. The snowflakes had thickened, helping to hide him from us; and I thought it likely that I'd heard his voice for the last time.

The raft seemed more and more determined to swing out into the stream and go down the falls. For fear it might pull us off our feet and drag us into the rapids, we sat in the shallows, water up to our waists, our feet wedged against rocks.

"I'll bet my way was best," Ogden muttered. "One of us ought to have *tried* to ride down on it. If the Major gets a stomach cramp when he's swimming to it—" He was silent. There wasn't much more to say.

At the edge of the pool the bushes moved apart, and Rogers, a dim figure through the steadily-falling snow, could be seen peering along the shore to the left and right, seeking, evidently, for a suitable position. Then he went back into the bushes, and reappeared nearer us, crawling out on a flat rock. With agonizing slowness he put down his musket, blanket, knapsack and powderhorn, and painfully undressed.

He crouched at the edge of the rock, staring up at the falls—a lonely, naked, helpless atom in that immensity of roaring white water, drifting snowflakes, screaking forest and towering dark hills. Then he held up his arm and waved.

We let go the rope and floundered to our feet. The raft swung slowly broadside to the current and moved downstream. When it reached the quick water, it bobbed on the white riffles; flung itself forward.

It rolled and rocked. Halfway down it nosed completely under: a surge of white foam swept it from end to end. It rose again, reeling and sliding in the surges, and seemed to fling itself breathlessly to the bottom of the long slope. It plunged heavily into the swirling pool, and hung there, tilted forward, half under water. We looked to see it fall apart; but with labored slowness it came to the surface, turning gently among the clots and streaks of froth.

Rogers lowered himself from the rock. He swam arduously, with awkward jerks, as if his rump strove to rise and force his head under. He stopped once, freed his face from gouts of foam,* and rolled on his side to look for the raft, which, again in the grip of a current, moved more rapidly.

gouts of foam: large, shapeless waves of foam

He altered his course and swam spasmodically on. He found himself so close to it that he clutched for a log—clutched and missed. He kicked again; got a hand on the raft: another hand. He hung there for a time, his chin on the edge, his legs and body carried beneath the logs by the current; and I, watching him, felt my muscles quake; for I knew that no mere human, with an icy torrent plucking at his starved and weakened limbs, could cling for long to those charred tree-trunks. As if in answer to my fears, he struggled sluggishly, hitched himself along with fumbling hands, gripped one of the branches we had left as uprights on the logs, and drew himself partly from the water, so that his upper body lay upon the raft—lay so long motionless, that I thought he was spent. Then we saw that he was making futile upward movements with his knee. It caught the edge eventually, and he squirmed aboard to lie flat.

"I never thought he'd make it!" Ogden whispered; and I, shaking all over, found that my tongue and throat were dry as chips.

Now Rogers had got to his knees, and we saw him unlash a paddle from the uprights, and begin to work slowly toward shore.

VI

Driftwood from Wattoquitchey Falls warmed us and kept us alive that night; and with the first faint grayness of that miserable last day of October—miserable and yet ever-memorable—we put Billy in the middle of the raft, with our blankets under and over him, and pushed out into midstream. The snow had ceased, and had been followed by a wind so bitter that it cut and slashed us like frigid knife-blades.

There were no more falls between Wattoquitchey and Number Four: no more quick water, Rogers said—no, there was nothing but the malignant cold, which seemed determined to finish what the French and the Indians had tried so hard to do to us.

But on both sides the intervals grew broader: the hills retreated; and though the glacial wind could thus howl at us unrestrained, we thought it had the voice of a raging demon of the wilderness, frantic to see us at last slipping from his grasp.

Out of his streaming eyes, Rogers stared at the widening intervals. "We're going to make it," he said. "We're going to make it!"

It was mid-afternoon when he seized Ogden by the arm. "Look!" he cried. "Look!" He doubled over with a cramp; but thus bent he pointed awkwardly, like an actor playing the part of a hunchback. On the river bank, a hundred yards ahead, two men with axes suddenly stood.

"Why," Ogden said incredulously, "it's people again!" But I don't think Rogers could speak at all, and I know I couldn't.

The two strange, strange figures, men that weren't skeletons, men that were clothed, men that swung axes easily in ruddy strength and health—those two unbelievable men saw us, and came back along the bank, hurrying toward us.

"Don't tell 'em anything," Rogers warned us huskily as we swung the raft in toward the shore. "I'll do the talking. Don't tell anyone a thing till we find out all about the dirty skunk that ran off with our food!"

One of the men splashed toward us, caught our rope of hazel switches and drew us to land.

"Where's Number Four?" Rogers asked.

They just stared.

"I'm Rogers," Rogers said. "Where's Number Four?"

"Rogers!" one of the men said, and a kind of horror was in his face. "You say you're Rogers?"

"I do!"

"I've often seen you," the man said, swallowing. "It's hard to believe!" He shook his head. "We heard you was dead, Major; and I guess it's true! You was! But anyhow, you're at Number Four, Major. It's right here, and we'll help you to the fort!"

With that, slipping and splashing in excitement, they gave us the unfamiliar help of muscular arms and got us off the raft, lifted Billy to the bank, put our belongings in a heap, and made the raft fast to the stake. They gawked at the burned ends of the logs and at the alder and hazel withes* that held them together, and kept staring at Rogers as if he'd been a hippogriff.*

withe: a tough twig used for binding things together

hippogriff: mythological figure with the wings, claws, and head of a griffin and the body and hindquarters of a horse

We sat down just beyond the water's edge and watched them as they made the raft fast.

"Happen to have anything to eat?" Rogers asked them whereupon, after another look at him, they sprang up the bank and departed, running. They were back in five minutes, bringing with them a bottle a third full of rum and a piece of bread the size of my fist. "That's all we got, Major," one said. "We're out chopping wood and et the rest, but there's plenty supplies at the fort. There's turnips and fresh pork."

Rogers broke the bread in four pieces. "Why, it's bread!" he said. He gave us our portions, took a mouthful of rum, then went over and looked at Billy. He poured a little rum between his lips. When Billy opened his eyes and coughed, he gave him the bread and passed us the bottle.

That mouthful of bread moistened by rum had incredible sweetness and savor. I could feel it moving warmly inside me, as though hastening to assure my cramped and aching stomach, my thumping heart, my laboring lungs and my shivering body that their long agony was over.

"Now we'll go up to the fort," Rogers told the staring woodcutters. "Guess maybe you'd better help us a little. Leave our stuff here: then come back for it. One of you can carry this Indian boy. Then we'll just lean on the two of you."

One of the men picked up Billy and carried him. The other gave Ogden and me each a shoulder, and Rogers staggered along, now and then bumping into the man who carried the Indian boy; thus we set off for the fort, which we could see, low and square, in the middle of its dismal, snowcovered clearing—that same peaceful clearing I had idly sketched on a warm September evening less than two months ago.

There was no sentry at the gate of the fort; no one on the small parade ground on which the snow had been trodden to dirty, frozen slush. Our helpers took us across the parade to the log barrack in the center. A squat tower of hewn plank rose from its northern end. The man on whom Ogden and I leaned pulled the latch-string of the door and kicked it open. In a broad stone fireplace opposite the door a fire burned, and at either end of the room were rows of bunks. In front of the fire a blanket was spread on the floor, and around it were a dozen Provincials, rolling dice.

They looked up. One said angrily, "Keep the door shut!"

"This here's Major Rogers," one of the woodcutters said in a voice that choked with excitement.

The Provincials got slowly to their feet and faced us, stared at us and frowned with unbelief, then seemed to see something terrifying.

"Who's in command of this fort?" Rogers said.

"We don't know his name, Major," a soldier said huskily. "We're strangers here."

"Go get him," Rogers ordered.

Three Provincials jumped together for the door at the end of the room, jostling and tripping in their haste.

Rogers walked drunkenly to a bench, and the staring soldiers fell away before him.

"Put Billy on the blanket and go back and get our muskets," Rogers told the woodcutters.

Ogden and I got to the bench with difficulty. The feel of a roof over my head and of a closed room, warmed by a fire, almost suffocated me.

The door at the end of the room burst open. A stolid-looking man in a wrinkled blue uniform peered at us, blinking. "Which?" he asked. "Which one?" he came to us. "They said Major Rogers! None of *you* are Major Rogers!"

"I'm Rogers," the Major said. "Now here: write down what I say. I can't repeat. What's your name?"

"Bellows," the officer said, "in charge of the King's stores." He clapped his hands to his pockets, looked confused, then hurried from the room. When he returned he had a pencil and paper. "We didn't know—" he stammered. "We heard—where did you—"

"Get canoes," Rogers said. "Load 'em with food. Send 'em up river. Mouth of the Ammonoosuc."

"These men are Provincials," Bellows said apologetically. "They're bound home. There's only—"

"Get settlers," Rogers said. "Good canoemen. Hire 'em!"

"It's pretty bad weather," Bellows said doubtfully. "Maybe when it clears off—"

Rogers rose wavering to his feet, then straightened himself to his full height and seemed to fill the room. In a strained, hoarse voice he said: "Today! Today! Now! Can't you realize there's a hundred Rangers at the mouth of the Ammonoosuc, starving! Get men and pay 'em! Get all the settlers into the fort! Call 'em in! Drum 'em up! I'll talk to 'em! Get started!"

Bellows stared at him wildly: rushed back to the door and shouted a name, adding, at the top of his lungs, "Assembly! Assembly!"

Three private soldiers tumbled into the room, one a drummer. At a gesture from Bellows he ran out on the parade ground, fumbling with his drum braces. His drum rolled and rumbled, sending chills down my spine.

To one of the other soldiers Bellows shouted, "Run to Mrs. Bellows. Get a pail of milk and a bottle of my rum."

"And some bread," Ogden said.

"All the bread she's got!" Bellows shouted.

Rogers sank down on the bench, rubbed his gaunt face with huge skeleton hands, ran his fingers through his hair. "Write an order for the food to go up river. What you got in this place?"

"Pork," Bellows said. "Fresh beef. Turnips."

"How much bread you got?"

"Not much," Bellows said. "These Provincials—"

"Let 'em go without! Put all the food you can find in those canoes, and send out for more. Send out for everything there is! Those men of mine are going to be fed, or I'll raid every house in the settlement!"

The drum rattled and rolled, rumbled and banged.

Bellows scribbled hastily on a sheet of paper and sent the third soldier flying from the barrack with it. There were people crowding in at the door, goggling at us.

Rogers raised his voice to be heard over the continuous rolling of the drum. "Tell me something," he said to Bellows. "Supplies of food were to meet us at the mouth of the Ammonoosuc. They were sent, weren't they?"

"Oh, yes," Bellows replied, and he looked frightened. "They were in charge of Lieutenant Stephens."

"So? What did he do with 'em?"

"He brought 'em back," Bellows said. "He waited several days; then he thought you and your command must have been wiped out—and he heard firing one morning and thought it might be French and Indians, so he decided he'd better start for home."

"Listen," Rogers said, and he spoke as much to the settlers and Provincials who had crowded in through the doorway as he did to Bellows. "We finished St. Francis for you. There isn't any more St. Francis, and you can begin to move up that way and clear the land and live in peace whenever you've a mind to. But this Lieutenant Stephens who got frightened and took our food away when we were firing muskets to show him we were coming—we'll have to have a settlement with him. He isn't here, is he?"

"No," Bellows said tremulously. "He's gone back to Crown Point. You'll be going that way, too, Major, I take it?"

"No, not till afterwards," Rogers answered in a choking voice.

The crowding people stared stupidly at him as he stood before them in the firelight, unbelievably gaunt, barefoot, covered with bruises, tattered strips of strouding* sagging around his legs. The shredded buckskin leggins hung loosely on his emaciated flanks; singular torn bits of garments concealed little of his ribs and bony chest: his hands were scarred, burned, sooty and pitch-stained from his labors with the raft.

strouding: coarse woolen cloth

"No, we'll see Lieutenant Stephens at Crown Point afterwards," Rogers said. "Now get me some beef—fat beef. I'm going back to Ammonoosuc myself."

About the Story

1. Captain Rogers is clearly the hero of this story. Cite passages that prove that statement.
2. Briefly describe the conflict Roberts emphasizes in this portion of his novel.
3. The narrator tells his story chronologically, dividing his narrative into units that reveal the increasingly desperate situation of Captain Rogers and his Rangers. What incidents serve as the crisis (major turning point for the main character) and the climax (moment of highest emotional intensity) of the plot?
4. Roberts's story presents the harsh side of winter. What images does Roberts use to convey the austerity of the season?
5. Near the end of the selection, what figure of speech does he often rely on to suggest nature's dangers?
6. At the end of the selection, most readers are surprised to hear that Rogers will return to Ammonoosuc. What in the story lets the reader know that this is consistent with Rogers's character?

Kenneth Roberts assumes that his readers will agree that the value of human life is so high that it is worth risking one's own life to protect someone else's. How could you use this story to question the evolutionary worldview, a worldview that says that the universe is governed by chance?

About the Author

Kenneth Roberts (1885–1957) was born in Maine and maintained a lifelong interest in that state. A skilled historian, Roberts collected information about New England's fierce battles, important political decisions, and minutiae of daily life. Unlike most historians, he did not present his findings in textbooks or treatises. He chose instead to transform the historical facts gleaned from his research into fascinating stories.

Roberts had a compelling style that was cultivated during his years of work as a newspaperman. As a journalist, Roberts wrote for such well-known periodicals as the *Saturday Evening Post* and *Life*. This journalistic background, coupled with his painstaking research, made him one of America's most talented historical novelists. Shortly before his death, he was awarded a Pulitzer Prize Special Citation in recognition of his novels' fostering interest in United States history. This selection may well reflect Roberts's personal experiences. As a member of the American Expeditionary Force Siberia during World War I, he was familiar not only with military life in hostile territory but also with both the deprivations and dangers of severe winters.

Mother to Son

LANGSTON HUGHES

Hughes is well-known for his ability to weave everyday vocal patterns and lively musical rhythms together. In this poem, which reads like a kindly parental admonition, Hughes uses dialect, informal language, and a strong metaphor to get his message across.

Well, son, I'll tell you:
Life for me ain't been no crystal stair.
It's had tacks in it,
And splinters,
And boards torn up,
And places with no carpet on the floor—
Bare.
But all the time
I'se been a-climbin' on,
And reachin' landin's,
And turnin' corners,
And sometimes goin' in the dark
Where there ain't been no light.
So boy, don't you turn back.
Don't you set down on the steps
'Cause you finds it's kinder hard.
Don't you fall now—
For I'se still goin', honey,
I'se still climbin',
And life for me ain't been no crystal stair.

About the Poem

1. What is the theme of Hughes's poem?
2. What implied metaphor does Hughes thread throughout "Mother to Son"?
3. Explain the meanings of the tenor and the vehicle in the poem's overall metaphor.
4. How does Hughes's language (dialect, colloquialisms, etc.) contribute to the poem's effect?
5. What do you think the speaker's worldview is? Do you agree or disagree with that worldview?

About the Author

Langston Hughes (1902–67) is best known for his musical verse rhythms infused with the jazz spirit of the Harlem Renaissance. His use of black dialect and syncopated speech patterns is suggestive of the blues music genre and popular folk ballads.

Hughes himself was influenced by two other American poetry icons: Paul Laurence Dunbar and Carl Sandburg. Both poets wrote using uniquely American voices: that of the African-American everyman and that of the working class. Hughes's poetry often looks and sounds like a sophisticated found poem fashioned from a scribbled note or transcribed from a fleeting conversation. However, the poems possess a flowing rhythm and metrical pattern beneath their seemingly haphazard and easy vernacular.

Hughes attended Lincoln University in Pennsylvania, where he received his degree in 1929. By the time of his graduation, Hughes was already a published author. He wrote widely—newspaper columns, song lyrics, and fiction. Writer Vachel Lindsay helped launch Hughes's career after he discovered Hughes working as a busboy in a Washington, DC, restaurant.

Later authors, such as Alice Walker, Gwendolyn Brooks, and others, have imitated and built upon Hughes's foundation of lively free verse and use of the vernacular, particularly of the African-American dialect.

The Soul's Dark Cottage

EDMUND WALLER

The following lines preface a volume of poetry written by Waller while in his eighties. They answer the objection that no one so old can write anything very much worth reading, especially anything poetic. Waller uses a metaphor to describe what happens to a person's soul and body as he grows older.

The soul's dark cottage, battered and decayed,
Lets in new light through chinks that time has made;
Stronger by weakness, wiser men become,
As they draw near to their eternal home.
Leaving the old, both worlds at once they view,
That stand upon the threshold of the new.

About the Poem

1. What two metaphors does Waller use in the poem?
2. What two biblical images does Waller use to evoke the realities of old age?
3. Do Waller's conclusions about old age reflect a biblical worldview? Explain your answer.

About the Author

Politics and poetry were the two great passions of Edmund Waller's (1606–87) life. Born into a wealthy family, Waller inherited a fortune when he was only ten years old. He entered the English parliament while still a teenager, and he spent most of his life involved with court society and party politics. Although his involvement in a political conspiracy led to banishment and fines, Waller eventually returned to court and resumed his role as a political moderate and peacemaker.

The poetry for which Waller was most famous in his day was *panegyric,* poetry written to praise someone, often a king or patron. For Waller, the writing of panegyric served not only as a suitable hobby for a courtly gentleman but also as a political tool for the promotion of ideas and opinions. Although Waller gained a reputation for supporting with panegyric anyone who happened to be in power, he also possessed great diplomatic skills and a strong desire to promote peace and harmony in a nation torn by petty strifes and political factions. His poetry displays this lifelong desire for reconciliation of extremes. Our selection comes from his *Divine Poems,* a collection of verse written in his later years.

The Windows

George Herbert

George Herbert, devout Anglican parson and lyric poet of the first rank, dedicated his poetic gifts to God. Before his early death, he completed a collection of lyric poems entitled *The Temple*. This collection represents Christian experience symbolically in terms of the structure and furnishings of an English church.

Lord, how can man preach thy eternal word?
  He is a brittle crazy* glass:
Yet in thy temple thou dost him afford
  This glorious and transcendent place,
  To be a window through thy grace.

But when thou dost anneal* in glass thy story,
  Making thy life to shine within
The holy Preacher's; then the light and glory
  More rev'rend grows, and more doth win:
  Which else shows watrish, bleak, and thin.

Doctrine and life, colors and light,* in one
  When they combine and mingle, bring
A strong regard and awe: but speech alone
  Doth vanish like a flaring thing,
  And in the ear, not conscience ring.

crazy: crazed, cracked
anneal: heat in order to add colors
The correspondences are reversed: doctrine (expository preaching) = light; life (Christ within the preacher) = colors.

About the Poem

1. What metaphor is developed throughout Herbert's poem? What is a metaphor called when it is developed beyond a sentence or one simple comparison?
2. Explain the overall metaphor of the poem as it is developed in each stanza.
3. In Herbert's day, most stained glass church windows depicted Bible characters or stories of past saints. How is that subject matter helpful in developing Herbert's metaphor?
4. Herbert begins the poem with a question. Summarize his answer to that question as found in the poem. Does his answer agree with the teaching of Scripture? Explain.

About the Author

George Herbert (1593–1633) is considered the author of the finest devotional poetry in English. His intellectual and searching poems are filled with inventive metaphors and sparkling wit, a dominant feature of the metaphysical poetry of his day. The metaphysical poets sought to answer philosophical questions about the world and the nature of existence, often in the form of love poems.

Herbert's primary goal in versification was neither wit nor eloquence. He believed that the use of literary devices and fine verse forms should be a means to the end of communicating holiness. Herbert viewed poetry as a means of reaching those who might otherwise not listen to the gospel. "A verse may find him who a sermon flies," he writes in "The Church Porch." As a result, Herbert's poems are notable in their simplicity and use of everyday objects such as collars, altars, and windows.

Herbert was a contemporary of John Donne, the preeminent metaphysical poet, who also wrote religious poetry. Herbert's mother, Magdalen, was Donne's patroness. With such an influential and intellectual mother, one would think that young George Herbert would have become a politician or scholar. Indeed he did study at Cambridge and held several positions there, including public orator, a stepping-stone for future employment at court. But he relinquished his position for the church at the behest of his mother. Much of Herbert's poetry reflects his struggle in giving up his worldly ambitions. His poetry is at once logical yet emotional, structured yet imaginative.

John 1

FROM THE BIBLE

John's unique and imaginative prologue (1:1–18) opens with powerful metaphors of Jesus. John evidently knew that, as author N.T. Wright said, "Metaphor consists in bringing two sets of ideas close together, close enough for a spark to jump, but not too close, so that the spark, in jumping, illuminates for a moment the whole area around, changing perceptions as it does so."† John's metaphors of word and light have been sparks illuminating Christians' view of our Lord for almost 2000 years. But there are other imaginative comparisons to be found in John 1. The literary tools you are learning will help you see things previously invisible in a familiar passage.

In the beginning was the Word, and the Word was with God, and the Word was God. The same was in the beginning with God. All things were made by him; and without him was not any thing made that was made. In him was life; and the life was the light of men. And the light shineth in darkness; and the darkness comprehended it not.

There was a man sent from God, whose name was John. The same came for a witness, to bear witness of the Light, that all men through him might believe. He was not that Light, but was sent to bear witness of that Light.

That was the true Light, which lighteth every man that cometh into the world. He was in the world, and the world was made by him, and the world knew him not. He came unto his own, and his own received him not. But as many as received him, to them gave he power to become the sons of God, even to them that believe on his name: Which were born, not of blood, nor of the will of the flesh, nor of the will of man, but of God.

And the Word was made flesh, and dwelt among us, (and we beheld his glory, the glory as of the only begotten of the Father,) full of grace and truth.

John bare witness of him, and cried, saying, This was he of whom I spake, He that cometh after me is preferred before me: for he was before me. And of his fulness have all we received, and grace for grace. For the law was given by Moses, but grace and truth came by Jesus Christ. No man hath seen God at any time, the only begotten Son, which is in the bosom of the Father, he hath declared him.

And this is the record of John, when the Jews sent priests and Levites from Jerusalem to ask him, Who art thou? And he confessed, and denied not; but confessed, I am not the Christ.

And they asked him, What then? Art thou Elias?

And he saith, I am not.

Art thou that prophet?

And he answered, No.

Then said they unto him, Who art thou? that we may give an answer to them that sent us. What sayest thou of thyself?

He said, I am the voice of one crying in the wilderness, Make straight the way of the Lord, as said the prophet Esaias.

And they which were sent were of the Pharisees. And they asked him, and said unto him, Why baptizest thou then, if thou be not that Christ, nor Elias, neither that prophet?

John answered them, saying, I baptize with water: but there standeth one among you, whom ye know not; He it is, who coming after me is

†N.T. Wright, The New Testament and the People of God (Minneapolis: Fortress, 1992), 40.

St. John the Baptist in the Wilderness. Antonio del Castillo y Saavedra (attr. to). From the Bob Jones University Collection

preferred before me, whose shoe's latchet* I am not worthy to unloose.

latchet: a strap of leather to fasten a shoe

These things were done in Bethabara beyond Jordan, where John was baptizing.

The next day John seeth Jesus coming unto him, and saith, Behold the Lamb of God, which taketh away the sin of the world. This is he of whom I said, After me cometh a man which is preferred before me: for he was before me. And I knew him not: but that he should be made manifest to Israel, therefore am I come baptizing with water.

And John bare record,* saying, I saw the Spirit descending from heaven like a dove, and it abode upon him. And I knew him not: but he that sent me to baptize with water, the same said unto me, Upon whom thou shalt see the Spirit descending, and remaining on him, the same is he which baptizeth with the Holy Ghost. And I saw, and bare record that this is the Son of God.

bare record: testified

Again the next day after John stood, and two of his disciples; And looking upon Jesus as he walked, he saith, Behold the Lamb of God!

And the two disciples heard him speak, and they followed Jesus. Then Jesus turned, and saw them following, and saith unto them, What seek ye?

They said unto him, Rabbi, (which is to say, being interpreted, Master,) where dwellest thou?

He saith unto them, Come and see.

They came and saw where he dwelt, and abode with him that day: for it was about the tenth hour.*

the tenth hour: 4:00 p.m.

One of the two which heard John speak, and followed him, was Andrew, Simon Peter's brother. He first findeth his own brother Simon, and saith unto him, We have found the Messias, which is, being interpreted, the Christ. And he brought him to Jesus.

And when Jesus beheld him, he said, Thou art Simon the son of Jona: thou shalt be called Cephas, which is by interpretation, A stone.

The day following Jesus would go forth into Galilee, and findeth Philip, and saith unto him, Follow me.

Now Philip was of Bethsaida, the city of Andrew and Peter. Philip findeth Nathanael, and saith unto him, We have found him, of whom Moses in the law, and the prophets, did write, Jesus of Nazareth, the son of Joseph.

And Nathanael said unto him, Can there any good thing come out of Nazareth?

Philip saith unto him, Come and see.

Jesus saw Nathanael coming to him, and saith of him, Behold an Israelite indeed, in whom is no guile!

Nathanael saith unto him, Whence knowest thou me?

Jesus answered and said unto him, Before that Philip called thee, when thou wast under the fig tree, I saw thee.

Nathanael answered and saith unto him, Rabbi, thou art the Son of God; thou art the King of Israel.

Jesus answered and said unto him, Because I said unto thee, I saw thee under the fig tree, believest thou? thou shalt see greater things than these.

And he saith unto him, Verily, verily, I say unto you, Hereafter ye shall see heaven open, and the angels of God ascending and descending upon the Son of man.

About the Passage

1. In this passage, John introduces three metaphors for Christ, some of which recur in other places in the New Testament. Find all three and give a brief possible meaning for each.
2. In this passage the author refers several times to a part of something to represent the whole object (synecdoche). Give two examples from the text.
3. What do you think the imaginative comparisons in the passage add to this portion of Scripture?
4. This passage ends with Christ's describing something that Nathanael will eventually see as a disciple—angels "ascending and descending upon the Son of Man." Jesus is referring to a dream given to Jacob in the Old Testament (Gen. 28). What is different about Christ's version here? What might that difference signify?

THINKING ZONE

In Matthew 19 and 20, Jesus twice makes the same statement describing the kingdom of God: "So the last shall be first, and the first last" (Matt. 20:16). His disciples are puzzled until the Lord explains that God's grace to men is best seen through His free gift of salvation rather than a person's earthly power, wealth, or prestige. In context, Jesus' point is clear; however, it is understandable that the disciples might be confused. On the surface, His statement doesn't seem to make sense, in part because Christ was making use of a literary paradox.

In literature, a **paradox** is a statement that seems to be self-contradictory but actually makes sense when understood in the right context. Writers use paradox to draw attention to important ideas or to make readers rethink their assumptions. In the disciples' case, they assumed that earthly blessings clearly signaled God's approval and support. Christ reversed that perception in an effort to emphasize its falsity. Not all who are rich or powerful are truly blessed of God, and some who are poor or lowly are counted high in God's service. Paradoxes like this one are sprinkled throughout literature, sometimes in the form of direct statements and sometimes implied in character or plot.

Many effective imaginative comparisons are paradoxical in nature. They compare two things that appear to have little in common or to be directly opposed to each other; nonetheless, the writer reveals similarities. A **conceit** is a particular type of comparison that is generally paradoxical. Conceits draw a striking parallel between two seemingly dissimilar things. They may be very brief, or they may be sustained and elaborate like an extended metaphor.

Some of the most famous conceits occur in the poetry of the seventeenth-century metaphysical poets. In metaphysical conceits, the poet usually compares things based on their abstract rather than their physical similarities. For example, in his "Holy Sonnet 14," John Donne compares himself to an occupied city that struggles to admit its true ruler (Christ). Physically, a person and a town have little in common, but the idea of a territory fought for by two people applies to both.

1. Which of the previous four works contains an obvious **paradox** about age? Describe this paradox and explain its meaning.
2. What paradoxical statement is found multiple times in John 1? What does it mean?
3. Which of the previous poems is built on a **conceit**? Briefly describe the conceit and its meaning. How is it paradoxical?

UNIT I REVIEW

Remember the Terms

Review the following terms from "Marks and Modes of Literature," "Imaginative Comparison," and the Thinking Zone pages. Be prepared to discuss their meanings and uses.

theme	parallelism	vehicle	synecdoche
figurative language	euphony	implied metaphors	personification
simile	cacophony	extended metaphors	apostrophe
metaphor	imagery	allegory	paradox
repetition	tenor	metonymy	conceit

Apply the Concepts

Answer the following questions about how the literary concepts you have studied are used in this unit.

1. At the end of Emily Dickinson's poem, "A Bird Came Down the Walk," the poet compares the bird's flight to a ship's sailing and butterflies' flying. What is Dickinson trying to communicate about the bird through these metaphors?
2. Identify the tenor and the vehicle in the following quotation by Emily Dickinson:

   I offered him a Crumb / And he unrolled his feathers / And rowed him softer home—

3. What effect does Dickinson's use of the pronouns *he* and *his* in "A Bird Came Down the Walk" have on the poem?
4. Explain the allegory in "The Nightingale and the Glowworm."
5. Which of the imaginative comparison techniques studied in Unit I most effectively enabled Twain to achieve humor in "What Stumped the Bluejays"?
6. What technique studied does the following quotation from "The Return of the Rangers" illustrate?

   "I've often seen you," the man said, swallowing. "It's hard to believe!" He shook his head. "We heard you was dead, Major; and I guess it's true! You was!"

7. What imaginary comparison studied does the following quotation from "The Return of the Rangers" illustrate?

   We hurriedly collected our rusty muskets, our soaked and tattered rags of blankets, and all our other accouterments that now were rubbish; then, taking Billy by his pipestem arms, we dragged him to the bank, where he lay all asprawl, no better than a shrivelled little red corpse.

8. In "The Return of the Rangers," Kenneth Roberts's vivid, excruciating details, as well as his portrayal of Captain Rogers's fixation with the waterfalls, serve what purpose in the story?
9. What is the theme of "Mother to Son"?
10. What does light represent in Waller's "The Soul's Dark Cottage"?
11. Relate the significance of Waller's having written "The Soul's Dark Cottage" when he was in his eighties.
12. In Herbert's poem "The Windows," the word *anneal* means to heat in order to add what?
13. How does the metaphorical aspect of the word *anneal* apply to the Christian?
14. How does the following quotation from John 1 exemplify paradox?

    He that cometh after me is preferred before me: for he was before me.

15. Do the following verses from John 1 contain an example of metonymy or of synecdoche? Explain.

    And the Word was made flesh, and dwelt among us, (and we beheld his glory, the glory as of the only begotten of the Father,) full of grace and truth.

Evaluate the Ideas

Identify each of the following statements as true or false. If false, rewrite the underlined portion of the statement to make it true.

16. In John 1, the examples of Christ as the Word, the Light, and the Lamb are examples of <u>simile</u>.
17. In "A Bird Came Down the Walk," the bird's unrolling its feathers illustrates <u>metonymy</u>.
18. In "The Spider and the Wasp," Petrunkevitch uses <u>many examples of metaphor and simile</u>.
19. "The Spider and the Wasp" is literature of <u>information</u>.
20. In Cowper's "The Nightingale and the Glowworm," "lamp" in the following line is the metaphor's <u>vehicle</u>.

    "Did you admire my lamp," quoth he, / "As much as I your minstrelsy"

21. The following quotation from Twain's "What Stumped the Bluejays" contains a <u>metaphor</u>.

    Well, at last he could hardly flop his wings, he was so tuckered out. He comes a-drooping down, once more, sweating like an ice-pitcher.

22. The following quotation from Twain's "What Stumped the Bluejays" contains <u>paradox</u>.

    "Well, you're a long hole, and a deep hole, and a mighty singular hole altogether—but I've started in to fill you, and I *will* fill you, if it takes a hundred years!"

23. The following quotation from "The Return of the Rangers" illustrates <u>imagery</u>.

> I joined Ogden, and together we clung to the rope. The raft plucked insistently at it, as if eager to be gone from us.

24. As illustrated in the following quotation, Kenneth Roberts's use of <u>parallelism</u> provides rhythm and movement, polishes his style, and accumulates realistic details, all of which aid his effective communication in the story.

> Then we inched a log to the bank, tumbled it to the shingle, and worried it into the stream.

25. Langston Hughes in his poem "Mother to Son" makes use of a <u>simile</u> to communicate his theme.
26. Herbert's "The Windows" is an <u>implied metaphor</u>.
27. In "The Windows" the "brittle crazy glass" is the <u>preacher</u>.
28. The following verse from John 1 contains an example of <u>allegory</u>.

> Hereafter ye shall see heaven open, and the angels of God ascending and descending upon the Son of man.

Write a Response

Completely answer each of the following questions.

29. Compare the purpose of personification in Twain's "What Stumped the Bluejays" and Cowper's "The Nightingale and the Glowworm."
30. "The Soul's Dark Cottage" and "Mother to Son" offer either insight or advice from the perspective of age. Summarize the advice or insight briefly and then judge its value.
31. Paraphrase the last stanza of "The Windows" by George Herbert.

> Doctrine and life, colors and light, in one
> When they combine and mingle, bring
> A strong regard and awe: but speech alone
> Doth vanish like a flaring thing,
> And in the ear, not conscience ring.

UNIT II

THREE MUSICIANS
Pablo Picasso

SOUND AND SYNTAX

Pablo Picasso (1881–1973) was a Spanish artist who worked in many different styles and media during his long career. He is one of the best-known artists of the twentieth century.

Picasso is remembered primarily as one of the founders of the cubism movement in art. Beginning around 1907, Picasso and his friend and fellow artist Georges Braque developed a style of painting that reduced the subject painted to its two-dimensional (flat) shapes and then presented multiple perspectives at once. They later softened their dependence on geometrical shapes and added textural elements such as collage, sometimes gluing paper or other materials onto the paintings.

In 1921, Picasso painted two versions of Three Musicians *while spending the summer in France. In both works, the oil painting mimics the flattened effect of a cut-and-pasted paper collage and exemplifies some of the important features of the synthetic cubist style.*

- What instrument is each musician playing? Do you recognize any of the costumes?
- Cubists often presented an object from several different angles at once. How many different angles of view did Picasso include in his depiction of the table?
- What do you like or dislike about Picasso's Cubist approach to his painting?
- Imagine Picasso had painted a realistic portrait of these musicians. How would your reaction to the painting differ from your current response?
- Instead of playing with lines and shapes, writers play with words to affect their readers. How might an author's choice or placement of words affect readers' responses to his art?

SOUND AND SYNTAX

A nursery rhyme, an eighteenth-century sonnet, a fast-food ad, the president's inaugural address—what could these diverse uses of language possibly have in common? Though they vary in audience, purpose, and significance, all make deliberate use of the sounds and syntax (word order) of language. Why?

From the time we are small children, we are captivated by the sounds and rhythms of language, not just by its messages. Consider a famous English nursery rhyme.

> Mary, Mary, quite contrary,
> How does your garden grow?
> With silver bells, and cockle shells,
> And pretty maids all in a row.

Clearly the ditty has little meaning for children who chant it. Its attraction lies, rather, in the repetition of sounds and in the rhythms created by its syntax. Adults also recognize the appeal of organized sound and syntax and use them to adorn all sorts of messages, from catchy commercial advertisements to official speeches.

Parallelism for Emphasis

As you read earlier, the principles of repetition and parallelism guide many of the techniques used to organize sound and syntax. Parallelism is frequently used to organize thought as well, a practice often reinforced by repeated syntax. These techniques serve to draw attention to important parts of a writer's message. They help to emphasize or clarify ideas and can set a mood that supports an author's message.

Though translation often eliminates techniques of sound, the English Bible offers many instances of parallelism and repetition in syntax and thought. A particularly beautiful and effective example is found in Christ's Sermon on the Mount. Though part of a longer discourse, this section has been granted a name of its own—the Beatitudes (Matt. 5:3–11)—because its syntactical structure draws attention to its weighty content. Each sentence repeats a two-part pattern of thought: the first part tells who will be blessed, and the second explains how they will be blessed. This parallelism of thought is reinforced by parallel syntax: each verse begins with "Blessed are" (followed by a type of person) and proceeds to "for they shall" (followed by a description of the reward). This structure compels a reader's attention and makes the passage stand out from the rest of the sermon. In addition, the book of Proverbs offers many fine examples of parallelism emphasizing differences. For instance, Proverbs 10:1 contrasts two types of sons: "A wise son maketh a glad father: but a foolish son is the heaviness of his mother." The syntax is obviously parallel, an arrangement that underscores the divergent messages.

Since the language of poetry is by definition more compressed than that of prose, it is no surprise that parallelism and patterned repetition—of sound, syntax, and thought—are more common in poetry than in prose. A poet carefully calculates the effects of each word and utilizes every aspect of language, including its structure and sounds, to convey the message. In contrast, patterns of sound and syntax in prose tend to be looser and less predictable, though they may certainly be present.

Parallelism for Rhythm

Parallelism and repetition are often used to create rhythm in poetry. Frequently this rhythm results in **meter**, a regular pattern of stressed and unstressed syllables. The individual units of these patterns are termed **poetic feet**. There are six main types, each referring to a different combination of stressed and unstressed syllables. **Iambic** is an unstressed syllable (˘) followed by a stressed syllable (´); **trochaic**, a stressed followed by an unstressed; **anapestic**, two unstressed followed by a stressed; and **dactylic**, a stressed followed by two unstressed. **Spondaic** and **pyrrhic** consist of two stressed syllables and two unstressed respectively. Poets generally maintain the same foot in a poem but may vary it for effect. A poem's line length is also important to identifying meter. A line containing two poetic feet is called dimeter; three make trimeter; four create tetrameter; five, pentameter; and so forth. Thus in **iambic pentameter**, the most common meter in English, each line contains five sets of one unstressed and one stressed syllable.

Depending on the combination of poetic foot and line length, meter can produce various moods, from a sonorous or majestic tone created by long, flowing lines to a more tense or uncomfortable atmosphere enforced by short, choppy lines.

Repetition in Rhyme

Next, **rhyme** is the most obvious form of sound repetition in poetry. Words rhyme when they show a similarity of sound from the vowel of the last accented syllable onward. In **perfect rhyme**, the type most commonly used, these syllables are exactly alike. **Slant rhyme** (or partial rhyme) pairs words that are similar but slightly mismatched in sound (e.g., *soul, sell*). **Eye rhyme** combines words that look alike but do not actually sound alike (e.g., *slow, vow*). Returning to the nursery rhyme, note that the final words of its second and fourth lines rhyme (*grow, row*). These illustrate **end rhyme**, or rhyme that falls at the end of a line. The middle and final words of lines one (*Mary, contrary*) and three (*bells, shells*) rhyme as well. These pairs demonstrate **internal rhyme**, rhyme occurring within a single line of poetry.

Three Types of Sound Repetition

Three additional forms of sound repetition appear frequently in poetry: alliteration, consonance, and assonance. Usually less noticeable than rhyme, they allow a writer to bolster his message more subtly. **Alliteration** is the repetition of initial consonant sounds. **Consonance** is the repetition of terminal and sometimes internal consonant sounds, and **assonance** is the repetition of vowel sounds. Each of these can flow through several lines, in some cases simultaneously. Consider the following example from Shakespeare's *Macbeth*. As Macbeth, a murderer and usurper, heads into a final battle for the kingdom, he hears that his wife has died. The following selection is part of his response. As you read, note the repeated sounds.

> Life's but a walking shadow, a poor player
> That struts and frets his hour upon the stage
> And then is heard no more: it is a tale
> Told by an idiot, full of sound and fury,
> Signifying nothing.

The alliteration and consonance formed using harsh and sibilant consonants like *t*, *p*, *f*, and *s* create cacophony that reinforces Macbeth's moral and emotional disintegration. The predominance of assonance using the various sounds of *o* and *u* create a depressed effect. At the same time, there is music in his speech: assonance and consonance using the *o*, *u*, *n*, and *l* sounds lend cadence to certain phrases and tie them together.

> As you read the selections in this unit, be alert to the use of these techniques. Above all, remember that the deliberate use of sound and syntax is meant to support meaning. Has an author used parallelism or repetition to organize his ideas? If he has employed alliteration, what might it emphasize? If a poem has meter, what effect might that rhythm have on the pace or mood of the poem? As noted above, skilled writers can adapt their styles to create a wide range of effects. Finally, remember that though a good ear for the sounds of poetry and prose is to some extent a gift from birth, you can also develop the ability by reading with attention to sound and sentence structure.

Who Has Seen the Wind?

Christina Rossetti

The poems of Christina Rossetti may seem simple on the surface, but they often convey profound spiritual truths. Rossetti achieved this seemingly effortless simplicity through careful craft, which allowed her to convey deep truths clearly and beautifully. In the following poem, Rossetti points out a paradox of nature and proceeds to resolve it. As you read, consider how Rossetti's resolution of this specific paradox might apply to other seeming contradictions in life.

Who has seen the wind?
    Neither I nor you:
But when the leaves hang trembling
    The wind is passing thro'.

Who has seen the wind?
    Neither you nor I:
But when the trees bow down their heads
    The wind is passing by.

About the Poem

1. Though we have never seen the wind, what are some proofs of its existence?
2. Identify the personification in the poem.
3. What kind of parallelism is found in the poem? Give one example.
4. What two metrical feet does Rossetti use most throughout the poem? Describe how her change in metrical foot coincides with a change in what she's saying.
5. What larger point about life does the poem make? Describe a spiritual truth that this theme illustrates.

About the Author

Probably best known for her poems "Goblin Market" and "In the Bleak Midwinter," Christina Rossetti (1830–94) was part of the famous and talented Rossetti family of England. Her father had been exiled from his native Italy because of his influence as a patriot and nationalistic poet. Her devout mother, formerly a governess, was an example of godly piety to her daughter Christina. Christina enjoyed an atmosphere of refined culture and education in her parents' home, where she remained all her life.

In the best traditions of lyric poetry, Rossetti's carefully crafted poems deal with the realities of life and death, the love of God and of others, and the joys and mysteries of nature. The sensitivity and depth of her writing are in part due to her many personal trials. Christina's family endured heavy financial worries, and after her father's death, the responsibilities of caring for her mother and aging maiden aunts greatly weighed upon her. Though two men close to Rossetti proposed marriage, neither shared her sturdy Christian faith and practice; thus, she chose to remain single. The loneliness she faced is often reflected in her poems. But stronger than her loneliness was her total confidence in and submission to her Lord. Rossetti filled her mind and heart with Scripture. She gained from it a unique appreciation of the sustaining and sacrificial love of God and extended that love to others through ministry work and her writing. Her poetry and uplifting devotional literature are the natural overflow of her complete dependence upon God.

Rattlesnake

Fray Angélico Chávez

In the following poem Fray Angélico Chávez makes imaginative comparisons to create startling images. He also plays with sound devices throughout, using them to unify his poem and reinforce its lively tone. Notice how the poet's perspective on his subject changes from stanza to stanza. In the first he observes; in the second he reacts.

Line of beauty scrawled alive
by God's finger on the sand,
diamond-patterned inlaid band
scrolling inward like a hive—

Stay away,
crawl-created,
articulated
coil of cloisonné!

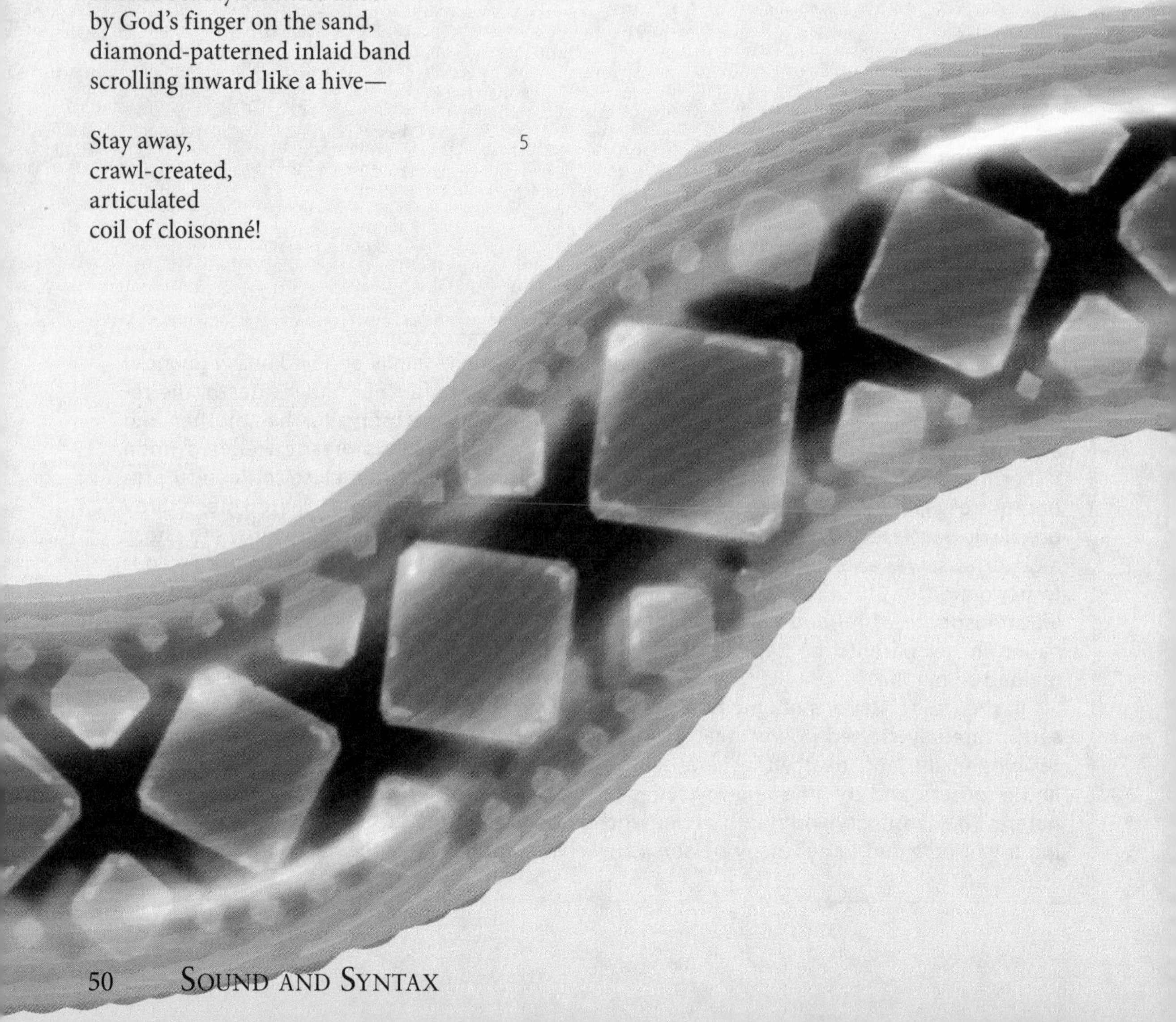

About the Poem

1. What two kinds of imaginative comparison does Chávez use? Give an example of each from the poem.
2. Name two types of sound devices (besides rhyme) that Chávez uses in the poem. Give an example of each from the poem.
3. Scan the meter of the poem. What meter does Chávez use throughout the first stanza? How do you think his change of meter in the second stanza affects the feeling conveyed by the poem?
4. Notice the last line of stanza one. How does this line prepare us for the first line of stanza two?
5. Imagine several other metaphors or similes of your own for a snake.

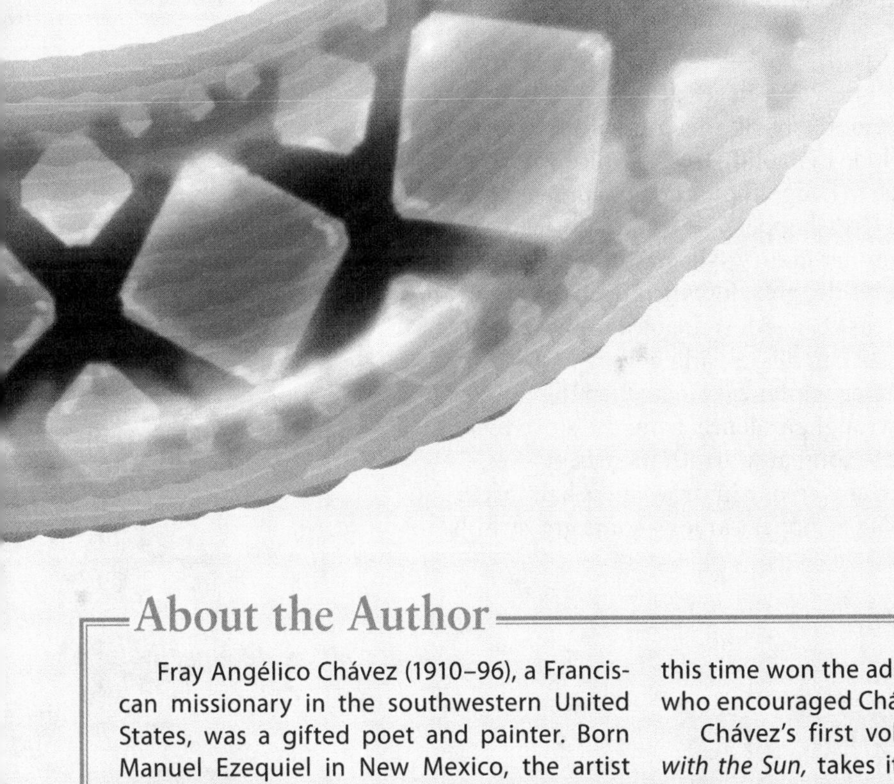

About the Author

Fray Angélico Chávez (1910–96), a Franciscan missionary in the southwestern United States, was a gifted poet and painter. Born Manuel Ezequiel in New Mexico, the artist was influenced early in life by his Catholic teachers. In 1937 he was ordained and took the religious name Fray Angélico in admiration of the fifteenth-century Italian religious painter.

Chávez worked in the Indian missions in the Southwest as well as among Spanish-speaking people. The poetry he wrote during this time won the admiration of area authors, who encouraged Chávez to publish.

Chávez's first volume of poetry, *Clothed with the Sun,* takes its name from a passage in Revelation. Like much of Chávez's poetry, it reflects both his familiarity with the Scripture and his artistic appreciation for the beauties of the southwestern desert. His poetry also reflects his sense of line and balance. "Rattlesnake" clearly illustrates Chávez's keen ability to create visual images that illustrate his appreciation of God's design in creation.

On the Grasshopper and the Cricket

John Keats

In this classic Italian-form sonnet, the British poet John Keats beautifully evokes the rhythms of nature to reveal a truth about human life. Though many poetic techniques appear throughout the poem, these seem so natural that they are easily overlooked. Here Keats makes the grasshopper (traditional symbol of idleness) into a poet, who ministers to others rather than only to itself. How does this portrayal differ from many people's view of poetry and art? In Keats's view, what do the arts offer the world?

The poetry of earth is never dead:
    When all the birds are faint with the hot sun,
    And hide in cooling trees, a voice will run
From hedge to hedge about the new-mown mead;
That is the Grasshopper's—he takes the lead
    In summer luxury,—he has never done
    With his delights; for when tired out with fun
He rests at ease beneath some pleasant weed.
The poetry of earth is ceasing never:
    On a lone winter evening, when the frost
    Has wrought a silence, from the stove there shrills
The Cricket's song, in warmth increasing ever,
    And seems to one in drowsiness half lost,
    The Grasshopper's among some grassy hills.

About the Poem

1. What is the dominant meter of Keats's poem?
2. There is one example of eye rhyme in the poem. What is it?
3. Besides rhyme, what three sound devices occur in the poem? Give one example of each.
4. How did Keats employ parallelism in the overall content of the poem?
5. The poem presents two scenarios, one in summer and one in winter. What about these situations is similar? What does the grasshopper's (or cricket's) song provide to others in both circumstances?
6. How does the similarity mentioned in question 5 apply to the arts?

About the Author

By the time he died at the age of twenty-five, John Keats (1795–1821) had produced an enormous amount of work that would later establish him among the most important of the English Romantic poets. Born into a lower-middle class family, Keats, unlike most prominent poets, attended neither Oxford nor Cambridge, but rather trained (successfully) as an apothecary and surgeon. In the realm of poetry, he was largely self-educated but by no means ignorant. However, his lack of upper-class education combined with his poetic originality (such as using informal language and unusually lush imagery) raised the hackles of prominent critics. During his brief career, his poetry was rarely appreciated.

Keats's short life was full of troubles, including financial difficulties, the loss of close family, and his own struggle with tuberculosis. But Keats's friends asserted that he was always cheerful and enthusiastic when discussing literature. "On the Grasshopper and the Cricket" resulted from a lively evening of such literary talk with his old schoolmaster Cowden Clarke and the controversial essayist Leigh Hunt. The poem was written during a contest between Keats and Hunt, which was motivated by the poets' observations concerning the grasshopper. Keats's "contest" poem was, like many other Romantic poems, a poem of association, that is, a poem in which one association evokes another. Like many of his poems, it also reflects a high regard for poetry and a subtle awareness of the rhythms and beauties of nature.

March for a One-Man Band

DAVID WAGONER

In the following poem, Wagoner does an excellent job of using sound and syntax to reinforce content. More than a description, it seems to be a performance, one in which the reader can see and hear the one-man band on the march. Try reading the poem a second time aloud to get the full effect of Wagoner's use of sound. As you read, note how the onomatopoeic words Wagoner inserts affect the rhythm of the poem.

He's *a boom a blat* in the uniform
Of an army *tweedledy* band *a toot*
Complete with medals *a honk* cornet
Against *a thump* one side of his lips
And the other stuck with *a sloop a tweet*
A whistle *a crash* on top of *a crash*
A helmet *a crash* a cymbal a drum
At his *bumbledy* knee and a *rimshot* flag
A click he stands at attention *a wheeze*
And plays the Irrational Anthem *bang.*

About the Poem

1. Identify at least two sound devices other than onomatopoeia that Wagoner uses in his poem.
2. Does the poem have a steady meter? How does the meter affect the overall impression of the poem and its subject?
3. Do you think the poet is entertained or annoyed by the performance of a one-man band?
4. Why do you think the poet used "Irrational Anthem" rather than "National Anthem"?

About the Author

Award-winning poet and novelist David Wagoner (b. 1926) was born in Massillon, Ohio, and received his education at Pennsylvania State University and Indiana University. While a student, he was greatly influenced by Theodore Roethke, professor and modern poet. Like Roethke, Wagoner went on to become both a university professor and a prolific writer, publishing ten novels and over twenty volumes of poetry. In addition to these activities, he served as the editor of *Poetry Northwest* for thirty-six years and as a Chancellor of the Academy of American Poets for twenty-one years. Currently he is a professor at the University of Washington.

Wagoner is well respected among modern poets for his ability to reanimate familiar or worn-out language, using the sound and the rhythm of words to paint dramatic scenes for his reader. His poems, which are a blend of the simple and the serious, display great energy. A common theme throughout much of his poetry is the relationship between man and nature: a speaker encounters nature and in the process learns something about himself or about man in general. In conjunction with this theme, Wagoner frequently addresses environmental concerns as well. Many of his novels mix this idealism with cynicism toward society. The social order becomes a bleak and corrupted place in which naive protagonists must struggle to retain their innocence or lose it in order to come to terms with society. Their experiences seem curiously disjointed, isolated, and absurd, much like the fumbling one-man band.

Foul Shot

EDWIN A. HOEY

Most narrative involves some kind of conflict. When the outcome of a conflict remains in doubt, the reader's curiosity and anxiety may rise to a level known as suspense. In the following narrative poem, Hoey draws a relatively brief conflict in minute detail in order to create suspense. How do the many uses of sound devices and parallelism included in the poem contribute to the creation of suspense?

With two 60's stuck on the scoreboard
And two seconds hanging on the clock,
The solemn boy in the center of eyes,
Squeezed by silence,
Seeks out the line with his feet,
Soothes his hands along his uniform,
Gently drums the ball against the floor,
Then measures the waiting net,
Raises the ball on his right hand,
Balances it with his left,
Calms it with fingertips,
Breathes,
Crouches,
Waits,
And then through a stretching of stillness,
Nudges it upward.

The ball
Slides up and out,
Lands,
Leans,
Wobbles,
Wavers,
Hesitates,
Exasperates,
Plays it coy
Until every face begs with unsounding screams—
And then

And then

And then,

Right before ROAR-UP,
Dives down and through.

About the Poem

1. What object is personified in the poem?
2. Identify examples of two types of sound devices used in the poem.
3. At what point in Hoey's poem does the outcome become clear?
4. Do you think Hoey was successful in building suspense in "Foul Shot"?
5. Identify one use of parallelism in the poem. How do instances such as these contribute to the poet's creation of suspense?

About the Author

Growing up in Chillicothe, Ohio, Edwin A. (Ted) Hoey (b. 1930) enjoyed playing outdoors with his brothers but could also often be found with his nose in a book. He majored in history at Swarthmore College and, after serving in the military during the Korean War, returned stateside to teach fifth grade for two and a half years at a private school on Long Island. Academically strong, Hoey's students wrote their own plays and then performed the parts.

Hoey wrote "Foul Shot" during his career at *READ* magazine, where he worked as writer and editor for almost forty years. Needing to fill a page, he drew on his memory as a spectator at a high school game at Chillicothe. The swish of the game-winning shot and roar of victory replayed in his mind's ear, and Hoey wrote "Foul Shot" in about sixty seconds. The poem was later published in *Reflections on a Gift of Watermelon Pickle . . . and Other Modern Verse*. To promote the book, *Scholastic, READ's* competition, disseminated copies of "Foul Shot" at a teachers' convention. Teachers carried the poem back to their classrooms. It has enjoyed continued popularity ever since.

Of his work at *READ,* Hoey said, "I enjoyed it. You were working with stories, with poems, with plays—ideas that were suddenly important. It was always interesting and fun to do."* Hoey also enjoyed the people with whom he worked. His legacy at *READ* continues through the NCTE Edwin A. Hoey Award, honoring not only the annual recipient but also Hoey, who, according to the citation, "brought limitless imagination and creativity to the pages of *READ* magazine."

*January 28, 2011, phone interview with BJU Press

THINKING ZONE

In poetry, meter and lines are an important way of organizing sound, syntax, and sense. However, they are not the only means of doing so. If a poet wishes to create divisions of thought that override poetic lines, he can do so in several ways. A person reading verse still tends to pause or stop at a natural break—for example, at the end of a sentence or a clause. When this natural pause comes at the end of a line of poetry, the lines are referred to as **end-stopped**. If the reader must run past the end of the line and into the next to find the natural pause or break (based on speech rhythm or sense) the lines illustrate **enjambment**. Enjambment allows a poet to emphasize the connection of ideas in two or more lines. In contrast, **caesura** is a break found within a line of poetry. The pause created by a caesura emphasizes a poet's break in thought. Often conventional punctuation marks coincide with a caesura, but not always.

Poets may also use meter to subtly emphasize connections or divisions in thought. For example, when the final syllable of a line is unstressed, it is referred to as a **feminine ending**. A final stressed syllable is called a **masculine ending**. These different endings may result naturally from the poetic foot chosen, or they may be created deliberately by the poet's varying his meter slightly. In any case, both tend toward certain effects: masculine endings are more likely when the idea of a line continues on to the next line, whereas feminine endings lend more closure to ideas or phrases. In addition, poets may create small variations in meter to create pauses or to aid the flow of thought. Spondaic and pyrrhic feet in particular are usually used for this purpose.

The following lines from Shelley's "Ozymandias" illustrate these terms.

"'My name is Ozymandias, king of kings:
Look on my works, ye mighty, and despair!'
Nothing beside remains. Round the decay
Of that colossal wreck, boundless and bare
The lone and level sands stretch far away."

Lines 1, 2, and 5 are end-stopped. Lines 3 and 4 illustrate enjambment. Lines 1 and 3 contain caesuras. Because all the lines end in stressed syllables, they are masculine, rather than feminine. These endings enhance the flow of thought, particularly in the last three lines.

1. Which two lines in Rossetti's poem "Who Has Seen the Wind?" illustrate **enjambment**? What does the enjambment emphasize?
2. Identify the one line (other than the final line) in "Rattlesnake" that is **end-stopped**. What purpose does this end-stop serve in contrast to the other lines of the poem?
3. Identify four lines containing a **caesura** in Keats's "On the Grasshopper and the Cricket."
4. Determine the lines in "On the Grasshopper and the Cricket" that illustrate **feminine endings**. Does the effect fit the overall tendency of feminine lines as mentioned above?
5. Are the line endings in Wagoner's "March for a One-Man Band" masculine or feminine? What do you think is the overall effect of these endings on the poem's flow?
6. What is the effect of Hoey's use of commas in the first twenty-four lines of "Foul Shot"?

A Gray Sleeve

Stephen Crane

Most famous for his Civil War novel, *The Red Badge of Courage*, Crane also wrote a collection of short stories set in the same time period. In this one, Union blue meets Confederate gray, but the real struggle proves not to be a military one. Crane is noted for his vivid evocations of his settings and of human psychology. Notice how he uses imaginative comparisons as well as devices of sound and syntax both to bring the setting and characters to life and to emphasize the story's tone.

1

"It looks as if it might rain this afternoon," remarked the lieutenant of artillery.

"So it does," the infantry captain assented. He glanced casually at the sky. When his eyes had lowered to the green-shadowed landscape before him, he said fretfully: "I wish those fellows out yonder would quit pelting at us. They've been at it since noon."

At the edge of a grove of maples, across wide fields, there occasionally appeared little puffs of smoke of a dull hue in this gloom of sky which expressed an impending rain. The long wave of blue and steel in the field moved uneasily at the eternal barking of the faraway sharpshooters, and the men, leaning upon their rifles, stared at the grove of maples. Once a private turned to borrow some tobacco from a comrade in the rear rank, but, with his hand still stretched out, he continued to twist his head and glance at the distant trees. He was afraid the enemy would shoot at him at a time when he was not looking.

Suddenly the artillery officer said, "See what's coming!"

Along the rear of the brigade of infantry a column of cavalry was sweeping at a hard gallop. A lieutenant, riding some yards to the right of the column, bawled furiously at the four troopers just at the rear of the colors. They had lost distance and made a little gap, but at the shouts of the lieutenant they urged their horses forward. The bugler, careering along behind the captain of the troop, fought and tugged like a wrestler to keep his frantic animal from bolting far ahead of the column.

On the springy turf the innumerable hoofs thundered in a swift storm of sound. In the brown faces of the troopers their eyes were set like bits of flashing steel.

The long line of the infantry regiments standing at ease underwent a sudden movement at the rush of the passing squadron. The foot soldiers turned their heads to gaze at the torrent of horses and men.

The yellow folds of the flag fluttered back in silken, shuddering waves, as if it were a reluctant thing. Occasionally a giant spring of a charger would rear the firm and sturdy figure of a soldier suddenly head and shoulders above his comrades. Over the noise of the scudding* hoofs could be heard the creaking of leather trappings, the jingle and clank of steel, and the tense, low-toned commands or appeals of the men to their horses. And the horses were mad with the headlong sweep of this movement. Powerful underjaws bent back and straightened so that the bits were clamped as rigidly as vises upon the teeth, and glistening necks arched in desperate resistance to the hands at the bridles. Swinging their heads in rage at the granite laws of their lives, which compelled even their angers and their

ardors to chosen directions and chosen paces, their flight was as a flight of harnessed demons.

scudding: swiftly and easily running

The captain's bay kept its pace at the head of the squadron with the lithe bounds of a thoroughbred, and this horse was proud as a chief at the roaring trample of his fellows behind him. The captain's glance was calmly upon the grove of maples whence the sharpshooters of the enemy had been picking at the blue line. He seemed to be reflecting. He stolidly rose and fell with the plunges of his horse in all the indifference of a deacon's figure seated plumply in church. And it occurred to many of the watching infantry to wonder why this officer could remain imperturbable and reflective when his squadron was thundering and swarming behind him like the rushing of a flood.

The column swung in a saber-curve toward a break in a fence, and dashed into a roadway. Once a little plank bridge was encountered, and the sound of the hoofs upon it was like the long roll of many drums. An old captain in the infantry turned to his first lieutenant and made a remark which was a compound of bitter disparagement of cavalry in general and soldierly admiration of this particular troop.

Suddenly the bugle sounded, and the column halted with a jolting upheaval amid sharp, brief cries. A moment later the men had tumbled from their horses and, carbines in hand, were running in a swarm toward the grove of maples. In the road one of every four of the troopers was standing with braced legs, and pulling and hauling at the bridles of four frenzied horses.

The captain was running awkwardly in his boots. He held his saber low, so that the point often threatened to catch in the turf. His yellow hair ruffled out from under his faded cap. "Go in hard now!" he roared, in a voice of hoarse fury. His face was violently red.

The troopers threw themselves upon the grove like wolves upon a great animal. Along the whole front of the woods there was the dry crackling of musketry, with bitter, swift flashes and smoke that writhed like stung phantoms. The troopers yelled shrilly and spanged* bullets low into the foliage.

spanged: banged

For a moment, when near the woods, the line almost halted. The men struggled and fought for a time like swimmers encountering a powerful current. Then with a supreme effort they went on again. They dashed madly at the grove, whose foliage, from the high light of the field, was as inscrutable as a wall.

Then suddenly each detail of the calm trees became apparent, and with a few more frantic leaps the men were in the cool gloom of the woods. There was a heavy odor as from burned paper. Wisps of gray smoke wound upward. The men halted; and, grimy, perspiring, and puffing, they searched the recesses of the woods with eager, fierce glances. Figures could be seen flitting afar off. A dozen carbines rattled at them in an angry volley.

During this pause the captain strode along the line, his face lit with a broad smile of contentment. "When he sends this crowd to do anything, I guess he'll find we do it pretty sharp," he said to the grinning lieutenant.

"Say, they didn't stand that rush a minute, did they?" said the subaltern.* Both officers were profoundly dusty in their uniforms, and their faces were soiled like those of two urchins.

subaltern: assisting officer

Out in the grass behind them were three tumbled and silent forms.

Presently the line moved forward again. The men went from tree to tree like hunters stalking game. Some at the left of the line fired occasionally, and those at the right gazed curiously in that direction. The men still breathed heavily from their scramble across the field.

Of a sudden a trooper halted and said: "Hello! there's a house!" Everyone paused. The men turned to look at their leader.

The captain stretched his neck and swung his head from side to side. "By George, it is a house!" he said.

Through the wealth of leaves there vaguely loomed the form of a large white house. These troopers, brown-faced from many days of campaigning, each feature of them telling of their placid confidence and courage, were stopped abruptly by the appearance of this house. There was some subtle suggestion—some tale of an unknown thing—which watched them from they knew not what part of it.

A rail fence girded a wide lawn of tangled grass. Seven pines stood along a driveway which led from two distant posts of a vanished gate. The blue-clothed troopers moved forward until they stood at the fence, peering over it.

The captain put one hand on the top rail and seemed to be about to climb the fence, when suddenly he hesitated and said in a low voice: "Watson, what do you think of it?"

The lieutenant stared at the house. "I don't know!" he replied.

The captain pondered. It happened that the whole company had turned a gaze of profound awe and doubt upon this edifice which confronted them. The men were very silent.

At last the captain swore and said: "We are certainly a pack of fools. Old deserted house halting a company of Union cavalry, and making us gape like babies!"

"Yes, but there's something—something—" insisted the subaltern in half a stammer.

"Well, if there's 'something—something' in there, I'll get it out," said the captain. "Send Sharpe clean around to the other side with about twelve men, so we will sure bag your 'something—something,' and I'll take a few of the boys and find out what's in the thing!"

He chose the nearest eight men for his "storming party," as the lieutenant called it. After he had waited some minutes for the others to get into position, he said "Come ahead" to his eight men, and climbed the fence.

The brighter light of the tangled lawn made him suddenly feel tremendously apparent, and he wondered if there could be some mystic thing in the house which was regarding this approach. His men trudged silently at his back. They stared at the windows and lost themselves in deep speculations as to the probability of there being, perhaps, eyes behind the blinds—malignant eyes, piercing eyes.

Suddenly a corporal in the party gave vent to a startled exclamation and half threw his carbine into position. The captain turned quickly, and the corporal said: "I saw an arm move the blinds—an arm with a gray sleeve!"

"Don't be a fool, Jones, now!" said the captain sharply.

"I swear—" began the corporal, but the captain silenced him

When they arrived at the front of the house, the troopers paused, while the captain went softly up the front steps. He stood before the large front door and studied it. Some crickets chirped in the long grass, and the nearest pine could be heard in its endless sighs. One of the privates moved uneasily, and his foot crunched the gravel. Suddenly the captain swore angrily and kicked the door with a loud crash. It flew open.

2

The bright light of the day flashed into the old house when the captain angrily kicked open the door. He was aware of a wide hallway carpeted with matting and extending deep into the dwelling. There was also an old walnut hat rack and a little marble-topped table with a vase and two books upon it. Farther back was a great venerable fireplace containing dreary ashes.

But directly in front of the captain was a young girl. The flying open of the door had obviously been an utter astonishment to her, and she remained transfixed there in the middle of the floor, staring at the captain with wide eyes.

She was like a child caught at the time of a raid upon the cake. She wavered to and fro upon her feet, and held her hands behind her. There were two little points of terror in her eyes, as she gazed up at the young captain in dusty blue, with his reddish, bronze complexion, his yellow hair, his bright saber held threateningly.

These two remained motionless and silent, simply staring at each other for some moments.

The captain felt his rage fade out of him and leave his mind limp. He had been violently angry, because this house had made him feel hesitant, wary. He did not like to be wary. He liked to feel confident, sure. So he had kicked the door open, and had been prepared to march in like a soldier of wrath.

But now he began, for one thing, to wonder if his uniform was so dusty and old in appearance. Moreover, he had a feeling that his face was covered with a compound of dust, grime, and perspiration. He took a step forward and said, "I didn't mean to frighten you." But his voice was coarse from his battle-howling. It seemed to him to have hempen fibers in it.

The girl's breath came in little, quick gasps, and she looked at him as she would have looked at a serpent.

"I didn't mean to frighten you," he said again.

The girl, still with her hands behind her, began to back away.

"Is there anyone else in the house?" he went on, while slowly following her. "I don't wish to disturb you, but we had a fight with some rebel skirmishers in the woods, and I thought maybe some of them might have come in here. In fact, I was pretty sure of it. Are there any of them here?"

The girl looked at him and said, "No!" He wondered why extreme agitation made the eyes of some women so limpid and bright.

"Who is here besides yourself?"

By this time his pursuit had driven her to the end of the hall, and she remained there with her back to the wall and her hands still behind her. When she answered this question, she did not look at him, but down at the floor. She cleared her voice and then said, "There is no one here."

"No one?"

She lifted her eyes to him in that appeal that the human being must make even to falling trees, crashing boulders, the sea in a storm, and said, "No, no, there is no one here." He could plainly see her tremble.

Of a sudden he bethought him that she continually kept her hands behind her. As he recalled her air when first discovered, he remembered she appeared precisely as a child detected at one of the crimes of childhood. Moreover, she had always backed away from him. He thought now that she was concealing something which was an evidence of the presence of the enemy in the house.

"What are you holding behind you?" he said suddenly.

She gave a little quick moan, as if some grim hand had throttled her.

"Oh, nothing—please. I am not holding anything behind me; indeed I'm not."

"Very well. Hold your hands out in front of you, then."

"Oh, indeed, I'm not holding anything behind me. Indeed I'm not."

"Well," he began. Then he paused, and remained for a moment dubious. Finally, he laughed. "Well, I shall have my men search the house, anyhow. I'm sorry to trouble you, but I feel sure that there is someone here whom we want." He turned to the corporal, who, with the other men, was gaping quietly in at the door, and said: "Jones, go through the house."

As for himself, he remained planted in front of the girl, for she evidently did not dare to move and allow him to see what she held so carefully behind her back. So she was his prisoner.

The men rummaged around on the ground floor of the house. Sometimes the captain called to them. "Try that closet." "Is there any cellar?" But they found no one, and at last they went trooping toward the stairs which led to the second floor.

But at this movement on the part of the men the girl uttered a cry—a cry of such fright and appeal that the men paused. "Oh, don't go up there! Please don't go up there!—ple—ease! There is no one there! Indeed—indeed there is not! Oh, ple—ease!"

"Go on, Jones," said the captain calmly.

The obedient corporal made a preliminary step, and the girl bounded toward the stairs with another cry.

As she passed him, the captain caught sight of that which she had concealed behind her back, and which she had forgotten in this supreme moment. It was a pistol.

She ran to the first step and, standing there, faced the men, one hand extended with perpendicular palm, and the other holding the pistol at her side. "Oh, please, don't go up there! Nobody is there—indeed, there is not! P-l-e-a-s-e!" Then suddenly she sank swiftly down upon the step and, huddling forlornly, began to weep in the agony and with the convulsive tremors of an infant. The pistol fell from her fingers and rattled down to the floor.

The astonished troopers looked at their astonished captain. There was a short silence.

Finally, the captain stopped and picked up the pistol. It was a heavy weapon of the army pattern. He ascertained that it was empty.

He leaned toward the shaking girl and said gently, "Will you tell me what you were going to do with this pistol?"

He had to repeat the question a number of times, but at last a muffled voice said, "Nothing."

"Nothing!" He insisted quietly upon a further answer. At the tender tones of the captain's voice, the phlegmatic* corporal turned and winked gravely at the man next to him.

phlegmatic: unemotional

"Won't you tell me?"

The girl shook her head.

"Please tell me!"

The silent privates were moving their feet uneasily and wondering how long they were to wait.

The captain said: "Please, won't you tell me?"

Then the girl's voice began in stricken tones, half coherent, and amid violent sobbing: "It was grandpa's. He—he—he said he was going to shoot anybody who came in here—he didn't care if there were thousands of 'em. And—and I know he would, and I was afraid they'd kill him. And so—and—so I stole away his pistol—and I was going to hide it when you—you—you kicked open the door."

The men straightened up and looked at each other. The girl began to weep again.

The captain mopped his brow. He peered down at the girl. He mopped his brow again. Suddenly he said: "Ah, don't cry like that."

He moved restlessly and looked down at his boots. He mopped his brow again.

Then he gripped the corporal by the arm and dragged him some yards back from the others. "Jones," he said, in an intensely earnest voice, "will you tell me what I am going to do?"

The corporal's countenance became illuminated with satisfaction at being thus requested to advise his superior officer. He adopted an air of great thought, and finally said: "Well, of course, the feller with the gray sleeve must be upstairs, and we must get past the girl and up there somehow. Suppose I take her by the arm and lead her—"

"What!" interrupted the captain from between his clenched teeth. As he turned away from the corporal, he said fiercely over his shoulder: "You touch that girl and I'll split your skull!"

3

The corporal looked after his captain with an expression of mingled amazement, grief, and philosophy. He seemed to be saying to himself that there unfortunately were times, after all, when one could not rely upon the most reliable of men. When he returned to the group he found the captain bending over the girl saying: "Why is it that you don't want us to search upstairs?"

The girl's head was buried in her crossed arms. Locks of her hair had escaped from their fastenings, and these fell upon her shoulder.

"Won't you tell me?"

The corporal here winked again at the man next to him.

"Because," the girl moaned—"because—there isn't anybody up there."

The captain at last said timidly: "Well, I'm afraid—I'm afraid we'll have to—"

The girl sprang to her feet again, and implored him with her hands. She looked deep into his eyes with her glance, which was at this time like that of the fawn when it says to the hunter, "Have mercy upon me!"

These two stood regarding each other. The captain's foot was on the bottom step, but he seemed to be shrinking. He wore an air of being deeply wretched and ashamed. There was a silence.

Suddenly the corporal said in a quick, low tone: "Look out, captain!"

All turned their eyes swiftly toward the head of the stairs. There had appeared there a youth in a gray uniform. He stood looking coolly down at them. No word was said by the troopers. The girl gave vent to a little wail of desolation, "Oh, Harry!"

He began slowly to descend the stairs. His right arm was in a white sling, and there were some fresh bloodstains upon the cloth. His face was rigid and deathly pale, but his eyes flashed like lights. The girl was again moaning in an utterly dreary fashion, as the youth came slowly down toward the silent men in blue.

Six steps from the bottom of the flight he halted and said, "I reckon it's me you're looking for."

The troopers had crowded forward a trifle and, posed in lithe, nervous attitudes, were watching him like cats. The captain remained unmoved. At the youth's question he merely nodded his head and said, "Yes."

The young man in gray looked down at the girl, and then, in the same even tone, which now, however, seemed to vibrate with suppressed fury, he said: "And is that any reason why you should insult my sister?"

At this sentence, the girl intervened, desperately, between the young man in gray and the officer in blue. "Oh, don't, Harry, don't! He was good to me! He was good to me, Harry—indeed he was!"

The youth came on in his quiet, erect fashion until the girl could have touched either of the men with her hand, for the captain still remained with his foot upon the first step. She continually repeated: "Oh, Harry! Oh, Harry!"

The youth in gray maneuvered to glare into the captain's face, first over one shoulder of the girl and then over the other. In a voice that rang like metal, he said: "You are armed and unwounded, while I have no weapons and am wounded; but—"

The captain had stepped back and sheathed his saber. The eyes of these two men were gleaming fire, but otherwise the captain's countenance was imperturbable. He said: "You are mistaken. You have no reason to—"

"You lie!"

All save the captain and the youth in gray started in an electric movement. These two words crackled in the air like shattered glass. There was a breathless silence.

The captain cleared his throat. His look at the youth contained a quality of singular and terrible ferocity, but he said in his stolid tone: "I don't suppose you mean what you say now."

Upon his arm he had felt the pressure of some unconscious little fingers. The girl was leaning against the wall as if she no longer knew how to keep her balance, but those fingers—he held his arm very still. She murmured: "Oh, Harry, don't! He was good to me—indeed he was!"

The corporal had come forward until he in a measure confronted the youth in gray, for he saw those fingers upon the captain's arm, and he knew that sometimes very strong men were not able to move hand nor foot under such conditions.

The youth had suddenly seemed to become weak. He breathed heavily and clung to the rail. He was glaring at the captain, and apparently summoning all his will power to combat his weakness. The corporal addressed him with profound straightforwardness: "Don't you be a fool!" The youth turned toward him so fiercely that the corporal threw up a knee and an elbow like a boy who expects to be cuffed.

The girl pleaded with the captain: "You won't hurt him, will you? He don't know what he's saying. He's wounded, you know. Please don't mind him!"

"I won't touch him," said the captain, with rather extraordinary earnestness; "don't you worry about him at all. I won't touch him!"

Then he looked at her, and the girl suddenly withdrew her fingers from his arm.

The corporal contemplated the top of the stairs, and remarked without surprise: "There's another of 'em coming!"

An old man was clambering down the stairs with much speed. He waved a cane wildly. "Get out of my house, you thieves! Get out! I won't have you cross my threshold! Get out!" he mumbled and wagged his head in an old man's fury. It was plainly his intention to assault them.

And so it occurred that a young girl became engaged in protecting a stalwart captain, fully armed, and with eight grim troopers at his back, from the attack of an old man with a walking stick!

A blush passed over the temples and brow of the captain, and he looked particularly savage and weary. Despite the girl's efforts, he suddenly faced the old man.

"Look here," he said distinctly, "we came in because we had been fighting in the woods yonder, and we concluded that some of the enemy were in this house, especially when we saw a gray sleeve at the window. But this young man is wounded, and I have nothing to say to him. I will even take it for granted that there are no others like him upstairs. We will go away, leaving your house just as we found it! And we are no more thieves and rascals than you are!"

The old man simply roared: "I haven't got a cow nor a pig nor a chicken on the place! Your soldiers have stolen everything they could carry away. They have torn down half my fences for firewood. This afternoon some of your accursed bullets even broke my windowpanes!"

The girl had been faltering: "Grandpa! Oh, grandpa!"

The captain looked at the girl. She returned his glance from the shadow of the old man's shoulder. After studying her face a moment, he said: "Well, we will go now." He strode toward the door, and his men clanked docilely after him.

At this time there was the sound of harsh cries and rushing footsteps from without. The door flew open, and a whirlwind composed of bluecoated troopers came in with a swoop. It was headed by the lieutenant. "Oh, here you are!" he cried, catching his breath. "We thought—Oh, look at the girl!"

The captain said intensely: "Shut up, you fool!"

The men settled to a halt with a crash and a bang. There could be heard the dulled sound of many hoofs outside the house.

"Did you order up the horses?" inquired the captain.

"Yes. We thought—"

"Well, then, let's get out of here," interrupted the captain morosely.

The men began to filter out into the open air. The youth in gray had been hanging dismally to the railing of the stairway. He was now climbing slowly up to the second floor. The old man was addressing himself directly to the serene corporal.

"Not a chicken on the place!" he cried.

"Well, I didn't take your chickens, did I?"

"No, maybe you didn't but—"

The captain crossed the hall and stood before the girl in rather a culprit's fashion. "You are not angry at me, are you?" he asked timidly.

"No," she said. She hesitated a moment, and then suddenly held out her hand. "You were good to me—and I'm—much obliged."

The captain took her hand, and then he blushed, for he found himself unable to formulate a sentence that applied in any way to the situation.

She did not seem to heed that hand for a time.

He loosened his grasp presently, for he was ashamed to hold it so long without saying anything clever. At last, with an air of charging an entrenched brigade, he contrived to say: "I would rather do anything than frighten or trouble you."

His brow was warmly perspiring. He had a sense of being hideous in his dusty uniform and with his grimy face.

She said, "Oh, I'm so glad it was you instead of somebody who might have—might have hurt brother Harry and grandpa!"

He told her, "I wouldn't have hurt 'em for anything!"

There was a little silence.

"Well, good-by!" he said at last.

"Good-by!"

He walked toward the door past the old man, who was scolding at the vanishing figure of the corporal. The captain looked back. She had remained there watching him.

At the bugle's order, the troopers standing beside their horses swung briskly into the saddle. The lieutenant said to the first sergeant: "Williams, did they ever meet before?"

"Hanged if I know!"

"Well, say—"

The captain saw a curtain move at one of the windows. He cantered from his position at the head of the column and steered his horse between two flower beds.

"Well, good-by!"

The squadron trampled slowly past.

"Good-by!"

They shook hands.

He evidently had something enormously important to say to her, but it seemed that he could not manage it. He struggled heroically. The bay charger, with his great mystically solemn eyes, looked around the corner of his shoulder at the girl.

The captain studied a pine tree. The girl inspected the grass beneath the window. The captain said hoarsely: "I don't suppose—I don't suppose—I'll ever see you again!"

She looked at him affrightedly and shrank back from the window. He seemed to have woefully expected a reception of this kind for his question. He gave her instantly a glance of appeal.

She said: "Why, no, I don't suppose we will."

"Never?"

"Why, no, 'tain't possible. You—you are a—Yankee!"

"Oh, I know it, but—" Eventually he continued: "Well, some day, you know, when there's no more fighting, we might—" he observed that she had again withdrawn suddenly into the shadow, so he said: "Well, good-by!"

When he held her fingers she bowed her head, and he saw a pink blush steal over the curves of her cheek and neck.

"Am I never going to see you again?"

She made no reply.

"Never?" he repeated.

After a long time, he bent over to hear a faint reply: "Sometimes—when there are no troops in the neighborhood—grandpa don't mind if I—walk over as far as that old oak tree yonder—in the afternoons."

It appeared that the captain's grip was very strong, for she uttered an exclamation and looked at her fingers as if she expected to find them mere fragments. He rode away.

The bay horse leaped a flower bed. They were almost to the drive, when the girl uttered a panic-stricken cry.

The captain wheeled his horse violently, and upon his return journey went straight through a flower bed.

The girl clasped her hands. She beseeched him wildly with her eyes. "Oh, please, don't believe it! I never walk to the old oak tree. Indeed I don't! I never—never—never walk there."

The bridle dropped on the bay charger's neck. The captain's figure seemed limp. With an expression of profound dejection and gloom he stared off at where the leaden sky met the dark green line of the woods. The long impending rain began to fall with a mournful patter, drop and drop. There was a silence.

At last a low voice said, "Well, I might—sometimes I might—perhaps—but only once in a great while—I might walk to the old tree—in the afternoons."

About the Story

1. Particularly in the first half of the story, Crane uses many metaphors, similes, and onomatopoeic words to evoke the scenes of battle. Find an example of each in the story.
2. The description of the cavalry's charge into the woods is especially full of sound devices. (See page 61, paragraphs 5–7.) Locate three examples of sound devices in this passage.
3. The literary term *anticlimax* refers to a sudden decline from the lofty to the ridiculous after a building up of suspense. Briefly explain how this story qualifies as anticlimactic.
4. Which character changes the most throughout the story? What do you think Crane wants to point out by this change?

About the Author

Stephen Crane (1871–1900) was the last of fourteen children born to a Methodist minister in New Jersey. Crane began writing early and by his teenage years had already published several articles. Such newspaper work would remain a helpful source of income throughout his career. After a stint at college (from which he never graduated), Crane struck out on his own, determined to become a serious writer.

For his first novel, he attempted to capture the reality of life for New York's downtrodden, going so far as to live in a poor neighborhood of the city for a year. Still, his attempts to privately publish and promote the novel were unproductive. Eventually, realist author Hamlin Garland recognized his talent and helped the struggling young writer gain the attention of the literary world.

Crane's second novel, *The Red Badge of Courage,* established his reputation as a leader in the modern realistic movement of American fiction. Considered by many to be one of the greatest war novels, *The Red Badge of Courage* presents a grim view of battle through the eyes of a young soldier, Henry Fleming. So accurate was Crane's portrayal of human psychology in the face of battle that critics at first believed the author must be a veteran. Like much of Crane's work, the novel is naturalistic fiction, presenting individuals as powerless in the face of a powerful but indifferent natural world. After this triumph, Crane continued to write but was never able to reach financial success. Worn down by traveling as a war correspondent and continually writing more fiction to pay the bills, Crane succumbed to tuberculosis at the age of twenty-eight.

Winter Ocean

John Updike

The following poem depicts the sea using sound devices and depends upon them to create its mood. The rhythm created also plays a part in reinforcing the mood of the poem. Note the picture and sounds of the sea that the poem creates in your mind. How does the poet achieve this effect using just words?

Many-maned scud*-thumper, tub
of male whales, maker of worn wood, shrub-ruster, sky-
    mocker, rave!
portly pusher of waves, wind-slave.

scud: wind-driven clouds and rain

About the Poem

1. What is the mood of Updike's poem?
2. Briefly describe how the overall sound devices of the poem relate to its mood.
3. Briefly describe how the overall rhythm of the poem reinforces its mood.

About the Author

Novelist, poet, short story writer, and critic, John Updike (1932–2009) had a writing career spanning six decades. A prolific writer, Updike said of himself in an interview in the *Paris Review*, "I write fairly rapidly if I get going. . . . If a thing goes, it goes for me, and if it doesn't go, I eventually stop and get off."[†] At his death at age 76, in addition to essays and reviews, Updike had written over twenty novels, over twelve short story collections, five children's books, and several books of poetry, one of which, *Endpoint*, was published posthumously.

Updike was a realist. He wrote about the everyday lives of ordinary people, capturing small town, middle-class, post–World War II America as he perceived it. A craftsman with impressive facility with language, Updike was noted for his rich and unusual writing style. In theme he often focused on Americans' attempts to fill the void left by the absence of traditional faith, an effort that included immorality and materialism, as illustrated in Updike's memorable character Harry "Rabbit" Angstrom of his "Rabbit" tetralogy. For his efforts Updike received many awards, including two Pulitzer Prizes for fiction (*Rabbit Is Rich* in 1981 and *Rabbit at Rest* in 1991), a distinction earned by only three other authors. Updike's poetry is often characterized as light and occasional verse. It covers a variety of topics and forms, has technical merit, and is highly accessible, demonstrating Updike's versatility.

[†]"John Updike: The Art of Fiction No. 43." Interview by Charles Thomas Samuels. *The Paris Review* 45 (Winter 1968): n.pag. Web. 14 March 2011.

Traveling Through the Dark

WILLIAM STAFFORD

This modern sonnet presents a moral dilemma. The setting and the nature of the dilemma are not uncommon: the speaker seems like an average person. But his reverence for life and strong sense of responsibility cause him to weigh his choices carefully. In keeping with this scenario, the poet's use of sound and syntax is subtle but nonetheless thoughtful.

Traveling through the dark I found a deer
dead on the edge of Wilson River road.
It is usually best to roll them into the canyon:
that road is narrow; to swerve might make more dead.
By glow of the tail-light I stumbled back of the car
and stood by the heap, a doe, a recent killing;
she had stiffened already, almost cold.
I dragged her off; she was large in the belly.
My fingers touching her side brought me the reason–
her side was warm; her fawn lay there waiting,
alive, still, never to be born.
Beside that mountain road I hesitated.
The car aimed ahead its lowered parking lights;
under the hood purred the steady engine.
I stood in the glare of the warm exhaust turning red;
around our group I could hear the wilderness listen.
I thought hard for us all—my only swerving—,
then pushed her over the edge into the river.

About the Poem

1. Identify one instance of slant rhyme found in the poem. Identify two other sound devices found in the poem.
2. Forms of the word *swerve* occur twice in the poem (lines 4 and 16). What universal human tendency does the second usage of the word allude to?
3. Does the title have additional meaning when you have finished reading the poem? Briefly explain your answer.
4. Does Stafford's message contradict a biblical worldview? Why or why not?
5. What would you have done had you faced the speaker's dilemma?

About the Author

William Edgar Stafford (1914–93) was born and reared in Kansas, where he enjoyed a happy childhood in the countryside and small rural towns. His love and respect for life, especially wildlife, was nurtured during these quiet years. A life-long pacifist, Stafford refused military service in World War II, choosing instead to serve in a public-works division. After the war's end, Stafford eventually turned to teaching in the English department of Oregon's Lewis and Clark College and completed his doctoral work in 1954. Not until 1962 did he publish his first significant volume of poetry, *Traveling Through the Dark*, but from then on, he continued to publish copious amounts of work, even serving as Poet Laureate in 1970.

Stafford received many awards and grants, most notably the 1963 National Book Award for Poetry for his *Traveling Through the Dark*. The presenters of this award to Stafford described his work as "both tough and gentle." These qualities are evident in our selection, the title poem from this book. The speaker in "Traveling Through the Dark" faces a moral dilemma and resolves it to the best of his ability. Nevertheless, his decision does not erase his sense of respectful awe before the forces of life and death he has encountered. Stafford generally stands apart from literary and political movements. In much of his poetry, he is a quiet yet independent voice of morality, often advocating that people reconnect with the natural world and what it has to teach.

I Have a Dream

Martin Luther King Jr.

The following address is generally acknowledged to be one of the greatest speeches of American history. Delivered on August 28, 1963, before a crowd of 250,000 people participating in the famous March on Washington, King's speech continues to inspire Americans today. A model of rhetorical skill, it is packed with rhetorical devices, from clever allusions to Lincoln's Gettysburg Address (the speech was delivered on the steps of the Lincoln Memorial) to classic examples of anaphora and metaphor. All are deftly geared to help communicate a clear message and inspire the audience to follow it. Indeed, it is a testament to King's oratorical gifts and skill that the speech's iconic eponymous passage was in fact an off-the-cuff addition.

I am happy to join with you today in what will go down in history as the greatest demonstration for freedom in the history of our nation.

Five score years ago, a great American, in whose symbolic shadow we stand today, signed the Emancipation Proclamation. This momentous decree came as a great beacon light of hope to millions of Negro slaves who had been seared in the flames of withering injustice. It came as a joyous daybreak to end the long night of their captivity.

But one hundred years later, the Negro still is not free. One hundred years later, the life of the Negro is still sadly crippled by the manacles* of segregation and the chains of discrimination. One hundred years later, the Negro lives on a lonely island of poverty in the midst of a vast ocean of material prosperity. One hundred years later, the Negro is still languished in the corners of American society and finds himself an exile in his own land. And so we've come here today to dramatize a shameful condition.

manacle: that which restrains

In a sense we've come to our nation's capital to cash a check. When the architects of our republic wrote the magnificent words of the Constitution and the Declaration of Independence, they were signing a promissory note to which every American was to fall heir. This note was a promise that all men, yes, black men as well as white men, would be guaranteed the "unalienable Rights" of "Life, Liberty and the pursuit of Happiness." It is obvious today that America has defaulted on this promissory note, insofar as her citizens of color are concerned. Instead of honoring this sacred obligation, America has given the Negro people a bad check, a check which has come back marked "insufficient funds."

But we refuse to believe that the bank of justice is bankrupt. We refuse to believe that there are insufficient funds in the great vaults of opportunity of this nation. And so, we've come to cash this check, a check that will give us upon demand the riches of freedom and the security of justice.

We have also come to this hallowed spot to remind America of the fierce urgency of Now. This is no time to engage in the luxury of cooling off or to take the tranquilizing drug of gradualism. Now is the time to make real the promises of democracy. Now is the time to rise from the dark and desolate valley of segregation to the sunlit path of racial justice. Now is the time to lift our nation from the quicksands of racial injustice to the solid rock of brotherhood. Now is the time to make justice a reality for all of God's children.

It would be fatal for the nation to overlook the urgency of the moment. This sweltering summer

of the Negro's legitimate discontent will not pass until there is an invigorating autumn of freedom and equality. Nineteen sixty-three is not an end, but a beginning. And those who hope that the Negro needed to blow off steam and will now be content will have a rude awakening if the nation returns to business as usual. And there will be neither rest nor tranquility in America until the Negro is granted his citizenship rights. The whirlwinds of revolt will continue to shake the foundations of our nation until the bright day of justice emerges.

But there is something that I must say to my people, who stand on the warm threshold which leads into the palace of justice: In the process of gaining our rightful place, we must not be guilty of wrongful deeds. Let us not seek to satisfy our thirst for freedom by drinking from the cup of bitterness and hatred. We must forever conduct our struggle on the high plane of dignity and discipline. We must not allow our creative protest to degenerate into physical violence. Again and again, we must rise to the majestic heights of meeting physical force with soul force.

The marvelous new militancy* which has engulfed the Negro community must not lead us to a distrust of all white people, for many of our white brothers, as evidenced by their presence here today, have come to realize that their destiny is tied up with our destiny. And they have come to realize that their freedom is inextricably* bound to our freedom.

---

militancy: aggressiveness
inextricably: inescapably

We cannot walk alone.

And as we walk, we must make the pledge that we shall always march ahead.

We cannot turn back.

There are those who are asking the devotees of civil rights, "When will you be satisfied?" We can never be satisfied as long as the Negro is the victim of the unspeakable horrors of police brutality. We can never be satisfied as long as our bodies, heavy with the fatigue of travel, cannot gain lodging in the motels of the highways and the hotels of the cities. We cannot be satisfied as long as the negro's basic mobility is from a smaller ghetto to a larger one. We can never be satisfied as long as our children are stripped of their self-hood and robbed of their dignity by signs stating: "For Whites Only." We cannot be satisfied as long as a Negro in Mississippi cannot vote and a Negro in New York believes he has nothing for which to vote. No, no, we are not satisfied, and we will not be satisfied until "justice rolls down like waters, and righteousness like a mighty stream."

I am not unmindful that some of you have come here out of great trials and tribulations. Some of you have come fresh from narrow jail cells. And some of you have come from areas where your quest for freedom left you battered by the storms of persecution and staggered by the winds of police brutality. You have been the veterans of creative suffering. Continue to work with the faith that unearned suffering is redemptive. Go back to Mississippi, go back to Alabama, go back to South Carolina, go back to Georgia, go back to Louisiana, go back to the slums and ghettos of our northern cities, knowing that somehow this situation can and will be changed.

Let us not wallow in the valley of despair, I say to you today, my friends.

And so even though we face the difficulties of today and tomorrow, I still have a dream. It is a dream deeply rooted in the American dream.

I have a dream that one day this nation will rise up and live out the true meaning of its creed: "We hold these truths to be self-evident, that all men are created equal."

I have a dream that one day on the red hills of Georgia, the sons of former slaves and the sons of former slave owners will be able to sit down together at the table of brotherhood.

I have a dream that one day even the state of Mississippi, a state sweltering with the heat of injustice, sweltering with the heat of oppression, will be transformed into an oasis of freedom and justice.

I have a dream that my four little children will one day live in a nation where they will not be judged by the color of their skin but by the content of their character.

I have a *dream* today!

I have a dream that one day, down in Alabama, with its vicious racists, with its governor* having his lips dripping with the words of "interposition"* and "nullification"*—one day right there in Alabama little black boys and black girls will be able to join hands with little white boys and white girls as sisters and brothers.

its governor: reference to then Alabama governor George Wallace

interposition: a doctrine by which a state opposes a federal law believed to encroach on its sovereignty

nullification: a state's refusing to enforce a federal law

I have a *dream* today!

I have a dream that one day every valley shall be exalted, and every hill and mountain shall be made low, the rough places will be made plain, and the crooked places will be made straight; "and the glory of the Lord shall be revealed and all flesh shall see it together."

This is our hope, and this is the faith that I go back to the South with.

With this faith, we will be able to hew out of the mountain of despair a stone of hope. With this faith, we will be able to transform the jangling discords of our nation into a beautiful symphony of brotherhood. With this faith, we will be able to work together, to pray together, to struggle together, to go to jail together, to stand up for freedom together, knowing that we will be free one day.

And this will be the day—this will be the day when all of God's children will be able to sing with new meaning:

My country 'tis of thee, sweet land of liberty, of thee I sing.

Land where my fathers died, land of the Pilgrim's pride,

From every mountainside, let freedom ring!

And if America is to be a great nation, this must become true.

And so let freedom ring from the prodigious hilltops of New Hampshire.

Let freedom ring from the mighty mountains of New York.

Let freedom ring from the heightening Alleghenies of Pennsylvania.

Let freedom ring from the snow-capped Rockies of Colorado.

Let freedom ring from the curvaceous slopes of California.

But not only that:

Let freedom ring from Stone Mountain of Georgia.

Let freedom ring from Lookout Mountain of Tennessee.

Let freedom ring from every hill and molehill of Mississippi.

From every mountainside, let freedom ring.

And when this happens, and when we allow freedom ring, when we let it ring from every village and every hamlet, from every state and every city, we will be able to speed up that day when *all* of God's children, black men and white men, Jews and Gentiles, Protestants and Catholics, will be able to join hands and sing in the words of the old Negro spiritual:

Free at last! Free at last!

Thank God Almighty, we are free at last!

About the Speech

1. King creates an extended metaphor to describe the situation prompting African Americans to protest in Washington. What is the basic metaphor? In terms of this metaphor, what problem is King targeting?
2. The following statement is one of the most famous and memorable lines from King's speech. Why do you think King used parallel syntax (prepositional phrases) and alliteration in this sentence?

   > "I have a dream that my four little children will one day live in a nation where they will not be judged by the color of their skin but by the content of their character."

3. King used a lot of repetition (of sounds, syntax, and sense) in his speech. This technique can quickly turn tedious when used extensively in written communication, but it is often highly effective in spoken (oral) communication. Why do you think this might be?
4. How do the ideas King expresses about freedom and equality compare with what the Bible has to say about these subjects?

King's literary skill played a role in carrying out God's moral will in American culture: King helped people see the evils of racism. What evils in society should Christians be concerned about today? Write a persuasive paragraph to make a point against one of those evils. In your answer consider using one of the literary techniques King used.

About the Author

Martin Luther King Jr. (1929–68) began life in Atlanta, Georgia, January 15, 1929, the son and grandson of Baptist preachers. Having skipped both ninth and twelfth grades, King entered Morehouse College early, where he was mentored by the college's president, Benjamin Mays, a man with a deep personal commitment to racial equality. After earning a degree in sociology from Morehouse, King advanced to Crozer Theological Seminary, where he was elected president of the student body. He earned a bachelor of divinity degree in 1951 and went on to earn a doctorate from Boston University.

King soon became a leader advocating reform for African Americans and co-founded the Southern Christian Leadership Conference in 1957. He would go on to become the most prominent symbol of the Civil Rights Movement, which successfully ended legal racial segregation in America.

King's advocacy of nonviolence and civil disobedience garnered influence with many but was controversial for others. While campaigning in 1963 to end segregation at lunch counters, King was jailed in Birmingham, Alabama, for ignoring an injunction prohibiting demonstrations. His famous "Letter from a Birmingham Jail" was written in response to a letter printed in the local newspaper, a letter questioning the timing and wisdom of his actions. King's response letter targeted a national audience and showcased his gift for communication and persuasive rhetoric.

The famous "I Have a Dream" speech eloquently articulated the vision for which King is most remembered and had a powerful effect on public opinion. The following year (1964) King became the youngest person ever to receive the Nobel Peace Prize.

Before his death King had shifted his focus to stopping the Vietnam War and ending poverty. Sadly, his efforts ended abruptly on April 4, 1968, when he was assassinated. The establishing in 1983 of a Martin Luther King Jr. Day, a federal holiday, attests to King's enduring place in history.

THINKING ZONE

Organizing the sounds and syntax of language was long considered primarily a tool of rhetoric. Originally focused on spoken language, the study of **rhetoric** reaches back to ancient Greek and Roman cultures, which prized the art of public speaking. Ancient rhetoric focused primarily on persuasive speech, promoting artful organization and style to achieve an intended effect. At times, the artfulness of a speech was as significant as the actual content. As a result, the field refined various devices of figurative language, which are today effectively used both in speechmaking and in literary prose and poetry.

One such device is the **rhetorical question**, a question asked, not to receive information, but to achieve an effect. The audience's mental affirmation of the question's obvious answer carries more impact than if the speaker or writer were to make the statement in a declarative sentence. The rhetorical question is often used in Scripture. In the Sermon on the Mount, for example, the Lord, having reminded the hearers of God's care for birds, asks, "Are ye not much better than they?" (Matt. 6:26) The unmistakable mental yes conveys God's great care for His children. Shelley's use of the device in his "Ode to the West Wind" has become one of the most famous rhetorical questions in English: "O, Wind, / If Winter comes, can Spring be far behind?" The answer communicates resounding hope that better things are ahead for those who persevere.

A speaker or writer using rhetorical devices is not trying to emulate the way people normally speak. The goal, rather, is to craft clear, memorable, and rhythmic lines. **Chiasmus**, one such rhetorical device, inverts parallel structure. Consisting of two grammatical units, chiasmus takes the elements of its first phrase, clause, or sentence and reverses them in its second. John F. Kennedy made use of this powerful tool in his 1961 inaugural address: "Ask not what your country can do for you; ask what you can do for your country." Another rhetorical device, **antithesis**, utilizes straightforward parallelism in two phrases or clauses to reinforce their contrast in meanings. An often quoted line from Pope's *Essay on Criticism* illustrates antithesis: "To err is human; to forgive, divine." The parallelism pleases the reader's ear in order to highlight the contrast in meaning.

Whereas chiasmus requires a crossover and antithesis, a contrast, anaphora requires repetition. **Anaphora** is the deliberate repetition of words or phrases at the beginnings of lines of poetry, grammatical units, or paragraphs. The effect of its skillful use is clearly illustrated in Lincoln's memorable Gettysburg Address, which declares, "We cannot dedicate, we cannot consecrate, we cannot hallow this ground." Sprinkled throughout more ordinary language, rhetorical devices sparkle as gems, focusing attention and crystallizing truth.

1. Which poem in this unit takes as its title a **rhetorical question**? How does that title qualify as a rhetorical question?
2. **Anaphora** and parallelism characterize much of Martin Luther King Jr.'s speech "I Have a Dream." What two sentences or phrases best showcase King's use of this device?
3. What device of **rhetoric** from this Thinking Zone is illustrated in the following quotation from "I Have a Dream"? More than one device applies. Choose the most specific answer.

   > I have a dream that my four little children will one day live in a nation where they will not be judged by the color of their skin but by the content of their character.

4. What rhetorical device from this Thinking Zone is illustrated in the following quotation from "I Have a Dream"?

   > Let freedom ring from every hill and molehill of Mississippi.
   > From every mountainside, let freedom ring.

UNIT II REVIEW

Remember the Terms

Review the following terms from the opening essay, "Sound and Syntax," and the Thinking Zone pages. Be prepared to discuss their meanings and uses.

meter	pyrrhic foot	internal rhyme	feminine ending
poetic feet	iambic pentameter	alliteration	masculine ending
iambic foot	rhyme	consonance	rhetoric
trochaic foot	perfect rhyme	assonance	rhetorical question
anapestic foot	slant rhyme	end-stopped	chiasmus
dactylic foot	eye rhyme	enjambment	antithesis
spondaic foot	end rhyme	caesura	anaphora

Apply the Concepts

Answer the following questions about how the literary concepts you have studied are used in this unit.

1. When Christina Rossetti says that "the trees bow down their heads" in her poem "Who Has Seen the Wind?" what literary device is she using?
2. The following lines from "Who Has Seen the Wind?" employ what type of poetic feet?

   But when the trees bow down their heads
   The wind is passing by.

3. Chávez's poem "Rattlesnake" makes use of many sound devices. What device (other than rhyme) is particularly evident in the following lines?

   crawl-created,
   articulated
   coil of cloisonné!

4. John Keats's poem "On the Grasshopper and the Cricket" is set up so that the first eight lines depict a grasshopper's summer contribution and the following six show a cricket's similar winter contribution. The information in both sections is presented in the same order, and the situations illustrate the same truth. This is an example of what kind of structure?
5. When Wagoner uses phrases like "*boom a blat*," "*a toot*," and "*a honk*" in his poem "March for a One-Man Band," he is using what sound device?
6. The following lines from Edwin Hoey's "Foul Shot" illustrate several sound and syntax devices studied in this unit. Name two of them.

   Lands,
   Leans,
   Wobbles,
   Wavers,
   Hesitates,
   Exasperates

7. Stephen Crane uses the sentence below to describe the captain in "A Gray Sleeve." What figure of speech does this sentence contain?

> He stolidly rose and fell with the plunges of his horse in all the indifference of a deacon's figure seated plumply in church.

8. Identify at least two examples of sound devices in the following paragraph describing the cavalry's charge into the woods from "A Gray Sleeve."

> The troopers threw themselves upon the grove like wolves upon a great animal. Along the whole front of the woods there was the dry crackling of musketry, with bitter, swift flashes and smoke that writhed like stung phantoms. The troopers yelled shrilly and spanged bullets low into the foliage.

9. Crane describes the horses hooves as a "swift storm of sound." What sound device is this an example of?
10. How do Crane's word choices reflect his worldview?
11. How does the rhythm of John Updike's poem "Winter Ocean" reinforce its mood?
12. William Stafford's "Traveling Through the Dark" uses what type of rhyme in lines 2 and 4?
13. What basic metaphor does Martin Luther King Jr. expand upon in his "I Have a Dream" speech?
14. Describe two effects of King's use of sound and syntax in his speech.
15. What is the primary syntactical device illustrated by the following passage, and what is the purpose King most likely had for using that device?

> Let freedom ring from the mighty mountains of New York.
> Let freedom ring from the heightening Alleghenies of Pennsylvania.
> Let freedom ring from the snow-capped Rockies of Colorado.
> Let freedom ring from the curvaceous slopes of California.

Evaluate the Ideas

Identify each of the following statements as true or false. If false, rewrite the underlined portion of the statement to make it true.

16. Rossetti's poem clearly reveals <u>what kinds of people have seen the wind</u>.
17. "Who Has Seen the Wind?" is a <u>free verse</u> poem.
18. The spiritual message of Rossetti's poem is that <u>intangible things are often best seen in their effects</u>.
19. When Fray Angélico Chávez describes the rattlesnake as "scrolling inward like a hive," he is using <u>metaphor</u>.
20. Chávez's lines "Stay away / crawl-created / articulated" illustrate <u>eye rhyme</u>.
21. The meter of "From hedge to hedge about the new-mown mead" from Keats's poem "On the Grasshopper and the Cricket" is <u>iambic pentameter</u>.
22. Wagoner's "March for a One-Man Band" is an example of a <u>perfect rhyme</u> poem.

23. Wagoner probably used the term "Irrational Anthem" in the last line because the poem makes no sense at all.
24. In Hoey's "Foul Shot" the object personified is the basketball.
25. The effect of Hoey's repetition of the words "And then" is dactylic rhyme.
26. Crane uses the literary device of personification in the following sentence from "A Gray Sleeve":

    Some crickets chirped in the long grass, and the nearest pine could be heard in its endless sighs.

27. In "A Gray Sleeve" the girl's character changes the most from the beginning of the story to the end.
28. When Updike refers to the ocean in winter as being a "tub of male whales," he is using assonance, rhyme, and exaggeration.
29. In "Traveling Through the Dark" Stafford says that the speaker "could hear the wilderness listen." This is an example of personification.
30. King's opinions about equality and freedom have some basis in biblical truth.

Write a Response

Completely answer each of the following questions.

31. Discuss the meaning of the line "I thought hard for us all—my only swerving" in "Traveling Through the Dark."
32. Discuss King's extensive use of repetition and parallelism in his "I Have a Dream" speech. Use examples from the speech for support.

UNIT III

THE ARMADA PORTRAIT OF QUEEN ELIZABETH I
George Gower

ALLUSION AND SYMBOL

The historical record offers little about English painter George Gower (c. 1539–1596) until 1573, when he appeared in London producing several works of a mature style. Apparently a well-established artist, he was patronized by wealthy, important people, including Queen Elizabeth I herself. In 1581 Gower was appointed Serjeant Painter to the Queen, serving until his death in 1596. His duties included painting and gilding coaches, furniture, palaces, and barges as well as decorating for festivities. His accomplishments range from a fountain and a clock at Hampton Court Palace to several famous portraits of the Queen, such as the one opposite.

Portraits of Elizabeth were generally intended less as likenesses than as images heavily laden with allusion and symbolism to influence public perception of her. A sieve, a pelican, the Tudor rose, the moon, pearls, ermine, the phoenix—these and more served as symbols projecting purity, unity, virginity, longevity, and motherly love to her subjects. Most of these alluded to biblical, historical, or mythological sources. Despite her richly elegant costume, the attention is drawn to Elizabeth's face, where Gower's technique and style precisely display her bold features and white complexion (sign of wealth and nobility). As in most of her portraits, Elizabeth appears young. Her unchanged face perpetuated an illusion of youth, reassuring subjects of the continuing stability of Elizabeth's reign.

- Note the title of the portrait. Specifically what is being depicted in the two scenes to the left and right of Elizabeth? Why does the painter allude to it in Elizabeth's portrait?
- Where is the Queen's right hand resting? What do you think this placement symbolizes?
- Identify two main impressions of Queen Elizabeth communicated by the portrait. How does it do so?

ALLUSION AND SYMBOL

You have now studied two marks of literature—imaginative comparison and the organized use of sound and syntax. With few exceptions, these will always be present in literature of a high caliber. Two additional modes of communication in literature are those of allusion and symbol. Though these need not appear in good literature, they are often present because of the rich possibilities they bring to a work.

Allusion

In **allusion**, a writer intentionally references persons, places, or things outside of the work itself, usually without specifically explaining them. As the following conversational statements exemplify, most often these references are to other works of literature or to history: "In her new boss, Sally met her nemesis." "At the last test, Jordan finally met his waterloo!" The first employs a literary allusion to Greek mythology. Nemesis was the goddess of retribution, particularly toward those suffering from excessive pride. The second draws on history, Waterloo being the battle at which Napoleon was finally conquered. But both allusions convey the same general idea—that Sally and Jordan have encountered their downfall within the specified settings.

Allusions can be either brief or extended, either stressed or so understated as to be nearly invisible. Often they overlap with imaginative comparisons (particularly metaphor and simile). Some reference only one aspect of their subject (e.g., the finality of the battle of Waterloo) or help create a certain tone (e.g., humor at comparing one's boss to a Greek goddess). Others carry subtle or complex ideas. For example, the title of the well-known play *A Raisin in the Sun* alludes to the poem "Harlem" (by Langston Hughes), in which the poet asks whether delayed dreams "dry up like a raisin in the sun." This literary allusion introduces and reinforces the play's main theme, the results of having one's dreams fulfilled or denied.

Allusions and Shared Knowledge

Allusions access an audience's communal knowledge and take advantage of well-known facts or associations between a topic and certain ideas or emotions. Like imaginative comparisons, they can compress many ideas into a short statement. The Lord Himself made use of allusion. His sermons and conversations repeatedly refer to what His hearers knew best—Israel's history and the Scriptures. In John 3:14–15, He tells Nicodemus, "As Moses lifted up the serpent in the wilderness, even so must the Son of man be lifted up: that whosoever believeth in him should not perish, but have eternal life." Christ's allusion to the brazen serpent (Num. 21:4–9) both illustrates His message and clarifies His attitude. The story directly parallels God's plan to save mankind, but His reference also accentuates God's loving commitment to His people. Just as He has saved them in the past, so He will in the future.

Writers using allusion anticipate readers with knowledge similar to their own. Remove this bond, and allusions can become difficult to decipher. English literature plainly demonstrates this process. For centuries educated persons were well-versed in the Bible and the ancient classics, so older literature abounds with allusions to both. Unfortunately, modern readers find many of these allusions impenetrable. To forestall this effect, authors writing for the broadest audiences tend to avoid allusions to current events or pop culture because they are less likely to translate across cultures or stand the test of time.

Symbol

As with allusion, the symbolic mode of writing serves to add another layer of meaning to the literal reading of a text. In common usage, a symbol is something (usually a picture) that represents something else. For example, in schoolwork, a check mark often symbolizes correctness while an *x* indicates an error. But a literary **symbol** signifies more: it is a person, place, thing, or idea within a narrative or poem that means something *in addition to* itself. It is both a literal object in the text and a window into further meaning beyond itself. For instance, in many Old Testament passages, the city of Babylon plays a part both as itself and as a symbol of sin and the kingdom of this world (i.e., human society that has no thought for Jehovah). This symbolism is perhaps most obvious in the story of Israel's Babylonian captivity. Since God's people rejected Him in favor of the world, He both literally and symbolically gave them up (for a time) to the full consequences of that decision.

Writers use symbols that recur throughout cultures or have a standard meaning within a set cultural group. For example, in world literature the seasons regularly evoke similar concepts (e.g., spring representing youth and beginnings). William Stafford's "Traveling Through the Dark" uses two such universal symbols: traveling suggests the course of one's life and darkness implies a state of ignorance or uncertainty. An example of a culturally specific symbol would be the combination of red, white, and blue: to Americans, it suggests the flag and patriotism.

More difficult to discern and interpret are symbols specific only to a particular literary work. For these, an author imbues an object with special meaning, usually deeply connected to specific themes he wishes to develop. As his story or poem proceeds, the object accumulates extra meaning through the way in which he handles it. For example, in Herman Melville's *Moby Dick*, the white whale (Moby Dick) gradually becomes a symbol with meanings pertinent to several themes. Some of these meanings are tied to the way different characters come to perceive him: to Captain Ahab, he is evil incarnate and must be killed. Other meanings are tied to the part Moby Dick plays in the larger conflicts of the novel. In one, he represents nature under siege by man. Thus, through the development of the plot, conflicts, and characters, Melville invests a simple animal with many meanings unique to the message of his novel.

Symbols and Imaginative Comparison

Well-known symbols are often applied in allusions and imaginative comparisons. For example, the phoenix is a mythical bird that at death would burst into flame and arise reborn from the ashes. Unsurprisingly, the creature came to symbolize rebirth, new beginnings, and, for Christians, the Resurrection. A modern allusion or comparison to the phoenix usually plays off this symbolic meaning rather than the actual creature of myth.

However, symbols should not be confused with imaginative comparisons, which convey a far more fixed meaning. For instance, objects or persons in allegories are not symbols: their meanings are definite, tightly constrained by the relationship between the literal story and its intended figurative meaning. Symbols instead communicate through rich implication: they are objects that, by their own properties, associations, and functions in the story, suggest a range of ideas transcending their literal role. Like the whale Moby Dick, they may speak to multiple subjects or themes simultaneously. Though they may embody a single broad idea (e.g., the sun as a symbol of life), the meaning of that concept to the text is often difficult to summarize in a simple statement.

Beyond question, to get the most out of our reading, especially of artistic writing and of the Scriptures, we must be sensitive to both the symbolic and allusive modes of communication. In each selection that follows, ask the following questions as you read: What additional information do any allusions communicate? What might they say about the author or his attitude? Are there any objects, actions, or characters that seem to stand for ideas larger than themselves? If so, how do these ideas contribute to the author's message? With practice, detecting these modes will become easier, and you may even come to enjoy deciphering the intricacies of good writing.

Cupid's Arrows

Rudyard Kipling

In many of his stories, Rudyard Kipling shows great sympathy for the young, particularly as they encounter the duties and constraints of adulthood. This brief tale reflects that attitude. Though it begins and ends in fairy-tale fashion, it also contains barbed, though humorous, commentary on the values of polite society. To reinforce his point, Kipling uses several classical and biblical allusions throughout.

Once upon a time there lived at Simla a very pretty girl, the daughter of a poor but honest District and Sessions Judge. She was a good girl but could not help knowing her power and using it. Her Mamma was very anxious about her daughter's future, as all good Mammas should be.

When a man is a Commissioner and a bachelor and has the right of wearing open-work jam-tart jewels in gold and enamel on his clothes, and of going through a door before every one except a Member of Council, a Lieutenant-Governor, or a Viceroy, he is worth marrying. At least, that is what ladies say. There was a Commissioner in Simla, in those days, who was, and wore, and did all I have said. He was a plain man—an ugly man—the ugliest man in Asia, with two exceptions. His was a face to dream about and try to carve on a pipe-head afterward. His name was Saggott—Barr-Saggott—Anthony Barr-Saggott and six letters to follow. Departmentally, he was one of the best men the government of India owned. Socially, he was like unto a blandishing* gorilla.

blandish: to persuade by flattery

When he turned his attentions to Miss Beighton, I believe that Mrs. Beighton wept with delight at the reward Providence had sent her in her old age.

Mr. Beighton held his tongue. He was an easy-going man.

A Commissioner is very rich. His pay is beyond the dreams of avarice—is so enormous that he can afford to save and scrape in a way that would almost discredit a Member of Council. Most Commissioners are mean;* but Barr-Saggott was an exception. He entertained royally; he horsed himself well; he gave dances; he was a power in the land; and he behaved as such.

mean: stingy

Consider that everything I am writing of took place in an almost prehistoric era in the history of British India. Some folk may remember years before lawn tennis was born when we all played croquet. There were seasons before that, if you will believe me, when even croquet had not been invented, and archery—which was revived in England in 1844—was as great a pest as lawn tennis is now. People talked learnedly about "holding" and "loosing," "steles," "reflexed bows," "56-pound bows," "backed" or "self-yew bows," as we talk about "rallies," "volleys," "smashes," "returns," and "16-ounce rackets."

Miss Beighton shot exquisitely over ladies' distance—sixty yards, that is—and was acknowledged the best lady archer in Simla. Men called her "Diana* of Tara-Devi."

Diana: Roman mythological goddess of the forest; associated with hunting

Barr-Saggott paid her great attention; and, as I have said, the heart of her mother was uplifted in consequence. Kitty Beighton took matters more calmly. It was pleasant to be singled out by a Commissioner with letters after his name, and to fill the hearts of other girls with bad feelings. But there was no denying the fact that Barr-Saggott was phenomenally ugly; and all his attempts to adorn himself only made him more grotesque. He was not christened "The Langur"—which means grey ape—for nothing. It was pleasant, Kitty thought, to have him at her feet, but it was better to escape from him and ride with the graceless Cubbon—the man in a Dragoon Regiment at Umballa—the boy with a handsome face, and no prospects.* Kitty liked Cubbon more than a little. He never pretended for a moment that he was anything less than head over heels in love with her; for he was an honest boy. So Kitty fled, now and again, from the stately wooings of Barr-Saggott to the company of young Cubbon, and was scolded by her Mamma in consequence. "But Mother," she said, "Mr. Saggott is such—such a—is so *fearfully* ugly, you know!"

prospects: hopes for advancement

"My dear," said Mrs. Beighton, piously, "we cannot be other than an all-ruling Providence has made us. Besides, you will take precedence of your own Mother, you know! Think of that and be reasonable."

Then Kitty put up her little chin and said irreverent things about precedence, and Commissioners, and matrimony. Mr. Beighton rubbed the top of his head; for he was an easy-going man.

Late in the season, when he judged that the time was ripe, Barr-Saggott developed a plan which did great credit to his administrative powers. He arranged an archery tournament for ladies, with a most sumptuous diamond-studded bracelet as prize. He drew up his terms skillfully, and every one saw that the bracelet was a gift to Miss Beighton, the acceptance carrying with it the hand and the heart of Commissioner Barr-Saggott. The terms were a St. Leonard's Round—thirty-six shots at sixty yards—under the rules of the Simla Toxophilite* Society.

toxophilite: one who loves archery

All Simla was invited. There were beautifully arranged tea tables under the deodars* at Annandale, where the Grand Stand is now; and, alone in its glory, winking in the sun, sat the diamond bracelet in a blue velvet case. Miss Beighton was anxious—almost too anxious—to compete. On the appointed afternoon all Simla rode down to Annandale to witness the Judgment of Paris turned upside down. Kitty rode with young Cubbon, and it was easy to see that the boy was troubled in his mind. He must be held innocent of everything that followed. Kitty was pale and nervous, and looked long at the bracelet. Barr-Saggott was gorgeously dressed, even more nervous than Kitty, and more hideous than ever.

deodars: cedars native to the Himalayas

Mrs. Beighton smiled condescendingly, as befitted the mother of a potential Commissioneress, and the shooting began, all the world standing in a semicircle as the ladies came out one after the other.

Nothing is so tedious as an archery competition. They shot, and they shot, and they kept on shooting, till the sun left the valley, and little breezes got up in the deodars, and people waited for Miss Beighton to shoot and win. Cubbon was at one horn of the semicircle round the shooters, and Barr-Saggott at the other. Miss Beighton was last on the list. The scoring had been weak, and the bracelet, with Commissioner Barr-Saggott, was hers to a certainty.

The Commissioner strung her bow with his own sacred hands. She stepped forward, looked at the bracelet, and her first arrow went true to a hair—full into the heart of the "gold"—counting nine points.

Young Cubbon on the left turned white, and Barr-Saggott smiled. Now horses used to shy when Barr-Saggott smiled. Kitty saw that smile. She looked to her left-front, gave an almost imperceptible nod to Cubbon, and went on shooting.

I wish I could describe the scene that followed. It was out of the ordinary and most

improper. Miss Kitty fitted her arrows with immense deliberation, so that every one might see what she was doing. She was a perfect shot; and her forty-six pound bow suited her to a nicety. She pinned the wooden legs of the target with great care four successive times. She pinned the wooden top of the target once, and all the ladies looked at each other. Then she began some fancy shooting at the white, which if you hit it, counts exactly one point. She put five arrows into the white. It was wonderful archery; but, seeing that her business was to make "golds" and win the bracelet, Barr-Saggott turned a delicate green like young water-grass. Next, she shot over the target twice, then wide to the left twice—always with the same deliberation—while a chilly hush fell over the company, and Mrs. Beighton took out her handkerchief. Then Kitty shot at the ground in front of the target, and split several arrows. Then she made a red—or seven points—just to show what she could do if she liked, and she finished up her amazing performance with some more fancy shooting at the target supports. Here is her score as it was pricked off:

	Gold	Red	Blue	Black	White	Total Hits	Total Score
Miss Beighton	1	1	0	0	5	7	21

Barr-Saggott looked as if the last few arrowheads had been driven into his legs instead of the target's, and the deep stillness was broken by a little snubby, mottled, half-grown girl saying in a shrill voice of triumph, "Then *I've* won!"

Mrs. Beighton did her best to bear up; but she wept in the presence of the people. No training could help her through such disappointment. Kitty unstrung her bow with a vicious jerk, and went back to her place, while Barr-Saggott was trying to pretend that he enjoyed snapping the bracelet on the snubby girl's raw, red wrist. It was an awkward scene—most awkward. Every one tried to depart in a body and leave Kitty to the mercy of her Mamma.

But Cubbon took her away instead, and—the rest isn't worth printing.

About the Story

1. Explain the classical allusion in the title.
2. Kitty's nickname is an allusion. What does it communicate about her?
3. What does the author seem to think of Kitty's choice? Give two supports for your answer from the text.
4. Were you in Kitty's situation, what do you think you would do or do differently?

About the Author

Born in Bombay, British writer Rudyard Kipling (1865–1936) grew up hearing folktales of India that would later influence his writing. Like many children of British colonials, he was sent to England for schooling at a young age, but his experience there was unhappy. After finishing, he returned to India in 1882 to work as a journalist in Lahore. There he began his career as a writer of fiction, and though he eventually returned to England, many of his works are set in colonial India.

Kipling was a versatile writer who penned excellent poems, novels, and short stories. A talented storyteller, his works appeal to readers of many ages and backgrounds. Though first famous for his stories and poems about British soldiers in India, he also wrote many works for children. In fact, his finest novel, *Kim*, is now considered a children's classic the world over. In addition to being the recipient of many other honors, in 1907 he became the youngest writer (and first British writer) ever to be awarded the Nobel Prize for literature.

Kipling was a firm supporter of the British Empire, a stance that affected much of his literature and for which he is often criticized. While he wrote much of India, his perspective is distinctly that of a British colonist rather than a native of India. Still, there is no denying the popular appeal of his works. Moreover, he is well-acknowledged as a master of the short story and a writer with an extraordinary gift for narrative.

Sir Francis Drake

Robert Hayman

One of England's greatest naval heroes was Sir Francis Drake. A commoner commissioned by Queen Elizabeth I to disrupt Spanish commerce and weaken Spain's power, he was wildly successful. During his famous voyage around the world (1577–80), Drake attacked Spanish ships and towns in the Americas, brought back an immense treasure in gold and precious stones, and earned a knighthood in the process. Today, his participation in the slave trade is rightly condemned; but in his own time, he was beloved by many for his exploits. The almost humorous despair of the poet adds luster to the portrait of his hero. Although the verse is a bit overdone, the poem has merit as the historical record of an encounter with a famous person.

The Dragon that our seas did raise his crest*
And brought back heaps of gold unto his nest,
Unto his foes more terrible than thunder,
Glory of his age, after-ages' wonder,
Excelling all those that excelled before—
It's feared we shall have none such any more—
Effecting all, he sole did undertake,
Valiant, just, wise, mild, honest, godly Drake.
This man when I was little I did meet
As he was walking up Totnes'* long street
He asked me whose I was. I answered him.
He asked me if his good friend were within.
A fair red orange in his hand he had;
He gave it me, whereof I was right glad,
Takes and kissed me, and prays, "God bless my boy,"
Which I record with comfort to this day.
Could he on me have breathéd with his breath
His gifts, Elias-like, after his death,
Then had I been enabled for to do
Many brave things I have a heart unto.
I have as great desire as e'er had he
To joy, annoy, friends, foes; but 'twill not be.

Dragon . . . crest: whose crest our seas did raise (*drake* is from the Latin *draco* for "dragon")

Totnes: a town on a hill above the river Dart about eight miles upriver from the seaport Dartmouth in Devonshire

About the Poem

1. In the first two lines of the poem, Hayman uses a pun on Drake's name (see gloss above) to create a metaphor. What is the metaphor?
2. To what events in Drake's life does the metaphor allude?
3. To what biblical character does Hayman allude? What does this allusion say about Drake?
4. Do you have a human hero you would like to emulate? If so, who is your hero, and what do you admire about him or her?

Sir Francis Drake

About the Author

Robert Hayman (1575–1629) was born in Devonshire, England. As a gentleman of the ruling class, he was expected to be skilled in the fine arts, including the art of composing verse. By 1621 he had earned a reputation as a poet of quality.

For a time, Hayman served as governor of the Harbour Grace settlement in Newfoundland, but by 1628 he had returned to England. After returning to his homeland, he published a book whose title is absurdly long. It reads in part as follows: "*Quodlibets*, lately come over from Britaniola, Old Newfoundland. Epigrams and other small parcels, both morall and divine. The first foure books being the authors owne. . . ." The collection included translations of John Owen, the epigrammatist, and François Rabelais, the French satirist. After his book was published, Hayman moved to British Guiana. No evidence exists that he ever returned to England.

Outta My Way, Grandpa!

Hugh O'Neill

Published in *Runner's World* in July of 2010, the following essay is both enjoyable and well-written. Full of self-deprecating humor, O'Neill's style is quite informal. Nonetheless, the marks of theme, imaginative comparison, and organized sound and syntax are strongly present. As you read, note how the author's use of allusion matches his informal style and enlivens his writing.

Halfway up the hill through the woods, I looked toward the crest and saw the bright sky at the top, a light calling me out of the darkness. On each side of me, runners moved, apparently effortlessly, past me. To my left, a girl, maybe 9 years old, powered her way up the grade. She smiled as though in apology. On my right charged a heavy-set guy pushing a baby-stroller with twins. I think one of the twins giggled—at me. But still, with a quarter-mile to go, I was perfectly positioned in my usual final-stretch-of-a-10-K position, sitting somewhere between 304th and 426th, poised to make my move.

At the top of the hill, we swooped left out onto a field. When I got a glimpse of the finish chute, I picked out my victim. Fifty yards ahead, wearing a red, white, and blue T-shirt, he was a small man with a ragged running style and some pepper in his pace. At that moment, he was, I'm sure, unaware that his dreams of finishing 367th were about to be dashed.

I reached deep and dropped the hammer.* Left. Right. Left. Right. I hummed the Rocky theme, the runners around me surely unaware of the drama that was unfolding. As the distance between me and my prey narrowed, once again, I was faced with one of the timeless ethical questions of running.

dropped the hammer: to dispense justice, i.e., made the decision to beat the man ahead of him

As large groups of runners—let's call them nonelite—head for the finish, exactly who are you allowed to blow by in the struggle for second-to-last place? Is there something less than sporting about busting it in the stretch to nip* your 10-year-old niece in a photo finish?

nip: snatch the victory from

In my racing history, I have been edged out in the final yards by all kinds of runners—antique men, pregnant women, pig-tailed girls, not to mention countless hyper-competitive 50-something guys like me. And every time I get caught with a stride or three to go, a little something inside me dies. I can't explain it. Somehow, I don't feel diminished by all the people who finished 29 minutes ago and who are now home having lunch. But the fourth-grader who beats me by a whisker really roasts my onions. I know I shouldn't have these feelings, but hey, God isn't finished with me yet.

The Debate of the Last 200 Yards is framed by two dueling sentiments. On the one hand, there is Kumbaya.* We're all back here in the pack trying to stay fit, enjoy the day, maybe raise a little money for the hospital. Who cares where we finish? But then there is this: It's vitally important that we achieve as high a ranking as possible. We need top scores in everything, from SAT scores decades ago to credit scores now. How else will we know who's winning? And if I can finish 307th instead of 308th, well then, that's exactly what I'm going to do!

Kumbaya: literally "Come by here" in the Gullah dialect

Left. Right. Left. Right. The spirit of Sly Stallone bolting through the streets of Philly pushed me forward. I was a puma.* Fierce. Determined. Inevitable. With 50 yards to go, something told my prey to look back over his shoulder, and we made eye contact. He was a dead man. With my last few strides, I pushed my sternum* past his.

puma: cougar or mountain lion
sternum: chest

As we crossed the finish line, a big celebratory crowd mobbed the guy. Five or six old men wearing the same patriotic shirt, a woman (his wife?) with a walker, five or six people my age, and a group of six or eight twenty-somethings who had devoted grandchildren written all over them. As I basked in the satisfaction of catching him, I noted that maybe he was older than I had thought. I squinted through my middle-aged presbyopia* to read the T-shirts the men were wearing. When I saw the words D-Day,* I felt a little queasy. There appeared to be a photographer arranging the gang for a photo.

presbyopia: an eye condition characterized by difficulty seeing objects up close
D-Day: June 6, 1944, massive Allied invasion in World War II

I steered clear of the local newspapers the next day. The phrases I most feared were "89 years old," "band of brothers," "cancer survivor," "inspiration to several generations." I don't mind admitting that this puma took no pleasure in that kill.

But the experience helped me to figure out the righteous point of view. Though I'm normally not a big motive guy—all that matters is what you do, not why you do it—in this case, motivation matters. If as you get your first glimpse of the finish chute, you center a *particular* runner in your crosshairs—as I did—and then proceed to track him down with your relentless predator stride, that's not a good thing.

If, on the other hand, you are inspired only by the sight of the finish line and you make an instant vow to cross the terrain between you and it as fast as you possibly can, and you just *happen* to blow past a fellow who earned his limp at Omaha Beach* so that you might draw the sweet breath of freedom, well, in that case, everybody in the vicinity of so singular an effort is enriched. Two identical actions—the first is corrupt, the second flirts with sacred. If Private Ryan just *happens* to be there as you challenge your weak mind and burning lungs, well, then you're not a thankless weasel at all. You're a different species entirely. You're a runner.

Omaha Beach: coast of Normandy, France, that was invaded by the Allies on D-Day

About the Essay

1. Beginning with the first paragraph, O'Neill injects a humorous note into his essay. How does he show that he's not taking himself too seriously?
2. Find two allusions in the text and explain their meanings in the essay. What emotional effect do most of these allusions have on the reader?
3. O'Neill presents his thesis using the inductive method—presenting specific evidence and then drawing a general conclusion from that evidence. What is his final conclusion about his topic?
4. The essayist makes the following statement: "Though I'm normally not a big motive guy—all that matters is what you do, not why you do it—in this case, motivation matters." How does that compare to 1 Corinthians 13:1–3 and a biblical worldview?
5. O'Neill's essay is well-written, but it is not (nor was it meant to be) literature that will last. Give two features that you think will limit the longevity of the essay.

About the Author

Hugh O'Neill was born and reared in New York City. Before beginning his career as a writer, he worked as an editor and publisher at Random House and Doubleday. He has written for many magazines, including *Reader's Digest*, *Glamour*, *Prevention*, and *Men's Health*, on a variety of topics—health, money, fashion, sports and fitness, medicine, and politics, among others. His resume also includes writing for television shows such as *The Cosby Show*. Father of a son and a daughter, O'Neill has authored three family books: *Here's Looking at You, Kids*; *Daddy Cool*; and *A Man Called Daddy*, all of which humorously offer advice on fatherhood. O'Neill resides in Princeton, New Jersey, with his son, daughter, and wife, Jody.

The Progress of Poesy

Matthew Arnold

Matthew Arnold, like many nineteenth-century poets, worried about the decline of his imaginative powers with old age. This poem pictures the life of a poet (or anyone else whose work depends on creative genius) as a search for water. Arnold subtly interweaves biblical allusions with universal symbols to suggest a deeper meaning to the images he describes.

Youth rambles on life's arid mount,
And strikes the rock, and finds the vein,
And brings the water from the fount,
The fount which shall not flow again.

The man mature with labor chops
For the bright stream a channel grand,
And sees not that the sacred drops
Ran off and vanished out of hand.

And then the old man totters nigh,
And feebly rakes among the stones.
The mount is mute, the channel dry;
And down he lays his weary bones.

About the Poem

1. What biblical allusion, basic to the poem's primary image, appears in the first stanza of Matthew Arnold's poem?
2. What does the fount symbolize in the context of the poem?
3. Given the symbolic meaning of the fount, what might creating a "channel grand" (stanza two) suggest?
4. What is Arnold's depiction of and attitude toward old age (his worldview)?

From a biblical worldview, write an answer to Arnold's attitude about old age.

About the Author

As a national inspector of schools, Matthew Arnold (1822–88) met hundreds of principals, teachers, and students. These conferences convinced him that English education was culturally barren. He concluded that literature, especially poetry, was the best way to incorporate spiritual concepts. Christians can agree with Arnold on this point, for Scripture is replete with poetic language that helps express and clarify complex truths. Unlike Arnold, however, Christians believe that the form of Scripture is subservient to the absolute truth of Scripture. Arnold held no such belief. Although he emphasized the value of poetic form, he was convinced that truth is relative—that it should change and develop as society changes and develops. Churchmen, therefore, who sought to stand for the absolute values of Scripture were subject to the poet's scorn.

Besides being a school inspector and poet, Arnold was also considered a successful professor and social critic. Yet despite his achievements, Arnold became dissatisfied toward the middle of his life. His thirtieth birthday brought him the sensation of being "three parts iced over." This despair toward aging is evident in "The Progress of Poesy."

maggie and milly and molly and may

E. E. Cummings

E. E. Cummings's poems are often easily recognized for his distinctive style. Cummings loved to play with language—from words themselves to grammar, punctuation, and syntax. As a result, his poems often possess a fresh, playful tone that overlays a nonetheless serious message. In this poem, he uses symbols to convey that what we are affects how we see life. What can we learn about each girl from her response to the seashore?

maggie and milly and molly and may
went down to the beach(to play one day)

and maggie discovered a shell that sang
so sweetly she couldn't remember her troubles,and

milly befriended a stranded star
whose rays five languid fingers were;

and molly was chased by a horrible thing
which raced sideways while blowing bubbles:and

may came home with a smooth round stone
as small as a world and as large as alone.

For whatever we lose(like a you or a me)
it's always ourselves we find in the sea

About the Poem

1. What are the four objects that the girls encounter? Pick one of these objects and explain what it seems to suggest about the little girl who encountered it.
2. Briefly explain why these four objects qualify as symbols.
3. What do you think Cummings means by the last line of the poem?
4. What do you think of Cummings's deviations from normal capitalization, punctuation, and spacing? How did they affect the mood and message of the poem for you?

About the Author

American poet E. E. Cummings (1894–1962) grew up in a happy home where reading and culture were highly valued. His Harvard education in Greek and the classics familiarized him with the elements of the best in literature. The effectiveness of Cummings's innovative style stems from this awareness of the traditional expectations his readers bring to poetry. He was able to defy those expectations in a way that communicates something to his readers. Though at first glance some of his poems appear to be simply letters or words scattered on the page, the unconventional format reinforces or clarifies his theme.

Our selection, "maggie and milly and molly and may," is one of Cummings's most understandable works. Many of his other poems are not only less accessible technically but also less acceptable philosophically. Some of Cummings's writings reflect a belief held by many modern authors: that espousing absolutes is damaging to individual creativity. Such an idea is grounded in pride, for it assumes that the God who created the desire for artistic expression in man failed to provide an acceptable outlet for such creativity. Poets such as John Milton, George Herbert, and John Donne prove the foolishness of such fears. As readers of literature we can, of course, recognize and appreciate the literary genius of Cummings and other modern poets. We should, however, reject the erroneous worldviews presented in many of their poems.

THINKING ZONE

Well-written literature often evokes strong emotions from readers. However, figuring out what an author wants us to do with these emotions can be tricky. If a story evokes despair, should we see it as a sign of the author's fatalism or as a device to indicate characters' wrong choices? The ability to distinguish between a story's atmosphere and its tone will help you answer such questions.

The **atmosphere** of a work is the overall emotion pervading it. Sometimes this mirrors the emotional or psychological state of the characters. At other times, characters seem unaware of the atmosphere: for example, in suspenseful writing, characters often remain oblivious to a foreboding mood so obvious to the reader.

In either case, authors use atmosphere to illustrate their themes. This approach may result in an atmosphere that the author does not actually encourage. For example, in her classic novel *Wuthering Heights*, Emily Brönte creates a dark and oppressive mood that mixes thwarted passions with anger, hatred, and regret. Brönte did not believe life must be so, but to understand her real meaning, a reader must also be able to discern her tone.

The **tone** of work (sometimes called the author's **voice**) is the attitude of the author toward his or her subject. Authors reveal their tone by the creative choices they make in a work. Their resolutions to conflicts, their sympathy for certain characters, their narrative comments—all of these show what they think is true. In Brönte's case, the resolution to *Wuthering Heights* decisively reveals her tone. She repudiates the attitudes and actions that have created the dark atmosphere, ending the characters' cycle of hatred and offering hope for renewal. While the novel's atmosphere is negative (emphasizing the destructiveness of these attitudes), the overall tone is positive.

Sometimes identifying tone is complicated by a **persona**, the person created by the author to tell the story. Though sometimes very much like the author, such narrators can also be distinctly different in personality and perspective; they may even express opinions that the author does not adhere to. Usually an author will reveal this differentiation in some way. For example, the narrator may espouse opinions or attitudes that are obviously flawed, letting the reader know that he or she is not to be fully trusted. Twain's eccentric narrator in "What Stumped the Bluejays" is a fine example: clearly he is telling a tall tale, because readers know that blue jays can't actually talk.

1. How can you tell that the narrator of "Cupid's Arrows" is a persona rather than Kipling's real voice?
2. What is Kipling's tone toward Kitty? Support your answer with details from the story.
3. In "Sir Francis Drake," how close is the persona to the poet's real tone? Briefly explain your answer.
4. Give a one-word description of the atmosphere of "Outta My Way, Grandpa!" How does that atmosphere help O'Neill convey his theme?
5. What is the atmosphere of Arnold's "The Progress of Poesy"?
6. Does Arnold's tone in the poem support its atmosphere? Explain your answer.

Afterglow

Jorge Luis Borges

Translated by Norman Thomas di Giovanni

In the following poem Argentine writer Jorge Luis Borges describes the final moments of a spectacular sunset. However, his reaction to that event is not the usual enjoyment of its beauty. Though Borges never directly states a moral, it becomes clear that for him, this event evokes a larger reality that he wishes his readers to contemplate.

Sunset is always disturbing
whether theatrical or muted,
but still more disturbing
is that last desperate glow
that turns the plain to rust
when on the horizon nothing is left
of the pomp and clamor of the setting sun.
How hard holding on to that light, so tautly drawn and different,
that hallucination which the human fear of the dark
imposes on space
and which ceases at once
the moment we realize its falsity,
the way a dream is broken
the moment the sleeper knows he is dreaming.

About the Poem

1. Borges describes a sunset in his poem. How does the title of the poem fit into that image?
2. Describe the atmosphere of Borges's poem.
3. What serves as the major symbol of the poem? What meaning does it suggest?
4. In your own words, explain the theme of the poem.
5. Borges describes a common human reaction. If a person trusts the God of the Bible, how would his or her reaction differ from what Borges describes?

About the Author

Born in Buenos Aires, Jorge Luis Borges (1899–1986) grew up in a middle-class family. He enjoyed a close relationship with his parents and younger sister, Norah. His father's library was made available to him early on, and Borges considered this access the most important experience in his life. He started writing at age six and, because his was a bilingual home, could read Shakespeare in English by age twelve.

In 1914 the family relocated to Geneva, Switzerland, where Borges's father received treatment for an eye disease that eventually claimed his sight. Borges inherited the disease, succumbing in time to the same fate. Once blind, Borges found that he more often wrote poetry because he could retain and modify the whole piece in his head.

After schooling in Geneva, Borges traveled to Spain, where he aligned himself with the avant-garde ultraist literary movement. In 1921 he returned to Argentina and began publishing poems, essays, and short stories. In addition, Borges's writing career included literary criticism, screenplays, and translations. His positions through the years included work as a librarian, a lecturer, and eventually a professor of literature at the University of Buenos Aires.

Borges's works have an element of unreality. They oppose nineteenth century realism/naturalism but combine realistic and fantastic elements, contributing to the genre of magical realism. Borges's first collection of short stories, *The Garden of Forking Paths*, combines text and maze. Though the work was successful, Borges did not receive the literary awards for it that many thought he would. He did, however, among other awards, receive the International Publishers' Prize and the Miguel de Cervantes Literature Award, Spain's highest literary honor. Though Borges was on the forefront of Latin American literature and its spread to the world at large, the Nobel Prize always eluded him, a fact that brought personal disappointment.

The Masque of the Red Death

Edgar Allan Poe

This tale comes close to being an allegory. However, the many possible interpretations of the story make it more accurately a highly symbolic narrative. It illustrates well Poe's philosophy of literature, which prioritizes the creation of effect. All the details are designed to reinforce the thrilling atmosphere Poe desired the tale to communicate. As you read, note how Poe creates that effect through imaginative comparisons, sound devices, and vivid descriptions.

The Red Death had long devastated the country. No pestilence had ever been so fatal, or so hideous. Blood was its Avatar* and its seal—the redness and the horror of blood. There were sharp pains, and sudden dizziness, and then profuse bleeding at the pores, with dissolution.* The scarlet stains upon the body and especially upon the face of the victim, were the pest ban which shut him out from the aid and from the sympathy of his fellowmen. And the whole seizure, progress and termination of the disease, were the incidents of half an hour.

Avatar: incarnation, manifestation
dissolution: death

But Prince Prospero was happy and dauntless* and sagacious.* When his dominions were half depopulated, he summoned to his presence a thousand hale and light-hearted friends from among the knights and dames of his court, and with these retired to the deep seclusion of one of his castellated* abbeys. This was an extensive and magnificent structure, the creation of the prince's own eccentric yet august* taste. A strong and lofty wall girdled it in. This wall had gates of iron. The courtiers, having entered, brought furnaces and massy hammers and welded the bolts. They resolved to leave means neither of ingress or egress to the sudden impulses of despair or of frenzy from within. The abbey was amply provisioned. With such precautions the courtiers might bid defiance to contagion. The external world could take care of itself. In the meantime it was folly to grieve, or to think. The prince had provided all the appliances of pleasure. There were buffoons,* there were improvisatori,* there were ballet dancers, there were musicians, there was Beauty, there was wine. All these and security were within. Without was the Red Death.

dauntless: fearless
sagacious: shrewd, wise
castellated: built like a castle
august: grand
buffoon: clown
improvisatori: musical improvisers

It was toward the close of the fifth or sixth month of his seclusion, and while the pestilence raged most furiously abroad, that Prince Prospero entertained his thousand friends at a masked ball of the most unusual magnificence.

It was a voluptuous* scene, that masquerade. But first let me tell of the rooms in which it was held. There were seven—an imperial suite. In many palaces, however, such suites form a long and straight vista,* while the folding doors slide back nearly to the walls on either hand, so that the view of the whole extent is scarcely impeded. Here the case was very different; as might have been expected from the duke's love of the *bizarre*.* The apartments were so irregularly disposed that the vision embraced but little more than one at a time. There was a sharp turn at every twenty or thirty yards, and at each turn a novel effect. To the right and left, in the middle of each wall, a tall and narrow Gothic window looked out upon a closed corridor which pursued the windings of the suite. These windows were of stained glass whose color varied in accordance with the prevailing hue of the decorations of the chamber into which it opened. That at the eastern extremity was hung, for example, in blue—and vividly blue were its windows. The second chamber was purple in its ornaments and tapestries, and here the panes were purple. The third was green throughout, and so were the casements. The fourth was furnished and lighted with orange—the fifth with white—the sixth with violet. The seventh apartment was closely shrouded in black velvet tapestries that hung all over the ceiling and down the walls, falling in heavy folds upon a carpet of the same material and hue. But in this chamber only, the color of the windows failed to correspond with the decorations. The panes here were scarlet—a deep blood color. Now in no one of the seven apartments was there any lamp or candelabrum* amid the profusion of golden ornaments that lay scattered to and fro or depended from the roof. There was no light of any kind emanating* from lamp or candle within the suite of chambers. But in the corridors that followed the suite, there stood, opposite to each window, a heavy tripod, bearing a brazier* of fire that projected its rays through the tinted glass and so glaringly illumined the room. And thus was produced a multitude of gaudy and fantastic appearances. But in the western or black chamber the effect of the firelight that streamed upon the dark hangings through the blood-tinted panes, was ghastly in the extreme, and produced so wild a look upon the countenances of those who entered, that there were few of the company bold enough to set foot within its precincts at all.

---

voluptuous: luxurious
vista: passage, scene
bizarre: odd, fantastic
candelabrum: a large, branched candlestick
emanating: issuing from
brazier: a metal pan holding burning coals

It was in this apartment, also, that there stood against the western wall, a gigantic clock of ebony. Its pendulum swung to and fro with a dull, heavy, monotonous clang; and when the minute hand made the circuit of the face, and the hour was to be stricken, there came from the brazen lungs of the clock a sound which was clear and loud and deep and exceedingly musical, but of so peculiar a note and emphasis that, at each lapse of an hour, the musicians of the orchestra were constrained to pause, momentarily, in their performance, to hearken to the sound; and thus the waltzers perforce ceased their evolutions; and there was a brief disconcert of the whole company; and, while the chimes of the clock yet rang, it was observed that the giddiest grew pale, and the more aged and sedate passed their hands over their brows as if in confused reverie or meditation. But when the echoes had fully ceased, a light laughter at once pervaded the assembly; the musicians looked at each other and smiled as if at their own nervousness and folly, and made whispering vows, each to the other, that the next chiming of the clock should produce in them no similar emotion; and then, after the lapse of sixty minutes (which embrace three thousand and six hundred seconds of the Time that flies), there came yet another chiming of the clock, and then were the same disconcert and tremulousness and meditation as before.

But, in spite of these things, it was a gay and magnificent revel. The tastes of the duke were peculiar. He had a fine eye for colors and effects. He disregarded the *decora** of mere fashion. His plans were bold and fiery, and his conceptions glowed with barbaric lustre. There are some who would have thought him mad. His followers felt that he was not. It was necessary to hear and see and touch him to be *sure* that he was not.

decora: Latin, dictates

He had directed, in great part, the movable embellishments of the seven chambers, upon occasion of this great fete;* and it was his own guiding taste which had given character to the masqueraders. Be sure they were grotesque. There were much glare and glitter and piquancy* and phantasm*—much of what has been since seen in *Hernani.** There were arabesque* figures with unsuited limbs and appointments.* There were delirious fancies such as the madman fashions. There was much of the beautiful, much of the wanton,* much of the bizarre, something of the terrible, and not a little of that which might have excited disgust. To and fro in the seven chambers there stalked, in fact, a multitude of dreams. And these—the dreams—writhed in and about, taking hue from the rooms and causing the wild music of the orchestra to seem as the echo of their steps. And, anon,* there strikes the ebony clock which stands in the hall of the velvet. And then, for a moment, all is still, and all is silent save the voice of the clock. The dreams are stiff-frozen as they stand. But the echoes of the chime die away—they have endured but an instant—and a light, half-subdued laughter floats after them as they depart. And now again the music swells, and the dreams live, and writhe to and fro more merrily than ever, taking hue from the many-tinted windows through which stream the rays from the tripods. But to the chamber which lies most westwardly of the seven, there are now none of the maskers who venture; for the night is waning away; and there flows a ruddier light through the blood-colored panes; and the blackness of the sable* drapery appals,* and to him whose foot falls upon the sable carpet, there comes from the near clock of ebony a muffled peal more solemnly emphatic than any which reaches their ears who indulge in the more remote gaieties of the other apartments.

fete: festival

piquancy: liveliness, charm

phantasm: a phantom or an illusion

Hernani: a romantic play by Victor Hugo (1802–85), presented in 1830.

arabesque: fanciful (in ballet a position in which the dancer extends one leg straight backward, one arm forward, and the other arm backward)

appointments: adornments

wanton: extravagant, unrestrained

anon: again

sable: black

appals: makes pale with fear, dismays

But these other apartments were densely crowded, and in them beat feverishly the heart of life. And the revel went whirlingly on, until at length there commenced the sounding of midnight upon the clock. And then the music ceased, as I have told; and the evolutions of the waltzers were quieted; and there was an uneasy cessation of all things as before. But now there were twelve strokes to be sounded by the bell of the clock; and thus it happened, perhaps, that more of thought crept, with more of time, into the meditations of the thoughtful among those who revelled. And thus, too, it happened, perhaps, that before the last echoes of the last chimes had utterly sunk into silence, there were many individuals in the crowd who had found leisure to become aware of the presence of a masked figure which had arrested the attention of no single individual before. And the rumor of this new presence having spread itself whisperingly around, there arose at length from the whole company a buzz, or murmur, expressive of disapprobation* and surprise—then, finally, of terror, of horror, and of disgust.

disapprobation: disapproval, condemnation

In an assembly of phantasms such as I have painted, it may well be supposed that no ordinary appearance could have excited such sensation. In truth the masquerade license of the night was nearly unlimited; but the figure in question had out-Heroded Herod, and gone beyond the bounds of even the prince's indefinite decorum. There are chords in the hearts of the most reckless which cannot be touched without emotion. Even with the utterly lost, to whom life and death are equally jests, there are matters of which no jest can be made. The whole company, indeed, seemed now deeply to feel that in the costume and bearing of the stranger neither wit nor propriety existed. The figure was tall and gaunt, and shrouded from head to foot in the habiliments* of the grave. The mask which concealed the visage was made so nearly to resemble the countenance of a stiffened corpse that the closest scrutiny must have had difficulty in detecting the cheat. And yet all this might have been endured, if not approved, by the mad revellers around. But the mummer* had gone so far as to assume the type of the Red Death. His vesture was dabbled in blood—and his broad brow, with all the features of the face, was besprinkled with the scarlet horror.

habiliments: clothing, attire
mummer: one who acts or plays in a mask or costume

When the eyes of Prince Prospero fell upon this spectral image (which with a slow and solemn movement, as if more fully to sustain its role, stalked to and fro among the waltzers) he was seen to be convulsed, in the first moment with a strong shudder either of terror or distaste; but, in the next, his brow reddened with rage.

"Who dares?" he demanded hoarsely of the courtiers who stood near him—"who dares insult us with this blasphemous mockery? Seize him and unmask him—that we may know whom we have to hang at sunrise, from the battlements!"

It was in the eastern or blue chamber in which stood the Prince Prospero as he uttered these words. They rang throughout the seven rooms loudly and clearly—for the prince was a bold and robust man, and the music had become hushed at the waving of his hand.

It was in the blue room where stood the prince, with a group of pale courtiers by his side. At first, as he spoke, there was a slight rushing movement of this group in the direction of the intruder, who at the moment was also near at hand, and now, with deliberate and stately step, made close approach to the speaker. But from a certain nameless awe with which the mad assumptions of the mummer had inspired the whole party, there were found none who put forth hand to seize him; so that, unimpeded, he passed within a yard of the prince's person; and, while the vast assembly, as if with one impulse, shrank from the centres of the rooms to the walls, he made his way uninterruptedly, but with the same solemn and measured step which had distinguished him from the first, through the blue chamber to the purple—through the purple to the green—through the green to the orange—through this again to the white—and even thence to the violet, ere a decided movement had been made to arrest him. It was then, however, that the Prince Prospero, maddening with rage and the shame of his own momentary cowardice, rushed hurriedly through the six chambers, while none followed him on account of a deadly terror that had seized upon all. He bore aloft a drawn dagger, and had approached, in rapid impetuosity,* to within three or four feet of the retreating figure, when the latter, having attained the extremity of the velvet apartment, turned suddenly and confronted his pursuer. There was a sharp cry—and the dagger dropped gleaming upon the sable carpet, upon which, instantly afterwards, fell prostrate in death Prince Prospero. Then, summoning the wild courage of despair, a throng of the revellers at once threw themselves into the black apartment, and, seizing the mummer, whose tall figure stood erect and motionless within the shadow of the ebony

clock, gasped in unutterable horror at finding the grave cerements* and corpse-like mask which they handled with so violent a rudeness, untenanted by any tangible form.

impetuosity: violent force
cerements: the winding sheet for a corpse

And now was acknowledged the presence of the Red Death. He had come like a thief in the night. And one by one dropped the revellers in the blood-bedewed halls of their revel, and died each in the despairing posture of his fall. And the life of the ebony clock went out with that of the last of the gay. And the flames of the tripods expired. And Darkness and Decay and the Red Death held illimitable* dominion over all.

illimitable: boundless

About the Story

1. What kind of atmosphere did Poe create in "The Masque of the Red Death"?
2. Give three details that Poe presents to reinforce the story's atmosphere.
3. The story pits Prince Prospero and his courtiers against the Red Death. What do you think each side symbolizes?
4. Given your answer to the previous question, what do you think the main theme of the story is?
5. Identify at least one additional symbol in the story and tell what that symbol represents.
6. Do you think Poe wants you to sympathize with Prince Prospero and his revelers? Why or why not?
7. Poe ends his story with the statement "And Darkness and Decay and the Red Death held illimitable dominion over all." Given the symbolic meaning of the story, how does his tone support or contradict a biblical worldview? (See especially Romans 6:9.)

About the Author

Perhaps one of the most intriguing authors in the American pantheon, Edgar Allan Poe (1809–49) lived a life that often seems just as dramatic as his writing. Orphaned within three years of his birth, he was reared by a wealthy couple, the Allans. Eventually, however, Poe's desire to be a writer resulted in a split with his foster father. Having dropped out of both the University of Virginia and West Point, the young Poe was jobless and penniless when his aunt offered him a home. There he met his cousin, Virginia, whom he eventually married (a practice not uncommon at the time). After ten years of marriage, Virginia died of tuberculosis in 1847, leaving Poe devastated. Nearly two years later, he disappeared for several days and resurfaced only to die of mysterious causes in a Baltimore hospital.

The victim of false biography after his death, Poe was long considered at best an eccentric and at worst a drug addict or a madman. Such is not the case. Known by his contemporaries primarily for his work as a critic, Poe was also a gifted and innovative writer who is today particularly famous for two "firsts": he was the first American writer to use only writing to support himself, and he is the originator of the detective story. As a literary author, he is studied for his literary theories, lyric poetry, and gripping short stories.

The Listeners

Walter de la Mare

Sometimes a story succeeds because of what it does not tell us. "The Listeners" teases our imaginations to supply missing details—or ponder the mystery. Notice that sometimes the less a story explains, the more it can suggest and symbolize.

"Is there anybody there?" said the Traveler,
Knocking on the moonlit door;
And his horse in the silence champed* the grasses
Of the forest's ferny floor.
And a bird flew up out of the turret,*
Above the Traveler's head:
And he smote upon the door again a second time;
"Is there anybody there?" he said.
But no one descended to the Traveler;
No head from the leaf-fringed sill

champ: to chew noisily

turret: a small tower

Leaned over and looked into his gray eyes,
Where he stood perplexed and still.
But only a host of phantom listeners
That dwelt in the lone house then
Stood listening in the quiet of the moonlight
To that voice from the world of men:
Stood thronging the faint moonbeams on their dark stair
That goes down to the empty hall,
Hearkening in an air stirred and shaken
By the lonely Traveler's call.
And he felt in his heart their strangeness,
Their stillness answering his cry,
While his horse moved, cropping the dark turf,
'Neath the starred and leafy sky;
For he suddenly smote on the door, even
Louder, and lifted his head:—
"Tell them I came, and no one answered,
That I kept my word," he said.
Never the least stir made the listeners,
Though every word he spake
Fell echoing through the shadowiness of the still house
From the one man left awake:
Aye, they heard his foot upon the stirrup,
And the sound of iron on stone,
And how the silence surged softly backward,
When the plunging hoofs were gone.

About the Poem

1. What information that you might expect to be given in a story does de la Mare withhold from his poem?
2. How does this withholding of information add to the poem?
3. De la Mare seems to suggest that this nameless, faceless Traveler might symbolize anyone. If so, what do you think the poet meant to represent by the Traveler's knocking on a door? What might that say about the message of the poem?

About the Author

Walter de la Mare (1873–1956) is a poet whose writing deals with the strange and the uncanny. Yet he cannot be compared with a writer such as Edgar Allan Poe, whose primary goal was to create an atmosphere of terror or strangeness. Instead, de la Mare explored the dreamy, imaginative side of existence as a means of discovering truth about life. His tone is gentler than Poe's. De la Mare wrote numerous poems for or about children. Yet they appeal to all ages with their lyricism and deceptively simple style.

De la Mare saw the universe as devoid of a caring, controlling God. To him, humanity suffers from the inexplicable action of "fate." In this respect, he strongly resembles Thomas Hardy (see pp. 324–26). De la Mare's rejection of Christianity was well known.

Nevertheless, de la Mare does make some valid observations about modern man. Although he was to all appearances a very ordinary, conservative Englishman, his mind was keenly aware of the spiritual as opposed to the strictly materialistic side of life. He shows insight into the connection between our sinful nature and our hidden imaginings, a relationship that the Scriptures long ago revealed.

A Piece of Chalk

G. K. Chesterton

In this masterful essay, G. K. Chesterton makes expert use of imaginative comparison, organized sound and syntax, allusion, and symbol. His tone is informal, even casual, seeming to wander here and there. Yet even these apparent detours help communicate his message in the end. In his hands, a boyhood experience recollected becomes emblematic of deep moral truth.

I remember one splendid morning, all blue and silver, in the summer holidays, when I reluctantly tore myself away from the task of doing nothing in particular, and put on a hat of some sort and picked up a walking stick, and put six very bright-colored chalks in my pocket. I then went into the kitchen (which, along with the rest of the house, belonged to a very square and sensible old woman in a Sussex village), and asked the owner and occupant of the kitchen if she had any brown paper. She had a great deal; in fact, she had too much; and she mistook the purpose and the rationale of the existence of brown paper. She seemed to have an idea that if a person wanted brown paper he must be wanting it to tie up parcels; which was the last thing I wanted to do; indeed, it is a thing which I have found to be beyond my mental capacity. Hence she dwelt very much on the varying qualities of toughness and endurance in the material. I explained to her that I only wanted to draw pictures on it, and that I did not want them to endure in the least; and that from my point of view, therefore, it was a question not of tough consistency, but of responsive surface, a thing comparatively irrelevant in a parcel. When she understood that I wanted to draw she offered to overwhelm me with note-paper, apparently supposing that I did my notes and correspondence on old brown paper wrappers from motives of economy.

I then tried to explain the rather delicate logical shade, that I not only liked brown paper, but liked the quality of brownness in paper, just as I liked the quality of brownness in October woods, or in the peat streams of the North. Brown paper represents the primal twilight of the first toil of creation, and with a bright-colored chalk or two you can pick out points of fire in it, sparks of gold, and blood-red, and sea-green, like the first fierce stars that sprang out of divine darkness. All this I said (in an off-hand way) to the old woman; and I put the brown paper in my pocket along with the chalks, and possibly other things. I suppose every one must have reflected how primeval and how poetical are the things that one carries in one's pocket; the pocketknife, for instance, the type of all human tools, the infant of the sword. Once I planned to write a book of poems entirely about the things in my pocket. But I found it would be too long; and the age of the great epics is past.

With my stick and my knife, my chalks and my brown paper, I went out on to the great downs.*I crawled across loose colossal contours that express the best quality of England, because they are at the same time soft and strong. The smoothness of them has the same meaning as the smoothness of great cart horses, or the smoothness of the beech tree; it declares in the teeth of our timid cruel theories that the mighty are merciful. As my eye swept the landscape, the landscape was as kindly as any of its cottages, but for power it was like an earthquake. The villages in the immense valley were safe, one could see,

for centuries; yet the lifting of the whole land was like the lifting of one enormous wave to wash them all away.

downs: long ridges of rolling hills in southern England

I crossed one swell of living turf after another, looking for a place to sit down and draw. Do not, for heaven's sake, imagine I was going to sketch from Nature. I was going to draw devils and seraphim, and blind old gods that men worshiped before the dawn of right, and saints in robes of angry crimson, and seas of strange green, and all the sacred or monstrous symbols that look so well in bright colors on brown paper. They are much better worth drawing than Nature; also they are much easier to draw. When a cow came slouching by in the field next to me, a mere artist might have drawn it; but I always get wrong in the hind legs of quadrupeds. So I drew the soul of the cow; which I saw there plainly walking before me in the sunlight; and the soul was all purple and silver, and had seven horns and the mystery that belongs to all the beasts. But though I could not with a crayon get the best out of the landscape, it does not follow that the landscape was not getting the best out of me. And this, I think, is the mistake that people make about old poets who lived before Wordsworth, and were supposed not to care very much about Nature because they did not describe it much.

They preferred writing about great men to writing about great hills; but they sat on the great hills to write it. They gave out much less about Nature, but they drank in, perhaps, much more. They painted the white robes of their holy virgins with the blinding snow, at which they stared all day. They blazoned the shields of their paladins* with the purple and gold of many heraldic sunsets. The greenness of a thousand green leaves clustered into the live green figure of Robin Hood. The blueness of a score of forgotten skies became the blue robes of the Virgin. The inspiration went in like sunbeams and came out like Apollo.*

paladins: champions of chivalry
Apollo: Roman god of the sun and of the arts

But as I sat scrawling these silly figures on the brown paper, it began to dawn on me, to my great disgust, that I had left one chalk, and that a most exquisite and essential chalk, behind. I searched all my pockets, but I could not find any white chalk. Now, those who are acquainted with all the philosophy (nay, religion) which is typified in the art of drawing on brown paper, know that white is positive and essential. I cannot avoid remarking here upon a moral significance. One of the wise and awful truths which this brown-paper art reveals, is this, that white is a color. It is not a mere absence of color; it is a shining and affirmative thing, as fierce as red, as definite as black. When (so to speak) your pencil grows red-hot, it draws roses; when it grows white-hot, it draws stars. And one of the two or three defiant verities of the best religious morality, of real Christianity for example, is exactly this same thing; the chief assertion of religious morality is that white is a color. Virtue is not the absence of vices or the avoidance of moral danger; virtue is a vivid and separate thing, like pain or a particular smell. Mercy does not mean not being cruel or sparing people revenge or punishment; it means a plain and positive thing like the sun, which one has either seen or not seen. Chastity does not mean abstention from sexual wrong; it means something flaming, like Joan of Arc. In a word, God paints many colors; but He never paints so gorgeously, I had almost said gaudily, as when He paints in white. In a sense our age has realized this fact, and expressed it in our sullen costume. For if it were really true that white was a blank and colorless thing, negative and noncommittal, then white would be used instead of black and grey for the funeral dress of this pessimistic period. We should see city gentlemen in frock coats of spotless silver linen, with top hats as white as wonderful arum lilies. Which is not the case.

Meanwhile, I could not find my chalk.

I sat on the hill in a sort of despair. There was no town nearer than Chichester at which it was even remotely probable that there would be such a thing as an artist's colorman. And yet, without white, my absurd little pictures would be as pointless as the world would be if there were no good people in it. I stared stupidly round, racking my brain for expedients. Then I suddenly stood up and roared with laughter, again and again, so that the cows stared at me and called a committee. Imagine a man in the Sahara regretting that he had no sand for his hourglass. Imagine a gentleman in mid-ocean wishing that he had brought some salt water with him for his chemical experiments. I was sitting on an immense warehouse of white chalk. The landscape was made entirely out of white chalk. White chalk was piled mere miles until it met the sky. I stooped and broke a piece off the rock I sat on: it did not mark so well as the shop chalks do; but it gave the effect. And I stood there in a trance of pleasure, realizing that this Southern England is not only a grand peninsula, and a tradition and a civilization; it is something even more admirable. It is a piece of chalk.

About the Essay

1. Find one of the allusions in Chesterton's essay and explain its meaning in the text.
2. Chesterton uses a number of imaginative comparisons throughout his essay. Find one example of simile and one of metaphor.
3. What rhetorical device has Chesterton used to emphasize his point in the following statement?

   But though I could not with a crayon get the best out of the landscape, it does not follow that the landscape was not getting the best out of me.

4. Chesterton uses two connected symbols that convey two different themes. Name one and explain the theme that it suggests.
5. Does Chesterton promote a Christian worldview in this essay? Explain your answer.

When Chesterton extolled white as the best color, he was not referring to skin color or people groups. (Every person may have a heart full of either darkness or light.) Use Chesterton's central point—"the chief assertion of religious morality is that white is a color"—to argue against racism. What you write should be an answer to someone who says, "I'm not racist because I've never done anything to hurt someone from a different ethnic group."

About the Author

G. K. Chesterton (1874–1936) was a man of great and varied talent. Enrolled in both college and art school, he finished neither. Nevertheless, he grew into a polished and prolific writer who engaged in a wide variety of genres—art and literary reviews, poetry, apologetics, and more. Chesterton began his life as an orthodox Anglican but converted to Catholicism in 1922; nonetheless, evangelical Protestants have consistently found his work engaging and helpful.

Having begun his career as a journalist, Chesterton wrote a column in the *Illustrated London News* that became a thirty-year-long platform for advocating Christian values. At the same time, he created a series of stories featuring amateur detective Father Brown, wrote a seminal biography of Charles Dickens, and became a leading Christian apologist with his books *Orthodoxy*, *Heretics*, and *The Everlasting Man*—to name only a few.

A brilliant social, political, and economic commentator, Chesterton was able to take deep philosophical questions and address them in a way ordinary people could understand. In a time of encroaching modernism, he fearlessly questioned the intellectuals of his day, deftly cutting to the heart of matters to reveal the hidden assumptions and contradictions in his opponents' arguments. Though possessed of such gifts as well as a larger-than-life personality, he was humble enough to retain the respect and even friendship of prominent thinkers with whom he strongly (and publicly) disagreed. Overall, his writing combines absolute values and depth of thought with optimism, wit, humor, and a love of paradox.

THINKING ZONE

Human life is characterized by conflict. Conflicts permeate our lives and choices, coming from forces both outside of us and within our own flawed nature. So it is not surprising that good literature requires some sort of conflict, whether physical, psychological, or symbolic, to catch our interest. Conflict brings a story alive and presents us with the situation's emotional stakes. Thus, wherever there is a tale to be told or a poem to be written, there is conflict.

Put simply, literary **conflict** is the opposition of two or more forces in a work. Though many conflicts take place between individual characters, they may also involve larger entities, such as nations or organizations. Depending on the players involved, a conflict is classified as either external or internal. **External conflicts** are those that occur between a character and an outside force (such as society or nature). "The Return of the Rangers" is such a story: one of the main conflicts of the story is between Captain Rogers and the wilderness. **Internal conflicts** are those that occur between a character and his own thoughts, emotions, or beliefs. "Traveling Through the Dark" is an example of internal conflict of a man and his beliefs.

Like many works of literature, Scripture intertwines both types of conflict. Consider, for example, the story of Gideon (Judges 6–8). In the midst of external conflicts between the Israelites and the Midianites, God calls Gideon to lead His people. A series of internal conflicts ensues in which Gideon struggles to be God's leader amid the external conflicts of war.

Conflict provides structure for an author's theme, letting a writer express his views on a subject. Whether prose or poetry, a work usually centers on its main conflict. The conflict may clearly dominate the work (as in many narratives), or it may remain implied in the background (as in many poems). In either case, how an author resolves the conflict communicates much about the way he views the topics under discussion. For example, the resolution to Gideon's story is victory for Israel and for Gideon: in context of the story, these resolutions show that God will be faithful to those who choose to trust Him.

1. Is the primary conflict of "The Masque of the Red Death" **internal** or **external**? Explain your answer.
2. Given the theme of the story, what does the resolution of that conflict communicate about Poe's beliefs?
3. On the symbolic level, what conflict does Borges's "Afterglow" explore? Is it external or internal? Explain.
4. Chesterton frames his essay "A Piece of Chalk" with a story. What is the simple external conflict of that story?
5. Chesterton uses this simple conflict as a platform to address a particular conflict of ideas going on at the time. What idea is he seeking to promote in the essay?

UNIT III REVIEW

Remember the Terms

Review the following terms from the opening essay, "Allusion and Symbol," and the Thinking Zone pages. Be prepared to discuss their meanings and uses.

allusion	tone	internal conflict
symbol	persona	external conflict
atmosphere	conflict	

Apply the Concepts

Answer the following questions about how the literary concepts you have studied are used in this unit.

1. How is the allusion in the title "Cupid's Arrows" relevant to the story?
2. Barr-Saggott's being christened "the Langur" is an example of what literary device?
3. The following lines from "Sir Francis Drake" are an example of what kind of rhyme?

   He asked me whose I was. I answered him.
   He asked me if his good friend were within.
4. O'Neill uses several allusions from history, literature, and pop culture in his essay "Outta My Way, Grandpa!" Discuss one of them.
5. Explain how the bones in "And down he lays his weary bones" from Arnold's "The Progress of Poesy" are an example of synecdoche.
6. Explain one of the symbols in Cummings's "maggie and milly and molly and may."
7. What is the atmosphere of Borges's "Afterglow"?
8. Identify three symbols from "The Masque of the Red Death" and discuss what the symbols mean in the story.
9. Give three details that reinforce the foreboding atmosphere of Poe's "The Masque of the Red Death."
10. What are two allusions that Poe makes in "The Masque of the Red Death"?
11. What is the primary conflict of "The Masque of the Red Death"?
12. What is the atmosphere of "The Listeners"? How does the author create that atmosphere?
13. Explain Chesterton's use of the color white as a symbol in "A Piece of Chalk."
14. What are the conflicts in "A Piece of Chalk"?

Evaluate the Ideas

Identify each of the following statements as true or false. If false, rewrite the underlined portion of the statement to make it true.

15. A theme of "Cupid's Arrows" is looks vs. influence as the prerequisite to marriage.
16. In "Cupid's Arrows" the arrow is a symbol of wealth and prestige.
17. "Sir Francis Drake" uses metaphor to compare the naval hero to a dragon.
18. Hayman uses a symbol when he wishes that Drake's "gifts, Elias-like" could have been passed along to him.
19. O'Neill's thesis in his essay "Outta My Way, Grandpa!" is that motivation matters.
20. O'Neill reveals an angry tone in "Outta My Way, Grandpa!"
21. Moses' striking the rock is the internal conflict that appears in the first stanza of Matthew Arnold's poem "The Progress of Poesy."
22. Arnold reveals a definitely pessimistic worldview in "The Progress of Poesy."
23. The atmosphere of "maggie and milly and molly and may" is primarily cheerful.
24. The major symbol of "Afterglow" is the horizon.
25. Poe's worldview in "The Masque of the Red Death" is revealed as a belief that death is frightening and inevitable.
26. When de la Mare repeats the similar phrases "Stood listening" and "Stood thronging" in "The Listeners," he is using the literary technique of chiasmus.
27. The phrase "the first fierce stars that sprang out of divine darkness" in Chesterton's "A Piece of Chalk" contains an allusion.
28. Chesterton's reflecting on "how primeval and how poetical are the things that one carries in one's pocket" contains examples of consonance and simile.

Write a Response

Completely answer each of the following questions.

29. What are the two major symbols in "The Masque of the Red Death"? Explain how these symbols relate to the story's theme.
30. Explain the symbolic conflict of Borges's "Afterglow."

UNIT IV

Whoever makes a DESIGN, without the Knowledge of PERSPECTIVE,
will be liable to such Absurdities as are shewn in this Frontispiece.

SATIRE ON FALSE PERSPECTIVE

William Hogarth

IRONY

As a young person, eighteenth-century English painter and engraver William Hogarth (1697–1764) observed life and enjoyed sketching people and street scenes. At age fifteen he was apprenticed to a silversmith, and by 1720 he had set up his own engraving business. Progressing to painting, Hogarth produced both conversation pieces, which feature small family groups in conversation or informal activity, and portraits. In his famous self-portrait Hogarth playfully invites comparisons by placing his pug dog, Trump, closely beside himself.

Hogarth is primarily known for his works (sometimes done in series) satirizing moral ills in society. His most famous, the series A Harlot's Progress *and* A Rake's Progress, *dramatize the downward spiral of the individuals depicted; each picture advances the main character further toward death and insanity respectively. Both satires were extremely popular and earned for Hogarth a certain degree of financial independence. A satirical series indicting upper-class marriages motivated by money followed (*Marriage a La Mode*).*

Satire on False Perspective *was produced to accompany a pamphlet on linear perspective. The caption reads, "Whoever makes a design without the knowledge of perspective will be liable to such absurdities as are shown in this Frontispiece."*

- ❋ To represent proper perspective, objects far away are drawn smaller than objects located nearer the observer. What two specific groups of objects in the picture violate this principle?
- ❋ Identify two impossibilities regarding the signpost and two connected with any of the men in the picture.
- ❋ How does Hogarth's engraving illustrate irony?
- ❋ In *Satire on False Perspective* Hogarth used intentional "mistakes" in order to teach. What other sources with which you are familiar use a similar strategy? Is this strategy effective?

IRONY

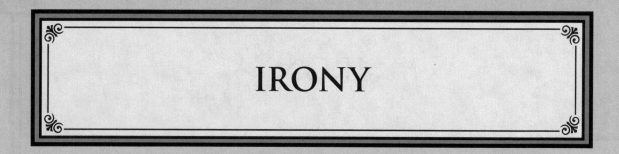

A strong theme throughout much of classic literature is the conflict between appearance and reality: the idea that what a person or situation appears to be is not always what it really is. Chesterton's "A Piece of Chalk" touches on this conflict in a moment late in the essay. In frustration, the boy Chesterton realizes he has forgotten to bring white chalk to draw with. Despondent, he searches for an alternative only to realize that he has an unlimited supply of white chalk literally at his feet: the very soil he is standing on consists of it. This sudden reversal—finding that what appeared to be inaccessible is in fact available in abundance—forms an example of the literary mode of irony.

Irony is a broad concept that underscores the paradoxical in language and in life. Put simply, **irony** refers to the use of language to convey meaning other than what is stated or to express a contradiction between what is expected to happen and what actually happens. In the ironic there is usually an element of contradiction asking readers (or characters) to read between the lines or deal with the unexpected. An author may appear to say one thing, when he really means another. A situation may seem likely to head in one direction but then take an entirely different tack. Though this discrepancy between meanings or between expectations and reality is at times revealed suddenly (as in Chesterton's essay), it is often meant to be clear all along to observant readers. For alert readers, the presence of irony, much like allusion and symbolism, draws attention to and further illustrates aspects of the author's message.

Types of Irony

First, **verbal irony** refers to a contrast between the literal interpretation of a statement and its implied meaning, with the implied level carrying the author's real meaning. Consider the example of Elijah in his confrontation with the prophets of Baal. After watching them call on Baal for an entire morning, Elijah taunts, "Cry aloud: for he is a god; either he is talking, or he is pursuing, or he is in a journey, or peradventure he sleepeth, and must be awakened" (1 Kings 18:27). Obviously Elijah does not really mean what he says. Rather, he is implying that their efforts are futile because a real god would have already responded. One particularly pervasive type of verbal irony is **sarcasm**, mock praise. Job 12:2 contains a rather humorous example. Frustrated with his friends' wrong-headed counsel, Job responds sarcastically saying, "No doubt but ye are the people, and wisdom shall die with you." In context it is clear that Job means just the opposite of what he says.

Second, an overarching feature of a work can sometimes generate two layers of meaning (one literal and one implied) throughout the entire work. This sustained verbal irony is termed **structural irony**. For example, an author may create a narrative persona with whom he does not actually agree. As a result, every opinion or statement by this narrator must be filtered through the knowledge of his obvious flaws in observation and judgment. Only then can the reader understand the author's implied personal viewpoint. And since the reader must continually evaluate this character's viewpoint, the writer can continually draw attention to the real-life issues the narrator reflects, countering the positions held by the character and making his own viewpoint look attractive in contrast. Such is the case with C. S. Lewis's famous *Screwtape Letters* (excerpted in this unit), which uses a demon as the narrator.

Next, **situational irony** contrasts what is reasonable to expect and what actually happens. Stephen Crane's "A Gray Sleeve" (Unit II) illustrates irony of situation in both its main character and its plot. The confident young captain appears unassailable, but he crumbles before a young woman. Similarly, the Union soldiers think they are heroically capturing the enemy, but in fact they end up cornering three helpless people. In both cases, neither the characters nor the readers expect events to proceed as they do. This gap between expectations and reality often creates humor. The Bible also provides many instances of situational irony. In Acts 12, believers gather together to pray for the release of Peter from prison. But when Rhoda, a young girl, answers the door to find Peter free outside, no one at first believes her. To the reader, the Christians' disbelief is disappointingly ironic. One would expect the Christians to pray believing that their prayers would, or at least could, be answered.

Finally, situational irony can sometimes be framed in a way that creates dramatic irony. In **dramatic irony** a reader or audience is aware of a plot development of which the character in the story is unaware. Usually, the character continues to act on expectations that the audience now knows will not be fulfilled. The author uses the resulting tension to highlight his message. Consider the example of Haman in the book of Esther. Haman builds a gallows to execute Mordecai, a Jew whom he hates, and comes to ask the king to sign the orders, expecting only agreement. Known to the readers but unbeknownst to Haman, the king owes Mordecai his life and wants to reward him. From Haman's perspective, subsequent events create situational irony. From the readers' more informed perspective, subsequent events create dramatic irony. This prior knowledge lets readers focus their attention on how Haman is thinking and behaving rather than on the unfolding events. With his ignorant boasting he seems almost a comic actor in a play, and his arrogance and petty cruelty stand fully revealed. The irony climaxes with the hanging of Haman on the very gallows he has built for Mordecai.

Uses of Irony

As you can see, most irony, whether situational or verbal, is based on incongruity. That is, it involves a contrast of some sort. Some irony, however, is based on ambiguity. A person may do or say something that has a wider significance than he or his observer realizes. In hindsight, many examples of foreshadowing are ironic. Alternatively, a character may make a statement of his beliefs or expectations that, in the light of later action, is shown to be far from true.

Irony can be very subtle. In fact, it can be downright difficult to recognize in written communication (which lacks vocal tones to help clue readers in). A writer dealing in verbal and structural irony in particular runs the risk of being very much misunderstood should readers fail to pick up on his real, implied meaning. Nonetheless, writers still use irony frequently because when it is done well, it forms an extremely powerful tool. Among other things, irony surprises us, amuses us, and can even satisfy our sense of justice (for instance, when the well-laid plans of villains such as Haman go awry).

The selections in this unit illustrate these types of irony. As you read, identify as many of them as you can. Evaluate the author's use of irony by asking yourself these questions: Is the irony serious or humorous or both? In cases of verbal irony, how does the writer signal the reader that what he is reading is in the ironic mode? What thought or theme does this irony serve to highlight?

The Golf Links Lie So Near the Mill

SARAH N. CLEGHORN

The following two poems illustrate the wide range of irony as a technique. While both poets use irony well, the overall mood and themes that irony contributes to in each poem differ considerably.

The golf links lie so near the mill
  That almost every day
The working children can look out
  And see the men at play.

About the Author

Born in Norfolk, Virginia, Sarah N. Cleghorn (1876–1959) lived there and in Minnesota before moving at age nine to Vermont, where she spent most of her life. She attended Radcliffe College, from which she received a bachelor's degree in literature and philosophy in 1896. Cleghorn's short stories and poems were often published in popular magazines, including *Scribner's*, *Harper's*, and *Atlantic Monthly*. Her writing reflects her rural upbringing in New England and her concerns as a social reformer. Beyond her vocation as an educator, Cleghorn worked for women's suffrage, equal rights, and prison reform and against child labor, among other issues. She called her earlier poems, those describing country life, "sunbonnets" and her later didactic poems, those concerned with social injustices, her "burning poems." In the introduction to her autobiography, *Threescore*, Robert Frost called Cleghorn "saint, poet—*and* reformer." In addition to poems and short stories, Cleghorn wrote three novels and a book of essays.

Jade Flower Palace

Tu Fu

Translated by Kenneth Rexroth

The following poem seems to describe a scene that Tu Fu encountered in his travels. He uses verbal irony to give his description a subtle message. Think about what the underlying meaning of the poem might be as you read.

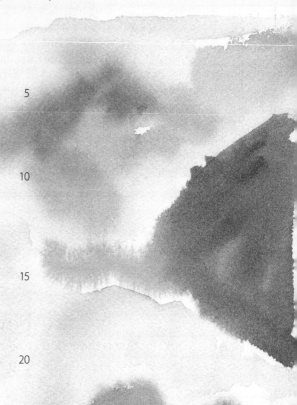

The stream swirls. The wind moans in
The pines. Gray rats scurry over
Broken tiles. What prince, long ago,
Built this palace, standing in
Ruins beside the cliffs? There are
Green ghost fires in the black rooms.
The shattered pavements are all
Washed away. Ten thousand organ
Pipes whistle and roar. The storm
Scatters the red autumn leaves.
His dancing girls are yellow dust.
Their painted cheeks have crumbled
Away. His gold chariots
And courtiers are gone. Only

A stone horse is left of his
Glory. I sit on the grass and
Start a poem, but the pathos of
It overcomes me. The future
Slips imperceptibly away.
Who can say what the years will bring?

About the Author

Chinese poet Tu Fu (also transliterated as Du Fu, 712–770) was born into a scholarly family. His education in Confucian classics was designed to prepare him for civil service, but he was thwarted in this ambition when he failed the civil service exam. In his subsequent travels, he met Li Bai, already a successful poet, and cultivated a friendship that had an impact on Tu Fu's artistic development.

Tu Fu lost an appointment to a minor governmental post when the An Lushan Rebellion began. This loss began a period characterized by an unhappy and itinerant lifestyle. At one point Tu Fu spent five years living in a thatched hut in the Sichuan province. The experience proved Tu Fu's making as a poet, however, for he wrote of what he saw, providing historical information through his poetry. Though living in poverty, he was happy and productive. Much of Tu Fu's later life was spent trying to secure a position to support his family.

Although Tu Fu received little recognition during his lifetime, he is now considered, along with Li Bai, one of the greatest Chinese poets. Almost 1,500 of his poems have survived, and his influence is significant. Tu Fu wrote about paintings, animals, calligraphy, domestic life, and other topics previously avoided in poetry. His poems reveal both patriotism and a compassion for the poor. Critics praise Tu Fu's poetry for technical excellence and innovation. He mastered all the poetic genres of his day, advanced many, and transformed the formal verse *lushi*, a particularly difficult style of poetry.

About the Poems

1. What emotion is the author striving to evoke in "The Golf Links Lie So Near the Mill"?
2. Which kind of irony does Cleghorn use in her poem? Explain.
3. Identify the theme of "Jade Flower Palace."
4. Identify the kind of irony present in "Jade Flower Palace."
5. What mood does Tu Fu create in "Jade Flower Palace"? Discuss whether you share the response of the poet (the persona) in the poem.
6. Explain how the use of irony in the two poems differs in terms of tone. How do the poets seem to feel about the people they examine?

Cleghorn wrote a poem to address a moral issue about which she felt strongly. List two situations in which this poem might be used to raise public awareness about child labor and to effect positive change.

The Grave Grass Quivers

MacKinlay Kantor

In the following short story, a relatively small act greatly influences the main conflict and its resolution. This incident drives the plot of the story and, through the irony involved, reinforces the main theme. However, in true detective-story fashion, its significance is not fully known until the end. At that point, certain previous statements become examples of ironic foreshadowing. To solve the mystery ahead of time, read carefully and stay alert for clues.

We were alone, out there in the soft spring sunshine. There was no one to disturb us. We dug silently, carefully.

The clinging black earth came up at every shovelful—moist and alive with richness of the prairies. We had been digging for ten minutes, when my shovel struck something. It struck again, and something cracked.

After that, it wasn't long before we began to uncover things. "Murdered," Doc said, once, and then he didn't talk anymore.

It began in Doc Martindale's office, which, as soon as he retired, was to be my office, on a cool spring afternoon in 1921.

"How's it going?" asked Doc.

"I guess it'll be pretty slow here, to live," I said, childishly.

"Not much excitement," agreed Doc. He went to the door and picked up a copy of the *Cottonwood Herald* which a boy had just tossed over the banisters. . . . "Yes, local news is slow, pretty slow. There's a sample of a Cottonwood thriller."

It told of the plans for Arbor Day. The children of the public schools were going to set out some trees as a memorial to the local boys who had died in the World War.

> . . . and selected as their choice, American elms. The trees will be planted on the Louis Wilson farm, above the Coon River. Mr. Wilson has agreed to donate a small plot of ground for this purpose. It is thought that these trees, standing on a high hill above the river and overlooking a majestic view of our city will be a fitting memorial.
>
> Ceremonies are to begin at 2 p.m., and it is urged that all local people attend. Rev. J. Medley Williams of the Baptist Church will deliver a—

Doc pulled his gray beard and laughed. "A few meetings, a church social, once in a while a fire or an auto accident! Once in a blue moon we have a divorce. Life comes—and goes—without much hullabaloo."

Then I had to laugh also, and a bit sheepishly. "I guess I'm rather silly. Of course those are the important things in most people's lives. But I would like to get called in on a nice, exciting murder once in a while!"

Doc was silent for a moment. He appeared to be thinking heavily, as if he had taken me seriously. "Murders," he said, after a moment. "Once before the war, a Mexican worker stabbed his wife. Then back in '96, an insane farmer shot his neighbor. But, come to think of it, those are the only murders we've ever had here in all my years of practice." He seemed much impressed. "Think of that, think of that! Only two murders since 1861."

"And who," I inquired idly, "was murdered in 1861?"

He tugged at his beard again, and cleared his throat. "Well," he said, slowly, "it was my father and my brother."

"Oh." And I scarcely knew what to say. "I'm sorry, Doctor, I—"

"No matter." He shrugged. "It's a long time. I was just a boy then."

My curiosity was aroused. "What are the details, Doctor? That is, if you don't—"

"Oh, I don't mind. . . . Sit down and take it easy." It was several minutes before he began to talk.

"My brother Titus—he was a lot older—had run away from home when he was small, and gone West with some folks. He didn't come back until the spring of '61. And when he came, what a time!"

He laughed his short, dry laugh.

"Titus had struck it rich. He had about seven thousand dollars in gold with him.

"Pa and Titus decided to take the gold to Hamilton. There was a sort of bank opened up there, and the folks were afraid to risk keeping so much money around home.

"They were pretty careful, too, and didn't tell around town much about what they'd planned. They started out at night, figuring to get clear away from Cottonwood and the settlers who knew them, before daylight. Pa and Titus were strapping big men. They looked very strong, setting up on the board laid across the plank wagon box, and Titus carried a navy revolver on his hip and a Sharps rifle across his knees."

Doc Martindale shifted his fat, bumpy body in his wide swivel chair. "And that," he said, "was the last we ever saw them.

"On the evening of the second day after my folks left," Doc Martindale continued, "a farmer from the Salt Creek neighborhood rode up in front of our house, and said that he had seen our team down in a clump of willows by Little Hell Slough, hitched to a wagon, and that the men folks were not with the wagon. The team had been dragging around, and tried to go home, but they got hung up in the willows."

Old Doc was silent for several minutes.

"That was a terrible night," he said, simply. "Before we all got down to Little Hell Slough—most of the neighbors were with us—we found the team in those willows, pretty muddy and hungry, and tangled up in the harness, too.

"None of the stuff in the wagon had been taken except—sure: the gold was gone. The blankets were still there, and Titus's rifle, but his navy revolver wasn't anywhere around. And there was no other sign of Pa and Titus.

"I drove Ma and the girls home, in that wagon. Ma sat there beside me on the board, stiff and solemn. Once she said, 'Georgie, if they're gone and gone for good, you'll get the man who did it. Won't you?' I began to cry, of course. I says, 'Yes, Ma. I'll take care of you always, Ma. . . . But if they're dead, it wasn't a man who killed 'em. It was men. One man wouldn't be a match for Titus alone.'"

Doc was buried in the thickening shadows of the office. I couldn't see his face any more.

"Then I went back with the men. We searched the river, up and down the hills around Cottonwood, too, clear down to the East Fork. And never found a thing.

"In that wagon there was just one clue—just one thing which made it certain in our minds that they were dead. That was a little spot of dried blood on the floor of the wagon, right behind the seat. About half as big as your hand. Seemed like, if they'd been shot off the wagon, there'd have been more blood. Then, too, the horses were a fairly young team and they might have cut loose and run away if any shooting had started.

"It was always the general opinion that the murderers had disposed of the bodies in the river. But, personally, I always hung to the idea that Titus and Pa were killed in some mysterious way, and their bodies buried. The fact is that the entire community searched for a week, and then gave it up. No other clue was ever discovered, and no further information of any kind was ever unearthed.

"I didn't quit searching for months. Eli Goble helped me, too; he worked like grim death. But we couldn't find a thing."

I asked, "Who was Eli Goble?"

There was a dull scraping of Doc's shoes on the floor. "Seems to me that you cashed a check this noon, boy. Where did you cash it?"

Somewhat perplexed, I told him. "At the bank across the street."

"Well, that's Eli Goble. And where are you living temporarily—until you can find rooms or an apartment to your liking?"

"At the—Oh, of course, Doctor. The Goble Hotel."

He chuckled. "Everything in this town's Goble, boy. He came here in '59 with a man named Goble, but that wasn't Eli's real name. He had heard that his folks came from Ohio, but didn't know anything about it. You see, his family was killed in the Mint Valley massacre, about 1840, and he had been kidnapped by the Indians. Lived with the Sioux until he was sixteen—could talk the language like a native, too. In fact, lots of folks used to think he was part Indian. But he wasn't. And during the search, he thought all the trailing experience he had had when among the Indians, might be of some account. But even that didn't help. We couldn't find a thing."

I said, slowly, "And he's rich, now?"

Doc sighed, and began to hunt around for the light switch. "Suspecting Eli Goble, are you?" He chuckled. "I don't believe anybody ever did, before. He never had a cent to his name for years after that. A few months later he enlisted in the army, served all through the war, and didn't come back here till 1867. In the meantime, through someone he met in the army, he had been trying to get track of his family. And eventually he succeeded. Found the original family, back in Ohio. He got what money was coming to him, brought it out here to Cottonwood, invested it carefully, and made good. He retained the name of Goble, for convenience's sake. Now he's almost ninety, but he's one of the richest men in the state, and one of the tightest. He never lets go of a nickel until the Goddess of Liberty yells for mercy."

The big yellow light hissed into being. It glared down on the white-enameled table, the glistening cabinets and instruments, the old desk and rows of books. Doc Martindale stood there in the middle of the office and nodded his head. "That's the story, boy. Real live mystery, just sixty years old this spring . . . ."

We were just putting on our hats, and Doc was struggling into his old brown slicker, when the telephone rang. Martindale took up the receiver. "Doctor Martindale speaking."

"Oh," he said, after a moment. "Well." And then he winked quickly at me above the telephone. "Did you use any of that stimulant I left last time? . . . Yes. I'm leaving the office, now, to go home, and I'll stop in. Yes."

He replaced the receiver on its hook. "Speak of the devil," he said. "Eli Goble's just had another heart attack. Nothing to get excited about. He has them frequently, but in between times he's up and down and around. We'll stop in to see him for a minute."

The Goble house was only a few minutes' drive from the main business streets. . . . Lights glowed from most of the windows, as we came up the sidewalk. "You can tell that Eli's flat on his back," said Doc. "If he was around, he wouldn't let them burn all that electricity."

The old man watched us from his pillow, with black-rimmed eyes, deeply sunk beneath the moldy fuzz of his eyebrows. . . . He was breathing heavily.

"Well, Eli. How do you feel? This is Dr. Patterson, Eli."

The old man seemed to glare broodingly at me.

"Don't feel—so—good," Goble managed with difficulty. "Plagued heart seems—like—played out on me."

Martindale began to open his bag. "Oh, nothing to worry about, Eli. We'll fix it up all right." He made a perfunctory* examination. "You'll feel better tomorrow, Eli. Sleep tight."

perfunctory: conducted routinely, with little interest or care

The old man mumbled and coughed; and we went down the shadowy stairway, through the gloomy, over-ornate hall, and out to the front door.

It was four o'clock the next afternoon when Doc Martindale and I arrived at the office, following a round of calls on widely separated cases. Beyond a few hasty reports to the girl whom Doc Martindale kept in his office during the mid-day hours, we had enjoyed no contact with the town of Cottonwood since 10 a.m.

When we returned in Doc's old touring car, it was to find the *Cottonwood Herald* spread on the table with plenty of black ink decorating the front page.

ELI GOBLE GIVES PARK TO CITY

Local Businessman and Pioneer Settler Decides on Memorial

Plans changed for Tomorrow's Dedication

At a special meeting of the city council this afternoon, it was unanimously agreed to accept the gift tendered by Eli Goble, revered Civil War veteran and early settler in Cottonwood, who today offered to give the town of Cottonwood some thirty acres of beautiful woodland, to be known as "Goble Memorial Park."

It is understood that Mr. Goble has been ill, and that is the reason for the delay in his plans.

"The grand old man of Crockett County" stipulated in the terms of his gift that the proposed Memorial Grove trees should be set out somewhere in the new park area. This necessitated a hasty change in plans. Instead of being planted on the north hill, on the Louis Wilson farm above the Coon River, the trees will be set out on the brow of the east hill, which is included in the thirty acres donated by Mr. Goble.

A big parade, forming in the city hall square, and proceeding across the east bridge toward the new park, will officially open Arbor Day ceremonies at two o'clock tomorrow afternoon. Following an invocation by Rev. J. Medley Williams, the Cottonwood city band will—

We leaned there, side by side with our hands upon the desk, and read that newspaper story.

Doc tapped the paper with his forefinger. "I'll go on record as saying," he declared, "that this is the first thing Eli Goble ever gave away in his life—at least the first thing in which there wasn't some chance of his getting value received out of it. And I don't see what he can get out of this, except glory. . . . Eli doesn't care a rap for glory. Listen to Editor Nollins calling him, 'the grand old man of Crockett County.' That's because Eli holds a mortgage on the *Herald* building."

Two patients drifted in for examination. When I left, an hour later, I looked back to see Doctor Martindale sitting there in his swivel chair, a tired hulk, still reading the *Cottonwood Herald*.

At five-thirty in the morning, Old Doc was beating on my door. I arose, startled, and feeling nothing short of peritonitis* or breech delivery could have made him summon me so insistently.

peritonitis: inflammation of the membrane lining the wall of the abdominal cavity

He came into the hotel room and waited while I threw on my clothes. "What is it?" I asked, between splashes of cold water.

"We're going out and do a little digging," he said.

I nodded. "Appendectomy? Or what?"

"Nothing so unimportant," Doc replied. And his eyes looked as if he had been awake all night—red-rimmed and circled. . . . "Real digging. No one will know where we are. If Mrs. Gustafson takes a notion to sink and die while we're away, she'll have to sink and die." He said it with seeming brutality. I was still too sleepy to press him for more details, or wonder what it was all about.

But when we got out to the curbing in front of the hotel, and I glanced into the rear seat of Doc's car, there lay two spades, a scoop-shovel and a pickax.

I turned with an exclamation of astonishment.

"Get in," said Doc. And I did, without any more words. He drove down Main Street, north on Kowa Avenue, and under the Burlington viaduct.* We seemed to be heading north of town. Two minutes later our car was making the Coon River bridge rattle and bang in every loose joint.

viaduct: several arches used to carry a road or railroad across a valley or over another road or railroad

"This is the Louis Wilson farm," said Doc. "Hm. I reckon we can turn here past the Cedar school, and drive down the lane past the timber."

At the furthest corner of the cornfield we climbed out, taking the shovels and ax with us. Doc was breathing hoarsely, but the strange pallor* had left his face. . . . His eyes were bright and intent; there was something almost furious in their gleam.

pallor: severe paleness

He led me through a fringe of oak timberland, skirting two brushy ravines, and coming out on a sloping knoll* where one solitary oak tree stood, stunted and twisted by many winds. The grass beneath our feet was coarse, tangled, flat-bladed. Native prairie sod, without a doubt. . . . Far away, a band of crows was circling over the river, cawing with faint and raucous* cries.

knoll: a small rounded hill

raucous: harsh; disorderly

"This is the north hill," said Doc. "There's the town."

It was a very high hill, this bald mound on which we stood. Beneath us the Coon River swung in a flat band of glistening brown.

The thin, brittle grass of the barren hill was tufted with hundreds of pale, lilac-pastel flowers. The blossoms grew short, fuzzy stems; the petals shaded from white to purple, with a heart of yellow in each flower.

"They're beautiful," I said, "I never saw anything like them before. What are they?"

"Wind-flowers. Easter flowers. Or I guess the more modern name is pasque-flower. Pretty things, aren't they? One of the earliest we have around here. . . . Well, I'm going to get busy."

Doc dropped the shovel he was carrying, and I was just as willing to relinquish the heavy load in my own arms. I went over and sat down against the gnarled oak tree, which was the only tree on all that bald, brownish hill. A million facts and statements and conjectures seemed boiling in my brain; I could make nothing out of them.

Before my eyes, Doc Martindale was behaving in a very strange manner. He was walking slowly in vague, indefinite circles, his eyes staring at the ground in front of him. Occasionally he would move up beyond the brow of the hill and sweep the surrounding area with his eyes. I had the strange notion that Doctor George Martindale, after unloading the sad story of his youth, had taken two days in going deliberately and completely insane.

He thrust a small piece of stick into the ground, moved away, surveyed the spot carefully, and then came back to set up another stick, several feet from the first. He repeated this process two more times. He now had an uneven rectangle, eight or ten feet long, marked at its corners by bits of stick. "We'll try it here," he said.

Without another word, he removed his coat, lifted the pickax, and sent its point into the ground.

I cried, "Wait a minute! Won't people down in the town see us up here?"

"They'll think we're cows or pigs," said Doc.

And, as I have said before, we were alone—out there in the thin sunshine of early morning. We dug silently. Neither of us spoke a word. After Doc had penetrated some two feet in depth, at one side of the rectangle, he moved out toward the middle of the space he had marked. I followed, with my shovel.

We had been digging for about ten minutes, when we began to find things.

"Murdered," said Doc.

We were finding them, picking out discolored relics from the rich earth where they had lain so long. Tibiae, ribs . . . phalanges . . . the rusty remains of an ancient revolver.

Doc straightened up, and spoke to me gently. His face was set and strained; it might have been cast in iron. "There's a sheet and a grain sack or two in the car," he said. "Will you go over and bring them?"

I was glad of the opportunity to get away for a few minutes. When I came back, Doc had most of the bones covered with his coat. The knees of his trousers were dark and earthy; he had been kneeling in the loose mold of the grave, picking out the smaller fragments.

"I want a witness," he said, shortly. "Take a look at this." From beneath the coat he withdrew a human skull and turned it slowly for me to see. There was a complete and noticeable fracture, such as might have been caused by a blow of a sharp ax. "The other is the same way," he added, and replaced the skull tenderly.

Then I spoke for the first time. "Can you identify them?"

"Easily," he said. "There's a pocket-piece, the revolver, and knives and things. . . . The pocket-piece is the best bet. It's engraved with Pa's name. Not corroded at all. I rubbed it up and could read the engraving."

Wisely, he made no attempt to identify or isolate the separate skeletons. The bones made awkward bundles, in the grain sacks. We worked slowly, carrying them and the shovels back to the car. I was too stunned by the grim reality to ask any questions. We went away and left that uneven black hole in the middle of the blooming wind-flowers.

Back in town, we went to Doc Martindale's garage, behind his little house on Omaha Street, and left the bundles there. Then we hurried to the office; fortunately there had been no phone calls at either house or office. It was after seven o'clock, yet I had no desire for breakfast.

Doc sat at his desk and thumbed through a stack of old letters and notebooks. "Clell Howard's living in Long Beach," he muttered. "Got his address somewhere. . . . And Eph Spokesman is with his niece out in Portland. I've got to send telegrams right away." Then, strangely enough, he seemed to discover me standing there. "You go around and look at Mrs. Gustafson and that greenstick fracture* and the little Walker boy; tell them I'm busy on an emergency case. Don't say a word to anybody."

greenstick fracture: a mild bone fracture, often found in the soft bones of children

"I won't," I promised.

He said, "And be sure you don't forget the parade. It forms at 2 p.m., at the city hall square. You'll want to see that." And then he turned back to his rummaging.

I had all of the bedfast patients bandaged and dosed and sprayed and examined before 1:30 p.m. At two o'clock I was standing, with a group of pleasant and gossipy citizens, on the steps of the Cottonwood city hall. The triangular "square" was blooming with the gay sweaters and dresses of hundreds of school children who darted wildly underfoot, seething and yelling in a mad half-holiday.

At twenty minutes after two, the crowd was somewhat impatient. There had been a large turn-out; the Boy Scouts were there, and the members of the American Legion, chafing and shifting in line. There was even a huge truck, splashed with vivid bunting, on which were the grove memorial elms all ready to be set out, their dirt-encrusted roots sticking from beneath the scarlet shimmer of flags, like so many claws.

This crowd was waiting for Eli Goble, albeit waiting impatiently. If a man was so kind as to give away thirty acres of land, one could at least expect him to show up for the dedication.

It was almost two-thirty before a big Cadillac touring car slid around the corner by Phillips' oil station, and the crowds in the vicinity began desultory* hand-clapping. Yes, it was Eli Goble. I could see that bearded, skeleton shape sitting hunched in the rear seat, a Navajo blanket across his knees. His narrow-eyed son, vice-president of the bank, was driving.

desultory: occurring randomly

Some fortunate fate had directed me to take up my station on those steps, above the mass of children. For I had a clear and unobstructed view of Doc Martindale, accompanied by a fat, pink-faced man who seemed very nervous emerging from a dark stairway across the street.

I vaulted over the concrete railing beside me, and shouldered through the knotted humanity. Once or twice I had a quick glance at Doc and the pink-faced man, over the heads of the crowd. They were walking rapidly toward the corner where the Goble car was parked; the pink-faced man was drawing a folded paper from his pocket, and he seemed more nervous than ever.

We reached the corner simultaneously. A benign citizen, who wore a white silk badge, "Chairman," fluttering from his coat, was leaning at the side of the car, conversing with Eli Goble and his son.

"Daniel," said Doc Martindale.

The chairman turned.

"Get up on the city hall steps," Doc directed him, "and announce to the crowd that Mr. Goble's physician refuses to allow him to participate in the exercises. Then get them started with their parade."

Daniel began to stammer and sputter.

"Go 'long with you," ordered Doc, firmly. He opened the door of the back seat, and he and the pink-faced man slid in beside Eli Goble. And then Doc saw me standing there. "Get in the front seat, Dr. Patterson," he called, and before I knew it, I was sitting beside Vincent Goble, who was too excited even to bow.

"I don't understand this," he said importantly. "You're carrying things off with a very high hand, Doctor Martindale. It is my father's wish that—"

Doc's lips were thin and firm beneath his scraggly beard. "You keep your mouth shut, Vincent," he said. Vincent Goble gasped. "Drive around the corner on Queen Street, out of this crowd, and pull up at the curb."

The younger man's face was flaming with rage, but he obeyed the command. The Cadillac purred ahead, past the corner, past the alley, past the crowd. A block away it drew up beside the curb.

Vincent Goble and I swung around to face the trio in the back. Eli Goble sat in the middle, clutching and contracting his hands against the red triangles of his Navajo blanket.

"Go ahead, Ed," said Doctor Martindale.

The little pink-faced man gasped apologetically, and fluttered the folds of the paper in his hand. He began a whispered jumble of phrases: "As sheriff of Crockett County, it is my duty to place you, Eli Goble, under arrest. You are charged with the murder of Titus Martindale, and William Martindale, on or about the twenty-fourth of April, in the year 1861—"

Vincent Goble snarled. The old man still sat there, motionless except for the parchment hands which twisted in his lap. "Ain't true," he managed to whisper. "It—ain't true."

"You cowards!" cried his son. The banker's face was livid. "You'd devil the very life out of an old man with some crazy superstition like that! You'd—"

Doc Martindale said, "Drive up to the sheriff's office, Vincent. We want to talk things over."

281

"I won't! I—"

Ed Maxon, the sheriff, gulped fearfully. "Yes, Mr. Goble. That's right. Have to ask you to bring your father up to my office."

And so, we went. Vincent, muttering beneath his breath, Doc Martindale silent as a tomb, Ed Maxon twisting and rubbing a damp hand around his collar. And Eli Goble sitting there under the blanket, his eyes like black caverns, saying: "I—never done it. You'll see. I never done—that."

"You saw the gold at the house. And made up your mind—"

"No."

"You followed them out there on the east prairie. Or maybe you were lying there, waiting for them."

"I never—done it."

"Say, Doctor Martindale! If my father should have another heart attack and die while you're questioning him—"

"Now, Mr. Goble, you—"

"I'm a physician, Vincent. And Eli's my patient. I'll look out for him if he starts to faint. . . . Eli, you killed them from ambush."

"I never. Never did."

"Then you left the bodies in the wagon, took the team, and drove out to the north hill. It was a long drive—must have taken hours to get out there. But you figured that nobody ever went up there, and it was away from the beaten track, and would be a good place to hide the bodies."

"I—I—George, I'm an old man. I—"

"Martindale! You—"

"Sit down, Vincent, and shut up. I'm not going to fool with anybody today. . . . Let's take your pulse, Eli. . . . Hm. Guess you can stand it. All right. You buried them out on the north hill. Maybe you drove the wagon back and forth over the grave—an Indian trick. Trick you learned from the Sioux. And probably you scattered lots of grass and brush around."

"No. *No.*"

"Titus had his gun strapped on; you left them in the ground, just as they were. You didn't take anything out of the wagon except those buckskin bags. Then you drove over by Little Hell Slough. You left the team there, and skinned out. Took the gold somewhere and hid it probably."

"Ain't so. Lie."

"Then you laid low, and waited to join in the search. You were clever, Eli. You helped me search, too. Oh, how we searched! We even went right across that north hill. But we never saw anything that looked like a grave. . . . You kept it covered up. Eli. You were smart."

"Don't. . . . Don't talk so—I can't—"

"You let my father alone!—"

"Now, Mr. Goble. Please. Control yourself. Please—"

"You concluded that seven thousand dollars was a big fortune. Well, it was. Worth waiting for. So you enlisted in the army, took your chances—I'll give you credit for nerve there, Eli—and turned up after the war with that story about finding your relatives and your family property back in Ohio. Yes, you were smart."

"I never—never done it."

"Why did you give this park to the city?"

"Mmmmm. I—"

"The *Herald* carried that Arbor Day announcement, night before last. And right away you had a heart attack. And the next morning you came out with that gift to the city. *Provided—*"

"Vincent. Vincent. Make 'em let me—"

"I'll—"

"Here, hold him!"

"I've got him. Now, Mr. Goble, you'll have to sit down."

"Don't be a fool, Vincent. This is true—all true. It's taken me sixty years to find out, but I've found out. . . . You gave that park to the city of Cottonwood, Eli Goble, *provided* that they set out the memorial grove over there, on the east hill, instead of the north hill. You didn't want anybody digging on the north hill, did you? It had never occurred to you to buy Louis Wilson's farm, so there wouldn't be a chance of people digging that ground up."

"No. . . . Don't talk so, George! . . . Old. I'm an old an'—"

"Well, it was the first thing you ever gave away, in your life. And it set me to thinking. I thought, 'Why didn't Eli want that memorial grove planted up there?' And then, I began to understand things. I went up there this morning. Doctor Patterson was with me—I have a witness to what I am now about to relate. He saw me dig; he saw me find things. I found *them*, Eli."

Vincent Goble was slumped forward, his head buried in his hands. Eli sat there in the sheriff's big chair, staring across the table. He seemed to be looking squarely through the opposite wall.

"They were murdered, Eli. Their skulls had been broken. A heavy, sharp blow at the back of each skull. I found them."

The old man's lips were gray and rubbery. He whispered, "No, I never done it. Can't prove it was me."

"A hatchet, Eli. Someone had thrown a hatchet—or maybe two hatchets, in quick succession. They were sitting on that wagon board, in the bright moonlight. It would have been easy for anyone who could throw a tomahawk."

Doc fumbled in the breast pocket of his coat, and brought out three folded squares of yellow paper. "I'll read to you all," he said calmly, "three telegrams. The first one I sent myself, early this morning, to Clell Howard, in Long Beach, California, and to Ephraim Spokesman in Portland, Oregon. . . . Remember those names, Eli? . . . Clell was mayor here, once. And Eph Spokesman—everybody knew him. Here's my telegram: 'Please reply by wire completely at my expense. During the old days at Cottonwood, what man was skillful at throwing a knife or hatchet? Search your recollection and reply at once.'

"Here's the first reply I got. It came from Ephraim Spokesman's niece. Came about eleven o'clock. You can read it for yourself, gentlemen. It says, 'Uncle Eph very sick but says man named Goble was only one who could throw a hatchet. Wants to hear full details why you ask.'

"Along about eleven-forty-five, I got a telegram from Clell Howard. Here it is: 'Hello old neighbor regards to you. Am almost ninety but recall perfectly how I lost five dollars betting Eli Goble couldn't stick hatchet ten times in succession in a big tree by Halsey blacksmith shop.' "

The room was perfectly still, except for the hoarse sputtering in Eli Goble's throat. "No," he whispered tremulously. "No."

Doc Martindale pointed to the further corner of the dusty old room. There was a table, which none of us had noticed before, and on that table was a white sheet, rumpled and bulky. . . . "Eli," said Doc, quietly. "They're over there. In the corner."

The aged man stiffened in his chair. His back arched up, the shoulders quaking; his claw hands seemed wrenching a chunk of wood from the table in front of him.

"Father!" his son cried.

Eli Goble shook his head, and dropped back in his chair, his deep-set eyes dull with a flat, blue light. "The dead," he whispered. "They found me. . . . They're in this room. I done it. I killed them. Titus and Bill. Yes. Yes."

Vincent Goble dropped down, his head buried in his arms, and began to sob—big, gulping sobs. The sheriff twisted nervously in his seat.

"George. You—you gonna send me to—prison? You gonna have them—hang me? I'm old . . . I done it. Yes."

Doc Martindale cleared his throat. "Yes, you are old, Eli. Lot older than I am. It's too late, now, to do anything about it. I told my mother I'd get the man, and—But I can't see what good it would do, now, to send you to jail or even try you for murder."

Sheriff Maxon wiped his forehead. "The law," he said shrilly, "the law must take its course! Eli Goble, you must—"

"No," said Old Doc derisively. "I'm running this show, Ed. Without me, without my testimony and the case I've built up, there isn't any show against Eli. I won't prosecute him, or furnish evidence."

Maxon shook his head and bit his lips.

"How much is your father worth?" asked Doc of Vincent Goble.

The banker lifted his face, on which the weary, baffled tears were still wet. "Couple of million, I guess."

"All yours," whispered Eli. "All yours. . . ."

"Maybe," Doc nodded. "Seven thousand dollars. Quite a nest egg in those days. Like fifty thousand, now. Or even more. . . . No, gentlemen. Money won't do me any good. It can't bring back Titus and my father. But it can still do good. Yes."

Eli Goble's eyes had closed, like dark windows on which ragged curtains had been drawn. "I've seen 'em—I've seen 'em. Always. Since I got old—they come back. . . . I had to give in. Yes."

"You'll go home," said Doc. "I'll give you something to put you to sleep. Then, after you have a little rest and get your strength back, you'll have a lawyer up at your house. . . . You will give, to this county in which you live, one million dollars for the purpose of founding and endowing a modern hospital, where every inhabitant can secure the best medical and surgical attention, free of charge. How does that sound?"

Head still buried in his arms, Vincent Goble nodded. His father had opened his eyes and was shivering, still staring through the blank wall ahead of him. "Yes. Anything. . . . I give—anything. But take me away. I want to go—home. . . . I'm old. I don't want to stay in—this room. I don't want to stay with—*them*."

After Eli Goble was in bed, and asleep, Doc and I came out into the damp warmth of the spring afternoon. Martindale looked ten years older than he did the day before. "After this," he said, "after everything is taken care of, I'll let things go. . . . You look after the practice beginning next Monday

Our feet sounded flat and talkative, echoing on the long sidewalk. "One thing," I said. "I can't understand how you found the place. I can see how you reasoned out the rest—about the grove and about Eli Goble's not wanting the trees planted up there. But how did you know where to dig? We could have been up there for days, turning the soil."

"Wind-flowers," he said quietly. "They were scattered all over that hill. Beautiful, like you said. . . . But I knew enough to dig where there were no wind-flowers. The grass on that hill looked pretty much alike, all over, but there weren't any flowers growing in that place I marked off. Those little purple flowers are funny. They grow on native soil. You can't get them to grow where the sod has ever been turned."

About the Story

1. How is Eli Goble's gift to the community ironic? What kind of irony does it exemplify?
2. At what point in the story do you begin to suspect Eli Goble?
3. Are you satisfied with the resolution of the story? Why or why not?
4. In the story Bill and Titus Martindale had been killed sixty years before Doc Martindale uncovered the truth and confronted the murderer. Identify a biblical principle that this story illustrates.

About the Author

The memories MacKinlay Kantor (1904–77) had of his boyhood in Webster, Iowa, furnished him with rich material for his writing. The sturdy values of small-town life infused his writing with a sense of idealism and a touch of nostalgia for better, simpler days. Some critics have been quick to classify Kantor's writing as sentimental and didactic. Regardless of this criticism, he still holds an important place in the development of the modern historical novel in America.

When Kantor was seventeen, his mother recruited his help in writing and editing the Webster newspaper. This internship kindled Kantor's writing ambitions and gave him needed experience. But success came slowly. For many years, the struggling writer held down numerous odd jobs to support his family while he wrote and researched. The freshness and immediacy in Kantor's narrative style, however, gave his fiction the universal appeal that eventually resulted in his success.

Although Kantor is not a Christian writer, his best characters are often sincere, decent citizens with traditional hopes and dreams. His most convincing characters learn the meaning of responsibility and sacrifice.

Scylla Toothless

ANONYMOUS

Epigrams have often been used for ironic mockery. What feature of Scylla is the real subject of the following one?

Scylla is toothless; yet when she was young,
She had both tooth enough, and too much tongue:
What should I now of Toothless Scylla say?
But that her tongue hath worn her teeth away.

About the Poem

1. What feature of Scylla is the real subject of the epigram?
2. Identify the particular kind of irony illustrated.
3. Does the use of humorous irony make you personally more receptive to the poem's implied caution?

Letter from a West Texas Constituent

J. B. Lee Jr.

Verbal irony, like symbolism, can extend throughout a work; in such cases, the work must be read entirely on an implied level. It would be difficult to pick out sentence examples of irony in the following letter. The entire letter is in the ironic mode. J. B. Lee Jr., "Potential Hog Raiser," is satirizing the federal government's farm subsidy program.

March 20, 1963

The Honorable Ed Foreman
House of Representatives
Congressional District # 16
Washington 25, D.C.

Dear Sir:

My friend over in Terebone Parish received a $1,000 check from the government this year for not raising hogs. So I am going into the not-raising hogs business next year.

What I want to know is, in your opinion, what is the best kind of farm not to raise hogs on and the best kind of hogs not to raise? I would prefer not to raise Razorbacks, but if that is not a good breed not to raise, I will just as gladly not raise any Berkshires or Durocs.

The hardest work in this business is going to be in keeping an inventory of how many hogs I haven't raised.

My friend is very joyful about the future of his business. He has been raising hogs for more than 20 years and the best he ever made was $400, until this year, when he got $1,000 for not raising hogs.

If I can get $1,000 for not raising 50 hogs, then will I get $2,000 for not raising 100 hogs? I plan to operate on a small scale at first, holding myself down to 4,000 hogs which means I will have $80,000 coming from the government.

Now, another thing: these hogs I will not raise will not eat 100,000 bushels of corn. So will you pay me anything for not raising 100,000 bushels of corn not to feed the hogs I am not raising?

I want to get started as soon as possible as this seems to be a good time of year for not raising hogs.

One thing more, can I raise 10 or 12 hogs on the side while I am in the not-raising-hog-business just enough to get a few sides of bacon to eat?

Very truly yours,
J.B. Lee, Jr.
Potential Hog Raiser

About the Letter

1. According to J. B. Lee Jr., how does the federal government's farm subsidy program work?
2. What are some clues that help you recognize that the entire letter is written in the ironic mode? Identify the kind of irony illustrated in the letter.
3. What is the point Mr. Lee is trying to make to "The Honorable Ed Foreman"?
4. Predict the letter's effect. If you were Ed Foreman, how would you reply to this letter from your constituent?

THINKING ZONE

Previously you looked at verbal irony, the contrast between the literal interpretation of a statement and its implied meaning, and at sarcasm, one type of verbal irony. Other types of verbal irony include hyperbole, understatement, and litotes, a special kind of understatement.

Hyperbole, or intentional exaggeration, is used for emphasis or effect. The student who announces "I'm starving" the hour before lunch may or may not know the term, but he is, nonetheless, using hyperbole. So is the student who laments that his book bag weighs a ton. Though we know he's not being truthful literally, he won't be accused of lying, and his obvious exaggeration may even garner some sympathy.

Authors also use hyperbole for effect. Hyperbole may be used to emphasize the importance of an incident. Referring to the minutemen's repulsion of the redcoats on April 19, 1775, Emerson in "The Concord Hymn" wrote the now famous exaggeration "shot heard round the world." Shakespeare used hyperbole to communicate the intense emotion and guilt felt by a murderer in *Macbeth*: "Will all great Neptune's ocean wash this blood / Clean from my hand? No, this my hand will rather / The multitudinous seas incarnadine, / Making the green one red." Most often hyperbole is used for humor. Mark Twain spoke hyperbolically in *A Connecticut Yankee in King Arthur's Court* when he wrote, "There did not seem to be brains enough in the entire nursery, so to speak, to bait a fishhook with."

Understatement, the opposite of hyperbole, is restraint or lack of emphasis for rhetorical effect. It is holding back and expressing less than what is true. Robert Frost employed the technique in "Birches" when he said, "One could do worse than be a swinger of birches." Indeed, one could do worse, for Frost has just described the pleasantness of momentary escape, briefly swinging high above life's cares before returning to start over. Jesus understated His meaning when He said of His disciples, "Ye are of more value than many sparrows" (Matt. 10:31). Because man is made in God's image (Gen. 1:26–28), and God has infinite worth, we know that humans are worth a great deal.

Litotes is a common form of understatement, one in which a statement asserts something by denying its contrary. "Mary is not as young as she used to be" really means that she's old. In the play *Cyrano de Bergerac*, Rostand's hero, Cyrano, and the beautiful Roxane reminisce concerning childhood, when they played together. Roxane asks, "Was I fair then?" to which Cyrano responds, "You were not ill to see!" Though not a straightforward answer, Cyrano's, nonetheless, affirms Roxane's childhood beauty. A biblical illustration of litotes is found in Paul's preaching at Ephesus where he created "no small stir" in the city (Acts 19:23). The implication is that Paul's preaching created an uproar. Certainly these specific types of verbal irony are valuable tools when put to good use by a skilled communicator.

1. Identify the specific kind of verbal irony illustrated in the following lines referring to Eli Goble in "The Grave Grass Quivers": "He never lets go of a nickel until the Goddess of Liberty yells for mercy." What does this quotation tell the reader about Goble's character?
2. In "Jade Flower Palace," Tu Fu says, "Ten thousand organ / Pipes whistle and roar." Identify the specific kind of verbal irony illustrated.
3. The following quotation is taken from "The Return of the Rangers" by Kenneth Roberts. Identify the specific kind of verbal irony illustrated.

   > Somewhere I have heard that after the first three days of fasting a man has no further desire for food, and that after thirty days he feels no discomfort whatever: that his brain is clear, his body pure, and his endurance almost unlimited. I suspect that statement in toto. I don't believe in the benefits of fasting, and ever since I tried it in the company of Major Robert Rogers on the St. Francis Expedition, I have been strongly opposed to it.

4. What line in Langston Hughes's "Mother to Son" uses **litotes?**

A Considerable Speck (Microscopic)

Robert Frost

The exaggerated seriousness with which the poet treats this trivial incident gives the poem its humorously ironic tone. Notice how Frost widens his topic in the final two lines.

A speck that would have been beneath my sight
On any but a paper sheet so white
Set off across what I had written there.
And I had idly poised my pen in air
To stop it with a period of ink
When something strange about it made me think.
This was no dust speck by my breathing blown,
But unmistakably a living mite
With inclinations it could call its own.
It paused as with suspicion of my pen,
And then came racing wildly on again
To where my manuscript was not yet dry;
Then paused again and either drank or smelt—
With loathing, for again it turned to fly.
Plainly with an intelligence I dealt.
It seemed too tiny to have room for feet,
Yet must have had a set of them complete
To express how much it didn't want to die.
It ran with terror and with cunning crept.
It faltered: I could see it hesitate;
Then in the middle of the open sheet
Cower down in desperation to accept
Whatever I accorded it of fate.
I have none of the tenderer-than-thou
Collectivistic regimenting love*
With which the modern world is being swept.
But this poor microscopic item now!
Since it was nothing I knew evil of
I let it lie there till I hope it slept.
I have a mind myself and recognize
Mind when I meet with it in any guise.
No one can know how glad I am to find
On any sheet the least display of mind.

Collectivistic regimenting love: socialistic liberal sentimentality

About the Poem

1. Specifically what kind of irony does Frost's poem illustrate? Explain the irony.
2. The target of the irony in Robert Frost's poem is not the "speck." What is it?
3. Compare "A Considerable Speck (Microscopic)" with "A Bird Came Down the Walk" (p. 6). In what way are the poems similar?
4. Frost mocked "collectivistic regimenting love," a love that arises not from one's heart but from one's political idea that the "little guy" should get preferential treatment. All the same, the author let the "little guy" live because, he said, he saw intelligence in him. Defend that decision from the standpoint of a Christian worldview.

About the Author

In his later years, Robert Frost (1874–1963) acquired the reputation of being not only New England's "poetic bard" but also America's official poet laureate. He was awarded four Pulitzer Prizes for poetry in his lifetime. His poetry avoids the moral coarseness of Walt Whitman and displays more traditional form than his contemporaries Carl Sandburg and E.E. Cummings.

Although his poetry was highly successful, his personal life was characterized by uncertainty and insecurity. Despite the aura of good-natured optimism he displayed in his public life, some of Frost's poems reveal a bleak and at times harsh side to the kindly pastoral poet.

Frost did not set forth his beliefs systematically, but we can discover much of his philosophy by examining his poems. In his writing, he frequently encouraged the use of human instinct as a moral guide. But he scoffed at the idea of an orderly worldview, so he had no good reason to trust the morality of human instincts.

Frost did tell us, however, his purpose for writing. In his *Collected Poems* he states that a poem "ends in a clarification of life— . . . a momentary stay against confusion." But as Frost readily admitted, writing is at best a "momentary stay" against the feelings of helplessness and chaos that are an outgrowth of the humanistic worldview.

The Day the Dam Broke

James Thurber

James Thurber published hundreds of humorous stories and essays drawing on his own experience. Many are critical of society, though usually in a playful way. Some are sheer fun. What kind of irony is present throughout the whole essay and creates its humorous tone?

The fact that we were all as safe as kittens under a cookstove did not assuage* in the least the fine despair and the grotesque desperation which seized upon the residents of the East Side when the cry spread like a grass fire that the dam had given way. Some of the most dignified, staid, cynical, and clear-thinking men in town abandoned their wives, stenographers*, homes, and offices and ran east. There are few alarms in the world more terrifying than "The dam has broken!" There are few persons capable of stopping to reason when that clarion cry strikes upon their ears, even persons who live in towns no nearer than five hundred miles to a dam.

assuage: diminish

stenographers: a person who takes dictation

The Columbus, Ohio, broken-dam rumor began, as I recall it, about noon of March 12, 1913. High Street, the main canyon of trade, was loud with the placid hum of business and the buzzing of placid businessmen arguing, computing, wheedling, offering, refusing, compromising. Darius Conningway, one of the foremost corporation lawyers in the Middle West, was telling the Public Utilities Commission in the language of Julius Caesar that they might as well try to move the Northern star as to move him. Other men were making their little boasts and their little gestures. Suddenly somebody began to run. It may be that he had simply remembered, all of a moment, an engagement to meet his wife, for which he was now frightfully late. Whatever it was, he ran east on Broad Street (probably toward the Maramor Restaurant, a favorite place for a man to meet his wife). Somebody else began to run, perhaps a newsboy in high spirits. Another man, a portly gentleman of affairs, broke into a trot. Inside of ten minutes, everybody on High Street, from the Union Depot to the Courthouse, was running. A loud mumble gradually crystallized into the dread word "dam." "The dam has broke!" The fear was put into words by a little old lady in an electric,* or by a traffic cop, or by a small boy: nobody knows who, nor does it now really matter. Two thousand people were abruptly in full flight. "Go east!" was the cry that arose—east away from the river, east to safety. "Go east! Go east! Go east!"

electric: electric automobile

Black streams of people flowed eastward down all the streets leading in that direction; these streams, whose headwaters were in the drygoods stores, office buildings, harness shops, movie theaters, were fed by trickles of housewives, children, servants, dogs, and cats, slipping out of the houses past which the main streams flowed, shouting and screaming. People ran out leaving fires burning and food cooking and doors wide open. I remember, however, that my mother turned out all the fires and that she took with her a dozen eggs and two loaves of bread. It was her plan to make Memorial Hall, just two blocks away, and take refuge somewhere in the top of it, in one of the dusty rooms where war veterans met and where old battle flags and stage scenery were stored. But the seething throngs shouting, "Go east!" drew her along and the rest of us with her. When grandfather regained full consciousness, at Parsons Avenue, he turned upon the retreating mob like a vengeful prophet and exhorted the men to form ranks and stand off the Rebel dogs, but at length he, too, got the idea that the dam had broken and, roaring "Go east!" in his powerful voice, he caught up in one arm a small child and in the other a slight clerkish man of perhaps forty-two and we slowly began to gain on those ahead of us.

A scattering of firemen, policemen, and army officers in dress uniforms—there had been a review* at Fort Hayes, in the northern part of town—added color to the surging billows of people. "Go east!" cried a little child in a piping voice, as she ran past a porch on which drowsed a lieutenant-colonel of infantry. Used to quick decisions, trained to immediate obedience, the officer bounded off the porch and, running at full tilt, soon passed the child, bawling, "Go east!" The two of them emptied rapidly the houses of the little street they were on. "What is it? What is it?" demanded a fat, waddling man who intercepted the colonel. The officer dropped behind and asked the little child what it was. "The dam has broke!" gasped the girl. "The dam has broke!" roared the colonel. "Go east! Go east!" He was soon leading, with the exhausted child in his arms, a fleeing company of three hundred persons who had gathered around him from livingrooms, shops, garages, backyards, and basements.

review: ceremonial presentation of troops

Nobody has ever been able to compute with any exactness how many people took part in the great rout of 1913, for the panic, which extended from the Winslow Bottling Works in the south end to Clintonville, six miles north, ended as abruptly as it began and the bobtail and ragtag and velvet-gowned groups of refugees melted away and slunk home, leaving the streets peaceful and deserted. The shouting, weeping, tangled evacuation of the city lasted not more than two hours in all. Some few people got as far as Reynoldsburg, twelve miles away; fifty or more reached the Country Club, eight miles away; most others gave up, exhausted, or climbed trees in Franklin Park, four miles out. Order was restored and fear dispelled finally by means of militiamen riding about in motor lorries bawling through megaphones: "The dam has *not* broken!" At first this tended only to add to the confusion and increase the panic, for many stampedes thought the soldiers were bellowing "The dam has now broken!" thus setting an official seal of authentication on the calamity.

All the time, the sun shone quietly and there was nowhere any sign of oncoming waters. A visitor in an airplane, looking down on the straggling, agitated masses of people below, would have been hard put to it to divine a reason for the phenomenon. It must have inspired, in such an observer, a peculiar kind of terror, like the sight of the *Marie Celeste*, abandoned at sea, its galley fires peacefully burning, its tranquil decks bright in the sunlight.

An aunt of mine, Aunt Edith Taylor, was in a movie theater on High Street when, over and above the sound of the piano in the pit (a W. S. Hart picture was being shown), there rose the steadily increasing tromp of running feet. Persistent shouts rose above the tromping. An elderly man, sitting near my aunt, mumbled something, got out of his seat, and went up the aisle at a dogtrot. This started everybody.

In an instant the audience was jamming the aisle. "Fire!" shouted a woman who always expected to be burned up in a theater, but now the shouts outside were louder and coherent. "The dam has broke!" cried somebody. "Go east!" screamed a small woman in front of my aunt. And east they went, pushing and shoving and clawing, knocking women and children down, emerging finally into the street, torn and sprawling. Inside the theater, Bill Hart was calmly calling some desperado's bluff and the brave girl at the piano played "Row! Row! Row!" loudly. Outside, men were streaming across the Statehouse yard, others were climbing trees, a

woman managed to get onto the "These Are My Jewels" statue, whose bronze figures of Sherman, Stanton, Grant, and Sheridan watched with cold unconcern the going to pieces of the capital city.

"I ran south to State Street, east on State to Third, south on Third to Town, and out east on Town," my Aunt Edith has written me. "A tall spare woman with grim eyes and a determined chin ran past me down the middle of the street. I was still uncertain as to what was the matter, in spite of all the shouting. I drew up alongside the woman with some effort, for although she was in her late fifties, she had a beautiful easy running form and seemed to be in excellent condition. 'What is it?' I puffed. She gave me a quick glance and then looked ahead again, stepping up her pace a trifle. 'Don't ask me, ask God!' she said.

"When I reached Grant Avenue, I was so spent that Dr. H. R. Mallory—you remember Dr. Mallory, the man with the white beard who looks like Robert Browning?—well, Dr. Mallory, whom I had drawn away from at the corner of Fifth and Town, passed me. 'It's got us!' he shouted, and I felt sure that whatever it was *did* have us, for you know what conviction Dr. Mallory's statements have always carried. I didn't know at the time what he meant, but I found out later. There was a boy behind him on roller-skates, and Dr. Mallory mistook the swishing of the skates for the sound of rushing water. He eventually reached the Columbus School for Girls, at the corner of Parsons Avenue and Town Street, where he collapsed, expecting the cold frothing waters of the Scioto to sweep him into oblivion. The boy on skates swirled past him and Dr. Mallory realized for the first time what he had been running from. Looking up the street, he could see no signs of water, but nevertheless, after resting a few minutes, he jogged on east again. He caught up with me at the Ohio Avenue, where we rested together. I should say that about seven hundred people passed us. A funny thing was that all of them were on foot. Nobody seemed to have had the courage to stop and start his car; but as I remember it, all cars had to be cranked in those days, which is probably the reason."

The next day, the city went about its business as if nothing had happened, but there was no joking. It was two years or more before you dared treat the breaking of the dam lightly. And even now, twenty years after, there are a few persons, like Dr. Mallory, who will shut up like a clam if you mention the Afternoon of the Great Run.

About the Essay

1. What is the tone of the essay?
2. List several incidents from the essay that could be labeled ironic.
3. Into which category do you think this essay should be placed: (1) among those written as "critical of society" or (2) among those written for sheer fun. Why?
4. What specific kind of irony is signaled by the first sentence and exists throughout "The Day the Dam Broke"? How does it add to the essay's overall effect?
5. Identify a point of contrast between the speaker in "A Considerable Speck (Microscopic)" and Dr. Mallory in "The Day the Dam Broke." Respond to this difference.

About the Author

The family of James Thurber (1894–1961) may have provided some of the material for which he became so well known. His father was a would-be actor and lawyer who worked intermittently as a politician and clerk. His mother was a practical joker with a fine sense of comedy. One of Thurber's two brothers accidentally injured young James's eye while playing a game of William Tell. The injury may have been what forced Thurber to turn his attention from sports to imaginative writing.

Thurber worked for over twenty-five years for *The New Yorker* magazine with friend and fellow contributor E. B. White. Thurber's stories and drawings were favorites for the readers. Thurber wrote in several genres including poetry, essay, children's books, drama, and screenplays. Today an annual Thurber prize is given to exceptional writers of American humor.

Thurber's balance between comic pleasure and serious intent established him as one of the most popular writers of the twentieth century. He often used his writing to expose life's absurdities and voice his displeasure in societal trends that stifled creativity and individuality. He especially despised the materialism fostered by the modern technological age. Thurber exposed the follies of mankind by using humor and imagination, two strong defenses against pride and the misuse of reason.

Earth

John Hall Wheelock

Though short, Wheelock's poem is highly effective, primarily because of the poet's use of irony. How does the contrast between the astronomer's message and his mood amplify the poem's irony and its theme?

"A planet doesn't explode of itself," said drily
The Martian astronomer, gazing off into the air—
"That they were able to do it is proof that highly
Intelligent beings must have been living there."

About the Author

John Hall Wheelock (1886–1978), American poet and editor, first experimented with poetry in grade school, transforming his Latin lessons into verse. His boyhood interest in poetry never left him, and he continued his literary activities until his death at age ninety-two. His poetry, pleasing in its rhythms, has a simple, lyric quality.

In his poem "Earth" Wheelock typifies the concern of many unregenerate but thoughtful men. Unfortunately, his other writings prove that his solutions to the problems facing a technological age came from a faulty worldview. Wheelock embraced the teachings of the Dutch philosopher Spinoza, a pantheist, who taught that man's reason could lead him not only to virtue but to ultimate perfection. Wheelock believed that the human understanding and cooperation embodied in a unified world system could protect us against the "irrational" tendencies of man. History, of course, has repeatedly proved such beliefs to be dangerously misguided.

At the Aquarium

Max Eastman

As in "Earth," the irony of Eastman's sonnet is aided by an air of calm observation. This attitude allows the poet and his readers to view humanity with more detachment than usual. The poem may be less caustic than Wheelock's, but it nonetheless makes a serious argument.

Serene the silver fishes glide,
Stern-lipped, and pale, and wonder-eyed;
As, through the agèd deeps of ocean,
They glide with wan and wavy motion.
They have no pathway where they go,
They flow like water to and fro.
They watch with never-winking eyes,
They watch with staring, cold surprise,
The level people in the air,
The people peering, peering there:
Who wander also to and fro,
And know not why or where they go,
Yet have a wonder in their eyes,
Sometimes a pale and cold surprise.

About the Poems

1. Can you state the message of Wheelock's poem directly in prose?
2. One advantage of irony over direct statement is that a reader can distance himself from what is being said. How is this advantage evident in "Earth"?
3. How does Eastman's poem cause the reader to look closely at himself?
4. What is ironic about Eastman's picture of the fish as the watchers at the aquarium?

About the Author

Max Eastman (1883–1969), American author and editor, spent his life trying to reconcile contradictory ideas. His first conflict was with organized religion. Eastman's mother, an ordained minister and outspoken feminist, left her son a heritage of inconsistency: she made him memorize Scripture but denied from the pulpit basic doctrines, such as the Trinity and the virgin birth. Eventually, Eastman completely rejected his family's "religion," proudly proclaiming himself a pagan.

At Columbia University, under the influence of the humanist educator John Dewey, Eastman denied the existence of absolute truth, asserting that man's reasoning powers should be used merely to better life here and now. He promoted socialism and communism, believing they emphasized human equality and individuality. However, his experiences, particularly with Stalinist communism (to which he lost friends), disillusioned him. Later in life, Eastman bitterly attacked most of the radical ideas he had promoted as a youth.

Eastman produced a great many works, most philosophical and political in nature, although only a few attain literary quality. He remained a life-long atheist, and both his life and his writings reveal man's failure to grapple successfully with a fallen world's problems apart from God. The irony of "At the Aquarium" echoes Eastman's view of life in the twentieth century.

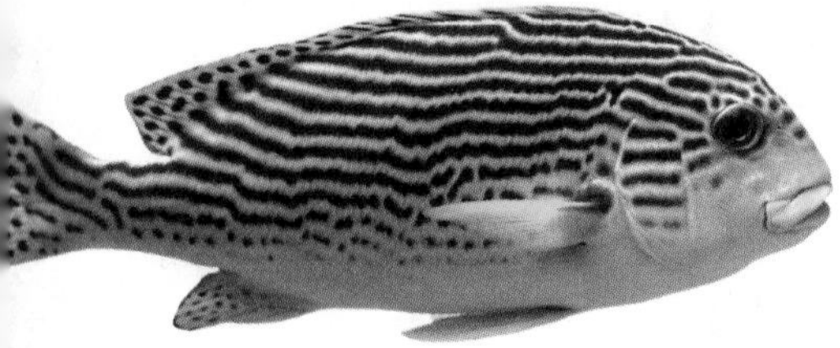

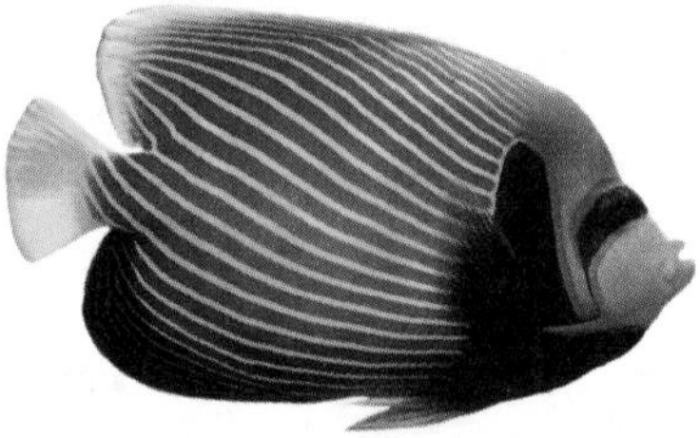

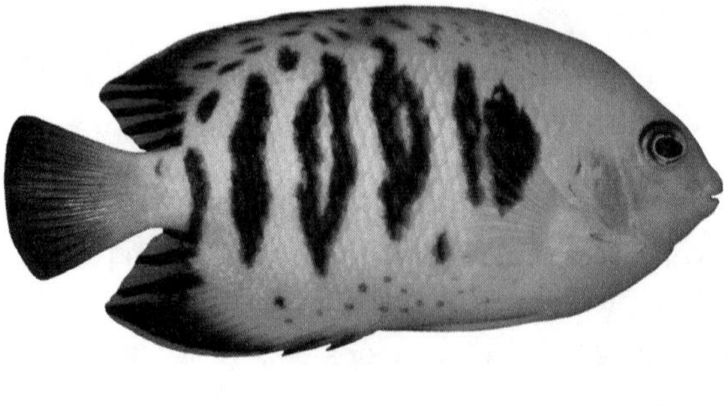

From *The Screwtape Letters*

C. S. Lewis

C. S. Lewis's *The Screwtape Letters* is an epistolary novel (one composed of fictional letters). The book explores humans' universal bent to stray from God, Satan's exploitation of that frailty, and God's intent to call man to Himself—all through the eyes of the most unexpected of narrators.

In the novel, Screwtape, a demon long in the service of Satan, is writing letters to his nephew Wormwood, a novice tempter. He advises Wormwood on the business of guiding "the patient," (a human soul) away from the fold of "the Enemy" (God) and into that of "Our Father Below" (Satan). Lewis intends the book to both delight and instruct, fortifying Christians against "the wiles of the devil."

Of course, the book must be interpreted while remembering who Lewis's narrator is (a fallen angel). Screwtape often presents human behavior as it really is—petty, irrational, self-interested, hypocritical. By relating human foibles through a demon whose business it is to take advantage of them, Lewis emphasizes the danger of these sins. In this way Lewis often agrees with his narrator.

On the other hand, Lewis rarely agrees with Screwtape's perspective on God. The demon continually questions God's motives for saving humans, believing God must have a hidden agenda. However, Lewis makes it clear that Screwtape's core difficulty is that he does not understand love. As a result, the demon's descriptions of sinful human nature and fulminations against "The Enemy" serve only to highlight the loving and generous nature of God.

The story begins *in medias res*, that is, in the middle of the action. As you read, remember that C. S. Lewis is writing to lay bare and counter ideas that are used to falsely undercut Christians' faith in and personal walk with Jesus Christ. What ideas is Lewis trying to refute? Have you encountered any of these in the world today? If so, how might Lewis's refutation of them apply to your experience?

Chapter I

My Dear Wormwood,

I note what you say about guiding our patient's reading and taking care that he sees a good deal of his materialist friend. But are you not being a trifle *naif*?* It sounds as if you supposed that *argument* was the way to keep him out of the Enemy's clutches. That might have been so if he had lived a few centuries earlier. At that time the humans still knew pretty well when a thing was proved and when it was not; and if it was proved they really believed it. They still connected thinking with doing and were prepared to alter their way of life as the result of a chain of reasoning. But what with the weekly press and other such weapons we have largely altered that. Your man has been accustomed, ever since he was a boy, to have a dozen incompatible philosophies dancing about together inside his head. He doesn't think of doctrines as primarily "true" or "false", but as "academic" or "practical", "outworn" or "contemporary", "conventional" or "ruthless". Jargon, not argument, is your best ally in keeping him from the Church. Don't waste time trying to make him think that materialism is *true*! Make him think it is strong, or stark, or courageous—that it is the philosophy of the future. That's the sort of thing he cares about.

naïf: naïve

The trouble about argument is that it moves the whole struggle onto the Enemy's own ground. He can argue too; whereas in really practical propaganda of the kind I am suggesting He has been shown for centuries to be greatly the inferior of Our Father Below. By the very act of arguing, you awake the patient's reason; and once it is awake, who can foresee the result? Even if a particular train of thought can be twisted so as to end in our favour, you will find that you have been strengthening in your patient the fatal habit of attending to universal issues and withdrawing his attention from the stream of immediate sense experiences. Your business is to fix his attention on the stream. Teach him to call it "real life" and don't let him ask what he means by "real".

Remember, he is not, like you, a pure spirit. Never having been a human (Oh that abominable advantage of the Enemy's!) you don't realise how enslaved they are to the pressure of the ordinary. I once had a patient, a sound atheist, who used to read in the British Museum. One day, as he sat reading, I saw a train of thought in his mind beginning to go the wrong way. The Enemy, of course, was at his elbow in a moment. Before I knew where I was I saw my twenty years' work beginning to totter. If I had lost my head and begun to attempt a defence by argument I should have been undone. But I was not such a fool. I struck instantly at the part of the man which I had best under my control and suggested that it was just about time he had some lunch. The Enemy presumably made the counter-suggestion (you know how one can never *quite* overhear What He says to them?) that this was more important than lunch. At least I think that must have been His line for when I said "Quite. In fact much too important to tackle at the end of a morning", the patient brightened up considerably; and by the time I had added "Much better come back after lunch and go into it with a fresh mind", he was already half way to the door. Once he was in the street the battle was won. I showed him a newsboy shouting the midday paper, and a No. 73 bus going past, and before he reached the bottom of the steps I had got into him an unalterable conviction that, whatever odd ideas might come into a man's head when he was shut up alone with his books, a healthy dose of "real life" (by which he meant the bus and the newsboy) was enough to show him that all "that sort of thing" just couldn't be true. He knew he'd had a narrow escape and in later years was fond of talking about "that inarticulate sense for actuality which is our ultimate safeguard against the aberrations* of mere logic". He is now safe in Our Father's house.

aberrations: deviations from normal

You begin to see the point? Thanks to processes which we set at work in them centuries ago, they find it all but impossible to believe in the unfamiliar while the familiar is before their eyes. Keep pressing home on him the *ordinariness* of things. Above all, do not attempt to use science (I mean, the real sciences) as a defence against Christianity. They will positively encourage him to think about realities he can't touch and see. There have been sad cases among the modern physicists. If he must dabble in science, keep him on economics and sociology; don't let him get away from that invaluable "real life". But the best of all is to let him read no science but to give him a grand general idea that he knows it all and that everything he happens to have picked up in casual talk and reading is "the results of modern investigation". Do remember you are there to fuddle* him. From the way some of you young fiends talk, anyone would suppose it was our job to *teach*!

Your affectionate uncle
Screwtape

fuddle: confuse

Chapter II

My Dear Wormwood,

I note with grave displeasure that your patient has become a Christian. Do not indulge the hope that you will escape the usual penalties; indeed, in your better moments, I trust you would hardly even wish to do so. In the meantime we must make the best of the situation. There is no need to despair; hundreds of these adult converts have been reclaimed after a brief sojourn in the Enemy's camp and are now with us. All the *habits* of the patient, both mental and bodily, are still in our favour.

One of our great allies at present is the Church itself. Do not misunderstand me. I do not mean the Church as we see her spread out through all time and space and rooted in eternity, terrible as an army with banners. That, I confess, is a spectacle which makes our boldest tempters uneasy. But fortunately it is quite invisible to these humans. All your patient sees is the half-finished, sham Gothic erection on the new building estate.* When he goes inside, he sees the local grocer with rather an oily expression on his face bustling up to offer him one shiny little book containing a liturgy* which neither of them understands, and one shabby little book containing corrupt texts of a number of religious lyrics, mostly bad, and in very small print. When he gets to his pew and looks round him he sees just that selection of his neighbours whom he has hitherto avoided. You want to lean pretty heavily on those neighbours. Make his mind flit to and fro between an expression like "the body of Christ" and the actual faces in the next pew. It matters very little, of course, what kind of people that next pew really contains. You may know one of them to be a great warrior on the Enemy's side. No matter. Your patient, thanks to Our Father Below, is a fool. Provided that any of those neighbours sing out of tune, or have boots that squeak, or double chins, or odd clothes, the patient will quite easily believe that their religion must therefore be somehow ridiculous. At his present stage, you see, he has an idea of "Christians" in his mind which he supposes to be spiritual but which, in fact, is largely pictorial. His mind is full of togas and sandals and armour and bare legs and the mere fact that the other people in the church wear modern clothes is a real—though of course an unconscious—difficulty to him. Never let it come to the surface; never let him ask what he expected them to look like. Keep everything hazy in his mind now, and you will have all eternity wherein to amuse yourself by producing in him the peculiar kind of clarity which Hell affords.

building estate: a primarily British term referring to a housing subdivision or apartment complex

liturgy: a prescribed form for public worship

Work hard, then, on the disappointment or anticlimax which is certainly coming to the patient during his first few weeks as a churchman. The Enemy allows this disappointment to occur on the threshold of every human endeavour. It occurs when the boy who has been enchanted in the nursery by *Stories from the Odyssey* buckles down to really learning Greek. It occurs when lovers have got married and begin the real task of learning to live together. In every department of life it marks the transition from dreaming aspiration to laborious doing. The Enemy takes this risk because He has a curious fantasy of making all these disgusting little human vermin into what He calls His "free" lovers and servants—"sons" is the word He uses, with His inveterate love of degrading the whole spiritual world by unnatural liaisons with the two-legged animals. Desiring their freedom, He therefore refuses to carry them, by their mere affections and habits, to any of the goals which He sets before them: He leaves them to "do it on their own." And there lies our opportunity. But also, remember, there lies our danger. If once they get through this initial dryness successfully, they become much less dependent on emotion and therefore much harder to tempt.

I have been writing hitherto on the assumption that the people in the next pew afford no *rational* ground for disappointment. Of course if they do—if the patient knows that the woman with the absurd hat is a fanatical bridge-player or the man with squeaky boots a miser and an extortioner—then your task is so much the easier. All you then have to do is to keep out of his mind the question "If I, being what I am, can consider that I am in some sense a Christian, why should the different vices of those people in the next pew prove that their religion is mere hypocrisy and convention?" You may ask whether it is possible to keep such an obvious thought from occurring even to a human mind. It is, Wormwood, it is! Handle him properly and it simply won't come into his head. He has not been anything like long enough with the Enemy to have any real humility yet. What he says, even on his knees, about his own sinfulness is all parrot talk. At bottom, he still believes he has run up a very favourable credit-balance in the Enemy's ledger by allowing himself to be converted, and thinks that he is showing great humility and condescension in going to church with these "smug", commonplace neighbours at all. Keep him in that state of mind as long as you can.

Your affectionate uncle
Screwtape

About the Letters

1. What kind of irony does Lewis create by choosing Screwtape as his main speaker?
2. In the following statement by Screwtape in Chapter I, what does Screwtape mean by "practical propaganda"? How is the statement ironic?

   > In really practical propaganda of the kind I am suggesting He [the Enemy] has been shown for centuries to be greatly the inferior of Our Father Below.

3. How does Screwtape want people to define "real life"? What does he have to gain from this definition?
4. In Chapter II, Screwtape mentions that Wormwood must endure "the usual penalties" for his patient's conversion and later talks of "the peculiar kind of clarity which Hell affords." In context, what impression of hell do these statements give you?
5. Screwtape points out that the spiritual reality of the church is easy to forget when humans look at the idiosyncrasies and flaws of its individual members. What does Screwtape's advice suggest is the answer to this problem?
6. What common human failure does Screwtape want Wormwood to take advantage of in the third paragraph of Chapter II? Give an example of this tendency from your own life.

Wormwood continues his efforts to trip the patient up, especially in his family relationships and prayer life. Then in Chapter V, World War II begins, to Wormwood's delight. Screwtape cautions Wormwood that wars tend to turn people's thoughts toward eternal matters. However, he encourages the young demon to take advantage of emotions such as anxiety and fear or distract the patient with extreme versions of patriotism or pacifism. At the same time, the patient falls into a spiritual slump, a circumstance that leads to Screwtape's next letter.

Chapter VIII

My Dear Wormwood,

So you "have great hopes that the patient's religious phase is dying away", have you? I always thought the Training College had gone to pieces since they put old Slubgob at the head of it, and now I am sure. Has no one ever told you about the law of Undulation?*

Undulation: the state of being like a wave in the water—up and down, up and down

Humans are amphibians—half spirit and half animal. (The Enemy's determination to produce such a revolting hybrid was one of the things that determined Our Father to withdraw his support from Him.) As spirits they belong to the eternal world, but as animals they inhabit time. This means that while their spirit can be directed to an eternal object, their bodies, passions, and imaginations are in continual change, for to be in time means to change. Their nearest approach to constancy, therefore, is undulation—the repeated return to a level from which they repeatedly fall back, a series of troughs and peaks. If you have watched your patient carefully you would have seen this undulation in every department of his life—his interest in his work, his affection for his friends, his physical appetites, all go up and down. As long as he lives on earth periods of emotional and bodily richness and liveliness will alternate with periods of numbness and poverty. The dryness and dulness [*sic*] through which your patient is now going are not, as you fondly suppose, your workmanship; they are merely a natural phenomenon which will do us no good unless you make a good use of it.

To decide what the best use of it is, you must ask what use the Enemy wants to make of it, and then do the opposite. Now it may surprise you to learn that in His efforts to get permanent possession of a soul, He relies on the troughs even more than on the peaks; some of His special favourites have gone through longer and deeper troughs than anyone else. The reason is this. To us a human is primarily food; our aim is the absorption of its will into ours, the increase of our own area of selfhood at its expense. But the obedience which the Enemy demands of men is quite a different thing. One must face the fact that all the talk about His love for men, and His service being perfect freedom, is not (as one would gladly believe) mere propaganda, but an appalling truth. He really *does* want to fill the universe with a lot of loathsome little replicas of Himself—creatures whose life, on its miniature scale, will be qualitatively like His own, not because He has absorbed them but because their wills freely conform to His. We want cattle who can finally become food; He wants servants who can finally become sons. We want to suck in, He wants to give out. We are empty and would be filled; He is full and flows over. Our war aim is a world in which Our Father Below has drawn all other beings into himself: the Enemy wants a world full of beings united to Him but still distinct.

And that is where the troughs come in. You must have often wondered why the Enemy does not make more use of His power to be sensibly present to human souls in any degree He chooses and at any moment. But you now see that the Irresistible and the Indisputable are the two weapons which the very nature of His scheme forbids Him to use. Merely to over-ride a human will (as His felt presence in any but the faintest and most mitigated* degree would certainly do) would be for Him useless. He cannot ravish. He can only woo. For His ignoble idea is to eat the cake and have it; the creatures are to be one with Him, but yet themselves; merely to cancel them, or assimilate them, will not serve. He is prepared to do a little over-riding at the beginning. He will set them off with communications of His presence which, though faint, seem great to them, with emotional sweetness, and easy conquests over temptation. But he never allows this state of affairs to last long. Sooner or later He withdraws, if not in fact, at least from their conscious experience, all those supports and incentives. He leaves the creature to stand up on its own legs—to carry out from the will alone duties which have lost all relish. It is during such trough periods, much more than during the peak periods, that it is growing into the sort of creature He wants it to be. Hence the prayers offered in the states of dryness are those which please Him best. We can drag our patients along by continual tempting, because we design them only for the tables, and the more their will is interfered with the better. He cannot "tempt" to virtue as we do to vice. He wants them to learn to walk and must therefore take away His hand; and if only the will to walk is really there He is pleased even with their stumbles. Do not be deceived, Wormwood. Our cause is never more in danger than when a human, no longer desiring, but still intending, to do our Enemy's will, looks round upon a universe from which every trace of Him seems to have vanished, and asks why he has been forsaken, and still obeys.

most mitigated: mildest

But of course the troughs afford opportunities to our side also. Next week I will give you some hints on how to exploit them.

Your affectionate uncle
Screwtape

In the intervening chapters, Wormwood succeeds in introducing his patient to several shallow but seemingly intellectual friends who drag him down, particularly through their flippant attitudes toward simple pleasures and spiritual realities. But the Holy Spirit woos the patient back with gentle conviction that the demon is powerless to stop. Screwtape suggests using the physical appetites to distract the patient or corrupting his newly gained spiritual growth. However, these efforts are hindered by two events: first, the patient falls in love with a girl who is a strong Christian. And second, Wormwood turns Screwtape in to hell's Secret Police for several statements he has made in his letters. The relationship between uncle and nephew begins to slowly break down. In addition, to the demons' consternation, the patient begins associating with the girl's family and friends who are also sincere and mature Christians.

Chapter XXV

My Dear Wormwood,

The real trouble about the set your patient is living in is that it is *merely* Christian. They all have individual interests, of course, but the bond remains mere Christianity. What we want, if men become Christians at all, is to keep them in the state of mind I call "Christianity And". You know—Christianity and the Crisis, Christianity and the New Psychology, Christianity and the New Order, Christianity and Faith Healing, Christianity and Psychical Research, Christianity and Vegetarianism, Christianity and Spelling Reform. If they must be Christians let them at least be Christians with a difference. Substitute for the faith itself some Fashion with a Christian colouring. Work on their horror of the Same Old Thing.

The horror of the Same Old Thing is one of the most valuable passions we have produced in the human heart—an endless source of heresies in religion, folly in counsel, infidelity in marriage, and inconstancy in friendship. The humans live in time, and experience reality successively. To experience much of it, therefore, they must experience many different things; in other words, they must experience change. And since they need change, the Enemy (being a hedonist at heart) has made change pleasurable to them, just as He has made eating Pleasurable. But since He does not wish them to make change, any more than eating, an end in itself, He has balanced the love of change in them by a love of permanence. He has contrived to gratify both tastes together on the very world He has made, by that union of change and permanence which we call Rhythm. He gives them the seasons, each season different yet every year the same, so that spring is always felt as a novelty yet always as the recurrence of an immemorial theme. He gives them in His Church a spiritual year; they change from a fast to a feast, but it is the same feast as before.

Now just as we pick out and exaggerate the pleasure of eating to produce gluttony, so we pick out this natural pleasantness of change and twist it into a demand for absolute novelty. This demand is entirely our workmanship. If we neglect our duty, men will be not only contented but transported by the mixed novelty and familiarity of snowdrops *this* January, sunrise *this* morning, plum pudding *this* Christmas. Children, until we have taught them better, will be perfectly happy with a seasonal round of games in which conkers* succeed hopscotch as regularly as autumn follows summer. Only by our incessant efforts is the demand for infinite, or unrhythmical, change kept up.

conkers: a children's game popular in Great Britain

This demand is valuable in various ways. In the first place it diminishes pleasure while increasing desire. The pleasure of novelty is by its very nature more subject than any other to the law of diminishing returns.* And continued novelty costs money, so that the desire for it spells avarice or unhappiness or both. And again, the more rapacious* this desire, the sooner it must eat up all the innocent sources of pleasure and pass on to those the Enemy forbids. Thus by inflaming the horror of the Same Old Thing we have recently made the Arts, for example, less dangerous to us than perhaps, they have ever been, "low-brow" and "high-brow" artists alike being now daily drawn into fresh, and still fresh, excesses of lasciviousness,* unreason, cruelty, and pride. Finally, the desire for novelty is indispensable if we are to produce Fashions or Vogues.

law of diminishing returns: economic concept meaning in context that the more one purchases of a particular good, the less pleasure one receives from it

rapacious: ravenous

lasciviousness: lust

The use of Fashions in thought is to distract the attention of men from their real dangers. We direct the fashionable outcry of each generation against those vices of which it is least in danger and fix its approval on the virtue nearest to that vice which we are trying to make endemic.* The game is to have them running about with fire extinguishers whenever there is a flood, and all crowding to that side of the boat which is already nearly gunwale* under. Thus we make it fashionable to expose the dangers of enthusiasm at the very moment when they are all really becoming worldly and lukewarm; a century later, when we are really making them all Byronic* and drunk with emotion, the fashionable outcry is directed against the dangers of the mere "understanding". Cruel ages are put on their guard against Sentimentality, feckless* and idle ones against Respectability, lecherous ones against Puritanism; and whenever all men are really hastening to be slaves or tyrants we make Liberalism* the prime bogey.

endemic: prevalent

gunwale: the top edge of the side of a vessel

Byronic: passionate, from George Gordon, Lord Byron, British Romantic poet

feckless: careless

Liberalism: a philosophy advocating individual rights and protections under law as well as social equality and rule by the consent of the governed (i.e., not American political liberalism)

But the greatest triumph of all is to elevate his horror of the Same Old Thing into a philosophy so that nonsense in the intellect may reinforce corruption in the will. It is here that the general Evolutionary or Historical character of modern European thought (partly our work) comes in so useful. The Enemy loves platitudes.* Of a proposed course of action He wants men, so far as I can see, to ask very simple questions; is it righteous? is it prudent? is it possible? Now if we can keep men asking "Is it in accordance with the general movement of our time? Is it progressive or reactionary? Is this the way that History is going?" they will neglect the relevant questions. And the questions they *do* ask are, of course, unanswerable; for they do not know the future, and what the future will be depends very largely on just those choices which they now invoke the future to help them to make. As a result, while their minds are buzzing in this vacuum, we have the better chance to slip in and bend them to the action we have decided on. And great work has already been done. Once they knew that some changes were for the better, and others for the worse, and others again indifferent. We have largely removed this knowledge. For the descriptive adjective "unchanged" we have substituted the emotional adjective "stagnant". We have trained them to think of the Future as a promised land which favoured heroes attain—not as something which everyone reaches at the rate of sixty minutes an hour, whatever he does, whoever he is.

Your affectionate uncle
Screwtape

platitudes: common expressions or clichés

About the Letters

1. According to Screwtape, the law of undulations refers to the naturally occurring ups ("peaks") and downs ("troughs") of human life in a fallen world and body. Why does the Enemy (God) "rely more" on the troughs than on the peaks?
2. According to Lewis, how do God's purpose for humans and Satan's purpose for humans differ?
3. In his introduction to *The Screwtape Letters,* Lewis points out that not everything Screwtape says is truthful, even from his own point of view. In Chapter VIII, Screwtape says that "the Enemy's determination to produce such a revolting hybrid was one of the things that determined Our Father to withdraw his support from Him." How is this statement untruthful, and why might Screwtape lie about this matter?
4. What specific biblical incident does Screwtape seem to allude to in the following statement?

   > Our cause is never more in danger than when a human, no longer desiring, but still intending, to do our Enemy's will, looks round upon a universe from which every trace of Him seems to have vanished, and asks why he has been forsaken, and still obeys.

5. In your own words, what does Screwtape find dangerous about the patient's new circle of friends? Do you agree that this is dangerous?
6. Screwtape gives three major results of being unsatisfied with the "Same Old Thing." In your own words, describe two of them and give a real-world example to illustrate one.

C. S. Lewis was the most influential and famous Christian apologist of the twentieth century. He is widely respected among non-Christians for his prose and widely beloved among Christians for his insights. Find a brief online biography of C. S. Lewis. What in Lewis's life do you think made him such an influential Christian apologist? What could you do to prepare yourself to become an effective apologist—maybe not someone as influential or incisive as Lewis, but someone worth hearing?

About the Author

British author and scholar C. S. Lewis (1898–1963), known to his friends as Jack, was born in Belfast, Ireland. He enjoyed a happy childhood with his parents and older brother, Warren, with whom he shared a close, lifelong friendship. But after their mother's death of cancer in 1908, both boys were sent to boarding school. Jack excelled academically and in 1916 won a scholarship to Oxford. Though his schooling was interrupted by frontline service in World War I, Lewis graduated with the highest honors in three separate fields of study. He taught at Oxford for twenty-nine years; then in 1955 he moved to Cambridge University, where he served as Professor of Medieval and Renaissance Literature until the year of his death.

Reared as a Protestant, Lewis by his early teens considered himself an atheist. But partly through the influence of J. R. R. Tolkien (friend and Oxford colleague) and other close friends, he converted to Christianity in 1931, joining the Anglican Church. Lewis famously called himself "the most . . . reluctant convert in all England," but once he made his decision, his wholehearted belief influenced his work profoundly. Beginning with his books *The Problem of Pain* (1940) and *The Screwtape Letters* (1942), Lewis earned an international reputation as a Christian apologist for the common man. He possessed an accessible style and often employed concrete analogies to explain complicated questions. Lewis authored many more such works, including *Mere Christianity* (texts of his BBC radio broadcasts) and *Surprised by Joy* (his spiritual autobiography), and many consider him the most influential Christian writer of his time. Today, he is probably best known for his fiction, including the *Chronicles of Narnia*, a classic series of fantasy novels for children, and his *Space Trilogy*. Both express Lewis's worldview, carrying strong Christian themes.

THINKING ZONE

The unit opener defines *irony* as a contradiction in what is expected to happen and what actually happens. It underscores the paradoxical in language and in life and is especially common in satire. **Satire** is corrective ridicule in literature or the holding up of vice and folly to ridicule with the purpose of improvement. Wit, sarcasm, and humor are also commonly used in satire, not as ends in themselves but as instruments to reach the ultimate goal of correction.

Satire ranges widely in tone, from humor and gentle mockery to outrage and harsh invective. Jonathan Swift used scorn-laden satire when he suggested in *A Modest Proposal* that Irish peasants sell their children as food for the tables of English lords, thereby both increasing trade and solving the problem of starvation in Ireland. Only the naïve took Swift's idea at face value. In reality, Swift was incensed at the plight of the poor and wrote to raise ire and force a solution.

The pun is yet another type of verbal irony. A **pun**, or play on words, creates duality of meaning through the use of words identical or similar in sound but different in meaning. Though often humorous, puns can be serious as well. In Scripture Joseph interpreted the dreams of Pharaoh's imprisoned butler and baker. Joseph speaks metaphorically to Pharaoh's butler: "Yet within three days shall Pharaoh lift up thine head, and restore thee unto thy place" (Gen. 40:13). Here the phrase *lift up thine head* means "exalt, raise to honor." Joseph uses the same phrase literally in explaining the beheading of Pharaoh's baker: "Yet within three days shall Pharaoh lift up thine head from off thee, and shall hang thee on a tree" (40:19). The narrative then brings these meanings together in a pun that carries both meanings at once: "And it came to pass the third day, which was Pharaoh's birthday, that he made a feast unto all his servants: and he lifted up the head of the chief butler and of the chief baker among his servants" (40:20).

Shakespeare punned often in his plays. In *Romeo and Juliet* lovesick Romeo trudges to Capulet's feast to try to forget Rosaline. Encouraged by Mercutio to dance, Romeo declines, declaring that Mercutio's shoes have "nimble soles," whereas he himself has a "soul of lead." The pun *sole/soul*—identical in sound, but different in meaning—conveys Romeo's excuse for not dancing—his heavy heart. Later in the play Mercutio, having been fatally stabbed, declares, "Ask for me tomorrow, and you shall find me a grave man." *Grave* is a play on words. As an adjective it means "serious"; as a noun it means "a place of burial," predicting that Mercutio will soon die.

Whereas a pun enables a writer to communicate multiple meanings at once, an **oxymoron** combines contradictory elements for effect. The word *bittersweet* is an oxymoron, as is the phrase *a definite possibility. Romeo and Juliet* affords many illustrations. For example, having professed their love, Romeo and Juliet are reluctant to separate. Juliet's expression of feeling contains what has become a well-known oxymoron: "Parting is such sweet sorrow." Juliet's love for Romeo will later be tested, however, eliciting from her a string of oxymorons, including "fiend angelical," "honorable villain," and "beautiful tyrant," expressions purposely crafted by Shakespeare to contradict. Certainly, great writers of all ages have written satire and have employed the pun and the oxymoron for effect.

1. Identify and explain the title of a work in Unit III that contains a **pun**.
2. What is satirical about "Letter from a West Texas Constituent"?
3. Find an example of an **oxymoron** in the first paragraph of "The Day the Dam Broke" by James Thurber.
4. How is *The Screwtape Letters* an example of **satire**? Support your answer.
5. Explain Lewis's satire in the following passage from *The Screwtape Letters*. What is Screwtape saying? Respond to the accuracy of Screwtape's assessment of Christians.

   > All you then have to do is to keep out of his mind the question "If I, being what I am, can consider that I am in some sense a Christian, why should the different vices of those people in the next pew prove that their religion is mere hypocrisy and convention?" You may ask whether it is possible to keep such an obvious thought from occurring even to a human mind. It is, Wormwood, it is! Handle him properly and it simply won't come into his head.

6. Write an original sentence containing a pun. The following words may serve as a springboard to your own creativity: *cents/sense, need/knead, patients/patience, class, dough, ground*, and *pants*.

UNIT IV REVIEW

Remember the Terms

Review the following terms from the opening essay, "Irony," and the Thinking Zone pages. Be prepared to discuss their meanings and uses.

irony
verbal irony
sarcasm
structural irony
situational irony
dramatic irony
hyperbole
understatement
litotes
satire
pun
oxymoron

Apply the Concepts

Answer the following questions about how the literary concepts you have studied are used in this unit.

1. For what purpose did Cleghorn write "The Golf Links Lie So Near the Mill"?
2. What kind of imaginative comparison does Tu Fu use in the following lines from his poem?

   Ten thousand organ / Pipes whistle and roar.

3. How do Cleghorn's and Tu Fu's poems differ in tone?
4. Give an example of foreshadowing from "The Grave Grass Quivers."
5. What type of irony does Goble's gift to the community exemplify within the story? Explain your answer.
6. The anonymous writer of "Scylla Toothless" uses what type of irony to convey his message? Explain your answer.
7. What is the real message of "Letter from a West Texas Constituent"?
8. What kind of imaginative comparison does Frost use throughout "A Considerable Speck (Microscopic)" in order to characterize the bug he describes?
9. Identify the type of irony Frost displays in the final two lines of the poem. Explain your answer.
10. Give an example of allusion from Thurber's essay "The Day the Dam Broke."
11. How does the tone of the speaker in "Earth" reinforce the message of the poem?
12. Describe the main irony of Eastman's poem, "At the Aquarium." What type of irony does it exemplify?
13. Does *The Screwtape Letters* qualify as a satire? Why or why not?
14. Screwtape refers to "that abominable advantage of the Enemy." In context, what is he alluding to? What Scripture passage is this allusion built on?

Evaluate the Ideas

Identify each of the following statements as true or false. If false, rewrite the underlined portion of the statement to make it true.

15. In "The Golf Links Lie So Near the Mill," Cleghorn uses <u>dramatic irony</u> to make her point.
16. The theme of "Jade Flower Palace" is <u>that the future is unpredictable</u>.
17. Tu Fu uses the rhetorical device of <u>antithesis</u> to sum up the theme of his poem.
18. In "The Grave Grass Quivers," the narrator's ignorance of Doc Martindale's discoveries helps create <u>foreshadowing</u>.
19. "Scylla Toothless" illustrates the techniques of <u>understatement</u> and <u>hyperbole</u>.
20. The skewed logic of "Letter from a West Texas Constituent" depends on <u>situational irony</u> for its effect on the reader.
21. "A Considerable Speck (Microscopic)" makes use of <u>iambic pentameter</u>.
22. In "The Day the Dam Broke," the readers' knowledge that the dam did not, in fact, break creates <u>dramatic irony</u> throughout the essay.
23. Overall, Thurber focuses his irony to create a <u>sarcastic but instructive</u> tone in "The Day the Dam Broke."
24. The final line of "Earth" contains a type of verbal irony known as <u>satire</u>.
25. Lines 4–8 of "At the Aquarium" contain an example of <u>anaphora</u>.
26. *The Screwtape Letters* forms a classic example of <u>structural irony</u>.
27. The following statement by Screwtape is an example of <u>chiasmus</u>:

    > We want cattle who can finally become food; He wants servants who can finally become sons. We want to suck in, He wants to give out. We are empty and would be filled; He is full and flows over.

28. One theme that Lewis visits multiple times is Screwtape's favorite method of undermining Christian faith: <u>distraction and misdirection</u>.

Write a Response

Completely answer each of the following questions.

29. Does the resolution of "The Grave Grass Quivers" conform to a biblical worldview of sin and its consequences? Explain your answer.
30. The speakers of "Jade Flower Palace" and "At the Aquarium" both observe certain ironies about human life. Contrast the tone of these observations. How does this tonal difference affect the theme of each poem?
31. Explain Lewis's concept of the law of undulation. Contrast how God and Satan use this process in people's lives. Illustrate your points with examples from the Bible.
32. How does Lewis's choice of narrator affect the tone and message of his work? Support your answer with examples from the text.

PART TWO

GENRES OF LITERATURE

In the first half of this book, you learned how to recognize literature by its marks and modes and discovered some purposes of those features. Now you will learn about some of the **genres** (recurring types or categories) that critics use to organize literature. These categories aid readers and critics in understanding, evaluating, and comparing various works. Genre is one element of literary criticism that can be difficult to navigate, largely because the criteria for defining genres vary in nature. Some genres are identified by the type of *content* in a work. Others are described based on the work's *form* (structure). Generally, whichever feature is more prominent to the purpose and message of a piece tends to take precedence when assigning genre.

The Basic Divisions of Genre

Every work of literature belongs to two primary genre continuums. Probably most familiar to you is the divide between **fiction** and **nonfiction**. Whereas fiction with its imaginative nature fits well within the artistic requirements of literature, nonfiction tends to focus on simply conveying information with less of an emphasis on artistry. Consequently, much (though not all) of true literature tends to fit into the genre of fiction. The second grouping includes three traditional genre divisions—**poetry**, **prose**, and **drama**. Note that while the divisions of fiction and nonfiction are based on the type of content in a work, these three divisions are based on the form of a given work. A close look reveals that these formal divisions, like many genres, overlap each other at various points. For instance, a *prose poem* offers features of both genres, *dramas* can be written in either prose or verse form, and *narrative* shows up in all three major genres. In addition, each straddles the fence of fiction and nonfiction, containing examples of both. Clearly the idea of genre is extremely flexible. Still, these categories remain generally useful for literary study.

Most literary compositions are part of several different genres at once. You might think of a work's genres as its family tree—each descending from one of the major genres. For an example, consider *The Screwtape Letters* from the previous unit. Lewis's piece first belongs to the genres of prose and fiction. Add to these facts its narrative nature and its length, and it falls into the genre of the novel as well. Finally, its form (a series of letters) marks it specifically as an epistolary novel. As you can see, each of these genres relates significant features of the book, with the final genre encompassing all the rest. A literary critic might choose to use one term or another based on what features of the text he wants to focus on.

The Purpose of Genre

The purpose of genres is twofold. First, genres are simply a way of organizing developments that have already occurred naturally in literature. It is difficult to say that anyone in particular invented prose, poetry, or drama, much less fiction or nonfiction. These categories simply describe types of literature that have existed throughout human history. More specific genres, such as detective fiction or the sonnet, are labeled only after they are widely used and defined within a culture's literature.

Second, to a certain degree, genre conventions represent an agreement between writers and their audience. Genres inform readers what to expect from a certain piece (whether in form or content) and provide a standard of judgment for critics. Are the events real or imagined? Is the piece meant to be read or performed? What themes is the writer likely to explore since he chose this particular genre? How well does he fulfill the requirements of his genre? Does he violate any of the rules? If he does, is the violation deliberate in order to make a point? These are all questions that genre distinctions may shed light on.

Take for an example several conventions of poetry. Poets create structured lines and organize these lines into stanzas. Informed readers understand that where a poet ends a line and which lines he groups together for a stanza are significant to the poem's meaning. These conventions help convey the poet's message. On the other hand, deviations from the expected conventions of a certain genre can add to a work's meaning as well. Consider the sonnet. Originally dedicated to strong declarations of romantic love, this form was used by Shakespeare to describe friendship and by George Herbert to explore religious themes. In each case, the poet's choice implied that his new subject was at least equally important and perhaps more important to him than the expected topic. In these ways, genres can provide a kind of communicative shorthand that authors can use and readers can understand.

Developments in Genre

While the distinctions pointed out by the genres of fiction and nonfiction, prose, poetry, and drama are fairly universal, a great many other genres are largely current only in a particular time and place. Some genres tend to cycle in and out of popularity depending on cultural fashions. Others fade from use altogether. But new genres also emerge through gradual changes or ground-breaking compositions. The once-popular *verse epistle* does not appear on a modern map of literature, nor do the long narrative poems (the *epic* and the *romance*) that once reigned supreme. Instead, new forms such as the *dramatic monologue* and the *novel* have arisen to take their places.

In the following four units, we will study some of today's most prevalent genres as well as several that have had great influence in a wide variety of cultures around the world. The *folktale* and the *epic* are both genres that had great currency in the ancient world. While some folktales maintain a lively presence in cultures around the world, many, like most epics, are relegated to the study of past literature. Today, *poetry*, *essays*, *short stories*, *novels*, and *dramas* form the bulk of contributions to artistic literature. These are relatively broad genres that contain numerous more specific genres within them. The selections in each unit will exhibit some of the variations possible within these overarching forms.

Like forms in any other creative discipline, genres simply provide a framework for writers. They need not constrain originality; in fact, an author's creative efforts can sometimes result in an entirely new genre. Generally, a writer chooses genres that work well with his own particular strengths as a writer. For example, Poe excelled at short stories but wrote no novels; Frost created many conventional poems but felt that free verse was overrated; Twain wrote plenty of prose but never seriously attempted poetry. And even when two writers use the same genre, the results can differ greatly. Few writings could be less similar than the novels of Charles Dickens and Henry James. Rules of convention and order do not always suffocate innovation. In fact, sometimes rules create new possibilities. So, as you study these genres, learn to see the possibilities. What do you like about short stories or poetry or dramas? How might a genre be uniquely suited to an author's gifts and message? And how do our expectations for a short story or a play affect how we respond to individual examples of the genre?

UNIT V

SAINT GEORGE FIGHTING THE DRAGON
Raphael

FOLKTALE AND EPIC

Art historians classify Italian artist Raffaello Sanzio (1483–1520), better known as Raphael, as one of three masters of the High Renaissance. Trained early on by his artist father, Raphael proved precociously talented and by age eighteen was considered a master artist. Four years in Florence, a center of art, led to further growth, and in 1508, Raphael was commissioned by Pope Julius II to paint frescos in four rooms of the Vatican. Today known as the Raphael rooms, they contain The School of Athens, *often considered Raphael's masterpiece. The artist spent the last twelve years of his life in Rome, where he died at the young age of thirty-seven. A painter without equal, he created a style characterized by balance, harmony, and serenity.*

Raphael painted the pictured cabinet piece at the request of the ruler of Urbino. Cabinet paintings were small works intended to be displayed in a small study or sitting room of a wealthy patron. This one depicts the legend of Saint George slaying a dragon. According to the legend, Saint George, a knight, rescued the daughter of a pagan king before she was sacrificed to a dragon. The painting portrays the ageless theme of good triumphing over evil, a topic illustrated again and again in the stories of folklore.

- What object is pictured broken in the painting? What details of the fight are conveyed by picturing this object?
- What else in the painting conveys the intensity of the struggle?
- What does picturing the maiden (the king's daughter) add to the theme and conflict of good versus evil?
- What is the maiden doing in the picture? What clues help you to answer?

FOLKTALE AND EPIC

To begin a study of genre, it seems logical to look at literature in its earliest forms, those of folklore. A culture's folklore is its general beliefs, customs, and stories passed along primarily by word-of-mouth. Most of the literary genres included have few formal requirements, but they are nonetheless powerful in their simplicity. They delighted listeners with their wit, imagination, and simple wisdom and helped to pass along a culture's history and way of life at a time when most people were illiterate. Both ancient and modern examples of these genres are still enjoyed by people of all ages today. Indeed, you likely have your own childhood memories of hearing such stories as you will study in this unit.

Folktales

One of the simplest folklore genres is the **folktale**, a short tale, usually anonymous, passed along by word-of-mouth. American folktales include everything from tall tales of Paul Bunyan to legends of Johnny Appleseed to fables of Brer Rabbit. Folktales can be sorted into subgenres that describe whether the stories were considered factual and what they were intended to do. However, some folktales may contain characteristics of more than one of the genres. In this unit, you will study three of the largest such genres: the fable, the fairy tale, and the myth.

One of the best-loved folktale genres, **fables** are brief fanciful stories that present a moral to teach character and life wisdom through practical examples. The stories are focused, embodying specific problems or dilemmas through the actions of the characters. The cleverness, common sense, or nobility of certain characters draws listeners' admiration while the foolishness or duplicity in others serves as a warning. The most common kind of fable is the *beast fable*, in which the characters are animals. The storyteller usually makes use of personalities associated with certain animals—for example, presenting the lion as the king of the forest or the fox as a wily trickster.

A second category of folktales is fairy tales. The label *fairy* can be misleading since often no fairies enter the story at all. Instead, **fairy tales** encompass a wide range of fictional stories set in an indefinite time and place and containing an element of the fantastic or magical. This element can extend from superstitions of quasi-religious origin to fairy godmothers or magical objects and creatures. Though fairy tales often teach clear moral boundaries, these lessons are very broad rather than focused and practical as in a fable. Usually, good characters are saintly and receive their due rewards while bad characters are unrelentingly evil and harshly punished. Fairy tales evoke a sense of wonder or sometimes of mystery, often reminding hearers of the beauty of goodness and the ugliness of evil.

Finally, **myths** are stories that explain specific aspects of life or the natural world, usually in terms of supernatural forces or beings. Together these stories form a culture's **mythology**, its explanation of how the world came to be as it is. Western literature owes a great debt to the shared mythology of ancient

Greece and Rome. Despite Rome's fall, Western scholars adopted Greek and Roman classics into the standard curriculum for educated persons. From these sources, Western authors drew many allusions, symbols, stock characters, and plotlines. Writers as diverse as Chaucer and Milton made liberal use of this heritage, and even today authors incorporate it in both popular and artistic literature.

Epics

Like the folktale, the epic originated in folklore. **Epics** are long, stylized narrative poems celebrating the deeds of a national or ethnic hero of legend. By convention, everything in epics is larger than life and full of significance: the setting is large, the hero is unusual both in his gifts and his national or historical importance, the supernatural is actively involved, and the story concerns superhuman actions usually in battle or on a difficult journey that must be made. In its treatment of this content—the difficulties the hero encounters, the choices the hero makes, and the consequences of those choices—the poem embodies its culture's values and beliefs. Epics usually address themes that are profoundly important to the human existence, including life and death, love, war, family, and friendship.

There are two types of epics: traditional and literary. Traditional epics sprang from the practice of oral poetry in societies where few people could read or write. Bards would recite or improvise poems at public or private events to entertain. Many of these poems told stories of past cultural events and heroes. Once a writing system became available, a poet who had mastered this tradition could use its stories and some of its forms to create poems of greater length and complexity than oral poets could recite. Such is the case with the *Iliad* and the *Odyssey*, perhaps the two greatest epics of Western culture. Other cultures produced traditional epics as well, from the ancient Mesopotamian *Epic of Gilgamesh* to the Indian *Ramayana*. Literary epics are those devised and written by individual poets in imitation of such traditional epics.

In addition to the four conventions of content, epics employ several conventions of form. First, the poet begins by stating the main topic of the epic and invoking the help of a guiding spirit to address his subject. Second, the poem begins *in medias res*, "in the middle," at some important point in the action. Third, it includes descriptive *catalogues* (lists), often of characters that audiences would recognize. Finally, it employs some of the verbal formulas of oral poetry, including epic similes and Homeric epithets.

Epic similes describe the vehicle of the comparison at considerable length, often more than is strictly necessary, while **Homeric epithets** are stock phrases that can be inserted to describe a particular person or thing that recurs in the poem. These served both as aids to memory and as a type of shortcut for both poet and reader. Perhaps the best-known epithet is of the Greek goddess Eos, whom Homer referred to as "rosy-fingered" since she brought the dawn. Bards could use these conventions without much thought, allowing them to focus their attention on upcoming actions in the poem. The overall style created by these conventions is deliberately formal and elevated, fitting the original cultural purpose of epics to pass along history and values.

Today the epic has largely been replaced by the novel, and folktales seem more often remembered than made. Yet the wonder and idealism of each can still enchant us. Their themes are often just as applicable to life today as thousands of years ago when they were first told. As a result, both genres remain popular as objects of literary study and continue to influence contemporary writing.

As you read, try to find the timeless elements in each selection. How are the characters in each selection similar to people you know? How are they different? What literary features do you still find in modern stories? Which literary features seem old-fashioned to you? Most important, how can you apply the theme or moral of each story to your own life?

The Ant and the Grasshopper

AESOP

Without doubt, Aesop's fables are the most widely known and beloved examples of the genre in Western culture. Typically, they are beast fables in which the animals talk, show human intelligence and stupidity, and suffer the consequences of their wise or unwise conduct. One of his most famous is the story of the ant and the grasshopper. Notice that the details of the narrative so clearly illustrate the moral that stating it at the end seems almost unnecessary.

One frosty autumn day an ant was busily storing away some of the kernels of wheat which he had gathered during the summer to tide him over the coming winter.

A grasshopper, half perishing from hunger, came limping by. Perceiving what the industrious ant was doing, he asked for a morsel from the ant's store to save his life.

"What were you doing all during the summer while I was busy harvesting?" inquired the ant.

"Oh," replied the grasshopper, "I was not idle. I was singing and chirping all day long."

"Well," said the ant, smiling grimly as he locked his granary door, "since you sang all summer, it looks as though you would have to dance all winter."

Moral: It is thrifty to prepare today for the wants of tomorrow.

About the Fable

1. Is the ant's response to the grasshopper cruel? Why or why not?
2. The Lord used the ant as an example. What biblical proverb summarizes the main thought or thesis of Aesop's moral fable?
3. Refer to Keats's view of the grasshopper in the poem "On the Grasshopper and the Cricket" (p. 52). Which grasshopper analogy do you think more accurate, Keats's or Aesop's?
4. Fables are supposed to teach practical life lessons. Give two specific applications of Aesop's moral for your own life (e.g., you should not wait until Thursday night to write a paper that is due Friday).

About the Author

Undisputed facts about the historical Aesop are hard to come by. Accounts of his life are often vague in detail or are clearly highly fictionalized. Traditionally, he is portrayed as a Greek slave who lived during the sixth century BC and who was noted for his story-telling abilities. Although we can be fairly certain that he indeed authored a number of moral tales like "The Ant and the Grasshopper," his reputation as the originator of the fable form lacks proof. It has been noted that this form appears in Egyptian manuscripts as early as the sixteenth century BC. Nonetheless, the Greeks, the Romans, and many others have liberally linked Aesop's name to moral tales of various origins. These facts, however, in no way diminish the lessons we can learn from the legendary "Aesopian" fables.

The Lion-Makers

Indian Folktale

translated by Charles Lanman

The following tale is part of an ancient Indian collection of stories known as the *Panchatantra*. Though today it is not the best-known of Indian texts, the *Panchatantra* made its way into Europe far earlier than many others, influencing writers as far back as medieval times. According to the text itself, the collection was meant to instruct three Brahman princes in how to live. Much like *The Arabian Nights*, this collection is strung together by a series of frame stories, tales that contain or introduce and organize other stories. The "Man-with-the-wheel" and the "Gold-magician" (who narrates this story) are both characters in the surrounding frame story. What lesson does the narrator want his listener to understand?

Even men of learning and noble birth are sometimes devoid of common-sense. For, true is the saying:

Book-learning people rightly cherish;
But gumption's* best of all to me.
Bereft of gumption you shall perish,
Like to the Lion-makers three.

gumption: in this context, common sense

"How was that?" said the Man-with-the-wheel. And the Gold-magician narrated:

In a certain place there dwelled four brahman youths in the greatest friendship. Three of them had got to the further shore of the ocean of science but were devoid of common-sense; while the fourth had common-sense only, and no mind for science. Now once upon a time these friends took counsel together, and said, "Of what profit is science, if we cannot go with it to some foreign country and win the favor of princes and make our fortune? Therefore to the Eastern Country let us go." And so it came to pass.

Now after they had gone a little way, the eldest spoke: "There is one among us, the fourth, who has no learning, but only common-sense; and a man can't get presents from kings by common-sense without learning. Not a whit will I give him of all that I gain; so let him go home." And the second said, "Ho there, Gumption! get you homeward, for you have no learning!" But the third made answer, "Alas, it is not fitting so to do: for we have played together since we were boys. So let him come along too. He's a noble fellow, and shall have a share in the riches that we win."

On then they went together, till in a jungle they saw the bones of a dead lion. Then spoke the first: "Ha! now we can put our book-learning to the test. Here lies some sort of a dead creature: by the power of our learning we'll bring it to life. I'll put the bones together." And that then he did with zeal. The second added flesh, blood, and hide. But just as the third was breathing the breath of life into it, Gumption stopped him and said, "Hold: this is a lion that you are turning out. If you make him alive, he will kill every one of us." Thereupon made answer the other, "Fie, stupid! is learning to be fruitless in my hands?" "Well, then," said Gumption, "just wait a bit till I climb a tree."

Thereupon the lion was brought to life. But the instant this was done, he sprang up and killed the three. Afterwards Gumption climbed down and went home.

Therefore, concluded the Gold-magician, therefore I say:

Book-learning people rightly cherish;
But gumption's best of all to me.
Bereft of gumption you shall perish,
Like to the Lion-makers three.

About the Story

1. State the moral of this story in your own words.
2. What character flaw led to the demise of the first three friends?
3. What are the narrator's feelings toward science and learning? Explain your answer.
4. Do you think the risks of education outweigh its benefits? Support your answer, referencing Proverbs 2:1–15.

As you have learned, fables present an important but practical truth through the choices of their characters and the consequences of those choices. In addition to entertaining people, fables were used to pass on community values. The Bible, as the source of all truth, provides truths needful for living righteously in God's eyes (2 Tim. 3:16–17). Choose a truth encapsulated in one or two verses of Scripture. Write a fable that helps illustrate that truth in a persuasive way.

The Tortoise and the Osprey

African Folktale

retold by Geraldine Elliot

The following story found in various folklore traditions of Africa hovers somewhere between fable and myth: it both teaches a practical moral lesson and explains why some natural occurrence is the way it is. Though the story does not directly state a moral, the events clearly reveal one primary theme. As you read, decide what you think the storyteller wants to teach you and be prepared to give your own moral.

"Why can't I fly?" grumbled Kamba, the Tortoise. "Or climb trees? Or . . ."

"For the very good reason that you weren't meant to!" snapped the Tortoise's wife, who had heard all this before and strongly disapproved of her husband's adventurous ambitions.

"But, my dear," he explained, "think what Prestige it would give us!" Tortoise had no idea what "Prestige" meant but he thought it sounded grand and he knew he was safe in trying it on his wife. It ought to impress her.

It did not impress her.

"What's 'Prestige' and why do you want it?" she demanded suspiciously.

"Oh, er . . . er . . . I thought you'd like it, my dear," he stammered lamely.

"Then you thought wrong. I'm quite content with things as they are, and I haven't time to waste talking about prestiges and things of that sort. Prestige indeed!" Tortoise's wife snorted with contempt and bustled off to her cooking-pots.

Kamba, the Tortoise, looked a little crushed, but only for a moment. The first few puffs of tobacco from his ancient pipe restored his confidence and before long he fell asleep in the hot sunshine, murmuring sadly to himself, "if only I could fly!"

The reason why Kamba yearned for this accomplishment was that he wished to visit his rich and noble friend, the Osprey. How the friendship came about it is hard to say, but no doubt the funny little Tortoise amused the Osprey who was a happy-go-lucky, kind-hearted bird, and he often used to drop in at the Tortoises' for a smoke and a chat before returning to his own home in the tree-tops. And as he was leaving he would always ask, "When are you going to pay us a visit, Kamba?" And Kamba would hurriedly say, "Well, not *this* week, Osprey, old friend, I'm afraid I am much too busy. But I'll come as soon as I can."

Now if only Tortoise had been honest enough to explain that he had no means of getting to Osprey's home, all would have been well. But Kamba thought that Osprey would despise

him if he were to say he could not fly, or climb trees or, in fact, do anything but crawl along the ground and that very slowly. So Tortoise went on hoping that he would find a way. The trouble was that he must find it soon. He could not put off the visit indefinitely, or Osprey would begin to wonder why. Then, too, there was the Chameleon who lived nearby who had guessed what was up and who now never missed an opportunity of jeering at Tortoise.

"Have you learnt to fly yet, Kamba?" he would call out. "Have you paid your call on Osprey?" And Tortoise did not know how to avoid him because he never saw him until he heard his voice.

It was the voice of the Chameleon that now roused him from his pleasant sleep.

"Pity you can't climb trees like me, isn't it, Kamba?" he was saying. He was disguised as a rock this morning and Tortoise had to look twice before he discovered him.

"It's a pity you've got such a long tongue!" retorted Kamba, and he moved off as fast as he could, found another sunny corner, and gave himself up to thought once more.

Suddenly an idea came to him. A brilliant idea! A splendid idea! Tortoise could hardly contain himself at the thought of it and crawled off at top speed to find his wife.

"What's the hurry?" she enquired as soon as she saw him.

"My dear, I have a wonderful idea! I think even you will be pleased with it," replied Tortoise and, as quickly as he could, he told her of his plan.

"H'm!" said Tortoise's wife. "It is not a bad idea . . . and it certainly would be polite to return the Osprey's many calls. And perhaps if you do, you will be more contented. Yes, I don't mind helping you this time. When do you expect Osprey to come here again?"

"I think he will come to-morrow," answered Tortoise. "So we must be prepared."

Sure enough, next morning the Osprey arrived, looking very fine and handsome. Tortoise's wife met him and said how sorry she was that her husband was out. He had had to go visiting, but he had left a present of tobacco for Osprey.

Osprey was delighted, politely said that it was very kind of Tortoise to have given him a present and added that he was sorry not to see him.

"I expect you will see him soon," said Kamba's wife, giving him a bundle of tobacco leaves. It was a very neat bundle, carefully tied up with twine. Osprey took it in his beak, spread his great wings and flew off.

Inside the bundle, of course, was Tortoise, and he was thinking to himself how well his plan had worked and how surprised and pleased Osprey would be to see him when he undid the tobacco leaves. But after a while Tortoise began to feel very hot and uncomfortable and he hoped that Osprey had not got much further to go. But it seemed that Osprey had. Tortoise became more and more unhappy. He decided he did not like flying, that he never would like flying. . . . At last, he could bear it no longer.

"Hi!" he called. "Put me down. I feel . . ."

He never finished his sentence for, at the sound of a voice coming from the middle of a bundle of tobacco leaves, Osprey opened his beak and let out a squawk of terror and his bundle dropped to the ground.

Luckily for Tortoise, Osprey had not been flying very high and the tobacco leaves helped to break his fall. Moreover, he landed on his back, where he had his hard shell to protect him, but it was a very bruised and shaken Tortoise who crept out of what had been the present-for-Osprey, and when he reached his home, he found that his shell was cracked in several places.

Tortoise's wife was not very sympathetic.

"Be thankful it wasn't worse," she said, when she had heard the sad story. "I never really approved of your foolish plan"—which wasn't quite true—"but now, perhaps, you'll be content to stay on the ground for the rest of your days," she finished up.

"Yes, my dear," said Tortoise humbly and crawled to his favorite place in the sun.

"Hullo!" said a clump of red aloes, in which Kamba eventually discovered the Chameleon. "I like your new shell. It *is* handsome with that criss-cross pattern on it."

Tortoise looked at Chameleon and saw that he was quite serious. He tried not to show his surprise as he answered in an off-hand manner, "It is smart, isn't it? I am so glad you like it. Good-bye" and he crept hurriedly back to his wife and told her what Chameleon had said.

"So you see," he chortled happily, "I think I've got Prestige after all!"

"Pouf!" said his wife. "I don't believe you know what it is!"

All this happened a very long time ago, and as Kamba was the father of all Tortoises, every one of them has criss-cross pattern cracks in his shell.

About the Story

1. What does Tortoise want in the story?
2. Within a work of literature, a *foil* is a character who emphasizes another character's opposing traits. Who is a foil for Tortoise in this story? Explain your answer.
3. In your own words, state the moral of this story.
4. What fact of nature does the story purport to explain?

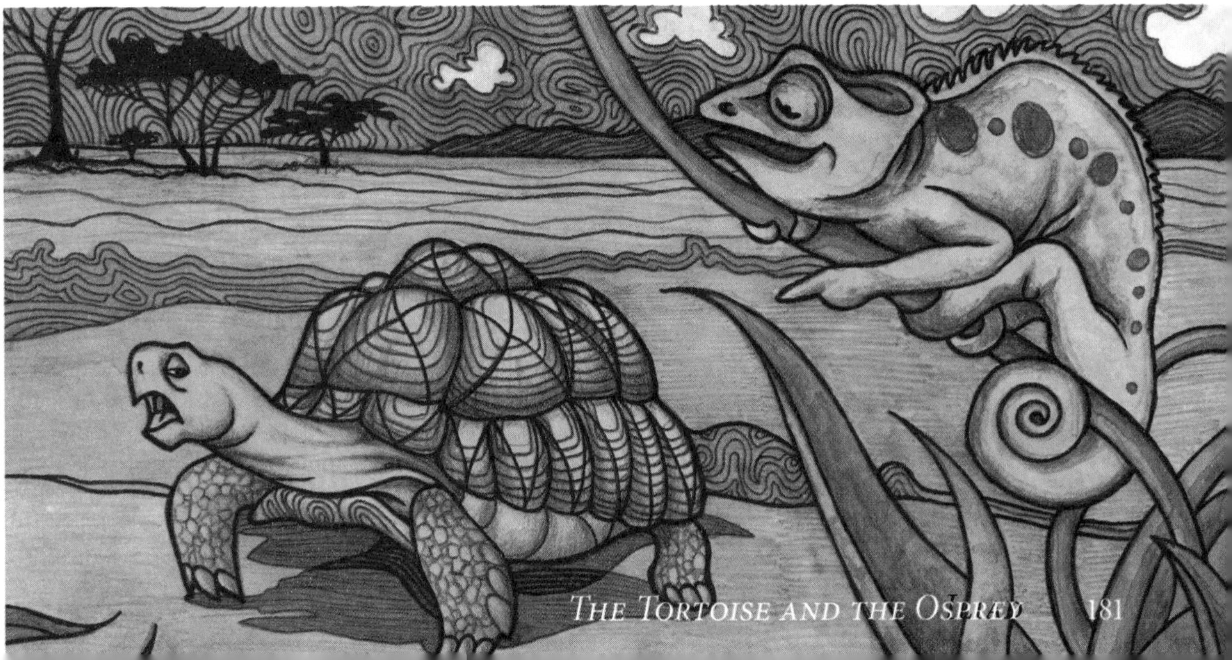

The Pumpkin Seeds

Korean Folktale

retold by Kim So-un

The following folktale is an example of a fairy tale retold for modern children. Though it is an ancient Korean tale, there are many European fairy tales that contain similar characters and events. Such similarities are found in folktales throughout the world. In literary criticism, these recurring character types, plot patterns, or images are often called **archetypes**, and many still appear in literature today. As you read, see whether you can pick out any archetypal characters or plot patterns from other fairy tales you know.

There once lived in the same village two brothers. The elder was greedy and miserly. The younger was a gentle and open-hearted man. The older brother lived in a great mansion and had everything he wanted. Yet he was always complaining, as if by habit, that he led a hard life. On the other hand, his younger brother was poor and lived a humble life. But he never once complained.

One spring, swallows from some faraway southern country came and made a nest under the eaves of the poor brother's house. By the time the early summer breeze was rippling the green rice seedlings, the swallow had hatched its eggs, and the nest was full of young birds. From morning to night, the baby birds made merry music under the eaves of the poor man's straw-thatched house. The kind-hearted younger brother placed a wide board under the nest to catch the baby birds, in case they fell from the nest to the ground below. The parent swallows busily carried food to their young and worked

hard to make them grow big. And they did grow big, with each passing day.

One day, while the parent birds were away looking for food, a large green snake slid down the roof of the hut. As it approached the swallow's nest, it raised its head and peered inside, as if to say, "Yum, yum! These young birds will make a tasty meal." The snake poised itself to strike, showing its fangs. Of course, the baby swallows had never seen such a horrible sight before. They flapped their small wings in fear and tried with all their might to fly away. But their wings were too weak. One little bird succeeded in taking off only to crash to the ground.

The young brother heard the commotion and came running out of the house. He saw the snake just in time and, with a great cry, chased it away.

The bird that had fallen from the nest had broken a leg. "Oh, you poor little thing," the brother said, "it must be painful." He gently lifted the bird from the ground, put medicine on its leg, and wound it carefully with a bit of white cloth.

Ten, twenty days passed. The baby swallow with the broken leg was soon well again. It was strong enough to fly now. It no longer needed to wait for its mother to bring it food. It swooped through the great sky, swiftly and freely, in search of insects and bugs.

Summer passed and autumn came. The swallows left for their winter home in the south. The swallow with the broken leg was now a big bird. Reluctantly, it too joined the migrating birds and left the village.

Early the next spring, the swallows came back to their old nest. They had traveled a long way, over seas and over mountains, but they had not forgotten their old home. The happy swallows swooped under the eaves of the straw-thatched hut. The humble hut of the younger brother again echoed to the merry chirping of birds.

The swallow that had broken its leg the year before also returned. As if to repay the young brother's kindness, it carried in its beak a pumpkin seed. The bird dropped the seed in a corner of the poor brother's yard, where it soon sprouted and shot forth a tendril that gradually climbed up to the roof of the poor man's home.

By autumn, three big pumpkins, so large that each made an armful, were ripening on the vine. The younger brother was overjoyed and cut down one pumpkin. "This is a rare thing to have such large pumpkins. One such pumpkin alone would be enough to feed many people. I must take some of it to the villagers." So thinking, the younger brother cut the pumpkin in two.

What should happen then! Out of the pumpkin trooped a host of carpenters. Some carried axes, some saws, some planes, and some hammers. Each carried some kind of tool. After the carpenters had all come out, there came a flow of building materials—timbers, planks, window frames, and doors. In a twinkling of an eye, the carpenters built a large mansion and then disappeared from sight.

The younger brother was completely dumbfounded at this strange and unexpected happening. He then began wondering what the other pumpkins might contain. He gingerly cut open the second pumpkin.

Out came a host of servants. There were farmhands too, with plows and spades and rakes. There were also maids, carrying water jugs on their heads, and seamstresses, with needles in their hands. When they had all come out, they lined up before the younger brother and, bowing deeply, said together, "Master, we are here to serve you. Please tell us what you would like us to do."

From the third pumpkin there flowed silver and gold in such quantities that the younger brother was completely dazed. Overnight, he became the richest man in the village, and soon he was the owner of vast lands, purchased with the money that had come from the third pumpkin.

The greedy older brother was totally green with envy. His every waking thought was how to become as wealthy as his younger brother. One day he came over to visit his brother, whom he had ignored for so long in the past. Slyly he asked, "Say, my dear brother, how did you manage to become so rich?"

The honest younger brother did not hide anything, but told him everything that had happened. The older brother, when he heard the story, thought greedily of a plan. As soon as early summer came the next year, he took a baby swallow from one of the nests in the eaves of his house and broke its leg. Then he put medicine on the broken leg, bound it with a piece of white cloth, and put the bird back into its nest. In autumn this swallow flew away to the south.

The older brother could scarcely contain his joy. "I've only to wait a short while longer. Then that swallow will return and bring me a pumpkin seed too."

Sure enough, the swallow whose leg had been broken on purpose returned the next spring to the elder brother's house and brought back a pumpkin seed in its mouth.

The older brother took the seed and planted it in a corner of his yard. Every day he gave it water and cried, "Hurry and grow big! Hurry and grow big!" He did not forget to mix a lot of manure into the ground where the pumpkin seed had been planted.

In time, out came a green sprout. It grew and grew, stretching its vine up over the roof. In time, too, three pumpkins took shape and ripened. The pumpkins were much larger than those that had grown at his younger brother's house.

"How lucky I am!" the older brother said. "Thank Heaven! Now everything is set. I shall be much richer than my younger brother." He could not help dancing about in joy and anticipation.

Finally, the time came and he cut the first pumpkin. But what should appear? Not carpenters, but a swarm of demons with cudgels in their hands.

"You inhuman and greedy monster! Now you'll get what you deserve!" the demons cried, and they began beating the older brother in turns.

After a while the demons disappeared. The older brother was all blue with bruises, but still he had not learned his lesson. "This time, for sure, I'll find much treasure," he thought, and cut open the second pumpkin.

But this time a host of money collectors came out crying, "Pay your debts! Pay your debts! If you don't we'll take away everything we can lay our hands on."

And they did! They grabbed everything in sight. In a flash, the older brother's home was completely emptied of all it contained, leaving only a shell.

The older brother cursed himself for having cut open the second pumpkin, but it was too late. And still he could not give up his dreams of an easy fortune. He stuck a knife into the third pumpkin and split it open. What should come out but a flood of yellow muddy water. It came bubbling out in an unending stream. It flowed in such quantities that soon his home, his garden, and his fields were covered with yellow mud.

The older brother finally could stand it no longer. With a cry of anguish he fled to the shelter of his younger brother's house.

The kind-hearted younger brother greeted him with open arms and treated him very well. The older brother suddenly realized how selfish and mean he had been. He became a humble and contrite man.

The younger brother gave his elder brother half of everything he had—paddies, fields, servants, and money—and from that time on the two lived on the most friendly of terms.

About the Story

1. Given the definitions of *fairy tales* and *fables* in the unit introduction, why do you think this story is better categorized as a fairy tale than as a fable?
2. In Korean culture family ties and responsibilities are extremely important. How might this important cultural belief influence how a listener would respond to the story, beginning in the first paragraph?
3. Did you find any archetypes in this story? List one possibility.
4. Does the story succeed in making good look lovely and bad, ugly? Is the worldview biblical?

Pandora

Greek Myth

retold by W. M. L. Hutchinson

One of the most famous stories of Greek mythology, the myth of Pandora's box is both a cautionary tale and a myth of explanation. Prometheus is one of the Titans, the gods who first ruled the earth and whom Zeus and his fellow Olympians overthrew. A very clever individual, he angers Zeus by stealing the secret of fire (which Zeus had taken) and giving it back to man. This is the story of Zeus's revenge on man. As you can see, the gods of Greek mythology were not always kind. In fact, they were often just as petty, selfish, and cruel as humans can be.

Now while Prometheus* comforted his heart with the thought of what mankind would be able to accomplish by means of fire, Zeus* sat pondering how he might frustrate that good gift with some countervailing evil. For it is a law to all the Immortals that none may take away what another has bestowed, nor could even he now deprive mortals of their new possession. He purposed, therefore, to send them some gift so baneful that they should be never free from misery their lives long, and thus to fill up the measure of his vengeance upon Prometheus.

Prometheus: Titan god who incurred the wrath of Zeus by giving mankind fire
Zeus: in Greek mythology, the ruler of the gods

After long thought, he called Hephaestus* to him and said, "Hephaestus, I have devised a new thing that has not its like in earth or heaven; now put forth all your skill, for you must forthwith make it according to the fashion I will tell you."

Hephaestus: Greek god of fire and blacksmiths

"Of what shall I make it?" asked Hephaestus.

"Of whatever you can find most fair," said Zeus. "Mingle together all things loveliest, sweetest, and best, but look that you also mingle therewith the opposites of each."

So Hephaestus took gold and dross,* wax and flint, pure snow and mud of the highways, honey and gall;* he took the bloom of the rose and the toad's venom, the voice of laughing water and the peacock's squall; he took the sea's beauty and its treachery; the dog's fidelity, the wind's inconstancy; the cruelty of the tiger and the mother-bird's heart of love. All these, and other contraries past number, he blended cunningly into one substance, and this he molded into the shape that Zeus described to him.

dross: impurities surfacing in molten metal
gall: bitterness

When it was finished Hephaestus looked upon his handiwork and said, "We have made no new thing, but the image of a goddess."

"Nay," said Zeus, "we have made the First Woman," and with that he breathed upon the image, and it lived, and looked upon them wonderingly, as one suddenly awakened.

Then he called all the Olympians to behold the First Woman, and they marveled at the beauty of her, for in truth she was fair as any goddess.

They cried that they would each offer her some gift on this her birthday, and so they did. The goddesses arrayed her in glorious apparel, Hephaestus decked her with jewels of cunning workmanship, and every god gave her some precious thing. Last of all, Zeus himself placed in her hands a casket of lustrous amber, richly overwrought with flowers and fruit of the pomegranate, and having two golden snakes for handles.

"Behold, Immortals," he said, "this new fair creature of my shaping thought, endowed with every earthly loveliness, laden with heaven's choicest treasures! Shall she not be named Pandora, All-Gifted? Seems she not even as a bride adorned for her husband? But she is no mate for an Olympian, for she is mortal; come, let us send her to wed with Epimetheus,* in token that we bear him no ill-will for his rebel brother's sake.

Epimetheus: brother to Prometheus

The Olympians were well pleased, for they knew not the guileful intent of Zeus, and straightway he bade Hermes lead Pandora to the house of Epimetheus, and say to him, "The King of Gods, in sign of his goodwill toward you, sends you this peerless bride, who brings with her in this casket such a dowry as he only can bestow."

So Hermes brought the First Woman to Arcadia.* Now when Epimetheus saw her beauty and heard why she was come, he could scarce contain himself for joy at his good fortune, and he received the bride with her casket into his house and wedded her that day, without once remembering the warning Prometheus gave him, not to take any gift from Zeus. But on the morrow it came back to his mind, and he repented of what he had done; for this was his nature, that he was never wise until too late. From this he had his name of Epimetheus, which means Afterthought, even as his brother was called Prometheus, that is, Forethought, because he was wise concerning things yet to come.

Arcadia: a region of ancient Greece

Epimetheus now reflected that the dowry Zeus had given his bride was doubtless meant to work him some deadly harm, and he asked Pandora if she knew what lay in her amber box.

"No, my husband," said she, "but I will fetch the box from our chamber, and we will open it and see. I long to know what the great King of the Immortals has bestowed on us."

"Bide here, Pandora," said the Titan, "and listen well to what I shall say. My mind misgives me that yonder casket holds some evil secret, and he who sent it is not a friend but a subtle enemy. I was warned erewhile* to take no gift at his hand, but in my folly I paid little heed. Now since what is done cannot be undone, and the gift is under my roof, here let it stay; but I charge you on your love and obedience, never open the casket. For whatever it holds can do us no mischief while we keep it fast shut, and it is itself so royal-rich and beautiful a thing that I have no heart to cast it away."

erewhile: previously

Pandora was glad that she might keep the wondrous box, and every day she viewed it with delight as it shone like translucent gold in the sunlight. But after a while she wearied of that pleasure and began to wonder more and more what might be hidden within it. Many a time, alone in her chamber, she sat gazing at the casket until longing to learn its secret so nearly overcame her that she arose and went hastily forth, vowing to look on it no more.

At last, in an accursed hour, she could resist her desire no longer; she laid her hand upon the lid and raised it gently—very gently, half fearful of what she might see. Quick as thought, out flew a swarm of tiny winged sprites, soaring and drifting upward like breeze-blown tufts of thistledown, and they vanished like a wreath of smoke through the open doorway.

With a startled cry Pandora closed the box—but, alas! too late; one glance had shown her it was empty, and she sat down and wept tears of disappointment. Now, had she known what she had done, she must have grieved a thousand times more bitterly, for the sprites

she had let loose were all the cares and woes and fell diseases that afflict mankind, and from that hour to this they fly abroad upon earth, pursuing hapless mortals from the cradle to the grave. Such was the dower* that the First Woman brought with her into the world.

dower: dowry

Epimetheus found his wife weeping, and she told him what had befallen, and he forgave her and said, "Half the fault is mine, because I left the casket in your keeping. It seems that it is as much a woman's nature to be overcurious as it is mine to be wise too late."

And he forbore to reproach her, although he now knew well enough by his power of afterthought what those sprites were. He asked Pandora if she was sure they had all escaped, and she said "Yes." But by and by she thought she would look again, and when she opened the casket, she saw there was still one left, clinging beneath the gold rim that held up the lid, with its rainbow wings drooping as if broken. And something told Pandora that the name of it was Hope.

What did Pandora do when she found Hope was left in the casket? She pitied the fairy thing, because it seemed half-dead, and she laid it in her bosom, to warm it back to life. But when she had cherished it for a while, Hope crept into her heart and made its abode there; and being comforted, it inhabits ever since the hearts of mortals.

About the Story

1. What two things did Zeus count on in order to make his plan work? What stereotypes about men and women does this plan reinforce?
2. How did Zeus mitigate his revenge?
3. What does this myth attempt to explain about life?
4. Do you think this is a satisfying explanation? How does the Bible address these facts?

Pyramus and Thisbe

Ovid

translated by Edith Hamilton

This Roman myth is one of explanation. Unusually, it focuses on human life rather than on gods or other supernatural forces. Like other stories told by Ovid in his collection *Metamorphoses*, the story proclaims the transformative power of love. It has often been referenced in subsequent literature, perhaps most famously by providing the basic plot pattern for one of Shakespeare's most famous plays. Can you guess which one?

Once upon a time the deep red berries of the mulberry tree were white as snow. The change in color came about strangely and sadly. The death of two young lovers was the cause.

Pyramus and Thisbe, he the most beautiful youth and she the loveliest maiden of all the East, lived in Babylon, the city of Queen Semiramis, in houses so close together that one wall was common to both. Growing up thus side by side they learned to love each other. They longed to marry, but their parents forbade. Love, however, cannot be forbidden. The more that flame is covered up, the hotter it burns. Also love can always find a way. It was impossible that these two whose hearts were on fire should be kept apart.

In the wall both houses shared there was a little chink. No one before had noticed it, but there is nothing a lover does not notice. Our two young people discovered it and through it they were able to whisper sweetly back and forth, Thisbe on one side, Pyramus on the other. The hateful wall that separated them had become their means of reaching each other. "But for you we could touch, kiss," they would say. "But at least you let us speak together. You give a passage for loving words to reach loving ears. We are not ungrateful." So they would talk, and as night came on and they must part, each would press on the wall kisses that could not go through to the lips on the other side.

Every morning when the dawn had put out the stars, and the sun's rays had dried the hoarfrost on the grass, they would steal to the crack and, standing there, now utter words of burning love and now lament their hard fate, but always in softest whispers. Finally a day came when they could endure no longer. They decided that that very night they would try to slip away and steal out through the city into the open country where at last they could be together in freedom. They agreed to meet at a well-known place, the Tomb of Ninus, under a tree there, a tall mulberry full of snow-white berries, near which a cool spring bubbled up. The plan pleased them and it seemed to them the day would never end.

At last the sun sank into the sea and night arose. In the darkness Thisbe crept out and made her way in all secrecy to the tomb. Pyramus had not come; still she waited for him, her love making her bold. But of a sudden she saw by the light of the moon a lioness. The fierce beast had made a kill; her jaws were bloody and she was coming to slake her thirst in the spring. She was still far enough away for Thisbe to escape, but as she fled she dropped her cloak. The lioness came upon it on her way back to her lair and she mouthed it and tore it before disappearing into the woods. That is what Pyramus saw when he appeared a few minutes later. Before him lay the bloodstained shreds of the cloak and clear in the dust were the tracks of the lioness. The

conclusion was inevitable. He never doubted that he knew all. Thisbe was dead. He had let his love, a tender maiden, come alone to a place full of danger, and had not been there first to protect her. "It is I who killed you," he said. He lifted up from the trampled dust what was left of the cloak and kissing it again and again carried it to the mulberry tree. "Now," he said, "you shall drink my blood too." He drew his sword and plunged it into his side. The blood spurted up over the berries and dyed them a dark red.

Thisbe, although terrified of the lioness, was still more afraid to fail her lover. She ventured to go back to the tree of the tryst, the mulberry with the shining white fruit. She could not find it. A tree was there, but not one gleam of white was on the branches. As she stared at it, something moved on the ground beneath. She started back shuddering. But in a moment, peering through the shadows, she saw what was there. It was Pyramus, bathed in blood and dying. She flew to him and threw her arms around him. She kissed his cold lips and begged him to look at her, to speak to her. "It is I, your Thisbe, your dearest," she cried to him. At the sound of her name he opened his heavy eyes for one look. Then death closed them.

She saw his sword fallen from his hand and beside it her cloak stained and torn. She understood all. "Your own hand killed you," she said, "and your love for me. I too can be brave. I too can love. Only death would have had the power to separate us. It shall not have that power now." She plunged into her heart the sword that was still wet with his life's blood.

The gods were pitiful at the end, and the lovers' parents too. The deep red fruit of the mulberry is the everlasting memorial of these true lovers, and one urn holds the ashes of the two whom not even death could part.

About the Story

1. What do you think is the main theme of the story?
2. What fact does the story explain?
3. The natural fact the story explains doesn't seem to be all that important. Why do you think this story nonetheless lasted and even now continues to be enjoyed?
4. Do you find Pyramus and Thisbe admirable? Why or why not?

THINKING ZONE

As you have seen in the folktales, **characters** (the persons or beings who perform the action of a story) are at any story's heart, no matter how simple the story. To gain the interest and attention of readers, a story must have a character possessing discernibly human qualities (good or bad), with desires, beliefs, and personality all his own. Lacking this, a story quickly loses its audience. For instance, beast fables have no human characters, but because the animals are given human traits and behavior, readers are able to relate to their conflicts and cares.

Characters are strongly intertwined with the conflicts of their story. They may initiate conflict or respond to it (or both, if they are in conflict with themselves). The main character, the one at the center of the main conflict, is the **protagonist**. Many times a protagonist will also have an **antagonist**, a character or force who opposes him. Usually, audiences identify with the protagonist; however, he or she need not be heroic just as the antagonist need not be villainous.

Figuring out which characters an author wants readers to approve of is important to understanding how he views the conflicts of his story. **Sympathetic characters** are those with whom the reader identifies or for whom the reader has favorable feelings. **Unsympathetic characters** are ones with whom the reader cannot identify or for whom the reader has strong feelings of dislike. These reactions are created by characters' attitudes and choices, shown through their words and actions. Of course, even sympathetic characters have character flaws or make wrong choices (just like people), but overall they retain the good will of their audience. It is these characters—the choices they make and the lessons they learn—that most clearly convey the author's perspective.

Many times a character's motivations dictate audience sympathy even more than his actions. **Character motivations** are the reasons characters behave as they do. Just like real people, characters may make bad choices with the best intentions, or they may do right with the very worst motivations. Readers must take these underlying reasons into account in deciding with whom the author sympathizes.

1. In Aesop's tale which is the **sympathetic character**? Briefly explain.
2. The four friends of "The Lion-Makers" are motivated by the desire for success. How does the narrator get readers to sympathize with one over the other three?
3. In "The Tortoise and the Osprey," what is Tortoise's motivation for his actions? How does this connect to the theme of the story?
4. How does "The Pumpkin Seeds" illustrate the importance of **character motivations**?
5. Both Pandora and Epimetheus have personal flaws that affect the outcome of "Pandora." Do you still sympathize with both? Why or why not?
6. Who are the **protagonists** and **antagonists** of "Pyramus and Thisbe"? With whom does the audience sympathize? Why?

From the *Iliad*

Homer

translated by Richmond Lattimore

Sing, goddess, the anger of Peleus' son Achilleus
and its devastation, which put pains thousandfold upon the Achaians,
hurled in their multitudes to the house of Hades strong souls
of heroes, but gave their bodies to be the delicate feasting
of dogs, of all birds, and the will of Zeus was accomplished
since that time when first there stood in division of conflict
Atreus' son the lord of men and brilliant Achilleus.

So begins one of the world's great epics, a work that has enthralled hearers and inspired writers for nearly three millennia. Most likely written during the eighth century BC, Homer's *Iliad* (meaning "song of Ilium," another name for the city of Troy) was quickly recognized for its artistic greatness. Western literature is littered with its influence, and each century sees multiple new translations published as scholars try their hand at bringing Homer's work to life. And this fact highlights the most amazing thing about the *Iliad*: people still want to read it. People still love this ancient song of the wrathful Achilles, the beauteous Helen, the well-beloved Hector, the doomed city of Troy, and the great warriors of old. Homer created a work that reaches something at the heart of any thoughtful reader, regardless of his time or place.

The setting of the *Iliad* is a war that took place in the twelfth century BC between the Trojans and the Achaeans (Greeks). According to legend, the war began when Paris, a prince of Troy, stole Helen from her husband, Menelaus, king of Sparta, and brought her back to Troy. Aphrodite assisted Paris, having promised him the love of the most beautiful woman in the world if he declared her the most beautiful in a contest between the goddesses Hera, Athena, and herself. In response to Helen's abduction, King Agamemnon (brother of Menelaus and king of Mycenae) gathered a heroic contingent of Greek warriors and set off to get her back. They landed on the beaches of Troy and spent the next ten years fighting to subdue the wealthy and strong-walled city. In the end, only Ulysses's scheme of the Trojan horse enabled them to defeat Troy.

The Iliad is set in the tenth and final year of the war when the Greek Achilles, the greatest warrior of either side, quarrels with Agamemnon over war prizes. As the first lines of the epic indicate, Achilles' anger motivates the ensuing tragedy. Feeling ill-used (with reason), Achilles refuses to fight. To no one's surprise, the Trojans, led by Hector (brother to Paris and oldest son of Troy's king Priam), soon make drastic inroads into the ranks of the Achaeans. Though the Achaeans, including Agamemnon, apologize to Achilles and beg him to return to battle, his anger is not entirely appeased. His young friend Patroclus, however, wishes to fight, and persuades a reluctant Achilles to let him. When Patroclus is killed by Hector, Achilles, in remorseful rage and grief, finally returns to the fighting. He kills Hector and mutilates the body by dragging it around with his chariot. His anger is only quieted when both the gods and Priam ask him to return Hector's body. The poem ends with Hector's funeral pyre, and though Troy has not yet fallen, readers understand that it is now only a matter of time.

Since little information about the real war has survived, it is sometimes difficult to know where truth ends and legend or pure fiction begins in Homer's story. It is probable that much of the plot is imagined. His vision of the war includes the supernatural influence of gods and goddesses, who play a great part in initiating the war and interfere at crucial moments throughout it: Zeus, the ruler of the gods, attempts to enforce the demands of fate and justice, but he sometimes succumbs to the petitions and manipulations of the other gods, many of whom take sides in the conflict. However, the poet's portrayal of war's brutalities and of humanity's response adds a note of realism that makes the epic relevant today. In fact, it is the human characters that stand out most in Homer's story. They are the ones who grab the audience's sympathies: they have the most to gain or to lose. Theirs is the duty and privilege to fight for family and most of all for glory.

The themes of the epic are varied and profound. The *Iliad* is a story of war in all its violence, degradation, pathos, and momentary beauties. Graphic details of battle abound. But this environment allows Homer to explore weighty questions of life. What is worth living for? How do you respond to death? Throughout the poem runs a fatalistic attitude that all things human must come to an end, whether individuals, cities, or civilizations: according to Homer, the only chance to live on is through great deeds, especially deeds on the battlefield. Achilles fully believes this, so when he is given the choice of a long and peaceful life or a short life full of glorious achievements in battle, he chooses the latter. By slaying Hector, he knowingly seals that fate. The downfall of Hector and Troy further illustrates this belief: though they are no more evil than Achilles, it is their time to end, just as all things mortal must end.

As you read the following excerpts from the epic, pay attention to its unique style. The narration is formal with little to indicate a personality behind the speaker. Instead, the characters take precedence, giving speeches almost like actors on a stage. The events and characters themselves are painted in lofty terms, their importance to the writer revealed by the interest of the gods and the characters' heroic nobility. Notice also that the poet uses what have since been termed homeric epithets and epic similes to fill out his descriptions and maintain a stately rhythm. Most important, try to look beyond the formal style and see the very real characters that Homer presents. Imagine yourself in their situations and you will find that in nearly three thousand years, humans have changed very little. In this truth is found the lasting charm and fascination of Homer's work.

Note that in Lattimore's translation of the *Iliad*, certain names are spelled differently than they commonly are in English. Thus *Achilles* becomes *Achilleus* and *Hector*, *Hektor*. This difference has no significant meaning, coming only from Lattimore's choice to transliterate the names from Greek rather than from Latin.

Hector and Andromache

The following is an unusual interlude in a story comprised mostly of battle. Here we see Hector not just as a warrior or a prince but also as a family man. The Trojans have been driven back to the city gates, and Hector goes into the city to bring his brother Paris back to the battle. He also takes the opportunity to speak to his wife and son, possibly for the final time. Unlike the Achaean warriors' families, his family is near the battle and will suffer dreadful consequences if Troy falls.

Then tall Hektor of the shining helm answered her: 'Do not, Helen,
make me sit with you, though you love me. You will not persuade me.
Already my heart within is hastening me to defend
the Trojans, who when I am away long greatly to have me.
Rather rouse this man [Paris], and let himself also be swift to action
so he may overtake me while I am still in the city.
For I am going first to my own house, so I can visit
my own people, my beloved wife and my son, who is little,
since I do not know if ever again I shall come back this way,
or whether the gods will strike me down at the hands of the Achaians.'*
So speaking Hektor of the shining helm departed
and in speed made his way to his own well-established dwelling,
but failed to find in the house Andromache* of the white arms;
for she, with the child, and followed by one fair-robed attendant,
had taken her place on the tower in lamentation, and tearful.
When he saw no sign of his perfect wife within the house, Hektor
stopped in his way on the threshold and spoke among the handmaidens:
'Come then, tell me truthfully as you may, handmaidens:
where has Andromache of the white arms gone? Is she
with any of the sisters of her lord or the wives of his brothers?
Or has she gone to the house of Athene,* where all the other
lovely-haired women of Troy propitiate the grim goddess?'
Then in turn the hard-working housekeeper gave him an answer:
'Hektor, since you have urged me to tell you the truth, she is not
with any of the sisters of her lord or the wives of his brothers,
nor has she gone to the house of Athene, where all the other
lovely-haired women of Troy propitiate the grim goddess,
but she has gone to the great bastion of Ilion,* because she heard that
the Trojans* were losing, and great grew the strength of the Achaians.
Therefore she has gone in speed to the wall, like a woman
gone mad, and a nurse attending her carries the baby.'
So the housekeeper spoke, and Hektor hastened from his home
backward by the way he had come through the well-laid streets. So
as he had come to the gates on his way through the great city,
the Skaian gates,* whereby he would issue into the plain, there

Achaians: (uh-KEE-enz) Greeks

Andromache: (an-DRAHM-uh-kee)

Athene: the Greek goddess of wisdom and warfare, also Athena

Ilion: Troy, also Ilium

Trojans: (TRO-jenz)

Skaian gates: the main gates of the city of Troy

at last his own generous wife came running to meet him,
Andromache, the daughter of high-hearted Eëtion;
Eëtion, who had dwelt underneath wooded Plakos,
in Thebe below Plakos, lord over the Kilikian people.
It was his daughter who was given to Hektor of the bronze helm.
She came to him there, and beside her went an attendant carrying
the boy in the fold of her bosom, a little child, only a baby,
Hektor's son, the admired, beautiful as a star shining,
whom Hektor called Skamandrios, but all of the others
Astyanax—lord of the city; since Hektor alone saved Ilion.
Hektor smiled in silence as he looked on his son, but she,
Andromache, stood close beside him, letting her tears fall,
and clung to his hand and called him by name and spoke to him: 'Dearest,
your own great strength will be your death, and you have no pity
on your little son, nor on me, ill-starred, who soon must be your widow;
for presently the Achaians, gathering together,
will set upon you and kill you; and for me it would be far better
to sink into the earth when I have lost you, for there is no other
consolation for me after you have gone to your destiny—
only grief; since I have no father, no honoured mother.
It was brilliant Achilleus* who slew my father, Eëtion,
when he stormed the strong-founded citadel of the Kilikians,
Thebe of the towering gates. He killed Eëtion
but did not strip his armour, for his heart respected the dead man,
but burned the body in all its elaborate war-gear
and piled a grave mound over it, and the nymphs of the mountains,
daughters of Zeus of the aegis*, planted elm trees about it.
And they who were my seven brothers in the great house all went
upon a single day down into the house of the death god,
for swift-footed brilliant Achilleus slaughtered all of them
as they were tending their white sheep and their lumbering oxen;
and when he had led my mother, who was queen under wooded Plakos,
here, along with all his other possessions, Achilleus
released her again, accepting ransom beyond count, but Artemis*

Achilleus: (uh-KILL-ee-oos) famous Greek warrior; also Achilles (uh-KILL-eez)

aegis: shield, representing protection

Artemis: goddess of the hunt

of the showering arrows struck her down in the halls of her father.
Hektor, thus you are father to me, and my honoured mother,
you are my brother, and you it is who are my young husband.
Please take pity upon me then, stay here on the rampart,
that you may not leave your child an orphan, your wife a widow,
but draw your people up by the fig tree, there where the city
is openest to attack, and where the wall may be mounted.
Three times their bravest came that way, and fought there to storm it
about the two Aiantes and renowned Idomeneus,
about the two Atreidai and the fighting son of Tydeus.
Either some man well skilled in prophetic arts had spoken,
or the very spirit within themselves had stirred them to the onslaught.'

Then tall Hektor of the shining helm answered her: 'All these
things are in my mind also, lady; yet I would feel deep shame
before the Trojans, and the Trojan women with trailing garments,
if like a coward I were to shrink aside from the fighting;
and the spirit will not let me, since I have learned to be valiant
and to fight always among the foremost ranks of the Trojans,
winning for my own self great glory, and for my father.
For I know this thing well in my heart, and my mind knows it:
there will come a day when sacred Ilion shall perish,
and Priam,* and the people of Priam of the strong ash spear.
But it is not so much the pain to come of the Trojans
that troubles me, not even of Priam the king nor Hekabe,*
not the thought of my brothers who in their numbers and valour
shall drop in the dust under the hands of men who hate them,
as troubles me the thought of you, when some bronze-armoured
Achaian leads you off, taking away your day of liberty,
in tears; and in Argos you must work at the loom of another,
and carry water from the spring Messeis or Hypereia,
all unwilling, but strong will be the necessity upon you;
and some day seeing you shedding tears a man will say of you:
"This is the wife of Hektor, who was ever the bravest fighter
of the Trojans, breakers of horses, in the days when they fought about Ilion."
So will one speak of you; and for you it will be yet a fresh grief,
to be widowed of such a man who could fight off the day of your slavery.
But may I be dead and the piled earth hide me under before I
hear you crying and know by this that they drag you captive.'

So speaking glorious Hektor held out his arms to his baby,
who shrank back to his fair-girdled nurse's bosom
screaming, and frightened at the aspect of his own father,
terrified as he saw the bronze and the crest with its horse-hair,
nodding dreadfully, as he thought, from the peak of the helmet.
Then his beloved father laughed out, and his honoured mother,
and at once glorious Hektor lifted from his head the helmet

Priam: (PRY-uhm)

Hekabe: (HEH-kuh-bee) wife of Priam, mother of Hektor, also Hecuba (HEH-kyu-buh)

C. W. Eckersberg. *Hector's Farewell to Andromache*. Painted in Rome 1813–16. 49, 1 x 34, 6 cm.
The Thorvaldsen Museum. Photographer Hans Petersen.

and laid it in all its shining upon the ground. Then taking
up his dear son he tossed him about in his arms, and kissed him,
and lifted his voice in prayer to Zeus and the other immortals:
'Zeus, and you other immortals, grant that this boy, who is my son,
may be as I am, pre-eminent among the Trojans,
great in strength, as am I, and rule strongly over Ilion;
and some day let them say of him: "He is better by far than his father",
as he comes in from the fighting; and let him kill his enemy
and bring home the blooded spoils, and delight the heart of his mother.'
So speaking he set his child again in the arms of his beloved
wife, who took him back again to her fragrant bosom
smiling in her tears; and her husband saw, and took pity upon her,
and stroked her with his hand, and called her by name and spoke to her:
'Poor Andromache! Why does your heart sorrow so much for me?
No man is going to hurl me to Hades,* unless it is fated,
but as for fate, I think that no man yet has escaped it
once it has taken its first form, neither brave man nor coward.
Go therefore back to our house, and take up your own work,
the loom and the distaff, and see to it that your handmaidens
ply their work also; but the men must see to the fighting,
all men who are the people of Ilion, but I beyond others.'
So glorious Hektor spoke and again took up the helmet
with its crest of horse-hair, while his beloved wife went homeward,
turning to look back on the way, letting the live tears fall.
And as she came in speed into the well-settled household
of Hektor the slayer of men, she found numbers of handmaidens
within, and her coming stirred all of them into lamentation.
So they mourned in his house over Hektor while he was living
still, for they thought he would never again come back from the fighting
alive, escaping the Achaian hands and their violence.

Hades: the mythological abode of the dead

About the Poem

1. Are Hector and his family close? How do you know?
2. How does Hector feel about the war he is fighting?
3. Does he believe he can win the war? Explain your answer.
4. Andromache is one of the few women who speak at length in the Iliad. What is her perspective on the war?
5. Why do you think Homer would include this scene in a story of battle?

The Death of Hector

The following excerpt is one of the iconic passages of the *Iliad*. After the death of Patroclus, Achilles finally returns to the field of battle. The Trojans, who have made many gains since he left, are driven back before his rage and many are killed. While Apollo (who supports the Trojans) distracts Achilles, the Trojans retreat through the gates of the city—all but Hector, who remains outside to fight Achilles. From atop the city walls, both his mother and father beg Hector to seek refuge within the city, knowing that no one can stand alone before Achilles. Hector refuses. The ensuing duel will decide the fate, not just of Hector, but of all Troy.

So these two* in tears and with much supplication called out
to their dear son, but could not move the spirit in Hektor,
but he awaited Achilleus as he came on, gigantic.
But as a snake waits for a man by his hole, in the mountains,
glutted with evil poisons, and the fell venom has got inside him,
and coiled about the hole he stares malignant, so Hektor
would not give ground but kept unquenched the fury within him
and sloped his shining shield against the jut of the bastion.
Deeply troubled he spoke to his own great-hearted spirit:
'Ah me! If I go now inside the wall and the gateway,
Poulydamas will be first to put a reproach upon me,
since he tried to make me lead the Trojans inside the city
on that accursed night when brilliant Achilleus rose up,
and I would not obey him, but that would have been far better.
Now, since by my own recklessness I have ruined my people,
I feel shame before the Trojans and the Trojan women with trailing
robes, that someone who is less of a man than I will say of me:
"Hektor believed in his own strength and ruined his people."
Thus they will speak; and as for me, it would be much better
at that time, to go against Achilleus, and slay him, and come back,
or else be killed by him in glory in front of the city.
Or if again I set down my shield massive in the middle
and my ponderous helm, and lean my spear up against the rampart
and go out as I am to meet Achilleus the blameless
and promise to give back Helen, and with her all her possessions,
all those things that once in the hollow ships Alexandros*
brought back to Troy, and these were the beginning of the quarrel;
to give these to Atreus' sons* to take away, and for the Achaians
also to divide up all that is hidden within the city,
and take an oath thereafter for the Trojans in conclave*
not to hide anything away, but distribute all of it,
as much as the lovely citadel keeps guarded within it;
yet still, why does the heart within me debate on these things?

these two: Priam and Hekabe, king and queen of Troy

Alexandros: another name for Paris, brother of Hektor

Atreus' sons: (uh-TRAY-oos) Agamemnon and Menelaos

in conclave: in a meeting of all the Trojans to reach official agreement

I might go up to him, and he take no pity upon me
nor respect my position, but kill me naked so, as if I were
a woman, once I stripped my armour from me. There is no
way any more from a tree or a rock to talk to him gently
whispering like a young man and a young girl, in the way
a young man and a young maiden whisper together.
Better to bring on the fight with him as soon as it may be.
We shall see to which one the Olympian grants the glory.'
 So he pondered, waiting, but Achilleus was closing upon him
in the likeness of the lord of battles, the helm-shining warrior,
and shaking from above his shoulder the dangerous Pelian
ash* spear, while the bronze that closed about him was shining
like the flare of blazing fire or the sun in its rising.
And the shivers took hold of Hektor when he saw him, and he could no longer
stand his ground there, but left the gates behind, and fled, frightened,
and Peleus'* son went after him in the confidence of his quick feet.
As when a hawk in the mountains who moves lightest of things flying
makes his effortless swoop for a trembling dove, but she slips away
from beneath and flies and he shrill screaming close after her

Pelian ash: ash wood grown on Mount Pelion

Peleus: (PEEL-ee-uhs) Achilles' father, king of the Myrmidons

Achilles statue at Corfu, Greece

plunges for her again and again, heart furious to take her;
so Achilleus went straight for him in fury, but Hektor
fled away under the Trojan wall and moved his knees rapidly.
They raced along by the watching point and the windy fig tree
always away from under the wall and along the wagon-way
and came to the two sweet-running well springs. There there are double
springs of water that jet up, the springs of whirling Skamandros.*
One of these runs hot water and the steam on all sides
of it rises as if from a fire that was burning inside it.
But the other in the summer-time runs water that is like hail
or chill snow or ice that forms from water. Beside these
in this place, and close to them, are the washing-hollows
of stone, and magnificent, where the wives of the Trojans and their lovely
daughters washed the clothes to shining, in the old days
when there was peace, before the coming of the sons of the Achaians.
They ran beside these, one escaping, the other after him.
It was a great man who fled, but far better he who pursued him
rapidly, since here was no festal beast, no ox-hide
they strove for, for these are prizes that are given men for their running.
No, they ran for the life of Hektor, breaker of horses.
As when about the turnposts racing single-foot horses
run at full speed, when a great prize is laid up for their winning,
a tripod* or a woman, in games* for a man's funeral,
so these two swept whirling about the city of Priam
in the speed of their feet, while all the gods were looking upon them.
First to speak among them was the father of gods and mortals:*
'Ah me, this is a man beloved whom now my eyes watch
being chased around the wall; my heart is mourning for Hektor
who has burned in my honour many thigh pieces of oxen
on the peaks of Ida with all her folds, or again on the uttermost
part of the citadel, but now the brilliant Achilleus
drives him in speed of his feet around the city of Priam.
Come then, you immortals, take thought and take counsel, whether
to rescue this man or whether to make him, for all his valour,
go down under the hands of Achilleus, the son of Peleus.'
Then in answer the goddess grey-eyed Athene spoke to him:
'Father of the shining bolt, dark misted, what is this you said?
Do you wish to bring back a man who is mortal, one long since
doomed by his destiny, from ill-sounding death and release him?
Do it, then; but not all the rest of us gods shall approve you.'
Then Zeus the gatherer of the clouds spoke to her in answer:
'Tritogeneia,* dear daughter, do not lose heart; for I say this
not in outright anger, and my meaning toward you is kindly.
Act as your purpose would have you do, and hold back no longer.'

Skamandros: river on the plain of Troy

tripod: a cauldron made with three feet and used in sacrifices

games: funeral games intended to honor a dead warrior

father of gods and mortals: Zeus

Tritogeneia: another name for Athena

The Iliad, Jean Leon Gerome (1824-1904)

So he spoke, and stirred on Athene, who was eager before this,
and she went in a flash of speed down the pinnacles of Olympos.
But swift Achilleus kept unremittingly after Hektor,
chasing him, as a dog in the mountains who has flushed from his covert
a deer's fawn follows him through the folding ways and the valleys,
and though the fawn crouched down under a bush and be hidden
he keeps running and noses him out until he comes on him;
so Hektor could not lose himself from swift-footed Peleion.*
If ever he made a dash right on for the gates of Dardanos*
to get quickly under the strong-built bastions, endeavouring
that they from above with missiles thrown might somehow defend him,
each time Achilleus would get in front and force him to turn back
into the plain, and himself kept his flying course next the city.
As in a dream a man is not able to follow one who runs
from him, nor can the runner escape, nor the other pursue him,
so he could not run him down in his speed, nor the other get clear.
How then could Hektor have escaped the death spirits, had not
Apollo, for this last and uttermost time, stood by him
close, and driven strength into him, and made his knees light?
But brilliant Achilleus kept shaking his head at his own people

Peleion: son of Peleus, Achilleus

gates of Dardanos: gates of the city of Troy

and would not let them throw their bitter projectiles at Hektor
for fear the thrower might win the glory, and himself come second.
But when for the fourth time they had come around to the well springs
then the Father balanced his golden scales, and in them
he set two fateful portions of death, which lays men prostrate,
one for Achilleus, and one for Hektor, breaker of horses,
and balanced it by the middle; and Hektor's death-day was heavier
and dragged downward toward death, and Phoibos* Apollo forsook him.
But the goddess grey-eyed Athene came now to Peleion
and stood close beside him and addressed him in winged words: 'Beloved
of Zeus, shining Achilleus, I am hopeful now that you and I
will take back great glory to the ships of the Achaians, after
we have killed Hektor, for all his slakeless fury for battle.
Now there is no way for him to get clear away from us,
not though Apollo who strikes from afar should be willing to undergo
much, and wallow before our father Zeus of the aegis.
Stand you here then and get your wind again, while I go
to this man and persuade him to stand up to you in combat.'
So spoke Athene, and he was glad at heart, and obeyed her,
and stopped, and stood leaning on his bronze-barbed ash spear. Meanwhile
Athene left him there, and caught up with brilliant Hektor,
and likened herself in form and weariless voice to Deïphobos.*
She came now and stood close to him and addressed him in winged words:
'Dear brother, indeed swift-footed Achilleus is using you roughly
and chasing you on swift feet around the city of Priam.
Come on, then; let us stand fast against him and beat him back from us.'
Then tall Hektor of the shining helm answered her: 'Deïphobos,
before now you were dearest to me by far of my brothers,
of all those who were sons of Priam and Hekabe, and now
I am minded all the more within my heart to honour you,
you who dared for my sake, when your eyes saw me, to come forth
from the fortifications, while the others stand fast inside them.'
Then in turn the goddess grey-eyed Athene answered him:
'My brother, it is true our father and the lady our mother, taking
my knees in turn, and my companions about me, entreated
that I stay within, such was the terror upon all of them.
But the heart within me was worn away by hard sorrow for you.
But now let us go straight on and fight hard, let there be no sparing
of our spears, so that we can find out whether Achilleus
will kill us both and carry our bloody war spoils back
to the hollow ships, or will himself go down under your spear.'
So Athene spoke and led him on by beguilement.
Now as the two in their advance were come close together,
first of the two to speak was tall helm-glittering Hektor:
Son of Peleus, I will no longer run from you, as before this

Phoibos: (FEE-buhs) a name for Apollo meaning "radiant," referring to his status as the sun god

Deïphobos: (dee-IF-o-buhs)

I fled three times around the great city of Priam, and dared not
stand to your onfall. But now my spirit in turn has driven me
to stand and face you. I must take you now, or I must be taken.
Come then, shall we swear before the gods? For these are the highest
who shall be witnesses and watch over our agreements.
Brutal as you are I will not defile you, if Zeus grants
to me that I can wear you out, and take the life from you.
But after I have stripped your glorious armour, Achilleus,
I will give your corpse back to the Achaians. Do you do likewise.'
Then looking darkly at him swift-footed Achilleus answered:
'Hektor, argue me no agreements. I cannot forgive you.
As there are no trustworthy oaths between men and lions,
nor wolves and lambs have spirit that can be brought to agreement
but forever these hold feelings of hate for each other,
so there can be no love between you and me, nor shall there be
oaths between us, but one or the other must fall before then
to glut with his blood Ares* the god who fights under the shield's guard.
Remember every valour of yours, for now the need comes
hardest upon you to be a spearman and a bold warrior.
There shall be no more escape for you, but Pallas Athene
will kill you soon by my spear. You will pay in a lump for all those
sorrows of my companions you killed in your spear's fury.'
So he spoke, and balanced the spear far shadowed, and threw it;
but glorious Hektor kept his eyes on him, and avoided it,
for he dropped, watchful, to his knee, and the bronze spear flew over his shoulder
and stuck in the ground, but Pallas Athene snatched it, and gave it
back to Achilleus, unseen by Hektor shepherd of the people.
But now Hektor spoke out to the blameless son of Peleus:
'You missed; and it was not, o Achilleus like the immortals,
from Zeus that you knew my destiny; but you thought so; or rather
you are someone clever in speech and spoke to swindle me,
to make me afraid of you and forget my valour and war strength.
You will not stick your spear in my back as I run away from you
but drive it into my chest as I storm straight in against you;
if the god gives you that; and now look out for my brazen
spear. I wish it might be taken full length in your body.
And indeed the war would be a lighter thing for the Trojans
if you were dead, seeing that you are their greatest affliction.'
So he spoke, and balanced the spear far shadowed, and threw it,
and struck the middle of Peleïdes' shield, nor missed it,
but the spear was driven far back from the shield, and Hektor was angered
because his swift weapon had been loosed from his hand in a vain cast.
He stood discouraged, and had no other ash spear; but lifting
his voice he called aloud on Deïphobos of the pale shield,

Ares: (AIR-eez) the god of war

and asked him for a long spear, but Deïphobos was not near him.
And Hektor knew the truth inside his heart, and spoke aloud:
'No use. Here at last the gods have summoned me deathward.
I thought Deïphobos the hero was here close beside me,
but he is behind the wall and it was Athene cheating me,
and now evil death is close to me, and no longer far away,
and there is no way out. So it must long since have been pleasing
to Zeus, and Zeus' son who strikes from afar, this way; though before this
they defended me gladly. But now my death is upon me.
Let me at least not die without a struggle, inglorious,
but do some big thing first, that men to come shall know of it.'
So he spoke, and pulling out the sharp sword that was slung
at the hollow of his side, huge and heavy, and gathering
himself together, he made his swoop, like a high-flown eagle
who launches himself out of the murk of the clouds on the flat land
to catch away a tender lamb or a shivering hare; so
Hektor made his swoop, swinging his sharp sword, and Achilleus
charged, the heart within him loaded with savage fury.
In front of his chest the beautiful elaborate great shield
covered him, and with the glittering helm with four horns

Athena the Defender by Leonidas Drosis (Academy of Athens)

he nodded; the lovely golden fringes were shaken about it
which Hephaistos had driven close along the horn of the helmet.
And as a star moves among stars in the night's darkening,
Hesper, who is the fairest star who stands in the sky, such
was the shining from the pointed spear Achilleus was shaking
in his right hand with evil intention toward brilliant Hektor.
He was eyeing Hektor's splendid body, to see where it might best
give way, but all the rest of the skin was held in the armour,
brazen and splendid, he stripped when he cut down the strength of
    Patroklos;
yet showed where the collar-bones hold the neck from the shoulders,
the throat, where death of the soul comes most swiftly; in this place
brilliant Achilleus drove the spear as he came on in fury,
and clean through the soft part of the neck the spearpoint was driven.
Yet the ash spear heavy with bronze did not sever the windpipe,
so that Hektor could still make exchange of words spoken.
But he dropped in the dust, and brilliant Achilleus vaunted above him:
'Hektor, surely you thought as you killed Patroklos* you would be
safe, and since I was far away you thought nothing of me,
o fool, for an avenger was left, far greater than he was,
behind him and away by the hollow ships. And it was I;
and I have broken your strength; on you the dogs and the vultures
shall feed and foully rip you; the Achaians will bury Patroklos.'
    In his weakness Hektor of the shining helm spoke to him:
'I entreat you, by your life, by your knees, by your parents,
do not let the dogs feed on me by the ships of the Achaians,
but take yourself the bronze and gold that are there in abundance,
those gifts that my father and the lady my mother will give you,
and give my body to be taken home again, so that the Trojans
and the wives of the Trojans may give me in death my rite of burning.'
But looking darkly at him swift-footed Achilleus answered:
'No more entreating of me, you dog, by knees or parents.
I wish only that my spirit and fury would drive me
to hack your meat away and eat it raw for the things that
you have done to me. So there is no one who can hold the dogs off
from your head, not if they bring here and set before me ten times
and twenty times the ransom, and promise more in addition,
not if Priam son of Dardanos should offer to weigh out
your bulk in gold; not even so shall the lady your mother
who herself bore you lay you on the death-bed and mourn you:
no, but the dogs and the birds will have you all for their feasting.'
    Then, dying, Hektor of the shining helmet spoke to him:
'I know you well as I look upon you, I know that I could not
persuade you, since indeed in your breast is a heart of iron.
Be careful now; for I might be made into the gods' curse

Patroklos: (puh-TRO-kluhs) Achilleus' dear friend killed by Hektor

Achilles Defeating Hector by Peter Paul Rubens

upon you, on that day when Paris and Phoibos Apollo
destroy you in the Skaian gates, for all your valour.'
He spoke, and as he spoke the end of death closed in upon him,
and the soul fluttering free of the limbs went down into Death's house
mourning her destiny, leaving youth and manhood behind her.
Now though he was a dead man brilliant Achilleus spoke to him:
'Die: and I will take my own death at whatever time
Zeus and the rest of the immortals choose to accomplish it.'
He spoke, and pulled the brazen spear from the body, and laid it
on one side, and stripped away from the shoulders the bloody
armour. And the other sons of the Achaians came running about him,
and gazed upon the stature and on the imposing beauty
of Hektor; and none stood beside him who did not stab him;
and thus they would speak one to another, each looking at his neighbour:
'See now, Hektor is much softer to handle than he was
when he set the ships ablaze with the burning firebrand.'
So as they stood beside him they would speak, and stab him.
But now, when he had despoiled the body, swift-footed brilliant
Achilleus stood among the Achaians and addressed them in winged words:
'Friends, who are leaders of the Argives* and keep their counsel:
since the gods have granted me the killing of this man
who has done us much damage, such as not all the others together
have done, come, let us go in armour about the city
to see if we can find out what purpose is in the Trojans,
whether they will abandon their high city, now that this man
has fallen, or are minded to stay, though Hektor lives no longer.
Yet still, why does the heart within me debate on these things?
There is a dead man who lies by the ships, unwept, unburied:
Patroklos: and I will not forget him, never so long as
I remain among the living and my knees have their spring beneath me.
And though the dead forget the dead in the house of Hades,
even there I shall still remember my beloved companion.
But now, you young men of the Achaians, let us go back, singing
a victory song, to our hollow ships; and take this with us.
We have won ourselves enormous fame; we have killed the great Hektor
whom the Trojans glorified as if he were a god in their city.'
He spoke, and now thought of shameful treatment for glorious Hektor.
In both of his feet at the back he made holes by the tendons
in the space between ankle and heel, and drew thongs of ox-hide through them,
and fastened them to the chariot so as to let the head drag,
and mounted the chariot, and lifted the glorious armour inside it,
then whipped the horses to a run, and they winged their way unreluctant.
A cloud of dust rose where Hektor was dragged, his dark hair was falling
about him, and all that head that was once so handsome was tumbled
in the dust; since by this time Zeus had given him over

Argives: the Greeks

to his enemies, to be defiled in the land of his fathers.
So all his head was dragged in the dust; and now his mother
tore out her hair, and threw the shining veil far from her
and raised a great wail as she looked upon her son; and his father
beloved groaned pitifully, and all his people about him
were taken with wailing and lamentation all through the city.
It was most like what would have happened, if all lowering
Ilion had been burning top to bottom in fire.
His people could scarcely keep the old man in his impatience
from storming out of the Dardarnian gates; he implored them
all, and wallowed in the muck before them calling on each man
and naming him by his name: 'Give way, dear friends,
and let me alone though you care for me, leave me to go out
from the city and make my way to the ships of the Achaians.
I must be suppliant to this man, who is harsh and violent,
and he might have respect for my age and take pity upon it

Achilles Fastens the Body of Hector to the Hearse by Master of Antiope

since I am old, and his father also is old, as I am,
Peleus, who begot and reared him to be an affliction
on the Trojans. He has given us most sorrow, beyond all others,
such is the number of my flowering sons he has cut down.
But for all of these I mourn not so much, in spite of my sorrow,
as for one, Hektor, and the sharp grief for him will carry me downward
into Death's house. I wish he had died in my arms, for that way
we two, I myself and his mother who bore him unhappy,
might so have glutted ourselves with weeping for him and mourning.'
So he spoke, in tears, and beside him mourned the citizens.
But for the women of Troy Hekabe led out the thronging
chant of sorrow: 'Child, I am wretched. What shall my life be
in my sorrows, now you are dead, who by day and in the night
were my glory in the town, and to all of the Trojans
and the women of Troy a blessing throughout their city. They adored you
as if you were a god, since in truth you were their high honour
while you lived. Now death and fate have closed in upon you.'
    So she spoke in tears but the wife of Hektor had not yet
heard: for no sure messenger had come to her and told her
how her husband had held his ground there outside the gates;
but she was weaving a web in the inner room of the high house,
a red folding robe, and inworking elaborate figures.
She called out through the house to her lovely-haired handmaidens
to set a great cauldron over the fire, so that there would be
hot water for Hektor's bath as he came back out of the fighting;
poor innocent, nor knew how, far from waters for bathing,
Pallas Athene had cut him down at the hands of Achilleus.
She heard from the great bastion the noise of mourning and sorrow.
Her limbs spun, and the shuttle dropped from her hand to the ground.
    Then she called aloud to her lovely-haired handmaidens: 'Come here.
Two of you come with me, so I can see what has happened.
I heard the voice of Hektor's honoured mother; within me
my own heart rising beats in my mouth, my limbs under me
are frozen. Surely some evil is near for the children of Priam.
May what I say come never close to my ear; yet dreadfully
I fear that great Achilleus might have cut off bold Hektor
alone, away from the city, and be driving him into the flat land,
might put an end to that bitter pride of courage, that always
was on him, since he would never stay back where the men were in numbers
but break far out in front, and give way in his fury to no man.'
    So she spoke, and ran out of the house like a raving woman
with pulsing heart, and her two handmaidens went along with her.
But when she came to the bastion and where the men were gathered
she stopped, staring, on the wall; and she saw him
being dragged in front of the city, and the running horses

dragged him at random toward the hollow ships of the Achaians.
The darkness of night misted over the eyes of Andromache.
She fell backward, and gasped the life breath from her, and far off
threw from her head the shining gear that ordered her headdress,
the diadem and the cap, and the holding-band woven together,
and the circlet, which Aphrodite* the golden once had given her
on that day when Hektor of the shining helmet led her forth
from the house of Eëtion, and gave numberless gifts to win her.
And about her stood thronging her husband's sisters and the wives of his brothers
and these, in her despair for death, held her up among them.
But she, when she breathed again and the life was gathered back into her,
lifted her voice among the women of Troy in mourning:
'Hektor, I grieve for you. You and I were born to a single
destiny, you in Troy in the house of Priam, and I
in Thebe, underneath the timbered mountain of Plakos
in the house of Eëtion, who cared for me when I was little,
ill-fated he, I ill-starred. I wish he had never begotten me.
Now you go down to the house of Death in the secret places
of the earth, and left me here behind in the sorrow of mourning,
a widow in your house, and the boy is only a baby
who was born to you and me, the unfortunate. You cannot help him,
Hektor, any more, since you are dead. Nor can he help you.
Though he escape the attack of the Achaians with all its sorrows,
yet all his days for your sake there will be hard work for him
and sorrows, for others will take his lands away from him.'

Aphrodite: (A-fruh-DY-tee) goddess of love and beauty

About the Poem

1. According to this excerpt, what motivates Hector to stay outside the walls and fight Achilles?
2. Why do you think Hector runs when he sees Achilles coming? How does this action affect your opinion of both characters?
3. Find and list two epic similes in the poem.
4. Does the gods' interference in this incident seem fair to you? What does Homer seem to think about it?
5. Given that the hero of an epic reflects the values of his culture, who better qualifies as the hero of the *Iliad*, Hector or Achilles? Support your answer from the story.
6. The *Iliad* addresses a common human question: If death is inevitable, then how does one live a meaningful life? What does that look like? To the ancient Greeks, the solution was to create a legacy of glorious deeds in combat. But what does a Christian solution to this problem look like? What might a Christian epic hero look like?

About the Author

Little is known of the Greek poet Homer. Many ancient sources claim that he was blind, but few agree on any other possible details of his life. Even his name may be a pseudonym. Though his birthplace and date are unknown, he is thought to have lived in the eighth century BC. Thus the legends he based the *Iliad* and the *Odyssey* on predate him considerably. But whatever the details of his life, his epics are literary treasures well worth reading. Study of them suggests that he was a master of the oral-formulaic poetry of ancient times: likely he constructed his epics from poems he had first polished and recited in verbal performances, as they reflect some of the styles and formulas of oral poetry. But Homer's epics clearly exceed the limitations of oral literature, being far more complex in plot and theme than oral poetry could sustain. Working in the budding medium of written literature, Homer unified and embellished the legendary accounts of the Trojan war and its heroes, and with his own artistic genius lifted the resulting poems into the realm of great literature. In the ranks of Western literature, his epics rightly hold a prominent place, both on their own artistic merits and by the significant contributions they have made to subsequent literature.

THINKING ZONE

All real people are complex and capable of change; however, fictional characters may or may not possess these two characteristics. In order to fully understand how characters contribute to an author's development of theme, you must learn to recognize the presence or absence of these qualities in each one.

Characters vary in complexity. **Flat characters** are those that lack complexity, being defined primarily by only one or two characteristics. Stereotypes are a somewhat negative example of flat characters, though they are certainly not the only kind. Flat characters can be very useful to authors, particularly when discussing the nature and effects of certain personality traits: for example, Aesop's grasshopper and ant are both flat characters. On the other hand, **round characters** are those who are complex in thought and behavior, with personal beliefs and desires that may even at times seem to conflict with each other. These characters are most like real people and help the author to portray a more nuanced view of life than flat characters allow.

Characters also vary in how much they change within a story. **Static characters** remain essentially the same throughout the story whereas **dynamic characters** change as the story progresses. Both types of characters can be useful in advancing the story's plot and exploring its theme. A static character who is morally good may serve as a norm by which to judge the behavior of other characters. A character who begins flawed or unlikable may learn and grow, thereby illustrating how people can change for the better. For example, the protagonist of a tragic story is often a **tragic hero**, a generally sympathetic character who usually falls into tragedy because of a personal character flaw, **his tragic flaw**: though he learns his lesson, he must still bear the consequences of his error. Authors often use characters of all four descriptions to develop the themes of their work.

1. For each of the four character types above, find a character from this unit's folktales that fits. Briefly explain your choice.
2. From what you have learned of the whole story of the *Iliad*, are the following characters **flat** or **round**, **static** or **dynamic**? (Each should have two labels.) Explain your answers.

   Achilles
   Hector
   Andromache
   Zeus

3. Who best qualifies as a **tragic hero** in the story? Explain your choice.
4. What is the hero's **tragic flaw**?

UNIT V REVIEW

Remember the Terms

Review the following terms from "Genres of Literature," "Folktale and Epic," the Thinking Zone pages, the headnotes, and the questions. Be prepared to discuss their meanings and uses.

genre
folktale
fable
beast fable
fairy tale
myth
mythology
epic
epic simile
homeric epithet
foil
archetype
characters
protagonist
antagonist
sympathetic character
unsympathetic character
character motivation
flat character
round character
static character
dynamic character
tragic hero
tragic flaw

Apply the Concepts

Answer the following questions about how the literary concepts you have studied are used in this unit.

1. What is true of the setting of most folktales, particularly fairy tales? What does this contribute to the author's message?
2. "The Ant and the Grasshopper" qualifies as what specific kind of fable? Why?
3. How does the fourth friend in "The Lion-Makers" earn readers' sympathy?
4. What kind of irony does the resolution of "The Lion-Makers" include? Explain.
5. In "The Tortoise and the Osprey," how do Tortoise's motivations contribute to the moral of the story?
6. In what way does the Tortoise's story fit in both the genre of fable and that of myth?
7. List two specific aspects or incidents of "The Pumpkin Seeds" that put it firmly in the fairy tale genre.
8. What two beliefs of Greek mythology does "Pandora" primarily describe?
9. How are character motivations important to the story "Pandora"?
10. What is the theme of "Pyramus and Thisbe"?
11. Explain how the content of the *Iliad* fits the four content conventions of epic form covered in the unit introduction.
12. List two examples of epic simile from the *Iliad*.
13. What theme does Homer highlight by including Hector's interactions with Andromache?
14. Explain how Hector's choice to fight Achilles highlights one of the three major themes of the story.

Evaluate the Ideas

Identify each of the following statements as true or false. If false, rewrite the underlined portion of the statement to make it true.

15. The lesson taught by a fable is known as its <u>thesis</u>.
16. The message of "The Ant and the Grasshopper" shows that <u>the ant</u> is at fault in the story's dilemma.
17. The narrator of "The Lion-Makers" agrees that science and learning are <u>useful</u>.
18. The character of Tortoise's wife is a foil to the <u>Osprey</u>.
19. In "The Pumpkin Seeds" the <u>injured bird</u> is an example of an archetype.
20. Zeus is <u>the antagonist</u> of "Pandora."
21. Both <u>Pandora</u> and <u>Epimetheus</u> are sympathetic characters.
22. "Pyramus and Thisbe" qualifies as a myth because it <u>includes gods and goddesses as main characters</u>.
23. The protagonists of "Pyramus and Thisbe" are best defined as <u>flat</u> and <u>static</u> characters.
24. <u>Hector</u> is the tragic hero of the *Iliad*.
25. Andromache is a <u>flat</u> and <u>static</u> character.
26. Epics are known for their <u>informal</u> style.
27. Hector believes that <u>Troy will eventually win the war</u>.
28. <u>Achilles' anger</u> drives the plot of the story.

Write a Response

Completely answer each of the following questions.

29. Compare and contrast the character of Zeus found in "Pandora" with that found in the *Iliad*.
30. What is Homer's tone toward both sides of the war (particularly as embodied in Hector and Achilles)? What beliefs about man's purpose does this tone reveal?

UNIT VI

TIGER IN A TROPICAL STORM (SURPRISED!)
Henri Rousseau

ESSAY AND SHORT STORY

French artist Henri Rousseau (1844–1910) painted in the Naïve or Primitive style. Born into a family of modest means, Rousseau never had the opportunity of formal training in art. Following high school, he worked in a lawyer's office and then served in the army before moving to Paris to take a job in the French customs office.

The recognition Rousseau sought for his work eluded him. Self-taught, Rousseau developed a unique style and technique. Lacking in accurate perspective and proportion, his work was often described as childish. Though he was ridiculed by the public and by critics, he persistently exhibited where permitted. Rousseau retired at age forty-nine to paint full time. Eventually, his persistence paid off, and Rousseau gained the respect of certain avant-garde painters, such as Picasso, whom he influenced.

Rousseau is best known for his jungle paintings, of which Tiger in a Tropical Storm (Surprised!)*, painted in 1891, was his first. These works are colorful, filled with lush vegetation and exotic creatures. Rousseau never personally saw a jungle. Rather, he studied the illustrations in books and frequented the Paris botanical gardens and zoo.*

- As with writers of short prose, artists often make every detail in their art count to convey a message. What details in Rousseau's painting communicate a sense of drama and excitement?
- Specifically what in the picture produces a strong sense of motion?
- Is the tiger surprised in Rousseau's depiction, or is prey outside the frame about to be surprised? What story do you read behind the tiger's expression? Is he frightened, or is he vicious?
- What do you notice about Rousseau's rendering of perspective in regard to the tiger?

ESSAY AND SHORT STORY

Among the three divisions of literature by form, prose is the most common both to read and to write. You are more likely to use prose than poetry when jotting a note to a family member, communicating an opinion about a particular issue, or writing a paper for a class. Likewise, prose usually makes up more of your daily reading than does poetry or drama. News articles, messages from friends, magazine stories, and novels—all fit within the broad genre of prose. The two short prose genres most frequently used in literature today are the essay and the short story.

Essay

As a student you are undoubtedly familiar with the term *essay* and have probably been assigned to write essays of various sorts. However, the genre encompasses much more than school assignments. An extremely versatile form, it is well-beloved by many serious writers, and when done well, easily rises to the level of literature.

As a literary genre the **essay** is a short prose composition that aims to discuss or explore a subject in an unsystematic or nontechnical way. It sacrifices the thoroughness of a scientific study in favor of expressing the author's opinions or thoughts on the matter at hand. The essayist has tremendous freedom both in content and form and can address virtually any topic in a variety of ways. From politics to picket fences, from debt to dolphins, from Verdi to video games—no topic is too complex or too mundane as long as it has sparked the interest of the essayist who has a point to express or a thesis to propound.

Essays divide broadly into two types, differing primarily in voice, tone, and structure. First, a **formal essay** possesses an impersonal but authoritative voice and a serious tone. Usually, the writer is well-versed in his topic and seeks to inform or persuade his audience regarding his position on it. Thus, he organizes his structure methodically to stress the logical train of thought. Many articles in serious journals fall into this category. For example, the scientific essay "The Spider and the Wasp" (Unit I) illustrates a formal essay, one which has clearly risen to the level of literature. In the past the formal essay dominated literary writing, but you are now more likely to encounter the second type, the informal essay.

The **informal** or **personal essay** is usually relaxed and unpretentious, stated in the author's own voice and addressed to an individual—to you, the reader, rather than to readers as a whole. This reader is taken into the confidence of the author, who shares some of his or her experience and thoughts in a more or less disconnected way. Typically, these essays begin with an anecdote and conclude with some kind of comment. This comment may relate to conduct or attitude or may be a general observation on life. Ranging in mood from vivacious to seriously reflective, keenly earnest to subdued, the essay may reenact a suspenseful experience or calmly reminisce. In any case, it has a point to make, one made all the more effectively because the reader is simultaneously taught and entertained. The informal essay's quirky movement—with sudden breaks in thought, parenthetical interruptions, and afterthoughts—may give it the appearance of an informal chat. But mere chat it is not. To the writer, the end is always in view. The randomness is only apparent.

Though literary essays vary between formal and informal, both kinds will usually include many of the elements of literature you have already studied. For example, G. K. Chesterton's "A Piece of Chalk" (Unit III) is a beautiful and well-crafted example of essay that contains multiple examples of irony, allusion, symbol, and imaginative comparison. In addition, Chesterton deftly makes use of syntax and sound devices to adorn his writing and emphasize his ideas.

Short Story

Whereas the essay is generally nonfictional, the **short story** is fictional prose. While real people or events may have inspired the author, a short story is essentially a product of the author's imagination. Though short narrative has a long history, encompassing everything from the factual biblical stories of Esther, Ruth, and Jonah to folktales and narrative ballads, it was not until the early 1800s that the short story emerged in the form we recognize today.

In its basic characteristics, the modern short story is much like the novel: the author combines imagined characters and actions to form a plot, a series of events arranged to produce a definite sense of movement toward a specific goal. The goal may be simply a resolution of conflict, but in literary novels and short stories, the author has a theme in mind as well. Both genres may focus on resolving either outward events or characters' internal conflicts. Thus, on the surface, the primary distinction of the short story is its shorter length. However, this one difference inevitably leads to others.

A short story contains the same basic elements that a novel does: setting, conflict, characters, theme, and tone. But all of these must be abbreviated or adjusted to achieve the desired effects within the genre's constraints. The setting cannot be described at length and therefore rarely varies greatly. In many cases, it works double time to convey the author's atmosphere and tone (see setting in Poe's "The Masque of the Red Death"). The cast of characters must be kept to a minimum, and the author must delineate the basic qualities of each in brief strokes or within events. Small statements, gestures, or looks become shorthand for broader meanings. Time is at a premium, so portions of the plot must be greatly compressed. The exposition and dénouement may be completed in a few sentences, and the action often focuses on only one incident. In the short story, nothing is extra; everything must count.

So why do writers willingly accept such constraints and choose the short story over the novel? And what is the appeal for readers? For readers, the short story is certainly easier to read, and the payoff of conflict resolved and theme communicated comes far more quickly than in a novel. For writers, the short story is perhaps more difficult to write well (creating an enjoyable challenge for some). However, it is also a logical choice for the author who wants to quickly highlight one idea or hammer one theme. Were the writer a photographer, his short story would be one meaningful image that comes sharply into focus versus the myriad snapshots in the gallery of the novel. As with the essayist, the skillful short story writer can delight or disturb, but he will rarely fail to get a response, for good literature always invites a response.

As you read the selections in this unit, notice the special features of the genre the author chose to use. How does the form of the work reveal or reinforce its theme? Can you spot the overall design the author uses to communicate the message? Does the genre seem to limit the author in any way? Do you think another genre would have been more effective? Aside from form, what other characteristics in the essay or story mark it as a work of literature?

How to Get Things Done

ROBERT BENCHLEY

If this essay, originally published in the *Chicago Tribune* in 1930, were not in the ironic mode, it might be entitled "Procrastination." Clearly, even professional writers such as the humorist Benchley sometimes find it hard to get down to the business of writing. As you read, notice the essay's informal nature with its chatty voice, humorous tone, and seemingly scattered delivery.

A great many people have come up to me and asked me how I manage to get so much work done and still keep looking so dissipated.* My answer is "Don't you wish you knew?" and a pretty good answer it is, too, when you consider that nine times out of ten I didn't hear the original question.

dissipated: used up, wasted

But the fact remains that hundreds of thousands of people throughout the country are wondering how I have time to do all my painting, engineering, writing and philanthropic work when, according to the rotogravure* sections and society notes I spend all my time riding to hounds, going to fancy-dress balls disguised as Louis XIV or spelling out *Greetings to California* in formation with three thousand Los Angeles school children. "All work and all play," they say.

rotogravure: newspaper section dedicated to photographs

The secret of my incredible energy and efficiency in getting work done is a simple one. I have based it very deliberately on a well-known psychological principle and have refined it so that it is now almost *too* refined. I shall have to begin coarsening it up again pretty soon.

The psychological principle is this: anyone can do any amount of work, provided it isn't the work he is supposed to be doing at the moment.

Let us see how this works out in practice. Let us say that I have five things which have to be done before the end of the week: (1) a basketful of letters to be answered, some of them dating from October, 1928, (2) some bookshelves to be put up and arranged with books (3) a haircut to get (4) a pile of scientific magazines to go through and clip (I am collecting all references to tropical fish that I can find, with the idea of some day buying myself one) and (5) an article to write for this paper.

Now. With these five tasks staring me in the face on Monday morning, it is little wonder that I go right back to bed as soon as I have had breakfast, in order to store up health and strength for the almost superhuman expenditure of energy that is to come. *Mens sana in corpore sano** is my motto, and, not even to be funny, am I going to believe that I don't know what the Latin means. I feel that the least that I can do is to treat my body right when it has to supply fuel for an insatiable mind like mine.

Mens sana in corpore sano: "sound mind in a sound body," quotation from Juvenal

As I lie in bed on Monday morning storing up strength, I make out a schedule. "What do I have to do first?" I ask myself. Well, those letters really should be answered and the pile of scientific magazines should be clipped. And here is where my secret process comes in. Instead of putting them first on the list of things which have to be done, I put them last. I practice a little deception on myself and say: "First you must write that article for the newspaper." I even say this out loud (being careful that nobody hears me, otherwise they would keep me in bed) and try to fool myself into really believing that I

must do the article that day and that the other things can wait. I sometimes go so far in this self-deception as to make out a list in pencil, with "No. 1. Newspaper article" underlined in red. (The underlining in red is rather difficult, as there is never a red pencil on the table beside the bed, unless I have taken one to bed with me on Sunday night.)

Then, when everything is lined up, I bound out of bed and have lunch. I find that a good, heavy lunch, with some sort of glutinous dessert, is good preparation for the day's work as it keeps one from getting nervous and excitable. We workers must keep cool and calm, otherwise we would just throw away our time in jumping about and fidgeting.

I then seat myself at my desk with my typewriter before me and sharpen five pencils. (The sharp pencils are for poking holes in the desk-blotter, and a pencil has to be pretty sharp to do that. I find that I can't get more than six holes out of one pencil.) Following this I say to myself (again out loud, if it is practical) "Now, old man! Get at this article!"

Gradually the scheme begins to work. My eye catches the pile of magazines, which I have artfully placed on a nearby table beforehand. I write my name and address at the top of the sheet of paper in the typewriter and then sink back. The magazines being within reach (also part of the plot) I look to see if anyone is watching me and get one off the top of the pile. Hello, what's this! In the very first one is an article by Dr. William Beebe, illustrated by horrifying photographs! Pushing my chair away from my desk, I am soon hard at work clipping. One of the interesting things about the Argyopelius, or "Silver Hatchet" fish, I find, is that it has eyes in its wrists. I would have been sufficiently surprised just to find out that a fish had wrists, but to learn that it has eyes in them is a discovery so astounding that I am hardly able to cut out the picture. What a lot one learns simply by thumbing through the illustrated weeklies! It is hard work, though, and many a weaker spirit would give it up half-done, but when there is something else of "more importance" to be finished (you see, I still keep up the deception, letting myself go on thinking that the newspaper article is of more importance) no work is too hard or too onerous* to keep one busy.

onerous: burdensome

Thus, before the afternoon is half over, I have gone through the scientific magazines and have a neat pile of clippings (including one of a Viper Fish which I wish you could see. You would die laughing). Then it is back to the grind of the newspaper article.

This time I get as far as the title, which I write down with considerable satisfaction until I find that I have misspelled one word terribly, so that the whole sheet of paper has to come out and a fresh one be inserted. As I am doing this, my eye catches the basket of letters.

Now if there is one thing that I hate to do (and there is, you may be sure) it is to write letters. But somehow, with the magazine article before me waiting to be done, I am seized with an epistolary* fervor which amounts to a craving, and I slyly sneak the first of the unanswered letters out of the basket. I figure out in my mind that I will get more into the swing of writing the article if I practice a little on a few letters. The first one, anyway, I really must answer. True, it is from a friend in Antwerp asking me to look him up when I am in Europe in the summer of 1929, so he can't actually be watching the incoming boats for an answer, but I owe something to politeness after all.

epistolary: associated with letters or the writing of letters

So instead of putting a fresh sheet of copy-paper into the typewriter, I slip in one of my handsome bits of personal stationery and dash off a note to my friend in Antwerp. Then, being well in the letter-writing mood, I clean up the entire batch. I feel a little guilty about the article, but the pile of freshly stamped envelopes and the neat bundle of clippings on tropical fish do much to salve my conscience. Tomorrow I will do the article, and no fooling this time either.

When tomorrow comes I am up with one of the older and more sluggish larks. A fresh sheet of copy-paper in the machine, and my name and address neatly printed at the top, and all before eleven A.M.! "A human dynamo" is the name I think up for myself. I have decided to write something about snake charming and am already more than satisfied with the title "These Snake-Charming People." But in order to write about snake charming, one has to know a little about its history, and where should one go to find history but a book? Maybe in that pile of books in the corner is one on snake charming! Nobody could point the finger of scorn at me if I went over to those books for the avowed purpose of research work for the matter at hand. No writer could be supposed to carry all that information in his head.

So, with a perfectly clear conscience, I leave my desk for a few minutes and begin glancing over the titles of the books. Of course, it is difficult to find any book, much less one on snake charming, in a pile which has been standing in the corner for weeks. What really is needed is for them to be on a shelf where their titles will be visible at a glance. And there is the shelf, standing beside the pile of books! It seems almost like a divine command written in the sky: "If you want to finish that article, first put up the shelf and arrange the books on it!" Nothing could be clearer or more logical.

In order to put up the shelf, the laws of physics have decreed that there must be nails, a hammer and some sort of brackets to hold it up on the wall. You can't just wet a shelf with your tongue and stick it up. And, as there are no nails or brackets in the house (or, if there are, they are probably hidden somewhere) the next thing to do is put on my hat and go out to buy them. Much as it disturbs me to put off the actual start of the article, I feel that I am doing only what is in the line of duty to put on my hat and go out to buy nails and brackets. And, as I put on my hat, I realize to my chagrin that I need a haircut badly. I can kill two birds with one stone, or at least with two, and stop in at the barber's on the way back. I will feel all the more like writing after a turn in the fresh air. Any doctor would tell me that.

So in a few hours I return, spick and span and smelling of lilac, bearing nails, brackets, the evening papers and some crackers and peanut butter. Then it's ho! for a quick snack and a glance through the evening papers (there might be something in them which would alter what I was going to write about snake charming) and in no time at all the shelf is up, slightly crooked but up, and the books are arranged in a neat row in alphabetical order and all ready for almost instantaneous reference. There does not happen to be one on snake charming among them, but there is a very interesting one containing some Hogarth prints and one which will bear even closer inspection dealing with the growth of the Motion Picture, illustrated with "stills" from famous productions. A really remarkable industry, the motion pictures. I might want to write an article on it sometime. Not today, probably, for it is six o'clock and there is still the one on snake charming to finish up first. Tomorrow morning sharp! Yes, *sir*!

And so, you see, in two days I have done four of the things I had to do, simply by making believe that it was the fifth that I *must* do. And the next day, I fix up something else, like taking down the bookshelf and putting it somewhere else, that I *have* to do, and then I get the fifth one done.

The only trouble is that, at this rate, I will soon run out of things to do, and will be forced to get at that newspaper article first thing Monday morning.

About the Essay

1. Identify two allusions in the essay.
2. Humorous exaggeration is often the first signal of the ironic mode. Where does irony first appear in the essay?
3. What specific kinds of irony can be found in "How to Get Things Done"?
4. Benchley's essay is informal. Would a formal essay have been more effective? Why or why not?

About the Author

American essayist Robert Benchley (1889–1945) had a genius for turning the frustrations of the average middle-class American into delightful comic material. He gained a solid reputation as a highly original humorist. His versatility and wit were evident even in his undergraduate days at Harvard, where Benchley employed his talent for humor in the school's plays and comic magazine. After college, Benchley took several unfulfilling jobs until his introduction into journalism on the staff of the *New York Tribune* in 1916.

After World War I, Benchley served as editor and contributor to a succession of well-known periodicals, eventually publishing fifteen collections of humorous essays written in his polished but informal style. He was also noted for his work on the stage and in film and radio. Despite his public success, however, Benchley never felt as if he had taken full advantage of his opportunities to excel as a writer. He resembled his own characters in his penchant for procrastination. But he always had time for people, and he had many devoted friends. Benchley's whimsical advice on "how to get things done" fits well with the challenging motto he kept over his desk: "The work can wait."

A Miserable Merry Christmas

LINCOLN STEFFENS

In this selection, Steffens recounts for us a boyhood experience that maintained its emotional impact for him even into adulthood. Interestingly, all but the last paragraph is written from a child's perspective. This autobiographical essay may at first seem purely narrative, but notice how Steffens manages to convey universal thoughts about children, mothers, and fathers, as well as the relationships between them all.

What interested me in our new neighborhood was not the school, nor the room I was to have in the house all to myself, but the stable which was built back of the house. My father let me direct the making of a stall, a little smaller than the other stalls, for my pony, and I prayed and hoped and my sister Lou believed that that meant that I would get the pony, perhaps for Christmas. I pointed out to her that there were three other stalls and no horses at all. This I said in order that she should answer it. She could not. My father, sounded,* said that someday we might have horses and a cow; meanwhile a stable added to the value of a house. "Someday" is a pain to a boy who lives in and knows only "now." My good little sisters, to comfort me, remarked that Christmas was coming, but Christmas was always coming and grownups were always talking about it, asking you what you wanted and then giving you what they wanted you to have. Though everybody knew what I wanted, I told them all again. My mother knew that I told God, too, every night, I wanted a pony, and to make sure that they understood, I declared that I wanted nothing else.

sounded: trying to learn how one feels about something

"Nothing but a pony?" my father asked.

"Nothing," I said.

"Not even a pair of high boots?"

That was hard. I did want boots, but I stuck to the pony. "No, not even boots."

"Nor candy? There ought to be something to fill your stocking with, and Santa Claus can't put a pony into a stocking."

That was true, and he couldn't lead a pony down the chimney either. But no: "All I want is a pony," I said. "If I can't have a pony, give me nothing, nothing."

Now, I had been looking myself for the pony I wanted, going to sales stables, inquiring of horsemen, and I had seen several that would do. My father let me "try" them. I tried so many ponies that I was learning fast to sit a horse. I chose several, but my father always found some fault with them. I was in despair. When Christmas was at hand I had given up hope of a pony, and on Christmas Eve I hung up my stocking along with my sisters, of whom, by the way, I now had three. I haven't mentioned them or their coming because, you understand, they were girls, and girls, young girls, counted for nothing in my manly life. They did not mind me either; they were so happy that Christmas Eve that I caught some of their merriment. I speculated on what I'd get; I hung up the biggest stocking I had, and we all went reluctantly to bed to wait till morning. Not to sleep; not right away. We were told that we must not only sleep promptly, we must not wake up till seven-thirty the next morning—or if we did, we must not go to the fireplace for our Christmas. Impossible.

We did sleep that night, but we woke up at 6 A.M. We lay in our beds and debated through the open doors whether to obey till, say, half-past six.

Then we bolted. I don't know who started it, but there was a rush. We all disobeyed; we raced to disobey and get first to the fireplace in the front room downstairs. And there they were, the gifts, all sorts of wonderful things, mixed-up piles of presents; only, as I disentangled the mess, I saw that my stocking was empty; it hung limp, not a thing in it, and under and around it—nothing. My sisters had knelt down, each by her pile of gifts; they were squealing with delight, till they looked up and saw me standing there in my nightgown with nothing. They left their piles to come to me and look with me at my empty place. Nothing. They felt my stocking: nothing.

I don't remember whether I cried at that moment, but my sisters did. They ran with me back to my bed, and there we all cried till I became indignant. That helped some. I got up, dressed, and, driving my sisters away, I went alone out into the yard, down to the stable, and there, all by myself, I wept. My mother came out to me by and by; she found me in my pony stall, sobbing on the floor, and she tried to comfort me. But I heard my father outside; he had come part way with her, and she was having some sort of angry quarrel with him. She tried to comfort me; besought me to come to breakfast. I could not; I wanted no comfort and no breakfast. She left me and went on into the house with sharp words for my father.

I don't know what kind of breakfast the family had. My sisters said it was "awful." They were ashamed to enjoy their own toys. They came to me, and I was rude. I ran away from them. I went around to the front of the house, sat down on the steps, and, the crying over, I ached. I was wronged, I was hurt—I can feel now what I felt then, and I am sure that if one could see the wounds upon our hearts, there would be found still upon mine a scar from that terrible Christmas morning. And my father, the practical joker, he must have been hurt, too, a little. I saw him looking out of the window. He was watching me or something for an hour or two, drawing back the curtain ever so little lest I catch him, but I saw his face, and I think I can see now the anxiety upon it, the worried impatience.

After—I don't know how long—surely an hour or two—I was brought to the climax of my agony by the sight of a man riding a pony down the street, a pony and a brand-new saddle, the most beautiful saddle I ever saw, and it was a boy's saddle; the man's feet were not in the stirrups; his legs were too long. The outfit was perfect; it was the realization of all my dreams, the answer to all my prayers. A fine new bridle, with a little curb bit. And the pony! As he drew near, I saw that the pony was really a small horse, what we called an Indian pony, a bay, with black mane and a tail, and one white foot and a white star on his forehead. For such a horse as that, I would have given, I could have forgiven anything.

But the man, a disheveled fellow with a blackened eye and a fresh-cut face, came along, reading the numbers on the houses, and, as my hopes—my impossible hopes—rose, he looked at our door and passed by, he and the pony, and the saddle and the bridle. Too much. I fell upon the steps, and having wept before, I broke now into such a flood of tears that I was a floating wreck when I heard a voice.

"Say, kid," it said, "do you know a boy named Lennie Steffens?"

I looked up. It was the man on the pony, back again, at our horse block.

"Yes," I sputtered through my tears. "That's me."

"Well," he said, "then this is your horse. I've been looking all over for you and your house. Why don't you put your number where it can be seen?"

"Get down," I said running out to him.

He went on saying something about "ought to have got here at seven o'clock; told me to bring the nag here and tie him to your post and leave him for you. But I got into a fight—and a hospital, and—"

"Get down," I said.

He got down, and he boosted me up to the saddle. He offered to fit the stirrups to me, but I didn't want him to. I wanted to ride.

"What's the matter with you?" he said angrily. "What you crying for? Don't you like the horse? He's a dandy, this horse. I know him of old. He's fine at cattle; he'll drive 'em alone."

I hardly heard, I could scarcely wait, but he persisted. He adjusted the stirrups, and then, finally, off I rode, slowly, at a walk, so happy, so thrilled, that I did not know what I was doing. I did not look back at the house or the man; I rode off up the street, taking note of everything—of the reins, of the pony's long mane, of the carved leather saddle. I had never seen anything so beautiful. And mine! I was going to ride up past Miss Kay's house. But I noticed on the horn of the saddle some stains like raindrops, so I turned and trotted home, not to the house but to the stable. There was the family, father, mother, sisters, all working for me, all happy. They had been putting in place the tools of my new business: blankets, currycomb, brush, pitchfork—everything, and there was hay in the loft.

"What did you come back so soon for?" somebody asked. "Why didn't you go on riding?"

I pointed to the stains. "I wasn't going to get my new saddle rained on," I said. And my father laughed.

"It isn't raining," he said. "Those are not raindrops."

"They are tears," my mother gasped, and she gave my father a look which sent him off to the house. Worse still, my mother offered to wipe away the tears still running out of my eyes. I gave her such a look as she had given him, and she went after my father, drying her own tears. My sisters remained and we all unsaddled the pony, put on his halter, led him to his stall, tied and fed him. It began really to rain; so all the rest of that memorable day we curried and combed that pony. The girls plaited his mane, forelock, and tail, while I pitchforked hay to him and curried and brushed, curried and brushed. For a change we brought him out to drink; we led him up and down, blanketed like a race horse; we took turns at that. But the best, the most inexhaustible fun, was to clean him. When we went reluctantly to our midday Christmas dinner, we all smelt of horse, and my sisters had to wash their faces and hands. I was asked to, but I wouldn't, till my mother bade me look in the mirror. Then I washed up—quick. My face was caked with the muddy lines of tears that had coursed over my cheeks to my mouth. Having washed away that shame, I ate my dinner, and, as I ate, I grew hungrier and hungrier. It was my first meal that day, and as I filled up on the turkey and the stuffing, the cranberries and the pies, the fruit and the nuts—as I swelled, I could laugh. My mother said I still choked and sobbed now and then, but I laughed, too; I saw and enjoyed my sisters' presents till—I had to go out and attend to my pony, who was there, really and truly there, the promise, the beginning, of a happy double life. And—I went and looked to make sure—there was the saddle, too, and the bridle.

But that Christmas, which my father had planned so carefully, was it the best or the worst I ever knew? He often asked me that; I never could answer as a boy. I think now that it was both. It covered the whole distance from brokenhearted misery to bursting happiness—too fast. A grownup could hardly have stood it.

About the Essay

1. What does Lennie say that he doesn't really mean? What is Lennie's response to an empty stocking at Christmas?
2. Steffens's title is a good illustration of what literary device?
3. Identify one type of irony illustrated in the story. Explain your answer.
4. What literary device illustrated in the quotation below gives readers hope for Lennie?

    > I saw [my father] looking out of the window. He was watching me or something for an hour or two, drawing back the curtain ever so little lest I catch him, but I saw his face, and I think I can see now the anxiety upon it, the worried impatience.

5. Imagine yourself as Lennie's father. Would you ever play a similar joke? Why or why not?

About the Author

In *Autobiography*, the book from which "A Miserable Merry Christmas" is taken, Lincoln Steffens (1866–1936) tells us of two of his greatest passions: horses and books. "As a boy I would ride far, far away to some spot, give my pony a long rope to swing round on, and let him feed on the grass, while I sat and did nothing but muse. I read a great deal. Finding that books fed my fancies, I would take one along, and finding a quiet nook, I read. And my reading always gave me something to be. I liked to change the hero I was to the same thing on horseback, and once wholly in the part, I would remount my pony and be Napoleon, or Richard the Lion-hearted, or Byron, so completely that any actual happening would wake me up dazed as from a dreaming sleep."

Steffens spent much of his adult life as a reporter and editor of such widely read magazines as the *New York Evening Post* and *McClure's*. But his name was also linked with the Muckrakers, a group of American writers in the early 1900s who endeavored to expose corruption in business and government. Steffens's influence and power were considerable. His impatience for change, however, caused him to join many others in their support of the fledgling Communist movement. Many well-meaning but naïve writers initially joined this movement, hoping it would accomplish the reforms for which they had so diligently worked.

Over ten years later, after much hardship and disillusionment, Steffens began his autobiography. His purpose in writing it was to give his son and others a chance to benefit from his lifetime of hard lessons. Steffen's initial title for the book, *A Life of Unlearning*, indicates the nature of those lessons.

An Old-Fashioned Iowa Christmas

Paul Engle

Unlike Steffens, Paul Engle includes in his topical essay the many pleasant aspects he remembers of family Christmases. Based on his general experiences, he puts forth a clear message. The central contrast is temporal: Christmas years ago and Christmas now. Obviously Engle prefers what he considers the good old days. He makes his preference clear in a statement repeated several times with slight modification. This statement also introduces the main units of the description. Within these units the organization is either spatial (city streets and country roads, barn and house) or temporal (before, during, and after dinner).

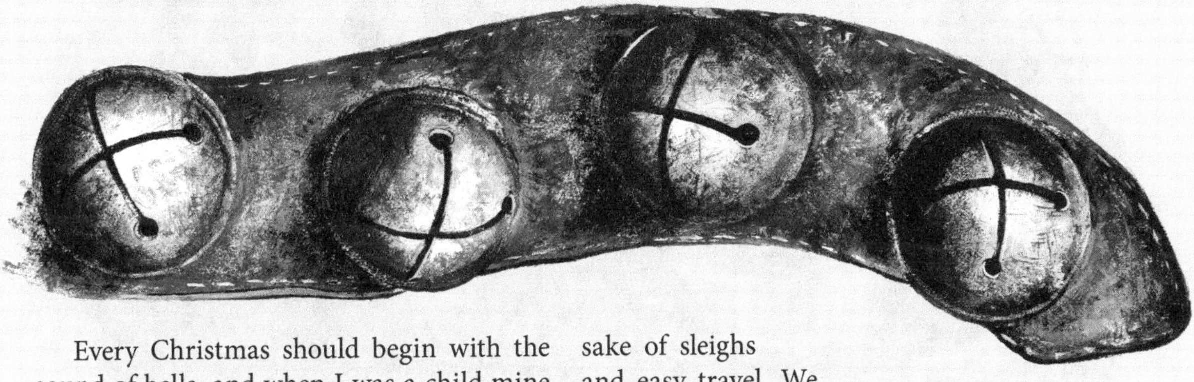

Every Christmas should begin with the sound of bells, and when I was a child mine always did. But they were sleigh bells, not church bells, for we lived in a part of Cedar Rapids, Iowa, where there were no churches. My bells were on my father's team of horses as he drove up to our horseheaded hitching post with the bobsled that would take us to celebrate Christmas on the family farm ten miles out in the country. My father would bring the team down Fifth Avenue at a smart trot, flicking his whip over the horses' rumps and making the bells double their light, thin jangling over the snow.

There are no such departures any more: the whole family piling into the bobsled with a foot of golden oat straw to lie in and heavy buffalo robes to lie under, the horses stamping the soft snow, and at every motion of their hoofs the bells jingling, jingling.

There are no streets like those any more: the snow sensibly left on the road for the sake of sleighs and easy travel. We could hop off and ride the heavy runners as they made their hissing, tearing sound over the packed snow. And along the streets we met other horses, so that we moved from one set of bells to another. There would be an occasional brass-mounted automobile laboring on its narrow tires and as often as not pulled up the slippery hills by a horse, and we would pass it with a triumphant shout for an awkward nuisance which was obviously not here to stay.

The country road ran through a landscape of little hills and shallow valleys and heavy groves of timber. The great moment was when we left the road and turned up the long lane on the farm. Near the low house on the hill, with oaks on one side and apple trees on the other, my father would stand up, flourish his whip, and bring the bobsled right up to the door of the house with a burst of speed.

There are no such arrivals any more: the harness bells ringing and clashing like faraway steeples, the horses whinnying at the horse in the barn and receiving a great, trumpeting whinny in reply, the dogs leaping into the bobsled and burrowing under the buffalo robes, a squawking from the hen house, a yelling of "Whoa, whoa," at the excited horses, boy and girl cousins howling around the bobsled, and the descent into the snow with the Christmas basket carried by my mother.

While my mother and sisters went into the house, the team was unhitched and taken to the barn to be covered with blankets and given a little grain. That winter odor of a barn is a wonderfully complex one, rich and warm and utterly unlike the smell of the same barn in summer: the body heat of many animals weighing a thousand pounds and more; pigs in one corner making their dark, brown-sounding grunts; milk cattle still nuzzling the manger for wisps of hay; horses eying the newcomers; oats, hay, and straw, tangy still with the live August sunlight; the sharp odor of leather harness rubbed with neat's-foot oil to keep it supple; the molasses-sweet odor of ensilage* in the silo where the fodder was almost fermenting. It is a smell from strong and living things, and my father always said it was the secret of health, that it scoured out a man's lungs. He would stand there, breathing deeply, one hand on a horse's rump, watching the steam come out from under the blankets as the team cooled down from their rapid trot up the lane. It gave him a better appetite, he argued, than plain fresh air, which was thin and had no body to it.

ensilage: fodder kept in a silo

A barn with the cattle and horses is the place to begin Christmas; after all, that's where the original event happened, and that same smell was the first air that the Christ Child breathed.

By the time we reached the house, my mother and sisters were wearing aprons and busying themselves in the kitchen, as red-faced as the women who had been there all morning. The kitchen was the biggest room in the house, and all family life save sleeping went on there. My uncle even had a couch along one wall where he napped and where the children lay when they were ill. The kitchen range was a tremendous black and gleaming one called a Smoke Eater, with pans bubbling over the holes above the fire box and a reservoir of hot water at the side, lined with dull copper, from which my uncle would dip a basin of water and shave above the sink, turning his lathered face now and then to drop a remark into the women's talk, waving his straight-edged razor, as if it were a threat, to make them believe him. My job was to go to the woodpile out back to split the chunks of oak and hickory and keep the fire burning.

It was a handmade Christmas. The tree came from down in the grove, and on it were many paper ornaments made by my cousins, as well as beautiful ones brought from the Black Forest* where the family originally lived. There were popcorn balls, paper horns with homemade candy, and apples from the orchard. The gifts tended to be hand-knit socks or wool ties or fancy crocheted "yokes" for nightgowns, tatted collars for blouses, doilies with fancy flower patterns for tables, and tidies* for chairs. Once I received a brilliantly polished cow horn with a cavalryman crudely but bravely carved on it. And there would usually be a cornhusk doll, perhaps with a prune or walnut for a face, and a gay dress of an old corset-cover scrap with its ribbons still bright. And there were real candles burning with real flames, every guest sniffing the air for the smell of scorching pine needles.

Black Forest: mountainous region in southwestern Germany

tidy: a decorative protective covering for the armrest or headrest of a chair

There are no dinners like that any more: every item from the farm itself, with no deep freezer, no car for driving into town for packaged food. The pies had been baked the day before, pumpkin, apple, and mince; as we ate them, we could look out the window and see the cornfield where the pumpkins grew, the trees from which the apples were picked. The bread had been baked that morning, heating up the oven for the meat, and as my aunt hurried by I could smell in her apron that freshest of all odors with which the human nose is honored—bread straight from the oven. There would be a huge brown crock of beans with smoked pork from the hog butchered every November.

There would be every form of preserve: wild grape from the vines in the grove, crab-apple jelly, wild blackberry and tame raspberry, strawberry from the bed in the garden, sweet and sour pickles with dill from the edge of the lane where it grew wild, pickles from the rind of the same watermelon we had cooled in the tank at the milk house and eaten on a hot September afternoon.

Cut into the slope of the hill behind the house, with a little door of its own, was the vegetable cellar, from which came carrots, turnips, cabbages, potatoes, squash. And of course there was the traditional sauerkraut, with flecks of caraway seed. I remember one Christmas Day when a ten-gallon crock of it in the basement, with a stone weighing down the lid, had blown up, driving the stone against the floor of the parlor.

All the meat was from the home place, too. Most useful of all was the goose—the very one which had chased me the summer before, hissing and darting out its bill at the end of its curving neck like a feathered snake. Here was the universal bird of an older Christmas: its down was plucked, washed, and hung in bags in the barn to be put into pillows; its awkward body was roasted until the skin was crisp as a fine paper; and the grease from its carcass was melted down, a little camphor added, and rubbed on the chests of coughing children. We ate, slept on, and wore that goose.

And of course the trimmings were from the farm, too: the hickory-nut cake made with nuts gathered in the grove after the first frost and hulled out by my cousins with yellowed hands; the black-walnut cookies, sweeter than any taste; the fudge with butternuts crowding it. In the mornings we would be given a hammer, a flatiron, and a bowl of nuts to crack and pick out for the homemade ice cream.

All families had their special Christmas food. Ours was called Dutch bread, made from a dough halfway between bread and cake, stuffed with citron and every sort of nut from the farm—hazel, black walnut, hickory, butternut. A little round one was always baked for me in a baking-soda can, and my last act on Christmas Eve was to put it by the tree so that Santa Claus would find it and have a snack—after all, he'd come a long, cold way to our house. And every Christmas morning, he would have eaten it. My aunt made the same Dutch bread and we smeared over it the same butter she had been churning from their own Jersey milk that same morning.

To eat in the same room where food is cooked—that is the way to thank the Lord for His abundance. The long table, with its different levels where additions had been made for the small fry,* ran the length of the kitchen. The air was heavy with odors, not only of food on plates but of the act of cooking itself along with the metallic smell of heated iron from the hard-working Smoke Eater, and the whole stove offered us its yet uneaten prospects of more goose and untouched pies. To see the giblet gravy made and poured into a gravy boat is the surest way to overeat its swimming richness.

small fry: young children

The warning for Christmas dinner was always an order to go to the milk house for cream, where we skimmed from the cooling pans of fresh milk the cream which had the same golden color as the flanks of the Jersey cows which had given it. The last deed before eating was grinding the coffee beans in the little mill, adding that exotic odor to the more native ones of goose and spiced pumpkin pie. Then all would sit at the table and my uncle would ask the grace, sometimes in German, but later, for the benefit of us ignorant children, in English:

Come, Lord Jesus, be our guest,
Share this food that you have blessed.

My aunt kept a turmoil of food circulating, and to refuse any of it was somehow to violate the elevated nature of the day. To consume the length and breadth of that meal was to suffer! But we all faced the ordeal with courage. Uncle Ben would let out his belt—a fancy Western belt with steer heads and silver buckle—with a snap and a sigh. The women managed better by always getting up from the table and trotting to the kitchen sink or the Smoke Eater or outdoors for some item left in the cold. The men sat there, grimly enduring the glory of their appetites.

After dinner, late in the afternoon, the women would make despairing gestures toward the dirty dishes and scoop up hot water from the reservoir at the side of the range. The men would go to the barn and look after the livestock. My older cousin would take his new .22 rifle and stalk out across the pasture with the remark, "I saw that fox just now, looking for his Christmas goose." Or sleds would be dragged out and we would slide in a long snake, feet hooked into the sled behind, down the hill and across the westward sloping fields into the sunset. Bones would be thrown to the dogs, suet* tied in the oak trees for the juncos* and winter-defying chickadees, a saucer of skimmed milk set out for the cats, daintily and disgustedly picking their padded feet through the snow, and crumbs scattered on a bird feeder where already the crimson cardinals would be dropping out of the sky like blood. Then back to the house for a final warming up before leaving.

suet: fatty tissue from the kidneys of cattle and sheep, used in cooking and making candles

juncos: North American birds of the genus *Junco*, having predominantly gray plumage

There was usually a song around the tree before we were all bundled up, many thanks all around for gifts, the basket loaded as when it came, more so, for leftover food had been piled in it. My father and uncle would have brought up the team from the barn and hooked them into the double shafts of the bobsled, and we would all go out into the freezing air of early evening.

And now those bells again as the horses, impatient from their long standing in the barn, stamped and shook their harness, my father holding them back with a soft clucking in his throat and a hard pull on the reins. The smell of wood smoke flavoring the air in our noses, the cousins shivering with cold, "Good-bye, good-bye," called out by everyone, and the bobsled would move off, creaking over the frost-brittle snow. All of us, my mother included, would dig down in the straw and pull the buffalo robes up to our chins. As the horses settled into a steady trot, the bells gently chiming in their rhythmical beat, we would fall half asleep, the hiss of the runners comforting. As we looked up at the night sky through half-closed eyelids, the constant bounce and swerve of the runners would seem to shake the little stars as if they would fall into our laps. But the one great star in the East never wavered. Nothing could shake it from the sky as we drifted home on Christmas.

About the Essay

1. The essay is organized by syntactically parallel topic sentences. List two.
2. Find two examples of simile in the essay.
3. Which of the five senses are represented in the essay's imagery? Which sense is especially emphasized?
4. Discuss the aspect of Engle's old-fashioned Christmas that made the biggest impression on you.

About the Author

In addition to prose, Paul Engle (1908–91) wrote poetry and drama. He also edited a variety of books and literary periodicals. His poetry is thought by many to be the successor of Walt Whitman's optimistic style. In over a dozen volumes of poetry, Engle expressed his deeply felt reactions to American life. The longer Engle wrote, the closer he came to the concentrated, powerful form he desired.

His best work, however, drew inspiration from his memories of life in Iowa and his belief in the values of the American Dream (prosperity through energetic effort). His sense of American idealism was attacked by critics accustomed to the cynicism and defeatism of contemporary American writing. Despite such criticism, however, Engle's straightforward style of writing and teaching garnered important awards. His influence on aspiring writers continued late in his life through his position as professor and director of creative writing at the University of Iowa and through his work in the university's famous Iowa Writers' Workshop.

Why the Leaves Turn Color in the Fall

Diane Ackerman

The following excerpt is taken from *A Natural History of the Senses*. Though basically explaining a natural phenomenon, this scientific essay, with its imaginative comparisons, sound devices, and concrete imagery, rises to the level of literature. Be alert for points where the essay deviates from science and enters the area of personal opinion. Does the essay make a point?

The stealth of autumn catches one unaware. Was that a goldfinch perching in the early September woods, or just the first turning leaf? A red-winged blackbird or a sugar maple closing up shop for the winter? Keen-eyed as leopards, we stand still and squint hard, looking for signs of movement. Early-morning frost sits heavily on the grass, and turns barbed wire into a string of stars. On a distant hill, a small square of yellow appears to be a lighted stage. At last the truth dawns on us: Fall is staggering in, right on schedule, with its baggage of chilly nights, macabre* holidays, and spectacular, heart-stoppingly beautiful leaves. Soon the leaves will start cringing on the trees, and roll up in clenched fists before they actually fall off. Dry seedpods will rattle like tiny gourds. But first there will be weeks of gushing color so bright, so pastel, so confettilike, that people will travel up and down the East Coast just to stare at it—a whole season of leaves.

macabre: frightful, ghastly

Where do the colors come from? Sunlight rules most living things with its golden edicts. When the days begin to shorten, soon after the summer solstice on June 21, a tree reconsiders its leaves. All summer it feeds them so they can process sunlight, but in the dog days of summer the tree begins pulling nutrients back into its trunk and roots, pares down, and gradually chokes off its leaves. A corky layer of cells forms at the leaves' slender petioles,* then scars over. Undernourished, the leaves stop producing the pigment chlorophyll,* and photosynthesis* ceases. Animals can migrate, hibernate, or store food to prepare for winter. But where can a tree go? It survives by dropping its leaves, and by the end of autumn only a few fragile threads of fluid-carrying xylem* hold leaves to their stems.

petioles: the stalk attaching a leaf to a stem
chlorophyll: green pigment found in plants
photosynthesis: the process by which plants produce food from sunlight
xylem: the woody, water-carrying tissue of plants

A turning leaf stays partly green at first, then reveals splotches of yellow and red as the chlorophyll gradually breaks down. Dark green seems to stay longest in the veins, outlining and defining them. During the summer, chlorophyll dissolves in the heat and light, but it is also being steadily replaced. In the fall, on the other hand, no new pigment is produced, and so we notice the other colors that were always there, right in the leaf, although chlorophyll's shocking green hid them from view. With their camouflage gone, we see these colors for the first time all year, and marvel, but they were always there, hidden like a vivid secret beneath the hot glowing greens of summer.

The most spectacular range of fall foliage occurs in the northeastern United States and in eastern China, where the leaves are robustly colored thanks in part to a rich climate. European maples don't achieve the same flaming reds as their American relatives, which thrive on cold nights and sunny days. In Europe, the warm, humid weather turns the leaves brown or mildly yellow. Anthocyanin, the pigment that gives apples their red and turns leaves red or red-violet, is produced by sugars that remain in the leaf after the supply of nutrients dwindles. Unlike the carotenoids, which color carrots, squash, and corn, and turn leaves orange and yellow, anthocyanin varies from year to year, depending on the temperature and amount of sunlight. The fiercest colors occur in years when the fall sunlight is strongest and the nights are cool and dry (a state of grace scientists find vexing to forecast). This is also why leaves appear dizzyingly bright and clear on a sunny fall day: The anthocyanin flashes like a marquee.

Not all leaves turn the same color. Elms, weeping willows, and the ancient ginkgo all grow radiant yellow, along with hickories, aspens, bottlebrush buckeyes, cottonweeds, and tall, keening poplars. Basswood turns bronze, birches bright gold. Water-loving maples put on a symphonic display of scarlets. Sumacs turn red, too, as do flowering dogwoods, black gums, and sweet gums. Though some oaks yellow, most turn a pinkish brown. The farmlands also change color, as tepees of cornstalks and bales of shredded-wheat-textured hay stand drying in the fields. In some spots, one slope of a hill may be green and the other already in bright color, because the hillside facing south gets more sun and heat than the northern one.

An odd feature of the colors is that they don't seem to have any special purpose. We are predisposed to respond to their beauty, of course. They shimmer with the colors of sunset, spring flowers, the tawny buff of a colt's pretty rump, the shuddering pink of a blush. Animals and flowers color for a reason—adaptation to their environment—but there is no adaptive reason for leaves to color so beautifully in the fall any more than there is for the sky or ocean to be blue. It's just one of the haphazard marvels the planet bestows every year. We find the sizzling colors thrilling, and in a sense they dupe us. Colored like living things, they signal death and disintegration. In time, they will become fragile and, like the body, return to dust. They are as we hope our own fate will be when we die; not to vanish, just to sublime from one beautiful state into another. Though leaves lose their green life, they bloom with urgent colors, as the woods grow mummified day by day, and Nature becomes more carnal, mute, and radiant.

We call the season "fall," from the Old English *feallan*, to fall, which leads back through time to the Indo-European *phol*, which also means to fall. So the word and the idea are both extremely ancient, and haven't really changed since the first of our kind needed a name for fall's leafy abundance. As we say the word, we're reminded of that other Fall, in the Garden of Eden, when fig leaves never withered and scales fell from our eyes. Fall is the time when leaves fall from the trees, just as spring is when flowers spring up, summer is when we simmer, and winter is when we whine from the cold.

Children love to play in piles of leaves, hurling them into the air like confetti, leaping into soft unruly mattresses of them. For children, leaf fall is just one of the odder figments of Nature, like hailstones or snowflakes. Walk down a lane overhung with trees in the never-never land of autumn, and you will forget about time and death, lost in the sheer delicious spill of color. Adam and Eve concealed their nakedness with a leaf, remember? Leaves have always hidden our awkward secrets.

But how do the colored leaves fall? As a leaf ages, the growth hormone, auxin, fades, and cells at the base of the petiole divide. Two or three rows of small cells, lying at right angles to the axis of the petiole, react with water, then come apart, leaving the petioles hanging on by only a few threads of xylem. A light breeze, and the leaves are airborne. They glide and swoop, rocking in invisible cradles. They are all wing and may flutter from yard to yard on small whirlwinds or updrafts, swiveling as they go. Firmly tethered to earth, we love to see things rise up and fly—soap bubbles, balloons, birds, fall leaves. They remind us that the end of a season is capricious, as is the end of life. We especially like the way leaves rock, careen, and swoop as they fall. Everyone knows the motion. Pilots sometimes do a maneuver called a "falling leaf," in which the plane loses altitude quickly and on purpose, by slipping first to the right, then to the left. The machine weighs a ton or more, but in one pilot's mind it is a weightless thing, a falling leaf. She has seen the motion before, in the Vermont woods where she played as a child. Below her the trees radiate gold, copper, and red. Leaves are falling, although she can't see them fall, as she falls, swooping down for a closer view.

At last the leaves leave. But first they turn color and thrill us for weeks on end. Then they crunch and crackle underfoot. They *shush*, as children drag their small feet through leaves heaped along the curb. Dark, slimy mats of leaves cling to one's heels after a rain. A damp, stuccolike mortar of semidecayed leaves protects the tender shoots with a roof until spring, and makes a rich humus. An occasional bulge or ripple in the leafy mounds signals a shrew or a field mouse tunneling out of sight. Sometimes one finds in fossil stones the imprint of a leaf, long since disintegrated, whose outlines remind us how detailed, vibrant, and alive are the things of this earth that perish.

About the Essay

1. In one sentence explain why leaves turn color.
2. Identify the type of imaginative comparison illustrated in the following quotation: "[Was that] a sugar maple closing up shop for the winter?" Find an additional example of this kind of imaginative comparison in the essay.
3. Identify the type of imaginative comparison illustrated in the following quotation: "The anthocyanin flashes like a marquee." Find an additional example of this kind of imaginative comparison in the first three paragraphs of the essay.
4. Ackerman uses the technical explanation of leaves turning color to comment on life and death. How does Ackerman view death? Do you agree with her assessment? Why or why not?
5. Respond to the following ideas in the essay: "Animals and flowers color for a reason—adaptation to their environment—but there is no adaptive reason for leaves to color so beautifully in the fall any more than there is for the sky or ocean to be blue. It's just one of the haphazard marvels the planet bestows every year." Do you concur?

About the Author

As a writer, Diane Ackerman (b. 1948) blends science and poetry in an easily accessible style. She began writing during her childhood, the first eight years of which were spent in Illinois, before the family's move to Pennsylvania. Later, Ackerman attended Pennsylvania State University, earning a BA in English. She subsequently earned an MFA, an MA, and then, in 1978, a PhD from Cornell University. In the years following Ackerman has taught at various universities, including Cornell, and has contributed to many periodicals, including *National Geographic, Discover, Parade,* and *The New Yorker.*

Ackerman has written more than a dozen books—some poetry and some nonfiction. Described as poet, essayist, and naturalist, she often communicates a child's sense of wonder in her writing. Poetry is sometimes found in her nonfiction works, and scientific topics thought unsuitable for poetry have occupied her poetry. Ackerman is best known for *A Natural History of the Senses.*

THINKING ZONE

At some point, you've probably heard someone say, "Everybody loves a good story!" But have you ever wondered what exactly makes a story good? At its base, a story is simply the relation of a sequence of events. But a truly good story, one that qualifies as literature, must have something more. A well-written narrative contains the structural element of plot.

In any narrative, whether prose, poetry, or drama, the plot in many ways molds the major elements of the work. Simply defined, **plot** is a series of events arranged to produce a definite sense of movement toward a specific goal. In other words, the incidents serve a common purpose: to further develop the conflicts, characters, and themes of the story. Character revelation and growth, conflict resolution, thematic meaning—all of these both motivate and benefit from the movement of the plot. In some complex narratives the author also weaves in a secondary plot strand, or **subplot**, that connects to the plot in location, time, or theme, but often centers on secondary characters. A master craftsman such as Dickens or Shakespeare may thread multiple subplots through the main plot of a novel or a play. However, subplots are rarely found in short stories because of the genre's brevity.

Many narrative works begin with an **exposition**, which introduces the reader to the setting, characters, and situation of the story. Modern short stories may, however, begin abruptly *in medias res* ("in the middle" of events). The **inciting incident**, an event that sets the conflict in motion, follows. The plot thickens with the **rising action**, various obstacles or complications that the central character must overcome, and leads to the **crisis**, the major turning point for the protagonist. This is the point at which something happens that affects the outcome of the story and determines the future of the protagonist. The crisis is not the same thing as the **climax**, the point at which the plot reaches the moment of highest emotional intensity for the reader (though the climax often coincides with the crisis or the dénouement). The events that unfold the results of the crisis and lead to the conclusion are known as the **falling action**. The **dénouement**, or resolution, is the final outcome of a story and the last element of the plot. The dénouement explains or settles the major complications, tying up any loose ends. Though plots may vary in how distinct these different stages are or how much time is spent on each, narratives of literary quality will always include plot as an integral unifying factor.

1. Identify the **crisis** and the **climax** of "A Miserable Merry Christmas."
2. Identify the part of the **plot** structure to which the following information belongs: The man on the pony should have arrived at 7:00 but had gotten into a fight and had gone to the hospital.
3. What is the conflict in "How to Get Things Done"? How is the conflict resolved, and what do you think of the conflict's resolution?
4. What is the **inciting incident** in "How to Get Things Done"?

The Sire de Maletroit's Door

ROBERT LOUIS STEVENSON

"The Sire de Maletroit's Door" is a delightful adventure set in fifteenth-century France. It is among the earliest examples of modern short fiction. In this story, Stevenson's characters and scenes are realistically drawn. His plot, however, is typical of the Romantic movement, relying on incidents that are emotionally dynamic rather than rationally controlled. As you read, note how Stevenson must compress his plot as well as his descriptions of setting, characters, and conflict. How might this story be different were it written in novel form?

Denis de Beaulieu was not yet two-and-twenty, but he counted himself a grown man, and a very accomplished cavalier into the bargain. Lads were early formed in that rough, warfaring epoch; and when one has been in a pitched battle and a dozen raids, has killed one's man in an honorable fashion, and knows a thing or two of strategy and mankind, a certain swagger in the gait is surely pardoned. He had put up his horse with due care, and supped with due deliberation; and then, in a very agreeable frame of mind, went out to pay a visit in the gray of the evening. It was not a very wise proceeding on the young man's part. He would have done better to remain beside the fire or go decently to bed. For the town was full of troops of Burgundy and England* under a mixed command; and though Denis was there on safe-conduct,* his safe-conduct was like to serve him little on a chance encounter.

Burgundy and England: The Duke of Burgundy, a Frenchman, was an ally of England for a time.

safe-conduct: the protection that a document of safe conduct provides a person passing through a military zone or occupied area

It was September, 1429; the weather had fallen sharp; a flighty, piping wind, laden with showers, beat about the township; and the dead leaves ran riot along the streets. Here and there a window was already lighted up, and the noise of men-at-arms, making merry over supper within, came forth in fits and was swallowed up and carried away by the wind. The night fell swiftly; the flag of England, fluttering on the spire top, grew even fainter and fainter against the flying clouds,—a black speck like a swallow in the tumultuous, leaden chaos of the sky. As the night fell the wind rose and began to hoot under archways and roar amid the tree-tops in the valley below the town.

Denis de Beaulieu walked fast and was soon knocking at his friend's door; but though he promised himself to stay only a little while and make an early return, his welcome was so pleasant, and he found so much to delay him, that it was already long past midnight before he said good-bye upon the threshold. The wind had fallen again in the meanwhile; the night was as black as the grave; not a star, nor a glimmer of moonshine, slipped through the canopy of cloud. Denis was ill acquainted with the intricate lanes of Chateau Landon; even by daylight he had found some trouble in picking his way; and in this absolute darkness he soon lost it altogether. He was certain of one thing only,—to keep mounting the hill; for his friend's house lay at the lower end, or tail, of Chateau Landon, while the inn was up at the head, under the great church spire. With this clue to go upon he stumbled and groped forward, now breathing more freely in the open places where there was a good slice of sky overhead, now feeling along the wall in stifling closes.* It is an eerie and mysterious position to be thus submerged in opaque blackness in an almost unknown town. The silence is terrifying in its possibilities. The touch of cold window bars to the exploring hand startles the man like a touch of a toad; the inequalities of the pavement shake his heart into his mouth; a piece of denser darkness threatens an ambush or a chasm in the pathway; and where the air is brighter, the houses put on strange and bewildering appearances, as if to lead him further from his way. For Denis, who had to regain his inn without attracting notice, there was real danger as well as mere discomfort in the walk, and he went warily and boldly at once, and at every corner paused to make an observation.

stifling closes: narrow passageways or alleys

He had been for some time threading a lane so narrow that he could touch a wall with either hand, when it began to open out and go sharply downward. Plainly this lay no longer in the direction of his inn, but the hope of a little more light tempted him forward to reconnoitre.* The land ended in a terrace with a bartizan wall,* which gave an outlook between high houses, as out of an embrasure,* into the valley lying dark and formless several hundred feet below. Denis looked down, and could discern a few tree-tops waving and a single speck of brightness where the river ran across a weir.* The weather was clearing up, and the sky had lightened, so as to show the outline of heavier clouds and the dark margin of the hills. By the uncertain glimmer the house on his left hand should be a place of some pretensions; it was surmounted by several pinnacles and turret-tops; the round stern of a chapel, with a fringe of flying buttresses,* projected boldly from the main block, and the door was sheltered under a deep porch carved with figures and overhung by two long gargoyles.* The windows of the chapel gleamed through their intricate tracery with a light as of many tapers, and threw out the buttresses and the peaked roof in a more intense blackness against the sky. It was plainly the mansion of some great family of the neighborhood, and as it reminded Denis of a town house of his own at Bourges, he stood for some time gazing up at it and mentally gauging the skill of the architects and the consideration* of the two families.

reconnoitre: to make a careful inspection of

bartizan wall: a small overhanging wall

embrasure: an opening in a wall for a door, window, or gun position

weir: a fence or dam placed in a stream or river to retain fish or divert the water

flying buttress: a masonry structure to brace a roof or arch

gargoyle: a grotesquely carved water spout projecting from a roof gutter

consideration: high regard or importance

There seemed to be no issue* to the terrace but the land by which he had reached it; he could only retrace his steps, but he had gained some notion of his whereabouts, and hoped by this means to hit the main thoroughfare and speedily regain the inn. He was reckoning without that chapter of accidents which was to make this night memorable above all others in his career; for he had not gone back above a hundred yards before he saw a light coming to meet him and heard loud voices speaking together in the echoing narrows of the lane. It was a party of men-at-arms going the night round with torches. Denis assured himself that they had all been making free with the wine-bowl and were in no mood to be particular about safe-conducts or the niceties of chivalrous war. It was as like as not that they would kill him like a dog and leave him where he fell. The situation was both inspiring and frightening. Their own torches would conceal him from sight, he reflected; and he hoped that they would drown the noise of his footsteps with their own empty voices. If he were but fleet and silent, he might evade their notice altogether.

issue: outlet

Unfortunately, as he turned to beat a retreat, his foot rolled upon a pebble; he fell against the wall with an ejaculation, and his sword rung loudly on the stones. Two or three voices demanded who went there—some in French, some in English; but Denis made no reply, and ran the faster down the lane. Once upon the terrace, he paused to look back. They still kept calling after him and just then began to double the pace in pursuit, with a considerable clank of armor and great tossing of the torchlight to and fro in the narrow jaws of the passage.

Denis cast a look around and darted into the porch. There he might escape observation, or—if that were too much to expect—was in a capital posture whether for parley* or defense. So thinking, he drew his sword and tried to set his back against the door. To his surprise it yielded behind his weight and, though he turned in a moment, continued to swing back on oiled and noiseless hinges until it stood wide open on a black interior. When things fall out opportunely for the person concerned, he is not apt to be critical about how or why, his own immediate personal convenience seeming a sufficient reason for the strangest oddities and revolutions in our sublunary* things; and so Denis, without a moment's hesitation, stepped within and partly closed the door behind him to conceal his place of refuge. Nothing was further from his thoughts than to close it altogether; but for some inexplicable reason—perhaps by a spring or a weight—the ponderous mass of oak whipped itself out of his fingers and clanked to, with a formidable rumble and a noise like the falling of an automatic bar.

parley: discussion
sublunary: of this earth

The round,* at that very moment, debouched upon the terrace* and proceeded to summon him with shouts and curses. He heard them ferreting* in the dark corners; the stock of a lance even rattled along the outer surface of the door behind which he stood; but these gentlemen were in too high a humor to be long delayed, and soon made off down a corkscrew pathway which had escaped Denis's observation, and passed out of sight and hearing along the battlements of the town.

round: group of soldiers making the night round
debouched . . . terrace: moved from the confined alley onto the terrace
ferreting: searching

Denis breathed again. He gave them a few minutes' grace for fear of accidents, and then groped about for some means of opening the door and slipping forth again. The inner surface was quite smooth,—not a handle, not a moulding, not a projection of any sort. He got his finger-nails round the edges and pulled, but the mass was immovable. He shook it, it was as firm as a rock. Denis de Beaulieu frowned and gave vent to a little noiseless whistle. What ailed the door, he wondered. Why was it open? How came it to shut so easily and so effectually after him? There was something obscure and underhand about all this, that was little to the young man's fancy. It looked like a snare in such a quiet by-street and in a house of so prosperous and even noble an exterior. And yet—snare or no snare, intentionally or unintentionally—here he was, prettily trapped; and for the life of him he could see no way out of it again. The darkness began to weigh upon him. He gave ear; all was silent without, but within and close by he seemed to catch a faint sighing, a faint sobbing rustle, a little stealthy creak—as though many persons were at his side, holding themselves quite still, and governing even their respiration with extreme slyness. The idea went to his vitals with a shock, and he faced about suddenly as if to defend his life. Then for the first time he became aware of a light about the level of his eyes and at some distance in the interior of the house—a vertical thread of light, widening toward the bottom, such as might escape between two wings of arras* over a doorway.

arras: a tapestry usually hung on the wall

To see anything was a relief to Denis; it was like a piece of solid ground to a man laboring in a morass*; his mind seized upon it with avidity,* and he stood staring at it trying to piece together some logical conception of his surroundings. Plainly there was a flight of steps ascending from his own level to that of this illuminated doorway, and indeed he thought he could make out another thread of light, as fine as a needle and as faint as phosphorescence, which might very well be reflected along the polished wood of a handrail. Since he had begun to suspect that he was not alone, his heart had continued to beat with smothering violence, and an intolerable desire for action of any sort had possessed itself of his spirit. He was in deadly peril, he believed. What could be more natural than to mount the staircase, lift the curtain, and confront his difficulty at once? At least he would be dealing with something tangible; at least he would no longer be in the dark. He stepped slowly forward with outstretched hands, until his foot struck the bottom step; then he rapidly scaled the stairs, stood for a moment to compose his expression, lifted the arras, and went in.

morass: soggy ground
avidity: eagerness

He found himself in a large apartment of polished stone. There were three doors, one on each of three sides, all similarly curtained with tapestry. The fourth side was occupied by two

large windows and a great stone chimney-piece, carved with arms of the Maletroits. Denis recognized the bearings and was gratified to find himself in such good hands. The room was strongly illuminated, but it contained little furniture except a heavy table and a chair or two, the hearth was innocent of fire, and the pavement was but sparsely strewn with rushes clearly many days old.

On a high chair beside the chimney, and directly facing Denis as he entered, sat a little old gentleman in a fur tippet.* He sat with his legs crossed and his hands folded, and a cup of spiced wine stood by his elbow on a bracket on the wall. His countenance had a strong masculine cast,—not properly human, but such as we see in the bull, the goat, or the domestic boar,—something equivocal* and wheedling, something greedy, brutal, and dangerous. The upper lip was inordinately full, as though swollen by a blow or a toothache; and the smile, the peaked eyebrows, and the small, strong eyes were quaintly and almost comically evil in expression. Beautiful white hair hung straight all round his head, like a saint's, and fell in a single curl upon the tippet. His beard and moustache were the pink of venerable sweetness. Age, probably in consequence of inordinate precautions, had left no mark upon his hands; and the Maletroit hand was famous. It would be difficult to imagine anything at once so fleshy and so delicate in design; the tapered, sensual fingers were like those of one of Leonardo's women; the fork of the thumb made a dimpled protuberance* when closed; the nails were perfectly shaped, and of a dead, surprising whiteness. It rendered his aspect tenfold more redoubtable* that a man with hands like these should keep them devoutly folded like a virgin martyr,—that a man with so intent and startling expression of face should sit patiently on his seat and contemplate people with an unwinking stare, like a god, or a god's statue. His quiescence* seemed ironical and treacherous, it fitted so poorly with his looks.

tippet: a scarf for the shoulders
equivocal: capable of misleading
protuberance: bulging
redoubtable: fear arousing
quiescence: inactivity

Such was Alain, Sire de Maletroit.

Denis and he looked silently at each other for a second or two.

"Pray step in," said the Sire de Maletroit. "I have been expecting you all the evening."

He had not risen, but he accompanied his words with a smile and a slight but courteous inclination of the head. Partly from the smile, partly from the strange musical murmur with which the sire prefaced his observation, Denis felt a strong shudder of disgust go through his marrow. And what with disgust and honest confusion of mind, he could scarcely get words together in reply.

"I fear," he said, "that this is a double accident. I am not the person you suppose me. It seems you were looking for a visit; but for my part, nothing was further from my thoughts—nothing could be more contrary to my wishes—than this intrusion."

"Well, well," replied the old gentleman indulgently, "here you are, which is the main point. Seat yourself, my friend, and put yourself entirely at your ease. We shall arrange our little affairs presently."

Denis perceived that the matter was still complicated with some misconception, and he hastened to continue his explanations.

"Your door," he began.

"About my door?" asked the other, raising his peaked eyebrows. "A little piece of ingenuity." And he shrugged his shoulders. "A hospitable fancy! By your own account, you were not desirous of making my acquaintance. We old people look for such reluctance now and then; when it touches our honor, we cast about until we find some way of overcoming it. You arrive uninvited, but believe me, very welcome."

"You persist in error, sir," said Denis. "There can be no question between you and me. I am a stranger in this countryside. My name is Denis damoiseau* de Beaulieu. If you see me in your house it is only—"

damoiseau: a young nobleman

"My young friend," interrupted the other, "you will permit me to have my own ideas on that subject. They probably differ from yours at the present moment," he added with a leer, "but time will show which of us is in the right."

Denis was convinced he had to do with a lunatic. He seated himself with a shrug, content to wait the upshot, and a pause ensued, during which he thought he could distinguish a hurried gabbling as of a prayer from behind the arras immediately opposite him. Sometimes there seemed to be but one person engaged, sometimes two; and the vehemence of the voice, low as it was, seemed to indicate either great haste or agony of spirit. It occurred to him that this piece of tapestry covered the entrance to the chapel he had noticed from without.

The old gentleman meanwhile surveyed Denis from head to foot with a smile, and from time to time emitted little noises like a bird or a mouse, which seemed to indicate a high degree of satisfaction. This state of matters became rapidly insupportable; and Denis, to put an end to it, remarked politely that the wind had gone down.

The old gentleman fell into a fit of silent laughter, so prolonged and violent that he became quite red in the face. Denis got upon his feet at once, and put on his hat with a flourish.

"Sir," he said, "if you are in your wits, you have affronted me grossly. If you are out of them, I flatter myself I can find better employment for my brains than to talk with lunatics. My conscience is clear; you have made a fool of me from the first moment; you have refused to hear my explanations; and now there is no power under God will make me stay here any longer; and if I cannot make my way out in a more decent fashion, I will hack your door in pieces with my sword."

The Sire de Maletroit raised his right hand and wagged it at Denis with the fore and little fingers extended.

"My dear nephew," he said, "sit down."

"Nephew!" retorted Denis, "You lie in your throat"; and he snapped his fingers in his face.

"Sit down, you rogue!" cried the old gentleman, in a sudden, harsh voice, like the barking of a dog. "Do you fancy," he went on, "that when I had made my little contrivance for the door I had stopped short with that? If you prefer to be bound hand and foot till your bones ache, rise and try to go away. If you choose to remain a free young buck, agreeably conversing with an old gentleman—why, sit where you are in peace, and God be with you."

"Do you mean I am a prisoner?" demanded Denis.

"I state the facts," replied the other. "I would rather leave the conclusion to yourself."

Denis sat down again. Externally he managed to keep pretty calm, but within, he was now boiling with anger, now chilled with apprehension. He no longer felt convinced that he was dealing with a madman. And if the old gentleman was sane, what had he to look for? What absurd or tragical adventure was he to assume?

While he was thus unpleasantly reflecting, the arras that overhung the chapel door was raised, and a tall priest in his robes came forth, and, giving a long, keen stare at Denis, said something in an undertone to Sire de Maletroit.

"She is in a better frame of spirit?" asked the latter.

"She is more resigned, messire," replied the priest.

"Now, the Lord help her, she is hard to please!" sneered the old gentleman. "A likely stripling—not ill-born—and of her own choosing, too! Why, what more would the jade* have?"

jade: willful young lady

"The situation is not usual for a young damsel," said the other, "and somewhat trying to her blushes."

"She should have thought of that before she began to dance! It was none of my choosing; but since she is in it, she shall carry it to the end." And then addressing Denis, "Monsieur de Beaulieu," he asked, "may I present you my niece? She has been waiting your arrival, I may say, with even greater impatience than myself."

Denis had resigned himself with a good grace—all he desired to know was the worst of it as speedily as possible; so he rose at once, and bowed in acquiescence. The Sire de Maletroit followed his example and limped, with the assistance of the chaplain's arm, toward the chapel door. The priest pulled aside the arras, and all three entered. The building had considerable architectural pretensions. A light groining* sprung from six stout columns, and hung down in two rich pendants from the center of the vault. The place terminated behind the altar in a round end, embossed and honeycombed with a superfluity* of ornament in relief, and pierced by many little windows shaped like stars, trefoils,* or wheels. These windows were imperfectly glazed, so that the night air circulated freely in the chapel. The tapers, of which there must have been half a hundred burning on the altar, were unmercifully blown about; and the light went through many different phases of brilliancy and semi-eclipse. On the steps in front of the altar knelt a young girl richly attired as a bride. A chill settled over Denis as he observed her costume; he fought with desperate energy against the conclusion that was being thrust upon his mind; it could not—it should not—be as he feared.

groining: curved edge formed at the meeting of two vaults
superfluity: excess
trefoil: architectural forms having the appearance of three leaflets

"Blanche," said the sire, in his most flute-like tones, "I have brought a friend to see you, my little girl; turn round and give him your pretty hand. It is good to be devout; but it is necessary to be polite, my niece."

The girl rose to her feet and turned towards the newcomers. She moved all a piece; and shame and exhaustion were expressed in every line of her fresh young face; she kept her eyes upon the pavement, as she came slowly forward. In the course of her advance her eyes fell upon Denis de Beaulieu's feet—feet of which he was justly vain, be it remarked, and wore in the most elegant accoutrement even while travelling. She paused—startled, as if his yellow boots had conveyed some shocking meaning—and glanced suddenly up into the wearer's countenance. Their eyes met; shame gave place to horror and terror in her looks; the blood left her lips; with a piercing scream she covered her face with her hands and sank upon the chapel floor.

"That is not the man!" she cried. "My uncle, that is not the man!"

The Sire de Maletroit chirped agreeably. "Of course not," he said; "I expected as much. It was so unfortunate you could not remember his name."

"Indeed," she cried, "indeed, I have never so much as set eyes upon him—I never wish to see him again. Sir," she said, turning to Denis, "if you are a gentleman, you will bear me out. Have I ever seen you—have you ever seen me—before this accursed hour?"

"To speak for myself, I have never had that pleasure," answered the young man. "This is the first time, messire, that I have met with your engaging niece."

The old gentleman shrugged his shoulders.

"I am distressed to hear it," he said. "But it is never too late to begin. I had little more acquaintance with my own late lady ere I married her; which proves," he added, with a grimace, "that these impromptu marriages may often produce an excellent understanding in the long run. As the bridegroom is to have a voice in the matter, I will give him two hours to make up for lost time before we proceed with the ceremony." And he turned toward the door, followed by the clergyman.

The girl was on her feet in a moment. "My uncle, you cannot be in earnest," she said. "I declare before God I will stab myself rather than be forced on that young man. The heart rises at it; God forbids such marriages; you dishonor your white hair. Oh, my uncle, pity me! There is not a woman in all the world but would prefer death to such a nuptial. Is it possible," she added, faltering—" is it possible that you do not believe me—that you still think this"—and she pointed at Denis with a tremor of anger and contempt—"that you still think this to be the man?"

"Frankly," said the old gentleman, pausing on the threshold, "I do. But let me explain to you once for all, Blanche de Maletroit, my way of thinking about the affair. When you took it into your head to dishonor my family and the name I have borne, in peace and war, for more than threescore years, you forfeited, not only the right to question my designs, but that of looking me in the face. If your father had been alive, he would have spat on you and turned you out of doors. His was the hand of iron. You may bless your God you have only to deal with the hand of velvet, mademoiselle. It was my duty to get you married without delay. Out of pure good-will I have tried to find your own gallant for you. And I believe I have succeeded. But Blanche de Maletroit, if I have not, I care not one jackstraw.* So let me recommend you to be polite to our young friend: for, upon my word, your next groom may be less appetizing."

jackstraw: thin stick used in the game of jackstraw

And with that he went out, with the chaplain at his heels; and the arras fell behind the pair.

The girl turned upon Denis with flashing eyes.

"And what, sir," she demanded, "may be the meaning of all this?"

"Heaven knows," returned Denis, gloomily. "I am a prisoner in this house, which seems full

of mad people. More I know not; and nothing do I understand."

He told her as briefly as he could. "For the rest," he added, "perhaps you will follow my example, and tell me the answer to all these riddles, and what is like to be the end of it."

She stood silent for a little, and he could see her lips tremble and her tearless eyes burn with a feverish luster. Then she pressed her forehead in both hands.

"Alas, how my head aches!" she said, wearily, "to say nothing of my poor heart! But it is due to you to know my story, unmaidenly as it must seem. I am called Blanche de Maletroit; I have been without father or mother for—oh! for as long as I can recollect, and indeed I have been most unhappy all my life. Three months ago a young captain began to stand near me every day in church. I could see that I pleased him; I am much to blame, but I was so glad that anyone should love me; and when he passed me a letter, I took it home with me and read it with great pleasure. Since that time he has written many. He was so anxious to speak with me, poor fellow! and kept asking me to leave the door open some evening that we might have two words upon the stair. For he knew how much my uncle trusted me." She gave something like a sob at that, and it was a moment before she could go on. "My uncle is a hard man, but he is very shrewd," she said at last. "He has performed many feats in war, and was a great person at court, and much trusted by Queen Isabeau in old days. How he came to suspect me I cannot tell; but it is hard to keep anything from his knowledge; and this morning, as we came from mass, he took my hand in his, forced it open, and read my little billet,* walking by my side all the while.

billet: short letter

"When he finished, he gave it back to me with great politeness. It contained another request to have the door left open; and this has been the ruin of us all. My uncle kept me strictly in my room until evening, and then ordered me to dress myself as you see me—a hard mockery for a young girl, do you not think so? I suppose, when he could not prevail with me to tell him the young captain's name, he must have laid a trap for him; into which, alas! you have fallen. I looked for much confusion; for how could I tell whether he was willing to take me for his wife on these sharp terms? He might have been trifling with me from the first, or I might have made myself too cheap in his eyes. But truly I had not looked for such a shameful punishment as this! I could not think that God would let a girl be so disgraced before a young man. And now I tell you all; and I can scarcely hope that you will not despise me."

Denis made her a respectful inclination.

"Madam," he said, "you have honored me by your confidence. It remains for me to prove that I am not unworthy of the honor. Is Messire de Maletroit at hand?"

"I believe he is writing in the salle* without," she answered.

salle: sitting room

"May I lead you thither, madam?" asked Denis offering his hand with his most courtly bearing.

She accepted it, and the pair passed out of the chapel, Blanche in a very drooping and shamefaced condition, but Denis strutting and ruffling in the consciousness of a mission, and the boyish certainty of accomplishing it with honor.

The Sire de Maletroit rose to meet them with an ironical obeisance.

"Sir," said Denis, with the grandest possible air, "I believe I am to have some say in the matter of this marriage; and let me tell you at once, I will be no party to forcing the inclination of this young lady. Had it been freely offered to me, I should have been proud to accept her hand, for I perceive she is as good as she is beautiful; but as things are, I have now the honor, messire, of refusing."

Blanche looked at him with gratitude in her eyes; but the old gentleman only smiled and smiled, until his smile grew positively sickening to Denis.

"I am afraid," he said, "Monsieur de Beaulieu, that you do not perfectly understand the choice I have offered you. Follow me, I beseech you, to this window." And he led the way to one of the large windows which stood open on the night. "You observe," he went on, "there is an iron ring in the upper masonry, and reeved through that a very efficacious rope. Now, mark my words: if you should find your disinclination to my niece's person insurmountable, I shall have you hanged out of this window before sunrise. I shall only proceed to such an extremity with the greatest regret, you may believe me. For it is not at all your death that I desire, but my niece's establishment in life. At the same time, it must come to that if you prove obstinate. Your family, Monsieur de Beaulieu, is very well in its way, but if you sprung from Charlemagne,* you should not refuse the hand of a Maletroit with impunity—not if she had been as common as the Paris road—not if she was as hideous as the gargoyle over my door. Neither my niece nor you, nor my own private feelings, move me at all in this matter. The honor of my house has been compromised; I believe you to be the guilty person, at least you are now in the secret; and you can hardly wonder if I request you to wipe out the stain. If you will not, your blood be on your own head! It will be no great satisfaction to me to have your interesting relics* kicking their heels in the breeze below my windows, but half a loaf is better than no bread, and if I cannot cure the dishonor, I shall at least stop the scandal."

Charlemagne: emperor who laid the basis for the Holy Roman Empire (742?–814)

relics: remains; corpse

There was a pause.

"I believe there are other ways of settling such imbroglios* among gentlemen," said Denis. "You wear a sword, and I hear you have used it with distinction."

imbroglios: disagreements

The Sire de Maletroit made a signal to the chaplain, who crossed the room with long, silent strides and raised the arras over the third of the three doors. It was only a moment before he let it fall again; but Denis had time to see a dusky passage full of armed men.

"When I was a little younger, I should have been delighted to honor you, Monsieur de Beaulieu," said Sire Alain; "but I am now too old. Faithful retainers are the sinews of age, and I must employ the strength I have. This is one of the hardest things to swallow as a man grows up in years, but with a little patience even this becomes habitual. You and the lady seem to prefer the salle for what remains of your two hours; and as I have no desire to cross your preference, I shall resign it to your use with all the pleasure in the world. No haste!" he added, holding up his hand, as he saw a dangerous look come into Denis de Beaulieu's face. "If your mind revolts against hanging, it will be time enough two hours hence to throw yourself out the window or upon the pikes of my retainers. Two hours of life are always two hours. A great many things may turn up in even as little a while as that. And, besides, if I understand her appearance, my niece has something to say to you. You will not disfigure your last hours by a want of politeness to a lady?"

Denis looked at Blanche, and she made him an imploring gesture.

It is likely that the old gentleman was hugely pleased at this symptom of an understanding, for he smiled on both and added sweetly, "If you will give me your word of honor Monsieur de Beaulieu, to await my return at the end of the two hours before attempting anything desperate, I shall withdraw my retainers and let you speak in greater privacy with mademoiselle."

Denis again glanced at the girl, who seemed to beseech him to agree.

"I give you my word of honor," he said.

Messire de Maletroit bowed and proceeded to limp about the apartment, clearing his throat the while with that odd musical chirp which had already grown so irritating in the ears of Denis de Beaulieu. He first possessed himself of some papers which lay upon the table; then he went to the mouth of the passage and appeared to give an order to the men behind the arras; and lastly he hobbled out through the door by which Denis had come in, turning upon the threshold to address a last smiling bow to the young couple, and followed by the chaplain with a hand-lamp.

No sooner were they alone than Blanche advanced toward Denis with her hands extended. Her face was flushed and excited, and her eyes shone with tears.

"You shall not die!" she cried, "you shall marry me after all."

"You seem to think, madam," replied Denis, "that I stand much in fear of death."

"Oh, no, no," she said, "I see you are no poltroon.* It is for my own sake—I could not bear to have you slain for such a scruple."

poltroon: horrible coward

"I am afraid," returned Denis, "that you underrate the difficulty, madam. What you may be too generous to refuse I may be too proud to accept. In a moment of noble feeling toward me, you forget what you perhaps owe to others."

He had the decency to keep his eyes on the floor as he said this, and after he had finished, so as not to spy upon her confusion. She stood silent for a moment, then walked suddenly away, and falling on her uncle's chair, fairly burst out sobbing. Denis was in the acme of embarrassment. He looked round, as if to seek for inspiration, and seeing a stool, plumped down upon it for something to do. There he sat, playing with the guard of his rapier, and wishing himself dead a thousand times over, and buried in the nastiest kitchen-heap in France. His eyes wandered round the apartment, but found nothing to arrest them. There were such wide spaces between the furniture, the light fell so badly and cheerlessly over all, the dark outside air looked in so coldly through the windows, that he thought he had never seen a church so vast, nor a tomb so melancholy. The regular sobs of Blanche de Maletroit measured out the time like the ticking of a clock. He read the device upon the shield over and over again, until his eyes became obscured; he stared into shadowy corners until he imagined they were swarming with horrible animals; and every now and again he awoke with a start, to remember that his last two hours were running, and death was on the march.

Oftener and oftener, as the time went on, did his glance settle on the girl herself. Her face was bowed forward and covered with her hands, and she was shaken at intervals by the convulsive hiccough of grief. Even thus she was not an unpleasant object to dwell upon, so plump and yet so fine, with a warm brown skin, and the most beautiful hair, Denis thought, in the whole world of womankind. Her hands were like her uncle's; but they were more in place at the end of her young arms, and looked infinitely soft and caressing. He remembered how her blue eyes had shone upon him, full of anger, pity, and innocence. And the more he dwelt on her perfections, the uglier death looked, and the more deeply was he smitten with penitence at her continued tears. Now he felt that no man could have the courage to leave a world which contained so beautiful a creature; and now he would have given forty minutes of his last hour to have unsaid his cruel speech.

Suddenly a hoarse and ragged peal of cockcrow rose to their ears from the dark valley below the windows. And this shattering noise in the silence of all around was like a light in a dark place, and shook them both out of their reflections.

"Alas, can I do nothing to help you?" she said, looking up.

"Madam," replied Denis, with a fine irrelevancy, "if I have said anything to wound you, believe me, it was for your own sake and not for mine."

She thanked him with a tearful look.

"I feel your position cruelly," he went on. "The world has been bitter hard on you. Your uncle is a disgrace to mankind. Believe me, madam, there is no young gentleman in all France but would be glad of my opportunity, to die in doing you a momentary service."

"I know already that you can be very brave and generous," she answered. "What I *want* to know is whether I can serve you—now or afterward," she added with a quaver.

"Most certainly," he answered, with a smile. "Let me sit beside you as if I were a friend, instead of a foolish intruder; try to forget how awkwardly we are placed to one another; make my last moments go pleasantly; and you will do me the chief service possible."

"You are very gallant," she added, with a yet deeper sadness "—very gallant—and it somehow pains me. But draw nearer, if you please; and if you find anything to say to me, you will at least make certain of a very friendly listener. Ah! Monsieur de Beaulieu," she broke forth—"ah! Monsieur de Beaulieu, how can I look you in the face?" And she fell to weeping again with a renewed effusion.

"Madam," said Denis, taking her hand in both of his, "reflect on the little time I have before me, and the great bitterness into which I am cast by the sight of your distress. Spare me, in my last moments, the spectacle of what I cannot cure even with the sacrifice of my life."

"I am very selfish," answered Blanche. "I will be braver, Monsieur de Beaulieu, for your sake. But think if I can do you no kindness in the future—if you have no friends to whom I could carry your adieus. Charge me as heavily as you can; every burden will lighten, by so little, the invaluable gratitude I owe you. Put in my power to do something more for you than weep."

"My mother is married again, and has a young family to care for. My brother Guichard will inherit my fiefs;* and if I am not in error, that will content him amply for my death. Life is a little vapor that passeth away, as we are told by the holy scriptures. When a man is in a fair way and sees all life open in front of him, he seems to himself to make a very important figure in the world. His horse whinnies to him; the trumpets blow and the girls look out of windows as he rides into town before his company; he receives many assurances of trust and regard,—sometimes by express in a letter, sometimes face to face, with persons of great consequence falling on his neck. It is not wonderful if his head is turned for a time. But once he is dead, were he as brave as Hercules or as wise as Solomon, he is soon forgotten. It is not ten years since my father fell, with many other knights around him, in a very fierce encounter, and I do not think that any one of them, nor as much as the name of the fight, is now remembered. No, no, madam, the nearer you come to it, you see that death is a dark and dusty corner, where a man gets into his tomb and has the door shut after him till the judgment day. I have a few friends just now, and once I am dead shall have none."

"Ah, Monsieur de Beaulieu!" she exclaimed, "you forget Blanche de Maletroit."

"You have a sweet nature, madam, and you are pleased to estimate a little service far beyond its worth."

"It is not that," she answered. "You mistake me if you think I am easily touched by my own concerns. I say so because you are the noblest man I have ever met,—because I recognize in you a spirit that would have made even a common person famous in the land."

"And yet here I die in a mousetrap, with no more noise about it than my own squeaking," answered he.

A look of pain crossed her face, and she was silent for a little while. Then a light came into her eyes, and with a smile she spoke again.

"I cannot have my champion think meanly of himself. Anyone who gives his life for another

fiefs: lands in a family estate

will be met in paradise by all the heralds and angels of the Lord God. And you have no such cause to hang your head. For—Pray, do you think me beautiful?" she asked, with a deep flush.

"Indeed, madam, I do," he said.

"I am glad of that," she answered heartily. "Do you think there are many men in France who have been asked in marriage by a beautiful maiden—with her own lips—and who have refused her to her face? I know you men would half despise such a triumph; but believe me, we women know more of what is precious in love. There is nothing that should set a person higher in his own esteem; and we women would prize nothing more dearly."

"You are very good," he said; "but you cannot make me forget that I was asked in pity and not for love."

"I am not so sure of that," she replied holding down her head. "Hear me to an end, Monsieur de Beaulieu. I know how you despise me; I feel you are right to do so; I am too poor a creature to occupy one thought of your mind, although, alas! you must die for me this morning. But when I asked you to marry me, indeed, and indeed, it was because I respected and admired you, and loved you with my whole soul, from the very moment that you took my part against my uncle. If you had seen yourself, and how noble you looked, you would pity rather than despise me. And now," she went on, hurriedly checking him with her hand, "although I have laid aside all reserve and told you so much, remember that I know your sentiments toward me already. I would not, believe me, being nobly born, weary you with importunities* into consent. I too have a pride of my own; and I declare if you should now go back from your word already given, I would no more marry you than I would marry my uncle's groom."

importunities: persistent requests

Denis smiled a little bitterly.

"It is a small love," he said, "that shies at a little pride."

She made no answer, although she probably had her own thoughts.

"Come hither to the window," he said with a sigh. "Here is the dawn."

And indeed the dawn was already beginning. The hollow of the sky was full of essential daylight, colorless and clean; and the valley underneath was flooded with a gray reflection. A few thin vapors clung in the coves of the forest or lay along the winding course of the river. The scene disengaged* a surprising effect of stillness, which was hardly interrupted when the cocks began once more to crow among the steadings.* Perhaps the same fellow who had made so horrid a clamor in the darkness, not half an hour before, now sent up the merriest cheer to greet the coming day. A little wind went bustling and eddying among the tree tops underneath the windows. And still the daylight kept flooding insensibly out of the east, which was soon to grow incandescent and cast up that red-hot cannon-ball, the rising sun.

disengaged: caused

steadings: farm buildings and outbuildings

Denis looked out over all this with a bit of a shiver. He had taken her hand, and retained it in his almost unconsciously.

"Has the day begun already?" she said; and then, illogically enough: "the night has been so long! Alas! what shall we say to my uncle when he returns?"

"What you will," said Denis, and he pressed her fingers in his.

She was silent.

"Blanche," he said, with a swift, uncertain, passionate utterance, "you have seen whether I fear death. You must know well enough that I would as gladly leap out of that window into the empty air as to lay a finger on you without your free and full consent. But if you care for me at all, do not let me lose my life in a misapprehension, for I love you better than the whole world;

and though I will die for you blithely, it would be like all the joys of paradise to live on and spend my life in your service."

As he stopped speaking a bell began to ring loudly in the interior of the house, and a clatter of armor in the corridor showed that the retainers were returning to their post, and the two hours were at an end.

"After all that you have heard?" she whispered, leaning toward him.

"I have heard nothing," he replied.

"The captain's name was Florimond de Champdivers," she said in his ear.

"I did not hear it," he answered, taking her in his arms and wiping away her tears.

A melodious chirping was audible behind, followed by a beautiful chuckle, and the voice of Messire de Maletroit wished his new nephew a good morning.

About the Story

1. Are the main characters sympathetic or unsympathetic? Why?
2. Which is the greater conflict in the story, the internal or the external? Justify your answer.
3. Did you find the ending satisfying? Why or why not?
4. Propose the possible significance of Blanche's name.
5. Analyze the following statement made by Blanche. Is her idea scriptural? "Anyone who gives his life for another will be met in paradise by all the heralds and angels of the Lord God."
6. Nineteenth-century Romanticism tended to emphasize an idealized picture of love similar to old ideas of courtly love and chivalry. This approach elevated certain noble aspects of love but rarely modeled the realities of everyday conflicts with loved ones. Through the characters of Blanche and Denis, what biblical ideals for love does Stevenson rightly elevate in his theme? (See especially John 15:12–13; 1 Cor. 13:1–8; Eph. 4:32; and Phil. 2:1–8.) What everyday applications of these truths does he leave out of his idealized portrayal of love?

About the Author

Scottish poet, essayist, and novelist Robert Louis Stevenson (1850–94) was the only child of Thomas and Margaret Balfour Stevenson, a prosperous Presbyterian couple. A sickly child for whom attending school was often difficult, Stevenson spent much time with his staunchly Calvinist nurse, Alison Cunningham (Cummy), who often read the Bible, Bunyan, and stories to Stevenson as he lay ill and bedridden. Perhaps these circumstances contributed to Stevenson's very early interest in storytelling and writing.

To follow in the family profession of building lighthouses, Stevenson entered the University of Edinburgh to study engineering. Here he abandoned both his religious upbringing and his course of study and declared his intent to become a man of letters. Because of his frail lungs and weak constitution, Stevenson often traveled to warmer climates and wrote about his travels. On one such trip to France, Stevenson met Fanny Vandegrift Osbourne, whom he married in 1880 in California. The next seven years were highly productive for the writer; during that time he produced the works for which he is best known—*Treasure Island, Kidnapped,* and *The Strange Case of Dr. Jekyll and Mr. Hyde.* After three years of traveling in the islands of the South Pacific, Stevenson purchased several hundred acres on a Samoan island, where he built an estate and lived until his unexpected death from a brain hemorrhage.

One of the most popular Victorian writers, Robert Louis Stevenson was an excellent storyteller who created characters—such as Jim Hawkins and Long John Silver—that capture the imagination. Though best known for adventure novels, Stevenson wrote capably in several other genres, including essays, short stories, poetry, and letters. Many believe *Weir of Hermiston*, the novel on which Stevenson was working when he died, would have been his masterpiece.

The Adventure of the Speckled Band

Sir Arthur Conan Doyle

"The Adventure of the Speckled Band" is in many ways a typical Conan Doyle detective story: Watson narrates how his friend, the master sleuth Sherlock Holmes, uses his extraordinary deductive powers to unravel a seemingly impossible mystery. This story, however, is more artfully constructed than other Holmes mysteries. Notice, for example, how quickly the author draws the reader into the conflict. Notice, too, how deftly he maintains a high level of suspense until the very end of his narrative.

On glancing over my notes of the seventy odd cases in which I have during the last eight years studied the methods of my friend Sherlock Holmes, I find many tragic, some comic, a large number merely strange, but none commonplace; for, working as he did rather for the love of his art than for the acquirement of wealth, he refused to associate himself with any investigation which did not tend towards the unusual, and even the fantastic. Of all these varied cases, however, I cannot recall any which presented more singular features than that which was associated with the well-known Surrey family of the Roylotts of Stoke Moran. The events in question occurred in the early days of my association with Holmes, when we were sharing rooms as bachelors in Baker Street. It is possible that I might have placed them upon record before, but a promise of secrecy was made at the time, from which I have only been freed during the last month by the untimely death of the lady to whom the pledge was given. It is perhaps as well that the facts should now come to light, for I have reasons to know that there were widespread rumors as to the death of Dr. Grimesby Roylott which tend to make the matter even more terrible than the truth.

It was early in April in the year '83 that I woke one morning to find Sherlock Holmes standing, fully dressed, by the side of my bed. He was a late riser, as a rule, and as the clock on the mantlepiece showed me that it was only a quarter past seven, I blinked up at him in some surprise, and perhaps just a little resentment, for I was myself regular in my habits.

"Very sorry to knock you up,* Watson," said he, "but it's the common lot this morning. Mrs. Hudson has been knocked up, she retorted upon me, and I on you."

knock . . . up: wake up (The phrase is derived from an old custom whereby a designated person awakened the people of a neighborhood by knocking at their doors.)

"What is it, then—a fire?"

"No; a client. It seems that a young lady has arrived in a considerable state of excitement, who insists upon seeing me. She is waiting now in the sitting room. Now, when young ladies wander about the metropolis at this hour of the morning, and knock sleepy people up out of their beds, I presume that it is something very pressing which they have to communicate. Should it prove to be an interesting case, you would, I am sure, wish to follow it from the outset. I thought, at any rate, that I should call you and give you the chance."

"My dear fellow, I would not miss it for anything."

I had no keener pleasure than in following Holmes in his professional investigations, and in admiring the rapid deductions, as swift as

intuitions, and yet always founded on a logical basis, with which he unraveled the problems which were submitted to him. I rapidly threw on my clothes and was ready in a few minutes to accompany my friend down to the sitting room. A lady dressed in black and heavily veiled, who had been sitting in the window, rose as we entered.

"Good-morning, madam," said Holmes cheerily. "My name is Sherlock Holmes. This is my intimate friend and associate, Dr. Watson, before whom you can speak as freely as before myself. Ha! I am glad to see that Mrs. Hudson had the good sense to light the fire. Draw up to it, and I shall order you a cup of hot coffee, for I observe that you are shivering."

"It is not cold which makes me shiver," said the woman in a low voice, changing her seat as requested.

"What, then?"

"It is fear, Mr. Holmes. It is terror." She raised her veil as she spoke, and we could see that she was indeed in a pitiable state of agitation, her face all drawn and gray, with restless, frightened eyes, like those of some hunted animal. Her features and figure were those of a woman of thirty, but her hair was shot with premature gray, and her expression was weary and haggard. Sherlock Holmes ran her over with one of his quick, all-comprehensive glances.

"You must not fear," said he soothingly, bending forward and patting her forearm. "We shall soon set matters right, I have no doubt. You have come in by train this morning, I see."

"You know me, then?"

"No, but I observe the second half of a return ticket in the palm of your left glove. You must have started early, and yet you had a good drive in a dogcart, along heavy roads, before you reached the station."

The lady gave a violent start and stared in bewilderment at my companion.

"There is no mystery, my dear madam," said he, smiling. "The left arm of your jacket is spattered with mud in no less than seven places. The marks are perfectly fresh. There is no vehicle save a dogcart which throws up mud in that way, and then only when you sit on the left-hand side of the driver."

"Whatever your reasons may be, you are perfectly correct," said she. "I started from home before six, reached Leatherhead at twenty past, and came in by the first train. Sir, I can stand this strain no longer; I shall go mad if it continues. I have no one to turn to—none, save only one, who cares for me, and he, poor fellow, can be of little aid. I have heard of you, Mr. Holmes; I have heard of you from Mrs. Farintosh, whom you helped in the hour of her sore need. It was from her that I had your address. Oh, sir, do you not think that you could help me, too, and at least throw a little light through the dense darkness which surrounds me? At present it is out of my power to reward you for your services, but in a month or six weeks I shall be married, with the control of my own income, and then at least you shall not find me ungrateful."

Holmes turned to his desk and, unlocking it, drew out a small casebook, which he consulted.

"Farintosh," said he. "Ah, yes, I recall the case; it was concerned with an opal tiara. I think it was before your time, Watson. I can only say, madam, that I shall be happy to devote the same care to your case as I did to that of your friend. As to reward, my profession is its own reward; but you are at liberty to defray whatever expenses I may be put to, at the time which suits you best. And now I beg that you will lay before us everything that may help us in forming an opinion upon the matter."

"Alas!" replied our visitor, "the very horror of my situation lies in the fact that my fears are so vague, and my suspicions depend so entirely upon small points, which might seem trivial to another, that even he to whom of all others I have a right to look for help and advice looks upon all that I tell him about it as the fancies of a nervous woman. He does not say so, but I can read it from his soothing answers and averted eyes. But I have heard, Mr. Holmes, that you can see deeply into the manifold wickedness of the human heart. You may advise me how to walk amid the dangers which encompass me."

"I am all attention, madam."

"My name is Helen Stoner, and I am living with my stepfather, who is the last survivor of one of the oldest Saxon families in England, the Roylotts of Stoke Moran, on the western border of Surrey."

Holmes nodded his head. "The name is familiar to me," said he.

"The family was at one time among the richest in England, and the estates extended over the borders into Berkshire in the north, and Hampshire in the west. In the last century, however, four successive heirs were of a dissolute and wasteful disposition, and the family ruin was eventually completed by a gambler in the days of the Regency.* Nothing was left save a few acres of ground, and the two-hundred-year-old house, which is itself crushed under a heavy mortgage. The last squire dragged out his existence there, living the horrible life of an aristocratic pauper; but his only son, my stepfather, seeing that he must adapt himself to the new conditions, obtained an advance from a relative, which enabled him to take a medical degree and went out to Calcutta, where, by his professional skill and his force of character, he established a large practice. In a fit of anger, however, caused by some robberies which had been perpetrated in the house, he beat his native butler to death and narrowly escaped a capital sentence. As it was, he suffered a long term of imprisonment and afterwards returned to England a morose and disappointed man.

Regency: the period (1811–20) when George III was declared incompetent and the Prince of Wales ruled as regent

"When Dr. Roylott was in India he married my mother, Mrs. Stoner, the young widow of Major-General Stoner, of the Bengal Artillery. My sister Julia and I were twins, and we were only two years old at the time of my mother's remarriage. She had a considerable sum of money—not less than £1000 a year—and this she bequeathed to Dr. Roylott entirely while we resided with him, with a provision that a certain annual sum should be allowed to each of us in the event of our marriage. Shortly after our return to England my mother died—she was killed eight years ago in a railway accident near Crewe. Dr. Roylott then abandoned his attempts to establish himself in practice in London and took us to live with him in the old ancestral house at Stoke Moran. The money which my mother had left was enough for all our wants, and there seemed to be no obstacle to our happiness.

"But a terrible change came over our stepfather about this time. Instead of making friends and exchanging visits with our neighbors, who had at first been overjoyed to see a Roylott of Stoke Moran back in the old family seat, he shut himself up in his house and seldom came out save to indulge in ferocious quarrels with whoever might cross his path. Violence of temper approaching to mania has been hereditary in the men of the family, and in my stepfather's case it had, I believe, been intensified by his long residence in the tropics. A series of disgraceful brawls took place, two of which ended in the police court, until at last be became the terror of the village, and the folks would fly at his approach, for he is a man of immense strength, and absolutely uncontrollable in his anger.

"Last week he hurled the local blacksmith over a parapet into a stream, and it was only by paying over all the money which I could gather together that I was able to avert another public exposure. He had no friends at all save the wandering gypsies, and he would give these vagabonds leave to encamp upon the few acres of bramble-covered land which represent the family estate, and would accept in return the hospitality of their tents, wandering away with them sometimes for weeks on end. He has a passion also for Indian animals, which are sent over to him by a correspondent, and he has at this moment a cheetah and a baboon, which wander freely over his grounds and are feared by the villagers almost as much as their master.

"You can imagine from what I say that my poor sister Julia and I had no great pleasure in our lives. No servant would stay with us, and for a long time we did all the work of the house. She was but thirty at the time of her heath, and yet her hair had already begun to whiten, even as mine has."

"Your sister is dead, then?"

"She died just two years ago, and it is of her death that I wish to speak to you. You can understand that, living the life which I have described, we were little likely to see anyone of our own age and position. We had, however, an aunt, my mother's maiden sister, Miss Honoria Westphail, who lives near Harrow, and we were occasionally allowed to pay short visits at this lady's house. Julia went there at Christmas two years ago, and met there a half-pay* major of marines, to whom she became engaged. My stepfather learned of the engagement when my sister returned and offered no objection to the marriage; but within a fortnight of the day which had been fixed for the wedding, the terrible event occurred which has deprived me of my only companion."

half-pay: one-half of regular pay, the amount of pay given an officer when retired or not on active duty

Sherlock Holmes had been leaning back in his chair with his eyes closed and his head sunk in a cushion, but he half opened his lids now and glanced across at his visitor.

"Pray be precise as to details," he said.

"It is easy for me to be so, for every event of that dreadful time is seared into my memory. The manor house is, as I have already said, very old, and only one wing is now inhabited. The bedrooms in this wing are on the ground floor, the sitting rooms being in the central block of the buildings. Of these bedrooms the first is Dr. Roylott's, the second my sister's, and the third my own. There is no communication between them, but they all open out into the same corridor. Do I make myself plain?"

"Perfectly so."

"The windows of the three rooms open out upon the lawn. That fatal night Dr. Roylott had gone to his room early, though we knew that he had not retired to rest, for my sister was troubled by the smell of the strong Indian cigars which it was his custom to smoke. She left her room, therefore, and came into mine, where she sat for some time, chatting about her approaching wedding. At eleven o'clock she rose to leave me, but she paused at the door and looked back.

"'Tell me, Helen,' said she, 'have you ever heard anyone whistle in the dead of night?'

"'Never,' said I.

"'I suppose that you could not possibly whistle, yourself, in your sleep?'

"'Certainly not. But why?'

"'Because during the last few nights I have always, about three in the morning, heard a low, clear whistle. I am a light sleeper, and it has awakened me. I cannot tell where it came from—perhaps from the next room, perhaps from the lawn. I thought that I would just ask you whether you had heard it.'

"'No, I have not. It must be those wretched gypsies in the plantation.'

"'Very likely. And yet if it were on the lawn, I wonder that you did not hear it also.'

"'Ah, but I sleep more heavily than you.'

"'Well, it is of no great consequence, at any rate.' She smiled back at me, closed my door, and a few moments later I heard her key turn in the lock."

"Indeed," said Holmes. "Was it your custom always to lock yourselves in at night?"

"Always."

"And why?"

"I think that I mentioned to you that the doctor kept a cheetah and a baboon. We had no feeling of security unless our doors were locked."

"Quite so. Pray proceed with your statement."

"I could not sleep that night. A vague feeling of impending misfortune impressed me. My sister and I, you will recollect, were twins, and you know how subtle are the links which bind two souls which are so closely allied. It was a wild night. The wind was howling outside, and the rain was beating and splashing against the windows. Suddenly, amid all the hubbub of the gale, there burst forth the wild scream of a terrified woman. I knew that it was my sister's voice. I sprang from my bed, wrapped a shawl round me, and rushed into the corridor. As I opened my door I seemed to hear a low whistle, such as my sister had described, and a few moments later a clanging sound, as if a mass of metal had fallen. As I ran down the passage, my sister's door was unlocked, and revolved slowly upon its hinges.

"I stared at it horror-stricken, not knowing what was about to issue from it. By the light of the corridor-lamp I saw my sister appear at the opening, her face blanched with terror, her hands groping for help, her whole figure swaying to and fro like that of a drunkard. I ran to her and threw my arms round her, but at that moment her knees seemed to give way and she fell to the ground. She writhed as one who is in terrible pain, and her limbs were dreadfully convulsed. At first I thought that she had not recognized me, but as I bent over her she suddenly shrieked out in a voice which I shall never forget, 'Oh Helen! Helen! It was the band! The speckled band!' There was something else which she would fain have said, and she stabbed with her finger into the air in the direction of the doctor's room, but a fresh convulsion seized her and choked her words. I rushed out, calling loudly for my stepfather, and I met him hastening from his room in his dressing gown. When he reached my sister's side she was unconscious, and though he sent for medical aid from the village, all efforts were in vain, for she slowly sank and died without having recovered her consciousness. Such was the dreadful end of my beloved sister."

"One moment," said Holmes; "are you sure about this whistle and metallic sound. Could you swear to it?"

"That was what the county coroner asked me at the inquiry. It is my strong impression that I heard it, and yet, among the crash of the gale and the creaking of an old house, I may possibly have been deceived."

"Was your sister dressed?"

"No, she was in her night dress. In her right hand was found the charred stump of a match, and in her left a matchbox."

"Showing that she had struck a light and looked about her when the alarm took place. That is important. And what conclusions did the coroner come to?"

"He investigated the case with great care, for Dr. Roylott's conduct had long been notorious in the county, but he was unable to find any satisfactory cause of death. My evidence showed that the door had been fastened upon the inner side, and the windows were blocked by old-fashioned shutters with broad iron bars, which were secured every night. The walls were carefully sounded and were shown to be quite solid all round, and the flooring was also thoroughly examined, with the same result. The chimney is wide, but is barred up by four large staples. It is certain, therefore, that my sister was quite alone when she met her end. Besides, there were no marks of any violence upon her."

"How about poison?"

"The doctors examined her for it, but without success."

"What do you think this unfortunate lady died of, then?"

"It is my belief that she died of pure fear and nervous shock, though what it was that frightened her I cannot imagine."

"Were there gypsies in the plantation at the time?"

"Yes, there are nearly always some there."

"Ah, and what did you gather from this allusion to a band—a speckled band?"

"Sometimes I have thought that it was merely the wild talk of delirium, sometimes that it may have referred to some band of people, perhaps to these very gypsies in the plantation. I do not know whether the spotted handkerchiefs which so many of them wear over their heads might have suggested the strange adjective which she used."

Holmes shook his head like a man who is far from being satisfied.

"These are very deep waters," said he; "pray go on with your narrative."

"Two years have passed since then, and my life has been until lately lonelier than ever. A month ago, however, a dear friend, whom I have known for many years, had done me the honor to ask my hand in marriage. His name is Armitage—Percy Armitage—the second son of Mr. Armitage, of Crane Water, near Reading. My stepfather has offered no opposition to the match, and we are to be married in the course of the spring. Two days ago some repairs were started in the west wing of the building, and my bedroom wall has been pierced, so that I have had to move into the chamber in which my sister died, and to sleep in the very bed in which she slept. Imagine, then, my thrill of terror when last night, as I lay awake, thinking over her terrible fate, I suddenly heard in the silence of the night the low whistle which had been the herald of her own death. I sprang up and lit the lamp, but nothing was to be seen in the room. I was too shaken to go to bed again, however, so I dressed, and as soon as it was daylight I slipped down, got a dogcart at the Crown Inn, which is opposite, and drove to Leatherhead, from whence I have come on this morning with the one object of seeing you and asking your advice."

"You have done wisely," said my friend. "But have you told me all?"

"Yes, all."

"Miss Roylott, you have not. You are screening* your stepfather."

screening: protecting

"Why, what do you mean?"

For answer Holmes pushed back the frill of black lace which fringed the hand that lay upon our visitor's knee. Five little livid spots, the marks of four fingers and a thumb, were printed upon the white wrist.

"You have been cruelly used," said Holmes.

The lady colored deeply and covered over her injured wrist. "He is a hard man," she said, "and perhaps he hardly knows his own strength."

There was a long silence, during which Holmes leaned his chin upon his hands and stared into the crackling fire.

"This is very deep business," he said at last. "There are a thousand details which I should desire to know before I decide upon our course of action. Yet we have not a moment to lose. If we were to come to Stoke Moran today, would it be possible for us to see over these rooms without the knowledge of your stepfather?"

"As it happens, he spoke of coming into town today upon some most important business. It is probable that he will be away all day, and that there would be nothing to disturb you. We have a housekeeper now, but she is old and foolish, and I could easily get her out of the way."

"Excellent. You are not averse to this trip, Watson?"

"By no means."

"Then we shall both come. What are you going to do yourself?"

"I have one or two things which I would wish to do now that I am in town. But I shall return by the twelve o'clock train, so as to be there in time for your coming."

"And you may expect us early in the afternoon. I have myself some small business matters to attend to. Will you not wait and breakfast?"

"No, I must go. My heart is lightened already since I have confided my trouble to you. I shall look forward to seeing you again this afternoon." She dropped her thick black veil over her face and glided from the room.

"It seems to me to be a most dark and sinister business."

"Dark enough and sinister enough."

"Yet if the lady is correct in saying that the flooring and walls are sound, and that the door, window, and chimney are impassable, then her sister must have been undoubtedly alone when she met her mysterious end."

"What becomes, then, of these nocturnal whistles, and what of the very peculiar words of the dying woman?"

"I cannot think."

"When you combine the ideas of whistles at night, the presence of a band of gypsies who are on intimate terms with this old doctor, the fact that we have every reason to believe that the doctor has an interest in preventing his stepdaughter's marriage, the dying allusion to a band, and, finally, the fact that Miss Helen Stoner heard a metallic clang, which might have been caused by one of those metal bars that secured the shutters falling back into its place, I think that there is good ground to think that the mystery may be cleared along those lines."

"But what, then, did the gypsies do?"

"I cannot imagine."

"I see many objections to such a theory."

"And so do I. It is precisely for that reason that we are going to Stoke Moran this day. I want to see whether the objections are fatal, or if they may be explained away. But what in the name of—!"

The ejaculation had been drawn from my companion by the fact that our door had been suddenly dashed open, and that a huge man had framed himself in the aperture. His costume was a peculiar mixture of the professional and of the agricultural, having a black top hat, a long frock coat, and a pair of high gaiters, with a hunting crop swinging in his hand. So tall was he that his

hat actually brushed the cross bar of the doorway, and his breadth seemed to span it across from side to side. A large face, seared with a thousand wrinkles, burned yellow with the sun, and marked with every evil passion, was turned from one to the other of us, while his deep-set, bile-shot eyes, and his high, thin, fleshless nose, gave him somewhat the resemblance to a fierce old bird of prey.

"Which of you is Holmes?" asked this apparition.

"My name, sir; but you have the advantage of me," said my companion quietly.

"I am Dr. Grimesby Roylott, of Stoke Moran."

"Indeed, Doctor," said Holmes blandly. "Pray take a seat."

"I will do nothing of the kind. My stepdaughter has been here. I have traced her. What has she been saying to you?"

"It is a little cold for the time of year," said Holmes.

"What has she been saying to you?" screamed the old man furiously.

"But I have heard that the crocuses promise well," continued my companion imperturbably.

"Ha! You put me off, do you?" said our new visitor, taking a step forward and shaking his hunting crop. "I know you, you scoundrel! I have heard of you before. You are Holmes, the meddler."

My friend smiled.

"Holmes, the busybody!"

His smile broadened.

"Holmes, the Scotland Yard Jack-in-office!"

Holmes chuckled heartily. "Your conversation is most entertaining," said he. "When you go out close the door, for there is a decided draught."

"I will go when I have had my say. Don't you dare to meddle with my affairs. I know that Miss Stoner has been here. I traced her! I am a dangerous man to fall foul of! See here." He stepped swiftly forward, seized the poker, and bent it into a curve with his huge brown hands.

"See that you keep yourself out of my grip," he snarled, and hurling the twisted poker into the fireplace he strode out of the room.

"He seems a very amiable person," said Holmes, laughing. "I am not quite so bulky, but if he had remained I might have shown him that my grip was not much more feeble than his own." As he spoke he picked up the steel poker and, with a sudden effort, straightened it out again.

"Fancy his having the insolence to confound me with the official detective force! This incident gives zest to our investigation, however, and I only trust that our little friend will not suffer from her imprudence in allowing this brute to trace her. And now, Watson, we shall order breakfast, and afterwards I shall walk down to Doctors' Commons,* where I hope to get some data which may help us in this matter."

Doctors' Commons: a place in London used as an official storage place for wills and other deeds

It was nearly one o'clock when Sherlock Holmes returned from his excursion. He held in his hand a sheet of blue paper, scrawled over with notes and figures.

"I have seen the will of the deceased wife," said he. "To determine its exact meaning I have been obliged to work out the present prices of the investments with which it is concerned. The total income, which at the time of the wife's death was little short of £1100, is now, through the fall in agricultural prices, not more than £750. Each daughter can claim an income of £250, in case of marriage. It is evident, therefore, that if both girls had married, this beauty would have had a mere pittance, while even one of them would cripple him to a very serious extent. My morning's work has not been wasted, since it has proved that he has the very strongest motives for standing in the way of anything of the sort. And now, Watson, this is too serious for dawdling, especially as the old man is aware that we are interesting ourselves in his affairs; so if you are ready, we shall call a cab and drive to Waterloo. I should be very much obliged if you would slip your revolver into your pocket. A handgun is an excellent argument with gentlemen who can twist steel pokers into knots. That and a toothbrush are, I think, all that we need."

At Waterloo we were fortunate in catching a train for Leatherhead, where we hired a trap* at the station inn and drove for four or five miles through the lovely Surrey lanes. It was a perfect day, with a bright sun and a few fleecy clouds in the heavens. The trees and wayside hedges were just throwing out their first green shoots, and the air was full of the pleasant smell of the moist earth. To me at least there was a strange contrast between the sweet promise of the spring and this sinister quest upon which we were engaged. My companion sat in the front of the trap, his arms folded, his hat pulled down over his eyes, and his chin sunk down upon his breast, buried in the deepest thought. Suddenly, however, he started, tapped me on the shoulder, and pointed over the meadows.

trap: small coach drawn by horses

"Look there!" said he.

A heavily timbered park stretched up in a gentle slope, thickening into a grove at the highest point. From amid the branches there jutted out the gray gables and high roof-tree of a very old mansion.

"Stoke Moran?" said he.

"Yes, sir, that be the house of Dr. Grimesby Roylott," remarked the driver.

"There is some building going on there," said Holmes; "that is where we are going."

"There's the village," said the driver, pointing to a cluster of roofs some distance to the left; "but if you want to get to the house, you'll find it shorter to get over this stile, and so by the foot path over the fields. There it is, where the lady is walking."

"And the lady, I fancy, is Miss Stoner," observed Holmes, shading his eyes. "Yes, I think we had better do as you suggest."

We got off, paid our fare, and the trap rattled back on its way to Leatherhead.

"I thought it as well," said Holmes as we climbed the stile, "that this fellow should think we had come here as architects, or on some definite business. It may stop his gossip. Good afternoon, Miss Stoner. You see that we have been as good as our word."

Our client of the morning hurried forward to meet us with a face which spoke her joy. "I have been waiting so eagerly for you," she cried, shaking hands with us warmly. "All has turned out splendidly. Dr. Roylott has gone to town, and it is unlikely that he will be back before evening."

"We have had the pleasure of making the doctor's acquaintance," said Holmes, and in a few words he sketched out what had occurred. Miss Stoner turned white to the lips as she listened.

"Good heavens!" she cried, "he has followed me, then?"

"So it appears."

"He is so cunning that I never know when I am safe from him. What will he say when he returns?"

"He must guard himself, for he may find that there is someone more cunning than himself upon his track. You must lock yourself up from him tonight. If he is violent, we shall take you away to your aunt's at Harrow. Now, we must make the best use of our time, so kindly take us at once to the rooms which we are to examine."

The building was of gray, lichen-blotched stone, with a high central portion and two curving wings, like the claws of a crab, thrown out on each side. In one of these wings the windows were broken and blocked with wooden boards, while the roof was partly caved in, a picture of ruin. The central portion was in little better repair, but the right hand block was comparatively modern, and the blinds in the windows, with the blue smoke curling up from the chimneys, showed that this was where the family resided. Some scaffolding had been erected against the end wall, and the stone work had been broken into, but there were no signs of any workmen at the moment of our visit. Holmes walked slowly up and down the ill-trimmed lawn and examined with deep attention the outsides of the windows.

"This, I take it, belongs to the room in which you used to sleep, the center one to your sister's, and the one next to the main building to Dr. Roylott's chamber?"

"Exactly so. But I am now sleeping in the middle one."

"Pending the alterations, as I understand. By the way, there does not seem to be any very pressing need for repairs at that end wall."

"There were none. I believe that it was an excuse to move me from my room."

"Ah! that is suggestive. Now, on the other side of this narrow wing runs the corridor from which these three rooms open. There are windows in it, of course?"

"Yes, but very small ones. Too narrow for anyone to pass through."

"As you both locked your doors at night, your rooms were unapproachable from that side. Now, would you have the kindness to go into your room and bar your shutters?"

Miss Stoner did so, and Holmes, after a careful examination through the open window, endeavored in every way to force the shutter open, but without success. There was no slit through which a knife could be passed to raise the bar. Then with his lens he tested the hinges, but they were of solid iron, built firmly into the massive masonry. "Hum!" said he, scratching his chin in some perplexity, "my theory certainly presents some difficulties. No one could pass these shutters if they were bolted. Well, we shall see if the inside throws any light upon the matter."

A small side door led into the whitewashed corridor from which the three bedrooms opened. Holmes refused to examine the third chamber, so we passed at once to the second, that in which Miss Stoner was now sleeping, and in which her sister had met her fate. It was a homely little room, with a low ceiling and a gaping fireplace, after the fashion of old country houses. A brown chest of drawers stood in one corner, a narrow white counterpaned* bed in another, and a dressing table on the left hand side of the window. These articles, with two small wicker-work chairs, made up all the furniture in the room save for a square of Wilton carpet in the center. The boards round and the paneling of the walls were of brown, worm-eaten oak, so old and discolored that it may have dated from the original building of the house. Holmes drew one of the chairs into a corner and sat silent, while his eyes traveled round and round and up and down, taking in every detail of the apartment.

counterpaned: covered with a bedspread

Where does that bell communicate with?" he asked at last, pointing to a thick bell-rope which hung down beside the bed, the tassel actually lying upon the pillow.

"It goes to the housekeeper's room."

"It looks newer than the other things?"

"Yes, it was only put there a couple of years ago."

"Your sister asked for it, I suppose?"

"No, I never heard of her using it. We used always to get what we wanted for ourselves."

"Indeed, it seemed unnecessary to put so nice a bell-pull there. You will excuse me a few minutes while I satisfy myself as to this floor." He threw himself down upon his face with his lens in his hand and crawled swiftly backward and forward, examining minutely the cracks between the boards. Then he did the same with the wood work with which the chamber was paneled. Finally he walked over to the bed and spent some time in staring at it and in running his eye up and down the wall. Finally he took the bell-rope in his hand and gave it a brisk tug.

"Why, it's a dummy," said he.

"Won't it ring?"

"No, it is not even attached to a wire. This is very interesting. You can see now that it is fastened to a hook just above where the little opening for the ventilator is."

"How very absurd! I never noticed that before."

"Very strange!" muttered Holmes, pulling at the rope. "There are one or two very singular points about this room. For example, what a fool a builder must be to open a ventilator into another room, when, with the same trouble, he might have communicated with the outside air!"

"That is also quite modern," said the lady.

"Done about the same time as the bell-rope?" remarked Holmes.

"Yes, there were several little changes carried out about that time."

"They seem to have been of a most interesting character—dummy bell-ropes, and ventilators which do not ventilate. With your permission, Miss Stoner, we shall now carry our researches into the inner apartment."

Dr. Grimesby Roylott's chamber was larger than that of his stepdaughter, but was as plainly furnished. A camp bed, a small wooden shelf full of books, mostly of a technical character, an armchair beside the bed, a plain wooden chair against the wall, a round table, and a large iron safe were the principal things which met the eye. Holmes walked slowly round and examined each and all of them with the keenest interest.

"What's in here?" he asked tapping the safe.

"My stepfather's business papers."

"Oh! you have seen inside, then?"

"Only once, some years ago. I remember that it was full of papers."

"There isn't a cat in it, for example?"

"No. What a strange idea!"

"Well, look at this!" he took up a small saucer of milk which stood on the top of it.

"No; we don't keep a cat but there is a cheetah and a baboon."

"Ah, yes, of course! Well, a cheetah is just a big cat, and yet a saucer of milk does not go very far in satisfying its wants, I dare say. There is one point which I should wish to determine." He squatted down in front of the wooden chair and examined the seat of it with the greatest attention.

"Thank you. That is quite settled," said he, rising and putting his lens in his pocket. "Hello! Here is something interesting!"

The object which had caught his eye was a small dog lash* hung on one corner of the bed. The lash, however, was curled upon itself and tied so as to make a loop of whipcord.

lash: leash

"What do you make of that, Watson?"

"It's a common enough lash. But I don't know why it should be tied."

"That is not quite so common, is it? Ah, me! It's a wicked world, and when a clever man turns his brains to crime it is the worst of all. I think that I have seen enough now, Miss Stoner, and with your permission we shall walk out upon the lawn."

I had never seen my friend's face so grim or his brow so dark as it was when we turned from the scene of this investigation. We had walked several times up and down the lawn, neither Miss Stoner nor myself liking to break in upon his thoughts before he roused himself from his reverie.

"It is very essential, Miss Stoner," said he, "that you should absolutely follow my advice in every respect."

"I shall most certainly do so."

"The matter is too serious for any hesitation. Your life may depend upon your compliance."

"I assure you that I am in your hands."

"In the first place, both my friend and I must spend the night in your room."

Both Miss Stoner and I gazed at him in astonishment.

"Yes, it must be so. Let me explain. I believe that that is the village inn over there?"

"Yes, that is the Crown."

"Very good. Your windows would be visible from there?"

"Certainly."

"You must confine yourself to your room, on pretence of a headache, when your stepfather comes back. Then when you hear him retire for the night, you must open the shutters of your window, undo the hasp,* put your lamp there as a signal to us, and then withdraw quietly with everything you are likely to want into the room which you used to occupy. I have no doubt that, in spite of the repairs, you could manage there for one night."

hasp: metal fastener

"Oh, yes, easily."

"The rest you will leave in our hands."

"But what will you do?"

"We shall spend the night in your room, and we shall investigate the cause of this noise which has disturbed you."

"I believe, Mr. Holmes, that you have already made up your mind," said Miss Stoner, laying her hand upon my companion's sleeve.

"Perhaps I have."

"Then for pity's sake, tell me what was the cause of my sister's death."

"I should prefer to have clearer proofs before I speak."

"You can at least tell me whether my own thought is correct, and if she died from some sudden fright."

"No, I do not think so. I think that there was probably some more tangible cause. And now, Miss Stoner, we must leave you, for if Dr. Roylott returned and saw us our journey would be in vain. Goodbye, and be brave, for if you will do what I have told you you may rest assured that we shall soon drive away the dangers that threaten you."

Sherlock Holmes and I had no difficulty in engaging a bedroom and sitting room at the Crown Inn. They were on the upper floor, and from our window we could command a view of the avenue gate, and of the inhabited wing of Stoke Moran Manor House. At dusk we saw Dr. Grimesby Roylott drive past, his huge form looming up beside the little figure of the lad who drove him. The boy had some slight difficulty in undoing the heavy iron gates, and we heard the hoarse roar of the doctor's voice and saw the fury with which he shook his clinched fists at him. The trap drove on, and a few minutes later we saw a sudden light spring up among the trees as the lamp was lit in one of the sitting rooms.

"Do you know, Watson," said Holmes as we sat together in the gathering darkness, "I have really some scruples as to taking you tonight. There is a distinct element of danger."

"Can I be of assistance?"

"Your presence might be invaluable."

"Then I shall certainly come."

"It is very kind of you."

"You speak of danger. You have evidently seen more in these rooms than was visible to me."

"No, but I fancy that I may have deduced a little more. I imagine that you saw all that I did."

"I saw nothing remarkable save the bell-rope, and what purpose that could answer I confess is more than I imagine."

"You saw the ventilator, too?"

"Yes, but I do not think that it is such a very unusual thing to have a small opening between two rooms. It was so small that a rat could hardly pass through."

"I knew that we should find a ventilator before ever we came to Stoke Moran."

"My dear Holmes!"

"Oh, yes, I did. You remember in her statement she said that her sister could smell Dr. Roylott's cigar. Now, of course that suggested at once that there must be a communication between the two rooms. It could only be a small one, or it would have been remarked upon at the coroner's inquiry. I deduced a ventilator."

"But what harm can there be in that?"

"Well, there is at least a curious coincidence of dates. A ventilator is made, a cord is hung, and a lady who sleeps in a bed dies. Does that not strike you?"

"I cannot as yet see any connection."

"Did you observe anything very peculiar about that bed?"

"No."

"It was clamped to the floor. Did you ever see a bed fastened like that before?"

"I cannot say that I have."

"The lady could not move her bed. It must always be in the same relative position to the ventilator and to the rope—or so we may call it, since it was clearly never meant for a bell-pull."

"Holmes," I cried, "I seem to see dimly what you are hinting at. We are only just in time to prevent some subtle and horrible crime."

"Subtle enough and horrible enough. When a doctor does go wrong he is the first of criminals. He has nerve and he has knowledge. Palmer and Pritchard were among the heads of their profession. This man strikes even deeper, but I think, Watson, that we shall be able to strike deeper still. But we shall have horrors enough before the night is over."

About nine o'clock the light among the trees was extinguished, and all was dark in the direction of the Manor house. Two hours passed slowly away, and then, suddenly, just at the stroke of eleven, a single bright light shone out right in front of us.

"That is our signal," said Holmes, springing to his feet; "it comes from the middle window."

As we passed out he exchanged a few words with the landlord, explaining that we were going on a late visit to an acquaintance, and that it was possible that we might spend the night there. A moment later we were out on the dark road, a chill wind blowing in our faces, and one yellow light twinkling in front of us through the gloom to guide us on our somber errand.

There was little difficulty in entering the grounds, for unrepaired breaches gaped in the old park wall. Making our way among the trees, we reached the lawn, crossed it, and were about to enter through the window when out from a clump of laurel bushes there darted what seemed to be a hideous and distorted child, who threw itself upon the grass with writhing limbs and then ran swiftly across the lawn into the darkness.

"Did you see it?" I whispered.

Holmes was for the moment as startled as I. His hand closed like a vise upon my wrist in agitation. Then he broke into a low laugh and put his lips to my ear.

"It is a nice household," he murmured. "That is the baboon."

I had forgotten the strange pets which the doctor affected.* There was a cheetah, too; perhaps we might find it upon our shoulders at any moment. I confess that I felt easier in my mind when, after following Holmes's example and slipping off my shoes, I found myself inside the bedroom. My companion noiselessly closed the shutters, moved the lamp onto the table, and cast his eyes round the room. All was as we had seen it in the daytime. Then creeping up to me and making a trumpet of his hand, he whispered into my ear again so gently that it was all that I could do to distinguish the words:

affected: had a liking for

"The least sound would be fatal to our plans."

I nodded to show that I had heard.

"We must sit without light. He would see it through the ventilator."

I nodded again.

"Do not go to sleep; your very life may depend upon it. Have your pistol ready in case we should need it. I will sit on the side of the bed, and you in that chair."

I took out my revolver and laid it on the corner of the table.

Holmes had brought up a long thin cane, and this he placed upon the bed beside him. By it he laid the box of matches and the stump of a candle. Then he turned down the lamp, and we were left in darkness.

How shall I ever forget that dreadful vigil? I could not hear a sound, not even the drawing of a breath, and yet I knew that my companion sat open-eyed, within a few feet of me, in the same state of nervous tension in which I was myself. The shutters cut off the least ray of light, and we waited in absolute darkness. From outside came the occasional cry of a night bird, and once at our very window a long drawn catlike whine, which told us that the cheetah was indeed at liberty. Far away we could hear the deep tones of the parish clock, which boomed out every quarter of an hour. How long they seemed, those quarters! Twelve struck, and one and two and three, and still we sat waiting silently for whatever might befall.

Suddenly there was a momentary gleam of a light in the direction of the ventilator, which vanished immediately, but was succeeded by a strong smell of burning oil and heated metal. Someone in the next room had lit a dark lantern. I heard a gentle sound of movement, and then all was silent once more, though the smell grew stronger. For half an hour I sat with straining ears. Then suddenly another sound became audible—a very gentle, soothing sound, like that of a small jet stream escaping continually from a kettle. The instant that we heard it, Holmes sprang from the bed, struck a match, and lashed furiously with his cane at the bell-pull.

"You see it, Watson?" he yelled. "You see it?"

But I saw nothing. At the moment when Holmes struck the light I heard a low, clear whistle, but the sudden glare flashing into my weary eyes made it impossible for me to tell what it was at which my friend lashed so savagely. I could, however, see that his face was deadly pale and filled with horror and loathing.

He had ceased to strike and was gazing up at the ventilator when suddenly there broke from the silence of the night the most horrible cry to which I have ever listened. It swelled up louder and louder, a hoarse yell of pain and fear and anger all mingled in the one dreadful shriek. They say that away down in the village, and even in the distant parsonage, that cry raised the sleepers from their beds. It struck cold to our hearts, and I stood gazing at Holmes, and he at me, until the last echoes of it had died away into the silence from which it rose.

"What can it mean?" I gasped.

"It means that it is all over," Holmes answered. "And perhaps, after all, it is for the best. Take your pistol, and we will enter Dr. Roylott's room."

With a grave face he lit the lamp and led the way down the corridor. Twice he struck at the chamber door without any reply from within. Then he turned the handle and entered, I at his heels, with the cocked pistol in my hand.

It was a singular sight which met our eyes. On the table stood a dark lantern with the shutter half open, throwing a brilliant light upon the iron safe, the door of which was ajar. Beside the table, on the wooden chair, sat Dr. Grimesby Roylott, clad in a long gray dressing gown, his bare ankles protruding beneath, and his feet thrust into red heelless Turkish slippers. Across his lap lay the short stock with the long lash which we had noticed during the day. His chin was cocked upward and his eyes were fixed in a dreadful rigid stare at the corner of the ceiling. Round his brow he had a peculiar yellow band, with brownish speckles, which seemed to be bound tightly round his head. As we entered he made neither sound nor motion.

"The band! the speckled band!" whispered Holmes.

I took a step forward. In an instant his strange headgear began to move, and there reared itself from among his hair the squat diamond-shaped head and puffed neck of a loathsome serpent.

"It is a swamp adder!" cried Holmes; "the deadliest snake in India. He has died within ten seconds of being bitten. Violence does, in truth, recoil upon the violent, and the schemer

falls into the pit which he digs for another. Let us thrust this creature back into its den, and we can then remove Miss Stoner to some place of shelter and let the county police know what has happened."

As he spoke he drew the dog-whip swiftly from the dead man's lap, and throwing the noose round the reptile's neck he drew it from its horrid perch and, carrying it at arm's length, threw it into the iron safe, which he closed upon it.

Such are the true facts of the death of Dr. Grimesby Roylott, of Stoke Moran. It is not necessary that I should prolong a narrative which has already run to too great a length by telling how we broke the sad news to the terrified girl, how we conveyed her by the morning train to the care of her good aunt at Harrow, of how the slow process of official inquiry came to the conclusion that the doctor met his fate while discreetly playing with a dangerous pet. The little which I had yet to learn of the case was told me by Sherlock Holmes as we traveled back next day. "I had," said he, "come to an entirely erroneous conclusion which shows, my dear Watson, how dangerous it always is to reason from insufficient data. The presence of the gypsies, and the use of the word 'band,' which was used by the poor girl, no doubt to explain the appearance which she had caught a hurried glimpse of by the light of her match, were sufficient to put me upon an entirely wrong scent. I can only claim the merit that I instantly reconsidered my position when, however, it became clear to me that whatever danger threatened an occupant of the room could not come either from the window or the door. My attention was speedily drawn, as I have already remarked to you, to this ventilator, and to the bell-rope which hung down to the bed. The discovery that this was a dummy, and that the bed was clamped to the floor, instantly gave rise to the suspicion that the rope was there as a bridge for something passing through the hole and coming to the bed. The idea of a snake instantly occurred to me, and when I coupled it with my knowledge that the doctor was furnished with a supply of creatures from India, I felt that I was probably on the right track. The idea of using a form of poison which could not possibly be discovered by any chemical test was just such a one as would occur to a clever and ruthless man who had had an Eastern training. The rapidity with which such a poison would take effect would also, from his point of view, be an advantage.

It would be a sharp-eyed coroner, indeed, who could distinguish the two little dark punctures which would show where the poison fangs had done their work. Then I thought of the whistle. Of course he must recall the snake before the morning light revealed it to the victim. He had trained it, probably by use of the milk which we saw, to return to him when summoned. He would put it through this ventilator at the hour that he thought best, with the certainty that it would crawl down the rope and land on the bed. It might or might not bite the occupant, perhaps she might escape every night for a week, but sooner or later she must fall victim.

"I had come to these conclusions before ever I had entered his room. An inspection of his chair showed me this: he had been in the habit of standing on it, which of course would be necessary in order that he should reach the ventilator. The sight of the safe, the saucer of milk, and the loop of whipcord were enough to finally dispel any doubts which may have remained. The metallic clang heard by Miss Stoner was obviously caused by her stepfather hastily closing the door of his safe upon its terrible occupant. Having once made up my mind, you know the steps which I took in order to put the matter to the proof. I heard the creature hiss as I have no doubt that you did also, and I instantly lit the light and attacked it."

"With the result of driving it through the ventilator."

"And also with the result of causing it to turn upon its master at the other side. Some of the blows of my cane came home and roused its snakish temper, so that it flew upon the first person it saw. In this way I am no doubt indirectly responsible for Dr. Grimesby Roylott's death, and I cannot say that it is likely to weigh very heavily upon my conscience."

About the Story

1. When Helen Stoner visits Holmes early one morning to solicit his help, what literary device does Doyle use to explain the reason for her visit?
2. What story element is introduced to divert readers' (and Holmes's) attention from the real cause of the crime?
3. Identify the surprises that Holmes finds upon examining Julia's room.
4. Did Holmes intend for the "speckled band" to attack Dr. Roylott? Respond to the story's ending.
5. List at least three characteristics that help make mysteries like "The Speckled Band" enjoyable to read.

About the Author

Sir Arthur Conan Doyle (1859–1930) was born in Edinburgh, Scotland. Though Doyle's father was given to alcoholism and depression, his mother loved books and was a gifted storyteller. Doyle demonstrated this same storytelling ability at the Jesuit prep school where he boarded as a boy. Later, Doyle completed medical studies at the University of Edinburgh and eventually set up private practice. He continued, however, to write while the practice grew, but he eventually gave up his practice to write full time.

Doyle wrote in many genres, including historical novel, drama, poetry, nonfiction, and science fiction. He is best known, however, for his detective fiction with his enduring characters Sherlock Holmes and Dr. John Watson, first introduced in *A Study in Scarlet*. Holmes brilliantly uses his powers of observation and deductive reasoning to solve crimes. The public loved the stories and clamored when Sir Conan Doyle "killed" Holmes in 1893. The character finally returned for good in 1901 in the sensation *The Hound of the Baskervilles*.

Doyle himself considered his other, more serious writing to be much more important than his fiction. For example, after serving as a doctor in the Boer War, Doyle wrote *The Great Boer War* and *The War in South Africa*, defending England's position in the war. He was later knighted for his efforts. He demonstrated character and honor and worked to ensure justice. Doyle died of heart disease at his home in Sussex, surrounded by his family. His gravestone in part reads "Patriot, Physician & Man of Letters." Doyle's works have been translated into more than fifty languages, and his popularity continues.

A Visit of Charity

Eudora Welty

On the surface "A Visit of Charity" is a relatively simple story. Beneath the surface, however, lies a deeper meaning. In the absence of much action, notice how Welty uses everything—the description of setting; the characters' appearances, movements, and statements; the literary tools of symbol, allusion, and imaginative comparison—to advance the atmosphere, tone, and theme of her story. Stay alert to these literary devices as you read.

It was mid-morning—a very cold, bright day. Holding a potted plant before her, a girl of fourteen jumped off the bus in front of the Old Ladies' Home, on the outskirts of town. She wore a red coat, and her straight yellow hair was hanging down loose from the pointed white cap all the little girls were wearing that year. She stopped for a moment beside one of the prickly dark shrubs with which the city had beautified the Home, and then proceeded slowly toward the building, which was of whitewashed brick and reflected the winter sunlight like a block of ice. As she walked vaguely up the steps she shifted the small pot from hand to hand; then she had to set it down and remove her mittens before she could open the heavy door.

"I'm a Campfire Girl. . . . I have to pay a visit to some old lady," she told the nurse at the desk. This was a woman in a white uniform who looked as if she were cold; she had close-cut hair which stood up on the very top of her head exactly like a sea wave. Marian, the little girl, did not tell her that this visit would give her a minimum of only three points in her score.

"Acquainted with any of our residents?" asked the nurse. She lifted one eyebrow and spoke like a man.

"With any old ladies? No—but—that is, any of them will do," Marian stammered. With her free hand she pushed her hair behind her ears, as she did when it was time to study Science.

The nurse shrugged and rose. "You have a nice *multiflora cineraria** there," she remarked as she walked ahead down the hall of closed doors to pick out an old lady.

multiflora cineraria: a winter annual with either purple, blue, white, red, or pink flowers

There was loose, bulging linoleum on the floor. Marian felt as if she were walking on the waves, but the nurse paid no attention to it. There was a smell in the hall like the interior of a clock. Everything was silent until, behind one of the doors, an old lady of some kind cleared her throat like a sheep bleating. This decided the nurse. Stopping in her tracks, she first extended her arm, bent her elbow, and leaned forward from the hips—all to examine the watch strapped to her wrist; then she gave a loud double-rap on the door.

"There are two in each room," the nurse remarked over her shoulder.

"Two what?" asked Marian without thinking. The sound like a sheep's bleating almost made her turn around and run back.

One old woman was pulling the door open in short, gradual jerks, and when she saw the nurse a strange smile forced her old face dangerously awry. Marian, suddenly propelled by the strong, impatient arm of the nurse, saw next the side-face of another old woman, even older, who was lying flat in bed with a cap on and a counterpane drawn up to her chin.

"Visitor," said the nurse, and after one more shove she was off up the hall.

Marian stood tongue-tied; both hands held the potted plant. The old woman, still with that terrible, square smile (which was a smile of welcome) stamped on her bony face, was waiting. . . . Perhaps she said something. The old woman in bed said nothing at all, and she did not look around.

Suddenly Marian saw a hand, quick as a bird claw, reach up in the air and pluck the white cap off her head. At the same time, another claw to match drew her all the way into the room, and the next moment the door closed behind her.

"My, my, my," said the old lady at her side.

Marian stood enclosed by a bed, a washstand, and a chair; the tiny room had altogether too much furniture. Everything smelled wet—even the bare floor. She held onto the back of the chair, which was wicker and felt soft and damp. Her heart beat more and more slowly, her hands got colder and colder, and she could not hear whether the old women were saying anything or not. She could not see them very clearly. How dark it was! The window shade was down, and the only door was shut. Marian looked at the ceiling. . . . It was like being caught in a robbers' cave, just before one was murdered.

"Did you come to be our little girl for a while?" the first robber asked.

Then something was snatched from Marian's hand—the little potted plant.

"Flowers!" screamed the old woman. She stood holding the pot in an undecided way. "Pretty flowers," she added.

Then the old woman in bed cleared her throat and spoke. "They are not pretty," she said, still without looking around, but very distinctly.

Marian suddenly pitched* against the chair and sat down in it.

pitched: stumbled

"Pretty flowers," the first old woman insisted. "Pretty—pretty . . ."

Marian wished she had the little pot back for just a moment—she had forgotten to look at the plant herself before giving it away. What did it look like?

"Stinkweeds," said the other old woman sharply. She had a bunchy white forehead and red eyes like a sheep. Now she turned them toward Marian. The fogginess seemed to rise in her throat again, and she bleated, "Who—are—you?"

To her surprise, Marian could not remember her name. "I'm a Campfire Girl," she said finally.

"Watch out for the germs," said the old woman like a sheep, not addressing anyone.

"One came out last month to see us," said the first old woman.

A sheep or a germ? wondered Marian dreamily, holding onto the chair.

"Did not!" cried the other old woman.

"Did so! Read to us out of the Bible, and we enjoyed it!" screamed the first.

"Who enjoyed it!" said the woman in bed. Her mouth was unexpectedly small and sorrowful, like a pet's.

"We enjoyed it," insisted the other. "You enjoyed it—I enjoyed it."

"We all enjoyed it," said Marian, without realizing that she had said a word.

The first old woman had just finished putting the potted plant high, high on the top of the wardrobe, where it could hardly be seen from below. Marian wondered how she had ever succeeded in placing it there, how she could ever have reached so high.

"You mustn't pay any attention to old Addie," she now said to the little girl. "She's ailing today."

"Will you shut your mouth?" said the woman in bed. "I am not."

"You're a story."

"I can't stay but a minute—really, I can't," said Marian suddenly. She looked down at the wet floor and thought that if she were sick in here they would have to let her go.

With much to-do the first old woman sat down in a rocking chair—still another piece of furniture!—and began to rock. With the fingers of one hand she touched a very dirty cameo pin on her chest. "What do you do at school?" she asked.

"I don't know . . ." said Marian. She tried to think but she could not.

"Oh, but the flowers are beautiful," the old woman whispered. She seemed to rock faster and faster; Marian did not see how anyone could rock so fast.

"Ugly," said the woman in bed.

"If we bring flowers—" Marian began, and then fell silent. She had almost said that if Campfire Girls brought flowers to the Old Ladies' Home, the visit would count one extra point, and if they took a Bible with them on the bus and read it to the old ladies, it counted double. But the old woman had not listened, anyway; she was rocking and watching the other one, who watched back from the bed.

"Poor Addie is ailing. She has to take medicine—see?" she said, pointing a horny finger at a row of bottles on the table, and rocking so high that her black comfort shoes lifted off the floor like a little child's.

"I am no more sick than you are," said the woman in bed.

"Oh, yes you are!"

"I just got more sense than you have, that's all," said the other old woman, nodding her head.

"That's only the contrary way she talks when *you all* come," said the first old lady with sudden intimacy. She stopped the rocker with a neat pat of her feet and leaned toward Marian. Her hand reached over—it felt like a petunia leaf, clinging and just a little sticky.

"Will you hush! Will you hush!" cried the other one.

Marian leaned back rigidly in her chair.

"When I was a little girl like you, I went to school and all," said the old woman in the same intimate, menacing voice. "Not here—another town. . . ."

"Hush!" said the sick woman. "You never went to school. You never came and you never went. You never were anything—only here. You never were born! You don't know anything. Your head is empty, your heart and hands and your old black purse are all empty, even that little old box that you brought with you you brought empty—you showed it to me And yet you talk, talk, talk, talk, talk all the time until I think I'm losing my mind! Who are you? You're a stranger—a perfect stranger! Don't you know you're a stranger? Is it possible that they have actually done a thing like this to anyone—sent them in a stranger to talk, and rock, and tell away her whole long rigmarole? Do they seriously suppose that I'll be able to keep it

up, day in, day out, night in, night out, living in the same room with a terrible old woman—forever?"

Marian saw the old woman's eyes grow bright and turn toward her. This old woman was looking at her with despair and calculation in her face. Her small lips suddenly dropped apart, and exposed a half circle of false teeth with tan gums.

"Come here, I want to tell you something," she whispered. "Come here!"

Marian was trembling, and her heart nearly stopped beating altogether for a moment.

"Now, now, Addie," said the first old woman. "That's not polite. Do you know what's really the matter with old Addie today?" She, too, looked at Marian; one of her eyelids drooped low.

"The matter?" the child repeated stupidly. "What's the matter with her?"

"Why, she's mad because it's her birthday!" said the first old woman, beginning to rock again and giving a little crow as though she had answered her own riddle.

"It is not, it is not!" screamed the old woman in bed. "It is not my birthday, no one knows when that is but myself, and will you please be quiet and say nothing more, or I'll go straight out of my mind!" She turned her eyes toward Marian again, and presently she said in the soft, foggy voice, "When the worst comes to the worst, I ring this bell, and the nurse comes." One of her hands was drawn out from under the patched counterpane—a thin little hand with enormous black freckles. With a finger which would not hold still she pointed to a little bell on the table among the bottles.

"How old are you?" Marian breathed. Now she could see the old woman in bed very closely and plainly, and very abruptly, from all sides, as in dreams. She wondered about her—she wondered for a moment as though there was nothing else in the world to wonder about. It was the first time such a thing had happened to Marian.

"I won't tell!"

The old face on the pillow, where Marian was bending over it, slowly gathered and collapsed. Soft whimpers came out of the small open mouth. It was a sheep that she sounded like—a little lamb. Marian's face drew very close, the yellow hair hung forward.

"She's crying!" She turned a bright, burning face up to the first old woman.

"That's Addie for you," the old woman said spitefully.

Marian jumped up and moved toward the door. For the second time, the claw almost touched her hair, but it was not quick enough. The little girl put her cap on.

"Well, it was a real visit," said the old woman, following Marian through the doorway and all the way out into the hall. Then from behind she suddenly clutched the child with her sharp little fingers. In an affected, high-pitched whine she cried, "Oh, little girl, have you a penny to spare for a poor old woman that's not got anything of her own? We don't have a thing in the world—not a penny for candy—not a thing! Little girl, just a nickel—a penny—"

Marian pulled violently against the old hands for a moment before she was free. Then she ran down the hall, without looking behind her and without looking at the nurse, who was reading *Field & Stream* at her desk. The nurse, after another triple motion to consult her wrist watch, asked automatically the question put to visitors in all institutions: "Won't you stay and have dinner with *us*?"

Marian never replied. She pushed the heavy door open into the cold air and ran down the steps.

Under the prickly shrub she stooped and quickly, without being seen, retrieved a red apple she had hidden there.

Her yellow hair under the white cap, her scarlet coat, her bare knees all flashed in the sunlight as she ran to meet the big bus rocketing through the street.

"Wait for me!" she shouted. As though at an imperial command, the bus ground to a stop.

She jumped on and took a big bite out of the apple.

About the Story

1. What details in the story shape the reader's impression of the facility in which the ladies live? What is your impression?
2. Explain the irony in the title. How does character motivation play a part in that irony?
3. What is the significance of the color of Marian's coat?
4. Identify the imaginative comparisons used in the following quotations. What is their effect in the story?

   > Behind one of the doors, an old lady of some kind cleared her throat like a sheep bleating.

   > Suddenly Marian saw a hand, quick as a bird claw, reach up in the air and pluck the white cap off her head.

5. Which object in the story is symbolic? Explain the symbolism.

About the Author

Eudora Welty (1909–2001) commands an undisputed place among the most accomplished American writers of fiction. Her fiction, set in the American South, reflects the culture and language, reproducing Southern idiom and expression. Her universal themes of family and community, however, transcend regional boundaries. In simple, elegant style incorporating humor and much detail, Welty brought to life a plethora of everyday characters, alike only in their humanity.

In her autobiography, *One Writer's Beginnings*, Welty shared the childhood that shaped her creative imagination. Her parents, Christian and Chestina Welty, provided a protective and nurturing home for her and her two younger brothers. Books were an integral part of that home, where any room was one in which to read or be read to. Early on she developed the art of listening and the power of observation, skills necessary to a writer.

Welty trained at Mississippi State College for Women and the University of Wisconsin. She then attended the Columbia Graduate School of Business. Following her father's death in 1931, Welty returned to Jackson, where she worked doing correspondent and publicity work until 1933, at which time she took a job with the Works Projects Administration. For three years she traveled the state, etching into her memory people, places, and stories. Welty's first published story, "Death of a Traveling Salesman," launched her writing career, which included both fiction and nonfiction. By the time of her death at age 92, Welty had attained wide recognition. Her awards include a Pulitzer Prize and honorary degrees from at least thirty-nine colleges and universities.

Civil Peace

Chinua Achebe

Achebe wrote this story after living through the Nigerian Civil War (1967–70). It is set during the immediate aftermath of the war, the same time in which it was written (1971). Most of us have not personally experienced war and its losses as Achebe did. However, you may have already experienced obstacles and difficulties of various degrees in life. As you read "Civil Peace," note how Jonathan responds to circumstances beyond his control. What lessons can you learn from him? Analyze how Achebe directs the elements of his story to create a brief but significant study of character.

Jonathan Iwegbu counted himself extraordinarily lucky. "Happy survival!" meant so much more to him than just a current fashion of greeting old friends in the first hazy days of peace. It went deep to his heart. He had come out of the war with five inestimable blessings—his head, his wife Maria's head and the heads of three out of their four children. As a bonus he also had his old bicycle—a miracle too but naturally not to be compared to the safety of five human heads.

The bicycle had a little history of its own. One day at the height of the war it was commandeered "for urgent military action." Hard as its loss would have been to him he would still have let it go without a thought had he not had some doubts about the genuineness of the officer. It wasn't his disreputable rags, nor the toes peeping out of one blue and one brown canvas shoe, nor yet the two stars of his rank done obviously in a hurry in biro,* that troubled Jonathan; many good and heroic soldiers looked the same or worse. It was rather a certain lack of grip and firmness in his manner. So Jonathan, suspecting he might be amenable* to influence, rummaged in his raffia bag and produced the two pounds with which he had been going to buy firewood which his wife, Maria, retailed to camp officials for extra stock-fish and corn meal, and got his bicycle back. That night he buried it in the little clearing in the bush where the dead of the camp, including his own youngest son, were buried. When he dug it up again a year later after the surrender all it needed was a little palm-oil greasing. "Nothing puzzles God," he said in wonder.

He put it to immediate use as a taxi and accumulated a small pile of Biafran* money ferrying camp officials and their families across the four-mile stretch to the nearest tarred road. His standard charge per trip was six pounds and those who had the money were only glad to be rid of some of it in this way. At the end of a fortnight* he had made a small fortune of one hundred and fifteen pounds.

biro: ballpoint pen
amenable: responsive
Biafran: relating to a region of southeastern Nigeria
fortnight: two weeks

Then he made the journey to Enugu and found another miracle waiting for him. It was unbelievable. He rubbed his eyes and looked again and it was still standing there before him. But, needless to say, even that monumental blessing must be accounted also totally inferior to the five heads in the family. This newest miracle was his little house in Ogui Overside. Indeed nothing puzzles God! Only two houses away a huge concrete edifice some wealthy contractor had put up just before the war was a mountain of rubble. And here was Jonathan's

little zinc house of no regrets built with mud blocks quite intact! Of course the doors and windows were missing and five sheets off the roof. But what was that? And anyhow he had returned to Enugu early enough to pick up bits of old zinc and wood and soggy sheets of cardboard lying around the neighborhood before thousands more came out of their forest holes looking for the same things. He got a destitute carpenter with one old hammer, a blunt plane and a few bent and rusty nails in his tool bag to turn this assortment of wood, paper and metal into door and window shutters for five Nigerian shillings or fifty Biafran pounds. He paid the pounds, and moved in with his overjoyed family carrying five heads on their shoulders.

His children picked mangoes near the military cemetery and sold them to soldiers' wives for a few pennies—real pennies this time—and his wife started making breakfast akara* balls for neighbors in a hurry to start life again. With his family earnings he took his bicycle to the villages around and bought fresh palm-wine which he mixed generously in his rooms with the water which had recently started running again in the public tap down the road, and opened up a bar for soldiers and other lucky people with good money.

akara: fried cakes made from black-eyed peas

At first he went daily, then every other day and finally once a week, to the offices of the Coal Corporation where he used to be a miner, to find out what was what. The only thing he did find out in the end was that that little house of his was even a greater blessing than he had thought. Some of his fellow ex-miners who had nowhere to return at the end of the day's waiting just slept outside the doors of the offices and cooked what meal they could scrounge together in Bournvita* tins. As the weeks lengthened and still nobody could say what was what Jonathan discontinued his weekly visits altogether and faced his palm-wine bar.

Bournvita: a malted chocolate beverage

But nothing puzzles God. Came the day of the windfall when after five days of endless scuffles in queues* and counterqueues in the sun outside the Treasury he had twenty pounds counted into his palm as ex-gratia* award for the rebel money he had turned in. It was like Christmas for him and for many others like him when the payments began. They called it (since few could manage its proper official name) egg-rasher.

queues: lines
ex-gratia: given as a favor

As soon as the pound notes were placed in his palm Jonathan simply closed it tight over them and buried fist and money inside his trouser pocket. He had to be extra careful because he had seen a man a couple of days earlier collapse into near-madness in an instant before that oceanic crowd because no sooner had he got his twenty pounds than some heartless ruffian picked it off him. Though it was not right that a man in such an extremity of agony should be blamed yet many in the queues that day were able to remark quietly at the victim's carelessness, especially after he pulled out the innards of his pocket and revealed a hole in it big enough to pass a thief's head. But of course he had insisted that the money had been in the other pocket, pulling it out too to show its comparative wholeness. So one had to be careful.

Jonathan soon transferred the money to his left hand and pocket so as to leave his right free for shaking hands should the need arise, though by fixing his gaze at such an elevation as to miss all approaching human faces he made sure that the need did not arise, until he got home.

He was normally a heavy sleeper but that night he heard all the neighborhood noises die down one after another. Even the night watchman who knocked the hour on some metal somewhere in the distance had fallen silent after knocking one o'clock. That must have been the last thought in Jonathan's mind before he was finally carried away himself. He couldn't have been gone for long, though, when he was violently awakened again.

"Who is knocking?" whispered his wife lying beside him on the floor.

"I don't know," he whispered back breathlessly.

The second time the knocking came it was so loud and imperious* that the rickety old door could have fallen down.

imperious: urgent; commanding

"Who is knocking?" he asked them, his voice parched and trembling.

"Na tief-man and him people," came the cool reply. "Make you hopen de door."* This was followed by the heaviest knocking of all.

"Na tief-man and him people. . . . Make you hopen de door": The man's dialect is a combination of English and his own language. When Jonathan asks who is knocking, the man answers, "The thief man and his people" and demands that Jonathan open the door.

Maria was the first to raise the alarm, then he followed and all their children.

"Police-o! Thieves-o! Neighbors-o! Police-o! We are lost! We are dead! Neighbors, are you asleep? Wake up! Police-o!"

This went on for a long time and then stopped suddenly. Perhaps they had scared the thief away. There was total silence. But only for a short while.

"You done finish?" asked the voice outside. "Make we help you small. Oya, everybody!"

"Police-o! Tief-man-so! Neighbors-o! we done loss-o! Police-o! . . ."

There were at least five other voices besides the leader's.

Jonathan and his family were now completely paralyzed by terror. Maria and the children sobbed inaudibly like lost souls. Jonathan groaned continuously.

The silence that followed the thieves' alarm vibrated horribly. Jonathan all but begged their leader to speak again and be done with it.

"My frien," said he at long last, "we don try our best for call dem but I tink say dem all done sleep-o . . . So wetin we go do now? Sometaim you wan call soja?* Or you wan make we call dem for you? Soja better pass police. No be so?"

soja: soldiers

"Na so!" replied his men. Jonathan thought he heard even more voices now than before and groaned heavily. His legs were sagging under him and his throat felt like sandpaper.

"My frien, why you no de talk again. I de ask you say you wan make we call soja?"

"No."

"Awrighto. Now make we talk business. We no be bad tief. We no like for make trouble. Trouble done finish. War done finish and all the katakata* wey de for inside. No Civil War again. This time na Civil Peace. No be so?

katakata: perhaps onomatopoeia for the sound of a gun

"Na so!" answered the horrible chorus.

"What do you want from me? I am a poor man. Everything I had went with this war. Why do you come to me? You know people who have money. We . . ."

"Awright! We know say you no get plenty money. But we sef no get even anini.* So derefore make you open this window and give us one hundred pound and we go commot. Orderwise we de come for inside now to show you guitar-boy like dis . . ."

anini: a Nigerian coin no longer used but originally worth one-tenth of a penny

A volley of automatic fire rang through the sky. Maria and the children began to weep aloud again.

"Ah, missisi de cry again. No need for dat. We done talk say we na good tief. We just take our small money and go nwayorly. No molest. Abi* we de molest?"

abi: Isn't that right?

"At all!" sang the chorus.

"My friends," began Jonathan hoarsely. "I hear what you say and I thank you. If I had one hundred pounds . . ."

"Lookia my frien, no be play we come play for your house. If we make mistake and step for inside you no go like am-o. So derefore . . ."

"To God who made me; if you come inside and find one hundred pounds, take it and shoot me and shoot my wife and children. I swear to God. The only money I have in this life is this twenty-pounds *egg-rasher* they gave me today. . ."

"Ok. Time de go. Make you open dis window and bring the twenty pound. We go manage am like dat."

There were now loud murmurs of dissent among the chorus: "Na lie de man lie; e get plenty money . . . Make we go inside and search properly well . . . Wetin be twenty pound? . . ."

"Shurrup!" rang the leader's voice like a lone shot in the sky and silenced the murmuring at once. "Are you dere? Bring the money quick!"

"I am coming," said Jonathan fumbling in the darkness with the key of the small wooden box he kept by his side on the mat.

At the first sign of light as neighbors and others assembled to commiserate* with him he was already strapping his five-gallon demijohn to his bicycle carrier and his wife, sweating in the open fire, was turning over akara balls in a wide clay bowl of boiling oil. In the corner his eldest son was rinsing out dregs of yesterday's palm-wine from old beer bottles.

commiserate: sympathize

"I count it as nothing," he told his sympathizers, his eyes on the rope he was tying. "What is egg-rasher? Did I depend on it last week? Or is it greater than other things that went with the war? I say, let *egg-rasher* perish in the flames! Let it go where everything else has gone. Nothing puzzles God."

About the Story

1. What is the source of the story's title? What is the significance of that title?
2. Identify an imaginative comparison and a sound device in the following quotation. Are these devices effective as used here?

   > "Na so!" replied his men. Jonathan thought he heard even more voices now than before and groaned heavily. His legs were sagging under him and his throat felt like sandpaper.

3. Readers learn about characters in three ways: (1) by what the character says, (2) by what the character does, and (3) by what other characters say about him or her. In which of these ways does the reader best learn about Jonathan? Describe Jonathan's character. Support your answer.
4. Is the protagonist in the story a static or a dynamic character?
5. Evaluate the tone of the story. Does Achebe admire Jonathan? Do you?
6. Formulate a theme for "Civil Peace."

Jonathan never overtly questions whether his circumstances are fair. Instead he responds, "Nothing puzzles God" and moves on with his life. What does he mean by this statement, and why do you think this idea helps him focus on the future? Imagine you are discussing Achebe's story with an unsaved friend. How could you use Jonathan's worldview to discuss the spiritual realities of life with your friend? What kinds of ideas might you cover in such a discussion?

About the Author

Chinua Achebe (b. 1930) is an influential African poet, novelist, and critic. The son of educated Christian parents, Achebe grew up in Ogidi in southeastern Nigeria, where his family belonged to the Igbo tribe. An excellent student, Achebe first attended Government College, followed by University College, where his course of study was history, theology, and English. Following graduation, Achebe initially taught and then went into broadcasting.

In 1959 Achebe published his first novel, *Things Fall Apart*, which introduced some of the major themes of his works and earned him international recognition. A sequel and additional novels followed. When the Nigerian Civil War (1967–70) erupted, Achebe backed the Igbo-led Republic of Biafra, serving as its ambassador until its defeat by Nigerian forces. During the war, Achebe wrote mainly poems, afterward publishing these in a collection entitled *Beware, Soul Brother*. Accepting a professorship at the University of Massachusetts Amherst in 1972, Achebe taught there for several years and then spent a decade at the University of Nigeria before returning to teach again in America. Unhappily, a car accident in 1990 left him paralyzed from the waist down. In addition to teaching, he continues to write and has published numerous creative, academic, and political works.

A serious student of Igbo culture, Achebe incorporates elements of his native culture into his writing, and his major themes examine how this culture has intersected with colonialism and Christianity. Although Achebe chooses to write in English, he changes word order and idiom to create an African style that communicates as much as possible the spoken language of the Igbo. Into this narrative Achebe weaves folktales and proverbs illustrating Igbo tradition. For his work Achebe has received many honorary degrees and several international awards, including the Man Booker International Prize in 2007.

THINKING ZONE

In the classic Japanese film *Rashomon*, police trying to solve a murder interview various witnesses. Each witness tells his version of events, but these differ so much that determining the truth is difficult. The film illustrates an important fact: perspective matters. A person's view of life depends on the vantage point—physical, spiritual, or emotional—from which he sees it. In similar fashion, writers can change a story almost beyond recognition simply by changing its point of view.

Literary **point of view** signifies the perspective from which the author presents the conflicts, characters, and events of a story. Generally, point of view is categorized by how much the narrator knows of events and of other characters' inner lives. Critics primarily distinguish between narrators who refer to all the characters in the third person (*she*, *he*, *they*) and those who speak from a first-person perspective (i.e., use the pronoun *I*). By choosing one over the other, an author may both expand and contract the kind of information that he is able to relate (or relate reliably) to his audience.

Third-person perspectives (of which there are two) offer the greatest liberty to relay information. In the **omniscient** point of view, the storyteller knows all. He can describe any setting, event, or conversation pertaining to the story and can even tell what every character is thinking and feeling. A narrator with a **limited-omniscient** viewpoint does the same, except he can "get inside the head" of only one character.

In contrast, a **first-person** narrator is a character in the story and can see, hear, feel, and know only what that character does. This approach limits access to information about events or other characters but deepens readers' knowledge of one character. A first-person narrator can be much easier to relate to since everything is seen from his perspective. But such narrators can also be unreliable: they may be deceived, blinded by prejudice, or limited by their distance from events or inability to understand what others are thinking. In any case, it is clear that an author's chosen point of view strongly influences the development of character, conflict, and theme as well as tone.

1. Which of the four short stories in this unit is narrated from a **first-person** perspective?
2. The remaining three stories are all written from which **point of view**?
3. In "The Sire de Maletroit's Door" how does the point of view chosen by the author affect readers' sympathy with the characters?
4. In "The Adventure of the Speckled Band" what is the advantage of having Watson rather than Holmes narrate the story?
5. Imagine that "A Visit of Charity" were narrated by one of the two old women. How would the story probably change?
6. Given Achebe's theme in "Civil Peace," why do you think he did not have Jonathan tell his own story?

UNIT VI REVIEW

Remember the Terms

Review the following terms from the opening essay, "Essay and Short Story," the Thinking Zone pages, and the headnotes. Be prepared to discuss their meanings and uses.

essay
formal essay
informal essay
short story
plot
subplot
exposition
inciting incident
rising action
crisis
climax
falling action
dénouement
point of view
omniscient point of view
limited-omniscient point of view
first-person point of view

Apply the Concepts

Answer the following questions about how the literary concepts you have studied are used in this unit.

1. From what point of view is "How to Get Things Done" written?
2. What kind of essay is "How to Get Things Done"?
3. In "A Miserable Merry Christmas" Lennie says, "If I can't have a pony, give me nothing, nothing." What kind of irony does his statement illustrate?
4. From what point of view is "A Miserable Merry Christmas" written?
5. How would you describe the tone of Engle's "An Old-Fashioned Iowa Christmas"?
6. In describing the goose and its uses, Engle makes use of two imaginative comparisons. Give one.
7. What imaginative comparison is illustrated in the following quotation? "Dry seedpods will rattle like tiny gourds."
8. Is "Why the Leaves Turn Color in the Fall" a formal or an informal essay?
9. What do Denis and Blanche symbolize in "The Sire de Maletroit's Door"?
10. In explaining Helen Stoner's reason for visiting Sherlock, Doyle makes use of what device to catch the reader up?
11. Holmes and Watson's vigil in the bedroom where Helen Stoner should have been sleeping is the culmination of what element in the short story?
12. In "A Visit of Charity" what do Marian's gift of a flower and her motives for giving it reveal about the story's title?
13. In "Civil Peace" Jonathan's ability both to keep and to use his bicycle for profit speaks to which of his character traits?

14. "In Civil Peace" Jonathan repeatedly expresses thanks for his family members' safety. What kind of imaginative comparison does he use in the way he refers to his family at these times?

Evaluate the Ideas

Identify each of the following statements as true or false. If false, rewrite the underlined portion of the statement to make it true.

15. "How to Get Things Done" is a parody.
16. Benchley's essay contains dramatic irony.
17. Lennie's sisters are indifferent to his plight on Christmas morning.
18. Currying, brushing, and feeding Lennie's horse and eating Christmas dinner are part of the narrative's dénouement.
19. "An Old-Fashioned Iowa Christmas" contains two allusions to Santa Claus.
20. The title "An Old-Fashioned Iowa Christmas" is a paradox.
21. Ackerman's essay "Why the Leaves Turn Color in the Fall" is strictly scientific.
22. In his reference to the brevity of life, Denis, in "The Sire de Maletroit's Door," alludes to a passage in the book of James.
23. "The Sire de Maletroit's Door" illustrates dramatic irony.
24. In "The Adventure of the Speckled Band," Dr. Roylott met and married Mrs. Stoner in India.
25. In "The Adventure of the Speckled Band," a bed clamped to the floor, a ventilator vented to another room, a fake bell-pull, and a glass of water are all clues that enabled Holmes to solve the mystery of the speckled band.
26. In "A Visit of Charity" Welty uses an imaginative comparison to describe Addie in terms of a bird.
27. Welty alludes to the fairy tale "Hansel and Gretel" in "A Visit of Charity."
28. In "Civil Peace," Achebe makes use of dialect to add to the realism of his characters.

Write a Response

Completely answer each of the following questions.

29. Discuss the irony inherent in the titles of "Civil Peace" and "A Visit of Charity."
30. Compare and contrast the two autobiographical essays on Christmas.

UNIT VII

THE PALACE OF WESTMINSTER
André Derain

POETRY

French artist André Derain (1880–1954) began his career by studying engineering but abandoned it to study painting. Along with Vlaminck and Matisse, Derain defined fauvism, a style of painting characterized by bright colors, broken brush strokes, and spontaneity. However, the movement was short lived. Around 1908 Derain's work underwent a shift to a postimpressionist style evidencing the influence of van Gogh and Cezanne. By the 1920s Derain had shifted again to catch the spirit of the day and was painting in more of a neoclassical style. He continued in this style until his death.

The Palace of Westminster *is among Derain's most popular paintings. It is one of thirty scenes of London painted at the request of art dealer Ambroise Vollard during one of three short visits to the city between March 1906 and February 1907. Though Vollard purchased all the paintings, he never exhibited them in Paris as he had intended, perhaps because the pieces represented such a departure from tradition. Though he admired them, they were somewhat shocking for the time, illustrating the aesthetic revolution of fauvism.*

- ❋ The picture depicts the Houses of Parliament in London. What famous landmark rising above the buildings helps to identify the location?
- ❋ Imagine yourself in the picture. What sounds do you hear or not hear?
- ❋ Why do you think Derain portrayed the color of the water in the foreground differently than that in the distance?
- ❋ How does Derain use both his choice of subject and his technique to evoke a mood?

POETRY

In the realm of literary writing, poetry is perhaps the hardest genre to understand completely. In many ways, it is impossible to explain exactly why a poem moves us, no matter how we analyze its parts and effects. But poetry is clearly worth taking time to appreciate, for it has formed and still does form a vital part of human culture in societies around the world. In both ancient and modern times, it has been the language of love and of sorrow, of song and of remembrance, of quiet meditation and sometimes of fierce condemnation. It is a great many things to a great many people, and by studying it, you can gain insight into the human mind and heart.

The Nature of Poetry

Much like prose, poetry is an extremely varied genre accommodating numerous subjects, purposes, and forms. In some ways, prose and poetry do overlap: the short story and the novel might be considered prose cousins to short narrative poems and the long poetic epics of the past, while lyric poetry often explores a poet's topic in the personal manner of the informal essay. Still, poetry and prose exhibit some obvious distinctions; for example, it would strike most readers as ludicrous to use poetic form to conduct conversations or convey simple factual information. Poetry is simply not meant for such a prosaic purpose.

But what exactly makes poetry, poetry? Concisely defined, **poetry** is artfully compressed thought resulting in the elevated expression of ideas. To achieve this compression without a loss of meaning, a poet employs all the subtle qualities of language alongside a highly organized structure. Thus, while many of the important elements of literature you studied in Units I–IV may be found in prose, they occur with far greater intensity (of frequency and purpose) in poetry. More importantly, a poet employs these with the intent to delight readers, not just with his ideas but also with the manner in which he expresses them. He uses language for both its meaning and its aesthetic qualities. Through imagery, sound devices, and symmetry, poetry appeals to our senses and to our love of beauty. It also puts a much higher premium on the intangible elements of imagination and emotion than does prose. Rather than simply telling us a truth, poets try to help us experience it.

Essentials of Poetry

Given the need for compression and the goal of creating delight, poets must carefully calculate imagery, word choices, and even the sounds and structure of a poem. Appreciative readers should take particular note of these four elements: they strongly affect the meaning, mood, and tone of the poem as well as the power of its expression.

First, good imagery is central to poetry. In most poems, imagery thrives in two forms: direct descriptions using **concrete language** (words appealing to one or more of the five senses) and references such as imaginative comparison, allusion, and symbol. As you have already studied, the latter three play off images, conscripting into the poet's service associations outside his poem. Unsurprisingly, poets make full use of this ability to compress depths and layers of meaning into a short space. But in either of these forms, imagery adds clarity and power to a poet's message, evoking readers' experiences to make the poet's ideas seem more tangible and applicable to life.

Poets also carefully calculate individual word choices. Whereas prose often emphasizes the denotative meaning of words, poetry depends on the **connotative**—that is, the implications and emotional overtones some words carry beyond their dictionary definitions. Such words subtly convey extra meanings (for example, the author's tone towards his subject). As a result, it is sometimes instructive to consider which word a poet could have but did *not* use at a particular point in his poem.

A third important element of poetry is its use of sound. As you have already studied at length in Unit II, certain sounds can add to a poem's aesthetic appeal while creating or enhancing mood, meaning, and emphasis (see euphony, cacophony, rhyme, alliteration, consonance, assonance, and onomatopoeia). Though rhyme is the sound device most identified with poetry, it is, in fact, not required. Far more important is the use of **rhythm** (the more or less regular recurrence of stressed syllables), a facet many consider the defining characteristic of poetry. Just as music employs rhythm to organize and emphasize sounds and to set a mood, so too can poetry. Even when a poem exhibits no set meter, some sort of cadence will exist to create emphasis, enforce mood, or help organize and connect various lines.

Finally, because of poetry's need for compression, structure contributes far more to meaning in a poem than in a prose work. The basic structural division of poetry—the line—is usually dictated by the demands of rhythm and content. Poets place individual words and sound devices into arrangements that emphasize the most important ideas, connect those ideas when necessary, and relate them in a rhythmically pleasing way. Lines themselves are further organized into **stanzas**, divisions of poems based on thought, meter, or rhyme and recognized by the number of lines they contain. Within and between specific lines or stanzas, repetition and parallelism of ideas or syntax often connect, contrast, or emphasize certain ideas. Together these features help create rhythm, emphasis, and coherence and enhance the meaning and beauty of the poem. In great poetry, such structural devices are not arbitrary. How a poet chooses to organize his words can have a great effect on how readers perceive his ideas.

Genres in Poetry

Though they often overlap, subgenres based on both content and form abound in poetry. Indeed, the high importance of poetic structure has led to more genres with strict formal demands than are found in prose or drama. From the ode to the rondeau to the ballad (and more), forms can help the poet direct his thoughts and artistic endeavors. Frost alluded to this function in his famed comment on free verse: to him it was "playing tennis with the net down."

Individual forms are usually capable of encompassing huge ranges in subject and mood. As a result, some have proven quite popular for many years, though they may undergo slight renovations to keep their currency. Genres based on content tend to fare better, being more flexible. For example, lyric poetry encompasses a huge number of poems because its requirements are relatively few: **lyric poems** are generally brief, expressing the personal views of a single speaker on a particular topic. This broad genre typifies poetry in many people's minds and will form the greater part of your study in this unit.

In poetry, the whole is often greater than the sum of its parts. Yet it is still important to try to appreciate the poet's entire message. Note the crafting of words, imagery, sounds, and structure. Why did the poet choose a certain word? How does the poem's main image contribute to the theme? What atmosphere or emphasis do the sounds of the poem create? Why are the lines and stanzas shaped as they are? Poetry best rewards readers who take the time to appreciate it fully. Christians can learn to appreciate the artistry of a poem even when they do not agree with the idea or worldview that the poet has expressed.

I will sing unto the Lord, for he hath triumphed gloriously

Exodus 15:1–18

Given poetry's pervasive presence in human culture, it is not surprising that the Scriptures abound with poems. While Psalms is the best known example, other books, especially the histories, contain some beautiful poems tucked within their narratives. The following example of lyric poetry was composed (by whom we do not know) to celebrate Israel's delivery from Pharaoh and his army at the Red Sea. Notice that, as with Hebrew poetry in general, the poem is structured around repetition and parallelism of thought and syntax rather than meter or rhyme.

I will sing unto the Lord, for he hath triumphed gloriously:
the horse and his rider hath he thrown into the sea.
The Lord is my strength and song, and he is become my salvation:
he is my God, and I will prepare him an habitation;
my father's God, and I will exalt him.
The Lord is a man of war:
the Lord is his name.
Pharaoh's chariots and his host hath he cast into the sea:
his chosen captains also are drowned in the Red sea.
The depths have covered them:
they sank into the bottom as a stone.
Thy right hand, O Lord, is become glorious in power:
thy right hand, O Lord, hath dashed in pieces the enemy.
And in the greatness of thine excellency thou hast overthrown them that rose up against thee:
thou sentest forth thy wrath, which consumed them as stubble.
And with the blast of thy nostrils the waters were gathered together,
the floods stood upright as an heap,
and the depths were congealed in the heart of the sea.
The enemy said, I will pursue, I will overtake, I will divide the spoil;
my lust shall be satisfied upon them;
I will draw my sword, my hand shall destroy them.

Thou didst blow with thy wind, the sea covered them:
they sank as lead in the mighty waters.
Who is like unto thee, O Lord, among the gods?
who is like thee, glorious in holiness, fearful in praises, doing wonders?
Thou stretchedst out thy right hand,
the earth swallowed them.
Thou in thy mercy hast led forth the people which thou hast redeemed:
thou hast guided them in thy strength unto thy holy habitation.
The people shall hear, and be afraid:
sorrow shall take hold on the inhabitants of Palestina.
Then the dukes of Edom shall be amazed;
the mighty men of Moab, trembling shall take hold upon them;
all the inhabitants of Canaan shall melt away.
Fear and dread shall fall upon them;
by the greatness of thine arm they shall be as still as a stone;
till thy people pass over, O Lord,
till the people pass over, which thou hast purchased.
Thou shalt bring them in, and plant them in the mountain of thine inheritance,
in the place, O Lord, which thou hast made for thee to dwell in,
in the Sanctuary, O Lord, which thy hands have established.
The Lord shall reign for ever and ever.

About the Poem

1. What is the theme of the poem?
2. Who is the clear hero of the poem? Name three qualities that this hero exhibits.
3. The speaker keeps retelling what the Lord did to the Egyptians. Why do you think the speaker repeats himself so much? What kind of atmosphere does this repetition create?
4. Much of the poet's repetition also exhibits parallel syntax. How does this parallelism add to the poem?
5. What rhetorical device does the poet use to turn the poem from a look at the past to a hope for future events?
6. The poet doesn't simply rejoice in the present triumph; he also uses it as the basis to anticipate future victories. How can we follow his example in our own spiritual lives?

Literature is a tool that can be used to spread God's words and God's kingdom to others, but it is also a marvelous tool for expressing your own thoughts and prayers to God—such as in a journal. Write a brief psalm of at least ten lines expressing thanksgiving to God for some of His blessings to you and hope for future blessings you anticipate from His Word. Use parallelism as exhibited in this poem.

Snow-Bound

JOHN GREENLEAF WHITTIER

In his famous description of a New England snowstorm, Whittier takes a narrative approach to his topic. Narrative poems form some of the oldest examples of poetry and are still popular today. They combine the beauties of poetic form with people's love of a good story, and just like prose stories, they can be used to communicate themes. Written in chronological order, Whittier's poem portrays the effects of the storm on the landscape and on human activity. Note how the setting shifts between indoors and outdoors with an attendant change in activity and atmosphere. How does Whittier's use of imagery in both of these settings reinforce the central conflict and themes of the poem?

The sun that brief December day
Rose cheerless over hills of gray,
And, darkly circled, gave at noon
A sadder light than waning moon.
Slow tracing down the thickening sky
Its mute and ominous prophecy,
A portent seeming less than threat,
It sank from sight before it set.
A chill no coat, however stout,
Of homespun stuff could quite shut out,
A hard, dull bitterness of cold,
That checked, mid-vein, the circling race
Of life-blood in the sharpened face,
The coming of the snowstorm told.
The wind blew east; we heard the roar
Of Ocean on his wintry shore,
And felt the strong pulse throbbing there
Beat with low rhythm our inland air.
Meanwhile we did our nightly chores,
Brought in the wood from out of doors,
Littered the stalls, and from the mows,*
Raked down the herd's-grass* for the cows:
Heard the horse whinnying for his corn;
And, sharply clashing horn on horn,
Impatient down the stanchion rows*
The cattle shake their walnut bows,*
While, peering from his early perch
Upon the scaffold's pole of birch
The cock his crested helmet bent
And down his querulous* challenge sent.
Unwarmed by any sunset light
The gray day darkened into night,

mows: storage places for hay or grain

herd's-grass: timothy hay or redtop

rows: posts used for controlling cattle

bows: collars attached to the stanchions

querulous: irritable, complaining

A night made hoary with the swarm
And whirl-dance of the blinding storm,
As zigzag, wavering to and fro
Crossed and recrossed the winged snow:
And ere the early bedtime came
The white drift piled the window-frame,
And through the glass the clothes-line posts
Looked in like tall and sheeted ghosts.

So all night long the storm roared on:
The morning broke without a sun;
In tiny spherule* traced with lines
Of Nature's geometric signs,
In starry flake, and pellicle,*
All day the hoary meteor fell;
And, when the second morning shone,
We looked upon a world unknown,
On nothing we could call our own.
Around the glistening wonder bent
The blue walls of the firmament,
No cloud above, no earth below,—
A universe of sky and snow!
The old familiar sights of ours
Took marvellous shapes; strange domes and towers
Rose up where sty or corncrib stood,
Or garden-wall, or belt of wood;
A smooth white mound the brush-pile showed,
A fenceless drift that once was road;
The bridle-post an old man sat*
With loose-flung coat and high cocked hat;
The well-curb had a Chinese roof;
And even the long sweep,* high aloof,
In its slant splendor, seemed to tell
Of Pisa's leaning miracle.*
A prompt, decisive man, no breath
Our father wasted: "Boys, a path!"
Well pleased, (for when did farmer boy
Count such a summons less than joy?)
Our buskins* on our feet we drew;
With mittened hands, and caps drawn low,
To guard our necks and ears from snow,
We cut the solid whiteness through.
And, where the drift was deepest, made
A tunnel walled and overlaid
With dazzling crystal: we had read
Of rare Aladdin's wondrous cave,*

spherule: miniature sphere

pellicle: small pellet

an old man sat: sat like an old man

long sweep: pole on a pivot with a bucket at one end to raise water from a well

Pisa's leaning miracle: Italy's famed leaning tower; the baptistry of the cathedral of Pisa

buskins: leather boots

Aladdin's wondrous cave: from *The Arabian Nights*; a secret cave wherein was hidden vast treasure

And to our own his name we gave,
With many a wish the luck were ours
To test his lamp's supernal* powers.
We reached the barn with merry din,
And roused the prisoned brutes within.
The old horse thrust his long head out,
And grave with wonder gazed about;
The cock his lusty* greeting said,
And forth his speckled harem led;
The oxen lashed their tails, and hooked,*
And mild reproach of hunger looked;
The horned patriarch of the sheep,
Like Egypt's Amun* roused from sleep,
Shook his sage head with gesture mute,
And emphasized with stamp of foot.
All day the gusty north wind bore
The loosening drift its breath before;
Low circling round its southern zone,
The sun through dazzling snow-mist shone.
No church bell lent its Christian tone
To the savage air, no social smoke
Curled over woods of snow-hung oak.

supernal: heavenly

lusty: cheerful, vigorous

hooked: moved their heads in a hooking motion

Egypt's Amun: Egyptian deity revered as king of the gods; also spelled *Amana* or *Amon*

A solitude made more intense
By dreary-voicéd elements,
The shrieking of the mindless wind,
The moaning tree-boughs swaying blind,
And on the glass the unmeaning beat
Of ghostly finger tips of sleet.
Beyond the circle of our hearth
No welcome sound of toil or mirth
Unbound the spell, and testified
Of human life and thought outside.
We minded* that the sharpest ear
The buried brooklet could not hear,
The music of whose liquid lip
Had been to us companionship,
And, in our lonely life, had grown
To have an almost human tone.
As night drew on, and, from the crest
Of wooded knolls that ridged the west,
The sun, a snow-blown traveller, sank
From sight beneath the smothering bank,

minded: took notice

We piled, with care, our nightly stack
Of wood against the chimney-back,—
The oaken log, green, huge, and thick,
And on its top the stout back-stick;
The knotty forestick* laid apart,
And filled between with curious art
The ragged brush; then, hovering near,
We watched the first red blaze appear,
Heard the sharp crackle, caught the gleam
On whitewashed wall and sagging beam,
Until the old, rude-furnished room
Burst, flower-like, into rosy bloom;
While radiant with a mimic flame
Outside the sparkling drift became,
And through the bare-boughed lilac-tree
Our own warm hearth seemed blazing free.
The crane and pendent trammels* showed,
The Turks' heads* on the andirons* glowed;
While childish fancy, prompt to tell
The meaning of the miracle,
Whispered the old rhyme: *"Under the tree,*
When fire outdoors burns merrily,
There the witches are making tea."

forestick: front log of a hearth fire

trammels: hanging pothooks

Turks' heads: turban-like ornaments

andirons: metal supports to hold logs in a fireplace

The moon above the eastern wood
Shone at its full; the hill-range stood
Transfigured in the silver flood,
Its blown snows flashing cold and keen,
Dead white, save where some sharp ravine
Took shadow, or the sombre green
Of hemlocks turned to pitchy black
Against the whiteness at their back.
For such a world and such a night
Most fitting that unwarming light,
Which only seemed where'er it fell
To make the coldness visible.
Shut in from all the world without,
We sat the clean-winged hearth about,
Content to let the north wind roar
In baffled* rage at pane and door,
While the red logs before us beat
The frost-line back with tropic heat;
And ever, when a louder blast
Shook beam and rafter as it passed,
The merrier up its roaring draught
The great throat of the chimney laughed;
The house dog on his paws outspread

baffled: frustrated, stymied

Laid to the fire his drowsy head,
The cat's dark silhouette on the wall
A couchant* tiger's seemed to fall;
And, for the winter fireside meet,*
Between the andirons' straddling feet,
The mug of cider simmered slow,
The apples sputtered in a row,
And, close at hand, the basket stood
With nuts from brown October's wood.

couchant: reclining
meet: appropriate

What matter how the night behaved?
What matter how the north wind raved?
Blow high, blow low, not all its snow
Could quench our hearth fire's ruddy glow.
O Time and Change!—with hair as gray
As was my sire's* that winter day,
How strange it seems, with so much gone
Of life and love, to still live on!
Ah, brother! only I and thou
Are left of all that circle now,—
The dear home faces whereupon
That fitful firelight paled and shone.
Henceforward, listen as we will,
The voices of that hearth are still;
Look where we may, the wide earth o'er,
Those lighted faces smile no more.
We tread the paths their feet have worn,
We sit beneath their orchard-trees,
We hear, like them, the hum of bees
And rustle of the bladed corn;
We turn the pages that they read,
Their written words we linger o'er,
But in the sun they cast no shade,
No voice is heard, no sign is made,
No step is on the conscious floor!
Yet Love will dream, and Faith will trust,
(Since He who knows our need is just,)
That somehow, somewhere, meet we must.
Alas for him who never sees
The stars shine through his cypress-trees!
Who, hopeless, lays his dead away,
Nor looks to see the breaking day
Across the mournful marbles play!
Who hath not learned, in hours of faith,
The truth to flesh and sense unknown,
That Life is ever lord of Death,
And Love can never lose its own!

sire's: father's

About the Poem

1. The central conflict of the poem's story is man against nature. What is Whittier's tone toward both sides? Briefly explain your answers.
2. What might be the theme of the poem?
3. Whittier includes a great deal of imagery in his poem. Answer the following questions regarding this facet of the poem.
   a. For both the indoor and outdoor settings, find an example of each of the following types of imaginative comparison: metaphor, simile, personification.
   b. Find three examples of concrete language in the first twenty lines of the poem.
   c. Find three examples of concrete language in the final twenty lines of the poem.
   d. What image forms the center of indoor life in contrast to the cold outdoors? How does this image add to the atmosphere of the setting?
4. How do you think Whittier's story would have been different if he had chosen to write the same events as a short story rather than a poem?

About the Author

John Greenleaf Whittier (1807–92) was born into a close-knit New England family known for its simple Quaker values. Although Whittier received little formal education, he completed nearly 150 poems and had become a recognized poet by the time he was twenty-one.

As a young man, Whittier earned the respect of his contemporaries while editing a number of weekly political and economic papers. This work brought him into close contact with well-known statesmen and abolitionists. As a Quaker, Whittier held a deeply ingrained belief in the social equality of all people. Thus, abolition was a vitally important cause for him. Using his literary skill, he produced countless poems and pamphlets in support of the emancipation of American slaves.

Although Whittier enjoyed great popularity as a reformist author, the writing of the timeless masterpiece "Snow-Bound" marks the beginning of his fame as a great literary figure. Not until Whittier was almost sixty did he attempt writing verse of high literary quality. "Snow-Bound," written in the poet's quiet old age, reflects the home-centered values he had always cherished. The style of the poem is simple but deeply moving; it displays much local color but is universal in its appeal to the imagination. The nostalgic themes in "Snow-Bound" proved a welcome balm for weary Americans recovering from the Civil War. The poem was an immediate literary and financial success.

In later life Whittier became something of an American institution, reflecting the idealistic side of the American heart and mind. In the approximately one hundred hymn texts written toward the end of his life, Whittier showed his religious devotion and gift for didactic writing. His enduring reputation as the voice of rural New England is well-merited.

Lady Clare

Alfred, Lord Tennyson

In the following narrative poem, Tennyson reveals his Romantic tendencies by nostalgically mimicking the ancient English ballad form. A genre of folklore, ballads were usually meant to be sung. They functioned both as entertainment and as a way of passing on a culture's worldview or its history. What universal theme about life does this poem explore? And what techniques does the poet use to render his telling of the story pleasing to his imagined audience?

It was the time when lilies blow,* blow: bloom
And clouds are highest up in air,
Lord Ronald brought a lily-white doe
To give his cousin, Lady Clare.

I trow* they did not part in scorn: trow: can imagine
Lovers long-betrothed were they:
They two will wed the morrow morn—
God's blessing on the day!

"He does not love me for my birth,
Nor for my lands so broad and fair;
He loves me for my own true worth,
And that is well," said Lady Clare.

In there came old Alice the nurse,
Said, "Who was this that went from thee?"
"It was my cousin," said Lady Clare,
"Tomorrow he weds with me."

"O God be thanked!" said Alice the nurse,
"That all comes round so just and fair:
Lord Ronald is heir of all your lands,
And you are *not* the Lady Clare."

"Are ye out of your mind, my nurse, my nurse,"
Said Lady Clare, "that ye speak so wild?"
"As God's above," said Alice the nurse,
"I speak the truth: you are my child.

"The old earl's daughter died at my breast;
I speak the truth, as I live by bread!
I buried her like my own sweet child,
And put my child in her stead."

"Falsely, falsely have ye done,
O mother," she said, "if this be true,
To keep the best man under the sun
So many years from his due."*

his due: the land that he rightfully should have inherited on the death of the infant heir

"Nay now, my child," said Alice the nurse,
"But keep the secret of your life,
And all you have will be Lord Ronald's,
When you are man and wife."

"If I'm a beggar born," she said,
"I will speak out, for I dare not lie.
Pull off, pull off, the brooch of gold,
And fling the diamond necklace by."

"Nay now, my child," said Alice the nurse,
"But keep the secret all you can."
She said, "Not so: but I will know
If there be any faith in man."

"Nay now, what faith?" said Alice the nurse,
"The man will cleave unto his right."
"And he shall have it," the lady replied,
"Though I should die tonight."

"Yet give one kiss to your mother dear,
Alas, my child, I sinned for thee."
"O mother, mother, mother," she said,
"So strange it seems to me."

"Yet here's a kiss for my mother dear,
My mother dear, if these be so,
And lay your hand upon my head,
And bless me, mother, ere I go."

She clad herself in a russet gown,*
She was no longer Lady Clare:
She went by dale,* and she went by down,*
With a single rose in her hair.

russet gown: gown of coarse brown homespun cloth
dale: valley
down: hill

The lily-white doe Lord Ronald had brought
Leaped up from where she lay,
Dropped her head in the maiden's hand,
And followed her all the way.

Down stepped Lord Ronald from his tower:
"O Lady Clare, you shame your worth!
Why come you dressed like a village maid,
That are the flower of the earth?"

"If I come dressed like a village maid,
I am but as my fortunes are:
I am a beggar born," she said,
"And not the Lady Clare."

"Play me no tricks," said Lord Ronald,
"For I am yours in word and in deed;
Play me no tricks," said Lord Ronald,
"Your riddle is hard to read."

O, and proudly stood she up!
Her heart within her did not fail;
She looked into Lord Ronald's eyes,
And told him all her nurse's tale.

He laughed a laugh of merry scorn:
He turned and kissed her where she stood:
"If you are not the heiress born,
And I," said he, "the next in blood—

"If you are not the heiress born,
And I," said he, "the lawful heir,
We two will wed tomorrow morn,
And you shall still be Lady Clare."

About the Poem

1. In what way does Tennyson's story seem like the fairy tales you studied in Unit V?
2. What is the theme of the poem? Explain your answer.
3. What kind of irony surfaces in the last line of the poem, and how does it reinforce the poem's theme?
4. What does the "lily-white doe" symbolize within the poem and how is that meaning reflected in its actions?
5. How does Tennyson use the rhythms of his poem to delight his readers? Address both meter and repetition in your answer.
6. If this were a real ballad, how do you think the meter and rhyme of the poem would have helped accomplish the last two purposes of the form listed in the headnote?

About the Author

Alfred, Lord Tennyson (1809–92), one of England's greatest Victorian poets, was born into a large family strained by the unhappiness, alcoholism, and mental instability of Tennyson's father. Despite these conditions, Tennyson received a rigorous early education from his father, while the Lincolnshire countryside offered his keen imagination a welcome diversion from study. In 1827, Tennyson left home to enter Trinity College at Cambridge University.

Tennyson's time at Cambridge (1827–31) marked a period of increased happiness. In 1829 he joined a club of undergraduate intellectuals, called the Apostles, who encouraged his pursuit of poetry. One fellow member, Arthur Henry Hallam, became both a great admirer of Tennyson's poetry and a dear friend. News of Hallam's sudden death in 1833 left Tennyson devastated, compounding his grief for his father's death (1831) and his doubts resulting from unfavorable reviews of his 1832 volume of poetry. The result—Tennyson did not publish again for a decade.

The year 1850 saw great changes in the poet's life: on June 1 he published *In Memoriam*, an elegy based on the death of Hallam, and two weeks later he married his long-time love interest, Emily Sellwood. The publication of *In Memoriam* finally gave Tennyson financial security. In addition to the acclaim for his new volume, he was appointed poet laureate, an office previously held by William Wordsworth. Amidst this stability (1856–74), Tennyson composed most of the poems that would form his most ambitious volume, *Idylls of the King* (1859).

As recognition of his poetry increased, Tennyson received honorary doctorates and was even ennobled in 1883 by Queen Victoria, elevating him to the position of baron. He died on October 6, 1892, leaving behind not only beautiful poetry, with its musical variations and vivid details, but also poetry that expresses the doubts and hopes of Victorian England.

Had I the Choice

Walt Whitman

American poet Walt Whitman rejected many of the traditional constraints of poetry, both of content and of form. Despite the initial controversy, he has become one of the most influential poets in the English language; indeed, many of the formal trends in modern poetry are a tribute to his innovations. Though he sometimes abandoned meter and rhyme altogether, Whitman never neglected rhythm or sound devices. Like many Romantics, he simply sought inspiration from nature, a fact he expresses in this poem.

Had I the choice to tally* greatest bards,
To limn* their portraits, stately, beautiful, and emulate at will,
Homer with all his wars and warriors—Hector, Achilles, Ajax,
Or Shakespeare's woe-entangled Hamlet, Lear, Othello—Tennyson's fair ladies
Meter or wit the best, or choice conceit* to wield in perfect rhyme,
    delight of singers;
These, these, O sea, all these I'd gladly barter,
Would you the undulation of one wave, its trick to me transfer,
Or breathe one breath of yours upon my verse,
And leave its odor there.

tally: duplicate
limn: draw
conceit: striking metaphor

About the Poem

1. Give two allusions that Whitman uses. What are their purposes within the poem?
2. According to the poem, what general poetic standard does Whitman reject? What ideal model does he want to emulate instead?
3. Does Whitman include any kind of meter or rhythm in his lines? If so, give an example.
4. Looking at Whitman's choice of line breaks, how might he have succeeded in emulating his ideal model?
5. What relatively unusual form of imaginative comparison does Whitman use beginning in line 7?

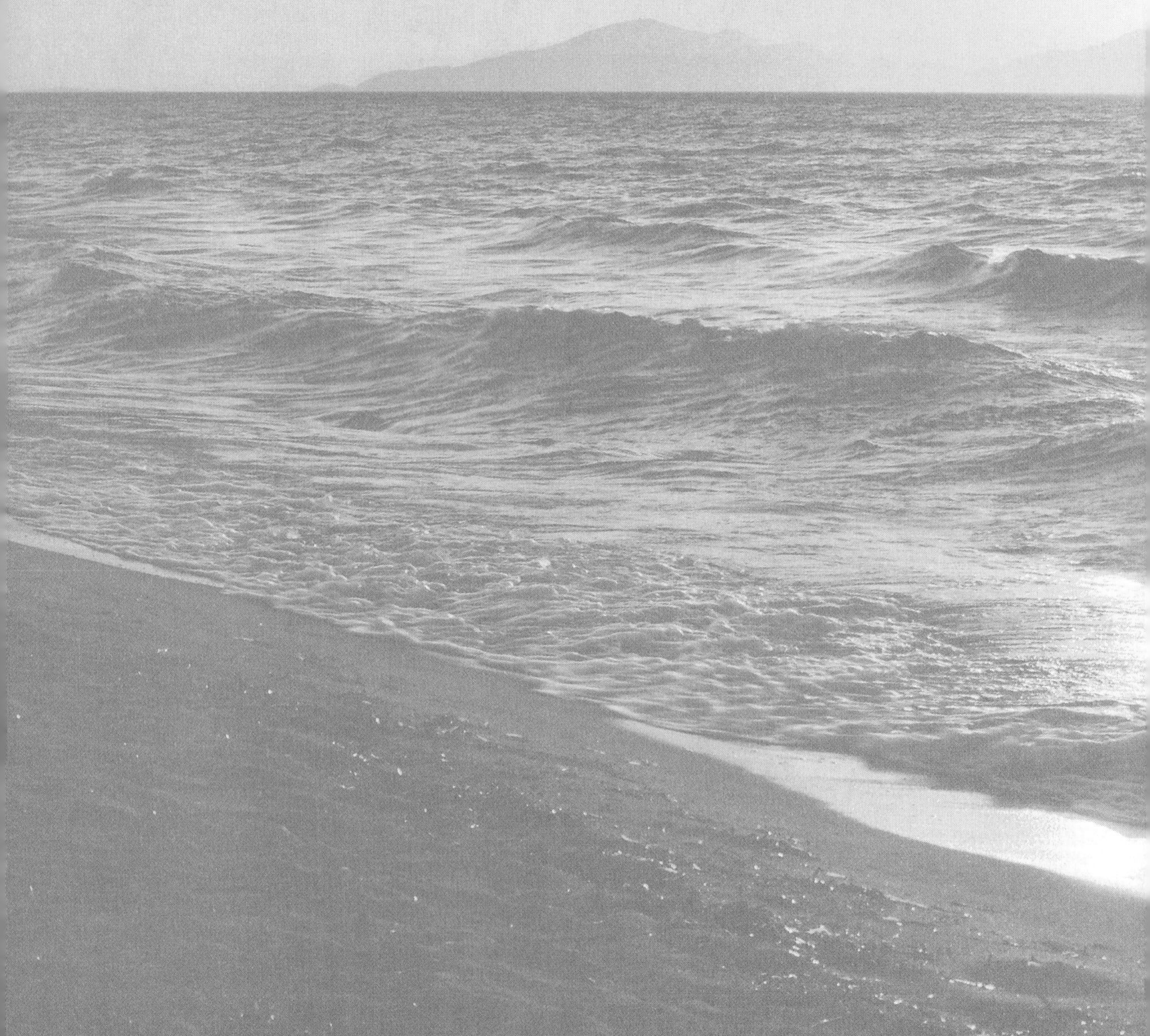

About the Author

By scope of influence, Walt Whitman (1819–92) can justly be called one of America's preeminent poets. His innovations in poetic language and structure provided a new voice for modern man, affecting all who came after. Born into a Quaker family, Whitman led an itinerant life, working at many jobs, from journalist to teacher to nurse during the American Civil War. Unfortunately, this fact and his rejection of restraints—literary, moral, and social—have lent his life a certain romantic mystique. His iconic status, however, should not blind us to the problems in his philosophy.

Whitman's poetry initially received decidedly mixed reviews: though Emerson hailed him as a rising poet, many others scorned his objectionable content. Yet his views of man and nature have been very influential. Whitman's humanistic idea that man forms his own moral compass and can be perfected through his own efforts is underscored in his egocentric poem "Song of Myself." These ideas permeate modern literature and society. Whitman believed that each individual must improve himself until death, when his soul returns to a cosmic Oversoul, or source of all life. A pantheist, Whitman possessed an ardent faith in nature as both a manifestation of deity and deity itself. His purpose in writing *Leaves of Grass*, his famous collection of poetry, was to build a bridge between his soul and nature, a bridge that would lead to ultimate truth. The poem "Song of Prudence" leaves no doubt as to Whitman's method of determining ultimate meaning and truth. In this poem he states, "Whatever satisfies souls is true. . . ."

Although we can appreciate the literary quality of many of Whitman's poems, we must, of course, be careful to evaluate their messages in light of scriptural principles. What a Christian would call sin Whitman dismisses as an excusable and inevitable result of failing to progress in the struggles of evolution. Unlike Whitman, Christians recognize that "there is a way which seemeth right unto a man, but the end thereof are the ways of death" (Prov. 14:12).

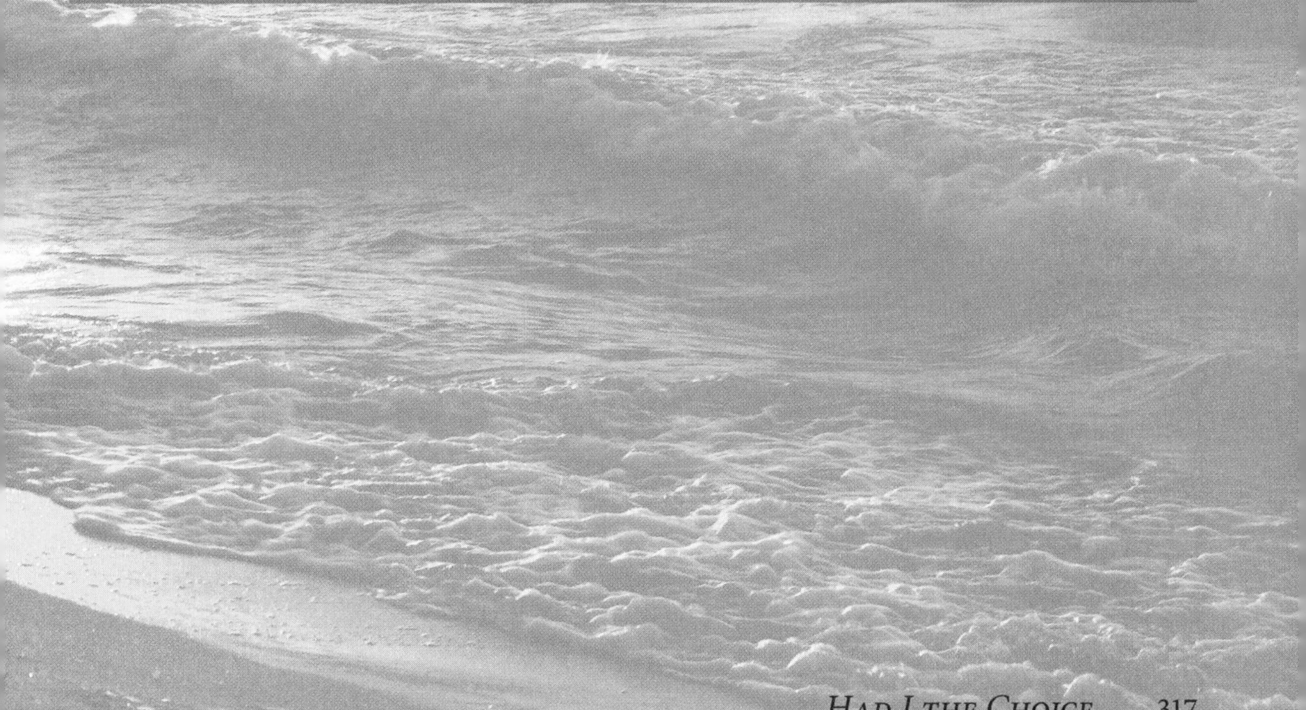

We Wear the Mask

Paul Laurence Dunbar

Though writing in the same era as Whitman, Dunbar made very different formal choices. The following poem is an example of a rondeau, a strict form that can be difficult to use, and it is to Dunbar's credit that his rendition flows naturally rather than sounding stilted. The poem is built around one central image that vividly illustrates Dunbar's theme. Have you ever felt what Dunbar describes here?

We wear the mask that grins and lies,
It hides our cheeks and shades our eyes,—
This debt we pay to human guile;
With torn and bleeding hearts we smile,
And mouth* with myriad subtleties.

Why should the world be over-wise,
In counting all our tears and sighs?
Nay, let them only see us, while
We wear the mask.

We smile, but, O great Christ, our cries
To thee from tortured souls arise.
We sing, but oh the clay is vile
Beneath our feet, and long the mile;
But let the world dream otherwise,
We wear the mask!

*mouth: to pretend, to deceive, to give a false impression in speaking

About the Poem

1. What is the central image of Dunbar's poem? What does this object hide (both literally and metaphorically)?
2. Which lines contain enjambment or caesura? Overall, how do these techniques affect your reading of the poem?
3. What meter is the poem written in? Which lines deviate from that meter and what is the effect of that change?
4. What is the overall atmosphere and tone of the poem? What are the reasons for this emotion?
5. Why do you think Dunbar chose the word *dream* rather than *think* or *believe* in line 14? What are the connotations of the word in context of the poem's theme?
6. How does the theme qualify as universal (applying to humans everywhere)? How did it apply specifically to Dunbar's experience as an African American in the nineteenth century?

About the Author

Paul Laurence Dunbar (1872–1906) developed an interest in poetry at a young age, writing and reciting his first poem at age twelve for an Easter church service. Growing up in Dayton, Ohio, he served as the editor of the school newspaper, published several of his poems in local newspapers, and also edited the *Tattler*, a newspaper for African Americans published and printed by Orville Wright.

Having no money to study law as he wished, Dunbar took a job as an elevator operator after graduation. While traveling up and down floors, Dunbar worked on the poems that would form his first collection, self-published in 1893. That same year he met the abolitionist Frederick Douglass, who gave Dunbar a position as clerk and the opportunity to read his poetry to large audiences.

Dunbar finally achieved literary prominence in 1895, when William Dean Howells, the leading literary critic of the day, favorably reviewed his collection *Majors and Minors*. A year later, Dunbar published *Lyrics of the Lowly Life,* which included "We Wear the Mask." In the introduction to the collection, Howells praised Dunbar's poetry for its understanding and expression of African-American culture and dialect, as seen in his "minor" poems.

Unlike Dunbar's dialect poems, "We Wear the Mask" exemplifies Dunbar's poems written in standard English, for which he most wanted recognition. Indeed, more recent criticism suggests that "We Wear the Mask" not only accurately describes the social injustice of racism but, more importantly, also becomes a lens through which the reader can view all of Dunbar's poetry.

The Panther

Rainer Maria Rilke

In the Jardin des Plantes, Paris*

A highly influential poet, Rilke was famous for his "thing" poems, in which he attempted to capture the essence of objects, lifting them from the natural world and elevating them to the place of symbol. Though strongly rooted in physical reality, Rilke's "thing" poems have much more to say than what meets the eye. What emotions or ideas does Rilke's picture of a panther evoke in you as you read the poem?

His vision, from the constantly passing bars,
has grown so weary that it cannot hold
anything else. It seems to him there are
a thousand bars; and behind the bars, no world.

As he paces in cramped circles, over and over,
the movement of his powerful soft strides
is like a ritual dance around a center
in which a mighty will stands paralyzed.

Only at times, the curtain of the pupils
lifts, quietly—. An image enters in,
rushes down through the tensed, arrested muscles,
plunges into the heart and is gone.

*Jardin des Plantes: a zoo in Paris

About the Poem

1. Identify two examples of imaginative comparison in the poem. Explain how the comparisons contribute to the poem's meaning.
2. Rilke, like the sculptor Rodin, tried to reveal the motion of the object he observed. What lines from the poem imply the motion of the poet's original model? What lines appear to work against this motion?
3. Rilke's use of imagery is often striking. What imagery can you find in the poem? How does the imagery enhance the reader's understanding?
4. Do you think the poem ends positively or negatively? Support your answer with details from the poem.
5. How well do you think Rilke evoked the object he observed? Consider answers to previous questions in your response.

About the Author

Arguably the greatest German-speaking poet of the modern period, Rainer Maria Rilke (1875–1926) was born in Prague, the only child of a coddling mother and a military-minded father. Rilke recalled his early years as a period of great unhappiness. Enrolled in military school after his parents separated, he was unsuited in constitution and temperament for military training and left to prepare for college. At nineteen, Rilke self-published his first book of poetry, but this and other early works demonstrated Rilke's immaturity as a writer, seeming overly romantic or sentimental.

Rilke traveled abroad for a time, taking a trip to Russia that would later influence his poetry heavily. Then in 1900, he joined a German artist colony and shortly thereafter met Clara Westholf, a sculptor, whom he married a year later. Unfortunately, the couple separated soon after the birth of their daughter, Ruth. At the colony Rilke wrote a majority of the poems that would form his first significant book of poetry—*The Book of Hours* (1905)—published later during his time in Paris. Employed in Paris as secretary to the famous sculptor Auguste Rodin, Rilke adopted Rodin's view of the artist as a craftsman: instead of waiting for inspiring ideas, the poet would seek out real objects and use language to bring them to life. Rilke's "thing" poems, of which "The Panther" is an example, developed from this new approach. Unlike his early mature poetry, which tends toward the mystical, Rilke's "thing" poems are anchored firmly in what can be seen.

In 1919, Rilke traveled to Switzerland for poetry readings and settled there for the rest of his life. There he completed his two masterpieces published in 1923: *Duino Elegies* and *Sonnets to Orpheus*. Both collections ensured Rilke's place among the most influential writers of the modern period. Just three years after their publication, Rilke died of leukemia on December 29, 1926.

THINKING ZONE

Poetry uses rhythm in a variety of ways, ranging from the regular patterns of meter to irregular patterns that achieve a desired rhythmic effect. The term ***verse*** refers to compositions written in meter.

Three verse forms summarize how poets include or deviate from rhyme and meter. The most common, **rhymed verse**, features both meter and end rhyme. These end rhymes often form a pattern, or **rhyme scheme**. To determine the rhyme scheme of a poem, label each new rhyming sound with a letter, beginning with *a* and continuing through the alphabet. Consider the rhyme scheme of the following sonnet, "Remember," by Christina Rossetti:

Remember me when I am gone away,	*a*
Gone far away into the silent land;	*b*
When you can no more hold me by the hand,	*b*
Nor I half turn to go yet turning stay.	*a*
Remember me when no more day by day	*a*
You tell me of our future that you planned:	*b*
Only remember me; you understand	*b*
It will be late to counsel then or pray.	*a*
Yet if you should forget me for a while	*c*
And afterwards remember, do not grieve:	*d*
For if the darkness and corruption leave	*d*
A vestige of the thoughts that once I had,	*e*
Better by far you should forget and smile	*c*
Than that you should remember and be sad.	*e*

The poem is an **Italian sonnet**, made of an octave (eight lines) and a sestet (six lines). As you can see, the rhyme scheme reinforces this division, switching to three new rhymes for the sestet. Labeling rhyme scheme can help you determine whether a poem follows a traditional form, such as a sonnet or ballad, or whether the poet has created his own pattern.

The second verse form differs only partially from rhymed verse; **blank verse** requires meter, specifically iambic pentameter, but forgoes rhyme. The use of iambic pentameter (the meter closest to the natural rhythms of English) and lack of rhyme give blank verse a conversational feel. For this reason, Shakespeare (among many others) used blank verse frequently, especially in the dialogue of his plays.

The last of the three forms, **free verse**, abandons regular meter and rhyme. The term *free verse*, however, may be somewhat misleading. Although free, in the sense of not being constrained by regular meter and rhyme, free verse still requires the poet to use both rhythm and structure in his writing. Walt Whitman was one of the first Americans to use free verse extensively and successfully. Indeed, he popularized the form to the point that a large portion of twentieth-century poetry was written in free verse.

1. Label the **rhyme scheme** of the first three stanzas of "Lady Clare" or "We Wear the Mask."
2. Which poem that you have read in this unit best qualifies as **free verse**?
3. Select two instances from the free verse poem that exhibit the poet's attention to rhythm. Be prepared to explain how the instances you chose achieve their effect.
4. Looking ahead to the play *Romeo and Juliet* by William Shakespeare, search for **blank verse** lines used in dialogue in act 1, scene 1 (pp. 350–59). Write down the page number(s), line numbers, and entire first line of the selection you have chosen.

Snow in the Suburbs

Thomas Hardy

Set in a peculiarly modern setting, the suburb, Hardy's poem nonetheless has a timeless appeal. In its imagery, nature's very real threat seems to grab the spotlight; no human action occurs until the final line. But when that action does occur, the real message of the poem becomes clear. Though the poem follows no set form, Hardy shapes the structure of it carefully: the line lengths, rhyme scheme, and stanza groupings are all significant to the poem's content. As you read, note the progression from impersonal descriptions of the inanimate to personal narrations of animate subjects. How does it help communicate the tone and theme of the poem?

Every branch big with it,
Bent every twig with it;
Every fork like a white web-foot;
Every street and pavement mute:
Some flakes have lost their way, and grope back upward, when
Meeting those meandering down they turn and descend again.
The palings* are glued together like a wall,
And there is no waft of wind with the fleecy fall.

palings: fence made of pointed pickets

A sparrow enters the tree,
Whereon immediately
A snow-lump thrice his own slight size
Descends on him and showers his head and eyes,
And overturns him,
And near inurns* him,
And lights on a nether twig, when its brush
Starts off a volley of other lodging lumps with a rush.

inurns: buries

The steps are a blanched slope,
Up which, with feeble hope,
A black cat comes, wide-eyed and thin;
And we take him in.

About the Poem

1. What is the rhyme scheme of the poem? Does this pattern indicate any connections between lines?
2. Why do you think Hardy made lines 5 and 6 so much longer than the other lines in the first stanza? Consider the content of both lines in your answer.
3. What two kinds of imaginative comparison are found in the first stanza? Give examples.
4. Hardy's skillful use of concrete language helps him paint a vivid image. What concrete words suggest silence and lack of movement in stanza one? How does Hardy use concrete language in stanza two to communicate movement?
5. Why is Hardy's choice of the word *inurn* humorous? What words in stanza three does he use to evoke sympathy?
6. How does Hardy's tone change between stanzas two and three?

About the Author

The son of a builder, English writer Thomas Hardy (1840–1928) grew up in a small village in Dorset County. His mother encouraged him in reading and scholarly pursuits, at which he excelled. Financially unable to attend college, Hardy apprenticed as an architect and worked in that field for many years, even while engaged in writing. A poet, playwright, and novelist, Hardy is perhaps best-known for novels such as *Far From the Madding Crowd*, *The Return of the Native*, and *Tess of the d'Urbervilles*. However, his poetry, written later in his life, was also quite influential in twentieth-century literature.

As a literary figure, Hardy was well-respected but controversial for his rejection of societal mores. Darwinism and naturalism heavily informed his writing, which abandoned a biblical worldview for one in which God and nature are unsympathetic forces. This dark view does not erase the fact that Hardy was a poet of great technical skill and emotional power. As readers of literature, we can appreciate the style and design of his work, especially his poetic works, without embracing his despair.

An enthusiastic outdoorsman, Hardy's keen appreciation of nature is evident in his writing. In many of his stories, weather and environment not only reflect the moods of the main characters, but also seem to control these characters' destinies. Although Hardy liked to present the harsher side of nature, he did have a tender heart toward suffering, seen in his promotion of efforts to prevent cruelty to animals. His pets appear in his poetry, and sometimes, as in "Snow in the Suburbs," they are the basis for memorable imagery.

High Flight

John Gillespie Magee Jr.

In this famous poem, Magee fulfills the most general demands of the Italian sonnet form, a lyric poem of fourteen lines written in iambic pentameter and combining an octave with a sestet. Yet Magee's take on this centuries-old form remains fresh, full to the brim with joy and vigor. Indeed, the experience he describes is, for him, almost a religious one. To do it justice, he ransacks metaphoric language and crams the poem with concrete imagery.

Oh, I have slipped the surly bonds of earth,
And danced the skies on laughter-silvered wings;
Sunward I've climbed and joined the tumbling mirth
Of sun-split clouds—and done a hundred things
You have not dreamed of—wheeled and soared and swung
High in the sunlit silence. Hov'ring there,
I've chased the shouting wind along and flung
My eager craft through footless halls of air.
Up, up the long delirious, burning blue
I've topped the wind-swept heights with easy grace,
Where never lark, or even eagle, flew;
And, while with silent, lifting mind I've trod
The high untrespassed sanctity of space,
Put out my hand, and touched the face of God.

About the Poem

1. What is the point of the poem?
2. How is the last metaphor appropriate to the poem's tone?
3. Identify an example of the following techniques:
   a. alliteration
   b. onomatopoeia
   c. personification
4. One specific tool of concrete language is synesthesia, the description of one sense experience in terms of another (e.g., a sunny tune). Find two examples of synesthesia in Magee's poem.
5. How does Magee's use of meter, enjambment, and caesura affect the flow of the poem?
6. What specifically do you think the author is trying to say in the last line of the poem? If the poet were writing from a biblical worldview, what biblical idea would the line allude to?

About the Author

John Gillespie Magee Jr. (1922–41) was born to Anglican missionaries in Shanghai, China. He was eventually sent to England for additional education at the Rugby School, where he won the school's poetry prize in 1938. In 1939 Magee visited America with his family but was unable to return to England because of the outbreak of war. His accomplishments earned him a scholarship to Yale in 1940, but Magee turned it down, choosing instead to enlist in the Royal Canadian Air Force because the United States had not yet officially entered the war. Upon graduating from flight training, Magee received orders to Digby, England, to engage the Nazis.

Late in the summer of 1941, while testing a new model of the fighter plane the Spitfire V, Magee began composing what would become the poem "High Flight." The nineteen-year-old pilot records his experience in a letter to his parents: "I am enclosing a verse I wrote the other day. It started at 30,000 feet, and was finished soon after I landed." Tragically, Magee's promising future was cut short just months after penning his poem when, on December 11, 1941, his plane crashed after a midair collision. In 1942, Archibald MacLeish, poet and Librarian of Congress, included Magee's sonnet in a "Faith and Freedom" exhibit, an action which helped to popularize the poem. Today, the poem is still treasured in both the Canadian and American air forces by aviators who affirm the beauty and message of Magee's words.

The Wise Old Apple Tree in Spring

ROBERT HILLYER

Instead of describing an object, an experience, or a situation, this lyric poem explores a decision the speaker has made and continues to make. Decisions recalled or in progress are among the most interesting subjects of lyric poetry, allowing the poet to explore beliefs that strongly affect how people live their lives. Here, the speaker explains his reasoning and in the process, conveys several deeply held convictions. How does Hillyer manage to apply this specific decision to all of human life?

The wise old apple tree in spring,
Though split and hollow, makes a crown
Of such fantastic blossoming
We cannot let them cut it down.
It bears no fruit, but honeybees
Prefer it to the other trees.

The orchard man chalks his mark
And says, "This empty shell must go."
We nod and rub it off the bark
As soon as he goes down the row.
Each spring he looks bewildered. "Queer,
I thought I marked this thing last year."

Ten orchard men have come and gone
Since first I saw my grandfather
Slyly erase it. I'm the one
To do it now. As I defer
The showy veteran's removal
My grandson nods his full approval.

Like mine, my fellow ancient's roots
Are deep in the last century
From which our memories send shoots
For all our grandchildren to see
How spring, inviting bloom and rhyme,
Defeats the orchard men of time.

About the Poem

1. Explain the decisions involving trees in "The Wise Old Apple Tree in Spring."
2. What do these decisions reveal about the poet's view of trees?
3. At the end of the poem, Hillyer universalizes his story; he makes it symbolize humans' struggle to balance beauty and functionality in the way we approach life and in the things we value or create. In this context, who do you think are the "orchard men of time"? What is a biblical view of their position?
4. Given the poet's tone in the story, which side of this conflict is he on? What does the poem reveal of the poet's view of life?

Given what the Bible reveals about beauty, can a Christian find value in the purely aesthetic (i.e., beautiful or artistic) aspects of poetry? Explain your answer.

About the Author

At a time when literature was undergoing great upheaval, Robert Hillyer (1895–1961) stood for conservative values in poetry. He distinguished himself early on as a student at Harvard, serving as editor of the *Harvard Monthly* and the *Harvard Advocate* and winning the school's Garrison Prize for poetry. Then his literary career was interrupted by World War I; he volunteered first as an ambulance driver and then as a soldier.

From 1919 until his death, Hillyer served with distinction as a professor of English in various universities, most notably Harvard. At the same time, he continued his own writing and won the Pulitzer Prize for Poetry in 1934 for his *Collected Verse*. Over the years, he maintained a heavy involvement in the American literary scene, participating in organizations such as The Poetry Society of America, The American Academy of Arts and Sciences, and The National Institute of Arts and Letters. In his positions he strongly advocated for the traditional literary values of beauty and order in poetry and against the extravagances of modern poetics. "The Wise Old Apple Tree in Spring" reflects Hillyer's conservative tone and temper, aptly illustrating his philosophy: poetry can and should keep alive that which is beautiful and worthwhile for the enjoyment of posterity.

Nightsong: City

Dennis Brutus

Well-known for his revolutionary stance against apartheid, South African poet Dennis Brutus was often less radical in his poetic forms. His early style was clearly influenced by traditional British poets and makes powerful use of established forms. Written during the 1960s, the following poem is a complex mix of frustration with and tender care for his country amid its great internal strife. Note the vivid use of connotative language and concrete imagery to describe the desperate state of the city's inhabitants.

Sleep well, my love, sleep well:
the harbour lights glaze over restless docks,
police cars cockroach through the tunnel streets

from the shanties creaking iron-sheets
violence like a bug-infested rag is tossed
and fear is immanent* as sound in the wind-swung bell;

the long day's anger pants from sand and rocks;
but for this breathing night at least,
my land, my love, sleep well.

immanent: existing within

About the Poem

1. What is the rhyme scheme of the poem?
2. What kind of ditty or song do the first and last lines of the poem remind you of?
3. Find two instances of imaginative comparison used in the poem.
4. What is the atmosphere of the poem, and what seems to be the poet's tone toward his subject?
5. Give an example of alliteration and of assonance. How does the poet's use of sound devices support the atmosphere of the poem?
6. What comfort might a Christian find during times like those described by Brutus? Support your answer with Scripture.

About the Author

South African Dennis Brutus (1924–2009) combined his role as poet with one as an outspoken activist. With ancestors of both African and European descent, he fell into the South African racial category of "colored," a group legally discriminated against under apartheid. Educated just before apartheid was instituted, he was a gifted student but could hope for little opportunity in his country.

Brutally imprisoned in the 1960s for his opposition to apartheid, Brutus spent time at the infamous Robben Island prison in a cell next to Nelson Mandela himself. During this time, his first volume of poetry, *Sirens, Knuckles, and Boots* (1963) was published. Brutus was finally released but then banished, eventually finding political asylum in the United States with his family. His years in America were spent writing, teaching at universities, and continuing his political activism from abroad. Brutus used sports (segregated in South Africa) in particular as an avenue to protest the policies of apartheid and was instrumental in getting South Africa barred from the Olympic games (1964–91) until the dismantling of apartheid. He was finally able to return to South Africa in the 1990s, and he remained there until his death.

Brutus's work was for many years banned in South Africa as his political concerns are quite evident in his poems. Despite their specific setting, Brutus's poems are connected to universal human experiences. Though his themes remained similar over the years, his style changed; his early work made full use of complex poetic forms and images, but Brutus later simplified his style to reach a broader audience with his message. He varied between ultra-simplicity of language and structure and a more balanced approach. "Nightsong: City" offers an example of formal complexity combined with a clear message.

Landscape with Cows

Rhina P. Espaillat

The following poem is another sonnet, clearly one of the most popular and enduring forms in English poetry. From addressing romantic love exclusively, the sonnet has grown to encompass all sorts of topics. Here Espaillat meditates on modern American life, with its fast pace and materialistic bent. Despite her adherence to form in meter, rhyme, and stanza, she maintains a casual, conversational manner, as if she were thinking aloud. Her internal monologue leads to a profound conclusion.

Cows, at their lumbering and stately pace,
rise from this roadside landscape, water, field
and early morning sky, not so much place
as attitude. Mist and crude rails have sealed
them in their all-but-changeless pose,
like founding fathers whom their myths embalm,
on meadows, captured, rapt, as in Corot's*
mute umbered* greens and shallow pools of calm.
The moment cannot last; already there's
the next billboard quickening appetites,
hawking aloud some need, somebody's wares,
some town approaching us with its delights
and deals and meretricious* urge to tease
us back into our natural unease.

Corot: French landscape painter (1796–1875)

umbered: having a brownish color

meretricious: garishly attractive

Landscape with Cows, Jean-Baptiste-Camille Corot, 1829. The State Hermitage Museum, St. Petersburg.

About the Poem

1. Give one allusion Espaillat makes in her poem.
2. Espaillat contrasts two settings in her poem. What are they and how do they differ for the speaker? Which do you think seems more real to her?
3. What is the theme of the poem?
4. In content, the Italian sonnet form exhibits a change in thought between the first eight and last six lines of the poem. How does this poem fit that pattern?
5. What are the connotative effects of the words *embalm* and *hawking*?
6. Espaillat mentions "our [humanity's] natural unease." In context of her theme, what does she mean by this statement? Is her assessment of human nature biblical? Explain your answer.

About the Author

Born in the Dominican Republic, Rhina Espaillat (b. 1932) began writing (in Spanish) at an early age. In 1939 her family was forced to leave the country for political reasons. They made their home in the United States, where Espaillat became a naturalized citizen. A graduate of Hunter College and Queens College, she served as an English teacher in the New York public school system for over fifteen years. Today, she continues to encourage writers through workshops and speaking engagements.

As a translator, Espaillat has gained particular attention for her Spanish renditions of Robert Frost's poetry. As a poet, Espaillat has published eleven collections of poetry, some award-winning. In 1998 *Where Horizons Go* garnered her the T. S. Eliot prize, and she has earned many other awards for both individual poems and her work as a whole. Espaillat is very active in the literary scene, championing a return to the traditional forms that she so masterfully uses in her poetry. In this role she has for many years headed a group of formalist poets known as the Powow River Poets. Her poetry is much admired for her natural and understated use of traditional forms. "Landscape with Cows" exemplifies this subtle approach. Though both rhyme and meter are present, a casual reader may initially overlook them since they do not override the conversational flow of her poem.

THINKING ZONE

As you learned in the unit opener, a stanza is a grouping of lines based on thought, meter, or rhyme. In print, stanzas are usually separated by a space. Most stanzas are designated by the number of lines they contain. The basic stanza forms are—in order from two lines to eight—couplet, triplet, quatrain, quintet, sestet, septet, and octave. These stanza patterns serve as building blocks for the various traditional forms that have developed over the centuries. The traditional forms referenced here illustrate how poets can use these stanza patterns.

In English the dominant stanza patterns are the couplet and the quatrain. The simplest of stanza forms, the **couplet** is a pair of successive lines that usually have the same rhyme (*aa*) and metrical length. Couplets that occur in iambic pentameter are known as **heroic couplets** because they were frequently used in heroic (epic) poems and dramas in the late seventeenth century. Eighteenth-century poets, such as Alexander Pope, used them abundantly. The couplet also appears as the last two lines of the **English sonnet** (*abab cdcd efef gg*). Shakespeare, who wrote numerous such sonnets, often used this couplet to conclude his thoughts. Couplets can also be grouped together with additional couplets or other stanza forms to create stanzas of varying lengths.

The **quatrain**, the most common stanza form in English, consists of four lines and has numerous variations in rhyme and meter. One common variation occurs in the ballad, which alternates tetrameter and trimeter lines and rhymes *abcb* or occasionally *abab*. Many quatrains alternate line length as the ballad does, but others preserve a uniform line length throughout. The English sonnet, for instance, features three quatrains in succession before the final couplet: each quatrain rhymes *abab* and all of its lines are iambic pentameter.

The triplet, sestet, and octave are also popular stanzas. The **triplet**, or tercet, consists of three lines that often share the same rhyme (*aaa*) and sometimes vary in length. Dante composed his *Divine Comedy* in triplets with rhymes linking each stanza together (*aba bcb cdc*, etc.). The **sestet** refers to any six-line stanza while the **octave** generally describes any eight-line stanza. Both stanzas allow for numerous variations in line length and rhyme scheme. Their best-known use, however, is in the Italian sonnet form, an octave comprising the first eight lines of the poem and the sestet, the last six.

1. Which two poems in Unit VII use **couplets** exclusively? Why do you think couplets work well in these poems?
2. Which of the two poems from question 1 has couplets that are further organized into **octaves** and a **quatrain**? What thought divisions does this arrangement emphasize? Why do you think a quatrain is more effective than an octave as the last stanza of the poem?
3. By rhyme scheme alone, which one of the sonnets in Unit VII most closely resembles an English sonnet (*abab cdcd efef gg*)?
4. Which poem in Unit VII is composed entirely of **sestets**? What smaller stanza units can be found within each sestet?
5. Which poem in Unit VII is composed entirely of **triplets** and which entirely of **quatrains**?
6. Which poem in Unit VII begins with a quintet?

UNIT VII REVIEW

Remember the Terms

Review the following terms from the opening essay, "Poetry," the Thinking Zone pages, and the headnotes. Be prepared to discuss their meanings and uses.

poetry	lyric poem	blank verse	quatrain
concrete language	verse	free verse	triplet
connotative language	rhymed verse	couplet	sestet
rhythm	rhyme scheme	heroic couplet	octave
stanza	Italian sonnet	English sonnet	

Apply the Concepts

Answer the following questions about how the literary concepts you have studied are used in this unit.

1. How would you describe the atmosphere of "I will sing unto the Lord, for he hath triumphed gloriously"?
2. What are two reasons that "I will sing unto the Lord, for he hath triumphed gloriously" qualifies as poetry?
3. What is the central image of the indoors in Whittier's "Snow-Bound"? What atmosphere does this image create?
4. Identify and briefly explain the significance of two of the symbols in Tennyson's "Lady Clare."
5. What was the original purpose of the ballad? How does "Lady Clare," though not a folk ballad itself, preserve some of the form's original purpose?
6. Identify two allusions in Whitman's "Had I the Choice" and explain their purpose in the poem.
7. How does Whitman generally imitate his poetic model in "Had I the Choice"?
8. What is the central image of Dunbar's "We Wear the Mask"? Explain the literal and metaphorical meaning of the symbol.
9. Explain the significance of the word *dream* in "We Wear the Mask."
10. Identify an example of imaginative comparison in Rilke's "The Panther" and explain its significance in the poem.
11. Identify two symbols from "The Panther" and explain what they represent.
12. Explain the differences between rhymed verse, blank verse, and free verse.
13. Identify four examples of concrete language from Hardy's "Snow in the Suburbs," two from stanza one and two from stanza two. Why does Hardy use this concrete language?
14. Why is it appropriate that Hardy's tone changes from stanza two to stanza three in "Snow in the Suburbs"?

15. Identify an example of the following techniques in Magee's "High Flight": alliteration, onomatopoeia, and personification.
16. Who are the "orchard men of time" in Hillyer's "The Wise Old Apple Tree in Spring"? What is the poet's tone toward them?
17. Identify two examples of imaginative comparison in Brutus's "Nightsong: City."
18. What are the two contrasting settings in "Landscape with Cows"? Which one does Espaillat seem to view as more realistic?
19. Which poem in Unit VII best qualifies as free verse?

Evaluate the Ideas

Identify each of the following statements as true or false. If false, rewrite the underlined portion of the statement to make it true.

20. "I will sing unto the Lord" is structured around meter and rhyme.
21. "I will sing unto the Lord" uses a rhetorical question to point toward the hopefulness of future events.
22. "Snow-Bound" is a lyric poem.
23. Whittier's tone toward the family in "Snow-Bound" is one of disapproval.
24. Tennyson's "Lady Clare" is a sonnet.
25. The final line of "Lady Clare" is an example of situational irony.
26. The strict meter of "Lady Clare" gives it a musical feel.
27. The overall tone of Dunbar's "We Wear the Mask" is one of happiness and praise.
28. When labeling rhyme scheme, use the same letter of the alphabet (beginning with *a*) for lines that rhyme.
29. The Italian sonnet form is made up of three quatrains and a couplet.
30. Shakespeare used rhymed verse in the dialogue of many of his plays because it is closest to the natural rhythms of English.
31. Hardy's choice of the word *inurns* in "Snow in the Suburbs" implies seriousness.
32. The phrase "laughter-silvered wings" from "High Flight" is an example of personification.

Write a Response

Completely answer each of the following questions.

33. Using information from the essay "Poetry" on pages 298–99, explain how poetry differs from prose. Illustrate your ideas from poems in the text.
34. Briefly state the universal themes of two poems from Unit VII and explain how each theme could apply to a situation in today's society. Support your applications with specific details and examples.
35. Poets often use stanza patterns to support the thought structure of a poem. Explain how one poem from Unit VII uses stanza patterns for structuring thought. Be sure to reference what stanza patterns are used and specifically how those stanza patterns support the poem's ideas.

UNIT VIII

ROMEO AND JULIET BEFORE FATHER LAWRENCE
Karl Ludwig Friedrich Becker

DRAMA

German history painter Karl Ludwig Friedrich Becker (1820–1900) knew as a boy that he wanted to paint. He initially studied under August von Kloeber at the Berlin Academy and later learned fresco painting under Peter von Cornelius and Heinrich Maria von Hess. A prize awarded by the Berlin Academy made it possible for Becker to study in Paris for a year, where he learned what were at the time modern color details and processes. The artist also spent two years in Rome studying Italian art collections. Becker finally found his painting niche, however, in Venice, where the vibrant colors of the Venetian masters enthralled him. His emulation of the magnificence of the Venetian and German Renaissance earned him success and fame. Becker's paintings are characterized by the brilliance and splendor of their colors. Because these colors are often displayed in the clothes of his characters, Becker has been called "Costume Becker." In addition to this rich color, historical accuracy and technical skill characterize his style.

- From what you know about Becker's style, what specifically identifies the painting as characteristic of his work?
- Which of the five senses other than sight does the picture especially evoke in you as a viewer? Support your answer with details from the painting.
- As in dramatic productions, Becker's painting uses the setting as well as the clothing, postures, and expressions of the people depicted to express what is happening. Even if you did not know the title, what would you think is happening in the picture? What specific details in the painting communicate the relationship between the young man and woman depicted?

DRAMA

Literary historians believe drama to be among the oldest of the genres. It probably has existed as long as man himself. Certainly it is among the most popular. Almost everyone at one time or another has helped act out a story. Children are born actors. They like to show as well as tell what happened at a birthday party or on the way home from school. Even adults enjoy skits, charades, masquerades, and other forms of play-acting and pretending. Performing the parts of characters, real or imagined, involves speaker and listener in the story more fully than can narrative alone.

Drama and Performance

Drama, stories consisting of action and dialogue for stage performance, strictly speaking becomes a literary genre only when deprived of one of its basic attributes. For drama requires actors and an audience. It is composed for performance and exists as a performance. Unless we are reading the rare **closet drama**, a play written to be read and not performed, what we read in print is only the actors' script. Unlike the more purely literary genres, drama requires more than just the text to succeed or even to exist. A director and set designer, actors, stage hands, costume designers and tailors—all must cooperate to bring a play before an audience. In plays being read as literature, the reader must perform all these functions if the play is to go on. He must stage the action in his mind, with appropriate sets, props, costumes, gestures, and vocal intonations. Today plays are more likely to be experienced mentally as a film than as a stage performance. But visualizing a stage with costumed actors, scenery, and props as our imaginary background may help us better understand some dramas, for each takes its shape from the expectations of the audience it was written for.

These expectations are influenced by the physical structure of the theaters to which the audience is accustomed. The modern "picture-frame stage" opens for the audience a window on a fictional world created by the author. The audience is, as it were, spying on life, and the characters are expected to behave realistically, as ordinary persons do. In contrast, the Elizabethan outdoor "platform stage," extending into the audience and rising in tiered balconies at the rear, tended to blur the line between actor and spectator. Spectators were physically close to the action and, in speeches directed or half-directed at them, were recognized as co-participants with the actors in the dramatic illusion.

> Thou seest we are not all alone unhappy:
> This wide and universal theater
> Presents more woeful pageants than the
>   scene
> Wherein we play in. (2.7.136–39)

These lines from Shakespeare's *As You Like It*, spoken by a banished duke to a bitter courtier, refer to the discovery of two hungry wanderers nearby in the forest. While the word *theater* literally denotes the world, it also, by the proper gesture, could be made to include the audience seated in the actual theater, whose circumstances included various degrees of good or of evil fortune. Or alternatively, half-facing the audience, the duke could be made to address both the courtier and the audience, assuring all present that others suffer as well as they. Today a similar effect may be achieved in **theater in the round** productions, where no walls exist and the audience's seating surrounds an inner circle where the action takes place. In any case, the audience is brought through the window or picture frame to mingle with the characters.

Genre Distinctions

As You Like It is a **comedy**, a drama that ends happily in contrast to a **tragedy**, a drama that ends unhappily. These terms hark back to Greek drama and delineate the two largest traditional categories within the genre. While these distinctions are generally helpful, they are not all-encompassing. Many subgenres, such as romantic comedy, satiric comedy, and comedy of manners, have since been created. Furthermore, some dramas do not quite fit into either category. For instance, Shakespeare blended the genres in tragicomedies, such as his *Merchant of Venice*. There, a serious threat (Shylock's cutting out Antonio's heart) dominates the ending until Portia's ingenuity leads to an unexpected reversal of circumstances and a happy ending.

Like any genre, drama has formal requirements. Most plays are divided into **acts**. These major divisions are then subdivided into **scenes**, units in which the setting is constant and the time continues uninterrupted. Acts often have a unifying theme or serve to accomplish particular movements in a plot or character arc. On the textual level, dramas may also be written in either prose or verse. Today prose dominates in drama writing. Consider film scripts; it would be the rare film script indeed that could succeed in verse form. But such was not always the case. In Shakespeare's time, audiences expected good playwrights to create scripts with elevated language using the figurative and rhetorical tools of literature.

Unsurprisingly, then, all the elements of literature we have studied are powerfully present in the play *Romeo and Juliet* by William Shakespeare. Notice that most of the play is in poetry—usually unrhymed but poetry nonetheless. Romeo, on finding Juliet beautifully preserved in death (she is only unconscious), exclaims:

> O my love, my wife,
> Death, that hath suck'd the honey of thy
> breath,
> Hath had no power yet upon thy beauty:
> Thou art not conquer'd; beauty's ensign yet
> Is crimson in thy lips and in thy cheeks,
> And death's pale flag is not advanced
> there. (5.3.91–96)

Romeo's words compare death to a bee and to a military conqueror. The face of Juliet is both a flower and a battlefield on which beauty is contending with death. The comparisons are rich in meaning. The Bible speaks of the sting of death (1 Cor. 15:55–56). Romeo expands the biblical metaphor into a compliment: Death, approaching Juliet, forgot to sting her. Distracted by the beauty of her face and the fragrance of her breath, it instead sucked the nectar of her breath (stopped her breathing). It kissed her and left her radiant as before. The paleness of death's horse in Revelation 6:8 is extended to death's military banner, the "ensign" of his advance. Beauty therefore has escaped death by both deception and force.

Imaginative comparison, sound devices, allusion, and irony—all abound in the play. In an example of dramatic irony, we the readers know of Romeo and Juliet's secret marriage, of which most of the characters are ignorant until the play's end. And before the end of scene one, the feud erupts and brings Capulet to the street in his nightgown, a symbol of violated domestic peace and dignity. As you read, look for these literary elements and be ready to enjoy your recognition of all you have studied. Observe, and learn how drama can masterfully bring together these elements to beautifully convey worthy and lasting themes.

The Tragedy of Romeo and Juliet

William Shakespeare

One of Shakespeare's most beloved plays, *Romeo and Juliet* appeals universally for its picture of young love tragically ended. The basic plot appears in the folklore of many cultures. Indeed, the myth "Pyramis and Thisbe" (found in Unit 5) is often cited as a precedent for the story. Shakespeare's audience would have been familiar with several versions, a fact he acknowledged by telling the play's ending in its beginning. Despite the familiarity of the story, however, Shakespeare infused his rendition with fully realized characters, complex themes, and literary beauty not seen in any previous English versions.

The predominant conflict of the play is external: Can genuine love win out against a society seemingly totally hostile to its survival? In developing this conflict, though, Shakespeare communicates several interlocking themes, most of which revolve around youth—its strengths and limitations, its dreams and disappointments, its dangers and splendors. Clearly, love in all its mystery and finality is a great theme of the play. Romeo abandons his initial infatuation with Rosaline for what is plainly meant to be a sincere love of Juliet. The wide differences between these loves are reflected in Romeo's subsequent changes in attitude and actions. These communicate something of Shakespeare's understanding of what love is and looks like.

In keeping with this theme, Shakespeare examines the strong passion of youth, a time in which the struggle to balance one's desires with one's reason, to do what is right or best rather than simply what one wants, is especially strong. Notice the frequent mention of tempering or temperance—that is, of balance and self-control. In many ways, the tragedies of the play ensue when characters succumb to the all-too-human tendency to let their strong emotions—whether of love or hate—drive their choices beyond reason's wise restraint. Such rashness in action creates unnecessary problems. "I stand on sudden haste," declares Romeo. "Wisely and slow," replies the Friar; "they stumble that run fast" (2.3.83–84).

Youth is also a time of crucial choices and decisions, the consequences of which often continue throughout life. Echoing common Renaissance themes, Shakespeare poses free-will choices against the idea of fate (an impersonal predestining force). Are our lives directed by chance and coincidence, or are we to some degree responsible? Who is to blame for the deaths of Romeo and Juliet? The feuding houses? Tybalt? the Friar? Romeo and Juliet themselves? Must a person accept responsibility for unwise behavior to which he was provoked? Can more than one person be responsible for an act?

In the midst of these themes, Shakespeare's tone is sometimes difficult to perceive. Advice given and choices made play a great part in revealing his tone toward different characters. Note the counsel each character gives. How does a person's advice reveal his or her character traits? If taken, how does that advice turn out in the action of the play? Does a character's age affect the advice he gives or takes? The play is in many ways about choosing and the need for wise judgment. But whether or not their behavior is always wise, Romeo and Juliet retain our sympathy because of their tender and self-sacrificing love for each other. In this way, the themes of the play come full circle.

About the Author

The facts of Shakespeare's life—what few we know—do very little to illuminate his writing. Born in Stratford, England, to a prominent merchant and later town official, William had the advantage of very good training in the village school. Taught by an Oxford graduate with a master's degree, the school offered the equivalent of an undergraduate major in the Latin classics today. Exactly when the teenaged William left Stratford for London and joined the Lord Chamberlain's players, we do not know. During the 1590s and 1610s (the main portion of his career) he averaged writing almost two plays a year while acting and helping administer the affairs of the company. The best of these plays are considered among the highest achievements of human art. They are also among the most interesting, as you will discover. As a stockholder as well as actor and playwright in his company, Shakespeare knew how important it was to please the nonliterary members of the audience as well as the highly educated minority. The performances had to entertain in order to show a profit. And all the evidence indicates they did.

Though we do not know much about Shakespeare's personal life, we do know a great deal about what he read, and that knowledge is much more important for our understanding of his writing. The curriculum of the Elizabethan "grammar school" (the grammar studied was, of course, Latin) was fairly well standardized, and reflections of his classroom reading appear constantly in his plays. Of the standard Latin works assigned, a favorite was the *Metamorphoses* of the Roman poet Ovid, a veritable library of classical mythology containing tales of miraculous changes. Ovid's story of Pyramus and Thisbe, the unfortunate eloping lovers of ancient Babylon, furnished the basic plot of *Romeo and Juliet* as well as of *A Midsummer Night's Dream*, written the same year (1595). Chief among the works with which Shakespeare was well acquainted was the Bible, read publicly every day in the Elizabethan church and school. Its influence shows in the abundance of biblical allusions and verbal echoes in the plays and in the reflection of biblical truth in their themes.

Characters

The Montague Household and Friends

Montague
Lady Montague
Romeo, their son
Balthasar, Romeo's servant
Benvolio, Montague's nephew and friend to Romeo
Mercutio, Romeo's friend and kinsman to Prince Escalus
Abram, servant

The Capulet Household and Friends

Capulet
Lady Capulet
Juliet, their daughter
Nurse, Juliet's attendant
Peter, Nurse's servant
Tybalt, Lady Capulet's nephew
Sampson, servant
Gregory, servant
Potpan, servant
Clown, servant
Old Capulet, Capulet's cousin
Paris, noble suitor to Juliet
Petruchio, a (mute) follower of Tybalt

Neutral Parties

Chorus
Escalus, Prince of Verona
Friar Lawrence, Franciscan priest, counselor to Romeo and Juliet
Friar John, Franciscan priest
An Apothecary of Mantua
Three musicians
Citizens of Verona; Gentlemen and Gentlewomen of both houses; Maskers, Torch-bearers, Pages, Guards, Watchmen, Servants, and Attendants

Setting

Place: Verona and Mantua, Italy
Time: Early Fourteenth Century

Act I

Prologue

Enter CHORUS.*

CHORUS Two households, both alike in dignity,
In fair Verona, where we lay our scene,
From ancient grudge break to new mutiny,*
Where civil* blood makes civil hands unclean.
From forth the fatal loins of these two foes
A pair of star-cross'd* lovers take their life;
Whose misadventur'd piteous overthrows*
Doth with their death bury their parents' strife.
The fearful passage* of their death-mark'd love,
And the continuance of their parents' rage,
Which, but their children's end, nought could remove,
Is now the two hours' traffic* of our stage;
The which if you with patient ears attend,
What here shall miss,* our toil shall strive to mend.*

Exit CHORUS.

Chorus: a single actor who summarizes in general terms the play and comments on its moral significance.
mutiny: fighting
civil: citizens'
star-cross'd: doomed by having been born under the wrong astrological signs
overthrows: fates
passage: course
traffic: subject
What . . . miss: What we perform inadequately
mend: make better (in future performances)

Scene I

Time: Sunday morning

Place: A public street in Verona

Jesting leads to quarreling between the servants of Capulet and Montague, rekindling an ancient feud. The Prince stills the commotion, sternly warning both houses not to break the peace again. Romeo's parents discuss with Benvolio their son's recent bizarre behavior. Romeo himself explains that he is scorned by one he loves, Rosaline.

Enter SAMPSON *and* GREGORY, *with swords and bucklers, of the house of Capulet.*

SAMPSON Gregory, on my word, we'll not carry coals.*

GREGORY No, for then we should be colliers.

SAMPSON I mean, and we be in choler,* we'll draw.*

GREGORY Ay, while you live, draw your neck out of collar.*

carry coals: take insults graciously
choler: anger
draw: make our swords ready
draw . . . collar: avoid being hanged

Sampson I strike quickly, being mov'd.

Gregory But thou art not quickly mov'd to strike.

Sampson A dog of the house of Montague moves me.

Gregory To move is to stir, and to be valiant is to stand; therefore, if thou art mov'd, thou run'st away.

Sampson A dog of that house shall move me to stand! I will take the wall* of any man or maid of Montague's.

Gregory That shows thee a weak slave, for weakest goes to the wall.* Draw thy tool, here comes two of the house of Montagues.

take . . . wall: force to the gutterside of the walk

goes . . . wall: yields

Enter two other servants, Abram *and* Balthasar.

Sampson My naked weapon is out. Quarrel, I will back thee.

Gregory How, turn thy back and run?

Sampson Fear me not.

Gregory No, marry,* I fear thee!

marry: indeed

Sampson Let us take the law of our sides, let them begin.

Gregory I will frown as I pass by, and let them take it as they list.*

list: choose

Sampson Nay, as they dare.

Gregory Do you quarrel, sir?

Abram Quarrel, sir? No, sir.

Sampson But if you do, sir, I am for you. I serve as good a man as you.

Abram No better?

Sampson Well, sir.

Enter Benvolio.

Gregory Say "better," here comes one of my master's kinsmen.

SAMPSON Yes, better, sir.

ABRAM You lie.

SAMPSON Draw, if you be men. Gregory, remember thy washing* blow.

They fight.

BENVOLIO Part, fools!
Put up your swords, you know not what you do.

Enter TYBALT.

TYBALT What, art thou drawn among these heartless hinds?*
Turn thee, Benvolio, look upon thy death.

BENVOLIO I do but keep the peace. Put up thy sword,
Or manage it to part these men with me.

TYBALT What, drawn and talk of peace? I hate the word
As I hate hell, all Montagues, and thee.
Have* at thee, coward!

washing: swashing, swordsmanlike

heartless hinds: cowards; also a pun on female deer (hinds) that have no male (hart) to protect them

Have: thrust

They fight. Enter three or four CITIZENS *with clubs or partisans.*

CITIZENS Clubs, bills,* and partisans!* Strike!
Beat them down! Down with the Capulets! Down with the Montagues!

bills: billhooks; curved blade on a handle used for clearing brush

partisans: broad-headed spears that were about nine feet long

Enter old CAPULET *in his gown, and his wife,* LADY CAPULET.

CAPULET What noise is this? Give me my sword, ho!

LADY CAP. A crutch, a crutch! Why call you for a sword?

CAPULET My sword, I say! Old Montague is come,
And flourishes his blade in spite of me.

Enter old MONTAGUE *and his wife,* LADY MONTAGUE.

MONTAGUE Thou villain* Capulet!— *(To* LADY MONTAGUE.*)* Hold me not, let me go.

villain: peasant, low-born fellow

LADY MON. Thou shalt not stir one foot to seek a foe.

Enter PRINCE ESCALUS *with his train.*

PRINCE Rebellious subjects, enemies to peace,
Profaners of this neighbor-stained steel—*
Will they not hear?—What ho, you men, you beasts!
That quench the fire of your pernicious rage
With purple fountains issuing from your veins—
On pain of torture, from those bloody hands
Throw your mistempered* weapons to the ground,
And hear the sentence* of your moved prince.
Three civil brawls, bred of an airy word,
By thee, old Capulet, and Montague,
Have thrice disturb'd the quiet of our streets,
And made Verona's ancient citizens
Cast by* their grave beseeming ornaments*
To wield old partisans, in hands as old,
Cank'red* with peace, to part your cank'red* hate;
If ever you disturb our streets again
Your lives shall pay the forfeit of the peace.
For this time all the rest depart away.
You, Capulet, shall go along with me,
And, Montague, come you this afternoon,

Profaners . . . steel: irreverent users of weapons, stained with neighbors' blood

mistempered: ill-forged

sentence: decision

Cast by: throw aside

ornaments: dignified apparel

Cank'red: rusted

cank'red: biting, corrosive

To know our farther pleasure in this case,
To old Free-town, our common judgment-place.
Once more, on pain of death, all men depart.

Exit all but MONTAGUE, LADY MONTAGUE, *and* BENVOLIO.

MONTAGUE Who set this ancient quarrel new abroach?*
Speak, nephew, were you by when it began?

abroach: astir

BENVOLIO Here were the servants of your adversary,
And yours, close fighting ere I did approach.
I drew to part them. In the instant came
The fiery Tybalt with his sword prepar'd,
Which, as he breath'd defiance to my ears,
He swung about his head and cut the winds,
Who, nothing hurt withal,* hiss'd him in scorn.
While we were interchanging thrusts and blows,
Came more and more and fought on part and part,
Till the Prince came, who parted either part.

withal: by it

LADY MON. O, where is Romeo? Saw you him today?
Right glad I am he was not at this fray.*

fray: brawl

BENVOLIO Madam, an hour before the worshipp'd sun
Peer'd forth the golden window of the east,
A troubled mind drave me to walk abroad,
Where, underneath the grove of sycamore
That westward rooteth from this city side,*
So early walking did I see your son.
Towards him I made,* but he was ware* of me,
And stole into the covert* of the wood.
I, measuring his affections by my own,
Which then most sought where most might not be found,*
Being one too many by my weary self,
Pursued my humor* not pursuing his,
And gladly shunn'd who gladly fled from me.

city side: side of the city
made: went
ware: wary, cautious
covert: protecting cover
where . . . found: i.e., sought privacy
humor: inclination

MONTAGUE Many a morning hath he there been seen,
With tears augmenting* the fresh morning's dew,
Adding to clouds more clouds with his deep sighs,
But all so soon as the all-cheering sun
Should in the farthest east begin to draw
The shady curtains from Aurora's* bed,
Away from light steals home my heavy son,
And private in his chamber pens himself,
Shuts up his windows, locks fair daylight out,
And makes himself an artificial night.
Black and portendous* must this humor* prove,
Unless good counsel may the cause remove.

augmenting: increasing
Aurora: goddess of the dawn
portendous: ominous
humor: disposition

BENVOLIO My noble uncle, do you know the cause?

MONTAGUE I neither know it, nor can learn of him.

BENVOLIO Have you importun'd* him by any means?

importun'd: pressed

MONTAGUE Both by myself and many other friends,
But he, his own affections' counsellor,
Is to himself (I will not say how true)
But to himself so secret and so close,
So far from sounding and discovery
As is the bud bit with an envious* worm
Ere he can spread his sweet leaves to the air
Or dedicate his beauty to the sun.
Could we but learn from whence his sorrows grow,
We would as willingly give cure as know.

envious: malicious, spiteful

Enter ROMEO.

BENVOLIO See where he comes. So please you step aside;
I'll know his grievance or be much denied.*

much denied: refused after much urging

MONTAGUE I would thou wert so happy* by the stay*
To hear true shrift.* Come, madam, let's away.

happy: fortunate
stay: lingering
shrift: confession

Exit MONTAGUE and LADY MONTAGUE.

BENVOLIO Good morrow, cousin.

ROMEO Is the day so young?

BENVOLIO But new strook nine.

ROMEO Ay me, sad hours seem long.
Was that my father that went hence so fast?

BENVOLIO It was. What sadness lengthens Romeo's hours?

ROMEO Not having that which, having, makes them short.

BENVOLIO In love?

ROMEO Out—

BENVOLIO Of love?

ROMEO Out of her favor where I am in love.

BENVOLIO Alas that love, so gentle in his view,
Should be so tyrannous and rough in proof!*

proof: experience

ROMEO Alas that love, whose view is muffled still,*
Should, without eyes, see pathways to his will!*
Where shall we dine? O me! what fray was here?
Yet tell me not, for I have heard it all:
Here's much to do with hate, but more with love.
Why then, O brawling love! O loving hate!
O any thing, of nothing first creat'd!*
O heavy lightness, serious vanity,
Misshapen chaos of* well-seeming forms,
Feather of lead, bright smoke, cold fire, sick health,
Still-waking sleep, that is not what it is!
This love feel I, that feel no love in this.*
Dost thou not laugh?

view . . . still: face is always covered

pathways . . . will: ways to accomplish what he wants

any . . . creat'd: All things were created by God out of nothing; ex nihilo.

Misshapen . . . of: that which is without shape made of

that . . . this: that have no love in return

BENVOLIO No, coz, I rather weep.

ROMEO Good heart, at what?

BENVOLIO At thy good heart's oppression.

ROMEO Why, such is love's transgression.
Griefs of mine own lie heavy in my breast,
Which thou wilt propagate to have* it press'd
With more of thine. This love that thou hast shown
Doth add more grief to too much of mine own.
Love is a smoke made with the fume of sighs,
Being purg'd,* a fire sparkling in lovers' eyes,
Being vex'd, a sea nourish'd with loving tears.
What is it else? a madness most discreet,
A choking gall,* and a preserving sweet.
Farewell, my coz.

propagate to have: increase by having

purg'd: rid of smoke (love is)

gall: bitterness

BENVOLIO Soft,* I will go along;
And if you leave me so, you do me wrong.

Soft: not so fast

ROMEO Tut, I have lost myself, I am not here:
This is not Romeo, he's some other where.

BENVOLIO Tell me in sadness,* who is that you love?

sadness: seriousness (Romeo deliberately misconstrues it as "heaviness of spirit," the usual meaning today.)

ROMEO What, shall I groan and tell thee?

BENVOLIO Groan? Why, no;
But sadly tell me, who.

ROMEO Bid a sick man in sadness make his will—
A word ill urg'd to one that is so ill!
In sadness, cousin, I do love a woman.

BENVOLIO I aim'd so near* when I suppos'd you lov'd.

ROMEO A right good mark man! And she's fair I love.

BENVOLIO A right fair mark, fair coz, is soonest hit.

ROMEO Well, in that hit you miss: she'll not be hit
With Cupid's arrow, she hath Dian's wit;*
O, she is rich in beauty, only poor
That, when she dies, with beauty dies her store.*

BENVOLIO Then she hath sworn that she will live chaste?*

ROMEO She hath, and in that sparing makes huge waste;
For beauty starv'd with* her severity
Cuts beauty off from all posterity.
She is too fair,* too wise, wisely too fair,
To merit bliss* by making me despair.
She hath forsworn* to love, and in that vow
Do I live dead that live to tell it now.

BENVOLIO Be rul'd by me, forget to think of her.

ROMEO O, teach me how I should forget to think.

BENVOLIO By giving liberty unto thine eyes:
Examine other beauties.*

ROMEO 'Tis the way
To call hers exquisite in question more.*
These happy masks that kiss fair ladies' brows,
Being black, puts us in mind they hide the fair.
He that is strooken blind cannot forget
The precious treasure of his eyesight lost.
Show me a mistress that is passing fair,*
What doth her beauty serve but as a note

aim'd . . . near: supposed so

Dian's wit: the mind of Diana, goddess of chastity

with . . . store: Her whole stock of beauty will die (she will leave no offspring to perpetuate her beauty).

chaste: unmarried

starv'd with: not reproduced because of

fair: (1) just (2) beautiful

merit bliss: earn her own salvation

forsworn: sworn not to

Examine . . . beauties: Take notice of other beautiful girls.

in . . . more: by comparing her beauty to others'

passing fair: surpassingly beautiful

Where I may read who pass'd* that passing fair?
Farewell, thou canst not teach me to forget.

pass'd: surpassed

BENVOLIO I'll pay that doctrine,* or else die in debt.*

pay . . . doctrine: teach (you) that lesson

in debt: without having fulfilled my obligations to you

Exeunt.

Scene II

Time: Sunday afternoon

Place: A street

Capulet responds encouragingly to Paris's request for Juliet's hand in marriage. He then sends a servant out to invite kinsmen and friends to a feast. Unable to read, the servant encounters Romeo, who reads the list for him. Learning that Rosaline is among the guests, Romeo is persuaded by Benvolio to go to the feast uninvited.

Enter CAPULET, COUNTY PARIS, and the CLOWN, Capulet's Servant.

CAPULET But Montague is bound* as well as I,
In penalty alike, and 'tis not hard, I think,
For men so old as we to keep the peace.

bound: pledged

PARIS Of honorable reckoning* are you both,
And pity 'tis you liv'd at odds so long.
But now, my lord, what say you to my suit?

reckoning: reputation

CAPULET But saying o'er what I have said before:
My child is yet a stranger* in the world,
She hath not seen the change of fourteen years;
Let two more summers wither in her pride,
Ere we may think her ripe to be a bride.

stranger: newcomer

PARIS Younger than she are happy mothers made.

CAPULET And too soon marr'd are those so early made.
Earth hath swallowed all my hopes but she;
She's the hopeful lady of my earth.*
But woo her, gentle Paris, get her heart,
My will to her consent is but a part;
And she agreed,* within her scope of choice
Lies my consent and fair according voice.*
This night I hold an old accustom'd feast,
Whereto I have invited many a guest,

hopeful . . . earth: (1) hope for which I exist, (2) heir to all I own, (3) person who will carry on my line

And . . . agreed: If she agrees

according voice: agreement

Such as I love, and you, among the store
One more, most welcome, makes my number more.
At my poor house look to behold this night
Earth-treading* stars that make dark heaven light.
Come go with me. *(To servant.)* Go, sirrah, trudge about
Through fair Verona; find those persons out
Whose names are written there, and to them say,
My house and welcome on their pleasure stay.*

Earth-treading: moving above the earth

on . . . stay: wait for their arrival

Exit with PARIS.

SERVANT Find them out whose names are written here! It is written that the shoemaker should meddle with his yard* and the tailor with his last,* the fisher with his pencil and the painter with his nets; but I am sent to find those persons whose names are here writ, and can never find what names the writing person hath here writ. I must to the learned. In good time!*

yard: cloth measuring tape

last: foot-shaped form for making or repairing shoes

In . . . time: What good timing!

Enter BENVOLIO *and* ROMEO.

BENVOLIO Tut, man, one fire burns out another's burning.
One pain is less'ned by another's anguish;
Turn giddy,* and be holp* by backward turning;*
One desperate grief cures with another's languish:
Take thou some new infection to thy eye,
And the rank poison of the old will die.

Turn giddy: become dizzy

holp: helped

backward turning: turning in reverse

ROMEO Your plantan* leaf is excellent for that.

plantan: plantain, a medicinal plant

BENVOLIO For what, I pray thee?

ROMEO For your broken shin.

BENVOLIO Why, Romeo, art thou mad?*

mad: insane

ROMEO Not mad, but bound more than a madman is;
Shut up in prison, kept without my food,
Whipt and tormented and—God-den,* good fellow.

God-den: good evening (used after noon)

SERVANT God gi'* god-den. I pray, sir, can you read?

gi': give you

ROMEO Ay, mine own fortune in my misery.

SERVANT Perhaps you have learn'd it without book.*

without book: by heart

But I pray, can you read any thing you see?

ROMEO Ay, if I know the letters and the language.

SERVANT Ye say honestly, rest you merry!*

rest you merry: farewell

ROMEO Stay, fellow, I can read.
(He reads the letter.) "Signior Martino and his wife and daughters; Count Anselme and his beauteous sisters; the lady widow of Vitruvio; Signior Placentio and his lovely nieces; Mercutio and his brother Valentine; mine uncle Capulet, his wife, and daughters; my fair niece Rosaline and Livia; Signior Valentio and his cousin Tybalt; Lucio and the lively Helena."
A fair assembly. Whither should they come?

SERVANT Up.

ROMEO Whither? To supper?

SERVANT To our house.

ROMEO Whose house?

SERVANT My master's.

ROMEO Indeed I should have asked thee that before.

SERVANT Now I'll tell you without asking. My master is the great rich Capulet, and if you be not of the house of Montagues, I pray come and crush* a cup of wine. Rest you merry!

crush: drink

Exit SERVANT.

BENVOLIO At this same ancient feast of Capulet's
Sups the fair Rosaline, whom thou so lovest,
With all the admired beauties of Verona.
Go thither, and with unattainted* eye
Compare her face with some that I shall show,
And I will make thee think thy swan a crow.

unattainted: unbiased

ROMEO When the devout religion of mine eye
Maintains such falsehood, then turn tears to fires;
And these, who, often drown'd, could never die,

Transparent heretics, be burnt for liars!
One fairer than my love! The all-seeing sun
Ne'er saw her match since first the world begun.

BENVOLIO Tut, you saw her fair, none else being by,
Herself pois'd* with herself in either eye;
But in that crystal scales let there be weigh'd
your lady's love against some other maid
That I will show you shining at this feast,
And she shall scant* show well that now seems best.

pois'd: balanced

scant: scarcely

ROMEO I'll go along not such sight to be shown,
But to rejoice in splendor of mine own.

Exeunt.

Scene III

Time: Sunday afternoon

Place: A room in Capulet's house

Lady Capulet and the Nurse encourage the hesitant Juliet to receive Paris's proposal favorably.

Enter LADY CAPULET and NURSE.

LADY CAP. Nurse, where's my daughter? Call her forth to me.

NURSE I bade her come. What, lamb! What, ladybird!*
Where's this girl? What, Juliet!

ladybird: sweetheart

Enter JULIET.

JULIET How now, who calls?

NURSE Your mother.

JULIET Madam, I am here; What is your will?

LADY CAP. This is the matter. Nurse, give leave a while,
We must talk in secret. Nurse, come back again;
I have remembr'ed me, thou's hear* our counsel.*
Thou knowest my daughter's of a pretty age.

thou's hear: thou shalt hear

counsel: private conversation

NURSE Faith, I can tell her age unto an hour.

LADY CAP. She's not fourteen.

NURSE I'll lay fourteen of my teeth—
And yet, to my teen* be it spoken, I have but four—
She's not fourteen. How long is it now
To Lammas-tide?*

teen: sorrow

Lammas-tide: August 1, a church festival in honor of harvest (and thus a symbol of early ripening); thus the action of the play is set in July

LADY CAP. A fortnight and odd days.

NURSE Even or odd, of all days in the year,
Come Lammas-eve at night shall she be fourteen,
Susan and she—God rest all Christian souls!—
Were of an age. Well, Susan is with God,
She was too good for me. But as I said,
On Lammas-eve at night she shall be fourteen,
That shall she, marry, I remember it well.
'Tis since the earthquake now eleven years,
And she was wean'd—I never shall forget it—

LADY CAP. Enough of this, I pray thee hold thy peace.

NURSE Peace, I have done. God mark thee to his grace!
Thou wast the prettiest babe that e'er I nurs'd.
An* I might live to see thee married once,
I have my wish.

An: if

LADY CAP. Marry, that "marry" is the very theme
I came to talk of. Tell me, daughter Juliet,
How stands your dispositions to be married?

JULIET It is an honor that I dream not of.

LADY CAP. Well, think of marriage now; younger than you,
Here in Verona, ladies of esteem,
Are made already mothers. By my count,
I was your mother much upon these years*
That you are now a maid. Thus then in brief:
The valiant Paris seeks you for his love.

much . . . years: about the same age

NURSE A man, young lady! Lady, such a man
As all the world—why, he's a man of wax.*

man of wax: perfect of feature, like a wax model

LADY CAP. Verona's summer hath not such a flower.

NURSE Nay, he's a flower, in faith, a very flower.

LADY CAP. What say you? Can you love the gentleman?
This night you shall behold him at our feast;
Read o'er the volume of young Paris' face,
And find delight writ there with beauty's pen;
Examine every married* lineament
And see how one another lends content;*
And what obscured in this fair volume lies
Find written in the margent* of his eyes.
This precious book of love, this unbound lover,
To beautify him only lacks a cover.*
The fish lives in the sea, and 'tis much pride
For fair without* the fair within* to hide.
That book in many's eyes doth share the glory,
That in gold clasps* locks in the golden story;
So shall you share all that he doth possess,
By having him, making yourself no less.
Speak briefly, can you like of Paris' love?

married: matched, symmetrical

content: substance (This phrase continues the book metaphor.)

margent: margin (which in books often supplied commentary)

cover: binding; i.e., the binding of marriage vows

fair without: outward beauty

fair within: inward beauty

gold clasps: (1) the lock of a book, (2) wedding rings

JULIET I'll look to like, if looking liking move;
But no more deep will I endart* mine eye
Than your consent gives strength to make it fly.

endart: shoot forth

Enter CLOWN.

CLOWN Madam, the guests are come, supper serv'd up, you call'd, my young lady ask'd for, the nurse curs'd in the pantry, and every thing in extremity. I must hence to wait; I beseech you follow straight.

Exit CLOWN.

LADY CAP. We follow thee. Juliet, the County* stays.*

County: Count, i.e., Paris

stays: waits for you

Exeunt.

Scene IV

Time: Sunday evening

Place: A street near Capulet's house

Masked, Romeo and his friends go to Capulet's feast in an exuberant, frolicsome mood.

Enter ROMEO, MERCUTIO, BENVOLIO, *with five or six other* MASKERS,* *and* TORCH-BEARERS.

ROMEO What, shall this speech be spoke for our excuse?*

BENVOLIO The date is out of such prolixity:*
We'll have no Cupid* hoodwink'd* with a scarf,
Bearing a Tartar's painted bow of lath,*
Scaring the ladies like a crow-keeper,*
Nor no without-book* prologue, faintly spoke
After the prompter, for our entrance;
But let them measure us by what they will,
We'll measure them a measure* and be gone.

ROMEO Give me a torch, I am not for this ambling;
Being but heavy,* I will bear the light.

MERCUTIO Nay, gentle Romeo, we must have you dance.

ROMEO Not I, believe me. You have dancing shoes
With nimble soles; I have a soul of lead
So stakes me to the ground I cannot move.

MERCUTIO You are a lover, borrow Cupid's wings,
And soar with them above a common bound.*

ROMEO I am too sore enpierced with his shaft
To soar with his light feathers and so bound
I cannot bound a pitch* above dull woe;
Under love's heavy burden do I sink.

MERCUTIO Give me a case* to put my visage in, *(Puts on a mask.)*
A visor for a visor! what care I
What curious eye doth cote* deformities?
Here are the beetle brows shall blush for me.

ROMEO A torch for me. Let wantons light of heart

maskers: those wearing masks, participants in either a masquerade or a masque

shall . . . excuse: Shall we have a presenter introduce us with a speech?

The . . . prolixity: Long introductions are outdated.

We'll . . . Cupid: boy dressed as Cupid (to present us)

hoodwink'd: blindfolded

Tartar's . . . lath: short, curved, lip-shaped archer's bow

crow-keeper: scarecrow

without-book: unmemorized

measure . . . measure: deal them out a dance

heavy: low in spirits

common bound: dancing leap

pitch: leap

case: mask

cote: take note of

Tickle the senseless rushes* with their heels.
For I am proverb'd with a grandsire phrase,*
I'll be a candle-holder and look on.*

rushes: floor covering
grandsire phrase: proverb, wise saying
I'll . . . on: I'll be an onlooker.

MERCUTIO Why, may one ask?

ROMEO I dreamt a dream tonight.

MERCUTIO And so did I.

ROMEO Well, what was yours?

MERCUTIO That dreamers often lie.

ROMEO In bed asleep, while they do dream things true.

MERCUTIO O then I see Queen Mab hath been with you.
She is the fairies' midwife, and she comes
In shape no bigger than an agot-stone*
On the forefinger of an alderman,*
Drawn with a team of little atomies*
Over men's noses as they lie asleep.
Her wagon spokes made of long spinners'* legs,

agot-stone: agate
alderman: member of the town council
atomies: tiny creatures
spinners': spider's

The cover of the wings of grasshoppers,
The traces of the smallest spider web,
The collars of the moonshine's wat'ry beams,
Her whip of cricket's bone, the lash of film,
Her wagoner a small grey-coated gnat,
Not half so big as a round little worm
Prick'd from the lazy finger of a maid.*
Her chariot is an empty hazel-nut,
Made by the joiner* squirrel or old grub,
Time out a' mind the fairies' coachmakers.
And in this state* she gallops night by night
Through lovers' brains, and then they dream of love;
O'er courtiers' knees, that dream on cur'sies* straight;*
O'er lawyers' fingers, who straight dream on fees;
O'er ladies' lips, who straight on kisses dream,
Which oft the angry Mab with blisters plagues,
Because their breaths with sweetmeats tainted are.
Sometime she gallops o'er a courtier's nose,
And then dreams he of smelling out a suit;*
And sometime comes she with a tithe-pig's tail*
Tickling a parson's nose as 'a lies asleep,
Then he dreams of another benefice.*
Sometime she driveth o'er a soldier's neck,
And then dreams he of cutting foreign throats,
Of breaches,* ambuscadoes,* Spanish blades,*
Of healths five fathom deep; and then anon*
Drums in his ear, at which he starts* and wakes,
And being thus frighted, swears a prayer or two,
And sleeps again.

the . . . maid: According to folklore, worms grew in the fingers of lazy girls.
joiner: carpenter
state: splendor
cur'sies: curtsies, bows
straight: immediately
smelling . . . suit: finding a client
tithe-pig's tail: tail of a pig used in payment of a church tithe
benefice: ecclesiastical appointment
breaches: breaking down
ambuscadoes: ambushes
Spanish blades: fine swords
anon: immediately
starts: jumps up

ROMEO Peace, peace, Mercutio, peace!
Thou talk'st of nothing.

MERCUTIO True, I talk of dreams,
Which are the children of an idle brain,
Begot of nothing but vain fantasy,
Which is as thin of substance as the air,
And more inconstant than the wind, who woos
Even now the frozen bosom of the north,
And, being anger'd,* puffs away from thence,
Turning his side to the dew-dropping south.

anger'd: i.e., because he cannot thaw the north

BENVOLIO. This wind you talk of blows us from ourselves:
Supper is done, and we shall come too late.

ROMEO: I fear, too early, for my mind misgives
Some consequence yet hanging in the stars
Shall bitterly begin his fearful date
With this night's revels,* and expire the term*
Of a despised life clos'd in my breast
By some vile forfeit of untimely* death.
But He that hath the steerage of my course
Direct my sail! On, lusty gentleman!

revels: merry making

expire the term: bring the end, in the sense of the forfeiture of an unpaid mortgage

untimely: premature

BENVOLIO: Strike, drum.

Exeunt.

Scene V

Time: Sunday evening

Place: A hall in Capulet's house

Capulet welcomes his guests and then chides Tybalt for being offended by the intrusion of Romeo and his friends. Unaware of each other's identity, Romeo and Juliet meet and fall in love.

SERVINGMEN come forth with napkins.

SERVANT 1: Where's Potpan, that he helps not to take away? He shift a trencher?* he scrape a trencher?

trencher: wooden platter

SERVANT 2: When good manners shall lie all in one or two men's hands, and they unwash'd too, 'tis a foul thing.

SERVANT 1: Away with the joint-stools,* remove the court-cubberd,* look to the plate.* Good thou, save me a piece of marchpane,* and, as thou loves me, let the porter let in Susan Grindstone and Nell.

joint-stools: folding stools

court-cubberd: sideboard

plate: silver flatware

marchpane: marzipan (molded cake made with almond paste)

Exit SERVANT 2.

Anthony and Potpan!

Enter ANTHONY and POTPAN.

ANTHONY: Ay, boy, ready.

SERVANT 1 You are look'd for and call'd for, ask'd for and sought for, in the great chamber.

POTPAN We cannot be here and there too. Cheerly, boys, be brisk a while, and the longer liver take all.*

longer . . . all: enjoy life while it lasts

Exeunt. Enter CAPULET, LADY CAPULET, JULIET, TYBALT, NURSE, SERVINGMEN, GENTLEMEN, LADIES, *and* MASKERS.

CAPULET Welcome, gentlemen! Ladies that have their toes
Unplagu'd with corns will have a bout* with you.
Ah, my mistresses, which of you all
Will now deny to dance? She that makes dainty,*
She I'll swear hath corns. Am I come near ye now?
Welcome, gentleman! I have seen the day
That I have worn a visor and could tell
A whispering tale in a fair lady's ear,
Such as would please; 'tis gone, 'tis gone, 'tis gone.
You are welcome, gentlemen! Come, musicians, play.

will . . . bout: dance a measure

makes dainty: refuses

Music plays, and they dance.

A hall, a hall!* Give room! And foot it, girls.
More light, you knaves, and turn the tables up*
And quench the fire, the room is grown too hot.
Ah, sirrah, this unlook'd-for sport comes well.
Nay, sit, nay, sit, good cousin Capulet,
For you and I are past our dancing days.
How long is't now since last yourself and I
Were in mask?

a hall: clear the floor

turn the tables up: stack the tables

OLD CAP. By'r lady, thirty years.

CAPULET What, man? 'tis not so much, 'tis not so much:
'Tis since the nuptial of Lucentio,
Come Pentecost* as quickly as it will,
Some five and twenty years, and then we mask'd.

Pentecost: church festival on the seventh Sunday after Easter

OLD CAP. 'Tis more, 'tis more. His son is elder, sir;
His son is thirty.

CAPULET Will you tell me that?
His son was but a ward* two years ago.

ward: minor

ROMEO (*To a Servingman.*) What lady's that which doth enrich the hand
Of yonder knight?

SERVANT 2 I know not, sir.

ROMEO O, she doth teach the torches to burn bright!
It seems she hangs upon the cheek of night
As a rich jewel in an Ethiop's ear—
Beauty too rich for use, for earth too dear!
So shows a snowy dove trooping with crows,
As yonder lady o'er her fellows shows.
The measure done, I'll watch her place of stand,
And touching hers, make blessed my rude hand.
Did my heart love till now? Forswear it, sight!
For I ne'er saw true beauty till this night.

TYBALT This, by his voice, should be a Montague.
Fetch me my rapier, boy. What dares the slave
Come hither, cover'd with an antic face,*
To fleer* and scorn at our solemnity?*
Now, by the stock and honor of my kin,
To strike him dead I hold it not a sin.

antic face: grotesque mask
fleer: mock
solemnity: celebration

CAPULET Why, how now, kinsman, wherefore storm you so?

TYBALT Uncle, this is a Montague, our foe;
A villain that is hither come in spite
To scorn at our solemnity this night.

CAPULET Young Romeo is it?

TYBALT 'Tis he, that villain Romeo.

CAPULET Content thee, gentle coz, let him alone,
'A bears him like a portly* gentleman;
And to say truth, Verona brags of him
To be a virtuous and well-govern'd youth.
I would not for the wealth of all this town
Here in my house do him disparagement;*
Therefore be patient, take no note of him;
It is my will, the which if thou respect,
Show a fair presence and put off these frowns,
An ill-beseeming semblance* for a feast.

portly: well-mannered
disparagement: disrespect
ill-beseeming semblance: inappropriate appearance

TYBALT It fits when such a villain is a guest.
I'll not endure him.

CAPULET He shall be endured.
What, goodman boy?* I say he shall, go to!*
Am I the master here, or you? Go to!
You'll not endure him! God shall mend my soul,
You'll make a mutiny among my guests!
You will set cock-a-hoop!* You'll be the man!

goodman boy: (a double insult) a goodman is a commoner; boy is a contemptuous term

go to!: come, come!

set cock-a-hoop: set everything in disorder

TYBALT Why, uncle, 'tis a shame.

CAPULET Go to, go to,
You are a saucy boy. Is't so indeed?
This trick* may chance to scathe* you, I know what.*
You must contrary* me! Marry, 'tis time.—*
Well said, my hearts!—You are a princox,* go,
Be quiet, or—More light, more light!—For shame,
I'll make you quiet, what!—Cheerly, my hearts!

trick: foolish behavior

scathe: harm

what: i.e., what will happen to you

contrary: be contrary to

'tis time: i.e., that you learned a lesson

princox: impudent boy

TYBALT Patience perforce* with willful choler meeting
Makes my flesh tremble in their different greeting.
I will withdraw, but this intrusion shall,
Now seeming sweet, convert to bitt'rest gall.

perforce: of necessity

Exit TYBALT.

ROMEO *(To Juliet.)* If I profane* with my unworthiest hand
This holy shrine,* the gentle fine is this:
My lips, two blushing pilgrims,* ready stand
To smooth that rough touch with a tender kiss.

profane: treat irreverently

This . . . shrine: Juliet's hand

pilgrims: those who for penance go on a journey to a holy place

JULIET Good pilgrim, you do wrong your hand too much,*
Which mannerly devotion shows* in this:
For saints have hands that pilgrims' hands do touch,
And palm to palm is holy palmers'* kiss.

wrong . . . much: accuse your hand of a sin it did not commit

Which . . . shows: i.e., which has shown

palmers: pilgrims, those who brought back palm boughs from a pilgrimage to Jerusalem

ROMEO Have not saints lips, and holy palmers too?

JULIET Ay, pilgrim, lips that they must use in pray'r.

ROMEO O then, dear saint, let lips do what hands do;
They pray—grant thou,* lest faith turn to despair.

grant thou: i.e., my request for a kiss

JULIET Saints do not move,* though grant* for prayers' sake.

move: insinuate an action

grant: they grant

ROMEO Then move not while my prayer's effect I take.
Thus from my lips, by thine, my sin is purg'd. *(Kissing her.)*

NURSE Madam, your mother craves a word with you.

ROMEO What is her mother?

NURSE Marry, bachelor,
Her mother is the lady of the house,
And a good lady, and a wise and virtuous.
I nurs'd her daughter that you talk'd withal.

ROMEO Is she a Capulet?
O dear account!* My life is my foe's debt.*

account: costly reckoning

my . . . debt: in my enemy's power

BENVOLIO Away, be gone, the sport is at the best.*

be . . . best: "Quit while you are winning."

ROMEO Ay, so I fear, the more is my unrest.

CAPULET Nay, gentlemen, prepare not to be gone,
We have a trifling foolish banquet towards.*
(They whisper in his ear.)
Is it e'en so? Why then I thank you all.
I thank you, honest gentlemen, good night.

towards: on the way

More torches here! Come on, then let's to bed.
(To Old Capulet.) Ah, sirrah, by my fay,* it waxes* late,
I'll to my rest.

fay: faith
waxes: grows

Exeunt all but JULIET *and* NURSE.

JULIET Come hither, nurse. What is yond gentleman?

NURSE The son and heir of old Tiberio.

JULIET What's he that now is going out of door?

NURSE Marry, that, I think, be young Petruchio.

JULIET What's he that follows here, that would not dance?

NURSE I know not.

JULIET Go ask his name: If he be married,
My grave is like to be my wedding-bed.*

My . . . wedding-bed: I'll go to my grave unmarried.

NURSE His name is Romeo, and a Montague,
The only son of our great enemy.

JULIET My only love sprung from my only hate!
Too early seen unknown, and known too late!
Prodigious birth of love it is to me
That I must love a loathed enemy.

NURSE What's this? what's this?

JULIET A rhyme I learnt even now
Of one I danc'd withal. *(One calls within, "Juliet!")*

NURSE Anon, anon!
Come let's away, the strangers all are gone.

Exeunt.

About the Play

1. What do the following quotations reveal about the older generation's attitude toward the ancient feud between the Montagues and the Capulets?
   a. Lady Montague to Montague, Scene I: "Thou shalt not stir one foot to seek a foe."
   b. Capulet to Paris, Scene II: "But Montague is bound as well as I, / In penalty alike, and 'tis not hard, I think, / For men so old as we to keep the peace."
   c. Capulet to Tybalt, Scene V: "Content thee, gentle coz, let him [Romeo] alone, / 'A bears him like a portly gentleman; / And to say truth, Verona brags of him / To be a virtuous and well-govern'd youth. / I would not for the wealth of all this town / Here in my house do him disparagement."
2. What do the following quotations reveal about the younger generation's attitude toward the ancient feud?
   a. Gregory to Sampson, Scene I: "Draw thy tool, here comes two of the house of Montagues. . . . / I will frown as I pass by and let them take it as they list."
   b. Tybalt to Benvolio, Scene I: "What, drawn and talk of peace? I hate the word / As I hate hell, all Montagues, and thee. / Have at thee, coward!"
   c. Capulet and Tybalt, Scene V: (Capulet) "Therefore, be patient, take no note of him; / It is my will, the which if thou respect, / Show a fair presence and put off these frowns, / An ill-beseeming semblance for a feast." (Tybalt) "It fits when such a villain is a guest. / I'll not endure him." (Capulet) "He shall be endured. / What, goodman boy? I say he shall, go to! / Am I the master here, or you? Go to!"
3. In light of these attitudes, who would you say is keeping the feud alive—the older or the younger generation?
4. How does Benvolio's attitude compare with the general attitude of the younger generation? Identify two instances in Act I that would support your answer.
5. Taking into account what others say about Romeo, Romeo's actions, and his dialogue, how would you describe his emotional state in Scene I? What causes him to be in this state emotionally?
6. Benvolio leads the audience to believe that Romeo's love is easily changeable. Given the events of Act I does Benvolio's assessment of Romeo seem correct? Explain.
7. Identify two puns (see definition of *pun* on p. 164).
8. Identify two metaphors or similes. Explain how each metaphor or simile contributes additional meaning to the surrounding passage.
9. Which character do you find most sympathetic so far? Why? Which character do you find least sympathetic? Why? Reference specific instances from Act I in your explanation.

Act II

Prologue

Enter CHORUS.

CHORUS Now old desire* doth in his death-bed lie,
And young affection gapes* to be his heir;
That fair* for which love groan'd for and would die,
With tender Juliet match'd is now not fair.
Now Romeo is belov'd and loves again,
Alike* bewitched by the charm of looks;
But to his foe suppos'd he must complain,*
And she steal love's sweet bait from fearful* hooks.
Being held a foe, he may not have access
To breathe such vows as lovers use* to swear,
And she as much in love, her means much less
To meet her new-beloved any where.
But passion lends them power, time means, to meet,
Temp'ring extremities* with extreme sweet.

Exit.

old desire: i.e., Romeo's infatuation with Rosaline

gapes: yearns

fair: beauty

Alike: equally

But . . . complain: i.e., he must attribute his love to his foe

fearful: dangerous

use: are accustomed

Temp'ring extremeties: moderating pain

Scene I

Time: Sunday evening (very late)

Place: Capulet's orchard

To escape the company of his friends, Romeo unwittingly enters Capulet's orchard. Cloaked in darkness, he listens as Mercutio and Benvolio, ignorant of Romeo's love for Juliet, jest about his love for Rosaline.

Enter ROMEO *alone.*

ROMEO Can I go forward when my heart is here?
Turn back, dull earth,* and find thy center* out.

Enter BENVOLIO *with* MERCUTIO. ROMEO *withdraws.*

dull earth: i.e., Romeo's body

center: i.e., Juliet is the center—the core—of his being

BENVOLIO Romeo! My cousin Romeo! Romeo!

MERCUTIO He is wise,
And on my life, hath stol'n him home to bed.

BENVOLIO He ran this way and leapt this orchard wall.
Call, good Mercutio.

MERCUTIO Nay, I'll conjure* too.
Romeo! humors! madman! passion! lover!
Appear thou in the likeness of a sigh!
Speak but one rhyme, and I am satisfied;
Cry but "Ay, me!" pronounce but "love" and "dove,"
Speak to my gossip Venus one fair word,
One nickname for her purblind son and heir,
Young Adam* Cupid, he that shot so trim,
When King Cophetua lov'd the beggar maid!*
He heareth not, he stirreth not, he moveth not,
The ape is dead, and I must conjure him.
I conjure thee by Rosaline's bright eyes,
By her high forehead and her scarlet lip,
That in thy likeness thou appear to us!

conjure: call up a spirit

Adam: an allusion to famed archer Adam Bell

When . . . maid: The ballad "King Cophetua and the Beggar Maid" calls Cupid "the blinded boy that shoots so trim."

BENVOLIO Come, he hath hid himself among these trees
To be consorted with* the humorous* night.
Blind is his love and best befits the dark.

be . . . with: keep company with

humorous: damp

MERCUTIO If love be blind, love cannot hit the mark.*
Romeo, good night, I'll to my truckle-bed,*
This field-bed is too cold for me to sleep.
Come, shall we go?

If . . . mark: an allusion to the naughty, blind Cupid who shoots arrows aimlessly

truckle-bed: trundle bed

BENVOLIO Go then, for 'tis in vain
To seek him here that means not to be found.

Exit with MERCUTIO.

Scene II

Time: Sunday evening (very late)

Place: Capulet's orchard

After Benvolio and Mercutio depart, Romeo overhears Juliet describing her love for him along with her fear of her family's opposition to their union. Gathering courage, he reveals his presence—and his love—to her. The two pledge their unending love and make plans to wed.

ROMEO *advances.*

ROMEO He jests at scars that never felt a wound.

Enter JULIET above at her window. ROMEO advances.

But soft, what light through yonder window breaks?
It is the east, and Juliet is the sun.
Arise, fair sun, and kill the envious moon,*
Who is already sick and pale with grief
That thou, her maid, art far more fair than she.
Be not her maid, since she is envious;
Her vestal livery* is but sick and green,
And none but fools* do wear it; cast it off.
It is my lady, O, it is my love!
O that she knew she were!
She speaks, yet she says nothing; what of that?
Her eye discourses,* I will answer it.
I am too bold, 'tis not to me she speaks.
Two of the fairest stars in all the heaven,
Having some business, do entreat her eyes
To twinkle in their spheres till they return.
What if her eyes were there, they in her head?
The brightness of her cheek would shame those stars,
As daylight doth a lamp; her eyes in heaven
Would through the airy region stream so bright
That birds would sing and think it were not night.
See how she leans her cheek upon her hand!
O that I were a glove upon that hand,
That I might touch that cheek!

moon: Diana, goddess of the moon and of chastity

vestal livery: maiden dress

fools: jesters, whose multicolored costumes included green

discourses: speaks

JULIET Ay me!

ROMEO She speaks!
O, speak again, bright angel, for thou art
As glorious to this night, being o'er my head,
As is a winged messenger of heaven
Unto the white up-turned wond'ring eyes
Of mortals that fall back to gaze on him
When he bestrides the lazy puffing clouds
And sails upon the bosom of the air.

JULIET O Romeo, Romeo, wherefore art thou Romeo?*
Deny thy father and refuse thy name;
Or, if thou wilt not, be but sworn my love,
And I'll no longer be a Capulet.

wherefore . . . Romeo: i.e., why are you called Romeo (and thus a Montague)

ROMEO *(Aside.)* Shall I hear more, or shall I speak at this?

JULIET 'Tis but thy name that is my enemy;
Thou art thyself, though not a Montague.*
What's Montague? It is nor hand nor foot,
Nor arm nor face, nor any other part
Belonging to a man. O, be some other name!
What's in a name? That which we call a rose
By any other name would smell as sweet;
So Romeo would, were he not Romeo call'd,
Retain that dear* perfection which he owes*
Without that title, Romeo. Doff* thy name,
And for thy name, which is not part of thee,
Take all myself.

though . . . Montague: i.e., though you were to change your name

dear: previous

owes: owns

Doff: discard

ROMEO I take thee at thy word.
Call me but love, and I'll be new baptiz'd;*
Henceforth I never will be Romeo.

be . . . baptiz'd: acquire a new name

JULIET What man art thou that thus bescreen'd in night
So stumblest* on my counsel?*

stumblest: overhears

counsel: private thoughts

ROMEO By a name
I know not how to tell thee who I am.
My name, dear saint, is hateful to myself,
Because it is an enemy to thee;
Had I it written, I would tear the word.

JULIET My ears have yet not drunk a hundred words
Of thy tongue's uttering, yet I know the sound.
Art thou not Romeo, and a Montague?

ROMEO Neither, fair maid, if either thee dislike.

JULIET How camest thou hither, tell me, and wherefore?
The orchard walls are high and hard to climb,
And the place death, considering who thou art,
If any of my kinsmen find thee here.

ROMEO With love's light wings did I o'erperch* these walls,
For stony limits cannot hold love out,
And what love can do, that dares love attempt;
Therefore thy kinsmen are no stop to me.

o'erperch: fly over

JULIET If they do see thee, they will murder thee.

ROMEO Alack, there lies more peril in thine eye
Than twenty of their swords! Look thou but sweet,
And I am proof against* their enmity.

JULIET I would not for the world they saw thee here.

ROMEO I have night's cloak to hide me from their eyes,
And but* thou love me, let them find me here;
My life were better ended by their hate,
Than death prorogued,* wanting of* thy love.

JULIET By whose direction foundst thou out this place?

ROMEO By love, that first did prompt me to inquire;
He lent me counsel, and I lent him eyes.
I am no pilot,* yet, wert thou as far
As that vast shore wash'd with the farthest sea,
I should adventure* for such merchandise.

JULIET Thou knowest the mask of night is on my face,
Else would a maiden blush bepaint my cheek
For that which thou hast heard me speak tonight.
Fain* would I dwell on form, fain, fain deny
What I have spoke, but farewell compliment!*
Dost thou love me? I know thou wilt say, "Ay,"
And I will take thy word; yet, if thou swear'st,
Thou mayest prove false: at lovers' perjuries*
They say Jove laughs. O gentle Romeo,
If thou dost love, pronounce it faithfully;
Or if thou thinkest I am too quickly won,
I'll frown and be perverse, and say thee nay
So* thou wilt woo, but else not for the world.
In truth, fair Montague, I am too fond,*
And therefore thou mayest think my behavior light,*
But trust me, gentleman, I'll prove more true
Than those that have more coying* to be strange.*
I should have been more strange, I must confess,
But that thou overheardest, ere I was ware,*
My true-love passion; therefore pardon me,
And not impute this yielding* to light* love,
Which the dark night hath so discovered.

ROMEO Lady, by yonder blessed moon I vow,
That tips with silver all these fruit-tree tops—

proof against: invulnerable to

but: if only

prorogued: delayed

wanting of: lacking

pilot: merchant-venturer

adventure: take a risk

Fain: gladly

compliment: social rules

perjuries: broken promises

So: so long as

fond: foolish

light: silly

coying: skill in acting coy

strange: distant, reserved

ware: aware

this yielding: my candor

light: insubstantial

JULIET O, swear not by the moon, th' inconstant moon,
That monthly changes in her circled orb,*
Lest that thy love prove likewise variable.

orb: orbit

ROMEO What shall I swear by?

JULIET Do not swear at all;
Or if thou wilt, swear by thy gracious self,
And I'll believe thee.

ROMEO If my heart's dear love—

JULIET Well, do not swear. Although I joy in thee,
I have no joy in this contract* tonight,
It is too rash, too unadvis'd,* too sudden,
Too like the lightning, which doth cease to be
Ere one can say it lightens. Sweet, good night!
This bud of love, by summer's ripening breath,
May prove a beauteous flow'r when next we meet.
Good night, good night! as sweet repose and rest
Come to thy heart as that within my breast!

contract: exchange of promises

unadvis'd: imprudent

ROMEO O, wilt thou leave me so unsatisfied?

JULIET What satisfaction canst thou have tonight?

ROMEO Th' exchange of thy love's faithful vow for mine.

JULIET I gave thee mine before thou didst request it;
And yet I would it were to give again.

ROMEO Would'st thou withdraw it? For what purpose, love?

JULIET But to be frank* and give it thee again,
And yet I wish but for the thing I have.
My bounty* is as boundless as the sea,
My love as deep; the more I give to thee,
The more I have, for both are infinite.

frank: freely generous

bounty: store of love

NURSE calls within.

I hear some noise within; dear love, adieu!
Anon, good nurse! Sweet Montague, be true.
Stay but a little, I will come again.

Exit JULIET *above.*

ROMEO O blessed, blessed night! I am afeard,
Being in night, all this is but a dream
Too flattering-sweet to be substantial.

Enter JULIET *above.*

JULIET Three words, dear Romeo, and good night indeed.
If that thy bent of love* be honorable,
Thy purpose marriage, send me word tomorrow,
By one that I'll procure* to come to thee,
Where and what time thou wilt perform the rite,
And all my fortunes at thy foot I'll lay
And follow thee my lord throughout the world.

bent . . . love: intentions with regard to love

procure: hire

NURSE *(Within)* Madam!

JULIET I come, anon.—But if thou meanest not well,
I do beseech thee—

NURSE *(Within)* Madam!

JULIET By and by, I come,—
To cease thy strife, and leave me to my grief.
Tomorrow will I send.

ROMEO So thrive my soul—

JULIET A thousand times good night!

Exit above.

ROMEO A thousand times the worse, to want* thy light.
Love goes toward love as schoolboys from their books,
But love from love, toward school with heavy looks.

want: lack

Retiring.

Enter JULIET *again above.*

JULIET Hist, Romeo, hist! O, for a falc'ner's voice,
To lure this tassel-gentle* back again!

tassel-gentle: tercel-gentle, or male hawk used in falconry by the nobility

Echo: a nymph who pined for her love until only her voice remained

Bondage is hoarse, and may not speak aloud,
Else would I tear the cave where Echo* lies,
And make her airy tongue more hoarse than mine,
With repetition of my Romeo's name. Romeo!

ROMEO It* is my soul that calls upon my name.
How silver-sweet sound lover's tongues by night,
Like softest music to attending ears!

It: i.e., Juliet

JULIET Romeo!

ROMEO My madam?

JULIET What a' clock tomorrow
Shall I send to thee?

ROMEO By the hour of nine.

JULIET I will not fail: 'tis twenty year till then.
I have forgot why I did call thee back.

ROMEO Let me stand here till thou remember it.

JULIET I shall forget, to have thee still* stand there,
Rememb'ring how I love thy company.

still: forever

ROMEO And I'll still stay, to have thee still forget,
Forgetting any other home but this.

JULIET 'Tis almost morning; I would have thee gone—
And yet no farther than a wanton's* bird,
That lets it hop a little from her hand,
Like a poor prisoner in his twisted gyves,*
And with a silken thread plucks it back again,
So loving-jealous of his liberty.

wanton's: spoiled child's

gyves: fetters

ROMEO I would I were thy bird.

JULIET Sweet, so would I,
Yet I should kill thee with much cherishing.
Good night, good night! Parting is such sweet sorrow,
That I shall say good night till it be morrow.*

morrow: morning

Exit above.

ROMEO Sleep dwell upon thine eyes, peace in thy breast!
Would I were sleep and peace, so sweet to rest!
Hence will I to my ghostly sire's* close cell,*
His help to crave and my dear hap* to tell.

Exit.

ghostly sire's: spiritual father's
close cell: small room
dear hap: good (or costly) fortune

Scene III

Time: Monday morning
Place: Friar Lawrence's cell

The meditations of Friar Lawrence are interrupted by Romeo, who announces his new love for Juliet. Once convinced of the genuineness of this affection, the Friar agrees to marry Romeo and Juliet secretly in the hope that their love will reconcile their families' hatred.

Enter FRIAR LAWRENCE *alone, with a basket.*

FRIAR L. The grey-ey'd morn smiles on the frowning night,
Check'ring the eastern clouds with streaks of light,
And flecked* darkness like a drunkard reels
From forth day's path and Titan's fiery wheels.*
Now ere the sun advance his burning eye,
The day to cheer and night's dank dew to dry,
I must up-fill this osier cage* of ours
With baleful* weeds and precious-juiced flowers.
O, mickle* is the powerful grace* that lies
In plants, herbs, stones, and their true qualities;
For naught so vile* that on the earth doth live
But to the earth some special good doth give;
Nor aught so good but, strain'd* from that fair use,*
Revolts from true birth,* stumbling on abuse.*
Virtue itself turns vice, being misapplied,
And vice sometime by action dignified.*

Enter ROMEO.

Within the infant rind* of this weak flower
Poison hath residence and medicine power;
For this, being smelt, with that part* cheers each part,*
Being tasted, stays* all senses with the heart.*
Two such opposed kings encamp them still*
In man as well as herbs, grace and rude will;
And where the worser is predominant,
Full soon the canker* death eats up that plant.

flecked: spotted
Titan's . . . wheels: the chariot of the sun god
osier cage: willow basket
baleful: poisonous
mickle: very great
powerful grace: gracious healing power
vile: held in low esteem
strain'd: forced
fair use: proper function
true birth: natural purpose
stumbling . . . abuse: falling into misuse
dignified: may become virtue
rind: bud
that part: the odor
part: i.e., of the body
stays: stops
with . . . heart: along with the heart
still: always
canker: destructive worm

ROMEO Good morrow, father.

FRIAR L. *Benedicite!**
What early tongue so sweet saluteth me?
Young son, it argues* a distempered* head
So soon to bid good morrow to thy bed.*
Care keeps his watch in every old man's eye,
And where care lodges, sleep will never lie;
But where unbruised* youth with unstuff'd* brain
Doth couch his limbs, there golden sleep doth reign.
Therefore thy earliness doth me assure
Thou art up-rous'd with some distemp'rature;*
Or if not so, then here I hit it right—
Our Romeo hath not been in bed tonight.

Benedicite: Bless you!
argues: reflects
distempered: disturbed
So . . . bed: to be up so early (at dawn)
unbruised: uninjured by the cares of life
unstuff'd: unburdened
distemp'rature: ailment

ROMEO That last is true—the sweeter rest was mine.

FRIAR L. God pardon sin! Was thou with Rosaline?

ROMEO With Rosaline? my ghostly father, no;
I have forgot that name, and that name's woe.

FRIAR L. That's my good son, but where hast thou been then?

ROMEO I'll tell thee ere thou ask it me again.
I have been feasting with mine enemy,
Where on a sudden one hath wounded me
That's by me wounded; both our remedies
Within my help* and holy physic* lies.
I bear no hatred, blessed man, for lo
My intercession likewise steads* my foe.

Within . . . help: power to heal
physic: medicine
steads: helps

FRIAR L. Be plain, good son, and homely* in thy drift,*
Riddling confession finds but riddling shrift.*

homely: simple
drift: current of meaning
shrift: absolution (declaration of forgiveness)

ROMEO Then plainly know my heart's dear love is set
On the fair daughter of rich Capulet.
As mine on hers, so hers is set on mine
And all combin'd, save what thou must combine
By holy marriage. When and where and how
We met, we woo'd, and made exchange of vow,
I'll tell thee as we pass, but this I pray,
That thou consent to marry us today.

FRIAR L. What a change is here!
Is Rosaline, that thou didst love so dear,
So soon forsaken? Young men's love then lies
Not truly in their hearts, but in their eyes.
The sun not yet thy sighs from heaven clears,*
Thy old groans yet ringing in mine ancient ears;
Lo here upon thy cheek the stain doth sit
Of an old tear that is not wash'd off yet.
If e'er thous wast thyself and these woes thine,
Thou and these woes were all for Rosaline.
And art thou chang'd? Pronounce this sentence* then:
Women may fall, when there's no strength in men.*

clears: dries

sentence: wise saying

Women . . . men: Women may be excused for fickleness when men are so weak.

ROMEO Thou chidst* me oft for loving Rosaline.

chidst: scolded

FRIAR L. For doting, not for loving, pupil mine.

ROMEO And badst me bury love.

FRIAR L. Not in a grave,
To lay one in, another out to have.

ROMEO I pray thee chide me not. Her I love now
Doth grace for grace and love for love allow;*
The other did not so.

Doth . . . allow: reciprocates my love

FRIAR L. O, she* knew well
Thy love did read by rote that could not spell.*
But come, young waverer, come go with me,
In one respect I'll thy assistant be;
For this alliance may so happy prove
To turn your households' rancor* to pure love.

she: Rosaline

did . . . spell: was imitative rather than genuine

rancor: hatred

ROMEO O, let us hence; I stand* on sudden haste.

stand: insist, am set

FRIAR L. Wisely and slow, they stumble that run fast.

Exeunt.

Scene IV

Time: Monday morning

Place: A street

Again the object of his friends' jesting, Romeo is met by Juliet's Nurse, who has been sent to confirm the young couple's wedding plans.

Enter BENVOLIO *and* MERCUTIO.

MERCUTIO Where should this Romeo be?
Came he not home tonight?

BENVOLIO Not to his father's; I spoke with his man.

MERCUTIO Why, that same pale hard-hearted wench, that Rosaline,
Torments him so, that he will sure run mad.

BENVOLIO Tybalt, the kinsman of old Capulet,
Hath sent a letter to his father's house.

MERCUTIO A challenge, on my life.

BENVOLIO Romeo will answer it.

MERCUTIO Any man that can write may answer a letter.

BENVOLIO Nay, he will answer the letter's master, how he dares, being dar'd.

MERCUTIO Alas, poor Romeo, he is already dead, stabb'd with a white wench's black eye, run through the ear with a love-song, the very pin* of his heart cleft with the blind bow-boy's butt-shaft;* and is he a man to encounter Tybalt?

BENVOLIO Why, what is Tybalt?

MERCUTIO More than Prince of Cats.* O, he's the courageous captain of compliments. He fights as you sing prick-song,* keeps time, distance, and proportion;* he rests his minim* rests, one, two, and the third in your bosom: the very butcher of a silk button,* a duellist, a duellist; a gentleman of the very first house,* of the first and second cause.* Ah, the immortal *passado*,* the *punto reverso*,* the *hay*!*

pin: peg at the center of an archery target

blind . . . shaft: blunt arrow used for practice, here associated with Cupid

Prince of Cats: The king of the cats in the folktale "Reynard the Fox" was named Tibalt.

as . . . prick-song: like a polished singer who sings by music, not rote

proportion: rhythm

minim: short

the . . . button: an expert swordsman, one able to pluck a button off his opponent's doublet

first house: best school (of fencing)

of . . . cause: ready on the earliest acceptable occasions for dueling

passado: forward thrust

punto reverso: backhanded thrust

hay: home thrust

BENVOLIO Here comes Romeo, here comes Romeo.

MERCUTIO Signor Romeo, *bon jour*! there's a French salutation to your French slop.* You gave us the counterfeit* fairly last night.

ROMEO Good morrow to you both. What counterfeit did I give you?

MERCUTIO The slip,* sir, the slip, can you not conceive?

ROMEO Pardon, good Mercutio, my business was great, and in such a case as mine a man may strain courtesy.*

ROMEO Here's a goodly gear!*

Enter NURSE and her servant PETER.

A sail, a sail!*

MERCUTIO Two, two: a shirt and a smock.*

NURSE Peter!

PETER Anon!*

NURSE My fan, Peter.

MERCUTIO Good Peter, to hide her face, for her fan's the fairer face.

NURSE Out upon you, what a man are you?

ROMEO One, gentlewoman, that God hath made, himself to mar.

NURSE By my troth, it is well said; "for himself to mar," quoth 'a! Gentlemen, can any of you tell me where I may find the young Romeo?

ROMEO I can tell you, but young Romeo will be older when you have found him than he was when you sought him. I am the youngest of that name, for fault of a worse.

NURSE If you be he, sir, I desire some confidence* with you.

BENVOLIO She will indite* him to some supper.

slop: sloppy trousers (Romeo has the neglectful appearance of a suffering lover.)

gave . . . counterfeit: (1) eluded us; (2) gave us false coins (slips)

slip: pun on counterfeit coins called slips

strain courtesy: break the rules of etiquette

gear: matter referring to Mercutio's jesting; equipment, clothing, referring mockingly to the Nurse's appearance

sail: a call indicating the appearance of a ship, in this case referring to the Nurse's size and outlandish regalia

shirt . . . smock: i.e., a man and a woman

Anon: right here

confidence: malapropism for conference, private conversation

indite: malapropism for invite, said in mockery

MERCUTIO Romeo, will you come to your father's? We'll to dinner thither.

ROMEO I will follow you.

MERCUTIO Farewell, ancient lady, farewell, (*singing*) "lady, lady, lady."

Exit MERCUTIO and BENVOLIO.

NURSE I pray you, sir, what saucy merchant* was this that was so full of his ropery?*

merchant: fellow

ropery: knavery, mischief

ROMEO A gentleman, nurse, that loves to hear himself talk, and will speak more in a minute than he will stand to* in a month.

stand to: apply himself manfully to (as in a fight or contest)

NURSE Scurvy knave!* Pray you, sir, a word: and as I told you, my young lady bid me inquire you out; what she bid me say, I will keep to myself. But first let me tell ye, if ye should lead her in a fool's paradise,* as they say, it were a very gross kind of behavior, as they say; for the gentlewoman is young; and therefore, if you should deal double with* her, truly it were an ill thing to be off'red to any gentlewoman, and a very weak dealing.

Scurvy knave: worthless rascal, spoken of Mercutio

lead . . . paradise: deceive her

deal double with: deceive

ROMEO Nurse, commend me* to thy lady and mistress. I protest* to thee—

commend me: give my regards

protest: affirm

NURSE Good heart, and, i' faith, I will tell her as much. O, she will be a joyful woman.

ROMEO What wilt thou tell her, nurse? Thou dost not mark* me.

mark: listen to

NURSE I will tell her, sir, that you do protest, which, as I take it, is a gentleman-like offer.

ROMEO Bid her devise
Some means to come to shrift* this afternoon,
And there she shall at Friar Lawrence' cell
Be shriv'd* and married. Here is for thy pains.*

shrift: confession

shriv'd: absolved (declared forgiven, reference to Catholic sacrament of penance)

pains: service (of carrying the message)

NURSE No, truly, sir, not a penny.

ROMEO Go to, I say you shall.

NURSE This afternoon, sir? Well, she shall be there.

ROMEO And stay, good nurse, behind the abbey wall.
Within this hour my man shall be with thee
And bring thee cords made like a tackled stair,*
Which to the high top-gallant* of my joy
Must be my convoy* in the secret night.
Farewell, be trusty, and I'll quit* thy pains.
Farewell, commend me to thy mistress.

tackled stair: rope ladder

top-gallant: highest mast of a ship

convoy: means of passage (to Juliet's chamber)

quit: requite, repay

NURSE Now God in heaven bless thee! Hark you, sir.

ROMEO What say'st thou, my dear nurse?

NURSE Is your man secret? Did you ne'er hear say,
"Two may keep counsel, putting one away"?*

Two . . . away: Two may keep a secret, subtracting one.

ROMEO 'Warrant thee,* my man's as true as steel.

'Warrant thee: I assure you

NURSE Well, sir, my mistress is the sweetest lady—O, O! when 'twas a little prating thing—O, there is a nobleman in town, one Paris, that would fain lay knife aboard;* but she, good soul, had as lieve* see a toad, a very toad, as see him. I anger her sometimes and tell her that Paris is the properer* man, but I'll warrant you, when I say so, she looks as pale as any clout* in the versal* world.

lay . . . aboard: claim Juliet

lieve: soon

properer: more handsome

clout: white cloth (cf. "as white as a sheet")

versal: universal, entire

ROMEO Commend me to thy lady.

NURSE Ay, a thousand times.

Exit ROMEO.

Peter!

PETER Anon!

NURSE Before, and apace.*

apace: quickly

Exeunt.

Scene V

Time: Monday noon
Place: Capulet's house

Juliet awaits the return of her tardy nurse, who teases her by revealing only gradually the information she has just received from Romeo.

Enter JULIET.

JULIET
The clock strook nine when I did send the nurse;
In half an hour she promised to return.
Perchance she cannot meet him—that's not so.
O, she is lame! Love's heralds should be thoughts,
Which ten times faster glides than the sun's beams,
Driving back shadows over low'ring* hills;
Therefore do nimble-pinion'd* doves draw Love,
And therefore hath the wind-swift Cupid wings.
Now is the sun upon the highmost hill
Of this day's journey, and from nine till twelve
Is three long hours, yet she is not come.
Had she affections and warm youthful blood,
She would be as swift in motion as a ball;
My words would bandy* her to my sweet love,
And his to me.
But old folks—many feign as they were dead,
Unwieldy,* slow, heavy, and pale as lead.
O, she comes!

low'ring: frowning

nimble-pinion'd: quick-winged (Venus's chariot was drawn by doves)

bandy: toss

Unwieldy: clumsy

Enter NURSE *and* PETER.

O honey nurse, what news?
Hast thou met with him? Send thy man away.

NURSE
Peter, stay at the gate.

Exit PETER.

JULIET
Now, good sweet nurse—why look'st thou sad?
Though news be sad, yet tell them merrily;
If good, thou shamest the music of sweet news
By playing it to me with so sour a face.

NURSE
I am a-weary, give me leave a while.
Fie, how my bones ache! What a jaunce* have I!

jaunce: jostling journey

JULIET I would thou hadst my bones, and I thy news.
Nay, come, I pray thee speak, good, good nurse, speak.

NURSE What haste! Can you not stay awhile?
Do you not see that I am out of breath?

JULIET How art thou out of breath, when thou hast breath
To say to me that thou art out of breath?
The excuse that thou dost make in this delay
Is longer than the tale thou dost excuse.
Is thy news good or bad? Answer to that.
Say either, and I'll stay the circumstance.*
Let me be satisfied, is't good or bad?

stay . . . circumstance: wait for the details

NURSE Well, you have made a simple choice, you know not how to choose a man. Romeo! No, not he. Though his face be better than any man's, yet his leg excels all men's; and for a hand and a foot and a body, though they be not to be talk'd on, yet they are past compare. He is not the flower of courtesy,* but I'll warrant him, as gentle as a lamb. Go thy ways, wench, serve God. What, have you din'd at home?

flower of courtesy: perfect gentleman

JULIET No, no! But all this did I know before.
What says he of our marriage? what of that?

NURSE O, how my head aches! What a head have I!
It beats as it would fall in twenty pieces.
My back a' t' other side—ah, my back, my back!
Beshrew* your heart for sending me about
To catch my death with jauncing up and down!

Beshrew: a curse on (said gently)

JULIET I' faith, I am sorry that thou art not well.
Sweet, sweet, sweet nurse, tell me, what says my love?

NURSE Your love says, like an honest* gentleman,
An' a courteous, and a kind, and a handsome,
And, I warrant, a virtuous—Where is your mother?

honest: honorable

JULIET Where is my mother! why, she is within,
Where should she be? How oddly thou repliest!
"Your love says like an honest gentleman,
'Where is your mother?'"

NURSE Is this the poultice* for my aching bones?
Henceforward do your messages yourself.

poultice: a warm compress for easing inflammation

JULIET Here's such a coil! Come, what says Romeo?

NURSE Have you got leave to go to shrift today?

JULIET I have.

NURSE Then hie* you hence to Friar Lawrence' cell,
There stays a husband to make you a wife.
Now comes the wanton* blood up in your cheeks,
They'll be scarlet straight at any news.*
Hie you to church, I must another way,
To fetch a ladder, by the which your love
Must climb a bird's nest soon when it is dark.
Go, I'll to dinner; hie you to the cell.

hie: hurry

wanton: unruly, impetuous

scarlet . . . news: You have always blushed easily.

JULIET Hie to high fortune! Honest nurse, farewell.

Exeunt.

Scene VI

Time: Monday afternoon
Place: Friar Lawrence's cell

Juliet meets Romeo and Friar Lawrence for the wedding.

Enter FRIAR LAWRENCE and ROMEO.

FRIAR L. So smile the heavens upon this holy act,
That after-hours with sorrow chide us not!

ROMEO Amen, amen! But come what sorrow can,
It cannot countervail* the exchange of joy
That one short minute gives me in her sight.
Do thou but close our hands with holy words;
Then love-devouring death do what he dare;
It is enough I may but call her mine.

countervail: equal

FRIAR L. These violent delights have violent ends
And in their triumph die like fire and powder,
Which as they kiss consume. The sweetest honey
Is loathsome* in his own deliciousness
And in the taste confounds* the appetite.

loathsome: repulsive

confounds: destroys

Therefore love moderately; long love doth so.
Too swift arrives as tardy as too slow.

Enter JULIET.

Here comes the lady. O, so light of foot
Will ne'er wear out the everlasting flint;*
A lover may bestride the gossamers*
That idles in the wanton summer air,
And yet not fall; so light is vanity.*

everlasting flint: hard stone (upon which Juliet walks)

gossamers: thin webs spun by spiders

vanity: empty, vain worldly pleasures

JULIET Good even* to my ghostly confessor.

even: evening

FRIAR L. Romeo shall thank thee, daughter, for us both.

JULIET As much* to him, else in his thanks too much.

As much: The same greeting

ROMEO Ah, Juliet, if the measure of thy joy
Be heap'd like mine and that* thy skill be more
To blazon* it, then sweeten with thy breath
This neighbor air and let rich music's tongue
Unfold the imagin'd happiness that both
Receive in either by this dear* encounter.

that: if

blazon: proclaim

dear: precious (with a secondary ominous meaning of costly)

JULIET Conceit,* more rich in matter than in words,
Brags of* his substance, not of ornament.
They are but beggars that can count their worth,
But my true love is grown to such excess
I cannot sum up sum* of half my wealth.

Conceit: thought

Brags of: takes pride in

sum . . . sum: calculate the sum

FRIAR L. Come, come with me, and we will make short work,
For by your leaves* you shall not stay alone
Till Holy Church incorporate two in one.

by . . . leaves: pardon me for insisting

Exeunt.

About the Play

1. Compare and contrast the love relationship of Romeo and Rosaline with that of Romeo and Juliet. Support your answer with quotations from the text.
2. What is Friar Lawrence's motivation for consenting to marry Romeo and Juliet?
3. What is the thematic significance of Friar Lawrence's statement, "Wisely and slow, they stumble that run fast"?
4. What do you think about Friar Lawrence's decision to marry Romeo and Juliet without their parents' consent?
5. How would you describe the Nurse? Defend your answer with specific quotations from the text.
6. What do you think about Mercutio's behavior so far? Is he an admirable character and a good friend to Romeo? Consider Mercutio's words and actions and what other characters say about him to support your answer.
7. Compare Friar Lawrence, who counsels Romeo, with the Nurse, who counsels Juliet. Which do you think is the better counselor? Support your answer with details from Act II.
8. If you were Romeo's friend or Juliet's friend, at what point in the story (so far) would you most like to insert yourself and bring Proverbs 13:20 to their attention?

THINKING ZONE

It may have surprised you to find that the classification of comedy does not depend on how funny a play is. Indeed, even tragedies can contain comic elements. To give the audience a rest from tragic events, playwrights employ **comic relief**, comic elements inserted into serious drama to relieve dramatic tension. This practice was very common in Elizabethan tragedies like Shakespeare's.

Hamlet provides an excellent illustration of comic relief. After the tragic deaths of Polonius and Ophelia, Shakespeare interjects a scene in which gravediggers banter hilariously as they prepare Ophelia's grave. Hamlet and Horatio approach and watch as one of the men tosses skulls from the grave, singing as he works. Hamlet's question "Whose grave's this, sirrah?" introduces an exchange of wit in which Hamlet puns on the word *lie* as the gravedigger previously did on the word *arms*.

Comedic elements may also serve to make a thematic point or to flesh out a character. In Rostand's *Cyrano de Bergerac*, the Viscount de Valvert deliberately provokes Cyrano, the hero, saying, "Sir, your nose is . . . hmm . . . it is very big!" In response, Cyrano launches into a series of clever insults Valvert could have made about Cyrano's famously enormous nose, demonstrating the inanity of Valvert's insult and delighting his audience with his verbal expertise. Choking with rage, Valvert shouts, "Base scoundrel! Rascally flat-footed lout!" Bowing as if the Viscount had introduced himself, Cyrano retorts, "Ah? And I—Cyrano-Savinien-Hercule De Bergerac."

The exchange aptly illustrates wit and repartee. Both are comic devices, though they may often make a serious point. **Wit** refers to a brief verbal expression that amuses listeners through a clever but unexpected turn of phrase or connection between ideas. Valvert's insult occasions a spectacular display of wit on Cyrano's part. Furthermore, the deft twisting of Valvert's name-calling is a classic example of **repartee** (a term borrowed from the sport of fencing), which refers to besting another's remark or turning it to one's own advantage in a contest of wits. Cyrano's use of both devices shows that he cannot be intimidated by status or peer pressure. This quality endears him to the audience and forms part of the play's theme.

1. Analyze Act II, Scene IV. What about the scene is humorous, justifying it as **comic relief**? Give two specifics. Consult the glosses.
2. How does the following exchange exemplify both **wit** and **repartee**?

   ROMEO: I dreamt a dream tonight.
   MERCUTIO: And so did I.
   ROMEO: Well, what was yours?
   MERCUTIO: That dreamers often lie.
   ROMEO: In bed asleep while they do dream things true.
3. Analyze Act I, Scene V, lines 93–107 and explain the wit.
4. You learned in the introduction that most of *Romeo and Juliet* is written in poetic form. Analyze Act I, Scene V, lines 93–107 again, this time as poetry, to discover the meter, the rhyme scheme, and the poetical form. Does the discovery impress you?

Act III

Scene I

Time: Monday afternoon

Place: A street

The young men of the opposing houses quarrel. When Romeo tries to ignore Tybalt's insults, Mercutio takes up the challenge. Romeo attempts to stop their fight, but in so doing, he obscures Mercutio's view of Tybalt, who then kills Mercutio and flees.

Enter MERCUTIO, BENVOLIO, PAGE, and MEN.

BENVOLIO I pray thee, good Mercutio, let's retire.
The day is hot, the Capulets are abroad,
And if we meet, we shall not 'scape a brawl;
For now, these hot days, is the mad blood stirring.

MERCUTIO Thou art like one of these fellows that, when he enters the confines of a tavern, claps me his sword upon the table and says, "God send me no need of thee!" and by the operation of the second cup draws* him on the drawer,* when indeed there is no need.

draws: i.e., draws his sword

drawer: tapster

BENVOLIO Am I like such a fellow?

MERCUTIO Come, come, thou are as hot a Jack in thy mood as any in Italy, and as soon mov'd to be moody,* and as soon moody to be mov'd.

moody: angry

BENVOLIO And what to?

MERCUTIO Nay, and there were two such, we should have none shortly, for one would kill the other. Thou? why, thou wilt quarrel with a man that hath a hair more or a hair less in his beard than thou hast. Thou wilt quarrel with a man for cracking nuts, having no other reason but because thou hast hazel eyes. What eye but such an eye would spy out such a quarrel? Thy head is as full of quarrels as an egg is full of meat,* and yet thy head hath been beaten as addle* as an egg for quarrelling. Thou hast quarrell'd with a man for coughing in the street, because he hath waken'd thy dog that hath lain asleep in the sun. Didst thou not fall out with a tailor for wearing his new

meat: food

addle: muddled, rotten

doublet* before Easter?* with another for tying his new shoes with old riband? And yet thou wilt tutor me from* quarrelling!

BENVOLIO: And* I were so apt to quarrel as thou art, any man should buy the fee-simple* of my life for an hour and a quarter.*

MERCUTIO: The fee-simple! O simple!

Enter TYBALT, PETRUCHIO, and others.*

BENVOLIO: By my head, here comes the Capulets.

MERCUTIO: By my heel, I care not.

TYBALT: Follow me close, for I will speak to them. Gentlemen, good e'en, a word with one of you.

MERCUTIO: And but one word with one of us? Couple it with something; make it a word and a blow.

TYBALT: You shall find me apt enough to that, sir, and you will give me occasion.

MERCUTIO: Could you not take some occasion without giving?

TYBALT: Mercutio, thou consort'st* with Romeo—

MERCUTIO: Consort! What, dost thou make us minstrels? And thou make minstrels of us, look to hear nothing but discords. Here's my fiddlestick;* here's that shall make you dance.

BENVOLIO:
We talk here in the public haunt of men.
Either withdraw unto some private place,
Or reason coldly of* your grievances,
Or else depart; here all eyes gaze on us.

MERCUTIO:
Men's eyes were made to look, and let them gaze;
I will not budge for no man's pleasure, I.

Enter ROMEO.

TYBALT: Well, peace be with you, sir, here comes my man.*

MERCUTIO: But I'll be hanged, sir, if he wear your livery.*

doublet: coat

before Easter: during Lent, when only dismal dress was allowed by the Catholic church

tutor me from: persuade me against

And: If

fee-simple: absolute ownership

an . . . quarter: i.e., a small sum, the pay for a small amount of work

Petruchio: a "ghost" character, or one whom Shakespeare intended to develop but wound up giving no lines

consort'st: (1) keep company, (2) perform music

fiddlestick: i.e., weapon (Mercutio draws his sword.)

reason . . . of: discuss calmly

my man: the man I'm looking for

livery: servant's uniform (Mercutio deliberately misinterprets *man* as *servant.*)

Indeed, go before to field,* he'll be your follower;
Your worship* in that sense may call him "man."

Tybalt Romeo, the love I bear thee can afford
No better term than this: thou art a villain.

Romeo Tybalt, the reason that I have to love thee
Doth much excuse* the appertaining rage*
To such a greeting. Villain am I none;
Therefore farewell; I see thou know'st me not.

Tybalt Boy, this shall not excuse the injuries
That thou hast done me; therefore turn and draw.

Romeo I do protest I never injured thee,
But love thee better than thou canst devise,*
Till thou shalt know the reason of my love,
And so, good Capulet—which name I tender*
As dearly as mine own—be satisfied.

Mercutio O calm, dishonorable, vile submission!
*Alla Staccato** carries it away.* *(He draws.)*
Tybalt, you rat-catcher,* will you walk?

Tybalt What wouldst thou have with me?

Mercutio Good King of Cats, nothing but one of your nine lives; that
I mean to make bold withal, and as you shall use me
hereafter, dry-beat* the rest of the eight. Will you pluck
your sword out of his pilcher* by the ears?*
Make haste, lest mine be about your ears ere it* be out.

Tybalt I am for you. *(Drawing.)*

Romeo Gentle, Mercutio, put thy rapier up.

Mercutio Come, sir, your *passado*.*

They fight.

Romeo Draw, Benvolio, beat down their weapons.
Gentlemen, for shame, forbear this outrage!
Tybalt, Mercutio, the Prince expressly hath
Forbid this bandying* in Verona streets.

go . . . field: arrive first at the site of a duel

your worship: term of polite address to a nobleman, used ironically by Mercutio to address Tybalt

excuse: justify the absence of

appertaining rage: appropriately angry response

devise: understand

tender: care for

Alla staccato: "with the thrust" (a scornful designation of Tybalt, the technical swordsman)

carries it away: wins

rat-catcher: i.e., Prince of Cats

dry-beat: bruise

pilcher: scabbard

by the ears: i.e., so reluctantly

it: i.e., your sword

passado: lunge

bandying: quarreling

ROMEO steps between them.

Hold, Tybalt! Good Mercutio!

TYBALT under ROMEO's arm stabs MERCUTIO. Exeunt TYBALT and his followers.

MERCUTIO I am hurt.
A plague a' both your houses! I am sped.*
Is he gone and hath nothing?*

sped: mortally wounded
nothing: no injury

BENVOLIO What, art thou hurt?

MERCUTIO Ay, ay, a scratch, a scratch, but, 'tis enough.
Where is my page? Go, villain,* fetch a surgeon.

villain: fellow

Exit PAGE.

ROMEO Courage, man, the hurt cannot be much.

Mercutio No, 'tis not so deep as a well, nor so wide as a church-door, but 'tis enough; 'twill serve. Ask for me tomorrow, and you shall find me a grave man. I am pepper'd,* I warrant, for this world. A plague a' both your houses! What! A dog, a rat, a mouse, a cat, to scratch a man to death! A braggart, a rogue, a villain that fights by the book of arithmetic!* Why came you between us? I was hurt under your arm.

pepper'd: shot to pieces

book of arithmetic: fencing text

Romeo I thought all for the best.

Mercutio Help me into some house, Benvolio,
Or I shall faint. A plague a' both your houses!
They have made worms' meat of me. I have it,
And soundly. To your houses!

Exit Mercutio and Benvolio.

Romeo This gentleman, the Prince's near ally,*
My very friend, hath got this mortal hurt
In my behalf; my reputation stain'd
With Tybalt's slander—Tybalt, that an hour
Hath been my cousin! O sweet Juliet,
Thy beauty hath made me effeminate,*
And in my temper* soft'ned valor's steel!*

ally: kinsman

effeminate: weak of will

temper: composition, make up

valor's steel: my courage

Enter Benvolio.

Benvolio O Romeo, Romeo, brave Mercutio is dead!
That gallant spirit hath aspir'd* the clouds,
Which too untimely here did scorn the earth.

aspir'd: risen to

Romeo This day's black fate on moe* days doth depend;*
This but begins the woe others must end.

moe: more

depend: extend its influence

Enter Tybalt.

Benvolio Here comes the furious Tybalt back again.

Romeo He gone in triumph, and Mercutio slain!
Away to heaven, respective lenity,*
And fire and fury be my conduct now!
Now, Tybalt, take the "villain" back again
That late thou gavest me, for Mercutio's soul
Is but a little way above our heads,

respective lenity: considerations of being mild

Staying* for thine to keep company.
Either thou or I or both must go with him.

Staying: waiting

TYBALT Thou wretched boy that didst consort him here
Shalt with him hence.

ROMEO This shall determine that.

(They fight; TYBALT falls.)

BENVOLIO Romeo, away, be gone!
The citizens are up and Tybalt slain.
Stand not amazed. The Prince will doom thee death
If thou are taken. Hence be gone away!

ROMEO O, I am fortune's fool!*

fool: plaything; the helpless victim of fortune

BENVOLIO Why dost thou stay?

Exit ROMEO. Enter CITIZENS.

CITIZEN 1 Which way ran he that kill'd Mercutio?
Tybalt, that murderer, which way ran he?

BENVOLIO There lies that Tybalt.

CITIZEN 1 Up, sir, go with me;
I charge thee in the Prince's name, obey.

Enter PRINCE, MONTAGUE, CAPULET, their WIVES and all.

PRINCE Where are the vile beginners of this fray?

BENVOLIO O noble Prince, I can discover* all
The unlucky manage of this fatal brawl:
There lies the man, slain by Romeo,
That slew thy kinsman, brave Mercutio.

discover: reveal

LADY CAP. Tybalt, my cousin! O my brother's child!
O Prince! O cousin! O husband! O, the blood is spill'd
Of my dear kinsman! Prince, as thou art true,
For blood of ours, shed blood of Montague.
O cousin, cousin!

PRINCE Benvolio, who began this bloody fray?

BENVOLIO Tybalt, here slain, whom Romeo's hand did slay!
Romeo that spoke him fair, bid him bethink*
How nice* the quarrel was, and urg'd withal*
Your high displeasure; all this, uttered
With gentle breath, calm look, knees humbly bowed,
Could not take truce with* the unruly spleen*
Of Tybalt, deaf to peace, but that he tilts
With piercing steel at bold Mercutio's breast,
Who, all as hot, turns deadly point to point
And, with a martial scorn, with one hand beats
Cold death aside, and with the other sends
It back to Tybalt, whose dexterity*
Retorts* it. Romeo he cries aloud,
"Hold, friends! Friends, part!" and swifter than his tongue
His agile arm beats down their fatal* points
And 'twixt them rushes; underneath whose arm
An envious* thrust from Tybalt hit the life
Of stout Mercutio, and then Tybalt fled;
But by and by comes back to Romeo,
Who had but newly entertain'd* revenge,
And to't they go like lightning, for, ere I
Could draw to part them, was stout Tybalt slain;
And as he fell, did Romeo turn and fly.
This is the truth, or let Benvolio die.

bethink: consider
nice: trivial
urg'd withal: emphasized also
take . . . with: calm
spleen: seat (bodily source) of anger
dexterity: skill
Retorts: returns
fatal: deadly
envious: malicious
entertain'd: thought of

LADY CAP. He is a kinsman to the Montague,
Affection makes him false; he speaks not true.
Some twenty of them fought in this black strife,
And all those twenty could but kill one life.
I beg for justice, which thou, Prince, must give:
Romeo slew Tybalt, Romeo must not live.

PRINCE Romeo slew him, he slew Mercutio;
Who now the price of his dear blood doth owe?

MONTAGUE Not Romeo, Prince: he was Mercutio's friend.
His fault concludes but what the law should end:
The life of Tybalt.

PRINCE And for that offense
Immediately we do exile him hence.
I have an interest* in your heart's proceeding.
My blood for your rude brawls doth lie a-bleeding;

interest: personal involvement (Mercutio was kinsman to the Prince.)

But I'll amerce* you with so strong a fine
That you shall all repent the loss of mine.
I will be deaf to pleading and excuses,
Nor tears nor prayers shall purchase out abuses;*
Therefore use none. Let Romeo hence in haste,
Else when he is found, that hour is his last.
Bear hence this body and attend our will;*
Mercy but murders,* pardoning those that kill.

amerce: punish (by fine)

purchase out abuses: pay for your transgressions

attend our will: come to hear my pronouncement of judgment

but murders: encourages others to murder

Exeunt.

Scene II

Time: Monday afternoon

Place: Capulet's house

Juliet, eagerly awaiting her husband's arrival at her chamber, is told by the Nurse that Romeo has murdered Tybalt and been banished. Torn between love for her husband and her cousin, she sends the Nurse to summon Romeo.

Enter JULIET alone.

JULIET Gallop apace, you fiery-footed steeds,
Toward Phoebus'* lodging; such a wagoner
As Phaeton* would whip you to the west*
And bring in cloudy night immediately.
Come, night, come, Romeo, come, thou day in night,
For thou wilt lie upon the wings of night,
Whiter than new snow upon a raven's back.
Come, gentle night, come, loving, black-brow'd night.
Give me my Romeo, and when he shall die,
Take him and cut him out in little stars,
And he will make the face of heaven so fine
That all the world will be in love with night
And pay no worship to the garish* sun.
O, I have bought the mansion of a love
But not possess'd it; and though I am sold,
Not yet enjoy'd. So tedious is this day
As is the night before some festival
To an impatient child that hath new robes
And may not wear them. O, here comes my nurse,

Phoebus': The sun's; Phoebus Apollo succeeded the Titan Helios as sun god.

Phaeton: The boy Phaeton insisted on driving the chariot (wagon) of his father, god of the sun, and thus destroyed himself.

whip . . . west: i.e., make the sun set

garish: gaudy

Enter NURSE, wringing her hands, with the ladder of cords in her lap.

And she brings news; and every tongue that speaks
But Romeo's name speaks heavenly eloquence.
Now, nurse, what news? What hast thou there? the cords
That Romeo bid thee fetch?

Nurse Ay, ay, the cords.

Juliet Ay, me, what news? Why dost thou wring thy hands?

Nurse Alack the day, he's dead, he's dead, he's dead!
We are undone, lady, we are undone!
Alack the day, he's gone, he's kill'd, he's dead!

Juliet Can heaven be so envious?*

envious: spiteful

Nurse Romeo can,
Though heaven cannot. O Romeo, Romeo!
Who ever would have thought it Romeo?

Juliet Hath Romeo slain himself? Say thou but ay,
And that bare vowel *I* shall poison more
Than the death-darting eye of cockatrice.*
I am not I, if there be such an ay,
Or those* eyes shut, that make thee answer ay.
If he be slain, say ay, or if not, no.
Brief sounds determine of* my weal or woe.

cockatrice: a mythical serpent that could kill by its glance
those: Romeo's
determine of: establish definitely

Nurse I saw the wound here on his manly breast.
A piteous corse,* a bloody, piteous corse,
Pale, pale as ashes, all bedaub'd in blood,
All in gore blood; I sounded* at the sight.

corse: corpse
sounded: swooned; fainted

Juliet O, break, my heart! Poor bankrout,* break at once!
To prison, eyes, ne'er look on liberty!
Vile earth,* to earth* resign;* end motion here
And thou and Romeo press one heavy bier!

bankrout: bankrupt
earth: Juliet's body
earth: the soil
resign: surrender

Nurse: O Tybalt, Tybalt, the best friend I had!
O courteous Tybalt, honest gentleman,
That ever I should live to see thee dead!

Juliet What storm is this that blows so contrary?
Is Romeo slaught'red? And is Tybalt dead?
My dearest cousin and my dearer lord?
Then, dreadful trumpet, sound the general doom,*

the . . . doom: universal judgment (Rev. 11:15)

Juliet and her Nurse (oil on canvas) (colour photo) by John Roddam Spencer Stanhope (1829–1908)
Private Collection/ By courtesy of Julian Hartnoll/ The Bridgeman Art Library
Nationality / copyright status: English / out of copyright

For who is living if those two are gone?

NURSE Tybalt is gone and Romeo banished;*
Romeo that killed him, he is banished.

banished: exiled, forced to leave his city by official decree

JULIET O Nurse, did Romeo's hand shed Tybalt's blood?

NURSE It did, it did. Alas the day, it did!
O serpent heart hid with a flow'ring* face!
Did ever dragon keep* so fair a cave?

flow'ring: fair

keep: dwell in

JULIET Beautiful tyrant! fiend angelical!
Dove-feather'd raven! wolvish ravening lamb!
Despised substance* of divinest show!*
Just opposite to what thou justly* seem'st,
A dimmed saint, an honorable villain!
O nature, what hadst thou to do in hell
When thou didst bower* the spirit of a fiend
In mortal paradise of such sweet flesh?
Was ever book containing such vile matter
So fairly bound? O that deceit should dwell
In such a gorgeous palace!

substance: reality

show: appearance

justly: rightly

bower: lodge

NURSE There's no trust,
No faith, no honesty in men, all perjur'd,
All forsworn,* all naught,* all dissemblers.*
Ah, where's my man? Give me some aqua-vitae.*
These griefs, these woes, these sorrows make me old.
Shame come to Romeo!

forsworn: disloyal, false

naught: wicked

dissemblers: hypocrites

aqua-vitae: a strong drink used as medicine

JULIET Blister'd be thy tongue
For such a wish! He was not born to shame.
Upon his brow shame is asham'd to sit;
For 'tis a throne where honor may be crown'd
Sole monarch of the universal earth.
O, what a beast was I to chide at him!

NURSE Will you speak well of him that kill'd your cousin?

JULIET Shall I speak ill of him that is my husband?
Ah, poor my lord, what tongue shall smooth thy name
When I, thy three-hours' wife, have mangled it?
But wherefore, villain, didst thou kill my cousin?
That villain cousin would have kill'd my husband.
Back, foolish tears, back to your native spring;

Your tributary drops belong to* woe,
Which you, mistaking, offer up to joy.*
My husband lives that Tybalt would have slain,
And Tybalt's dead that would have slain my husband.
All is comfort; wherefore weep I then?
Some word there was, worser than Tybalt's death
That murder'd me; I would forget it fain,
But O, it presses to my memory
Like damned* guilty deeds to sinners' minds:
"Tybalt is dead, and Romeo is banished."
That "banished," that one word "banished"
Hath slain* ten thousand Tybalts. Tybalt's death
Was woe enough if it had ended there;
Or if sour woe delights in fellowship*
And needly* will be rank'd with other griefs,
Why followed not when she said, "Tybalt's dead,"
Thy father or thy mother, nay, or both,
Which modern* lamentation might have moved?
But with a rearward* following Tybalt's death,
"Romeo is banished," to speak that word
Is father, mother, Tybalt, Romeo, Juliet,
All slain, all dead: "Romeo is banished!"
There is no end, no limit, measure, bound
In that word's* death; no words can that woe sound.
Where is my father and my mother, nurse?

Your . . . to: you should function in

joy: i.e., the occasion of Romeo's survival

damned: damnable

Hath slain: Carries the emotional force of the deaths of

delights in fellowship: ushers in other woes

needly: of necessity

modern: moderate, not excessive

rearward: rear guard (literally a group of soldiers that follow)

that word's: i.e., Romeo's

Nurse Weeping and wailing over Tybalt's corse.
Will you go to them? I will bring you thither.

Juliet Wash they his wounds with tears? Mine shall be spent,*
When* theirs are dry, for Romeo's banishment.
Take up those cords. Poor ropes, you are beguil'd,*
Both you and I, for Romeo is exil'd.

spent: used up

When: i.e., Only when

beguil'd: cheated

Nurse Hie to your chamber. I'll find Romeo
To comfort you. I wot* well where he is.
Hark ye, your Romeo will be here at night.
I'll to him; he is hid at Lawrence's cell.

wot: know

Juliet O, find him! Give this ring to my true knight
And bid him come to take his last farewell.

Exeunt.

Scene III

Time: Monday afternoon

Place: Friar Lawrence's cell

Friar Lawrence informs Romeo of his banishment and tries to console him. The Nurse also informs Romeo of Juliet's predicament and gives him a ring from Juliet.

Enter FRIAR LAWRENCE.

FRIAR L. Romeo, come forth, come forth, thou fearful man.
Affliction is enamor'd of* thy parts,*
And thou art wedded to calamity.

enamor'd of: charmed by

parts: good features, qualities

Enter ROMEO.

ROMEO Father, what news? What is the Prince's doom?*
What sorrow craves acquaintance at my hand?*
That I yet know not?

doom: judicial decision, sentence

craves . . . hand: waits to make acquaintance

FRIAR L. Too familiar
Is my dear son with such sour company!
I bring thee tidings of the Prince's doom.

ROMEO What less than doomsday is the Prince's doom?

FRIAR L. A gentler judgment vanish'd* from his lips—
Not body's death but body's banishment.

vanish'd: escaped

ROMEO Ha, banishment? Be merciful: say "death";
For exile hath more terror in his look,
Much more than death. Do not say "banishment"!

FRIAR L. Here from Verona art thou banished.
Be patient, for the world is broad and wide.

ROMEO There is no world without* Verona's walls
But purgatory, torture, pain itself.
Hence "banished" is banish'd from the world,
And world's exile is death. Then "banished"
Is death mistermed. Calling death "banished,"
Thou cut'st my head off with a golden axe
And smilest upon the stroke that murders me.

without: outside

Friar L. O deadly sin! O rude unthankfulness!
Thy fault our law calls death;* but the kind Prince,
Taking thy part, hath rush'd* aside the law
And turn'd that black word "death" to "banishment."
This is dear mercy, and thou seest it not.

Thy . . . death: According to our laws, you have committed a capital offense.
rush'd: pushed

Romeo 'Tis torture and not mercy. Heaven is here
Where Juliet lives, and every cat and dog
And little mouse, every unworthy thing
Live here in heaven and may look on her,
But Romeo may not. More validity,*
More honorable state, more courtship lives
In carrion* flies than Romeo. They may seize
On the white wonder of dear Juliet's hand
And steal immortal blessing from her lips,
Who, even in pure and vestal modesty,
Still* blush, as thinking their own kisses* sin.
But Romeo may not; he is banished.
This may flies do, but I from this must fly.
They are free men, but I am banished.
And sayest thou yet that exile is not death?
Hadst thou no poison mix'd, no sharp-ground knife,
No sudden mean* of death, though ne'er so mean,*
But "banished" to kill me? "Banished"?
O friar, the damned use that word in hell;
Howling attends it. How hast thou the heart,
Being a divine,* a ghostly confessor,
A sin-absolver, and my friend profess'd,
To mangle me with that word "banished"?

validity: dignity
carrion: flesh-eating
Still: continually
kisses: contact with each other
mean: means
mean: base, lowly
divine: learned clergyman

Friar L. Then fond* madman, hear me a little speak.

fond: foolish

Romeo O, thou wilt speak again of banishment.

Friar L. I'll give thee armor to keep off that word:
Adversity's sweet milk, philosophy,
To comfort thee though thou art banished.

Romeo Yet "banished"? Hang up philosophy!
Unless philosophy can make a Juliet,
Displant* a town, reverse a prince's doom,
It helps not, it prevails not. Talk no more.

Displant: transplant

Friar L. O then I see that madmen have no ears.

Romeo How should they when that wise men have no eyes?

Friar L. Let me dispute* with thee of thy estate.*

dispute: discuss
estate: situation

Romeo Thou canst not speak of that thou dost not feel.
Wert thou as young as I, Juliet thy love,
An hour but married, Tybalt murdered,
Doting like me and like me banished,
Then mightest thou speak; then mightest thou tear thy hair
And fall upon the ground as I do now,
Taking the measure of* an unmade grave.

Taking . . . of: measuring for

Nurse knocks within.

Friar L. Arise; one knocks. Good Romeo, hide thyself.

Romeo Not I, unless the breath of heartsick groans
Mist-like infold* me from the search of eyes.

infold: obscure, hide

Knock.

Friar L. Hark how they knock!—Who's there?—Romeo, arise;
Thou wilt be taken.—Stay a while!*—Stand up!

Stay a while: Wait a moment!

Loud knock.

Run to my study by and by! Good man,
What simpleness* is this? I come, I come!

simpleness: foolishness

Knock.

Who knocks so hard? Whence come you? What's your will?

Nurse Let me come in, and you shall know my errand.
I come from Juliet.

Friar L. Welcome then!

Enter Nurse.

Nurse O holy friar, O, tell me, holy friar,
Where's my lady's lord? Where's Romeo?

Romeo in Friar Laurence's Cell, illustration to 'Romeo and Juliet' Act III, Scene 3 (w/c & pencil on board) by William Hatherell (1855–1928)

FRIAR L. There on the ground, with his own tears made drunk.

NURSE O, he is even in my mistress' case,
Just in her case, O woeful sympathy!*
Piteous predicament! Even so lies she,
Blubb'ring and weeping, weeping and blubb'ring.
Stand up, stand up, stand, and* you be a man.
For Juliet's sake, for her sake rise and stand.
Why should you fall into so deep an O?*

sympathy: affinity

and: if

O: groaning fit

ROMEO Nurse!

NURSE Ah, sir, ah, sir, death's the end of all.

ROMEO Spakest thou of Juliet? How is it with her?
Doth not she think me an old* murderer,
Now I have stain'd the childhood of our joy
With blood removed but little from her own?*
Where is she? And how doth she? And what says
My conceal'd* lady to our cancell'd love?

old: hardened

removed . . . own: i.e., of her cousin Tybalt

conceal'd lady: secret wife

NURSE O, she says nothing, sir, but weeps and weeps
And now falls on her bed and then starts up
And Tybalt calls and then on Romeo cries
And then falls down again.

ROMEO As if that name,
Shot from the deadly level* of a gun,
Did murder her as that name's cursed hand
Murder'd her kinsman? O, tell me, friar, tell me,
In what vile part of this anatomy
Doth my name lodge? Tell me that I may sack*
That hateful mansion.

level: aim

sack: destroy

He offers to stab himself, and the NURSE snatches the dagger away.

FRIAR L. Hold thy desperate hand!
Art thou a man? Thy form cries out thou art;
Thy tears are womanish; thy wild acts denote
The unreasonable fury of a beast.
Unseemly* woman in* a seeming* man
And ill-beseeming* beast in seeming both,*
Thou hast amaz'd me! By my holy order*
I thought thy disposition better temper'd.*

Unseemly: improper

in: in the form of

seeming: what seems to be a

ill-beseeming: unnatural

seeming both: seeming to be both (woman and beast)

holy order: priestly vows

temper'd: made up

Hast thou slain Tybalt? Wilt thou slay thyself
And slay thy lady that in thy life lives
By doing cursed hate upon thyself?
Why railest thou on thy birth, the heaven and earth?*
Since birth and heaven and earth all three do meet
In thee at once, which thou at once wouldst lose.
Fie, fie, thou shamest thy shape, thy love, thy wit,*
Which* like a usurer* abound'st in all
And usest none in that true use* indeed
Which should bedeck thy shape, thy love, thy wit.
Thy noble shape is but a form of wax,*
Digressing* from the valor of man;
Thy dear love sworn but hollow perjury,
Killing that love which thou hast vow'd to cherish;
Thy wit, that ornament to shape and love,
Misshapen* in the conduct* of them both,*
Like powder in a skilless soldier's flask,*
Is set afire by thine own ignorance
And thou dismemb'red with thine own defense.*
What, rouse thee, man! Thy Juliet is alive,
For whose dear sake thou was but lately dead:*
There art thou happy.* Tybalt would kill thee,
But thou slewest Tybalt: there art thou happy.
The law that threaten'd death becomes thy friend
And turns it to exile: there art thou happy.
A pack of blessings light upon thy back;
Happiness courts thee in her best array,
But like a mishaved* and sullen wench,
Thou frownst upon thy fortune and thy love.
Take heed, take heed, for such die miserable.
Go get thee to thy love as was decreed;*
Ascend her chamber; hence and comfort her.
But look thou stay not till the watch be set,*
For then thou canst not pass to Mantua,
Where thou shalt live till we find a time
To blaze* your marriage, reconcile your friends,*
Beg pardon of the Prince, and call thee back
With twenty hundred thousand times more joy
Than thou went'st forth in lamentation.
Go before, nurse; commend me to thy lady,
And bid her hasten all the house to bed,
Which heavy sorrow makes them apt unto.*
Romeo is coming.

heaven and earth: i.e., soul and body

wit: intelligence

Which: for you

usurer: moneylender charging high interest (Usury was illegal in Shakespeare's England.)

that . . . use: the way in which God intended it to be used

form of wax: wax figure, a shell without a manly substance

Digressing: turning aside

Misshapen: deformed

conduct: guidance

them both: i.e., shape (appearance) and love

flask: powder horn

defense: means of defense

thou . . . dead: you wished to die

happy: fortunate

mishaved: misbehaved

decreed: planned

watch be set: guard be posted and the city gates shut

blaze: announce

friends: relations (kin and in-laws)

apt unto: likely to do

NURSE O how I could have stay'd here all the night
To hear good counsel. O, what learning is!
My lord, I'll tell my lady you will come.

ROMEO Do so, and bid my sweet prepare to chide.

NURSE offers to go and then turns again.

NURSE Here, sir, a ring she bid me give you, sir.
Hie you, make haste, for it grows very late.

ROMEO How well my comfort is reviv'd by this!

Exit NURSE.

FRIAR L. Go hence; good night; and here stands all your state:*
Either be gone before the watch is set
Or by the break of day disguise from hence.
Sojourn* in Mantua. I'll find out* your man,
And he shall signify from time to time
Every good hap* to you that chances* here.
Give me thy hand. 'Tis late; farewell; good night.

here . . . state: your well-being depends entirely on this

Sojourn: reside

find out: locate

hap: happening

chances: occurs

ROMEO But that a joy past joy calls out on me,
It was a grief so brief to part with thee.
Farewell.

Exeunt.

Scene IV

Time: Monday evening
Place: Capulet's house

The Capulets make plans with Paris for Juliet's marriage.

Enter CAPULET, LADY CAPULET, and PARIS.

CAPULET Things have fall'n out, sir, so unluckily
That we have had no time to move our daughter.*
Look you, she lov'd her kinsman Tybalt dearly,
And so did I. Well, we were born to die.
'Tis very late; she'll not come down tonight.

move our daughter: persuade our daughter to accept your proposal

I promise you, but for your company
I would have been abed an hour ago.

Paris These times of woe afford no times to woo.
Madam, good night. Commend me to your daughter.

Lady Cap. I will, and know her mind early tomorrow.
Tonight she's mewed up to* her heaviness.

mewed up to: shut up with (Mews were houses in which hawks slept.)

Paris begins to exit, but Capulet calls him again.

Capulet Sir Paris, I will make a desperate tender*
Of my child's love. I think she will be rul'd
In all respects by me; nay more, I doubt it not.
Wife, go you to her ere you go to bed;
Acquaint her here of my son* Paris' love.
And bid her—mark you me?—on We'n'sday next—
But soft, what day is this?

desperate tender: bold offer

son: future son-in-law

Paris Monday, my lord.

Capulet Monday! Ha, ha! Well, We'n'sday is too soon.
A' Thursday let it be—a' Thursday, tell her,
She shall be married to this noble earl.
Will you be ready? Do you like this haste?
We'll keep not great ado*—a friend or two,
For hark you, Tybalt being slain so late,
It may be thought we held him carelessly,
Being our kinsman, if we revel much.
Therefore we'll have some half a dozen friends
And there an end. But what say you to Thursday?

ado: hustle and bustle

Paris My lord, I would that Thursday were tomorrow.

Capulet Well, get you gone; a' Thursday be it then.
Go you to Juliet ere you go to bed;
Prepare her, wife, against this wedding day.
Farewell, my lord. Light to my chamber, ho!
Afore me! It is so very late that we
May call it early by and by. Good night.

Exeunt.

Romeo and Juliet, Benjamin West, 1778

Scene V

Time: Early Tuesday morning

Place: Juliet's balcony

Romeo and Juliet bid each other farewell as he leaves for exile in Mantua. Lady Capulet at first encourages Juliet to marry Paris, but when she fails to embrace the idea, Capulet angrily insists that she follow his wishes in the matter. The Nurse loses Juliet's respect when she counsels her to ignore her marriage to Romeo and marry again.

Enter Romeo *and* Juliet *aloft at the window.*

Juliet Wilt thou be gone? It is not yet near day.
It was the nightingale and not the lark
That pierc'd the fearful hollow of thine ear.
Nightly she sings on yond pomegranate tree.
Believe me, love, it was the nightingale.

ROMEO It was the lark, the herald of the morn,
No nightingale. Look, love, what envious streaks*
Do lace the severing clouds in yonder east.
Night's candles are burnt out, and jocund* day
Stands tiptoe on the misty mountain tops.
I must be gone and live or stay and die.

streaks: i.e., early morning light
jocund: merry

JULIET Yond light is not daylight; I know it, I.
It is some meteor that the sun exhales*
To be to thee this night a torchbearer
And light thee on thy way to Mantua.
Therefore stay yet; thou need'st not to be gone.

exhales: gives off

ROMEO Let me be ta'en; let me be put to death;
I am content so thou wilt have it so.
I'll say yon grey is not the morning's eye;
'Tis but the pale reflex* of Cynthia's* brow;
Nor that is not the lark whose notes do beat
The vaulty* heaven so high above our heads.
I have more care* to stay than will to go.
Come, death, and welcome! Juliet wills it so.
How is't, my soul?* Let's talk; it is not day.

reflex: reflection
Cynthia's: the moon's
vaulty: arched
care: desire
soul: i.e., Juliet

JULIET It is, it is! Hie hence, be gone, away!
It is the lark that sings so out of tune,
Straining harsh discords and unpleasing sharps.*
Some say the lark makes sweet division.*
This doth not so, for she divideth us.
Some say the lark and loathed toad change eyes;*
O now I would they had chang'd voices too,
Since arm from arm that voice doth us affray,*
Hunting thee hence with hunt's-up* to the day.
O now be gone; more light and light it grows.

sharps: shrill sounds
division: variations on a melody
change eyes: exchange eyes, or fall in love
affray: frighten away
hunt's-up: a song to waken hunters or newlyweds, who customarily had a formal hunt on the morning after their wedding

ROMEO More light and light, more dark and dark our woes!

Enter NURSE hastily.

NURSE Madam!

JULIET Nurse?

NURSE Your lady mother is coming to your chamber.
The day is broke;* be wary; look about.

is broke: has dawned

Exit.

JULIET Then, window, let day in and let life out.

ROMEO Farewell, farewell! One kiss, and I'll descend.

He goes down.

JULIET Art thou gone so, my lord, my love, my friend!
I must hear from thee every day in the hour,
For in a minute there are many days.
O, by this count I shall be much in years
Ere I again behold my Romeo!

ROMEO Farewell!
I will omit* no opportunity
That may convey my greetings, love, to thee.

omit: fail to take advantage of

JULIET O, think'st thou we shall ever meet again?

ROMEO I doubt it not, and all these woes shall serve
For sweet discourses* in our times to come.

discourses: subjects of conversation

JULIET Husband, I have an ill-diving* soul!
Methinks I see thee now, thou art so low,
As one dead in the bottom of a tomb.
Either my eyesight fails or thou lookest pale.

ill-diving: full of evil premonitions

ROMEO And trust me, love, in my eye so do you;
Dry* sorrow drinks* our blood. Adieu, adieu!

Dry: thirsty
drinks: dries up

Exit.

JULIET: O Fortune, Fortune, all men call thee fickle.
If thou art fickle, what dost thou with him
That is renown'd for faith? Be fickle, Fortune;
For then I hope thou wilt not keep him long
But send him back.

LADY CAP. *(Within.)* Ho, daughter, are you up?

JULIET Who is't that calls? It is my lady mother.
Is she not down so late, or up so early?
What unaccustom'd cause* procures* her hither?

unaccustom'd cause: unusual circumstance
procures: brings

She goes down from the window. Enter LADY CAPULET.

Lady Cap. Why, how now, Juliet?

Juliet Madam, I am not well.

Lady Cap. Evermore weeping for your cousin's death?
What, wilt thou wash him from his grave with tears?
And if thou couldst, thou couldst not make him live;
Therefore have done. Some grief shows much of love,
But much of grief shows still some want of wit.*

want of wit: lack of intelligence

Juliet Yet let me weep for such a feeling* loss.

feeling: deeply felt

Lady Cap. So shall you feel the loss but not the friend
Which you weep for.

Juliet Feeling so the loss,
I cannot choose but ever weep the friend.

Lady Cap. Well, girl, thou weep'st not so much for his death
As that the villain lives which slaughter'd him.

Juliet What villain, madam?

Lady Cap. That same villain Romeo.

Juliet *(Aside.)* Villain and he be many miles asunder.—
God pardon him! I do with all my heart,
And yet no man like* he doth grieve my heart.

like: as much as

Lady Cap. That is because the traitor murderer lives.

Juliet Ay, madam, from the reach of these my hands.
Would none but I might venge my cousin's death!

Lady Cap. We will have vengeance for it; fear thou not.
Then weep no more. I'll send to one in Mantua,
Where that same banish'd runagate* doth live,
Shall give him such an unaccustom'd dram*
That he shall soon keep Tybalt company;
And then I hope thou wilt be satisfied.

runagate: renegade

unaccustom'd dram: poison

Juliet Indeed I never shall be satisfied
With Romeo till I behold him—dead—
Is my poor heart so for a kinsman vex'd.
Madam, if you could find out but a man

To bear a poison, I would temper it,
That Romeo should upon receipt thereof
Soon sleep in quiet. O how my heart abhors
To hear him nam'd and cannot come to him
To wreak the love I bore my cousin
Upon his body* that hath slaughter'd him.

Upon his body: upon the body of him

Lady Cap. Find thou the means, and I'll find such a man.
But now I'll tell thee joyful tidings, girl.

Juliet And joy comes well in such a needy time.
What are they, I beseech your ladyship?

Lady Cap. Well, well, thou hast a careful* father, child,
One who, to put thee from thy heaviness,*
Hath sorted out a sudden* day of joy
That thou expects not nor I look'd not for.

careful: considerate

heaviness: grief

sudden: imminent

Juliet Madam, in happy time, what day is that?

Lady Cap. Indeed, my child, early next Thursday morn
The gallant, young, and noble gentleman,
The County Paris, at Saint Peter's Church
Shall happily make thee there a joyful bride.

Juliet No; at Saint Peter's Church or any place
He shall not make me there a joyful bride.
I wonder at this haste, that I must wed
Ere he that should be husband comes to woo.
I pray you tell my lord and father, madam,
I will not marry yet, and when I do, I swear
It shall be Romeo, whom you know I hate,
Rather than Paris. These are news indeed!

Lady Cap. Here comes your father; tell him so yourself
And see how he will take it at your hands.

Enter Capulet and Nurse.

Capulet When the sun sets, the earth doth drizzle dew,
But for the sunset of my brother's son
It rains downright.
How now, a conduit,* girl? What, still in tears?
Evermore show'ring? In one little body

conduit: fountain

Thou resemblest a bark,* a sea, a wind;
For still thy eyes, which I may call the sea,
Do ebb and flow with tears. The bark thy body is,
Sailing in this salt flood; the winds, thy sighs,
Who, raging with thy tears and they with them,
Without a sudden calm* will overset
Thy tempest-tossed body. How now, wife?
Have you delivered to her our decree?

bark: any sailing vessel

Without . . . calm: unless they (the winds) suddenly calm

Lady Cap. Ay, sir, but she will none, she gives you thanks.*
I would the fool were married to her grave!

she . . . thanks: i.e., she replies, "No, thanks."

Capulet Soft, take me with you;* take me with you, wife.
How, will she none? Doth she not give us thanks?
Is she not proud?* Doth she not count her* blest,
Unworthy as she is, that we have wrought*
So worthy a gentleman to be her bride?*

take . . . you: explain to me what you mean

proud: overjoyed

her: herself

wrought: gotten

bride: bridegroom

Juliet Not proud you have, but thankful that you have.
Proud can I never be of what I hate,
But thankful even for hate that is meant love.

Capulet How now, how now, chopp'd logic!* What is this?
"Proud" and "I thank you" and "I thank you not,"
And yet "not proud," mistress minion* you?
Thank me no thankings nor proud me no prouds,
But fettle* your fine joints 'gainst* Thursday next
To go with Paris to Saint Peter's Church,
Or I will drag thee on a hurdle* thither.
Out, you green-sickness carrion!* Out, you baggage,
You tallow* face!

chopp'd logic: faulty reasoning

minion: impudent, spoiled girl

fettle: prepare

'gainst: for

hurdle: frame for carrying criminals to execution

green-sickness carrion: anemic flesh

tallow: pale

Lady Cap. Fie, fie. What are you mad?

Juliet Good father, I beseech you on my knees,
Hear me with patience but to speak a word.

She kneels down.

Capulet Hang thee, young baggage! Disobedient wretch!
I tell thee what: get thee to church a' Thursday,
Or never after look me in the face.
Speak not, reply not, do not answer me!
My fingers itch.* Wife, we scarce thought us blest

My . . . itch: I have an overwhelming urge to thrash her.

That God had lent us but this only child,
But now I see this one is one too much
And that we have a curse in having her,
Out on her, hilding!*

hilding: good-for-nothing

Nurse God in heaven, bless her!
You are to blame, my lord, to rate* her so.

rate: berate, scold

Capulet And why, my Lady Wisdom? Hold your tongue,
Good Prudence. Smatter* with your gossips.* Go!

Smatter: chatter

gossips: old-women friends

Nurse I speak no treason.

Capulet Peace, you mumbling fool!
Utter your gravity* o'er a gossip's bowl,
For here we need it not. Day, night, early, late,
At home, abroad, still* my care hath been
To have her match'd; and having now provided
A gentleman of noble parentage,
Of fair demesnes,* youthful and nobly train'd,
Stuff'd, as they say, with honorable parts,
Proportion'd as one's thought would wish a man,
And then to have a wretched puling* fool,
A whining mammet,* in her fortunes tender,*
To answer, "I'll wed not; I cannot love;
I am too young, I pray you pardon me."
But and you will not wed, I'll pardon you.*
Graze where you will; you shall not house with me.
Look to't, think on't, I do not use* to jest.
Thursday is near; lay hand on heart; advise.*
And you be mine, I'll give you to my friend;
And you be not, hang, beg, starve, die in the streets;
For by my soul I'll ne'er acknowledge thee,
Nor what is mine shall never do thee good.
Trust to't, bethink you; I'll not be forsworn.

gravity: advice

still: always

demesnes: domains, estates

puling: whimpering

mammet: doll, puppet

in . . . tender: young and vulnerable in her fate

I'll . . . you: used ironically as "I'll excuse you from the house"

do not use: am not accustomed

advise: think it over

Exit.

Juliet Is there no pity sitting in the clouds
That sees into the bottom of my grief?
O sweet my mother, cast me not away!
Delay this marriage for a month, a week,
Or if you do not, make a bridal bed
In that dim monument* where Tybalt lies.

monument: tomb

Lady Cap. Talk not to me, for I'll not speak a word.
Do as thou wilt, for I have done with thee.

Exit.

Juliet O nurse, O nurse, how shall this be prevented?
My husband is on earth, my faith* in heaven.
How shall that faith return again to earth
Unless that husband send it me from heaven
By leaving earth?* Comfort me, counsel me!
Alack, alack, that heaven should practice strategems*
Upon so soft a subject as myself!
What say'st thou? Has thou not a word of joy?
Some comfort, nurse.

faith: marriage vows

How . . . leaving earth: How can I marry again unless my present husband dies?

strategems: devious schemes

Nurse Faith, here it is.
Romeo is banished, and all the world* to nothing
That he dares ne'er come back to challenge you,
Or if he do, it needs must be by stealth.*
Then since the case so stands as now it doth,
I think it best you married with the County.
O, he's a lovely gentleman!
Romeo's a dish-clout* to him.* An eagle, madam,
Hath not so green, so quick, so fair an eye
As Paris hath. Beshrow* my very heart,
I think you are happy in this second match,
For it excels your first; or if it did not,
Your first is dead, or 'twere as good he were
As living here* and you no use of him.

all the world: I'll bet the world

stealth: covert means

dish-clout: dishrag

to him: compared to him

Beshrow: a curse upon

here: i.e., on earth

Juliet Speak'st thou from thy heart?

Nurse And from my soul too,
Else beshrew them both.

Juliet Amen!

Nurse What?

Juliet Well thou hast comforted me marvelous much.
Go in and tell my lady I am gone,
Having displeas'd my father, to Lawrence's cell
To make confession and to be absolv'd.

Nurse Well, I will, and this is wisely done.

Exit.

Juliet *(She looks after the nurse.)*
Ancient damnation! O most wicked fiend!
Is it more sin to wish me thus forsworn
Or to dispraise my lord with that same tongue
Which she hath prais'd him with above compare
So many thousand times? Go, counselor.
Thou and my bosom* henceforth shall be twain.*
I'll to the friar to know his remedy.
If all else fail, myself have power to die.

bosom: innermost thoughts
twain: separated

Exit.

About the Play

1. Contrast Benvolio with the following characters:
   a. Romeo
   b. Mercutio
   c. Tybalt
2. What does Mercutio's speech on page 402, lines 90–96, tell you about him?
3. How might the circumstances surrounding Romeo's fight with Tybalt seem fateful? How much is Romeo responsible for?
4. Describe Juliet's dilemma in Scene II.
5. What do Juliet's parents believe to be the cause of her excessive grief?
6. Describe Romeo's reaction to the Prince's pronouncement of banishment.
7. What do you think of his reaction?
8. What does the Nurse counsel Juliet to do regarding Paris? What do you think of her counsel?
9. Capulet advances the date of Juliet's marriage to Paris to help ease her grief over Tybalt's death. Evaluate Capulet's and Lady Capulet's responses to Juliet's refusal. How would you respond if you were Juliet's parents?

Act IV

Scene I

Time: Tuesday
Place: Friar Lawrence's cell

Paris makes arrangements with Friar Lawrence for his wedding to Juliet. She pays passing courtesies to Paris upon his departure and then entreats the Friar to help her escape her marriage to him. Friar Lawrence formulates the potion plan.

Enter FRIAR LAWRENCE *and* PARIS.

FRIAR L. On Thursday, sir? The time is very short.

PARIS My father Capulet will have it so,
And I am nothing slow to slack his haste.*

nothing . . . haste: not hesitant myself so I am not given to slowing him down

FRIAR L. You say you do not know the lady's mind?
Uneven* is the course; I like it not.

Uneven: irregular

PARIS Immoderately she weeps for Tybalt's death,
And therefore have I little talk'd of love,
For Venus smiles not in a house of tears.
Now, sir, her father counts it dangerous
That she do give her sorrow so much sway
And in his wisdom hastes our marriage
To stop the inundation* of her tears,
Which, too much minded* by herself alone,
May be put from her by society.*
Now do you know the reason for this haste?

inundation: flood

minded: thought about

society: companionship (i.e., that of Paris)

FRIAR L. *(Aside.)* I would I knew not why it should be slowed.—
Look, sir, here comes the lady toward my cell.

Enter JULIET.

PARIS Happily met, my lady and my wife!

JULIET That may be, sir, when I may be a wife.

PARIS That may be, must be, love, on Thursday next.

JULIET What must be shall be.

FRIAR L. That's a certain text.

PARIS Come you to make confession to this father?

JULIET To answer that, I should* confess to you.

should: would need to

PARIS Do not deny to him that you love me.

JULIET I will confess to you that I love him.

PARIS So will ye, I am sure, that you love me.

JULIET If I do so, it will be of more price,*
Being spoke behind your back, than to your face.

price: value

PARIS Poor soul, thy face is much abus'd with tears.

JULIET The tears have got small victory by that,

For it was bad enough before their spite.

PARIS Thou wrong'st it more than tears with that report.

JULIET That is no slander, sir, which is a truth,
And what I spake, I spake it to* my face.

to: concerning

PARIS Thy face is mine, and thou hast sland'red it.

JULIET It may be so, for it is not mine own.
Are you at leisure, holy father, now,
Or shall I come to you at evening mass?

FRIAR L. My leisure serves me, pensive* daughter, now.
My lord, we must entreat* the time alone.

pensive: sad
entreat: beg to have

PARIS God shield* I should disturb devotion!*
Juliet, on Thursday early I will rouse ye;
Till then adieu, and keep this holy kiss.

shield: forbid
devotion: prayers

Exit.

JULIET O, shut the door, and when thou hast done so,
Come weep with me, past hope, past cure, past help!

FRIAR L. O Juliet, I already know thy grief.*
It strains me past the compass* of my wits.
I hear thou must, and nothing may prorogue* it,
On Thursday next be married to this County.

thy grief: the cause of thy grief
compass: boundary
prorogue: postpone

JULIET Tell me not, friar, that thou hearest of this
Unless thou tell me how I may prevent it.
If in thy wisdom thou canst give no help,
Do thou but call my resolution wise,
And with this knife I'll help it presently.*
God join'd my heart and Romeo's, thou our hands,
And ere this hand, by thee to Romeo's seal'd,
Shall be the label* to another deed*
Or my true heart with treacherous revolt
Turn to another,* this shall slay them both.*
Therefore out of thy long-experienc'd time,
Give me some present counsel, or, behold,
'Twixt my extremes* and me this bloody knife
Shall play the umpeer,* arbitrating that

presently: immediately
label: seal
deed: legal document
another: i.e., man
both: i.e., hand and heart
extremes: dire plight
umpeer: umpire

Which the commission* of thy years and art*
Could to no issue* of true honor bring.
Be not so long to speak. I long to die,
If what thou speak'st speak not of remedy.

commission: authority
art: skill
issue: outcome, conclusion

FRIAR L. Hold, daughter! I do spy a kind of hope,
Which craves as desperate an execution*
As that is desperate which we would prevent.
If rather than to marry County Paris,
Thou hast the strength of will to slay thyself,
Then is it likely thou wilt undertake
A thing like death to chide away this shame,
That cop'st with* Death himself to scape from it;
And if thou darest, I'll give thee remedy.*

craves . . . execution: necessitates a course of action
That . . . with: (a plan) that deals with
remedy: the plan

JULIET O, bid me leap, rather than marry Paris,
From off the battlements* of any tower
Or walk in thievish ways,* or bid me lurk
Where serpents are; chain me with roaring bears,
Or hide me nightly in a charnel house*
O'ercover'd quite with dead men's rattling bones,
With reeky* shanks and yellow chapless* skulls;
Or bid me go into a new-made grave
And hide me with a dead man in his shroud—
Things that, to hear them told, have made me tremble—
And I will do it without fear or doubt,
To live an unstain'd wife to my sweet love.

battlements: top wall
thievish ways: places where thieves lurk
charnel house: storage place for bones of the dead
reeky: stinking
chapless: jawless

FRIAR L. Hold then. Go home, be merry, give consent
To marry Paris. We'n'sday is tomorrow;
Tomorrow night look that thou lie alone;
Let not the nurse lie with thee in thy chamber.
Take thou this vial, being then in bed,
And this distilling* liquor* drink thou off,
When presently through all thy veins shall run
A cold and drowsy humor;* for no pulse
Shall keep his native progress* but surcease.*
No warmth, no breath shall testify thou livest.
The roses in thy lips and cheeks shall fade
To paly ashes, thy eyes' windows* fall
Like death when he shuts up the day of life.
Each part, depriv'd of supple government,*
Shall, stiff and stark and cold, appear like death,
And in this borrowed likeness of shrunk death
Thou shalt continue two and forty hours,

distilling: permeating
liquor: liquid
humor: moisture
native progress: natural progression
surcease: cease
eyes' windows: i.e., eyelids
supple government: control of movement

And then awake as from a pleasant sleep.
Now when the bridegroom in the morning comes
To rouse thee from thy bed, there art thou dead.
Then as the manner of our country is,
In thy best robes, uncovered on the bier,
Thou shalt be borne to that same ancient vault
Where all the kindred of the Capulets lie.
In the meantime, against* thou shalt awake
Shall Romeo by my letters know our drift,*
And hither shall he come, an' he and I
Will watch thy waking, and that very night
Shall Romeo bear thee hence to Mantua.
And this shall free thee from this present shame,
If no inconstant toy,* nor womanish fear,
Abate thy valor* in the acting it.

against: before
drift: purpose
inconstant toy: wavering fancy
Abate ... valor: lessen your courage

JULIET Give me, give me! O, tell me not to fear!

FRIAR L. Hold, get you gone. Be strong and prosperous
In this resolve.* I'll send a friar with speed
To Mantua with letters to thy lord.

resolve: decision

JULIET Love give me strength! and strength shall help afford.*
Farewell, dear father!

afford: (me) carry out the deed

Exeunt.

Scene II

Time: Tuesday, near night

Place: A hall in Capulet's house

Capulet prepares for Juliet's marriage to Paris on Thursday but moves the date up to Wednesday when Juliet, returning from the Friar's cell, pretends to yield to his will.

Enter CAPULET, LADY CAPULET, NURSE, and SERVANTS.

CAPULET So many guests invite as here are writ.

Exit SERVANT 1.

Sirrah, go hire me twenty cunning* cooks.

cunning: expert

SERVANT 2 You shall have none ill, sir, for I'll try if they can lick their fingers.

CAPULET How canst thou try them so?*

try . . . so: discern their ability by such a test

SERVANT 2 Marry, sir, 'tis an ill cook that cannot lick his own fingers; therefore he that cannot lick his fingers goes not with me.

CAPULET Go, be gone.

Exit SERVANT 2.

We shall be much unfurnish'd* for this time.
What, is my daughter gone to Friar Lawrence?

unfurnish'd: unprepared

NURSE Ay, forsooth.*

forsooth: indeed

CAPULET Well, he may chance to do some good on her.
A peevish* self-will'd harlotry* it is.

peevish: silly

harlotry: good-for-nothing girl

Enter JULIET.

NURSE See where she comes from shrift with a merry look.

CAPULET How now, my headstrong, where have you been gadding?*

gadding: rambling about

JULIET Where I have learnt me to repent of sin
Of disobedient opposition
To you and your behests,* and am enjoin'd*
By holy Lawrence to fall prostrate here
To beg your pardon. *(She kneels down.)* Pardon, I beseech you!
Henceforward I am ever rul'd by you.

behests: commands

enjoined: directed (with authority)

CAPULET Send for the County; go tell him of this:
I'll have this knot knit up tomorrow morning.

JULIET I met the youthful lord at Lawrence's cell,
And gave him what becomed* love I might,
Not stepping o'er the bounds of modesty.

becomed: befitting

CAPULET Why, I am glad on't; this is well; stand up.
This is as't should be. Let me see the County;
Ay, marry, go, I say, and fetch him hither.
Now, afore God, this reverend holy friar,
All our whole city is much bound to him.

JULIET Nurse, will you go with me into my closet*
To help me sort such needful ornaments
As you think fit to furnish me tomorrow?

closet: private room

LADY CAP. No, not till Thursday; there is time enough.

CAPULET Go, nurse, go with her: we'll to church tomorrow.

Exeunt JULIET and NURSE.

LADY CAP. We shall be short in our provision:*
'Tis now near night.

provision: i.e., for the wedding feast

CAPULET Tush, I will stir about,
And all things shall be well, I warrant thee, wife;
Go thou to Juliet, help to deck up her.
I'll not to bed tonight; let me alone;*
I'll play the housewife for this once. What ho!
They are all forth. Well, I will walk myself
To County Paris, to prepare him up
Against* tomorrow. My heart is wondrous light,
Since this same wayward girl is so reclaim'd.

let . . . alone: allow me to take care of everything

Against: for

Exeunt.

Scene III

Time: Tuesday evening
Place: Juliet's chamber

After her mother and the Nurse leave her alone for the night, Juliet takes the potion prepared by Friar Lawrence.

Enter JULIET and NURSE.

JULIET Ay, those attires are best, but, gentle nurse,
I pray thee leave me to myself tonight,
For I have need of many orisons*
To move the heavens to smile upon my state,
Which, well thou knowest, is cross* and full of sin.

orisons: prayers

cross: perverse

Enter LADY CAPULET.

Lady Cap. What, are you busy, ho? Need you my help?

Juliet No, madam, we have cull'd* such necessaries
As are behooveful* for our state* tomorrow.
So please you, let me now be left alone
And let the nurse this night sit up with you,
For I am sure you have your hands full all,
In this so sudden business.

cull'd: selected
behooveful: suitable
state: ceremony

Lady Cap. Good night.
Get thee to bed and rest, for thou hast need.

Exit Lady Capulet and Nurse.

Juliet Farewell! God knows when we shall meet again.
I have a faint* cold fear thrills* through my veins,
That almost freezes up the heat of life.
I'll call them back again to comfort me.
Nurse!—What should she do here?
My dismal* scene I needs must act alone.
Come, vial.
What if this mixture do not work at all?
Shall I be married then tomorrow morning?
No, no, this shall forbid it. Lie thou there.

faint: that which produces faintness
thrills: that pierces
dismal: dreadful

Laying down her dagger.

What if it be a poison which the friar
Subtly hath minist'red to have me dead,
lest in this marriage he should be dishonor'd
Because he married me before to Romeo?
I fear it is, and yet methinks it should not,
For he hath still* been tried* a holy man.
How if, when I am laid into the tomb,
I wake before the time that Romeo
Come to redeem me? there's a fearful point!
Shall I not then be stifled* in the vault,
To whose foul mouth no healthsome air breathes in,
And there die strangled ere my Romeo comes?
Or if I live, is it not very like
The horrible conceit* of death and night
Together with the terror of the place—
As in a vault, an ancient receptacle,
Where for this many hundred years the bones

still: always
tried: proved
stifled: suffocated
conceit: fantastic thought

Of all my buried ancestors are pack'd,
Where bloody Tybalt, yet but green* in earth,
Lies fest'ring in his shroud, where, as they say,
At some hours in the night spirits resort—
Alack, alack, is it not like that I,
So early waking—what with loathsome smells,
And shrikes* like mandrakes* torn out of the earth,
That living mortals, hearing them, run mad—
O, if I wake, shall I not be distraught,
Environed with all these hideous fears,
And madly play with my forefathers' joints
And pluck the mangled Tybalt from his shroud,
And in this rage, with some great kinsman's bone,
As with a club, dash out my desp'rate brains?
O, look! methinks I see my cousin's ghost
Seeking out Romeo, that did spit* his body
Upon a rapier's point. Stay, Tybalt, stay!
Romeo, Romeo, Romeo! Here's drink—I drink to thee.

green: newly buried

shrikes: shrieks

mandrakes: a plant with a forked root thought to resemble a man; it was said to shriek when pulled out of the earth, causing the hearer to go insane or die.

spit: impale

She falls upon her bed, within the curtains.

Scene IV

Time: Early Wednesday morning

Place: A hall in Capulet's house

Capulet and the servants complete the wedding preparations.

Enter Lady Capulet and Nurse with herbs.

LADY CAP. Hold, take these keys and fetch more spices, nurse.

NURSE They call for dates and quinces in the pastry.*

pastry: pantry

Enter Capulet.

CAPULET Come, stir, stir, stir! The second cock hath crowed;
The curfew bell hath rung, 'tis three a' clock.
Look to the bak'd meats, good Angelica:
Spare not for cost.

LADY CAP. Go, you cot-queen,* go,

cot-queen: man who does woman's work

Get you to bed. Faith,* you'll be sick tomorrow
For this night's watching.*

Faith: indeed

watching: staying awake

CAPULET No, not a whit*. What, I have watch'd ere now
All night for lesser cause, and ne'er been sick.

not a whit: not in the least

Exeunt LADY CAPULET and NURSE.

CAPULET A jealous hood,* a jealous hood!

hood: person

Enter three or four SERVANTS with spits and logs and baskets.

SERVANT 1 Things for the cook, sir, but I know not what.

CAPULET Make haste, make haste.

Exit SERVANT 1.

Sirrah, fetch drier logs.
Call Peter, he will show thee where they are.

SERVANT 2 I have a head, sir, that will find out logs,
And never trouble Peter for the matter.

Exit SERVANT 2.

CAPULET Thou shalt be logger-head. Good faith, 'tis day.
The County will be here with music straight,
For so he said he would. *(Music plays within.)* I hear him near.
Nurse! Wife! What ho! What, nurse, I say!

Enter NURSE.

Go waken Juliet, go and trim her up;
I'll go and chat with Paris. Hie, make haste,
Make haste; the bridegroom he is come already.
Make haste, I say.

Exeunt.

Frederic Leighton, Britain, 1830–1896, *The feigned death of Juliet* 1856-58, Rome, Paris & London, oil on canvas 113.6 x 175.2 cm. Elder Bequest Fund 1899. Art Gallery of South Australia, Adelaide

Scene V

Time: Early Wednesday morning

Place: Juliet's chamber

The Nurse discovers Juliet's "death," and great lamentation follows. The Friar assures Juliet's family and Paris of God's providence; and the musicians, turning from wedding to funeral song, jest with Peter.

Enter NURSE *above.*

NURSE Mistress! what, mistress! Juliet!—Fast,* I warrant her, she:—
Why, lamb! why, lady! fie, you slug-a-bed!
Why, love, I say! madam! sweetheart! why, bride!
What, not a word? How sound is she asleep!
I needs must wake her. Madam, madam, madam!

Fast: fast asleep

Draws back the curtains around Juliet's bed.

What, dress'd and in your clothes and down again?
I must needs wake you. Lady, lady, lady!
Alas, alas! Help, help! my lady's dead!
O, weraday,* that ever I was born!
Some aqua-vitae, ho! My lord! my lady!

weraday: alas

Enter LADY CAPULET.

LADY CAP. What noise is here?

NURSE O lamentable day!

LADY CAP. What is the matter?

NURSE Look, look! O heavy day!

LADY CAP. O me, O me, my child, my only life!
Revive, look up, or I will die with thee!
Help, help! Call help.

Enter CAPULET.

CAPULET For shame, bring Juliet forth; her lord is come.

NURSE She's dead, deceased; she's dead, alack the day!

LADY CAP. Alack the day, she's dead, she's dead, she's dead!

CAPULET Ha! let me see her. Out alas, she's cold:
Her blood is settled, and her joints are stiff;
Life and these lips have long been separated.
Death lies on her like an untimely frost
Upon the sweetest flower of all the field.

NURSE O lamentable day!

LADY CAP. O woeful time!

CAPULET Death, that hath ta'en her hence to make me wail,
Ties up my tongue and will not let me speak.

Enter FRIAR LAWRENCE *and* PARIS *with* MUSICIANS.

FRIAR L. Come, is the bride ready to go to church?

CAPULET Ready to go but never to return.—
O son, the night before thy wedding day
Hath Death lain with thy wife. There she lies.
Death is my son-in-law, Death is my heir;
My daughter he hath wedded. I will die
And leave him all: life, living,* all is Death's.

living: possessions

PARIS Have I thought long* to see this morning's face,
And doth it give me such a sight as this?

thought long: been impatient

LADY CAP. Accurs'd, unhappy, wretched, hateful day!
Most miserable hour that e'er time saw
In lasting labor of his pilgrimage!
But one, poor one, one poor and loving child,
But one thing to rejoice and solace in,
And cruel Death hath catch'd* it from my sight!

catch'd: taken

NURSE O woe! O woeful, woeful, woeful day!
Most lamentable day, most woeful day
That ever, ever I did yet behold!
O day, O day, O day, O hateful day!
Never was seen so black a day as this.
O woeful day, O woeful day!

PARIS Beguil'd,* divorced, wronged, spited, slain!
Most detestable Death, by thee beguil'd,
By cruel, cruel, thee quite overthrown!
O love, O life! Not life, but love in death!

Beguil'd: cheated

CAPULET Despis'd, distressed, hated, martyr'd, kill'd!
Uncomfortable* time, why cam'st thou now
To murder, murder our solemnity?*
O child, O child! my soul, and not my child!
Dead art thou! Alack, my child is dead,
And with my child my joys are buried.

Uncomfortable: comfortless

solemnity: celebration

FRIAR L. Peace, ho, for shame! Confusion's cure lives not
In these confusions.* Heaven and yourself
Had part in this fair maid; now heaven hath all,
And all the better is it for the maid.
Your part in her you could not keep from death,
But heaven keeps his part in eternal life.
The most you sought was her promotion,*

confusions: disorder

promotion: translation to heaven

For 'twas your heaven she should be advanc'd.
And weep ye now, seeing she is advanc'd
Above the clouds as high as heaven itself?
O, in this love* you love your child so ill
That you run mad, seeing that she is well.
She's not well married that lives married long,
But she's best married that dies married young.
Dry up your tears and stick your rosemary*
On this fair corse,* and as the custom is,
And in her best array, bear her to church;
For though fond nature bids us all lament,
Yet nature's tears are reason's merriment.*

in . . . love: by showing your love through such lamentation

rosemary: fragrant herb whose sprigs symbolized remembrance and were strewn at both funerals and weddings

corse: corpse

nature's . . . merriment: The human side of man mourns for that which makes his reason rejoice.

CAPULET All things that we ordained festival*
Turn from their office to black funeral:
Our instruments to melancholy bells;
Our wedding cheer* to a sad burial feast;
Our solemn hymns to sullen dirges* change;
Our bridal flowers serve for a buried corse;
And all things change them to the contrary.

ordained festival: intended for our festivities

cheer: food

dirges: funeral songs

FRIAR L. Sir, go you in, and, madam, go with him;
And go, Sir Paris. Every one prepare
To follow this fair corse unto her grave.
The heavens do low'r* upon you for some ill;*
Move them no more by crossing their high will.

low'r: frown

ill: sin

Exit all but NURSE and MUSICIANS, casting rosemary on Juliet and shutting the curtains.

MUSICIAN 1 Faith, we may put up our pipes* and be gone.

put . . . pipes: These musicians are string players, not pipers.

NURSE Honest good fellows, ah, put up, put up,
For well you know this is a pitiful case.

Exit NURSE.

MUSICIAN 1 Ay, by my troth, the case may be amended.*

amended: (1) The instrument case might well be repaired. (2) The situation can be made better.

Enter PETER.

PETER Musicians, O musicians, "Heart's ease,"* "heart's ease"!
O, and you will have me live, play "Heart's ease."

"Heart's ease": the name of a popular tune

MUSICIAN 1 Why "Heart's ease"?

PETER O, musicians, because my heart itself plays "My heart is full." O, play me some merry dump* to comfort me.

MUSICIAN 1 Not a dump we; 'tis not time to play now.

PETER You will not then?

MUSICIAN 1 No.

PETER I will then give it you soundly.

MUSICIAN 1 What will you give us?

PETER No money, on my faith, but a gleek;* I will give you the minstrel.*

MUSICIAN 1 Then will I give you the serving-creature.

PETER Then will I lay the serving-creature's dagger on your pate.* I will carry no crotchets.* I'll *re* you, I'll *fa** you. Do you note* me?

MUSICIAN 1 And you *re* us and *fa* us, you note* us.

MUSICIAN 2 Pray you put up your dagger and put out* your wit.

PETER Then have at you with my wit! I will dry-beat you with an iron wit and put up my iron dagger. Answer me like men:
"When griping griefs the heart doth wound,
And doleful dumps the mind oppress,
Then music with her silver sound"—
why "silver sound"? Why "music with her silver sound"? What say you, Simon Catling?*

MUSICIAN 1 Marry, sir, because silver hath a sweet sound.

PETER Pretty! What say you, Hugh Rebeck?*

MUSICIAN 2 I say "silver sound," because musicians sound* for silver.

PETER Pretty too! What say you, James Soundpost?*

MUSICIAN 3 Faith, I know not what to say.

dump: sad tune

gleek: gibe, witty taunt

give . . . minstrel: call you rascals

pate: head

crotchets: (1) quarter notes, (2) fanciful notions

re, fa: puns on notes of the scale

note: observe, also pun on musical notes

note: make music of

put out: exhibit

Simon Catling: name suggestive of a lute string, which was made of cat gut

Hugh Rebeck: name suggestive of a three-stringed instrument, prototype of the violin

sound: make music

James Soundpost: name suggestive of a component part of a stringed instrument

PETER O, I cry you mercy,* you are the singer; I will say* for you. It is "music with her silver sound," because musicians have no gold for sounding*:
"Then music with her silver sound
With speedy help doth lend redress."*

cry . . . mercy: beg your pardon
say: speak
sounding: speaking
redress: aid

Exit.

MUSICIAN 1 What a pestilent knave is this same!

MUSICIAN 2 Hang him, Jack! Come, we'll in here; tarry for the mourners and stay*dinner.

stay: stay for

Exeunt.

About the Play

1. How much time has passed since the opening of the play?
2. How does the speed of passing time change in the play? What is the significance of this change?
3. Re-read Juliet's soliloquy in Scene III (lines 14–58). What fears does Juliet have? What kind of conflict do these fears indicate? How do they affect your view of Juliet?
4. Juliet illustrates her fears by placing a dagger beside her. What does this action foreshadow?
5. Plot out Romeo's and Juliet's actions and reactions up to this point.
6. Review these actions and reactions. If you had to identify one tragic flaw in the young lovers, what would it be?
7. How has fate affected their circumstances?
8. What is a biblical view of the concept of fate (an impersonal force that orders events)? According to the Bible, how responsible is every person for his or her choices? Support your answers with Bible references.

Act V

Scene I

Time: Thursday

Place: A street in Mantua

Balthasar informs Romeo of Juliet's "death." Refusing to be separated from his love, Romeo persuades an apothecary to sell him illegal poison.

Enter ROMEO.

ROMEO If I may trust the flattering truth of sleep,*
My dreams presage* some joyful news at hand.
My bosom's lord* sits lightly in his throne,
And all this day an unaccustom'd spirit
Lifts me above the ground with cheerful thoughts.
I dreamt my lady came and found me dead—
Strange dream, that gives a dead man leave* to think—
And breath'd such life with kisses in my lips
That I reviv'd and was an emperor.
Ah me, how sweet is love itself possess'd,*
When but love's shadows* are so rich in joy!

the . . . sleep: i.e., exaggeratedly favorable dreams

presage: foretell

bosom's lord: i.e., the heart

gives . . . leave: permits a dead man

how . . . possess'd: love itself is possessed of such sweetness

love's shadows: dreams of love

Enter BALTHASAR, *Romeo's man, booted.*

News from Verona! How now, Balthasar?
Dost thou not bring me letters from the friar?
How doth my lady? Is my father well?
How fares my Juliet? That I ask again,
For nothing can be ill if she be well.

BALTHASAR Then she is well, and nothing can be ill:
Her body sleeps in Capel's monument,
And her immortal part with angels lives.
I saw her laid low in her kindred's vault,
And presently took post* to tell it you.
O, pardon me for bringing these ill news,
Since you did leave it for my office,* sir.

took post: engaged relays of fast horses

office: duty

ROMEO Is it e'en so? Then I defy you, stars!
Thou knowest my lodging: get me ink and paper,
And hire post horses; I will hence tonight.

BALTHASAR I do beseech you, sir, have patience.
Your looks are pale and wild and do import*
Some misadventure.*

import: indicate, show the possibility of

misadventure: misfortune

ROMEO Tush, thou art deceiv'd.
Leave me, and do the thing I bid thee do.
Hast thou no letters to me from the friar?

BALTHASAR No, my good lord.

ROMEO No matter. Get thee gone,
And hire these horses; I'll be with thee straight.

Exit BALTHASAR.

Well, Juliet, I will lie with thee tonight.
Let's see for means.* O mischief, thou art swift
To enter in the thoughts of desperate* men!
I do remember an apothecary—
And hereabouts 'a dwells—which late I noted
In tatt'red weeds,* with overwhelming brows,*
Culling of simples;* meager* were his looks,
Sharp misery had worn him to the bones;
And in his needy shop a tortoise hung,
An alligator stuff'd, and other skins
Of ill-shap'd fishes, and about his shelves
A beggarly account* of empty boxes,
Green earthen pots, bladders,* and musty seeds,
Remnants of packthread* and old cakes of roses*
Were thinly scattered, to make up a show.
Noting this penury,* to myself I said,
"An' if a man need a poison now,
Whose sale is present death* in Mantua,
Here lives a caitiff* wretch would sell it him."
O, this same thought did but forerun* my need,
And this same needy man must sell it me.
As I remember, this should be the house.
Being holiday, the beggar's shop is shut.
What ho, apothecary!

means: a way to accomplish the aforementioned purpose

desperate: those devoid of hope

weeds: clothes

with . . . brows: giving a frowning appearance

Culling . . . simples: selecting medicinal herbs

meager: poor

beggarly account: pitifully small collection

bladders: pouches

packthread: twine

cakes . . . roses: roses pressed for the making of perfume

penury: poverty

is . . . death: subjects the seller to immediate capital punishment

caitiff: miserable

forerun: go before

Enter APOTHECARY.

APOTHECARY Who calls so loud?

ROMEO
Come hither, man. I see that thou art poor.
Hold, there is forty ducats;* let me have
A dram of poison, such soon-speeding gear*
As will disperse itself through all the veins
That the life-weary taker may fall dead
And that the trunk may be discharg'd of breath
As violently as hasty powder fir'd
Doth hurry from the fatal cannon's womb.

ducats: gold coins
soon-speeding gear: fast-acting stuff

APOTHECARY
Such mortal* drugs I have, but Mantua's law
Is death to any he that utters* them.

mortal: lethal
utters: sells

ROMEO
Art thou so bare and full of wretchedness,
And fearest to die? Famine is in thy cheeks,
Need and oppression starveth in thy eyes,
Contempt and beggary hangs upon thy back;*
The world is not thy friend, nor the world's law,
The world affords no law to make thee rich;
Then be not poor, but break it,* and take this.

Contempt . . . back: Contemptible poverty is evident in thy poor clothing.
it: i.e., the law

APOTHECARY
My poverty, but not my will, consents.

ROMEO
I pay thy poverty, and not thy will.

APOTHECARY
Put this in any liquid thing you will
And drink it off, and if you had the strength
Of twenty men, it would dispatch you straight.*

dispatch . . . straight: kill you immediately

ROMEO
There is thy gold, worse poison to men's souls,
Doing more murder in this loathsome world
Than these poor compounds that thou mayest not sell.
I sell thee poison; thou hast sold me none.
Farewell! Buy food, and get thyself in flesh.*

get . . . flesh: fatten yourself

Exit APOTHECARY.

Come, cordial* and not poison, go with me
To Juliet's grave, for there I must use thee.

cordial: restorative drink; literally a stimulant to the heart (used ironically here)

Exit.

Scene II

Time: Thursday evening

Place: Friar Lawrence's cell

Friar John, just returned from Mantua, reports that a quarantine has prevented his delivering to Romeo the message that Juliet's "death" is only temporary. Friar Lawrence quickly leaves to go to the tomb so that he can be with Juliet until Romeo arrives.

Enter FRIAR JOHN.

FRIAR J. Holy Franciscan friar! brother, ho!

Enter FRIAR LAWRENCE.

FRIAR L. This same should be the voice of Friar John.
Welcome from Mantua! What says Romeo?
Or, if his mind be writ, give me his letter.

FRIAR J. Going to find a barefoot brother out,
One of our order, to associate* me,
Here in this city visiting the sick,
And finding him, the searchers of the town,*
Suspecting that we both were in a house
Where the infectious pestilence* did reign,
Seal'd up the doors and would not let us forth,
So that my speed to Mantua there was stay'd.*

associate: go with (the Franciscan toward Mantua)
searchers . . . town: quarantine officers
pestilence: plague
stayed: delayed

FRIAR L. Who bare my letter then to Romeo?

FRIAR J. I could not send it—here it is again—
Nor get a messenger to bring it thee,
So fearful were they of infection.

FRIAR L. Unhappy fortune! By my brotherhood,*
The letter was not nice* but full of charge,
Of dear import, and the neglecting it
May do much danger. Friar John, go hence,
Get me an iron crow,* and bring it straight
Unto my cell.

brotherhood: office as a friar
nice: trivial
iron crow: crowbar

FRIAR J. Brother, I'll go and bring it thee.

Exit.

FRIAR L. Now must I to the monument alone;
Within this three hours will fair Juliet wake.
She will beshrew me much that Romeo
Hath had no notice of these accidents;*
But I will write again to Mantua,
And keep her at my cell till Romeo come—
Poor living corse, clos'd in a dead man's tomb!

accidents: dire events

Exit.

Scene III

Time: Late Thursday evening

Place: The Capulets' tomb

Paris encounters Romeo, who he assumes has come to desecrate the grave of Tybalt. In self-defense Romeo kills Paris. Purposing to join Juliet in death, Romeo drinks poison and dies just moments before Juliet awakens. Friar Lawrence fails in his attempt to persuade Juliet to flee with him. Seeing Romeo dead, Juliet, too, kills herself. Watchmen discover what has happened at the Capulet monument. The Prince reconstructs the tragic events of the deaths of Paris, Romeo, and Juliet and then denounces the hate of the Capulets and Montagues that has brought their children to such a lamentable end. The penitent Capulet and Montague are reconciled, and each promises to erect a gold statue in memory of the other's child and in token of the death of their vile enmity.

Enter PARIS, *and his* PAGE *with flowers, sweet water, and a torch.*

PARIS Give me thy torch, boy. Hence, and stand aloof.
Yet put it out, for I would not be seen.
Under yond yew trees lay thee all along,*
Holding thy ear close to the hollow ground;
So shall no foot upon the churchyard tread,
Being loose, unfirm, with digging up of graves,
But thou shalt hear it. Whistle then to me
As signal that thou hearest something approach.
Give me those flowers. Do as I bid thee, go.

all along: stretched out

PAGE *(Aside.)* I am almost afraid to stand alone
Here in the churchyard, yet I will adventure.*

adventure: take the risk (of doing so)

PAGE *retires.* PARIS *strews the tomb with flowers.*

Sweet flower, with flowers thy bridal bed I strew—
O woe, thy canopy is dust and stones!—
Which with sweet water nightly I will dew,
Or wanting that, with tears distill'd by moans.
The obsequies* that I for thee will keep
Nightly shall be to strew thy grave and weep.

obsequies: rites for the dead

Page whistles.

The boy gives warning, something doth approach.
What cursed foot wanders this way tonight,
To cross* my obsequies and true love's rite?
What, with a torch? Muffle me, night, awhile.

cross: thwart

Paris retires.

Enter Romeo and Balthasar with a torch, a mattock, and a crow of iron.

ROMEO Give me that mattock and the wrenching iron.
Hold, take this letter; early in the morning
See thou deliver it to my lord and father.
Give me the light. Upon my life I charge thee,
Whate'er thou hearest or seest, stand all aloof,*
And do not interrupt me in my course.
Why I descend into this bed of death
Is partly to behold my lady's face,
But chiefly to take thence from her dead finger
A precious ring, a ring that I must use
In dear employment;* therefore hence, be gone.
But if thou, jealous, dost return to pry
In what I farther shall intend to do,
By heaven, I will tear thee joint by joint,
And strew this hungry churchyard with thy limbs.
The time and my intents are savage wild,
More fierce and more inexorable* far
Than empty* tigers or the roaring sea.

aloof: aside

dear employment: urgent business

inexorable: unyielding

empty: hungry

BALTHASAR I will be gone, sir, and not trouble ye.

ROMEO So shalt thou show me friendship. Take thou that;
Live and be prosperous, and farewell, good fellow.

BALTHASAR *(Aside.)* For all this same, I'll hide me hereabout.
His looks I fear,* and his intents I doubt.*

fear: am anxious about

doubt: suspect

ROMEO Thou detestable maw,* thou womb of death,
Gorg'd with the dearest morsel of the earth,
Thus I enforce thy rotten jaws to open
And in despite* I'll cram thee with more food.

maw: mouth (of the tomb)

in despite: for spite

ROMEO opens the tomb.

PARIS This is that banish'd haughty Montague,
That murd'red my love's cousin, with which grief
It is supposed the fair creature died,
And here is come to do some villainous shame
To the dead bodies. I will apprehend* him.

apprehend: arrest

PARIS comes forward.

Stop thy unhallowed toil,* vile Montague!
Can vengeance be pursued further than death?
Condemned villain, I do apprehend thee.
Obey and go with me, for thou must die.

unhallowed toil: unholy work

ROMEO I must indeed and therefore came I hither.
Good gentle youth, tempt not a desp'rate man.
Fly hence and leave me; think upon these gone,*
Let them affright thee. I beseech thee, youth,
Put not another sin upon my head,
By urging* me to fury:* O, be gone!
By heaven, I love thee better than myself,
For I come hither arm'd against myself.
Stay not, be gone; live; and hereafter say
A madman's mercy bid thee run away.

these gone: i.e., the dead

urging: provoking

fury: rage

PARIS I do defy thy conjurations,*
And apprehend thee for a felon here.

conjurations: appeals

ROMEO Wilt thou provoke me? Then have at thee, boy!

They fight.

PAGE They fight! I will go call the watch.*

watch: watchmen

Exit.

PARIS O, I am slain! *(Falls.)* If thou be merciful,
Open the tomb, lay me with Juliet.

Paris dies.

ROMEO In faith, I will. Let me peruse* this face:
Mercutio's kinsman, noble County Paris!
What said my man,* when my betossed soul
Did not attend* him as we rode? I think
He told me Paris should* have married Juliet.
Said he not so? or did I dream it so?
Or am I mad, hearing him talk of Juliet,
To think it was so? O, give me thy hand,
One writ with me in sour misfortune's book!
I'll bury thee in a triumphant grave.
A grave? O no, a lanthorn,* slaught'red youth;
For here lies Juliet, and her beauty makes
This vault a feasting presence* full of light.
Death, lie thou there, be a dead man interr'd.*

peruse: examine closely

man: servant (Balthasar)

attend: pay attention to

should: was to

lanthorn: lantern

feasting presence: brightly lit, festive hall

by . . . interr'd: i.e., buried by one who is himself about to die

Romeo lays Paris in the tomb.

How oft when men are at the point of death
Have they been merry, which their keepers* call
A lightning before death! O how may I
Call this lightning?* O my love, my wife,
Death that hath suck'd the honey of thy breath,
Hath no power yet upon thy beauty:
Thou art not conquer'd; beauty's ensign* yet
Is crimson in thy lips and in thy cheeks,
And death's pale flag is not advanced* there.
Tybalt, liest thou there in thy bloody sheet?
O, what more favor can I do to thee,
Than with that hand that cut thy youth in twain*
To sunder* his that was thine enemy?
Forgive me, cousin! Ah, dear Juliet,
Why art thou yet so fair? Shall I believe
That unsubstantial* Death is amorous
And that the lean abhorred monster keeps
Thee here in dark to be his paramour?
For fear of that, I still will stay with thee,
And never from this palace of dim night
Depart again. Here, here will I remain
With worms that are thy chambermaids; O, here
Will I set up my everlasting rest,
And shake the yoke of inauspicious* stars
From this world-wearied flesh. Eyes, look your last!

keepers: jailers

lightning: an uplifting of the spirits said to occur before death

ensign: military banner

advanced: raised

cut . . . twain: caused you to die

sunder: cut off

unsubstantial: having no bodily form

inauspicious: hostile

Arms, take your last embrace! and lips, O you
The doors of breath seal with a righteous kiss,
A dateless bargain* to engrossing* death!
Come, bitter conduct,* come, unsavory guide!
Thou desperate pilot, now at once run on
The dashing rocks thy seasick weary bark!
Here's my love! *(He drinks.)* O true apothecary!
Thy drugs are quick. Thus with a kiss I die.

dateless bargain: unending contract
engrossing: all-encompassing
conduct: conductor, guide

ROMEO dies.

Enter FRIAR LAWRENCE with lanthorn, crow, and spade.

FRIAR L. Saint Francis be my speed!* how oft tonight
Have my old feet stumbled at graves!* Who's there?

BALTHASAR Here's one, a friend, and one that knows you well.

speed: aid
Have . . . graves: Such was thought an evil omen in Shakespeare's day.

FRIAR L. Bliss be upon you! Tell me, good my friend,
What torch is yond, that vainly lends his light
To grubs and eyeless skulls? As I discern,
It burneth in the Capels' monument.

BALTHASAR It doth so, holy sir, and there's my master,
One that you love.

FRIAR L. Who is it?

BALTHASAR Romeo.

FRIAR L. How long hath he been there?

BALTHASAR Full half an hour.

FRIAR L. Go with me to the vault.

BALTHASAR I dare not, sir.
My master knows not but I am gone hence,
And fearfully did menace* me with death
If I did stay to look on his intents.

menace: threaten

FRIAR L. Stay then; I'll go alone. Fear comes upon me.
O, much I fear some ill unthrifty* thing.

unthrifty: unlucky

BALTHASAR As I did sleep under this yew tree here,
I dreamt my master and another fought,
And that my master slew him.

FRIAR L. Romeo!

FRIAR stoops and looks on the blood and weapons.

Alack, alack, what blood is this, which stains
The stony entrance of this sepulchre?
What mean these masterless and gory swords
To lie discolor'd by this place of peace?

Enters the tomb.

Romeo, O, pale! Who else? What, Paris too?
And steep'd* in blood? Ah, what an unkind* hour
Is guilty of this lamentable chance?
The lady stirs.

steep'd: soaked
unkind: cruel

JULIET rises.

JULIET O comfortable* friar! Where is my lord?
I do remember well where I should be,
And there I am. Where is my Romeo?

comfortable: comfort-giving

Noise within.

FRIAR L. I hear some noise, lady. Come from that nest
Of death, contagion, and unnatural sleep.
A greater power than we can contradict*
hath thwarted our intents. Come, come away.
Thy husband in thy bosom there lies dead;
And Paris too. Come, I'll dispose of thee
Among a sisterhood of holy nuns.
Stay not to question, for the watch is coming.
Come go, good Juliet, *(noise again)* I dare no longer stay.

A . . . contradict: i.e., Providence

Exit.

JULIET Go get thee hence, for I will not away.
What's here? A cup clos'd in my true love's hand?
Poison, I see, hath been his timeless* end.
O churl,* drunk all, and left no friendly drop
To help me after?* I will kiss thy lips;
Haply* some poison yet doth hang on them,
To make me die with restorative.

timeless: untimely

churl: miser; stingy person

help . . . after: allow me to follow you in death

Haply: perhaps

She kisses ROMEO.

Thy lips are warm.

WATCH. 1 *(Within.)* Lead, boy, which way?

JULIET Yea, noise? Then I'll be brief. O happy dagger,

Snatching ROMEO's dagger.

This is thy sheath; *(stabs herself)* there rust, and let me die.

Falls on Romeo's body and dies.

Enter Paris's PAGE and WATCH.

PAGE This is the place, there where the torch doth burn.

WATCH. 1 The ground is bloody; search about the churchyard.
Go, some of you, whoe'er you find attach.*

attach: arrest

Exeunt some WATCHMEN.

Pitiful sight! here lies the County slain,
And Juliet bleeding, warm, and newly dead,
Who here hath lain these two days buried.
Go tell the Prince, run to the Capulets,
Raise up the Montagues; some others search.

Exeunt others.

We see the ground whereon these woes* do lie,
But the true ground* of all these piteous woes*
We cannot without circumstance descry.*

woes: woeful creatures
ground: cause
woes: woeful events
descry: discern

Enter some of the WATCH with Romeo's man, BALTHASAR.

WATCH. 2 Here's Romeo's man; we found him in the churchyard.

WATCH. 1 Hold him in safety* till the Prince come hither.

safety: security

Enter FRIAR LAWRENCE and another WATCHMAN.

WATCH. 3 Here is a friar, that trembles, sighs, and weeps.
We took this mattock and this spade from him,
As he was coming from the churchyard's side.

WATCH. 1 A great suspicion.* Stay* the friar too.

suspicion: cause for suspicion
Stay: detain

Enter the PRINCE and ATTENDANTS.

PRINCE What misadventure is so early up,
That calls our person from our morning rest?

Enter CAPULET, LADY CAPULET, and others.

CAPULET What should it be that they so shriek abroad?

LADY CAP. O, the people in the street cry "Romeo,"
Some "Juliet," and some "Paris," and all run
With open outcry toward our monument.

PRINCE What fear is this which startles in your ears?

WATCH. 1 Sovereign, here lies the County Paris slain,
And Romeo dead, and Juliet, dead before,
Warm and new kill'd

PRINCE Search, seek, and know how this foul murder comes.

WATCH. 1 Here is a friar, and slaughter'd Romeo's man
With instruments upon them, fit to open
These dead men's tombs.

CAPULET O heavens! O wife, look how our daughter bleeds!
This dagger hath mista'en, for lo his house*
Is empty on the back of Montague*
And is mis-sheathed in my daughter's bosom!

house: i.e., sheath

on . . . Montague: Men conventionally wore daggers on their backs.

LADY CAP. O me, this sight of death is as a bell
That warns my old age to a sepulchre.

Enter MONTAGUE and others.

PRINCE Come, Montague, for thou art early up
To see thy son and heir now early down.

MONTAGUE Alas, my liege, my wife is dead tonight;
Grief of my son's exile hath stopp'd her breath.
What further woe conspires against mine age?

PRINCE Look and thou shalt see.

MONTAGUE O thou untaught!* what manners is in this,
To press* before thy father to a grave?

untaught: ill-mannered

press: rush forward

PRINCE Seal up the mouth of outrage* for a while,
Till we can clear these ambiguities
And know their spring, their head, their true descent,*
And then will I be general of your woes*
And lead you even to death. Meantime forbear,
And let mischance be slave to patience.
Bring forth the parties of suspicion.

mouth . . . outrage: violent outcry

descent: origin

general . . . woes: your leader in mourning these woes

FRIAR L. I am the greatest, able to do least,
Yet most suspected, as the time and place

Doth make against me, of this direful murder;
And here I stand both to impeach* and purge*
Myself condemned and myself excus'd.*

impeach: accuse

purge: exonerate

Myself . . . excus'd: I am both guilty and innocent

PRINCE Then say at once what thou dost know in this.

FRIAR L. I will be brief, for my short date of breath*
Is not so long as is a tedious tale.
Romeo, there dead, was husband to that Juliet,
And she, there dead, that Romeo's faithful wife.
I married them, and their stol'n marriage day
Was Tybalt's dooms-day, whose untimely death
Banish'd the new-made bridegroom from this city,
For whom, and not for Tybalt, Juliet pin'd.
You, to remove that siege of grief from her,
Betroth'd and would have married her perforce*
To County Paris. Then comes she to me,
And with wild looks bid me devise some mean
To rid her from this second marriage,
Or in my cell there would she kill herself.
Then gave I her (so tutor'd by my art*)
A sleeping potion, which so took effect
As I intended, for it wrought on her
The form of death. Meantime I writ to Romeo,
That he should hither come as this* dire night
To help take her from her borrowed grave,
Being the time the potion's force should cease.
But he which bore my letter, Friar John,
Was stayed by accident,* and yesternight
Return'd my letter back. Then all alone,
At the prefixed hour of her waking,
Came I to take her from her kindred's vault,
Meaning to keep her closely* at my cell,
Till I conveniently could send to Romeo.
But when I came some minute ere the time
Of her awakening, here untimely lay
The noble Paris and true Romeo dead.
She wakes, and I entreated her come forth
And bear this work of heaven with patience.*
But then a noise did scare me from the tomb,
And she, too desperate, would not go with me,
But as it seems, did violence on herself.
All this I know, and to the marriage
Her nurse is privy;* and if aught in this
Miscarried* by my fault, let my old life

short . . . breath: brief remaining lifespan

perforce: by compulsion

art: skill with herbs

as this: this very

stayed . . . accident: delayed by chance

closely: secretly

patience: fortitude

privy: knowledgeable (concerning these secret matters)

Miscarried: went wrong

Be sacrific'd some hour before his time
Unto the rigor of severest law.

PRINCE We still have known thee for a holy man.
Where's Romeo's man? what can he say to this?

BALTHASAR I brought my master news of Juliet's death,
And then in post* he came from Mantua
To this same place, to this same monument.
This letter he early bid me give his father,
And threaten'd me with death, going in the vault,
If I departed not and left him there.

PRINCE Give me the letter. I will look on it.
Where is the County's page that rais'd the watch?
Sirrah, what made your master* in this place?

PAGE He came with flowers to strew his lady's grave,
And bid me stand aloof, and so I did.
Anon comes one with light to ope the tomb,
And by and by my master drew on him,
And then I ran away to call the watch.

PRINCE This letter doth make good the friar's words,
Their course of love, the tidings of her death;
And here he writes that he did buy a poison
Of a poor 'pothecary and therewithal
Came to this vault, to die and lie with Juliet.
Where be these enemies? Capulet! Montague!
See what a scourge* is laid upon your hate,
That heaven finds means to kill your joys* with* love.
And I, for winking at* your discords too
Have lost a brace of* kinsmen. All are punish'd.

CAPULET O brother Montague, give me thy hand.
This is my daughter's jointure,* for no more
Can I demand.

MONTAGUE But I can give thee more,
For I will raise her stature in pure gold,
The whiles* Verona by that name is known,
There shall no figure at such a rate* be set,
As that of true and faithful Juliet.

in post: speedily, by horse

made . . . master: did your master do

scourge: punishment

kill . . . joys: (1) kill your children, (2) make you unhappy, i.e., punish you

with: by means of

winking at: closing my eyes to

a . . . of: two (Mercutio and Paris)

jointure: wifely inheritance (as a result of Romeo's death, i.e., the reconciliation of Montague with Capulet)

whiles: as long as

rate: (1) value, (2) cost

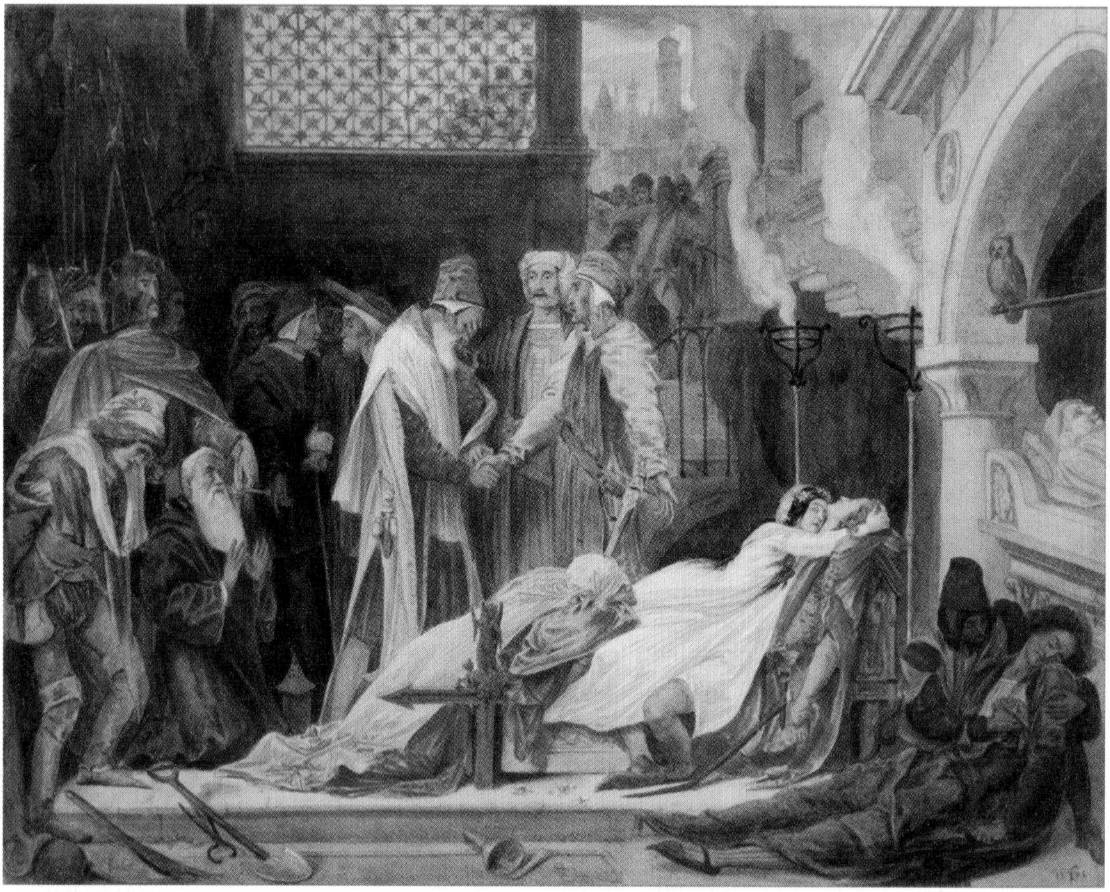

The Reconciliation of the Montagues and the Capulets, c. 1854 (w/c, bodycolour and gum over graphite on paper) by Frederic Leighton (1830–96). © Yale Center for British Art, Paul Mellon Fund, USA/ / The Bridgeman Art Library Nationality / copyright status: English / out of copyright

CAPULET As rich shall Romeo's* by his lady's lie,
Poor sacrifices of our enmity!*

PRINCE As glooming* peace this morning with it brings;
The sun, for sorrow, will not show his head.
Go hence to have more talk of these sad things;
Some shall be pardon'd, and some punished.
For never was a story of more woe
Than this of Juliet and her Romeo.

Exeunt.

Romeo's: a statue of Romeo
enmity: hatred, hostility
glooming: cloudy

About the Play

1. How is Romeo's dream at the beginning of Act V ironic in light of what follows immediately after it?
2. There are several "coincidences" in the plot. Identify at least two of these coincidences. How do these support the themes of fate and of haste? How might Shakespeare have intended these coincidences to affect our sympathy for the lovers?
3. What does Romeo decide to do when he hears of Juliet's "death"? Is this decision surprising when we consider previous characterization of Romeo? Provide two specific examples from the play to support your answer.
4. What happens to Romeo's mother?
5. The Prince's final speech mentions pardon and punishment. Should Friar Lawrence be pardoned or punished? Should the apothecary be pardoned or punished? Who do you think is ultimately guilty of the deaths of Romeo and Juliet? Explain.
6. Philip Sidney once said that the purpose of literature is "to delight and to instruct." The value of *Romeo and Juliet* as entertaining drama is clear. But how does the play also "instruct"? List at least three things the drama teaches us.
7. Read 1 Corinthians 13:3–13. Choose three characteristics of love and explain how Romeo and Juliet's love either violates or exhibits these characteristics. Use specific instances from the play to support your answer.

Drama is a genre uniquely suited to showing, not just telling, what truth looks like in action. As a result, it can be a powerful tool for Christians. Choose one quality of biblical love listed in 1 Corinthians 13. Write a dramatic scene in which the dialogue and action combine to reveal how that quality works out in real life relationships. (The quality need not be specifically mentioned in the scene). Follow script formatting and include stage directions and a cast list.

THINKING ZONE

Like some novels, some dramas contain **prologues** and **epilogues**. In dramas, these are short speeches, addressed directly to spectators by an actor. Both direct the audience in certain ways. Prologues, set at the beginning, may introduce themes or characters and describe the setting or events preceding the play. Epilogues may summarize, comment, recap theme, or otherwise give a finishing touch.

Consider Thornton Wilder's *The Matchmaker.* In this play, Horace Vandergelder, wealthy and widowed, solicits Dolly Levi's help in finding a wife. Vandergelder is "willing to risk a little security for a certain amount of adventure." Dolly plans a trip to New York ostensibly to introduce Horace to the perfect match. In reality, she designs to be the match. At the same time Cornelius and Barnaby, workers at Vandergelder's store, head to New York for adventure. Comical high jinks ensue, including mistaken identities and kidnapping. In the end, not one, but three couples plan to marry, and Barnaby gives an epilogue stating the moral of the play.

> Oh, I think it's about . . . I think it's about adventure. The test of an adventure is that when you're in the middle of it, you say to yourself, "Oh, now I've got myself into an awful mess; I wish I were sitting quietly at home." And the sign that something's wrong with you is when you sit quietly at home wishing you were out having lots of adventure. What we would like for you is that you have just the right amount of sitting quietly at home, and just the right amount of—adventure!*

Two other conventions unique to drama include the soliloquy and the aside. The **soliloquy** is a speech in which a character who believes himself to be alone discloses his innermost thoughts, often revealing his motives or mental state. Perhaps the most famous example is Hamlet's "To be or not to be" soliloquy. In an **aside,** a character briefly discloses his thoughts in the presence of other characters who by convention do not hear him. In Shakespeare's time, stages that extended into the audience created an intimacy between actor and audience that made the aside seem very natural. Understanding these conventions enables modern audiences to more fully enjoy such dramas.

1. Reread the **prologue** to Act I of *Romeo and Juliet*. What functions of a prologue does it illustrate? What information included might annoy a first-time audience?
2. Does *Romeo and Juliet* have an **epilogue**? Explain your answer.
3. Who in Act IV speaks in an **aside**, and what is said? Who, though present in the scene, does not hear, and why should he or she not hear?
4. Reread Juliet's **soliloquy** in Act IV, Scene III. What is the general idea it conveys, and how realistic is it? Can you identify with Juliet?

*Wilder, Thornton. *The Matchmaker in Three Plays*. New York: HarperPerennial Modern Classics, 2006. 415. Print.

UNIT VIII REVIEW

Remember the Terms

Review the following terms from the opening essay, "Drama," and the Thinking Zone pages. Be prepared to discuss their meanings and uses.

drama	act	prologue
closet drama	scene	epilogue
theater in the round	comic relief	soliloquy
comedy	wit	aside
tragedy	repartee	

Apply the Concepts

Answer the following questions about how the literary concepts you have studied are used in this unit.

1. One of the themes of *Romeo and Juliet* is fate versus free will. What phrase in the prologue to Act I identifies the influence of fate?
2. What theme is addressed in the following lines?

   Though I do joy in thee,
   I have no joy of this contract tonight.
   It is too rash, too unadvis'd, too sudden,
   Too like the lightning, which doth cease to be
   Ere one can say it lightens.

3. For Montague "to raise [Juliet's] statue in pure gold" and for Capulet to raise one "as rich" of Romeo forms what part of the plot structure?
4. Identify the lovers' tragic flaw.
5. Who delivered the following lines, and to whom do they refer?

   O, she doth teach the torches to burn bright!
   It seems she hangs upon the cheek of night
   As a rich jewel in an Ethiop's ear—
   Beauty too rich for use, for earth too dear!

6. What sound device is illustrated in the first line above? What type of figurative language do the second and third lines illustrate? What rhetorical device organizes the last line, and what type of verbal irony does it include?
7. What object does Juliet place beside her bed before taking the potion, why does she do so, and what literary device do her action and its reason illustrate?
8. To whom does Romeo allude when he uses the phrase "the envious moon" prior to Juliet's balcony soliloquy?

9. What is the meaning of the following famous line spoken by Juliet? "O Romeo, Romeo, wherefore art thou Romeo?"
10. When Juliet sends her Nurse to Romeo to find out the location and time of her marriage ceremony, what function does the young men's mockery of the Nurse play in the midst of a tragic story?
11. Of Romeo's friends Benvolio and Mercutio, which character is more sympathetic and which is less? Explain your answers.
12. What type of verse is much of the play written in?
13. What literary effect is enhanced by the increasing speed of the plot in Acts IV and V?
14. Given the definition of *soliloquy*, what is unusual about Juliet's famous soliloquy in the balcony scene of Act II?

Evaluate the Ideas

Identify each of the following statements as true or false. If false, rewrite the underlined portion of the statement to make it true.

15. At the end of the balcony scene, in which Romeo and Juliet profess their love for each other, Juliet delivers the following lines: "Good night, good night! Parting is such sweet sorrow, / That I shall say good night till it be morrow." The lines contain a famous example of wit.
16. The embedded sonnet at the beginning of Act II is also a prologue.
17. Though *Romeo and Juliet* contains wit, repartee, and comic relief, it is a tragedy because of its ending.
18. In *Romeo and Juliet*, the feud is primarily kept alive by the older generation.
19. Shakespeare intends Romeo and Juliet's love to be an example of infatuation.
20. The following lines delivered by Benvolio address an important theme in *Romeo and Juliet*: "Wisely and slow; they stumble that run fast."
21. That Romeo, in attempting to stop a fight, blocked Mercutio's view and enabled Tybalt to stab Mercutio is an example of situational irony.
22. Mercutio's statement "Ask for me tomorrow, and you shall find me a grave man" illustrates litotes.
23. Romeo argues that it was the lark that Juliet and he heard outside the window.
24. The audience learns in a soliloquy that Juliet will not follow the Nurse's advice to marry Paris.
25. Juliet's speech in response to the Nurse's news that Tybalt is dead and that Romeo has killed him primarily displays external conflict.
26. Capulet's reaction to Romeo's presence at the party indicates his desire to see the feud continue.

27. The aside seemed more natural in the Elizabethan theater than in modern theater because the stages of that time extended into the audience.
28. Romeo's response to the Prince's decree of banishment evidences the character quality of immaturity.

Write a Response

Completely answer two of the following questions.

29. Lady Capulet and the Nurse serve as foils to Juliet. Discuss the attitudes of Lady Capulet and the Nurse in regard to love and marriage. Does Juliet ultimately adopt their attitudes?
30. Discuss how Shakespeare develops the theme of haste through the words and actions of the characters. What is Shakespeare's tone toward their hasty actions?
31. Shakespeare complements his characterization of Romeo by surrounding him with other young men who are similar to him in certain respects and different from him in others. Compare and contrast Romeo's character with that of Benvolio, Mercutio, Tybalt, and Paris.
32. Discuss Shakespeare's recurring use of the imagery of light and darkness (and day and night) in the play. Comment on its function in several scenes as well as its overall effect in the play.

Glossary of Literary Terms

A

abstract concept. A concept that cannot be perceived by the five senses but must instead be discussed in general terms by describing the image's attributes or its effects upon a concrete subject.

act. A major division in the action of a play.

action. What a **character** does.

adaptation. A rewritten version of an author's work that has been changed for reasons such as length or readability.

allegory. A type of **extended metaphor** that forms a story with two levels of meaning, a literal and an implied.

alliteration. The repetition of initial consonant sounds.

allusion. A reference within a work to something else, usually history or another artistic work.

analogy. A detailed comparison of one thing to another dissimilar thing.

anapestic foot. **Poetic foot** that contains two unstressed and then one **stressed syllable**.

anaphora. The repetition of words or phrases at the beginnings of lines of poetry or grammatical units.

anecdote. A short narrative of a single interesting or amusing incident.

antagonist. A force or **character** who struggles against the **protagonist**.

antithesis. A rhetorical device that uses syntactical **parallelism** in two adjacent phrases or clauses to emphasize their contrasting meanings.

apostrophe. A speaker or writer's directly addressing an absent person, abstraction, or inanimate object.

archetype. Character types, plot patterns, or images that recur throughout world literature.

aside. A stage device in which a character briefly discloses his thoughts in the presence of other characters who by convention do not hear him.

assonance. The repetition of similar vowel sounds in a series of words.

atmosphere. The mood or emotion that the reader is supposed to share with the **characters**.

authorial intent. The reason an author composed his or her work.

autobiographical essay. A short selection written by the author about his experience(s) and focused on a particular event or happening.

B

ballad. A narrative poem often derived from folklore and originally intended to be sung or recited.

biographical sketch. A brief descriptive **biographical** essay. See also **sketch**.

biography. A **nonfiction** account in which the author tells the true events that make up the life of a real individual other than himself.

blank verse. Unrhymed **iambic pentameter**.

C

cacophony. The use of words that are harsh or dissonant in sound.

caesura. A pause in the middle of a line of **poetry**, usually indicated by a mark of punctuation.

character. A person or being who performs the action of the story.

character flaw. An incidental weakness or serious moral fault that a **character** reveals through the story.

character motivation. See **motivation**.

character trait. How a **character** thinks or acts.

chiasmus. Two parallel phrases, clauses, or sentences in which the second reverses the elements of the first, inverting the parallel structure.

chronological order. The order in which events actually occur in a story.

cinquain. A five-line **poem** whose first line contains one stressed syllable; the second, two; the third, three; and the fourth, four. The fifth line, like the first, has only one stressed syllable.

cliché. A phrase, **idiom**, or expression that has become so overused that it often detracts from rather than contributes to a story.

cliffhanger. Suspenseful situations strategically placed throughout different parts or chapters of a longer work.

climax. The point at which the **plot** reaches the moment of highest emotional intensity.

closet drama. A play written to be read and not performed.

comedy. Drama that focuses on light-hearted matters such as courtship and love and that may also be satirical.

comic relief. Comic elements inserted into serious **drama** to relieve dramatic tension.

conceit. a type of comparison that draws a striking parallel between two seemingly dissimilar things.

concrete language. Words that appeal to one or more of the five senses.

conflict. The opposition of two or more **characters** or forces; the three main conflicts are *man against a greater force*, *man against man*, and *man against himself*.

conflict resolution. The opposing forces in a particular conflict come to grips with the issues at hand.

connotative meaning. The meaning of a word plus all of its implications and emotional associations.

consonance. The repetition of terminal consonant sounds (as in "bi*t* . . . figh*t* . . . le*t*") and, more rarely, of internal consonants that creates extra emphasis on the words involved.

context. The influence of factors surrounding a work of literature that may provide additional insight into its meaning.

couplet. A pair of rhymed lines.

crisis. The major turning point for the main **character**; the point at which something happens that affects the outcome of the story and determines the future of the main character.

criticism. The analysis of a literary work.

D

dactylic dimeter. See **dactylic foot** and **dimeter**.

dactylic foot. Poetic foot that contains one stressed and then two unstressed syllables.

denotative meaning. The exact definition of a word as found in a dictionary.

dénouement. See **resolution.**

description. Writing that seeks to aid the reader in seeing or feeling whatever the author is trying to convey.

detective fiction. Fiction with a recurring **character** (a detective) who investigates and solves a crime that often stretches a reader's interest and thinking to the limit.

developing character. A **character** who changes as the story progresses.

dialect. Dialogue written to reflect qualities of a character's speech.

dialogue. A conversation between **characters**.

diary. See **journal**.

dimeter. A line of **verse** consisting of two metrical feet.

direct characterization. Type of character description in which straightforward details tell the reader about the **character.**

drama. Literature written to be acted.

dramatic irony. A type of **irony** in which the reader is aware of a **plot** development of which the **characters** of the story are unaware.

dramatic monologue. A literary form, usually **poetry**, in which a single **character** speaks either to himself or to another character.

dramatist. See **playwright.**

dynamic character. A changing or **developing character**.

E

end rhyme. **Rhyme** that occurs at the ends of corresponding lines of **poetry**.

end-stopped lines. Lines of **poetry** that end with a natural pause indicated by punctuation.

English sonnet. **Poetry** whose thought is usually distributed over three **quatrains** with a concluding **couplet**, the whole rhyming *ababcdcdefefgg.*

enjambment. A poetic device in which lines flow past the end of one verse line and into the next with no punctuation at the end of the first verse line.

epic. A long stylized **narrative poem** celebrating the deeds of a great national or ethnic hero of legend.

epic simile. A type of **simile** common in traditional epics in which the vehicle of the comparison is described at considerable length.

epilogue. An addition to a story's ending that expounds on the fortunes of the main **character** or on the significance of the story's conclusion. In drama, a short speech occurring at the end of the play in which an actor directly addresses the audience, often to summarize or comment on the play's theme.

essay. A work that seeks to state a point of view, discuss a subject, or persuade a reader to accept an argument.

euphemism. A mild, indirect, or vague term that substitutes for a harsh, blunt, or offensive one.

euphony. The use of words whose sounds are pleasant and musical to the ear.

explicit theme. **A theme** stated outright within a work of literature.

exposition. The part of a story's **plot** that introduces the reader to the **setting**, the **characters**, and the situation.

extended metaphor. A **metaphor** that is developed beyond a single sentence or comparison.

external conflict. **Conflict** that occurs between a **character** and an outside force (such as society or nature).

eye rhyme. Word pairs that are spelled alike but pronounced differently.

F

fable. A brief fanciful story that embodies a particular **moral**.

fairy tale. A folktale set in an indefinite time and place and containing an element of the fantastic or magical.

falling action. The events that unfold the results of the **crisis** and lead to the conclusion.

feminine ending. In **poetry**, a line ending in which the final syllable is unstressed.

fiction. A work that contains events and **characters** invented by the author.

figurative language. An artful deviation from literal speech.

first-person point of view. The point of view in which the narrator, as one of the story's characters, refers to himself as I throughout the piece.

flashback. A reference to events that occurred before the action of the main story or to action that occurred before the time that the **narrator** is speaking.

flat character. A **character** with little individuality whose mindset the reader knows little about.

foil character. A **character** used to emphasize another character's opposing traits within a work.

folklore. The collective term for the tales and myths passed along primarily by word of mouth within a society or culture.

folktale. A short tale passed along by word of mouth throughout a given culture.

foot. See **poetic foot.**

foreshadowing. Hinting at events that will occur later within a story.

formal essay. A type of **essay** in which the writer adopts an impersonal, authoritative tone and models highly organized structure.

frame story. A story that contains another story or an introductory story from which another story springs.

free verse. Poetry with no set **meter** or **rhyme**.

G

genre. A type or category of literature.

H

haiku. A seventeen-syllable poem about nature, composed of three lines of five, seven, and five syllables. Example: "Daffodils in spring / Lift their golden trumpets and / Breathe a melody."

hero/heroine. A male or female **protagonist** who behaves virtuously within a story.

heroic couplet. A pair of rhyming lines written in **iambic pentameter**.

historical fiction. A fictional story that employs authentic historical **characters** or **settings**.

Homeric epithet. A stock phrase inserted to describe a particular person or thing that recurs in a poem, generally in an epic.

humor. A genre that seeks to amuse the reader through wordplay, irony, or other means.

hyperbole. A type of obvious **overstatement** used by writers to make a point.

I

iamb. A type of **poetic foot** that contains one unstressed syllable followed by one **stressed syllable** (also known as an *iambic foot*).

iambic foot. Poetic foot consisting of one unstressed and one **stressed syllable**, in that order.

iambic pentameter. Meter with five **iambs** in each line of a poem.

idiom. An expression that is unique to itself and cannot be defined from the meanings of the individual words (e.g., *pass the buck*).

imagery. Descriptive words or phrases that appeal to sense perceptions in order to create an impression.

implicit theme. A **theme** that is not stated outright but must be discerned from the details that the author includes in the work.

implied metaphor. Metaphors conveyed indirectly.

inciting incident. The incident that sets the events of the **conflict** in motion.

indirect characterization. Type of characterization in which the reader must infer character traits from information shown by the author.

informal essay. A type of **essay** in which the writer adopts a friendly or conversational tone with the reader (also known as a *personal essay*).

in media res. Latin literary term meaning "in the middle of events" and referring to the practice of starting a story in the midst of the action.

internal conflict. Conflict that occurs between a character and his own thoughts, emotions, or beliefs.

internal rhyme. Rhyme that occurs between words within a single line of **poetry**.

irony. The use of language to convey meaning other than what is stated or a contradiction in what is expected to happen and what actually happens.

Italian sonnet. Poetry whose first eight lines (an **octave**, rhyming *abbaabba*) form a distinct unit of thought and whose last six lines (a **sestet**, rhyming variously with two or three new **rhymes**) form another.

J

journal. An informal daily record of a person's life.

L

limited-omniscient point of view. Viewpoint of a narrative in which the narrator tells the story in third person but "gets inside" only *one* of the characters, usually the central character.

literal meaning. A standard definition of a word or expression.

litotes. A form of **understatement** that expresses a positive statement by denying its opposite, e.g., *That girl is no slacker.*

local color. Recreates the dress, **dialect**, geography, social practices, and general **worldview** of a specific region.

lyric poem. A brief poem expressing the personal views of a single speaker on a particular topic.

M

masculine ending. In **poetry**, a line ending in which the final syllable is stressed.

memoir. A type of **nonfiction** that recounts a personal recollection of the author.

metaphor. An imaginative comparison consisting of the stated or implied equivalence of two dissimilar things.

meter. The regular pattern of stressed and unstressed syllables.

metonymy. An expression in which a related thing stands for the thing itself.

monologue. An extended speech or piece of writing in which a single **character** reveals his thoughts.

moral. A simple statement that sums up a truth about life.

moral tone. Application of a person's philosophy through the ethics that the individual embraces.

motivation. The reason that a **character** behaves as he or she does.

myth. A folktale that explains a specific aspect of life or the natural world, usually in terms of supernatural forces or beings, and that was at one time held to be true within a certain cultural group.

mythology. A collection of myths forming a particular culture's explanation of how the world came to be as it is.

N

narrative poem. A poem that tells a story.

narrator. The individual telling the story to the reader.

nonfiction. Prose that tells of real people and events.

normative character. The **character**, sometimes called simply the norm, who models and articulates the author's ethics throughout the story.

novel. An extended work of fictional **prose**.

novella. A prose work of medium length, longer than a **short story** yet shorter than a **novel**.

O

octave. A **stanza** of eight lines.

omniscient viewpoint. The narrator tells his story in third person, and as the storyteller he "knows all."

onomatopoeia. The use of words that sound like what they mean (e.g., *hiss*, *buzz*).

oral tradition. The audible means by which much **folklore** and **mythology** was transferred from person to person before the prevalent use of written language.

overstatement. The exaggeration of details surrounding the events of a story.

oxymoron. Brief phrases that combine contradictory elements for effect (e.g., *sweet sorrow*).

P

parable. A brief story told to illustrate or clarify a truth, often biblical in nature.

paradox. A statement that seems to be self-contradictory yet actually makes sense when understood in the right context.

parallelism. Similarity in the structure of two or more phrases, clauses, or sentences.

perfect rhyme. Agreement of sounds from the last stressed vowel sound onward, with a difference in the immediately preceding consonant sounds.

persona. The person created by the author to tell the story, affecting the way a story is told.

personification. Giving human characteristics to something that is not human.

perspective. The author's mental view or outlook that influences his account of a story.

persuasion. Argument that motivates the listener to change not only his ideas but also his actions.

play. See **drama.**

playwright. The author of a **drama** or play.

plot. A series of events arranged to produce a definite sense of movement toward a specific goal.

plot twist. A **plot** development that violates the reader's expectations.

poetic foot. The specific combination of two or three stressed and/or unstressed syllables that predominantly repeats throughout the poem's lines.

poetic justice. The term given to the reward or punishment that a **character** receives for his virtue or vice within a story.

poetry. Artfully compressed thought resulting in the elevated expression of ideas.

point of view. The perspective or angle from which a story is told.

prologue. An introduction to a literary work. In drama, a short speech at the beginning of the play in which an actor directly addresses the audience, often to introduce the setting, themes, or characters.

propaganda. Literature plainly written to persuade the reader to espouse the author's position on a significant issue of his time.

prose. Writing that resembles speech and differs from **poetry**, such as a **short story** or an **essay**.

prose poem. Writing that unites the two most basic literary forms, drawing on both the meterless structure of **prose** and the sensory images, sound devices, and compressed speech of **poetry**.

protagonist. The main **character** of a story.

proverb. A brief but wise saying.

pun. A type of **wordplay** in which the author combines two word meanings within a sentence.

pyrrhic foot. **Poetic foot** that has two unstressed syllables.

Q

quatrain. A **stanza** or poem of four lines.

R

refrain. A line or group of lines repeated throughout a poem.

repartee. Besting another's remark or turning it to one's own advantage in a contest of wits.

repetition. In **poetry**, the act of creating patterns by repeating not only sounds but also words, lines, **meter**, or syntax.

resolution. The final outcome of a story and the last element of the **plot** (also known as the *dénouement*) in which the major complications are explained or settled.

rhetoric. The art of public speaking.

rhetorical question. A question asked, not to receive information, but to achieve an effect.

rhyme. Two or more words having identical sounds in the last stressed vowel and all of the sounds following that vowel.

rhymed verse. Verse having **end rhyme** and regular **meter**.

rhyme scheme. The pattern of **rhyme** sounds in a poem or in a **stanza** of poetry.

rhythm. A regular pace or beat.

rising action. The events that follow the **inciting incident** and lead up to the **crisis** in a story.

round character. A **character** who is complex and often undergoes changes in his actions and thoughts.

S

sarcasm. A type of **irony** that takes the form of mock praise.

satire. Corrective ridicule of some object of scorn usually outside of the literature itself.

scansion. The process of identifying the two major features of **meter** in a particular poem.

scene. In a **drama**, a subdivision of an **act** that does not contain a change of time or place.

sestet. A **stanza** of six lines.

setting. The time, place, and way of life in which the action of the story occurs.

shaped poem. A poem that rarely follows any specific **stanza** or **verse** form but is shaped in an image that supports the subject of the poem.

short story. A brief work of prose **fiction**.

simile. A comparison of two unlike objects using *like* or *as*.

situational irony. A type of **irony** in which a story's events violate normal expectations.

sketch. A brief descriptive **essay**.

slant rhyme. **Rhyme** between two words with similar but slightly mismatched sounds (e.g., *star* and *door*).

soliloquy. In drama, a form of speech in which a **character** who believes himself to be alone discloses his innermost thoughts.

sonnet. A **lyric poem** of fourteen lines. The two most common types of sonnet are the **Italian** (or Petrarchan) and the **English** (or Shakespearean).

spondaic foot. Poetic foot that repeats two **stressed syllables**.

stage directions. Instructions for lighting, movement, and action included within a **drama** script.

stanza. Divisions of a poem based on thought, **meter**, or **rhyme** and usually recognized by the number of lines they contain.

static character. A **character** who remains essentially the same throughout the story.

stream of consciousness. A type of writing in which the author attempts to reproduce the flow of thoughts in a character's mind with little attention to grammar or logic.

stressed syllable. A syllable that receives greater emphasis when read.

structural irony. Sustained **verbal irony** that generates two layers of meaning, one literal and one implied, throughout the entire work.

style. An author's manner of expression in **prose** or **verse**, in written or oral discourse.

subplot. A secondary **plot** within a piece of literature that accompanies the main plot yet is lesser in importance or significance.

surprise ending. A **plot twist** at the end of a story.

suspense. Reader anxiety resulting from the author's withholding of **plot** details.

symbol. A person, place, thing, or idea within a narrative or poem that means something in addition to itself.

sympathetic character. A **character** with whom the reader identifies or for whom the reader has favorable feelings.

synecdoche. Using a part of something to stand for the whole.

synesthesia. Describing one sense experience in terms of another.

T

tenor. In a **metaphor**, the original subject which the metaphor seeks to describe.

theater in the round. A drama presentation in which the stage is completely surrounded by the audience.

theme. A recurring or emerging idea in a work of literature.

third-person point of view. The **point of view** in which the narrator refers to the **characters** as *he*, *she*, or *it*.

tone. The attitude of an author toward his or her subject.

traditional forms. Established poetic patterns requiring specific organization and techniques and sometimes also a specific type of content.

tragedy. A literary work in which the flaws of the protagonist cause him tremendous suffering, eventually resulting in a catastrophe, or disastrous conclusion.

tragic flaw. In a **tragedy**, the most significant personal flaw that triggers the **tragic hero's** downfall.

tragic hero. The **protagonist** in a tragedy.

triplet. A **stanza** of three lines that usually share the same **rhyme** (also known as a tercet).

trochaic foot. **Poetic foot** that contains a stressed and then an unstressed syllable.

U

understatement. The representation of something as less important than it truly is.

universal theme. Ideas about life that are found throughout world literature because they can be understood by people of all times and places.

unsympathetic character. A **character** with whom the reader cannot identify or for whom the reader has strong feelings of dislike.

V

vehicle. In a **metaphor**, the image the **tenor** of the metaphor is being compared to.

verbal irony. **Irony** occurring when a speaker's meaning differs from what he or she expresses in words.

verse. A composition written in **meter**.

verse forms. In poetry, specific combinations of **rhyme** and **meter**.

villain. An evil or cruel **antagonist**.

W

wit. A brief verbal expression that amuses listeners through a clever but unexpected turn of phrase or connection between ideas.

word play. Witty or clever verbal exchange.

worldview. The philosophical viewpoint from which a person examines the world and draws conclusions.

Index

Entries in SMALL CAPITALS refer to artists and authors. Entries in *italics* refer to titles of paintings and literary selections. Entries in **bold** refer to literary terms.

M

N

O

P

Q

R

S

T

U

V

W

Illustrators

The Nightingale and the Glowworm Holly Hannon
What Stumped the Bluejays from ***A Tramp Abroad*** Paula Cheadle
The Return of the Rangers Del Thompson
Who Has Seen the Wind? Kathy Pflug
A Gray Sleeve Del Thompson
Outta My Way, Grandpa! Del Thompson
maggie and milly and molly and may Paula Cheadle
The Masque of the Red Death Kathy Pflug
Jade Flower Palace Paula Cheadle
The Grave Grass Quivers Kathy Pflug
Scylla Toothless Del Thompson
Letter from a West Texas Constituent Kathy Pflug, Del Thompson
The Day the Dam Broke Tim Davis, Del Thompson
From ***The Screwtape Letters*** Del Thompson
The Lion-Makers Nichole Radin, Paula Cheadle
The Tortoise and the Osprey Beau Jackson
The Pumpkin Seeds Paula Cheadle
Pandora Courtney Godbey Wise
Pyramus and Thisbe Kathy Pflug
A Miserable Merry Christmas Paula Cheadle
The Sire de Maletroit's Door Paula Cheadle, Courtney Godbey Wise
The Adventure of the Speckled Band Dave Schuppert
A Visit of Charity Kathy Pflug
Lady Clare Dave Schuppert
We Wear the Mask Del Thompson
High Flight Preston Gravely

Photograph Credits

The following agencies and individuals have furnished materials to meet the photographic needs of this textbook. We wish to express our gratitude to them for their important contributions.

Alamy
Andrew Wyeth office
Art Gallery of South Australia
Art Resource
Associated Press
BigStock
BJU Photo Services
The Bridgeman Art Library
Fotolia
Getty Images
The Granger Collection
iStockphoto
Library of Congress
Media Bakery
NASA
Shutterstock
The State Hermitage Museum
Kathleen Stocker
SuperStock
Thinkstock
The Thorvaldsen Museum
Wikimedia Commons
123RF

Cover

©iStockphoto.com/iSebastian

Front Matter

©iStockphoto.com/iSebastian i; Digital Image © The Museum of Modern Art/Licensed by SCALA / Art Resource, NY / Christian's World, 1948 tempera © Andrew Wyeth vii; The Granger Collection, New York viii; © SuperStock / SuperStock ix, xviii; William Hogarth/Wikimedia Commons/Public Domain x; Imagno/Hulton Archive/Getty Images xi; Henri Rousseau/Wikimedia Commons/Public Domain xii; © Tomas Abad / Alamy xiii; Karl Ludwig Friedrich Becker/Public Domain xiv; ©iStockphoto .com/ooyoo xx

Unit 1

© The Museum of Modern Art/Licensed by SCALA/ Art Resource, NY / Christian's World, 1948 tempera © Andrew Wyeth 2; Getty Images/iStockphoto/ Thinkstock 6; ©iStockphoto.com/Okea 8; Getty Images/Hemera Technologies/PhotoObjects.net/ Thinkstock 9; © Bjenks/Wikimedia Commons/CC 3.0 10; © Tony Wills/Wikimedia Commons/GNU 1.2 CC 2.5 11; ©iStockphoto.com/BartCo 32; Getty Images/Hemera/Thinkstock 34; © iStockphoto.com/ dlewis33 35, 36; St. John the Baptist in the Wilderness. Antonio del Castillo y Saavedra (attr. to). From the Bob Jones University Collection 38

Unit 2

The Granger Collection, New York 44; © James W. Porter/Corbis/Media Bakery 54; © iStockphoto.com/ bigstevemac 56; Getty Images/iStockphoto/Thinkstock 70; © iStockphoto.com/diephosi 72; Stringer/ AFP/Getty Images 75

Unit 3

© SuperStock / SuperStock 84; Stock Montage/ Archive Photos/Getty Images 93; Getty Images/ iStockphoto/Thinkstock 97, 110; Getty Images/ Jupiterimages/Comstock/Thinkstock / Getty Images /iStockphoto/Thinkstock 102

Unit 4

William Hogarth/Wikimedia Commons/Public Domain 120; Library of Congress 124; ©iStockphoto .com/Giorgio Fochesato / Getty Images/iStockphoto/ Thinkstock 144; NASA/JPL-Caltech/T. Pyle (SSC) 150; ©iStockphoto.com/antos777 151; Getty Images/ iStockphoto/Thinkstock 152 (all)

Unit 5

Imagno/Hulton Archive/Getty Images 170; ©The Metropolitan Museum of Art/Art Resource, NY 197; The Thorvaldsen Museum. Photographer Hans Petersen 199; Panos Karapanagiotis/Shutterstock .com 202; © Christie's Images Ltd. / SuperStock 204; ©iStockphoto.com/Stefanos Kyriazis 207; Peter Paul Rubens/The Bridgeman Art Library/Getty Images 209; Leonid Bogdanov/SuperStock/Getty Images 211; ©iStockphoto.com/Eduard Andras 213

Unit 6

Henri Rousseau/Wikimedia Commons/Public Domain 218; AP Photo 223; ©iStockphoto.com/ooyoo 239; © Tom Till/Superstock 241; 4594189/123RF 288; © africa - Fotolia.com 290; ©imagebroker.net/SuperStock 291

Unit 7

© Tomas Abad / Alamy 296; ©iStockphoto.com/Stephen Roberts 305; Hemera Technologies/Photos.com/Thinkstock 306; Getty Images/iStockphoto/Thinkstock 315, 316–17; © John Warden/SuperStock 321; DmitryP/BigStock.com 325; ©iStockphoto.com/clu 330; ©imagebroker.net/SuperStock 332; The State Hermitage Museum, St. Petersburg 335

Unit 8

Karl Ludwig Friedrich Becker/Public Domain 340; BJU Photo Services 345, 350, 352, 361, 365, 371, 384, 394, 401, 424, 429, 446, 453; Charles Edouard Delort /Public Domain 377; Private Collection/ By courtesy of Julian Hartnoll/ The Bridgeman Art Library 407; © Birmingham Museums and Art Gallery/ The Bridgeman Art Library 413; Kathleen Stocker 418; Art Gallery of South Australia, Adelaide 438; © Yale Center for British Art, Paul Mellon Fund, USA/ / The Bridgeman Art Library 460